D1740909

1 MONTH OF
FREE
READING

at
www.ForgottenBooks.com

By purchasing this book you are eligible for one month membership to ForgottenBooks.com, giving you unlimited access to our entire collection of over 1,000,000 titles via our web site and mobile apps.

To claim your free month visit:
www.forgottenbooks.com/free932544

ISBN 978-0-260-17313-3
PIBN 10932544

T
Agric
S
I

International Review of the ...
Practice of Agriculture

INTERNATIONAL INSTITUTE OF AGRICULTURE

BULLETIN OF THE BUREAU OF

AGRICULTURAL INTELLIGENCE AND

OF PLANT-DISEASES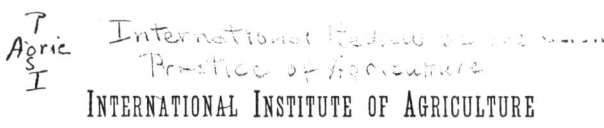

2nd YEAR - NUMBER 4

APRIL 1911

ROME 1911 PRINTED AT THE INSTITUTE'S PRINTING OFFICE

CONTENTS

LIVE STOCK BREEDING. — AVICULTURE. BEEKEEPING. — SILK PRODUCTION. — FISHERIES AND GAME. ANIMAL INDUSTRIES.

THE INTERNATIONAL INSTITUTE OF AGRICULTURE

The International Institute of Agriculture was established under the International Treaty of June 7th, 1905, which was ratified by 40 Governments. Eight other Governments have since adhered to the Institute.

It is a Government Institution in which each Country is represented by delegates. The Institute is composed of a General Assembly and a Permanent Committee.

The Institute, confining its operations within an international sphere, shall:

a) Collect, study, and publish as promptly as possible statistical, technical, or economic information concerning farming, vegetable and animal products, the commerce in agricultural products, and the prices prevailing in the various markets;

b) Communicate to parties interested, also as promptly as possible, the above information;

c) Indicate the wages paid for farm work;

d) Make known the new diseases of vegetables which may appear in any part of the world, showing the territories infected, the progress of the diseases, and, if possible, the remedies which are effective;

e) Study questions concerning agricultural co-operation, insurance, and credit in all their aspects; collect and publish information which might be useful in the various countries for the organisation of works connected wrth agricultural co-operation, insurance and credit;

f) Submit to the approval of the Governments, if there is occasion for it, measures for the protection of the common interests of farmers and for the improvement of their conditions, after having utilized all the necessary sources of information, such as the wishes expressed by international or other agricultural congresses or by congresses of sciences applied to agriculture, or agricultural societies, academies. learned bodies, etc:

The Institute publishes: *a*) a Monthly Bulletin of Agricultural Statistics; *b*) a Monthly Bulletin of Agricultural Intelligence and Diseases of Plants; *c*) a Monthly Bulletin of Economic and Social Intelligence.

It has also published a volume on " The Organization of Agricultural Statistical Services in the Several Countries ", and a volume on " Statistics of Cultivated Areas and of Vegetable and Animal Production in the Adhering Countries " (an Inventory drawn up from documents published by Governments), and " Studies upon the present condition of Agricultural Association in certain countries (2 vols) ".

Officers of the Institute
and List of the Delegates to the Permanent Committee.

President: Marquess RAFFAELE CAPPELLI, *Delegate of Italy*

Vice-President : M. LOUIS-DOP, *Delegate of France.*

General Secretary: Prof. PASQUALE JANNACCONE.

Delegates of the adhering States to the Permanent Committee.

	States adhering to the Institute	Groups in which adhering States are classified	Names and Rank of the Delegates
1	Germany . . .	I	Dr. T. MUELLER, Privy Councillor.
2	Argentine Rep. .	I	E. PORTELA, Minister Plenipotentiary of the Argentine Rep. to H. M. the King of Italy
3	Austria	I	Chev. V. DE POZZI, Government Councillor.
4	Hungary	I	E. DE MIKLÓS DE MICLOSVÁR, Member of the House of Magnates, late Secretary of State for Agriculture.
5	Belgium	IV	O. BOLLE.
6	Brazil	I	His Excell. A. FIALHO, Minister Plenipotentiary of Brazil to H. M. the King of Italy.
7	Bulgaria	III	D. RIZOFF, Minister Plenipotentiary of Bulgaria to H. M. the King of Italy,
8	Chile	I	S. ALDUNATE BASCUÑAN, Minister Plenipotentiary of Chile to H. M. the King of Italy.
9	China	I	TCHAO HI-TCHIOU, Secretary to the Imperial Chinese Legation.
10	Costa-Rica . . .	V	R. MONTEALEGRE, Minister Plenipotentiary of Costa-Rica to H. M. the King of Italy.
11	Cuba	V	C. M. DE CESPEDES QUESADA, Minister Plenipotentiary of Cuba to H. M. the King of Italy.

	States adhering to the Institute	Groups in which the adhering States are classified	Names and Rank of the Delegates
12	**Denmark**	IV	H. H. KONOW, Secretary to the Danish Legation to the Italian Government.
13	**Ottoman Empire**	I	Dr. MEHMED DJEMIL BEY.
14	**Egypt**	II	B. CHIMIRRI, Delegate af Eritrea and Italian Somaliland.
15	**Ecuador**	V	LOUIS-DOP, Delegate of France.
16	**Spain**.	I	AUGUSTE ECHEVERRIA, Agricultural Engineer.
17	**United States** . .	I	DAVID LUBIN.
18	**Ethiopia**	V	Prof. G. CUBONI, Director of the Station of Vegetable Pathology of Rome.
19	**France**	I	LOUIS-DOP, Vice-President of the Institute.
20	**Algeria**	V	LOUIS-DOP, Delegate of France.
21	**Tunis**.	V	LOUIS-DOP, Delegate of France.
22	**Great Britain & Ireland**	I	H. G. DERING Counsellor to the British Embassy to the Italian Government.
23	**Australia**	IV	. . . .
24	**Canada**	II	Hon. A. BOYER, Senator.
25	**British India** . .	II	Sir EDWARD BUCK, K. C. S. I.
26	**New Zealand** . .	IV	H. G. DERING, Delegate of Great Britain and Ireland.
27	**Mauritius** . . .	V	H. G. DERING. Delegate of Great Britain and Ireland.
28	**Greece**	IV	A. CARAPANOS, Chargé d'affaires of Greece to the Italian Government.
29	**Italy**	I	Marquess R. CAPPELLI, Vice-President of the Chamber of Deputies, President of the Istitute.
30	**Eritrea and Italian Somaliland**	IV	B. CHIMIRRI, Member of Parliament.

States adhering to the Institute	Groups in which the adhering States are classified	Names and Rank of the Delegates
31 Japan	I	SHINOOH IMAI, Second Secretary to the Imperial Japanese Embassy to the Italian Government.
32 Luxemburg . . .	V	O. BOLLE, Delegate of Belgium.
33 Mexico	II	G. A. ESTEVA, Minister Plenipotentiary of Mexico to H. M. the King of Italy.
34 Montenegro . . .	V	G. VOLPI, Director General of the Monopolies of the Kingdom.
35 Nicaragua. . . .	V	V. E. BIANCHI, Consul General of Nicaragua at Rome.
36 Norway.	IV	Dr. G. FJELSTAD, Landowner.
37 Holland	IV	H. DE WEEDE, Minister Plenipotentiary of Holland to H. M. the King of Italy.
38 Peru	V	Dr. M. M. MESONES,
39 Persia	IV	A. DEL GALLO, Marquess of ROCCAGIOVINE.
40 Portugal	IV	LUIZ FILIPPE DE CASTRO, Professor of the Institute of Agriculture at Lisbon.
41 Roumania. . . .	I	G. C. NANO, Minister Plenipotentiary of Roumania to H. M. the King of Italy.
42 Russia	I	His Ex. G ZABIELLO, Consul General of Russia in Rome.
43 Salvador	V	A. BALLO, Acting Consul General of Salvador at Genoa.
44 San Marino . . .	V	His Excell. L. LUZZATTI, Minister of State of the Kingdom of Italy.
45 Servia	III	B. I. SOUBOTITCH, Secretary to the Servian Legation to the Italian Government.
46 Sweden	IV	G. V. T. DE STRÄLE, Councillor to the Swedish Legation to the Italian Government.
47 Switzerland . . .	IV	J. B. PIODA, Minister Plenipotentiary of Switzerland to H. M. the King of Italy.
48 Uruguay	V	. . . .

The information contained in some of the abstracts dealing with Canada has been most kindly placed at the disposal of the Institute by the Government of the Dominion.

The Canadian abstracting is by Mr. J. K. Doherty, the able chief of the Canadian Bureau of Correspondence with the International Institute of Agriculture.

AGRICULTURAL INTELLIGENCE

NB. The Intelligence contained in the present Bulletin has been taken exclusively from the books, periodicals, bulletins, and other publications which have reached the Library of the International Institute of Agriculture in Rome during the month of April 1911.

The Bureau assumes no responsibility with regard to the opinions and the results of experiments outlined in the Bulletin.

The Editor's notes are marked (Ed.).

Development of Agriculture in Different Countries. — Scientific Institutions. — Education in Agriculture and Forestry. — Experimentation. — Biography. — History of Agriculture.

MEKOVIÉ (Austrian Consul). **Agriculture in Montenegro**. — *Berichte der k.k. Oester.-Ung. Konsularämter*, Montenegro-Antivari, pp. 1-15 Wien, 1910.

1079

Montenegro

In Montenegro there are extensive barren tracts. There are however productive regions where maize, wheat, barley and some rye are cultivated, but even in the best years not sufficient for local consumption. Few vegetables are grown. Potatoes are generally cultivated but might be made much more productive ; in some years they have been exported to Dalmàtia.

Montenegro produces excellent pears, apricots, cherries, almonds, lemons and figs, but in no great quantity. Wine is produced in abundance, but is not of good quality.

Great pains have been taken to stimulate the culture of olives, which prosper along the coast, between Antivari and Dulcigno. About 9000 quintals of olives are produced, and the surplus over home consumption is exported to Servia and Albania.

Tobacco culture has developed admirably since the monopoly was entrusted to an Italian administration. Turkish seed has been introduced, selected and improved under Italian supervision. The *Balcha*, *Danica* and *Nemanja* are excellent varieties, much appreciated abroad. The Italian Society has 520 hectares (1284.4 acres) under tobacco, with an average production of 750 kg. per hectare, (670 lbs per acre) bringing in annually about 3 500 000 frs. (£ 140 000) The exportation is chiefly to Dresden, and to France and Belgium.

20

The cattle are not remarkable; the horses are small and the oxen of inferior breeds. Much cheese is produced, and the butter is excellent. On the markets of Niksic and Podgoritza, from 5000 to 6000 sheep are sold; the entire exportation of sheep goes to Italy. In order to protect the forests, of which there are few, the breeding of goats has been limited; they are all exported to Italy. Poultry-rearing might be carried on successfully in the country; eggs are exported to Ragusa, in Dalmatia.

1080　　Van den Steen (Belgian Consul). **Agriculture in Switzerland.** (La situation agricole suisse). — *Recueil Consulaire*, T. 152, 3ᵉ Livraison, pp. 110-332. Bruxelles, 1911.

Switzerland　　Switzerland is naturally adapted for cattle raising and sylviculture. Meadows and pastures together occupy 75 % of the total productive area, and arable land only 11.7 %. The cultivation of cereals occupies about 200 000 hectares (494 000 acres).

The production of potatoes has reached 8 400 000 quintals, grown chiefly in the Cantons of Berne, Fribourg and Vaud. About 20 000 quintals of sugar-beet are grown, and are all bought by the sugar-factory of Aarberg.

Tobacco is grown in the Cantons of Vaud and Fribourg, on about 400 hectares, producing annually about 12 000 quintals.

Vines cover a total of about 24 794 hectares (61 241.18 acres), but do not grow in the Cantons of Uri, Unterwald and Appenzell. The production of wine varies between 1 200 000 and 1 300 000 hectolitres. The most celebrated wines are: Dézaley de Lavaux, Yvorne (Vaud), Neuchâtel, Neftenbach, Hallau (Schaffhausen) and Goldwändler (Argau). With help from the Government, the vineyards destroyed by phylloxera have been reconstituted, but the surface under vines diminishes yearly.

Fruit is grown everywhere, especially in the Canton of Thurgau and in part of the Canton of Berne. The number of fruit trees is estimated at 14 millions and their annual produce at 60 million francs (£ 2 400 000). A great quantity of preserves are made at Lenzbourg, Rorschach, Saxon and Minusio.

In 1900 forests covered 29 % of the total area of Switzerland. In the Jura they cover from 31 % to 41 % of the productive soil. Their annual production is calculated at 40 million francs, (£ 1 600 000), and it is not enough for the home consumption.

Cattle-raising and the allied industries are closely connected with the growing of forage crops. Alpine pastures cover about

1 100 000 hectares (2 717 000 acres), and it is here that the strength
and endurance and build of Swiss cattle are developed.

There are now about 1 ½ million head of cattle in Switzerland. Of these, two races have been brought to remarkable
perfection :

    1) The brown race, in the central region and the Grisons ;
    2) The white race with : a) yellow markings, (*Simmenthal*) ;
b) black markings, (*Friburg*).

A Swiss cow is calculated to yield on an average 2650 litres
of milk per year. Of the total production of milk in Switzerland,
about 10 400 000 hectolitres are consumed fresh ; 6 840 000 are used
in cheese-making ; 3 340 000 in the rearing industry ; and 986 000
in the manufacture of condensed milk.

The following table shows, in millions of francs, the total production in all branches of the dairy industry in 1907 and 1908 :

	1907	1908
Fresh milk	1 839	2 159
Fresh butter	92	47
Condensed milk	31 445	27 103
Cheese	54 183	54 128
Sugar of milk	13	1
Farine lactée	2 784	2 536
	90 356	85 974

The importation of dairy produce in 1909 was valued at
13 390 000 francs (£ 535 600). Condensed milk is made at Vevey,
Payene, Neuenegg, Cham, and Guin ; sterilised milk chiefly at
Stalden (Emmenthal) and at Utzenstorf.

The native Swiss cattle are all bred for dairy purposes, cattle
are imported for the meat market.

Since 1887 efforts have been made by the Government and by
the Cantons to revive the breeding of horses, and several stud-
farms have been established. There is but one Swiss breed of
horses, that of the Franches-Montagnes, the centre for which is
Saignelégier, in the Bernese Jura.

Efforts are also made to improve the breeds of pigs and to
increase their numbers.

The white goats of Saanen, the goats of Oberhasli and of the
Toggenburg are celebrated.

Sheep are only raised in the high pastures inaccessible to cows.
Notwithstanding the encouragement given, poultry-raising makes

little progress. Bee-keeping flourishes ; there are about 250 000 hives. The silk-worm industry would do well'in the Canton Ticino. The lakes and streams of Switzerland are generally full of fish.

One great factor in Swiss agricultural development is the high level of professional agricultural instruction (1).

1081

TAHY von TAHVAR (Austrian Consul). **Agriculture in the Province of Novi Bazar.** — *Berichte der k. k. Oester- Ung. Konsularämter,* pp. 1-19. Wien, 1910.

Ottoman Empire : Novi Bazar

In Novi Bazar and the neighbouring Albanian provinces agriculture is improving, but the wooden plough and other primitive implements are still used. Wheat, barley, rye and especially maize are grown, as well as beans, French beans, cabbages, potatoes and tomatos. Onions and cabbages are exported to Salonika. A good deal of fruit is grown, and walnuts, apples and plums are exported. Tobacco is grown for home consumption only.

Cattle-raising is one of the most important industries, but modern methods and modern forage plants are still unknown, and the cattle live in the open fields, and are put to work too young. The breeding of horses has deteriorated. The following are the figures for the exportation from Novi Bazar and the surrounding Albanian provinces in 1901 :

Cereals.	28 144 quintals
Fruit	2 534 »
Onions	5 787 »
Cattle	28 400 head
Hides	1 399 quintals
Cheese from ewe's milk . . .	2 467 »
Wood	42 642 »

The walnuts are sent to America and the apples to Rumania. Cattle are exported, via Salonika, to Egypt, Sicily and Malta. Besides hides of cattle the skins of sheep and goats, of foxes, wild cats, sables, badgers, wolves and bears are exported.

---

(1) See No. 1102 of this *Bulletin.*   (*Ed.*).

ZAMBAUR (Austrian Consul). **Agriculture in Northern Albania.** —   1082
Berichte der k. k. Oester- Ung. Konsularämter, pp. 1-28, Wien, 1910.

In Northern Albania, especially round Scutari, maize chiefly   Ottoman
is cultivated and forms the common food. The production varies   Empire:
between 34 and 35 million kg. (74 800 000 lbs and 82 000 000 lbs),   Albania
and sometimes a good deal is exported, principally to Montenegro.
About 5 million kg. of wheat are produced and part is annually
exported to Montenegro and Southern Albania. The total production of barley and oats is about 1 500 000 kg. (3 300 000 lbs)
the barley is given to the army horses. In some years the production of hay is very great.
The tobacco is excellent and abundant, being free from all
Government control.
Vines are not well managed and were ruined by cryptogamic
diseases. But last year a yield of 10 000 000 kg. (22 000 000 lbs.)
of grapes was obtained, and vine culture seems to be reviving.
Olive oil is produced, sumach is also grown.
There is a fair exportation of hides. Poultry-raising and the
exportation of eggs are increasing.
There are fine forests, but the want of roads has rendered
exploitation impossible hitherto, notwithstanding the efforts of some
Italian contractors.

Agricultural and Irrigation Developments in Andalusia. *The Times*   1083
(Engineering Supplement). No. 321. p. 21. London, April, 19, 1911.

The Province of Seville is one of the richest agricultural dis-   Spain:
tricts in Spain. In addition to cereals and all kinds of garden   Andalusia
produce, oranges and olives are grown in large quantities, and the
conditions of soil and climate are favourable for the cultivation of
mulberries, for silk, tobacco, and cotton.
Yet large tracts of ground are barren, which might be fertile,
and agricultural distress is chronic. The sole reason is want of water.
To remedy this state of things, a Committee of engineers was
appointed by the Government to study the possibility of irrigation.
Of the scheme proposed by the chief engineer and adopted by
the Government, the most important part is the construction of
a canal in ten sections, having a total length of 247 km. (167 miles),
which will take the water of the Guadalquivir at Palma del Rio,
and distribute it over a total area of 80 600 hectares (199 082 acres).
To supplement the river water in dry seasons, when the stream is

low, six reser voirs will be constructed in convenient valleys, with a total available capacity of about 260 000 000 cub. met. (340 600 000 cub. yds.). On the right bank five short canals will be made, having a total length of 93 km. (58.125 miles) each fed by its own reservoir. These reservoirs will have a total capacity of 81 000 000 c. m. (106 110 000 cub. yds.), and will together irrigate an area of about 40 sq. miles. The continuous supply of the whole system of six canals will be 33 087 litres (58 233.12 pints) a second. The total cost of the proected works is estimated at 40 500 000 pesetas. (£ 1 620 000).

1084   J. DAUTREMER (French Consul). **The Yangtse.** (La grande artère de la Chine, le Yangtseu), in-8°, pp. 295 + map. Paris. E. Guilmoto, ed.

China   This book gives an account of the geography, ethnography, customs, religion, government, commerce, natural resources and industries of the basin of the Yangtse. It contains an historical summary of the commercial relations between China and Europe ; an account of agriculture in the provinces of Kiangsu, Hupeh, Anhwei, Kiangsi, Hunan, Kwei Chau, Szechwan, and Yünnan ; information on customs tarifs, postal service, corporations and secret societies in China, together with some account of Europeans and Japanese on the Yangtse Kiang.

The same crops, chiefly rice, are grown in all the provinces in the Yangtse basin, where the mass of the population is agricultural. The immense, well-watered plains are very fertile. In the provinces of the Upper Yangtse the mountain slopes are terraced, and the rice fields thus formed are irrigated from high reservoirs whence the water flows from field to field until it reaches the valley. Besides rice, maize is grown, sweet potatoes (1), earth-nuts, different sorts of haricot beans, melons, water-melons, Jerusalem artichokes, the water-chestnut (2), cabbages, turnips, carrots etc.

In these regions there are buffaloes, used for field work, zebus, sheep and ponies. Poultry do extremely well. Pig raising here, as all over China, is very common, as pork and rice are the staple

---

(1) *Batatas edulis.*   (*Ed.*).

(2) The kernel of *Trapa bispinosa*, Roxb. is a common article of food in the regions where it grows in India. It is rich in starch, and like the chestnut in flavour ; it is eaten cooked or raw.

See WATT, *Dict. of the Economic Products of India*, vol. VII, part. IV, p. 73. London-Calcutta, 1893.   (*Ed.*).

foods in China. Hares, pheasants, and roebuck abound, but the Chinese do not touch game.

The Yangtse and its affluents are literally full of fish, which are found even in the ditches in the rice-fields, for the Chinese breed fish. In spring, sturgeons and shad go up the Yangtse, sturgeons as far as Hankow and Kieukiang; the shad only as far as Shanghai. Carp and eels are the commonest fish.

The richest provinces in this part of China are Kiangsu, Kiangsi, Anhwei and Szechwan; the provinces of Hupeh, Hunan, Kweichau and particularly Yünnan are poor.

The silk markets are at Shanghai and Canton. The finest silks come from Chêhkiang, Shantung, and Canton; those of Chêhkiang and Canton are from silk-worms fed on mulberry leaves; those of Shantung from silkworms fed on the leaves of a kind of oak, which give a brown colour to the silk (1). The Chinese judge silk by its whiteness, suppleness and fineness, and often, to give it a good appearance, they dress it with rice-water mixed with lime, with the result that when it arrives in Europe it constantly breaks in winding. The silk of Chêhkiang is prepared in the province of Kiangsu, specially at Nankin. There are many silk factories with European machinery at Shanghai and other towns.

The cultivation of the opium poppy is prohibited, by Imperial order, throughout the Empire, and since the agreement with Great Britain, the importation of Indian opium decreases gradually, so that in time it will be entirely suppressed (2).

Tea grows everywhere, but the best quality comes from the hills of the provinces of Hupeh, Kiangsi, Fukien and Chêh-kiang. cotton and ramie are grown in the Yangtse valley.

Hides of cattle, buffaloes and goats form an important export, the preparation of which is not without danger, as anthrax decimates cattle in the Yangtse valley.

In the province of Hupeh the principal products are: rice, of which in some parts there are two harvests in the year; wheat and cotton in the northern part, hemp, ramie, and sesame, tea, which is the chief product of the district of Ohe-nan-Fu; the lac tree (*Rhus vernicifera*) and rhubarb, in the mountainous western parts of the province; haricot beans, indigo, tobacco, sorghum, maize and millet.

---

(1) *Antheraea yamamai*, Guér. Ménc. See remarks on *Antheraea* by Sir GEORGE WATT, *The Silk of India* (*Ibid.*, Vol. VI, Part. III, p. 69). (*Ed.*).

(2) In 1909, the importation of Opium into China was valued at £.4 654 295. *The Statesman's, Yearbook*, 1911, p. 699. (*Ed.*).

The potato, introduced by Italian missionaries, forms, together with the sweet potato, the staple food of the peasants in the mountains of the western part of this province. The centre of the silk-worm industry is Ta-Yang.

In the province of Hunan, rice is grown, especially in the plains round Lake Tong-Ting and in the Siang valley ; cotton, in all the northern part of the province ; tobacco, of superior quality but very strong in nicotine, especially in the district of Tcheng-Tcheou ; indigo, and very superior tea. The annual exportation of black tea is worth from 20 to 25 million francs (£ 800 000 — £ 1 000 000) ; green tea is also grown in Hunan, and a little silk is produced.

Hunan and Yünnan are the only provinces in China where there are forests that are exploitable.

In the province of Kweichau ramie is largely cultivated. Horses and cattle are raised in considerable numbers.

The province of Szechwan exports pigs' bristles, musk (about 600 kg. (1320 lbs) annually), rhubarb, both wild and cultivated, white insect wax (1) (to the value of about 300 000 taëls annually), yellow wax, gall-nuts, and hides (2).

Great progress has been made of late years in sericulture. The provincial Bureau of Agriculture sells, on request, silkworm « seed » imported from Hang-chou, Soochou and Japan. This « seed » is distributed gratuitously in all the schools where sericulture is taught. Premiums are offered annually by the authorities for the production of silk of superior quality.

The province of Szechwan exports vegetable tallow, extracted from the seed of *Stillingia sebifera* (Euphorbiacea).

Chinese money and weights. — An Imperial Decree of May 24, 1910, prescribes that the unit of currency shall be the silver piastre and the standard shall be silver until further orders ; subsidiary coins will be pieces of 50, of 25 and 10 cents (3) etc.

---

(1) Called also Chinese Wax. It is produced by an insect parasite, *Ceroplastes ceriferos,* on the young branches of *Terminalia Arjuna.* WATT, *Dict. of the Economic Products of India,* Vol. V, p. 459. London-Calcutta, 1891.

(2) The haikwan, or customs täel was equal in value in 1909 to 31 ¼ d = 3.13 frcs. (*The Statesman's Year-Book,* 1911, p. 702 London, Macmillan, 1911. (*Ed.*).

(3) The cent is worth at present, at Hankow, 0.0375 fr. which would make the piastre worth 3.75 fr. See p. 12 of this *Bulletin.* (*Ed.*).

The units of weight are the following (1) :

Chinese name	European name	Value in metrical weights	English weights
Tan . . .	Picul	60 kg.	133 ⅓ lbs avoirdupois
Chin . . .	Catty	600 ' gr. $\left(\frac{1}{100}$ of a tan$\right)$	1 ⅓ lbs avoirdupois
Liang , .	Tael	37.5 » $\left(\frac{1}{16}$ of a chin$\right)$	1 ⅓ oz. avoirdupois
Chi'en . .	Mace	3.75 » $\left(\frac{1}{10}$ of a liang$\right)$	
Fên . .	Candaren	0.375 » $\left(\frac{1}{10}$ of a chien$\right)$	
Li	Cash	0.0375 » $\left(\frac{1}{10}$ of a fën$\right)$	

The *meou*, (about 600 m²) and the *king* (about 100 *meou*) are the principal surface measures. The *li*, common unit of length, varies from 500 to 650 metres between Northern and Southern China.

MAZZOLANI. **Agriculture in the Province of Yünnan.** (L'Agricultura nella provincia dell' Yünnan). — *Boll. Soc. Geografica italiana,* N. 4, pp. 476-504, Roma, Aprile, 1911.

1085

China:
Yünnan

The climate of Yünnan is partly tropical, partly temperate, and the soil is very varied. The chief crop is rice, of which the following are some of the varieties: *lo-mi, nan-mi, tong-iao-mi, he-lo-mi, siao-mi,* and *hong-mi.* The last, (red rice) is the most cultivated, because it resists the irregularity of the summer water supply. It is cultivated, not only in the valleys, but also on the terraced hill-sides. In some irrigated localities, two rice-crops are obtained in the year. Sometimes the rice fields are left fallow for 2 or 3 years.

Winter and summer-wheat are grown. The grain is small, and the flour makes good bread, but it does not rise much. Maize is grown on a large scale ; the grain is small and whitish. Oats are also grown, and earthnuts, haricots, beans, pumpkins, potatoes, peas, carrots, celery etc. Foreign horticultural seeds give excellent produce of fine quality.

Cotton and hemp are not much grown, but tobacco cultivation is spreading everywhere. Tea is mostly of middling quality, but

(1) The English equivalents of Chinese weights are those established by treaty between Great Britain and China. The *Chih* of 14 ¹/10 English inches has been adopted as the legal standard of length. *The Statesman's Yearbook for 1911,* p. 703. (*Ed.*).

is very good in the district of Pueul. Bee-keeping is diminishing, because of the cultivation of the poppy, poisonous to bees. Sugar-cane grows everywhere. Medicinal plants are numerous. Musk is sold for 6 or 7 times its weight in silver. The mountains are wooded with pines, firs, oaks, ilex etc.

Horses are numerous; they are small but strong and enduring. The mules are excellent and larger than the horses. Donkeys are not much used. The cattle are small, except in the neighbourhood of Linngan; they are yoked with buffaloes in the rice-fields, and also serve as beasts of burden. The cows do not give much milk; goats are numerous; and sheep very fine, of good quality and not very large. Pigs are raised in great numbers; their meat is not firm when from breeds in the plains, but in the mountains the pork is considered the best in all the Empire.

Ducks, geese, pigeons, and fowls are reared; our common fowl is even found wild in Yünnan.

1086   **Agriculture in Japan.** *The Producer's Review, Perth,* Western Australia. March, 20, 1911.

Japan   The Department of Agriculture in Tokyo has published a work of 132 pages entitled « Outlines of Agriculture in Japan ». It states that of a total population of 51 000 000, about 31 000 000 or 60 per cent are engaged in, or dependent upon agriculture. The farms are generally small. Anyone who possesses more than 75 acres of land is regarded as a large landed proprietor; an ordinary land-owner's estate does not exceed 25 acres. Tenants' rents are by no means low, the rent ranging from 44 per cent to 37 per cent of the gross products of the farm. Were it not for the fact that crops are raised twice, thrice and even four times a year, tenants would fail. Their farms vary in size from 1.96 acres to 3.68 acres, on which they support a household consisting sometimes of six members. To some extent they have to rely on subsidiary occupations, such as making mats, baskets, paper and bamboo articles, such work being done at night   Seventy per cent of the farmers cultivate less than 2 acres and only 3 per cent cultivate more than 7 acres. Rice of course is the principal crop ; then come the following products, given in order of importance : barley and wheat, raw silk, vegetables and fruits, beans, sweet potatoes, and animal products.

An interesting chapter on Agricultural administration shows that the Japanese Government are alive to the advantages of educating and assisting the farmers. Cooperation amongst farmers is encouraged and financial assistance is given in the holding of farms and in the sale of produce. Stringent measures are taken for the prevention of disease in animals, and for the destruction of insect and fungus pests, an army of inspectors being appointed to see that effect is given to legislation. It is pointed out that the future of agriculture in Japan is highly promising and that at an early date the import of cereals will no longer be necessary.

HOMERY. **Agriculture in Newfoundland.** (L'agriculture à Terre-Neuve). — *Rapports commerciaux: Terre-Neuve*, N. 940, pp. 1-22. Paris, 1911.

1087

Forest industry has developed very remarkably in Newfoundland. The manufacture of paper from wood pulp, which was begun only a few years ago, progresses very rapidly. The factories at Grand Falls cover an immense area of land and forest in the midst of which rises a whole town.

Newfoundland

The soil is not fertile, but the Government makes every effort to improve agriculture, by distributing good seed, bringing over agricultural instructors, and forming agricultural societies. It is now hoped that the prosperity of the island will no longer depend entirely on the fishing industry (1).

G. MURRAY. **Agriculture in S. Vincent, W. I.** *Brit. Colonial Reports-Annual*, N. 668, St. Vincent - Report for 1909-1910, pp. 1-26, February 1911. London.

1088

Owing to the comparatively low prices received for cotton in 1908 the area under this crop in 1909 was reduced. According to a rough estimate, prepared by the Cotton Inspector, in the early part of 1910 not more than 2000 acres were put under cotton as compared with an estimated area of nearly 3000 acres in 1908. The area in which cotton can be cultivated is limited, practically, to the coast lands. Every effort is being made by the Agricultural Department

Windward Isles : St. Vincent

(1) Compare with :
Forestry in Newfoundland and Labrador. Journ. of the Roy. Society of Arts. London. N. 2994, 1910.
ED. MORRIS. *What the railroads are doing to open up Newfoundland.* The American Review of Reviews, July 1910, p. 51.   (*Ed.*).

to induce planters and small growers to devote more attention to
the burning of old cotton stalks, and to crop rotations ; they are
also urged to grow more leguminous plants for green-manuring
and to utilise all available manures, such as bushes, grasses etc.
and cotton seed. It is satisfactory to note the annual improvement
in cultivation and the evident desire on the part of the growers to
assimilate all the scientific and expert information given by the
Agric. Department.

In the St. Vincent Grenadines, notably in Union, Canonan and
Mayrean, the common Marie Galante type of cotton is grown. It
is cultivated as a perennial. In several of the other islets, Requia,
Mustique, Battowia, and Balliceaux, the cultivation of Sea Island
cotton has been taken up exclusively, and with very satisfactory
results.

Arrowroot again heads the list in regard to area under cultivation,
and also in regard to export value, which showed an increase of
100 000 francs (£ 4 000) over 1908. The « St. Vincent Arrowroot
Growers' and Exporters' Association has been formed, with headquarters in Kingstown, for the promotion and encouragement of
the arrowroot industry.

The export figures in sugar show an increase of about £ 1633.
Most of the sugar grown is on the Canib estates. Elsewhere in the
Colony it is only cultivated in small quantities for the purpose of
making rum. The soil and climate of St. Vincent are no doubt as
suitable for the growth of sugar as any other of the West Indian
Islands. The cultivation of the cacao tree has never been taken
up very heartily since the hurricane of 1908, when a large number
of trees were destroyed.

The efforts to demonstrate the working of implemental tillage
have been so successful, that planters are now systematically im
porting and using agricultural implements.

1089   VINCART. (Belgian Consul at Caracas) **Agriculture in Venezuela.**
(Le développement agricole au Vénézuéla). — *Recueil Consulaire*,
T. 152, 5ᵉ Livr. pp. 356-396. Bruxelles, 1911.

Venezuela   Venezuela comprises three distinct regions, the coasts, the mountains, and the plains, each with its own climate. There are lands
at different altitudes suited to every culture, from wheat to spices.
Agriculture is still old-fashioned and limited to the growing, for

exportation, of coffee and cacao. The land suitable for agriculture covers about 350 000 square kilometres, and the great *llanos* of the interior, where cattle-raising is carried on, cover about 400 000 square kilometres.

Venezuela has great natural resources. Cacao flourishes in the warm regions near the sea and coffee in the temperate regions up to an altitude of 1600 metres. Sugar-cane is also grown, and tobacco, maize, wheat, cotton, bananas, and a great variety of tropical fruits.

The value of the cacao and coffee exported in 1909-1910 was 54 ½ million francs (£ 2 180 000); of the India-rubber from the Orenoco forests, 14 millions (£ 560 000), and of the cattle hides, 8 millions (£ 320 000) ; these are the four great staples of Venezuelan exportation.

Maize is grown on a large scale, the grain serving for the *arrepas* or maize bread; cut green it forms the principal forage of the horses, mules and donkeys. Wheat is grown on the temperate slopes of the Andes, and yields a fine quality of flour rich in gluten. Sugar-cane succeeds almost every where on sufficiently moist or irrigated land. The varieties most cultivated are the native *Criolla*, *Salangore*, *Otahiti* and *Batavia*, this last especially for making rum. Distilling rum and spirits are important industries.

Tobacco does well, but is grown without much care. The cultivation of cotton has begun to develop lately, and that of ramie has been introduced round Valencia.

Bananas are being more extensively grown and might become a very important export. A North-American Company has bought land near Lake Maracaïbo for the purpose of growing bananas.

Next to the Argentine Republic, Venezuela possesses the widest extent of grazing lands in South America. Cattle-raising was once more prosperous than it is now. A British Company has however been formed for cold-storage of meat, and at Barrancas, on the Orenoco, a factory has been opened for the preparation of meat-extracts. Cattle hides are a sufficiently important export.

The immense forests on the Orenoco contain every sort of fine woods for cabinet-making, medicinal and tan-producing plants, and trees and lianas from which rubber can be extracted. At present they furnish mahogany, cedar, ebony, and guayacum. The balsam and the wood of the copahu tree, kola nuts, cinchona bark, Tonquin beans, or Sarrapia, are also exported.

The most important forest products are India rubber, of which, in 1909-1910, 32 700 kg. (71 940 lbs) were exported ; and balata gum (1), of which 1 996 000 kg. (4 391 200 lbs.) were exported. For tanning purposes dividivi is exported and a small quantity of mangrove bark.

1090

YVES HENRY. **Agriculture in the Mono Region, Dahomey.** — (Etude économique de la région du Mono, Dahomey). *L'Agriculture pratique des pays chauds*, 11ᵉ année, N. 96, pp. 194-205. Paris, mars, 1911.

French West Africa: Dahomey

This region, lying between the rivers Mono and Cuffo and Lake Ahémé, has been studied to ascertain whether its agricultural possibilities and present modes of transport would justify the construction of a railway. The present elements of traffic are the annual crops, of maize, earth-nuts and manioc, and the products of the oil-palm. The region forms part of two river basins and is subject to periodical inundations. The soils suitable for cultivation belong to three different formations, of varying value:

1) The soil «de barre» a superficial formation, forms the greater part of the cultivated land. In the Sahué country it varies very much in value; and while in the western and southern parts of the plateau the soil is excellent, in the east it is unfertile. On the Locossa Parahué it seems more homogeneous and more fertile, and is light, permeable, and often rich in humus.

2) Alluvial soils deposited by the Mono in its immediate neighbourhood. These recent deposits are inundated during part of the year and form very deep sandy and organic loam, of great fertility.

3) Plastic clay, covering the greater part of the depression, which forms, to the north of the Sahué plateau, an immense marsh in the rainy season.

The total extent of soil fit for cultivation is calculated at 75 000 (185 250 acres) hectares, of which 50 000 (123 500 acres) may be classed as fertile, and very fertile; and 25 000 hectares (61 750 acres) as average and middling.

Palms cover about 13 000 ha. (32 110 acres) growing in thick plantations, generally connected with villages, especially in the Athiémé Locossa region. The fertile alluvial soils are particularly adapted to the oil-palm.

The population, in this region of the Mono, is calculated to be about 50 000.

---

(1) *Balata*: rubber produced by *Mimusops*, a genus of Sapotaceae. The principal exports from Venezuela in 1909 had the following values in *bolivars* (1 bolivar is approximately equal to 1 franc): Coffee, 39 736 538 bolivars; Cocoa, 18 073 477; Balata and Rubber 8 468 280; Hides, 7 148 430; Cattle 1 160 367 bolivars. *The Statesman's Yearbook, 1911*, p. 1323. *(Ed.)*.

The production of maize that might be exported may be calculated at 15 000 tons approximately ; there might be also an important traffic in yams and manioc, but no precise data exist as to probable quantities. Taking the 13 000 hectares under palm trees as a guide, the palm kernels may be calculated át 10 500 tons, and the oil at 3 500 tons. The principal traffic would thus be :

	15 000	tons of maize,
	10 500	» palm-kernels.
	3 500	» palm-oil.
Total	29 000	tons.

The actual traffic amounts to 5000 tons, only about a sixth of the possible production. The Mono is an intermittent river, only utilisable for transport during floods ; bought produce has therefore to be stored, with consequent loss of time and money. The industry and commerce of this fertile region are thus completely paralysed by the deficiency of roads and means of communication.

P. Dussert. **Agriculture in Mayotte and the Comoro Islands.** (L'Agriculture à Mayotte et aux Comores). — *L'Agriculture pratique des pays chauds*, 11ᵉ année, N. 96, pp. 206-214. Paris, Mars 1911.   **1091**

The Comoro Islands and Mayotte cover about 260 000 hectares. (642 200 acres) These islands are in the early stage of colonisation, when a harmonious and profitable relation has still to be established between colonists and natives. Sugar, vanilla, perfume plants, fibre plants, tobacco, oil-producing plants, and India rubber are all grown, and should in time make these islands a prosperous colony.   **Mayotte and Comoro Islands**

Mr. Dussert gives the exportation figures for Mayotte, from 1903 to 1908, which show that from 21 to 27 thousand kg. (46 000 lbs to 59 000 lbs) of vanilla are regularly exported, and sugar, coffee, rum and cacao in smaller quantities. In 1908,6 755 litres (11 888.8 pints) of perfume essences were exported, and 59 275 litres (104 324 pints) of rum.

Anjouan also possesses the necessary elements for prosperous agriculture ; provided that energetic measures be taken against deforestation, and that no pretext be given to the natives to emigrate. Coffee and cloves might be grown with profit. In 1908, 2 691 kg. (5 920 lbs) of vanilla and 262 596 kg. (577 711 lbs) of sugar were exported (1).

---

(1) The island of Anjouan possesses numerous wild varieties of the genus *Citrus* See 855 of this *Bulletin*, March, 1911.

The little island of Moheli has soil like that of Mayotte, but is gradually being ruined by deforestation. It exported in 1908 11 360 kg. (24 992 lbs) of vanilla, 94 200 cocoa-nuts, 28 250 kg. (62 150 lbs) of manioc, etc.

Grand Comore has an area of about 105 000 hectares (259 350 acres), of which 35 000 (86 450 acres) are covered by recent lava streams from the crater of Kartala, where only scanty grass grows here and there. Forests cover 19 000 hectares (46 930 acres). A mountainous region of extinct volcanoes covers 25 000 hectares (61 750 acres) in the north and 2 000 hectares (4 940 acres) in the extreme south. The really fertile land lies along the coast and is from 2 to 5 kilometres (1.25 to 3.125 miles) wide. This belt covers about 40 000 hectares (98 800 acres), half of which are included in the lava streams above mentioned. In the east and south-east the soil is remarkably fertile. The flora of this island is rich in Rubiaceae ; the coffee of the Comoro Islands is *Coffea Humblotiana*, in which there is no caffeine. The wild vine abounds in the forests, and nearer the coast wild cotton is found.

The forests have considerable influence on the climate ; twice as much rain falls on the wooded mountain mass of Kartala as falls on the grassy slopes of the mountains in the north. The soil of the northern coast belt is too light for cereals, but the sugar-cane does very well there and sago-palm abounds.

Notwithstanding its " golden belt " of fertile soil, its 60 000 inhabitants, and its very healthy climate, Grand Comore, owing to the idleness of the natives, does not rise above a certain economic mediocrity. In 1908, 293 785 kg. (646 327 lbs) of physic nuts (1) and 50 100 coco nuts were exported.

---

(1) The physic nut is the seed of *Jatropha Curcas*, L. (French: *Médicinier de Barbades* or *Gros pignon d'Inde*) an Euphorbiaceous shrub of 1 to 2 metres in height, which grows in South America, India, and on the west coast of Africa. These seeds yield a fixed oil, with the same medicinal properties as the croton, though less pronounced. Great quantities are imported into Europe for soap-manufacture and lighting purposes.

See DUJARDIN-BEAUMETZ et EGASSE, *Les Plantes Médicinales*. Paris, 1889 p. 384.

Arnaudon and Ubaldini found 37 % of oil in physic-nuts containing 72 % of water.

In India, *Jatropha Curcas* in grown especially on the Coromandel Coast and in Travancore. Besides its medicinal uses the oil of the seeds is said to be used especially in the manufacture of certain transparent soaps, for dressing woollen cloths and as a good drying oil.

The leaves of *Jatropha Curcas* appear to be sometimes used in Assam to feed eri silk-worms when *Ricinus* leaves are scarce. GEO. WATT, *Dict of the Economic Products of India*, London, 1890, vol. IV. p. 545.   (*Ed.*).

RUSSELL. **The Development of Agriculture in Uganda.** *Brit. Colonial Reports Annual,* No. 670; Uganda Report for 1909-1910, pp. 1-42. London. February, 1911.

1092

The agricultural export trade from Uganda is increasing, especially that of cotton, hides, and rubber. The trade in chillies revived considerably during the year, and the export of ground nuts, ghee (clarified butter) and sesame seed was the highest ever known. The export of rubber, hides and goat skins was also the highest on record. The total quantity of rubber exported was 47 tons. The rubber is chiefly obtained from the West African rubber tree (*Funtumia elastica*). Amongst new articles of export which appear for the first time are bees-wax, cotton seed oil, and sesame oil.

Uganda

The total number of plants distributed by the Botanical Department during 1910 was 160 679, being 102 217 in excess of last year's distribution. The demand for Para rubber and cacao seeds from trees in the Botanic Gardens greatly exceeded the supply. Large numbers of seeds, principally of Para rubber, were imported direct by planters.

The Para rubber trees grow well and more quickly than Funtumia trees. The Castilloa rubber tree grows well, but it is subject to the attacks of a weevil (*Inesida leprosa* Tal.). *Manihot Glaziowii* grows very rapidly. Two new varieties, *Manihot dichotoma* and *Manihot pianhyensis* have been introduced : the former has made exceedingly rapid growth, and a few trees will be already productive in another year. The sisal fibre of Uganda is of excellent quality and readily saleable. The cultivation of *Mazzaqua* Maize has been a failure. It promises best in the two districts where a further experiment is to be carried out. The bees-wax industry promises to be a success, especially in the Masindi district.

Three assistant superintendents who have had experience in cotton-growing in Egypt, the United States and Ceylon were appointed to the Cotton Department. In 1908,56 tons of cotton seed were distributed by the Government, 35 tons of which were *Black Battler*, the rest was *Upland* seed. Variety, cultural and manurial tests have been commenced in selected plots throughout the Protectorate, but these tests are not sufficiently advanced to permit any definite statement of results.

Another important branch of the work now being carried on is the visiting of the various districts by the officers of the Cotton Department for the purpose of giving practical demonstrations to native growers. The rapidly increasing desire on the part of the na-

21

tives to cultivate cotton shows that the work which is being done in this direction is already bearing fruit. In the year 1904-05 the export of cotton amounted to 10 tons; in 1909-10 it was 2116 tons.

1093   F. MAIN. **Sanitary Regulations for Rice-Culture.** (La réglementation des rizières et l'état sanitaire dans les pays de riziculture). — *Journ. d'Agriculture tropicale*, No. 117, pp. 71-73. Paris, 31 mars, 1911.

Spain.
Italy.

After rapidly reviewing Spanish and Italian legislation for the protection of farmers and work-people exposed to fevers by the stagnation of water in rice fields, Mr. Main observes that this question will not be solved by hampering rice-growing, but by making rice fields healthy. He recalls the important communication of Professor Golgi at the Congress for Rice-culture at Pavia in 1906, and the many publications on the subject in the last years, especially in the United States. Prof. Golgi observes that malaria diminishes in rice-growing countries with the progress of sanitation and improved methods of culture, consisting principally in the substitution of running for stagnant water. When this is secured through better agricultural instruction and by the cooperation of irrigation companies and a public water supply, there need be no appeal to Boards of Health for protection against rice fields.

1094   **Paris Bureau for the Study of India Rubber.** (Création d'un service d'études du caoutchouc à Paris). — *Bulletin de l'Office Coloniale*, No. 40, pp. 119-121. Melun, avril, 1911.

International
Service:
Paris

The International Bureau of the Scientific and International Association for Colonial and Tropical Agriculture, in connection with the Colonial Office and Colonial Garden of Paris, has organised a service for the investigation of all questions connected with India-rubber. This service is divided into two Sections, the one for scientific and industrial investigation, the other for bibliographical documentation and for economic and cultural studies. The latter section besides collecting all documents and papers connected with rubber, also acts as an Intelligence Office for giving information to the public.

Butter-Control during 1910 in Holland. (Les stations de contrôle des beurres en 1910). — *Laiterie et Elevage*, 6ᵉ année, N. 8, p. 62. Louvain, avril, 1911.

1095

Netherlands

By the 31st. December, 1910, the total number of producers connected with the Stations for butter-control in the Netherlands was 880 ; the annual production of controlled butter is 43 405 000 kg. *i. e.* Assen, 3 900 000 kg. ; Deventer, 10 512 400 kg. ; Eindhoven, 5 150 000 kg. ; the Hague; 3 500 000 kg. ; Groningen, 2 000 000 kg.; Leenwarden, 14 333 600 kg.; Maestricht, 3 834 000 kg. and Middelburg, 155 000 kg, (1).

Union of the Agricultural Experiment Stations in Austria. (Gründung eines Verbandes der landw. Versuchsstationem in Oesterreich. — *Zeitschrift für das landw. Versuchswesen*, XIII, J. H. 9, pp. 755-757, H. 12, pp. 943-949; pp. 950-956. Wien, September, Dezember 1910.

1096

Austria

The German Agricultural Experiment Stations have long formed a Union for the better organising of their work; hitherto no such Union existed in Austria. It was suggested in 1897, but the institution of the Zeitschrift or Review of Agricultural Experimentation in Austria was the only result. In December 1910, fresh efforts were made, and the Union of the Austrian Experiment Stations was founded, with the following objects:

1. The laying down of rules for sampling and for analytical investigations.

2. The undertaking and carrying out of experiments, enquiries and other technical researches, according to one common plan.

3. Combating proceedings considered unfair or otherwise prejudicial to agriculture.

4. Exchange of ideas among the Agricultural Exp. Stations.

---

(1) The well organised butter control in the Netherlands, by favouring the production of butter of good and uniform quality, must contribute to the growing exportation of Dutch butter. The exportation of butter from the Netherlands in 1907 was valued at 29 397 000 guilders, and in 1908 at 33 072 000 guilders. (12 guilders = 1 £.; 1 kg. = 2.204 lb). The value of the butter exportation from the Netherlands is about double that of cheese exports. *The Statesman's Yearbook* for 1910, p. 1039. (*Ed.*).

5. The institution of umpires for settling questions of analysis and other professional differences.

For the furtherance of these objects the following methods have
been adopted :

1. Periodical meetings for the discussion of questions interesting the Union.

2. The editing and encouraging of publications.

3. A closer connection with land-owners, farmers and other
persons interested in agriculture.

It has also been decided to publish monthly, in the official
Review of the Union, reports on the more important observations
of members, to be communicated to the agricultural press. The
data will be furnished: by Dr Czavek for forage, by Dr Piez for fertilizers; by Dr Kornrauth for vegetable pathology and harmful
insects and for methods of control ; and by the Vienna Seed-Control
Station for seeds.

By the end of 1910, 17 Stations were included in the Austrian
Union, with a total of 73 members. Under the title, *Mitteilungen
des Verbandes der landwirtschaftlichen Versuchsstationen in Oesterreich*
it has already published (January and February 1911) reports on
Bernard Phosphate, « Phosphatose » (a French precipitated phosphate for cattle), an adulterated sulphate of ammonia, and the
forage called « Z. Futter ».

1097   M.P. PAPAGEORGIOU. **Hellenic Royal Society of Agriculture** — (La
Société Royale d'Agriculture Hellénique). — *Annales de Gem-
bloux*, p. 89. Bruxelles, 1er févr. 1911.

Greece   Agriculture is the principal source of prosperity in Greece, and
presents a great variety of products: raisins, wine, silk, olives, oil, honey, cereals, tobacco, cotton, sesame and other industrial cultures.
Fruits are in great variety: citrus fruits, grapes, figs, almonds, walnuts, chestnuts, pistachio nuts etc. Mules, horses, donkeys, cattle, pigs
sheep and goats are raised and there is some production of cheese
and butter. Bees are kept. But all these cultures and industries are
little developed, and require improvement and financial impulse.

With a view to developing and improving the agriculture of
the country, George I, King of the Hellenes, founded the *Royal Agricultural Society* in 1901.

An Administrative Council, composed of 36 members, chiefly
country land-owners and men with scientific, agricultural and industrial knowledge, form the active nucleus of the Society.

Generous donors at once came forward and the Government gives annual subsidies,so that the Society is now in a position to render real service to the agriculture of the country.

The Society has at present three Agricultural Stations; at Khalandry, near Athens; at Aigion, in the Peloponnesus, near Patras; and at Pharsala, in the centre of the vast grain-growing plains of Thessaly.

The Station at Khalandry is chiefly for arboriculture; several thousand fruit trees, mulberry trees for sericulture, etc. are distributed yearly in all the provinces of the kingdom. A great variety of trees are collected and studied at this Station. A special department for sericulture, and for silkworm rearing is annexed to this Station.

The Station at Aigion is also arboricultural, with some specialisation for citrus fruits, and for improving the culture of raisin grapes.

The Station at Pharsala is of recent institution. Its special province is the culture of cereals, tobacco etc. It attends to the breeding of an early wheat, resistant to drought and to the scorching west wind, called *Livas*, from which crops often suffer.

These Stations study the acclimatisation of new economic plants, such as *Chloris Gayana* (a forage plant for dry regions) (1), the *Caravonica* cotton plant, and Egyptian and American varieties of cotton; varieties of barley for malt, etc.

The Hellenic Agricultural Society has also annexed to these Agricultural Stations stud stations where are kept pure-bred Arab stallions, donkeys from Cyprus for mule-breeding, of special importance to the country, Yorkshire and Berkshire boars, rams from the islands of Chios, Skopelos and Zante, Maltese and Angora rams. Some of the stallions are sent at the covering season round the districts where horses are bred. Stud books are kept.

Honey is an important product in Greece; and the Society opened a School of Bee-keeping in 1901, at Khalandry, under the direction of W.G. Toufexis. This school has given an important impulse to the industry, and already a great number of frame-hives, are in use. The Khalandry school has succeeded in organising agricultural statistics in the country.

In its offices at Athens the Society has organised: 1. a Service for Agricultural Information on all agricultural questions: Field work, stock-breeding, arboriculture, sericulture, olive oil production, vineculture and wine-making, bee-keeping, raisin production, determina-

---

(1) On experiments with *Chloris Gayana*, see this Bulletin Nov. 1910. p. 58. and Febr. 1911, n. 446.

tion of crop diseases and methods for prevention and control, land-reclamation, etc.

2. A Service of Agricultural Statistics, collected with the cooperation of the mayors, teachers, agriculturists, etc. This service is becoming gradually more important, as hitherto the agricultural statistics were very defective.

3. A permanent Exhibition of agricultural implements and produce. Through the Society agricultural machines and implements and seed may be obtained at a reduction.

4. The Society issues a Bulletin and occasional leaflets.

Annual Agricultural Shows, are organised, such as the Cheese Show last October, which has given an impulse towards improvement in cheese making.

Direct encouragement is given to all kinds of agricultural institutions, and the Society has instituted Committees for propaganda in the different parts of Greece.

Finally, the Society takes up questions of general agricultural utility and by presenting reports to Government helps to forward the interests of agriculture.

1098

P. J. BROUNOV. **The Russian Bureau of Agricultural Meteorology. Meteorological Critical Periods and Crop-growing. Agricultural Forecasting.** (Kratkii Otcerk Dieiatelnosti Meteorologhitceskago Biuro sa Vremia Ego Sutstcestvovaniéa). — S. Peterburg, 1910.

Russia

The Russian Bureau of Agricultural Meteorology began its work, in 1896, by organising, at the national exhibition of Nixegorod, a section for agricultural meteorology. A number of diagrams and data were here brought together on the relation existing between meteorological factors and the life of cultivated plants.

The study of this material showed the existence, for each plant, of a " critical period, " which varies according to climate, soil, methods of culture, etc. ; and on the presence of a particular group of meteorological factors during this critical period depends the success or failure of the crop. For instance: for the most important meteorological factor, *rain*, the critical period for wheat and rye is immediately after sowing ; for buckwheat, during flowering. Hence the utility of determining exactly this period in different parts of Russia, in order to regulate the choice of early or late varieties, of fertilisers (for instance, potassium nitrate hastens ripening), of time for sowing, etc., enabling the farmer to make the critical period coincide with the time of year most favourable to the life of the plant.

The answers, filled in by private persons, to sets of questions put by the Meteorological Bureau furnished too few and too uncertain data for so complex an undertaking. M. Brounov therefore, in 1907, organised a network of meteorological Agricultural Stations throughout the Empire. In these Stations the action of meteorological factors on the soil, on the growth of cultivated plants and on the life of domestic animals is studied.

In each Station an uninterrupted series of observations is carried out: on the modes of growth of cultures in the experimental field ; on the moisture of the soil and of the atmosphere ; on actinometry, evaporation, rainfall, penetration of frost in the soil, etc.

In 1904 the Bureau began to arrange the material supplied by the Stations, and in 1908 published a first work: " The action of meteorological factors on the growth of oats in the Tchernoziom, or " black soils, " the more important conclusions in which are here summarised ;

1. The " critical period " for oats, in relation to rain, comes on all black soils at the moment immediately preceding the appearance of the inflorescence.

2. During the first period of vegetation, cold does not hurt the crop; indeed, by prolonging the period of vegetation, cold strengthens the plant and raises the yield.

3. Frosts, and cold in general, do no harm during the first period, but become dangerous after the appearance of the shoots; the later they occur, the greater the danger. When the stools are already formed, a fall of temperature to —5° C is always fatal.

4. Observations on soil moisture are a good guide, better than rainfall observations, in regard to crop forecasts. If the soil moisture falls below 10 to 14 % before the appearance of the inflorescence the effect is always harmful.

5. The conditions of climate, and therefore the growth of oats, are not uniform all over the black-soil region, which from this point of view may be divided into an eastern and a western zone.

6. In the western zone, the abundant June rains are very favourable to the growth of oats; but the farther towards the east the more uncertain becomes the forecast for this crop.

Wheat, rye, millet and maize have been studied from the same point of view.

Not only on plants but also on domestic animals atmospheric changes have an influence. " The action of meteorological factors on the composition of cows' milk in Siberia " has been studied by M. Jefremov ; he found by numerous methodical observations that thunder storms in summer and tempests in winter reduce the fat-content of milk by 0.2 to 1 %.

The critical period is determined by calculating the average value of constant factors ; and these averages must serve as a guide in choice of varieties and of methods of culture best suited to given conditions. Weather forecasts determined by these data may be valuable to the farmer, enabling him to hasten or delay operations, and to protect his crops against foreseen dangers.

A method of forecasts has gained ground in Russia, based upon observations on the colours of the sky at twilight and at dawn, the forms of the clouds, etc. The Bureau has published some interesting notes on this subject: *Weather forecasts according to the colours of the atmosphere.*

The Bureau has also published numerous studies on the action of climate on soil, according to which Russia has been divided into geographico-agricultural zones. An atlas of agricultural meteorology has been published, besides many papers on the character and causes of meteorological phenomena that are harmful to agriculture. These papers, drawn up in clear language and distributed among the rural population, enable them to be on their guard against frosts, black fogs and other meteorological dangers.

1099   F. CHARLAN. **Experimental Stations for the Growing - of Tobacco in Canada.** — *Department of Agriculture, Ottawa, Canada. Tobacco Division Bulletin.* N. A-9, Ottawa, Ont., April, 1910.

Canada :
Quebec
Ontario

Considering the rapid growth of tobacco culture in Canada within the last few years, and the good prospects for the Canadian product, which will henceforth be admitted in the manufactures of the Dominion on equal footing with its foreign competitors, the Dominion Minister of Agriculture established in 1909 experimental tobacco growing stations in the chief districts where this industry is carried on. Their object is to study how tobacco culture can be made more profitable in Canada; to demonstrate the value of proper methods; to create improved strains, and produce seeds, for general distribution in Canada; and to test new foreign varieties.

There are now three experimental stations. Two are in the province of Quebec, one at St. Jacques l'Achigan (county of Montcalm) the other at St. Césaire (county of Rouville). They cover about ten acres each. The third is in the province of Ontario, about a mile from Harrow (county of Essex) ; it covers an area of about twenty-seven acres.

These stations are placed in the centre of the different tobacco-growing districts, each under different climatic conditions. At the present time Quebec produces chiefly pipe tobaccos, of the « seed leaf », type, while Ontario grows pipe and chewing tobaccos of the « Burley » type. Experiments with Virginia tobacco have been carried on in the county of Essex during the last few years and special attention was given to this variety at the Harrow Station. A three-years rotation, comprising tobacco, grain, and clover, has been started to restore the fertility of these lands long considered as inexhaustible. Special attention was given to better aeration of the seed-beds. Experiments showed that good results may be obtained from the combined use of farm manure and commercial fertilizers. A new variety has been introduced, which will be pretty generally grown in the province of Quebec as soon as the quantity of seed harvested is sufficient for general distribution. The Hybrid Comstock × Sumatra, started in 1908 at St. Césaire by Mr Chevalier, superintendent of the Quebec stations, is much larger in size and a heavier yielder than the Comstock Spanish ; the leaf has a finer texture and a better shape ; it is also earlier and more easily cured. This tobacco is sure to become the special type of the province of Quebec, for it seems to be adapted to a great variety of soils. On the comparatively heavy loam of the St. Jacques station, the texture of the product was as fine as on the light loams of St. Césaire. Experiments will be continued in Quebec on the following types : For « wrappers », the Hybrid Comstock × Sumatra; for « fillers », Hazlewood or other Cuban varieties ; for cut tobaccos (pipe and cigarette) Big Ohio. Grown on suitable soils, these varieties will ensure the prosperity of the tobacco growers. The St. Césaire Station is situated in a comparatively new district where the land is in better condition for the growing of tobacco than in the northern district. The summer is milder and the rainfalls are more frequent and more regular. The proportion of light soils is also greater, at least in those parts where the growing of tobacco has been carried on.

In 1909 the varieties grown at the St. Césaire station were : the Comstock Spanish, the Brewer Hybrid, and the Hazlewood.

The county of Essex in South Ontario where the Harrow Station is situated is largely given to the growing of Burley ; this is a large heavy yielding tobacco rather slow in maturing. The climatic conditions of that part of Canada are very favourable to it, and the growing of the Burley is one of the most prosperons industries in South Ontario. A few black tobaccos are grown on a small scale by a few planters. Some aromatic varieties, suitable for « fillers » (Cuban, Hazlewood, Big Havana) were tested this year at this

Station. The Virginia variety, of relatively recent introduction and requiring a special curing process demands like the Burley, a long and warm summer to become sufficiently ripe, but it requires an entirely different soil. The soil must be sandy, or slightly gravelly, very permeable, and contain as small a proportion of lime as possible. Soils of this nature are sometimes met with in the southern part of the county of Essex, but they must be carefully selected.

The Virginia will not only give the grower as good cash returns as the Burley if not better, but grown on a moderate scale in place of the latter, it will enable the grower to avoid the over-production of Burley which has occured in some years. It will fill a real want of the Canadian manufactures, and although the product obtained is sometimes only second grade, it will nevertheless always be able to replace the same product at present imported from the Southern States. The chief characteristic of the flue-cured Virginias is their bright colour obtained and fixed by a special process.

1100   **Report of the Botanic Station of Dominica.** — *Nature*, London, March 16, 1911.

Leeward
Isles:
Dominica
From the Report of the Botanic Station and Agricultural School of Dominica for 1909-1910 it appears that more than 79 000 plants were sent out during the year as well as large numbers of seeds. The experiments with economic plants include, among others, trials with spineless limes, varieties of citrus plants, Para rubber, and grafted cacao. The lime industry appears to be well established, and the conditions of production are steadily improving. Para rubber continues to do well in the wet districts of the island. Much remains to be done in improving the cacao industry; it is considered that the yield might be considerably higher if better methods were more generally used.

1101   **The Experimentation in the Oasis of Gafsa, Tunis.** (Le Jardin d'essais dans l'Oasis de Gafsa). — *La Quinzaine Coloniale*, N. 7, p. 245 Paris, 10 avril 1911.

Tunis:
Gafsa
The Tunisian Department of Agriculture has laid out an experimental field of 1.26 hectares in the Oasis of Gafsa with a training school annexed. The experiments will be made with market-garden produce and fruit trees, in order to lead the natives to cultivate varieties, that would find a ready market in the country. At pre-

sent the inhabitants of the oasis grow chiefly a poor sort of apricot which they dry in the sun and sell occasionally. There are numerous groves of olives in the oasis, of inferior quality and badly managed. The experiments should be the more convincing, seeing that the water for irrigation will be taken from a well with water of inferior quality to that of the *Oued* used by the natives.

HENNET. **Agricultural Instruction in the Canton of Berne, Switzerland.** 1102
— (Das landw. Unterrichtswesen im Kanton Bern). - *Mitteilungen der Fachberichterstatter des k. k. Ackerbau-ministeriums*, N. 7, pp. 49-52. Wien, 1911.

There are in Switzerland 243 710 agricultural holdings of over 0.5 **Switzerland** hectares. For every 244 farms there is 1 pupil attending the agricultural schools. Excluding the farms below 3 hect., there is 1 pupil for every 144 farms.

A project for agricultural instruction on a large scale has been presented in the Canton of Berne. This Canton has already: an Agricultural School at Rütti, with a two years course; a Winter School, also at Rütti, with branches at Langenthal and Munsingen; a French Winter School at Porrentruy and a Dairy School for cheese-making, at Rütti. The Canton contributes besides: to the School for Pomology, Vine-culture and Horticulture at Wädenswil; to the School for Horticulture at Châtelaine-Genève and to the School of Gardening for Women at Niederlenz.

By the proposed law the Canton of Berne must maintain the Annual School of Agriculture, the School for Cheese-making and as many Winter schools as may be necessary. The Canton must also provide for special courses of agricultural instruction, for travelling teachers, for inspectors in the dairy and breeding industries, and for the education of technical experts in agriculture and dairying.

The Annual Agricultural School has developed considerably since the institution of winter schools. The pupils receive complete practical instruction.

The law provides for the institution of markets for breeding animals and cattle for the butcher, and for seeds; for agricultural shows, etc. (1).

(1) On the expenditure in Switzerland for Agricultural Education, See this Bulletin, No. 1080 and No. 1, Jan. 1911. (*Ed.*).

1108   ALPERA. **Rural Schools in Spain.** (La Escuela Rural en España) *Boletin Oficial de la Camara del Ampurdan*, n. 257, p. 83. Figueras 15 de Marzo de 1911.

Spain   In studying the organisation of rural Schools in Spain, Mr. Alpera proposes that agricultural instruction be rendered obligatory to all boys and girls, and that the teaching be done by means of a garden annexed to each School. Itinerant teaching is proposed with the institution throughout the country of agricultural museums and lending libraries.

1104   **Agricultural School in Yucatan.** — *Bulletin of the Pan-American Union.* Vol. XXXII, N. 1, p. 171. Washington. Jan., 1911.

Mexico :
Yucatan   The Ministry of " Fomento ' (*i. e.* Agriculture and Commerce) acting conjointly with the Governor of Yucatan, is about to establish an agricultural school in the State of Yucatan. This step is in accordance with the movement for the founding of these schools throughout the Mexican Republic, so that the vast area of vacant land in Mexico may be made more productive.

In connection with the agricultural school there will be a department for instruction in the various crafts. The entire institution will be known as the Lorenzo Ancona Castillo School, and will be in charge of a president to be elected annually.

It is hoped that the school may be in operation by next winter (1).

1105   **Promoting Agriculture in Tunis.** — (Enseignement agricole et distribution de graines en Tunisie). *Dépêche Tunisienne.* Tunis, 22. févr. 1911.

Tunis   The scheme for agricultural experimentation, by the Direction of Agriculture, provides for field experimentation and for the agricultural education of the natives. A Mohammedan teacher must assist in itinerary lecturing and in the distribution of seeds.

---

(1) For the labour and cultural conditions of Yucatan, see : JOHN KENNETH TURNER, *Mexico*, London, 1911. See also *The Nation*, London, April 29, 1911, p. 172.   (*Ed.*).

R. Chierici. **Value of a Sicilian Vineyard, with Vines grafted**   **1106**
on American Stocks. (Calcolo del Capitale-Terra di un ettaro
di vigneto su legno americano in Sicilia nelle zone litoranee della
Val di Noto). — *L'Agricoltura Italiana*, Anno XXXVII, fasc. 694,
pp. 193-203. Pisa, 16 Aprile, 1911.

The writer observes that the technical and economic conditions   Italy:
of Sicilian vine-growing are radically transformed since the appear-   Sicily
ance of phylloxera.   Vineyards are now nearly all reconstituted
in Sicily, and the writer, after studying those of the coast region
of the Val di Noto, finds that valuation of the new vineyards
must be based on quite different data from the old.   The new data
must refer to:
   a) the cost of planting the American stocks, of grafting, and
of the care entailed ;
   b) the shorter time to be allowed for the vegetation cycle
of the vine, and therefore for the period of variation in the revenue.
   Calculations were made for five different stations, taking into
consideration : that the annual cost of cultivation and plantation
remains constant, whatever may be the sale price of the products ;
that the yearly deductions, within certain limits, may be calculated
at a constant percentage ; finally taking 15 frs. as the average sale
price, per hectolitre, of sweet wine.   These calculations show the
net receipts per hectare to be 184.44 frs. and the value represented
by the land 3688 frs. per hectare.
   Comparing the results obtained with 10 frs. and with 15 frs.
as the value of the hectolitre, it is seen that for every extra franc
on the sale price of the wine, from 10 frs. upwards, the net receipts increase by 22.236 fr. and the land-value by 444.72 frs. per
hectare.

Improving Farms in New York State. — New York Land Bulletins.   **1107**
American Agriculturist, New York, April 8, 1911.

   The New York State Department of Agriculture undertook five   United
years ago the work of reclaiming neglected or deserted farms of the   States:
State.   New York
   Descriptions of 2 500 such farms were gathered and published
in a first Bulletin stating the prices.   Up to January 1, 1911,
$ 6 200 000 have been paid to owners of farms sold through the
publicity afforded by the Department ; and $ 3 000 000 to owners

of non-advertised farms by persons who had been attracted by the descriptions published in the bulletins.

According to the fifth Bulletin there are now 1 100 farms for sale or hire in New York State. These aggregate 148 170 acres and the owners value them at $ 4 734 742, an average of $ 31.75 an acre.

During 1910 Commissioner Pearson received no less than 14 000 letters from western farmers inquiring about these farms. These show that the advantages of raising meat and fruit are being recognised as well as the importance of pastures.

The soil for apples cannot be excelled in any part of the country and millions of fruit trees have recently been planted in the Susquehanna and Hudson valleys. Some of the best fruit lands are in Schoharie county and can be had for $ 20 an acre. The new State Bulletin contains descriptions of purchaseable farm land in 50 of the 61 counties of the State.

Agriculture.
Agricultural Physics, Chemistry, and Botany.

1108   L. LINDET. **Selective Power of Vegetable Cells in Presence of Dextrose and Levulose.** — (Sur le pouvoir électif des cellules végétales vis-à-vis du dextrose et du lévulose). *C. R. de l'Acad. des Sciences*, T. 152, No. 12. 20 Mars, 1911, pp. 775 Paris.

France   The writer showed, in 1900, that the cells in the leaves and stalks of beet, in contact with the two sugars which constitute inverted saccharose, absorb in preference dextrose, when the conditions are especially favourable to respiration, the dextrose being decomposed; on the other hand levulose serves especially to form new cellular tissue. Similar results have been obtained by Mr. Lindet in studying the selective power of yeast cells, of germinating embryos and of aerobic fungi. Yeast can vegetate both in dextrose and in levulose solutions, levulose appearing more favourable to growth and reproduction, while dextrose is decomposed and oxidised.

Studying the vegetation of embryos of barley and of haricot beans, grown on cotton wool soaked with Raulin's nutritive solution (1), it was shown that if this solution contains inverted sucrose, the seedlings decompose dextrose more rapidly than levulose. If, on the other hand, the Raulin solution contains only levulose, or only dextrose, it is seen that the weight of shoots and rootlets developed in the levulose solution is about double the weight of the seedlings grown in the dextrose solution, when these dry weights are referred to the same weight of sugar that has been decomposed.

Similar conclusions are reached with cultures of aerobic fungi, as *Aspergillus niger*, *Penicillium glaucum*, and *Leuconostoc*. For growth and reproduction, the fungi prefer levulose, while dextrose is consumed in respiration. If cultivated in Raulin's solution, containing inverted sugar, these moulds at first decompose dextrose and levulose about equally; but gradually, as the mould extends over the surface, and as aerobic conditions become dominant, the dextrose is rapidly decomposed, in a proportion that is about 2.5 the quantity of the levulose decomposed at the same time. It is levulose that contributes chiefly and directly to increase the dry weight of the mould crop.

L. MASSOL. **Action of Ultra Violet Rays on Starch.** — (Action des radiations ultraviolettes sur l'amidon). *C. R. de l'Acad. des Sciences*, T. 152, N. 13, pp. 902-904. Paris, 27 mars, 1911.   1109

Solutions containing 2 % to 1 % of soluble starch (prepared by heating ordinary starch for 3 hours at a temperature of 150° C.) were exposed to the action of a mercury vapour lamp, and it was seen that the starch rapidly loses the property of giving the blue reaction with iodine, while it increases in reductive action on Fehling's solution, passing through the same degrees of trasformation observed when starch changes to sugar under the influence of diastase. The reducing sugar thus formed, under the action of ultra-violet rays, appears to be maltose. This transformation must be due solely to photo-chemical action, for the temperature of the solutions exposed to the mercury lamp did not rise above 30° C.   France

(1) Raulin's solution is prepared by dissolving in 1500 grams of water, the following compounds, in grams: Sugar, 70 ; Tartaric acid, 4 ; Ammonium nitrate, 4 ; Ammonium phosphate, 0.60 ; Potassium carbonate, 0.60 ; Magnesium carbonate, 0.40 ; Ammonium sulphate 0.25 ; Zinc sulphate, 0.07 ; Ferrous sulphate, 0.07 ; Potassium silicate, 0.07.   (*Ed.*).

1110   G. ANDRE'. **Variation in Dry matter and Distribution of Mineral Constituents and of Nitrogen in an Annual Plant.** — Conservation des matières salines chez une plante annuelle ; répartition de la matière sèche, des cendres totales et de l'azote). — *C. R. de l'Acad. des Sciences*, T. 152, n. 12, pp. 777-780. Paris, 20 mars, 1911.

France

These experiments were made on the poppy (*oeillette, Papaver somniferum*), determining the variations in the dry weight of the plant, in the total ash, and in the quantity of nitrogen during successive periods of growth .These investigations led to the following conclusions:

1). The absolute dry weight of all the organs increases regularly; only in the case of the leaves a slight diminution was observed, due to increased respiratory action.

The absolute weight of total ash also increases regularly in all the parts of the plant, except in the leaves, where a slight diminution, of about 5 %, is observed in the last period of growth.

2) The weight of total nitrogen in the roots increases at first till July 13th, then continues to diminish till August 9th, the nitrogen evidently emigrating towards the stalks and the flowers. On August 23rd a new increase of nitrogen in the root, up to a maximum, is observed ; this proves that the plant has continued to absorb nitrogen from the soil, and to accumulate it in its organism, even when fructification is nearly accomplished.

The relative weight of nitrogen regularly decreases during growth, increasing only towards August 23rd. In the stalks the absolute quantity of nitrogen goes on increasing till the end of vegetation, although the relative weight of this element continues regularly to diminish.

In the leaves of the poppy, the absolute weight of nitrogen increases until the time of flowering (13th July), then diminishes till the end of vegetation. The relative weight of nitrogen in the leaves diminishes regularly during all the life of the plant.

In the fruits the absolute weight of nitrogen increases very rapidly during ripening, but its relative weight varies slightly.

The migratory variations of phosphoric acid are more regular than those observed in the case of nitrogen. The variations in the quantities of potash appear to follow very closely on those of nitrogen.

G. ANDRÉ. **Conservation of Saline Constituents and their Distribu-**   **1111**
tion in an Annual Plant. — (Conservation des matières sa-
lines chez une plante annuelle ; répartition des éléments fixes).
C. R. de l'Acad. des Sciences, T. 152, N. 14, pp. 865-967. Paris,
3 avril, 1911.

As in the preceding paper, the observations were made on the   **France**
poppy, in the following periods of its growth : I.) June 13th 1910 ;
II.) June 28th, during budding ; III.) July 13th, during flowering ;
IV.) August 9th, when the fruits were nearly ripe ; V.) August 23rd,
at complete maturity. The organs examined separately were the
roots, the stems, the leaves, and the fruits, in each of which, during
the five periods of growth the dry weight, phosphoric acid, and
potash and other mineral constituents were determined.

Some of the conclusions are given in the preceding paper. The
absolute weights of calcium and magnesium increase regularly in all
the organs. As in the case of nitrogen, during all its vegetation, the
poppy has lost none of its fixed constituents. Some saline constituents, however, may be carried away by leaching, or rather by
exosmosis. The conditions that affect the exosmosis of some alkaline
constituents of plants are not yet well understood.

DANGEARD. **On Chlorophyll Assimilation in the Cyanophyceae.** —   **1112**
(Sur le conditions de l'assimilation chlorophyllienne chez les
Cyanophycées). *C. R. de l'Acad. des Sciences*, T. 152, N. 14,
pp. 967-969. Paris, 3 Avril, 1911.

By means of changes in growth, it is possible to obtain a photo-   **France**
graphic registration of the rays which produce chlorophyll-synthesis (1).

This method has been applied to organisms in which chlorophyll is mixed with other pigments, as in some Cyanophyceae (*Oscil-
laria* and *Phormidium*). It has been proved that with these algae
there is no maximum of growth within the limits of the green rays ;
in the case of Phormidium growth is especially favoured near the
infra-red limit of the spectrum.

The Cyanophyceae therefore utilise for growth the orange and the
infra-red rays : a step in the direction of the Sulphurariae. In the
case of Sulphurariae, the Sulphur algae, the dark heat rays beyond
the line A of Frauenhofer attract the algae and are doubtless utilised
for their growth.

(1) See this *Bulletin*, Feb. 1911, N. 382.   (*Ed.*).

1113   F. Kövessi. **On the Question of the Assimiliation of free Atmo-spheric Nitrogen by means of special Hairs in Plants.** — (Nouvelles recherches sur la prétendue utilisation de l'Azote de l'Air par certains poils spéciaux des plantes). *C. R. de l'Acad. des Sciences*, T. 152, N. 13, pp. 888-890. Paris, 27 mars, 1911.

Hungary   Mr. Jamieson and, later, Messrs. Zemplèn and Roth, observed on certain plants special hairs to which they attribued the properties of absorbing the free nitrogen of the air and producing albuminoid matter.

    Preceding researches of Mr. Kövessi (*C. R. de l'Acad. des Scienc.*, T. 159, p. 56, 1909) did not confirm this opinion. On two sets of plants, one set cultivated in the open air, and the other in an atmosphere from which nitrogen was excluded, these hairs showed the same development and produced exactly the same reactions.

    By still more rigorous experiments, made with cuttings of *Robinia Pseudacacia, Robinia hispida, Ribes Grossularia, Aesculus Hippocastanum, Acer platanoides, Acer pseudoplatanus*, Mr. Kövessi has again shown that these hairs behave in exactly the same way in free air and in pure oxygen, whence he concludes :

    1) The hairs on cultivated plants, whether in the open air, or in an atmosphere from which nitrogen is excluded, develop in exactly the same way. The same may be said of the special hairs studied by Messrs. Jamieson, Zemplèn and Roth ;

    2) Hairs taken from organs of the same age and state of development, when treated with the reagents that show the presence of albuminoids, gave exactly the same results ;

    3) These experiments sufficiently prove that the nitrogen in these albuminoid substances is not derived from the air.

1114   F. Scurti and G. Tommasi. **On the Formation of Fatty Matter in Olives.** — (Sulla formazione del grasso nei frutti oleaginosi). *Rendiconti della Società Chimica Italiana*, Serie II. Vol. III, fasc. IV. Roma, 1 Aprile, 1911.

Italy   Experiments have shown that the fatty matters formed in oil-fruits, such as olives, have neither the same origin nor the same biological function as the reserve materials in oily seeds. In fact, in green berries there is no migration of carbohydrates to justify the idea that their fatty acids are formed at the expense of carbohydrates. It has been proved by direct experiment that the fatty matter is not formed until after the fruit is completely developed.

Some olives were gathered on August 3rd., when no bigger than peas, and exhausted in ether, which only extracted mere traces of fats and remarkable quantities of oleanol, a waxy alcohol of which the molecule contains 31 atoms of carbon. The olives of a second gathering, 15 days later, contained oleanol in association with non-saturated fatty acids (oleic and linoleic) and saturated fatty acids. At the third gathering it was found that the fatty matter in the fruit is composed chiefly of the oil, which, by the 6th gathering, on October 20th, had acquired its normal properties.

It is thus seen that the formation of the fatty matter in the meso-carp of the olive is not analogous to the process in oily seeds. In the olive-berry the flesh seems to be an organ for the secretion of the waxy alcohol above-mentioned, which is an elaboration product of the leaves. This alcohol is destroyed as the fruit ripens. It is by a process of demolition of the molecule of these compounds so rich in carbon, transforming themselves successively into fatty acids, that the neutral fatty matter is finally formed.

E. VASSALLO. **Injecting of Plants with Mineral and Organic Substances.** — (Comportamento delle sostanze organiche ed inorganiche negli organismi vegetali) *Gazzetta Chimica Italiana*, Anno XLI, fasc. II and III, pp. 342-352. Roma, 17 Aprile, 1911.   1115

To facilitate research on the activity and the transformations of certain substances in plants, the writer began a series of experiments with specially constructed apparatus that enabled him to cause the absorption, under pressure, of solutions of these substances by roots.   Italy

The root is laid bare with precaution, the tip cut off and the indiarubber tube of the apparatus applied to the section and tied in place. The apparatus is a pump with a reservoir containing the solutions to be injected.

It was ascertained that all the liquid injected was absorbed and remained in the plant, without filtering out of the root tissues.

The first experiments showed that vigorous roots can support a pressure of more than 80 cm. of mercury. A plant may be made to absorb a large quantity of liquid by this means, and one important advantage of the system is that it admits of experiments being carried out upon plants in normal physiological conditions and large enough to yield considerable experimental data. The writer has already ascertained that the power of absorption increases with the diameter of the root injected and is highest when the activity of the plant is at its maximum.

1116   O. V. LIPPMANN. **Appearance of d. Galactose in Ivy-Berries.** —
(*Ber. chem. Ges.* XLIII, p. 3611, 1910). *Journ. de Pharmacie et de Chimie,* 103e année, 7e Série, T. III, N. 7, p. 358. Paris, 1er Avril, 1911.

Germany   After a sharp night frost in dry weather, after an autumn characterised by a constant high temperature, a mass of ivy presented a remarkable appearance. The most projecting berries, which had been most exposed to the frost, were covered with a white, brilliant substance which proved, on examination, to be d-galactose. Free sugar had hitherto been rarely found, and not with certainty, in ivyberries.

1117   N. IVANOFF. **Action of Stimulants on Plant Respiration.** (Die Wirkung der nützlichen und schädlichen Stimulatoren auf die Atmung der lebenden und abgetödeten Pflanzen). *Bio-chemische Zeitschrift,* 52 B. 1 H., pp. 94-96. Berlin, 1911.

Russia   It is known that the respiration of living plants is stimulated not only by nutritive matter but also by poisons. The identity of the result springs doubtless from different chemical reactions of the cells. In the first instance there is a reaction to nutrition, in the second, to poisoning. While the difference cannot be observed on living plants, the writer was able to observe it on dead plants.

Thus useful stimulating phosphates exert no influence on the respiration of living plants, but increase it in dead plants. Poisons, on the contrary, which are harmful stimulants, sometimes strongly excite the respiration of living plants, while on dead plants they either have no action, or they distinctly prevent respiration (quinine, urethane, according to the experiments of W. Palladin).

Thus, by eliminating the active principle that regulates living protoplasm it becomes more easy to determine clearly the stimulants useful or harmful to vegetable respiration.

1118   E. P. SANDSTEN. **Some Conditions which Influence the Germination and Fertility of Pollen.** *Twenty-fifth and Twenty-sixth Annual Reports of the Agricultural Experiment Station of the University of Wisconsin.* Research Bulletin N. 4 8vo, pp.VII + 52 + 228, (149-172). Madison, 1910.

United States: Wisconsin   This work is confined principally to a study of the pollen grain as affected by various external conditions, together with a brief presentation of its purely botanical relations. The principal conclusions arrived at may be summarized as follows :

1) The first noticeable change in the germination of the pollen grain is the swelling of the grain due to the absorption of water ; the rate of absorption depends on the temperature, concentration of the culture media and in some cases upon sunshine. The greater the concentration the less rapid is the absorption and germination. In these experiments the presence of diastase and invertase has been confirmed both in the pollen grains and in the tissues of the style and stigma.

2) Most pollen grains will germinate in a solution of cane sugar. The degree of concentration differs with the different species of plants. It is possible that this fact may to some extent be a barrier against a promiscuous cross-fertilization in Nature and in horticultural practice.

3) The vitality of pollen is not seriously affected by temperatures ranging from 25° to 55° C., in a dry atmosphere. Temperatures under 25° seriously interfere with germination. A temperature from 70° to 80° C. in a saturated atmosphere is fatal to the pollen of the peach, apple and plum. At a temperature of 40° to 50° C., in a saturated atmosphere, the pollen grains burst open in consequence of the rapid absorption of water and the number of burst grains increases with the temperature. This bursting of pollen grains actually takes place in masses of apple and plum pollen during warm spring rains. Freezing temperatures ranging from — 1.° 5 to — 1.° C. were not seriously injurious to the pollen of apple, pear and plum, while less than 50 per cent of peach and apricot pollen were killed by these low temperatures. The pistils of the species named were more susceptible to the low temperatures than pollen. Temperatures ranging from — 1.° 5 to 0° C. killed pistils.

4) Sunshine had little or no effect on the germination of pollen, or upon the growth of the pollen tube, in most plants. But the germination and growth of the pollen of the tomato is decidedly retarded by cloudy weather, and also the anthers of the tomato require a certain amount of sunshine for the proper development of the pollen. The same is true in several species of *Lilium*.

5) Bad culture and insufficient manuring in orchards greatly injures the production and fertility of pollen.

6) The longevity of apple, pear and plum pollen depends on the conditions in which it is kept. If kept in a dry place at a temperature ranging from 7° to 26° C., apple pollen can be kept for six months or longer, while only a small amount of plum pollen germinated after being kept for six months. Pollen may be safely

shipped from one part of the country to another without losing vitality or fertility.

7) Under favorable conditions it requires 9 to 32 hours for the pollen tube of apples, plums and cherries to reach the ovary when placed on the stigma. The stigma of apple flowers is receptive from 4 to 6 days, whether pollinated or not. Continuous rainy weather for days would probably prevent fecundation and result in the total failure of the crop.

1119   LUCIEN DANIEL. **Biometric Study of the Offspring of Grafted and Ungrafted Haricot Beans.** (Etude biométrique de la descendance de Haricots greffés et de Haricots francs de pied). *C. R. de l'Acad. des Sciences,* T. 152, N. 15, pp. 1018-1020. Paris, 10 avril, 1911.

France   In order to see whether the influence of the stock was perceptible in the offspring of black Belgian haricot beans grafted on the large white beans of Soissons, Mr. Daniel sowed in 1909, and again in 1910, seed from grafted plants. He formed five lots, of 1008 seeds each, and measured them in length, width and thickness. Comparing them with control seed of black Belgian ungrafted haricot beans, he found :

1) The degree of variation is the same as regards thickness, being sometimes smaller for the width ; sometimes greater and sometimes less for the length.

2) The dominant characters remained the same for width and thickness, and the graft seemed to have fixed the average type.

3) Speaking generally, the graft produced individual cases of variation, but the prevalent variation was sufficiently consistent to be attributed entirely to the influence of the stock on the offspring of the graft.

4) The diminution in size, noticed in the seeds of the grafted haricots, is very marked in their offspring.

As regards size of seed, therefore, a character acquired in consequence of grafting showed itself in these experiments to be remarkably hereditary.

1120   H. TEDIN. **Is the Proportion between Skin and Cotyledons specific in Peas ?** (Är skalhalten hos ärter en sortegenskap ?). *Sveriges Utsädesförenings Tidskrift,* A. XXI, H. 2, pp. 72-77. Malmö, 1911.

Sweden   In order to determine whether the relative weight of the skin of peas to their cotyledons is a hereditary character, Mr. Tedin examined 27 samples of 15 varieties of peas, 13 of which were of *Pisum* *sativum* and 2 of *Pisum arvense*. Except the variety *Victoria*, they were all pedigree varieties, raised at Svalöf. In 12 yellow varieties the differences were very slight ; in 2 others the differences for peas of the same sample were greater than for two different varieties, which shows that possible hereditary character will be difficult to discover.

In the *Concordia* variety Mr. Tedin observed a higher proportion of skin, due perhaps to the flattened form of these peas. The higher proportion of skin in field peas seems a specific quality.

The author confirms the relationship established by Fruwirth (1), that the smaller the pea the heavier is its skin. This, however, is only true among the individuals of a pure strain. The author states that this relationship is of no use in selection.

A. J. CELINZEV. **Criteria for the Establishment in Russia of Stations for Plant-Breeding**. — (Ob .orientirovanii Seleksionnekh Rabot po Economiceskim Raionam Selskago Khosiaistva). *Khosiaistvo (The Home)*, VI G., N. 9, pp. 263-269. Kiev, 3 mars, 1911.

1121

A lengthy article in which the conditions of European Russia are studied with a view to the establishment of Stations for Plant-Breeding. Russian territory is divided into eight different zones, according to the different conditions of the soils and of the development of agriculture. The writer especially recommends that besides the study of cereals attention be given to all kinds of forage crops, the importance of which is becoming daily greater in Russia.

Russia

F. B. GUTHRIE. **Testing Flours and breeding Wheats for « Strength ». The Present Position of the Flour Question**. (A paper read before the Sixth Federal Convention of Master Bakers of Australia, Sydney, October, 1910). *Agricultural Gazette of N. S. W.* Vol. XXII Part. 2, Sydney, February 2, 1911·

1122

The present position of the flour question may be summed up briefly in the statement that wheats that yield a strong flour, are not produced in quantities sufficient to supply the demand, coming especially from English millers, and command in consequence a high

Australia:
New South
Wales

---

(1) K. FRUWIRTH. *Das Schalengewicht der Hülsenfruchten, etc.* Fühling's Landw. Zeitung, 1898, h. 12.

price. In the principal wheat-producing countries, the United States, Canada, and India and in England itself, systematic efforts are being made to raise varieties possessing this important characteristic of flour strength in addition to other desirable qualities.

The Home-grown Wheat Committee appointed by the National Association of British and Irish Millers, consisting of practical millers and farmers, makes its chief object that of testing British wheats, and scientific experiments have been undertaken in the laboratories of Rothamsted and of Cambridge University. The same Association, after its recent meeting at Chester, passed a resolution affirming the desirability of establishing a National Cereal Selection Station.

Australia has done pioneering work in this direction, Mr. Wm. Farrer was the first to see the importance of selecting wheat for strength; he realised the value of wheats of the Fife class in perpetuating this characteristic and he relied on cross-fertilisation and selection rather than on selection alone in order to produce the required results.

In order to place the problem on a satisfactory basis, the British Home-grown Wheat Committee has arrived at the following definition of flour-strength: as « The capacity to make a big well raised loaf». What exactly determines this important quality is not accurately known and the only reliable test of the strength of a flour is its actual behaviour on baking. Several factors have been suggested as being responsible for strength of flour, such as the quantity of gluten, its chemical nature, amounts of sugar, of mineral constituents; but so far none of them have provided a satisfactory solution of the problem. The only test that has proved satisfactory is the « water-absorbing capacity » of the flour. Mr. Farrer's strong-flour wheats were submitted to this test, and were retained or rejected according as they gave flour of high water-absorbing power or not.

This quality in wheat is to some extent affected by environment, by the nature of the soil and climate, and particularly by the kind of weather during the ripening period of the grain. A hot and dry summer which rapidly ripens the grain after it is formed always increases flour strength. This flour strength is however an inherent characteristic of certain varieties, and soft wheats, though they may become stronger under hot and dry conditions, never attain the flour strength of the harder varieties. Flour strength is an inherited characteristic, and can be bred for just as colour, stiffness of straw, stooling, beards etc. can be bred for. It would appear that strength and weakness are Mendelian pairs and the breeding of strong-flour wheats becomes, in competent hands, an operation which can be regulated in the same manner as other characters.

Strength does not appear to be affected by manuring. Even nitrogenous fertilisers, which might be expected, by increasing the protein matter, to also increase the strength, appear to have no effect in this respect. It is doubtful whether any very great advantage is to be gained by breeding for increased gluten content alone. But flour-strength is almost invariably associated with fairly high gluten-content.

There is very little to choose in nutritive value between bread from strong or from weak flour ; but a given quantity of hard or strong flour provides more nutrition in the form of bread than does the same quantity of weak flour. (1).

P. REMLINGER. **On the Carriage to Great Distances of Samples of Water for Bacteriological Analysis.** — (Transport à grande distance des échantillons d'eau destinés à l'analyse bactériologique). *C. R. de l'Acad. des Sciences*, T. LXX, N. 12, pp. 468-469. Paris, 31 mars, 1911.

1123

The carriage of samples of water to great distances for bacteriological analysis is so difficult as to be sometimes not practicable. Mr. Remlinger succeeded several times in having water sent from Constantinople to Châlons, in France, and in analysing it before the multiplication of the germs set in.

France

Without having recourse to ice, which entails difficulties, this result was secured by adding sea-salt to the samples of water in the proportion of 10 %.

E. KAYSER. **Researches on the Extract of Beer Yeast.** — (Recherches sur le suc de la levure de bière). *See this Bulletin*, No. 1262.

1124
France

Nitro-culture for inoculating Lucerne and Clovers. (Press. Bulletin). *The Farmer's Advocate*, London, Ontario, April 6, 1911.

1125

During every season since 1905 the Bacteriological Laboratory of the Ontario Agricultural College has sent out to farmers bacteria cultures for inoculating seed of alfalfa and several clovers in order to aid in ensuring a more vigorous growth. Experience has shown that the most satisfactory method of inoculation is to apply the bacteria directly to the seed before sowing.

Canada :
Ontario

Last year there were 3375 of these bacteria cultures sent to 1881 farmers, and of 771 who returned reports, two thirds stated that the

(1) See this Bulletin, December 1910 p. 333 and January 1911, No. 93.
(*Ed.*).

inoculation of the seed had aided in securing a better crop. During
the present season the College will send cultures for the inoculation
of the following kinds of seeds : alfalfa, red or mammoth clover,
alsike clover, white clover, crimson clover, vetches, peas, beans, and
sweet ·peas. Each kind of seed requires a different bacteria culture.
The cultures are sent by post with full instructions for their use.

1126

L. RUDAUY. **Rainfall in France during 1910.** — (La pluie en France
en 1910). *La Géographie*, XXIII, N. 3, pp. 200-203. Paris,
10 mars, 1911.

France

The year 1910 was remarkably wet in France. In the following
table the rainfall for 1910 is compared with the average values,
the figures being those of the French Central Meteorological
Bureau. The places named are in widely different parts of France
and are in different physical conditions.

Locality	Rainfall in 1910 mm.	Average annual Rainfall mm.
Perpignan	559.4	501
Paris (Parc St. Maur)	750.3	565
Marseille	812.3	567
Toulouse	775.2	666
Dunkerque	669.9	716
Nantes	1045.7	wanting
Ste. Honorine du Fary (Calvados) . .	1062.0	wanting
Lyon	923.2	814
Brest	966.6	824
Bordeaux	1061.0	848
Besançon	1484.1	1108
Pic du Midi	2118.0	1490
Mont Ventoux	1455.1	1544
Puy de Dôme	2549.2	1586

1127

J. A. PULMAN. **Action of Weather and Moisture in Soil on the
Growth of Buckwheat.** (Opiti nad Vliianiem Meteorologhitceskikh
Uslovii na Proisrastanie Grecikhi). *Exegodnik Glavnago Upra-
vlenia Semlieustroistva i Semledielia po Departamentu Semledielia.
(Year-Book of the Administration of Rural Organisation and
Agriculture, Department of Agriculture).* G. III, pp.67-69. Peter-
burg. 1910.

Russia

Independently of the time of sowing and of the nature of the soil, if
there is sufficient rain in the period between the flowering and the for-

mation of the grain the yield will be good. In experiments at the Station of Borodizk this period was divided into two parts, the second beginning with the formation of the grain, the following correspondence being observed between the harvest and the weather:

During bad years, when the harvest was not more than 18 *pud*.

	1st half	2nd half
Temperature in the 24 hours	20.°1 C	21.°1 C
Nebulosity, %	42	42
Total rainfall, mm.	14.0	8.2

During good years, when the harvest varies between 40 and 80 *pud*.

	1st half	2nd half
Temperature in the 24 hours	18.°4 C	19.°3 C
Nebulosity, %	60	63
Total rainfall, mm.	34.2	39.0

When, after favourable conditions up to the period of flowering, the weather becomes too dry there will be a large production of straw but little grain. In the opposite case, the yield in straw will be less, that in grain higher.

Numerous pot experiments were made to determine the action of soil- moisture on the growth of buckwheat. The following table gives the results:

	Number of Pots			
	I	II	III	IV
Soil-moisture, % :				
From flowering to formation of grain . . .	34	34	25	24
From formation to maturity of grain . . .	24	34	34	24
Total crop, grams	3.90	5.74	3.62	3.27
» straw, »	2.30	2.70	1.90	1.50
» chaff »	0.75	0.98	0.36	0.57
» grain »	0.85	2.06	1.36	1.20
Number of good, ripe grains	40	96	60	53
Proportion % between weight of chaff and of ripe grain	53	67	80	67

Given constant moisture in the two periods, the greater the moisture, the higher the yield. The maximum is given by a constant moisture of 34%. During the second or flowering period, a reduction of moisture from 34% to 24% has a bad effect on the yield; but an increase of moisture from 24% to 34% at the same period gives a considerable increase of grain.

1128   J. A. Pulman. **Buckwheat and Frost**. (Opeti s Grecikhi).) - *Exegodnik Glavnago Upravlenia Semlieustroistva i Semliedielia po Departamentu Semliedielia, (Year-Book of the Administration of Rural Organisation and Agriculture, Department of Agriculture)*, G. II, pp. 70-71. Peterburg, 1910.

Russia   Temperatures of - 1° and - 2° C. do no harm to buckwheat seedlings, but at - 2.5° the tenderest leaves begin to suffer; at- 4° nearly all the plants are damaged, and at - 6° they are killed.

Observations have shown :

a) that seedlings at 3 days old are more sensitive to cold than at 5 days;

b) that when the thickness of sowing is equal, more damage is done on moist soil;

c) that by selection more resistant varieties may be obtained.

By sowing buckwheat before April 25 through a long series of years, the Experiment Station at Borodzk has produced a type that resists — 4° C. and has already been grown with success in various localities in the Government of Kursk.

1129   G. A. Pulman. **Effect of Weather on the Growth of Oats and Millet.** (Vliianie Meteorologhiceskikh Uslovii na Proisrastanie Ovza, Prosa i Grecikhi). Exegodnik Glavnago Upravlenia Semlienstroistva i Semledielia po Dep. Semledielia. (*Yearbook of the Administration of Rural Organisation and Agriculture Department of Agriculture*), G. III, pp. 71-74. Peterburg.

Russia   Diagrams are given determining the influence on vegetation of different meteorological conditions, as atmospheric temperatures, cloudiness, rain-fall. These diagrams point to the following conclusions:

OATS. — 1) In years of good harvest, during the 10 days preceding formation of the ear there was abundant rain, rather low temperature and a cloudy sky.

2) In years of bad harvest, during the same period there was very little rain, the temperature was rather high and the sky clear.

3) Up to this period, whatever the outer conditions, the growth of the oats is uniform and slow; but after the formation of the ears, up to harvest, they grow rapidly in favourable years. Rain is the most important factor, and the critical period is within the 10 days preceding the formation of the ears, generally in June.

MILLET. - In the period between the formation of the leaves and the appearance of the flower, temperature is the most important fac-

tor, and should not fall below 18°. C., the optimum being between 19°
and 22.° Severe cold delays the appearing of the flower, and delay
is always an indication of a bad crop.

As regards rain, if, in the 20 days between flowering and the
ripening of the grain, the rainfall is below 30 mm. the yield will be
below average.

Rumanian Soils. (Les sols de la Roumanie). — *Revue Scientifique*,   **1130**
49 année, N. 16, p. 503. Paris, 22, avril, 1911.

The Geological Institute of Bucarest has lately published a geo-   **Rumania**
logical map, signed by Mr. Murgoci, scale 1 : 2 500 000, representing
fourteen types of soil. The following table gives these types,
with the maximum and minimum content of physical and chemical
elements, according to Murgoci :

ANALYSIS OF TYPICAL RUMANIAN SOILS (%).

FORMATION	Mechanical Analysis Diameter of particles					Chemical Analysis						Observations
	About 1 m/m	1 to 1/4 m/m	Less than 1/4 m/m	Clay	Humus	Loss by desiccation	Humic Acid	Lime, CaO	Phosphoric Acid, P2 O5	Nitrogen	Potash, K2 O	
I. Steppe soils:	Max							Max				
Dry steppe, } light yellow loam......... {	—	—	—	—	—	5.5	1.1	2.8	0.2	0.2	0.18	
Dry steppe, } reddish .... loam......... {	0.2	1	60	37	4	6	1.5	2	0.4	0.2	0.27	On Russian frontier
Tchernoziom, brown colour	0.15	3.6	57	6	5	6	—	2	0.23	0.16	0.37	The most extensive
Tchernoziom common (Russian).	—	—	—	—	8	8	—	—	0.1	0.27	0.5	
Tchernoziom, decomposed .	—	8	48	45	2	7	1 8	1.9	—	0.27	—	
II. Forest soils:												
Brown oak-forest soils . . .	—	10	50	36	4	5	1.1	0.8	0.1	0.17	—	
Podzol: pale sand with oak and beech forests.	1.3	1.6	44	54	2	6	—	0.1	0.04	0.16	0.15	One analysis
III. Soils on rocks *in situ*:												
Stony forest soils of the Carpathians.	1.4	8	46	46	—	5	1.5	0.4	—	0.17	—	
Terra rossa, red soil of the West (Permian-Trias).	—	—	—	—	—	—	—	—	—	—	—	Very limited
IV. Recent silt soils:												
Danube silt	—	—	—	—	—	8.5	—	3	0.13	0.3	0.3	
Alluvium from large rivers.	Coast dunes, salt soils and lakes, swamps. (Lacoviste).											

1131   T. L. LYON AND J. A. BIZZELL.. **Relation of Certain Crops to the Nitrate Content of Soils.** (J. Franklin Institute 171, 1-16 pp. 205-220 1911). *Journal of the Society of Chemical Industry,* No. 5, Vol. XXX, London, March 15, 1911.

Great Britain   Experiments made with Timothy grass, maize, potatoes, oats, millet and soy beans showed that on the same soil the amount of nitrate present was different for each crop. At different stages of growth there was a characteristic relationship between the crop and the soil's nitrate content. During the most active growing period, nitrates were more abundant in the soil under maize than in the same soil when uncultivated ; at the same period the nitrate content was higher under a mixture of maize and millet than under millet alone, though the amount of crops obtained was about the same in the two cases. Apparently nitrification is stimulated by some processes connected with the active growth of plants, particularly of maize. Part of its nitrogen is however obtained by the maize plant in some other form than nitrates; and the amount of nitrate was higher at the time when the crop was taking most nitrogen from the soil than in the later stages of growth under both maize and oats, although the nitrates ·in the uncropped soil were decreasing. Under maize, oats, and millet, the nitrate failed to increase late in the season, when the absorption of nitrogen had practically ceased, although the amount of nitrate in the uncropped soil. was increasing rapidly. Apparently plants during their later period of growth exert a retarding influence on nitrification.

Changes in the moisture content or in the temperature of the soil under crops during the growing period had but little effect in the amount of nitrate present.

On the other hand on uncropped soil a marked increase in nitrates followed an increase of moisture in September.

The large differences in the nitrates under the crops studied are attributed to inherent differences between plants of different species in their stimulating influence on nitrification, or the reverse.

1182   A. CONTINO. **Manganese in Italian Soils.** (Sulla quantità di manganese in alcuni terreni italiani). *Le stazioni Sper. Agr. Italiane,* Vol. XLIX, f. 1, pp. 51-54, Modena, 1911.

Italy   In analysing 21 samples of soils from South Italy and 2 from North Italy, Mr. Contino found a minimum of 0.03, and a maximum of 0.485, or an average of 0.17 of oxide of manganese (Mn_3O_4).

Soils in other countries have given similar results. If one kilogram of soil contains on an average 1 gram of this oxide, a hectare would contain a far greater quantity than is generally recommended in ordinary manuring, and which is necessary to plants. Manganese compounds in the soil must act chiefly as catalysers.

J. A. PULMAN. **Action of Soil-Moisture on the Growth of Oats.** — (Vliianie Vlaxnosti Potcvi na Uroxai Ovzà). - *Exegodnik Glavnago Upravlenia Semlieustroistva i Semledielia po Departamentu Semledielia. (Year-Book of the Administration of Rural Organisation and Agriculture. Department of Agriculture)*, G. III, pp. 74-75. Peterburg, 1910 (1).

1188

Numerous experiments have been made in pots at the Borodizk Station, to observe the action of soil-moisture on the growth of oats between the appearance of the ear and the setting of the grain. This may be called the « critical period » of oats with regard to the factor *moisture*. The following table gives the results of these experiments:

Russia

Number of pots		10	14	11	13
Soil Moisture %	from germination to maturity	34	34	24	24
	from appearance of ear to setting of grain	34	24	24	34
Weight of grain, grams,		2.00	1.58	1.88	1.80
Weight of straw, »		2.06	1.17	1.15	1.49
Weight of chaff, »		0.80	0.54	0.49	0.61
Total crop, »		4.86	3.29	3.52	3.90
Number of Grains	large and well formed	64	39	47	56
	small,	17	28	41	27
Total number of grains		81	67	88	83
Length of stalk, centimetres		58	56	39	47
» of panicle		14	13	11	15
Total length of plant		72	70 (?)	50	62
Number of well developed stalks		3	2	4	3
» » imperfectly developed stalks		4	4	1	1
Total number of stalks		7	6	5	5

This table shows: 1) that the optimum is given by a constant humidity of 34; 2) with a decrease in moisture from 34 to 24, coming exactly at the « critical period », the yield diminishes by 32 %; 3) if the moisture rises from 24 to 34%, at this period, there is an increase of 11% on the average yield; 4) the number of the seeds is higher with a constant moisture of 24, but in size the seeds are much reduced.

---

(1) Compare with the experiments on buckwheat: this *Bulletin*, No. 1127
(*Ed.*)

1184   **Land-Drainage in Montenegro.** (Montenegrinische Entwässerungsarbeiten). *Report of Austrian Consul. Oesterreichische Monatsschrift für den Orient,* N. 3, p. 43.   Wien, März, 1911.

Montenegro   Two Italian engineers have presented a project for the drainage
of the marshy area which extends between Dulcigno and the river
Bojana.   The Montenegro Government has ceded the land in question
for 30 years to the Society undertaking the work of drainage.

1185   **Irrigation Project for Andalusia in Spain.** (Projet d'irrigation en
Spain   Andalousie). *See N.* 1083 *of this Bulletin.*

1186   **Extensive Irrigation Scheme in Mexico.** — *Bulletin of the Pan-
American Union.* Washington, Jan. 1911. p. 167.

Mexico   On the initiative of the Mexican Agricultural Department of the
Ministry of « Fomento » a plan has been completed for the organization of a Federal service of irrigation throughout the Republic.   The
Government is about to invest large sums of money in building
great reservoirs for collecting the waters now going to waste.

The country will be divided into ten zones, preference being given
to such districts as promise the greatest success and the best returns.

It is believed that at least 10 000 000 hectares of land can be
reclaimed and made among the most productive in the Republic.
The report made to the Ministry of « Fomento » indicates that the
amount of irrigated land would increase the annual agricultural production of the country by 300 000 000 dollars and in addition to
this increase of agricultural resources, irrigation would make the
crops of these regions practically certain each year.

1187   **Irrigation Work in South Argentine, in the Neuquen Valley.** *Bulletin of the Pan-American Union.* Washington, Jan. 1911, p. 143.

Argentina   The President of the Argentine Republic has recently approved
the contract entered into between the Minister of Public Works and
the Buenos Aires Great Southern Railway Co. for the execution of
irrigation works in the valleys of the Neuquen River and the Rio
Negro.

According to the terms of the contract the company is merely
the constructor of the works, while the Department of Public Works
will prepare the plans and appoint the technical staff.

The works to be executed by the Great Southern Railway Co. are those comprised in the first section of the zone of the valleys, *i. e.*, between Lake Pellegrini and the Chinchinales station. A dam is to be thrown across the Neuquen River and an intake canal will be cut at this point for the irrigation works. In connection with this dam there is to be a canal for the diversion of the flood waters into a large natural basin, known as the « Cuenca Vidal ».

M. AUFRAY. **Amounts of Ammonia and Nitric Acid in Rain-water**   **1188**
in Tonking. (*Bull. Econ.*, Hanoi-Haiphong, 1909 12, 595-616).
Journal of the Chemical Society. Abs. ü 224. London, March
1911.

The amounts of nitrogen as ammonia or as nitrates were estimated   French
in 123 samples of rain-water, collected in the Botanic Gardens, Hanoi,   Indo-China
from April 1902 to March 1905, and in 313 samples collected from
June 1906 to September 1909 in an open space in the middle of the
same town. Assuming the composition of the samples to represent
approximately the whole rainfall, the average amounts of nitrogen per
million and the total amounts per acre for the six years would be as
follows :

		N. per million.		N. per acre (lbs.)		
	Rainfall. inches	as ammonia.	as nitrates.	as ammonia.	as nitrates.	Total.
1902-3	90.55	0.71	0.66	14.74	13.42	28.21
1903-4	59.68	0.99	0.88	13.34	10.89	24.23
1904-5	84.72	0.64	0.43	12.25	8.26	20.51
1906-7	49.92	0.54	0.36	6.13	4.06	10.19
1907-8	57.91	0.33	0.27	4.39	3.54	7.93
1908-9	77.72	0.23	0.15	4.04	2.65	6.64

or, in metric measures :

		N. per hectare (kgr.)		
	Rainfall. mm.	as ammonia.	as nitrates.	Total.
1902-3	2299.9	16.50	15.08	31.59
1903-4	1412.8	14.94	12.19	27.13
1904-5	2151.8	83.72	9.25	22.97
1906-7	1267.9	6.86	4.54	11.41
1907-8	1470.9	4.91	3.96	8.88
1908-9	1974.0	4.52	2.96	7.49

Of the total rainfall, about 82 % falls from May to October and this contains about 84 % of the total nitrogen (1).

1139   K. STÖRMER. **Influence of Straw on the Nitrogen in Green Manure** (Versuche über die Beeinflussung der Wirkung des Gründüngungs-Stickstoff durch Zugabe von Stroh). — *Fühling's Landw. Zeitung*, 60 J. H. 6, pp. 185-198. Stuttgart, 15 März, 1911.

Germany: Württemberg   The writer recalls the fact that the utilisation of the nitrogen contained in green manure is relatively slight: from 25 to 40 %. As a continuation of preceding researches, Mr. Störmer has studied the influence of straw, which is rich in carbo-hydrates, on the utilisation of the nitrogen in green manure, the slight results of which would be due to the fact that decomposition takes place in a substratum too rich in albuminoids.

Three series of experiments were carried out, from 1905 to 1907, at the Leipzig Agricultural Institute. Field experiments with oats, and with summer wheat; pot experiments with oats and with mustard. These experiments were made in heavy soils; others, in pots, were in light soils. All the field-plots received per hectare: 1.5 qls. 40 % salts of potash; 2 qls. superphosphates; 20 qls. lime; 0.5 qls. nitrate of sodium. The green manure was a mixture of beans and vetches, in the proportion of 1.5 ql. per *are*, and the action of straw was studied in the five following lots, each 1 *are* in size:

1) not treated; 2) chopped wheat-straw 0.5 ql. per are; 3) long wheat-straw, 0.5 ql.; 4) green manure and chopped straw, 5) green manure and long straw 0.5 ql.

From these experiments Mr. Störmer observed that:

1) The addition of straw to green manure, whether in the field or in pots, with heavy or light soils, does not favour the utilisation of the nitrogen of the green manure.

2) It would rather appear that straw has really a fixing effect on a part of the nitrogen. During the first year, in fact,

---

(1) Compare with: J. W. LEATHER. *Composition of Indian Rain and Dew*. Mem Dpt. of Agric. India: Chem. Series. 1906, I, No. I, 11. Also Journ. Chem. Soc. 1906, Abstr. II, 487.

J. B. BRUNNICH. *Fertilising Value of Rainwater*. Ann. Rpt. Dept. of Agriculture, Queensland. 1908-09 59-60. Journ. Chem. Soc. 1910. Abstr. II, 647 - Brünnich's determinations were done in Brisbane, Cairns, Kamerunga, Roma, and other parts of Queensland.　　　　　　　　　　(*Ed.*).

the utilisation of nitrogen is lowered; the second year this loss may be made good, although there is no increase in the utilisation of the nitrogen.

3) Treatment with straw alone has always reduced the yield, both in dry matter and in nitrogen, both in the field and in pots, during the first year, except when the straw is given in minimum quantities. In general the action of straw .was more evident the smaller it was chopped. In the pot-experiments there was an after-effect the second year, but not compensating the loss in dry matter and in nitrogen during the first year.

4) The utilisation of the nitrogen of the green manure was highest when no straw was added. The results, showing the nitrogen in the straw and in the wheat harvested, were the following:

    a) in heavy soil, in the field 14.0 % 1st year

                         0.0 % 2nd »

      »   »   » in pots . . 40.0 % 1st »

                         0.0 % 2nd »

    b) in light soil, and in pots. 40.0 % 1st »

Note the difference between the field and the pot experiments. The second year M. Störmer treated a part of the light soil, in pots, with carbon di-sulphide, almost doubling the utilisation of nitrogen, which reached its maximum with green manure and chopped straw. He comes to the conclusion that in the decomposition of nitrogenous matter in the soil, part of the nitrogen passes into the atmosphere.He recommends the use of well-matured farm- manure only, which should be turned in like green manure in late autumn, or in early spring; and the avoidance, as much as possible of undecomposed straw.

A. Müntz and E. Lainé. **On Loss of Nitrogen during Filtration of Sewage through Bacterial Beds.** (Sur les pertes d'azote au cours de l'épuration de l'eau d'égout pâr les lits bactériens). *C. R. de l'Acad. des Sciences*, T. 152, N. 13, pp. 822-826, Paris, 27 mars, 1911.

1140

The loss of nitrogen which takes place during the filtration of sewage on bacterial beds is on an average from 50 to 60 %, sometimes 70 %. The study of this question entails researches into the causes of this loss, and the forms under which it takes place.

France

There is a close relation between the proportion of organic matter present in the sewage water and the loss of nitrogen. When
there is no organic matter and all the nitrogen is in the form of salts
of ammonia, the loss of nitrogen is little or none. The loss of free
nitrogen must be attributed to the organic matter ; and this elimination together with the destruction of the organic matter itself,
may be compared to combustion by fire, during which in the same
way carbon is eliminated as carbonic acid, and nitrogen as free
nitrogen.

The greater part of the micro-organisms which destroy organic
matter act in this way. But it is not only nitrifying organisms which
produce sewage purification ; for when they act alone they cause the
nitrification of nitrogen and do not set free nitrogen gas. Considering
the quantities of nitrified nitrogen and of free nitrogen formed by
sewage-water in its passage over the bacterial beds, it is easy to see
(from the point of view of the destruction of nitrogenous matter,
which is the element of pollution most to be feared) the most effectual action is due to combustion agents, unless the nitrates formed
pass through a series of successive reductions to the state of free
nitrogen.

Experiments were made by adding known quantities of potassium nitrate to sewage-water in course of purifying. Any reducing
action would extend to the nitrate introduced. This took place ; and
the results showed that notwithstanding aeration, there is a perceptible reduction of the nitrates formed. But the loss of nitrogen in
this way is much less than results from the direct combustion of the
organic matter and of the ammonia itself. Denitrification is all the
more rapid the greater the quantity of organic matter.

In no case was the nitrogen of the nitrates used to form organic
matter or ammonia. The action of the micro-organisms was therefore limited to using the oxygen of the nitric acid, without using its
nitrogen. This reduction is direct and complete ; for the passing
through the stage of nitrites has not been verified.

1141 GYÀRFÀS. **Drill-Manuring in Hungary.** — (Weitere Erfolge der
Drilldüngung in Ungarn). *Deutsche Landwritschaftliche Presse*,
N. 17, pp. 193-195, Berlin, 1 März, 1911.

Hungary Experiments in manuring in lines are giving good results in Hungary. The fertiliser was spread by a drill constructed at Losonc, in
Hungary, and called Record II. The following table shows the results

per hectare, obtained on the Vilke property, by manuring experiments with summer barley, oats, winter-rye and winter wheat :

	Fertiliser	Total Production	Surplus compared with unmanured soil	Surplus compared with soil manured by scattering
For 1 hectare of Summer Barley.				
Manure	kg.	kg.	kg.	kg.
Unmanured	—	1392	—	—
Superphosphate, scattered	345	2038	646	—
» drilled in	115	2167	775	129
» »	182	2148	746	110
» »	230	2107	715	69
» »	390	1923	531	—
» »	345	2038	646	
For 1 hectare of Oats.				
Unmanured	—	1508		
Superphosphate, scattered,	345	1415	—	—
» drilled in	115	1725	217	310
» »	182	1702	194	287
» »	230	1587	79	172
» »	300	1599	91	184
» »	345	1541	33	126
For 1 hectare of Winter Rye.				
Unmanured	—	1185	—	
Superphosphate, scattered,	345	1300	115	—
» drilled in	115	1408	223	108
» »	182	1631	446	331
» »	230	1610	425	310
For 1 hectare of Winter Wheat.				
Unmanured	—	1323	—	—.
Superphosphate, scattered,	345	1369	43	—
» drilled in	115	1564	241	195
» »	182	1748	425	379
» »	230	1723	400	354

Phosphate Deposits in Egypt. (Report of the Brit. Chamb. of Comm. of Egypt). *The Board of Trade Journal.* — N. 746, p. 573. London. March, 1911.

1142

During the course of the Geological Survey of Egypt, begun in 1896, extensive phosphate deposits were discovered, ranging in colour from a light grey to a yellowish brown, and composed mainly of fossil bones, such as the vertebrae and teeth of fishes, together with coprolites and carbonate of lime. Varying quantities of silica and silicates of iron and aluminium are also present.

Egypt

Nile Valley deposits. — Deposits have been discovered in the Nile valley at Sebahia, south of Esneh, and on the top of the plateau called Jebel El Qurm. The nearest point of these deposits to the railway is some 10 km. away, and it is stated that at small cost a light railway could be laid by which the phosphates could be brought down to the Nile. Samples yielding 70 per cent. of tribasic phosphate were obtained from the deposits at Sebahia. Deposits in the neighbourhood of Qena, or Keneh, extend over a length of 25 km. from the base of Jebel Serrai and the southern end of Abu Had, with an average breadth of 1 km. There are apparently large deposits of low grade phosphates here but phosphates giving up to 70 per cent. of tricalcium phosphate have not as yet been found. Very little systematic prospecting, however, has been done.

Red Sea Hills deposits. — Phosphate-bearing beds occur on the east slope of the Red Sea Hills in the Duwi Hills, and near Wadi Safaja, whence there is a good track to the sea, at a place where the water close to the shore is 13 fathoms deep. It is understood that preparations are being made to work these deposits on a large scale, and that a light· railway is now being constructed. The phosphate bed also reappears a little south of Qossier, (Kosseir) but overlaid by thick strata of limestone.

Dakhla Oasis deposits. — Phosphate deposits occur throughout the Dakhla oasis, extending from the extreme west at Qasr Dakhla to the extreme east at Tenid, a distance of over 50 km. The average thickness of the bed is between 2 and 3 metres. Throughout the desert margin, bordering the cultivated lands at Qasr Dakhla, Birbaya, Rashida and Hindan, these beds could be worked with great facility.

It would appear that the average of the out-cropping rock in the Egyptian phosphate deposits contains between 40 and 50 per cent. of tricalcium phosphate, but occasional samples have returned up to over 70 per cent. Localities which are being carefully worked over give promise of producing considerable quantities of rock averaging over 60 per cent of phosphate.

1148   J. Grandvoinnet. **Experiments with Potassic Fertilisers in France.** — (Essais d'engrais potassiques en 1910 dans le Département de l'Ain). *Journal d'Agric. pratique,* N. 11, pp. 337-338. Paris, 16 mars, 1911.

France   Experiments with potassic fertilisers were carried out, in 1910, in the Department of the Ain, in 30 fields with different crops, but principally with potatoes and maize, as required by the Paris Bureau for the Study of Fertilisers. The results obtained with potatoes were all good, although the damp season induced rot. It may be said that in fields manured with potassium sulphate the damage caused by rot was reduced from 30 or 40% to 10%. The average return for an outlay of about 30 frs. on fertilisers was from 100 to 200 frs.

Although the year was very unfavourable to maize, the net return for an outlay of 50 frs. on potassium sulphate was 70 frs.

In an experiment with wheat it was found that the potassium sulphate had raised the weight of the hectolitre from 75 kg. to 78.50 kg.: equivalent to an increase in market value of 75 centimes per quintal.

In vineyards, potassic fertilisers induced a better ripening (*aoûtement*) of the wood. Thus, notwithstanding the exceptionally damp and unfavourable season of 1910, the vintage results were satisfactory.

A. BAUMANN. **Liming and Lime Fertilisers in Peat Soils.** (Kulturversuche auf den Versuchsfeldern der k. Moorkulturanstalt, Moorkulturstation Bernau. Kalkung und Kalkdüngung im Hochmoor.). *Landw. Jahrb. für Bayern,* 1 J. N. 3. pp. 154-160. Munchen, 1911.

1144

Germany

The writer recalls preceding researches, according to which what is called the humic acidity of peat-moss depends on the absorbing power of the cellular membranes of the mosses forming the peat: a power exerted not only on alkaline substances, but also on acids. This generally occurs in peats and in clays poor in nutritive matter.

From his own experiments, Mr. Baumann would infer that liming peat-land in high proportions (2000 kg. and more of lime per hect.) is a great mistake: 1st because of the expense; 2nd because lime entails a series of difficulties, both in South and North Germany.

Mr. Baumann therefore recommends the following rules for bringing peat moss under culture :

1) Avoid all liming, especially with quick lime. The application of 1000 kg. per hectare does no harm, but is generally useless.

2) Liberally apply phosphatic and potassic manures during the first year. The phosphatic fertilisers should be rich in lime : mineral phosphates containing about 20 % of phosphoric acid and consequently 250 to 300 kg. of phosphoric anhydride per hect., and 500 to 600 kg. of lime. The potassic manure should consist of concentrated salts (salts at 40 %, or potassium sulphate and magnesium at 29 %), or of potassic mixtures containing no free acid.

3) When possible, crop with potatoes the first two years, in order to cause rapid decomposition in the soil.

1145   E. CHANCRIN AND A. DESRIOT. **Sulphur as Fertilizer for Potatoes and**
            Beet. (Action du Soufre comme engrais sur le développement
            des Pommes de terre et des Betteraves). *Journ. d'Agr. pratique*
            N. 14, pp. 427-429. Paris, 6 avril, 1911.

France   Having noticed that potatoes treated with sulphur for " Galle '
            gave a very abundant crop, the writers made experiments to ascertain
            whether the good crop was due merely to absence of disease, or to the
            direct action of sulphur on the tubers. The results obtained at the
            School of Gennetines (Allier) France, are given in the following table,
            the figures representing the weight of crops in kilograms per hectare:

Plots.	Potatoes: Kgr. per hectare		
	Without sulphur.	250 kg. sulphur.	500 kg. su'phur.
1, 5, 9, Unmanured	10 000	10 580	10 810
2, 6, 10, Superphosphate	12 400	12 450	12 520
3, 7, 11, Superph. & potassium sulph. . .	12 700	12 962	13 444
4, 8, 12, Superph., potass. sulph., sodium nitrate	13 060	14 338	16 036

The variety of potato was *Eléphant.*
The same experiments were made with beets, *Jaune ovoïde des*
Barres and *Jaune géante de Vauriac.*   The results obtained at Genne-
tines were the following:

Plots.	Beets: Kgr. per hectare		
	Without sulphur.	250 kg. sulp'ur	500 kg. sulphur.
1, 5, 9, Unmanured	25 500	26 050	27 250
2, 6, 10, Superphoshate	30 010	32 100	35 000
3, 7, 11, Superph. potassium sulph.	33 037	35 250	38 694
4, 8, 12, Superph., potass. sulph., sodium nitrate	45 805	47 018	49 990

All the plots treated with sulphur produced a higher yield. The
same experiments carried out at the School of Beaume (Côte d'Or)
France, gave results pointing the same way.
            Without giving a definite explanation of the action of sulphur,
the writers think that its effects are of the same kind as those
obtained in sterilising the soil by heat, by carbon disulphide or boric
acid. In any case, these experiments of one year only are worth
repeating, as the result might be of practical value.

Field Crops. — Industrial Crops. — Horticulture. Arboriculture.

O. Manetti. **Eritrea Food Grains.** (Ricerche analitiche sulle ca-   **1146**
riossidi dei cereali eritrei). *L'Agricoltura Coloniale* — V. anno,
N. 3, pp. 100-113, Firenze, 31, Marzo 1911.

The food grains examined were : « Dura » *Sorghum vulgare*   **Eritrea**
Pers., *Andropogon Sorghum* Brot ; « Dagussa » *Eleusine coracana*
Gaertn., *Eleusine tocussa* Fres., *Eleusine aegyptiaca* Dest.; « Taff »
Eragrostis abyssinica, Lk.; « Bultuc » *Pennisetum spicatum*, Kolan,
Pennisetum tiphoideum, Rich.

The first two are natives of India, where they are still found to
a considerable extent, while the others are indigenous to Abyssinia (1).

The « dura » is cultivated over large regions of Eritrea at different altitudes, from sea level to 2309 m., the yield being very
irregular. It is nearly always cultivated for food, being little used
as fodder.

Dagussa is cultivated for the manufacture of beer ; Dr J. Baldrati
reports that its starch content is as much as 80 %, which ranks
it among the best cereals for the starch factory and the distillery.

Taff is cultivated at altitudes above 400 m., and yields as much
as 100 times the seed. Its cultivation is similar to that of barley. It is
used for food, and the straw as fodder for cattle.

Bultuc is less cultivated; the flour is employed in the preparation
of a porridge and for the manufacture of beer ; the grains are used
in the starch factory and in the distillery.

Colour of the grain. The colour of the grain in some samples of
dura varied from wine red to grayish white. The varieties studied
were very much mixed ; the purest were the « uarda », with white
grains, and the « uot ferat », with red grains ; the dura of the Baza
was a mixture, in about equal parts, of red and white.

The four types of dagussa examined were genuine mixtures of
three known varieties, brown, red and white.

The « fengel » type was mainly formed of brown grains and so
was one of the types of « gobezé ».

Four samples of taff examined were a mixture of red and white
grains; the « uaffe » contained 67 % of red grains while the « gezené »
and the « scimase » were on the contrary formed respectively of 88

---

(1) Compare, A. H. Church, *Food Grains of India.* 1886 and Geo. Watt,
Dict. of the Economic Products of India.   (*Ed.*).

and 96 % of white grains and the « cengher » had an equal mixture of red and white.

Bultuc is yellowish, verging towards a brownish green.

Dimensions of the grains:

Dura . . . . { 4.20 - 4.80 mm. long
{ 2.70 - 2.90 mm. wide

Bultuc . . . . { 3.10 - 3.90 mm. long
{ 1.60 - 2.00 mm. wide

Dagussa . . . . { 2.20 - 2.60 mm. long
{ 1.35 - 1.80 mm. wide

Taff. . . . . { 1.40 - 2.00 mm. long
{ 0.85 - 1.00 mm. wide

Volume, weight, density. — The results given below represent the average of several weighings :

GRAINS	Average Weight of 100 grains	Weight of 1 hectol.	Volume, of 1 quintal average
	gr.	kg.	Hl.
Dura.	2.512	77-78	1.320
Dagussa.	0.200	82-83	1.210
Taff.	0.033	88	1.125
Bultuc.	0.690	79	1.260

The following table gives the composition of these Eritrean grains :

GRAINS	Proteids	Fibre	Fatty Matters	Starch etc.	Nutritive ratio
Dura	9.17	0.40	4.45	46.60	6.40
Dagussa	4.24	0.37	0.83	55.52	13.57
Taff.	11.70	0.25	2.32	48.49	4.62
Bultuc	8.25	0.22	2.79	50.36	6.90

It would be interesting to experiment on the value of dagussa for starch factories and breweries, as well as the bread-making qualities of dura and taff.

White and Yellow Maize in Rhodesia. — *The Rhodesia Agricultural*   **1147**
Journal, Salisbury, Febr. 1911, pp. 404-406.

In order to obtain definite information as to whether white or   **Rhodesia**
yellow maize is more profitable for export, four samples of Rhodesian
maize were recently forwarded for examination and report to the
London Corn Exchange, as well as to the most prominent corn dealers
in England. In all cases the maize was reported to be of excellent
quality and the samples were placed in the following order ·
    Choice Hickory King or *Large Flat White* commanding a pre-
mium of about 6 d. per quarter (480 lbs) over any of the others. *F. A.
Q. Hickory* and *Choice Boone County* of about equal value and yellow
maize about equal in value to *F. A. Q. Hickory* or *Boone County*,
but on some markets worth 3 d. to 6 d. per quarter less.
    Messrs. Fear, Colebrook & Co. of Southampton write : « If there
were a very large import of the white flat maize and a comparatively
small import of the yellow flat maize the latter would command
quite as good a price as the former; but with such a small general
import as we usually have from South Africa we think the white
would as a rule be worth more than the yellow ».
    According to Messrs. John Jackson & Co. of Glasgow: « For export
purposes we suggest that the Rhodesian farmer will certainly obtain
better results by growing white maize. The reason for this is that
the supplies of white maize available for the United Kingdom and
the Continental markets are limited to certain parts of the United
States of America, South Africa, the Argentine, the Danubian provinces and South Russia, so that the competition in it is certain at all
times to be more intense. Of course the value of white maize will
be governed more or less by the value of yellow, but for certain purposes white maize will bring a substantial premium. South African
and Rhodesian maize are eminently suited for the commercial requirements of Great Britain and it is all a matter of price. The Rhodesian grower will require to compete with other maize growing
countries, but he certainly has an advantage in his quality being of
a higher standard than the maize from the United States of America
and, as we have said, for certain purposes, to that from South Russia,
the Danubian Provinces and the Argentine; and judging by the size
and colour of the berry he is extremely fortunate in the climate and
the soil ».
    It thus appears that the English trade is expecting better prices
to be realised for white than yellow maize, and the use of white
maize for manufacturing purposes is being extended and will thereby
bring about an increased demand.

As regards production, it was shown in certain experiments carried out by the Mississippi Experiment Station in seven different States that when 217 white varieties were grown in comparative trials with 273 yellow, the advantage in yield of the former was at the rate of about two and a half bushels or 150 lbs. per acre. On referring to the variety trials carried out at the Government Experiment Farm, Potchefstroom, Transvaal, and extending over several seasons, it will be seen that of the ten heaviest croppers, five are white varieties and five yellow. It would therefore appear that there is little or no difference between the average cropping powers of yellow and white maize, provided that they are grown under equally favourable conditions.

1148   T. BENINI. (From Mansoura) **Rice and the Salt Soils of Egypt.**
              (Culture egiziane, il riso). — *L'Agricoltura Coloniale*, anno V,
              pp. 19-22, Firenze, Gennaio, 1911.

Egypt   The cultivation of rice is one of the means adopted in Egypt in controlling salt in soils. This culture is begun in April and finished at the end of November. Five or six varieties of rice are used, according to the saline conditions of the soil.

The saltest soils, when first put under cultivation, are adapted for the coarser and later varieties of rice, to be sown not later than April 15th.

The *Panicum aquaticum* often precedes the rice, but it is generally better to well leach the soil in Autumn. The « barari » (abandoned) lands should be first improved and levelled. When it is desired to obtain the maximum leaching effect the ground is formed into fields, 25 m. by 100 m. surrounded by ditches, where the infiltration water drains off to the nearest canal.

After the embankments in the rice-fields have been strengthened to prevent any leakage, the soil should be levelled with the « lawate » harrow, so that the water should lie equally all over the field.

During the first period of vegetation the water should be frequently renewed. This is necessary in strongly saline soils, and delay may cause considerable damage to the rice, a crop that on saline soils requires abundance of water and great care on the part of the farmer. Rice-diseases are less harmful than elsewhere when the soil is saline.

The yield varies from 15 to 60 quintals of paddy. Paddy is sold at the field per hectare by the « daribe » of 945 kg.

H. PAUL. **Forage Plants Manuring Experiments.** (Kulturversuche auf den Versuchsfelden der K. Moorkulturanstalt. Moorkultur-station Bernau, Wiesen und Weiden in Hochmoor). — *Jahrbuch Landw. für Bayern,* I Jahrgang, N. 3, pp. 168-176, München, 1911.

1149

The following results were obtained from the manuring of pure cultivations of forage plants with 30 kg. of nitrate of sodium in a peaty soil:

Germany

	Crop per hectare				Extra crop per hect. with nitrogen	
	Green		Dry			
	With nitrogen	Without nitrogen	With nitrogen	Without nitrogen	Green	Dry
	Kg.	Kg.	Kg.	Kg.	Kg.	Kg.
Agrostis alba	11 400	9 000	4 389	2 537	2 400	1 852
Anthoxanthum odoratum .	5 200	2 600	1 776	888	2 600	888
Festuca arundinacea. . .	7 300	4 600	—	—	2 700	—
Festuca pratensis. . . .	6 100	2 800	—	—	3 300	—
Festuca rubra	7 400	2 600	2 890	1 097	4 800	1 793
Festuca ovina	7 400	2 800	2 760	1 120	4 600	1 640
Phleum pratense	11 400	5 800	3 775	2 102	5 600	1 673
Glyceria fluitans	4 500	2 700	1 397	798	1 800	599
Phalaris arundinacea . .	9 500	5 000	3 179	1 651	4 500	1 528
Holcus lanatus	6 200	3 400	1 550	788	2 800	762
Aira flexuosa	9 100	5 000	2 962	1 893	4 100	1 069
Poa nemoralis	10 500	6 000	4 075	2 411	4 500	1 664
Poa pratensis	7 700	5 100	2 785	1 975	2 600	810

The results obtained in meadows with the different manures show their influence on the quality of the crop:

	Farm manure		Horse manure		Sheep manure		Artificial Fertilisers	
	1st cut	2nd cut	1st cut	2nd cut	1st cut	2nd cut	1st cut	2nd cut
Grasses (per cent). .	78.8	57.2	93.3	78.4	82.8	72.0	93.1	81.1
Leguminous Plants (per cent)	15.2	31.2	3.2	13.8	9.4	19.9	3.2	6.8
Total Hay Crop Kgr. per hectare	3 430	2 680	3 160	2 580	2 895	2 555	3 790	2 065

Each field received per hectare 10 000 kg. of farm manure, and the deficiency in phosphoric acid and potash was made up by 60 or 120 kg. of chalky calcium phosphate (*Kreide Phosphat*) and salts of potash. Field 98 received only phosphates and salts of potash, and as nitrogen fertiliser, nitrate of soda corresponding to 20 kg. nitrogen per hectare.

1150   **The *Chloris Gayana* or Rhodes Grass in Sicily.** *Boll. R. Orto Botanico e Giardino Coloniale* di Palermo. Anno IX, N. 4, pp. 192-193.

Italy: The *Chloris Gayana* is a perennial grass which resembles
Sicily   *Cynodon Dactylon* and spreads very rapidly by its long stolons. Its main quality is resistance to drought, so that it is one of the best fodder plants for summer in dry hot regions. In spite of drought it keeps its green colour much longer than any other grass and as soon as the rain falls it begins to throw out vigorous shoots.

This plant, which is known in the Transvaal under the name of Rhodes grass, is found throughout the whole of Central and South Africa, from Senegal to Eritrea and Cape Colony; it has been successfully introduced into Australia and recently into Algeria.

Experiments in the Colonial Garden of Palermo have demonstrated its adaptability to the climate of Sicily, where it may be recommended as a summer fodder plant (1).

1151   TRABUT. **Turkestan Lucerne in Algeria.** *Journal d'Agriculture pratique,* N. 12, pp. 375-376. Paris, Mars 23, 1911.

Algeria   Mr. Trabut, who has been making experiments with the Turkestan Lucerne since 1900 at the Botanical Station of Algiers, (2) does not think it desirable for the moment to substitute this lucerne of extreme climates for the lucernes which have been acclimatised in various countries, and especially in the temperate zones. It would be more interesting to undertake a methodical and connected study of the innumerable forms of *Medicago sativa ;* for each region, there is a kind which is more particularly adapted to it,

---

(1) For experiments made in New Zealand, see this *Bulletin*, November, 1910, p. 58.

(2) See this *Bull*. Feb. 1911, N. 445, and March, 1911, N. 811.   (*Ed.*)

and it is a mistake to think that the same varieties would give the best yields anywhere. It is necessary to select, according to the climate and soil, the variety capable of giving the best results and the maximum profit. Each farm should select by planting the lucerne in spaced rows, and by only keeping for seed the plants which are most developed, the shoots of which may be used as slips in order to fix the variety.

P. LIEBAU. **Comparative Experiments with Red Clovers of different**   1152
Origin. (Anbauversuche mit Rotklee verschiedener Herkunft).
— *Illustrierte Landw. Zeitung*, 31 J., Nos. 24-25, pp. 233-234, and
246-247. Berlin, 25-29 März 1911.

The following are the results of experiments with *Trifolium*   Germany
pratense made at the High Agricultural School of Berlin. The clovers were on triple plots, in 1906-7 and 1908-10.

Origin	Total crop of dry substance, qs. per hectare and per cent of the total crop of 1909 and 1910 produced in the first and second year respectively.		
	1906	1909 and 1910	1909-1910
Silesia . . .	46.07	138.93 1st year 46 %.	2nd year 54 %
Styria . . .	48.26	138.09 » 44	» 56
France . . .	49.08	106.35 » 43	» 57
England . . .	51.52	103.01 » 41.5	» 58.5
Bohemia . . .	47.62	121.03 » 43	» 57
Hungary. . .	47.45	127.76 » 44.5	» 55.5
Galicia . . .	46.39	134.52 » 44	» 56
Russia . . .	44.62	131.58 » 39.5	» 60.5
Livonia . . .	—	140.03 » 42.7	» 57.3

The crop is seen to be considerably superior in the second year.

D. M. DONALD. **Accidental Introduction into Australia of** *Trifo-*   1153
lium fragiferum **and of** *Paspalum ovatum*, **two Useful Plants**
Gardeners' Chronicle March 4th, 1911, p. 139. London

The « Strawberry Clover » (*Trifolium fragiferum*) was introduced   **Australia**
accidentally into Victoria from Ireland.   **Victoria**
Having been used as packing material, it was subsequently thrown out into a farmyard belonging to the Hon. Mr. Irving.
Soon after, a plant of this clover (hitherto unknown in the country) appeared on the spot, and as the species proved more drought-resisting than other clovers, it was perpetuated, and is now, the writer believes, cultivated extensively throughout Victoria (1).

_____

(1) *Trifolium fragiferum* grows spontanewly in Italy. G. ARCANGELI
Flora Italiana, Torino, 1894, p. 498. ·   (*Ed.*).

The introduction of *Paspalum ovatum* into New South Wales was on somewhat similar lines. In 1890, a packet of the seed of this grass was sent thither from Victoria, in the hope that it would succeed better under the subtropical conditions prevailing there.

Mr. E. Seccombe of Wollongbar sowed about ½ oz. of the seed, and in 1891, said he did not think much of it. In 1892 however, he sent a specimen of grass to be identified, stating that he found it stood drought exceptionally well. The plant proved to be *Paspalum ovatum*, which sold, a year after, at £ 1 per lb., owing to its wonderful properties as a forage grass.

1154   G. JOSA. **Experiments with Vetch Varieties in Molise (Southern Italy).** (Le varietà di veccia da foraggio e il commercio del seme). — *Giorn. di Agric. della Domenica*, Anno XXI, N. 23, p. 18. 1 fig. Piacenza, 26 Marzo, 1911.

Italy:
Molise   The cultivation of vetches for fodder has developed considerably in Italy, there being several varieties for autumn and spring sowing, adapted to different local conditions. The following are the results of comparative experiments with different Italian varieties:

Varieties of vetch	Crop calculated as hay per hectare
White	28 qs.
Black Piacenza.	39 »
Modena . . . . , . .	42 »
Black Ravenna	48 »
Gray Ravenna	57 »
Abruzzi (Roccaraso)	35 »
With greenish seed	23 »

There would thus be a difference in the production of hay varying from 7 to 29 qs. per hectare, according to the variety sown and this without considering the last variety.

Farmers should prefer seed produced in their own or in neighbouring farms. In trade the different varieties and origins of vetch seed should be distinguished.

Abruzzi vetch was severely attacked by *Septoria Viciae* Sept. (1).

---

(1) *Septoria* (family of *Sphaerodiacae*) are a numerous group of imperfect fungi often living as parasites on spots on leaves, but seldom causing serious damage. (Cfr. DELACROIX and MAUBLANC. *Maladies parasitaires des plantes cultivées*, p. 392, Paris, J. B. Baillière & Fils). *(Ed)*.

W. M. Esten. **Maize Silage in Connecticut.** — *The Connecticut Far-* 1155
mer. New Haven, Conn. March. 11, 1911.

The importance of silage is recognized by farmers in general United
and dairymen in particular. In Connecticut more maize is raised States:
for the silo than for other purposes. The siloing develops in the Connecticut
maize flavours and aromas which are much relished by cattle. The
term maize, or corn, means here the whole maize plant with the
ears included. The conditions for fermentation of maize into silage
are four : A sufficient temperature, exclusion of air, sugar, and sugar
fermenting organisms.

In the lower part of the stalk the amount of sugar in maize.
is from 1 to 1 ½ per cent. Very soon after filling a silo an increase of temperature is noticed. The cause of this is not definitely understood. Some would place the cause in the residual activity
of the living cells, others in the activities of micro-organisms.

The exclusion of air is necessary for the acid-bacteria to prevail.
Where air is present the fermentation is alkaline, and the acid-bacteria seem to play no part in the fermentation. The fermentation
of silage takes from 4 to 10 days, in which time most of the acid
is produced (1).

After this period there is a very slow acid accumulation for
several weeks. In every silage the sugar entirely disappears. The
list of acids found in silage is a long one, and illustrates the com-
plexity of the fermentation and ripening processes.

During the warmest part of the year silage spoils very rapidly
where it comes in contact with air. Spoiled silage is a dangerous
food. Besides tainting the milk and upsetting the digestion of the
cow, it often becomes poisonous. To avoid this, it is necessary to
feed off each day from 1 ½ to 2 inches. If this is done the silage
has no time to change or ferment much.

---

(1) Whether sour silage or sweet silage results from the operation is determined mainly by the temperature at which fermentation takes place within
the mass of herbage. Silage is sour or sweet according to the presence or
absence of acid, chiefly acetic acid. When " sweet " silage is produced it is
due to the higher temperature having killed the living organisms which, under
conditions of less heat, set up an acid fermentation. W. Fream. *Elements
of Agriculture*, London, 1910.

For the fermenting organisms that act in ensilage and for the conditions
that favour their activity, see: F. Lafar, *Technischen Mykologie*, Jena, 1908,
vol. II, p. 332. (*Ed.*).

The tall narrow silo is better than the broad low one. The loss is much less.

If the herd be large enough, two silos of different diameters are of great economic convenience, the large one being used for winter feed and the small one for summer. Another advantage is in filling. One will be settling while the other is being filled.

A round wooden-stave silo is the best and can be made to last as long as a wooden building, by soaking the wood in some preservative, by applying asphalt or tar to the bottom, and to the staves to the height of a few feet, and by keeping the outside surface well painted.

The best wooas for a silo are western red cedar and western fir. A silo 18 feet in diameter will feed 42 animals. The maize which will contain the most nutriment per acre is the one to grow for silage purposes. Taking two extremes, the *Leaming* variety grows a high percentage of grain on the cob, while the *Eureka* grows a high stalk full of leaves but very little grain.

The maturity of the maize presents one of the most important factors connected with silage. This one factor alone will determine whether there will be one third of it lost in the silo or only $1/20$.th Immature maize has more juice, which is easily pressed out and runs away from the silo: a complete loss. Furthermore, immature maize has more sugar which has to be entirely turned to acid, and a very sour silage is the result. Some of the proteins are also changed to undesirable compounds, which do not appear in matnre maize.

On the other hand, matured maize has gained in total nutriments, of a more stable nature, less likely to be broken down by fermenting agencies.

If maize does not blossom in Connecticut by the 20th of July, it will not be likely to develop completely. The period in which maize will grow in Connecticut is not much over 120 days, between May 20th and September 20th.

Inoculation with pure cultures of acid-bacteria showed that silage could be made in 24 hours. About 3 000 tons of maize were treated by inoculation, producing silage without any disagreable odour, and with a saving of three to four weeks.

« Cotton Famine » in European Iudustry relatively to the   1156
general Increase of Cotton Production. (Die Baumwollefrage,
Denkschrift über Produktion und Verbrauch von Baumwolle.
Massnahmen gegen die Baumwollnot). — *Veröffentlichungen
des Reichskolonialamtes*, N. 1, pp. VIII + 341, Jena, 1911.

Insufficient cotton production, while the requirements of the   German
cotton industry increase, produces in Europe what is called the   Colonies
« Cotton Famine ». There is some danger that eventually the cotton industry should leave Europe to pass to those countries where
the raw material is produced.

If all the inhabitants of the globe were to wear cotton, 42 000 000
bales of cotton would be required. Meanwhile the world's total cotton
demand for the year 1909-1910 is estimated at 17 030 511 bales,
while the actual total production varies from 15 000 000 to 19 000 000
bales, distributed as follows :

United States	59.8 %
British India	21.8 »
Egypt	5.5 »
Russia	4.3 »
China	3.6 »
Brazil	2.2 »
Other countries	3.0 »

The industrial development is meanwhile growing apace out
of Europe.

The increase of spindles, from 1890 to 1910, was 91.8 % in
the United States and 79.4 % in British India, while it was only
54.6 % in Europe.

It becomes therefore very important to find out what are the
productive capacities of all the different cotton centres of the world,
and to stimulate cotton production in all those countries where
cotton con be grown.

It is useless to expect the present production centres to improve the future conditions of the European cotton industry.
Without speaking of the United States, any future increase in Asia
would always be largely absorbed by the markets there. In the
same way, Russia would absorb its own production in Central
Asia, where the institution of numerous experimental stations and
other measures taken by the Russian Ministry of Agriculture are
developing the cotton industry. In South America also, even if
the difficulties of hand labour and capital could be surmounted,

the increase of production would be absorbed by the local demand. The same may be said for Australia, in proportion as the soil and climate may allow the extension of cotton planting.

For the use of the cotton industry in Europe there remains only Africa, where Egypt alone up to the present has an important place in the world's cotton market. But the production of Egypt is restricted to an irrigated centre, and limited by the continuous increase in the value of the soil, which will cause the substitution of more intensive cultivations than that of cotton. The whole remainder of Africa must be looked upon for the future as the principal Colonial territory that can furnish cotton to the European industrial states. These states are making every effort to introduce and develop cotton cultivation in the regions most suited, in order to remedy the pressing scarcity of raw material from which their textile industries are suffering. At the same time, each European nation is taking every commercial or political step possible for securing the cotton production of its Colonies as a national industry.

Thus Germany is taking the proper measures for continuously developing the cotton cultivation in her Colonies, not only in the interest of her industries, but also in the interest of the working and middle classes.

In German East Africa, the Indian cotton (*Gossypium herbaceum*) has been introduced, and in the interior the Peruvian cotton (*G. peruvianum*). At Togo the Sea-Island cotton (*G. Barbadense*) and also a hybrid between the Sea Island and Peruvian. In Kamerun there have been for a long time several kinds of cotton, introduced probably by Arab influence. In South-West Africa, in Amboland, there are a few plantations, probably due to missionaries.

Since 1903 some plantations of Egyptian cotton have been made in German East Africa, with excellent results ; but the cotton there is liable to various diseases, owing to the fact that the seed bought in Egypt has to adapt itself to totally new conditions. Hence the establishment of the Cotton Station of Mpanganya in German East Africa for the production of local seed. The Egyptian varieties succeeded best; then came the American Upland (*G. hirsutum*) ; while the Caravonica failed entirely. The cultivation is still carried on chiefly by natives, for whose benefit the Cotton School at Mpanganya has been created and a fixed wage guaranteed. The large plantations were much developed in 1908. At present there are 12 Companies with 85 000 hectares. There are also 3500 hectares cultivated in European plantations of less importance. In Togo, cotton production is much in the hands of the natives, who require the tactful treatment which is only possible when they are understood. In German South-West Africa and in Kamerun, little has been done for cotton production, and not much remains to be done in the German territories of the Pacific.

Generally speaking, it may be said that the German Colonies offer favourable conditions for the cultivation of cotton ; in certain regions the conditions are even excellent. One of the greatest difficulties is that due to the periods of drought, especially in East Africa and in Togo; but artificial irrigation is possible in the former. It is generally advisable that the small native cultivations should be allowed to develop side by side with the large European plantations, which should be directed according to the rules of modern agriculture. The substitution of the plough for the spade, together with the extension of railways, will largely contribute to the economical development in tropical Africa.

It is desirable that special experimental stations should be organised by the State in the German African Colonies. Those stations should attend to:

The choice and cultivation of cotton varieties adapted to the different conditions of the soil and climate, special attention being given to the earliness of the varieties, their resistance to disease, the quality and quantity of the crops and of seed production.

The determination of suitable methods of cultivation, tillage of the soil by hand and by animal traction. Irrigation and fertiliser experiments. Determination of the best rotations and subsidiary cultivations. The study and control of parasites. Agricultural training of planters and natives.

These are the objects provided for by the Convention of March 14th, 1910 between the German Imperial Colonial Office and the Colonial Economic Committee. The effect will be to extend cotton cultivation experiments and increase the available resources, for investigating and improving all the conditions connected with the production of cotton, the Colonial Administration having thus to organise a State Experimental Administration.

By the afore-mentioned Convention, the Imperial Colonial Office is connected with the Organisation of the Colonial Economic Committee in Germany and with its proper representatives in the Colonies, in order that the work may proceed in a uniform and disciplined manner.

The German nation has a general interest, as have all other industrial nations, in encouraging the cultivation of cotton in the Colonies ; and this is why State aid is necessary in addition to private efforts. The following is a comparison of the expenditure

	£	£
Great Britain . . .	470 000	1 005 000
Germany. . . .	85 000	215 000
France . . . ˙ .	45 000	45 000

These figures show that the money expended by England has already given satisfactory results.

The publication of the *Reichkolonialamt* on the Cotton Question gives useful bibliographical indications at the end of each chapter. In Appendix are some special reports on the causes of the " Cotton Famine ", and on Cotton production in North America and in other countries.

1157   C. TROPEA. **Cotton Cultivation in Italy.** (Sulla possibilità di esten-
dere le colture cotoniere in Italia). *Bollettino del R. Orto Botanico e Giardino Coloniale di Palermo*, Anno IX, N. 4, pp. 169-179.

**Italy :
Sicily
Sardinia**

The present condition of the market tends to encourage cotton cultivation in Italy. In Sicily there used to be thousands of hectares of cotton plantations; but American competition greatly reduced this culture in Sicily, where the small area now under cotton is cultivated with very primitive methods.

Cotton could be grown in Sicily on two extensive plains, one irrigated, that of Catania, and the other dry, that of Terranuova. If these two regions were to resume the cultivation of cotton, adopting modern methods, the quantity of cotton necessary for Italian industry would be assured.

Without counting Sicily and Sardinia, where it is now admitted that cotton gives a satisfactory yield, it will be as well to study what other parts of Italy might be utilised for this cultivation.

Mr. Tropea has made a comparison between the climates of Bulgaria and Italy. He gives tables of the average monthly temperature and of the rainfall at the Agronomic Station of Sadovo, which show that the greater part of Italy has an average temperature superior to that of Bulgaria, and that the rainfall is also more abundant.

Italian climatic conditions are therefore more suitable for cotton production than Bulgarian, where cotton is cultivated over very extensive areas, and where a still greater extension is predicted. The lands bordering the Mediterranean could grow especially those cotton varieties that flourish under similar climatic conditions in Bulgaria and Turkestan.

Cotton Cultivation in Tunis. (La culture du Cotonnier en Tunisie)   1158
La Dépêche Tunisienne, XXIII année, N. 7491, Tunis, mars 2, 1911.

The Research Section of the Agricultural Association of Tunis,   Tunis
at its meeting on March 1st, examined the question of Cotton growing in Tunis.

Mr. Barrion reported that the first attempts had been very encouraging. Some planters also spoke of the good results obtained. Mr. Gounot pointed out how prosperous this cultivation is near Bizerta, where the natives have grown cotton from time immemorial Seeds of different varieties of cotton will be distributed throughout the country,

G. C. DUDGEON. **Assil Cotton in Egypt.** *Nature,* vol. 86, London.   1159
March 30, 1911, pag. 144.

Mr. G. C. Dudgeon, General Director of the Agricultural Depart-   Egypt
ment in Cairo, in a letter to the Editor of *Nature,* writes : A form of cotton has been produced by selection in the field from superior growths of Mit Afifi, which is said to be a pure strain and similar to the Mit Afifi of twenty years ago. This form is known by the name of « Assil, » meaning « of pure original strain »

In order to prevent all mistakes, and that the new variety may not be confounded with the existing impure Mit Afifi, it is recommended that the former be for the present referred to as « Assil Afifi ».

Substitutes for Cotton. (Plantes capables de produire des succédanés   1160
du Coton). — *La Quinzaine Coloniale,* N. 7, p. 239, 10 Avril 1911. Paris.

At the meeting of the *Kolonial-Wirtschaftliches Komitee* of   German
Berlin, Mr. Hulfeld advised that measures be taken to promote the   Colonies

cultivation of certain plants capable of affording substitutes for cotton (*Kapok* and *Calotropis*) (1) :

Fibre plants should be systematically collected and studied and tried in experimental fields. Publications on fibre plants should be distributed and encouragement given to the cultivation of these plants and the testing of their fibres.

1161   **Irish Flax growing Industry.** (Minutes of Evidence, Appendices and Index ; Report) *Dep. of Agric. and Techn. Instruction for Ireland*, pp. XII + 505, 23, Dublin, 1911.

United
Kingdom :
Ireland

The following is a summary of the chief conclusions and recommendations of the Irish Committee on Flax culture :

1) The area planted in flax in Ireland has been gradually decreasing for several decades. Twelve years ago it reached the minimum, but since that period there has been a slight increase.

2) The extent of the areas planted in flax has always fluctuated considerably so that statistics on the crops are of little use in drawing conclusions as to the future of this cultivation.

3) The following considerations would suggest that the cultivation of flax may be extended and continued in certain districts :

a) In Ulster, which was the centre of the industry, the decrease is less marked than in the other provinces.

b) In other countries, there has been a simultaneous decrease in the area under flax. At present flax fibre is rare, a fact which will undoubtedly cause an increase in the cultivation of flax in the various parts of the world.

c) Irish flax possesses in a special degree the qualities of strength and fitness for spinning, which make it nearly indispensable in certain branches of the Irish spinning industry.

d) There will probably be an increased demand for Irish flaxes if the price of cotton keeps as high as it has been of late.

4) While there have been several causes for the decline in the cultivation of flax, the most striking is the speculative character of the crops due to the uncertainty in prices and production.

---

(1) *Calotropis gigantea*, or *Asclepias gigantea*. An Asclepiad cultivated in the East Indies, extensively in Equatorial Africa, besides being cultivated in Egypt, where it is known under the name of "Aschur". The woody bark furnishes a long, fine, silky tow which is not very strong and is used for stuffing cushions and for manufacturing sewing and weaving thread as well as fine stuffs.

HEUZÉ, *Les plantes industrielles*, p. 208, Paris 1893.   (*Ed.*).

5) Irish flax has an intermediate position between that of Courtrai, which is ranked highest, and that of Russia, which is lowest.

6) In regard to the uncertainty of the yields, it seems that success in the cultivation of flax is due rather to the adaptation to the soil, to the seasons, and the quality of the seed than to the application of fertilisers.

7) The quality of the seed influences greatly the success of the cultivation. There are great differences between the different stocks of seeds which come from Russia and Holland. It is often doubtful whether the seeds thus imported have been specially selected for the production of fibres of a superior quality, the object for which flax is cultivated in Ireland

8) The opinion that the Riga flax-seed is suitable for light soils and the Dutch seed for heavy soils, is not borne out by experiments made by the Irish Department of Agriculture, nor has it been justified by the experience of the best farmers.

9) The Irish Department of Agriculture ought to undertake experiments on a large scale to find out whether better seeds can be produced from the Irish plantations than those which come from abroad, adopting a similar method of selection to that employed successfully for cereals.

10) The quality and the product of fibre is greatly influenced by the method of retting used. The great variability in the character of the ponds and the quality of the water in which the flax is steeped increases the difficulty of ensuring uniform results.

11) The Irish Department of Agriculture ought to undertake investigations for the solution of the retting problem.

12) Although it is possible to find a river, lake or canal in Ireland where the flax could be properly and uniformly retted, the great difficulty of drying and the lack of middlemen to buy the standing crop are serious obstacles to the adoption of the Courtrai system of retting.

13) If a syndicate were to be formed for the purpose of buying and retting the flax according to the Courtrai system or some other good artificial method, the Department of Agriculture, without accepting financial responsibility would be ready to give advice and technical instruction on the cultivation and drying of flax.

14) There is undoubtedly still some progress to be made in tilling ; but it may be said to be well done in Ireland on the whole. Bad retting and a want of care in the other operations carried out before the plants are consigned to the factory are to a

great extent the cause of the numerous defects generally attributed to the tilling.

15) There is no evidence to confirm the frequently expressed opinion that the decrease in the cultivation of flax should be attributed to a perceptible change in the climate in Ireland.

16) The emptying of the water which has been used for retting flax, into the rivers and small watercourses causes great damage to fish, especially by the destruction of fry.

17) In cases where the water cannot be run on the fields to be absorbed, the difficulty might be solved by means of evacuation dams.

18) The Irish Department of Agriculture ought to make experiments in the method of evacuating, purifying and chemically treating the flax water, and studying the action of this water in various dilutions on the life of fish.

19) Consecutive experiments on the cultivation, manuring and treatment of flax, as well as on the varieties of seed, should be studied and carried out by the Department of Agriculture according to the advice of the Consultive Flax Committee.

20) The Irish Department of Agriculture ought, lastly, to get together an expert staff for the practical cultivation, treatment and sale of flax, and should put this staff at the disposal of groups of producers.

1162   **The Cultivation of Flax in France. Flax Competition for 1911.** (La culture du Lin en France. Concours linier). *L'Engrais*, N. 11, p. 297, Lille, 17, March 1911.

France   The French Flax Committee is organising a Flax Competition for the year 1911 in all the Departments of France.

The cultivators to whom they appeal are those who have planted an experiment field in flax of at least 75 *ares* (about 2 acres) and have made some comparative studies of seed or of manure.

Special rewards will be given to those assistant instructors who may have succeeded in planting flax on a large scale in their own or neighbouring districts.

The programme of the competition will be sent on request by Mr. Albert Durand, Secretary of the Flax Committee, 6 Rue Faidherbe, Lille.

1163   **Hemp-Culture in Madagascar.** (La culture du Chanvre à Madagascar). — *La Quinzaine Coloniale*, N. 7, p. 247, Paris, 10 April 1911.

Madagascar   Hemp grows very readily in various regions of Madagascar, especially in the province of Vakinankaratra, where some satisfactory experiments have been carried out. At present no business is done in hemp, on account of the defective method of preparation. Some native retters are to be sent to the districts where the plant is cultivated, in order to teach the method of treating hemp.

A. BELLUCCI, AND T. VALBUSA. **Sugar-beet Culture Experiments**   **1164**
in Italy. (Esperienze sulla coltivazione della barbabietola zuccherina nella Provincia di Ravenna) *Cattedra ambulante d'Agric. per la Prov. di Ravenna*. pp. 54 + figs. Ravenna 1911.

These experiments were made near Ravenna during 1910, in a   Italy
fertile alluvial soil.

The following are the chief results;

1) The varieties of Sugar beet which gave good results were the *Schlieckmann, orig. No. 2*, the *Rittergut No.* 15,(husked), the M. Deutsch B.A. 3 (No. 4), the *Rabbethge & Giesecke*, the *X. W. No. 21*; then come the *Vilmorin Andr. & C.A. No. 8 and 9*, the Buszczynski and the Lazynski N. 27; and lastly the Indigenous No. 45.

2) The varieties in which the proportion of sugar remained most constant and highest after the September rains were the *Schlieckmann*, the *Vilmorin*, the *M. Deutsch* and the *Rittergut*.

3) The quantity of beets produced, within certain limits, is in direct ratio to the early sowing, decreasing gradually and constantly with late sowing.

4) The proportion of sugar, and still more the purity of the juice, in respect. to early or late sowing, follows the same lines as the production, with some rare exceptions.

5) Reasonably early sowing is preferable to late sowing.

6) March is the best month for sowing beet in the district of Ravenna.

7) Late sowing may sometimes give good results when the season is favourable.

8) In the fresh and deep soil where the experiments were made, the production did not vary directly with the space between the seeds.

9) The sugar content, with the exception of the first plot, underwent a slight but gradual decrease from the plots sown at fair distances apart (35 × 25, 40 × 20) to those sown at greater distances.

10) The purity of the juice followed the same lines as the sugar content, in regard to sowing,

11) The increase in production due to potash fertilisers did not pay, the soil being naturally rich in potash. Kainite gave better results than any other potash fertiliser.

12) The addition of potash salts in all cases increased the sugar content of the beets:

13) Potassium sulphate increased the purity of the juice.

14) Chloride of potassium and kainit decreased the purity of the juice.

The minimum rainfall in these Ravenna experiments occurred in May and August, the maximum in September.

The absolute maximum of sugar content was 22.50%, with a juice purity maximum of 91.35%. The average maximum of sugar content was 18.93%, and of purity 87.74 %.

1165

F. G. KRAUSS. **Peanuts in Hawaii.** (Hawaii Agricultural Experiment Station; Honolulu) Press Bulletin N. 28, pp. 11 + 2 pls.

Hawaii

There are two more or less distinct types of peanuts. Under Hawaiian conditions, the « bunch » type grows into an erect, compact bush 8 to 24 inches (20 to 60 cm) high with an equal spread of foliage; the « running » or « flat » type is decumbent and spreading, rarely more than 1 foot (30 cm) high, and in some varieties attains a spread of fully 5 feet (1.52 metres) in diameter. The first type is best adapted where the crop of nuts is the principal object; the second is preferable for fodder or green manuring.

Except for an occasional small planting made by Chinese and Japanese gardeners, very little has been done to develop peanut as a field crop in Hawaii. Experiments conducted by the Hawaii Agricultural Experiment Station, show that the peanut would deserve extensive planting in the islands.

The yields of peanuts obtained by the Station and cooperative experimental plantings for the years 1908, 1909 and 1910, are summarized in the following table:

VARIETY OF PEANUT (Arachis hypogaea)	Calculated to average acre yields			Highest Acre Yield (lbs)	Lowest Acre Yield (lbs)	Days to Maturity
	Green Weight Whole peanut (lbs)	Cured Weight Nuts (lbs)	Cured Weight Tops (lbs)			
Spanish.	10 454	1 728	1 835	3 858	564	168
Bunch Jumbo . . .	8 961	1 881	1 950	3 225	837	158
Running Jumbo . .	14 439	2 077	2 256	4 729	675	158
Virginia Creeping . .	—	2 026	2 205	2 489	920	157
Bunch Virginia (Sport).	16 803	2 249	2 714	4 130	832	173

The best results appear invariably to have been obtained on light soils with moderate moisture.

Under several years culture in Hawaii, the peanut has much improved, bearing larger and heavier kernels.

The following are the average yields, in number per plant, of sound, well-matured nuts taken from a large number of select plants used for breeding purposes: Spanish 145; Bunch Jumbo 184; Running Jumbo 208; Virginia Creeping 219; and Virginia Bunch 190. Numerous selections of Virginia Creeping having yielded 250 and more sound nuts. The green weight of such plants has averaged something over 10 lbs (4 530 kg) each, and the cured pods have run about 250 seeds per pound as against 325 pods per pound (620 seeds as against 710 pods per kg) of the imported stock. A single plant of the sport Bunch Virginia, has yielded 280 nuts, weighing 1 pound 3 ounces (538 gr.).

CL. GRIMME. **An Oily Fruit of Guatemala.** (Un fruit oléagineux du Guatemala) (Chem. Rev. d. Fett. u. Harz. Ind. 1910, p. 158) *Journal de Pharmacie et de Chimie*, 103 année, 7 Serie, Tome IIIe, N. 7e, p. 358, Paris, April 1, 1911.

1166

Guatemala

This fruit, which is not yet determined from the botanical point of view, resembles the cherry, and belongs to the Simarubaceae, perhaps to the *Picramnia Carpinterae* Polack. The stone has the appearance of a coffee bean, but is very soft.

Extraction by ether gave 75.98% of a solid, crystallized fat, with the following characters:

Melting point.	50° to 52°
Index of acidity	3.6
Iodine number	63.9
Refraction index	1.4624 at 50° C.
Saponification index	156.2
Non-saponified matters	1.74%

This fat contained 96.3% of fatty acids, having the following characters.

Melting point.	56° to 57°
Saturation index	192
Molecular weight	292.5
Refraction index	1.4538 at 70° C.
Iodine number	87

The residue after ether extractions contained 35.23 % of protein.

1167

The Tea Industry in Russia. (L'industrie du Thè en Russie) — *Feuille d'Informations du Ministère de l'Agriculture*, XV année, n. 11 p. 4, Paris, March 14, 1911.

**Russia
Caucasus**

The cultivation of tea in the Caucasus (1) is the object of investigation and encouragement by the Russian Ministry of Agriculture.

To Colonel A. Solovtzeff, who was awarded a first Prize in 1896 at the International Exhibition at Nijni-Novgorod, belongs the merit of having placed this industry on a firm footing.

From some information reprinted in the *Feuille d'Informations* from the Bulletin of the French Chamber of Commerce at Constantinople, it appears that a complete crop is not obtainable until the plants are from 7 to 8 years old.

The first picking is, as a rule, done at the end of the fourth year; and three or four cuttings are made each year. The crop per hectare is about 3 200 lbs of green leaves which would make about 740 lbs of dry leaves.

The sale price on the spot is 50 centimes (5 d.) per lb (409 gr.). and the price of a pound of tea at St. Petersburg, including all expenses, is 2.35 Frs. (1 s. 10 d.).

. According to the analyses of Trans-Caucasian soils made by Professor Kzassunnoff and others, there are from 28 000 to 33 000 hectares of land which are suitable for tea cultivation in the districts of Batum, to the west of Kontais, and to the south of Sukhum. This area might yield annually from 21 to 26 million lbs of tea, which could easily be sold in Russia, as she imports annually 144 million lbs of tea.

1168

Experimental Work at Tobacco growing Stations in Canada. *Bulletin* No. A-9, *Tobacco Division, Department of Agriculture*, Ottawa, Canada, p. 51.

Canada

This Bulletin has three divisions. The first contains a statement of the object of the three Experimental Stations organized in Canada, chiefly for the growing of tobacco, together with a brief analysis of the results already obtained. Parts 2 and 3, prepared by officers in charge of the Stations, present a report of work done and progress made. Complete instructions are given for preparing the soil, planting, cultivating and harvesting the crop,

---

(1) See this Bulletin N. 2, Dec. 1910, p. 263.

together with notes on varieties of tobacco, methods of manuring etc·
Twelve half-tone illustrations serve to give a clear understanding
of the text in regard to a subject comparatively new to Canadian
farmers.

F. CHARLAN. **Tobacco Growing in British Columbia.** *Bulletin*   1169
No. A-10, *Tobacco Division, Department of Agriculture*, Ottawa, Canada, p. 15.

This Bulletin contains a summary of observations made by   Canada:
Mr Charlan, Canadian Chief of the Tobacco Division, during a trip   British
in the Province of British Columbia. The possibilities of tobacco-   Columbia
growing from a purely agricultural standpoint are discussed. Advice
is given for the guidance of beginners on the proper method of
tobacco cultivation.

F. CHARLAN. **Financial Situation of the Tobacco Growers in Ca-**   1170
nada. *Dep. of Agric. Tobacco Division, Bulletin* N. A-11 p. 12,
Ottawa, Canada January, 1911.

In Canada, perhaps more than anywhere else, tobacco growing   Canada:
has justified its reputation for being a profitable industry.   Quebec
In the Quebec centres the yields have long been limited to 1000   Ontario
to 1200 pounds per acre. In years when high prices prevail, a gross
revenue of $ 100 per acre is for from being exceptional. The cost of
production, including the personal work of the farmer and his family,
seldom exceeds $ 45 to $ 50 per acre. The net profit is then about
fifty dollars per acre. An experienced grower can easily obtain
heavier yields and realize as much as $ 75 per acre and even more.
The brillant prospects opened to the tobacco grower by Canadian
legislation will probably encourage him to modify his rather antiquated methods of culture. It will then be possible for him to increase
his net average yield to $ 75 and even to $ 100 per acre in certain cases.
Under such conditions tobacco culture becomes one of the most profitable industries.
In Ontario, owing to the variety most generally grown (Burley)
the yields are much heavier than in the province of Quebec. When
in both these provinces more attention is given to the soil, it will
be possible to maintain the average between 1500 and 2000 pounds
per acre. At this rate, if the market price is 9 cents per pound (it is
actually from 10 to 11 cents), the net profit per acre will be from $ 80
to $ 100.

It is admitted by American growers engaged in the experiments
undertaken in Canada, or who have visited its tobacco-growing centres, that this branch of Agriculture is nowhere as prosperous as it is
in Canada. The immigrant with capital might well be advised that
it is one of the most profitable in which he could invest his money.

1171

ARDOUIN-DUMAZET. **Hop Gardens in French Flanders** (Les hou-
blonnières de la Flandre française). — *Journ. d'Agric. pratique*,
N. 14, pp. 439-441, Paris, 6 Avril 1911.

France:
Flanders

There are some hop gardens in the Cambrésis which cover
an area of 500 hectares; in this region the plants are trained on
wooden poles, whereas in Flanders, on the borders of Belgium, iron
wire frames are used. The Flemish hop region includes only about
600 or 700 hectares in the cantons of Steenwoorde and Bailleul; its
main production centre is Boeschèpe. The fields are surrounded
with tall poles bent outwards joined together at the top by thick
iron wires; thinner wires are drawn from these towards the ground
near the stocks of the hop plants, which are 2 metres apart.
The Boeschèpe mark is considered the best. The association
of the hop-planters dates from March 15th, 1859. A Commission
nominated by the planters superintends the packing of the hops
into bags and examines the quality of the product. These measures
enable the farmers of Boeschèpe to keep up their mark and to
obtain a high price on the market: 50 fr. per quintal of 50 kg.
As soon as they are gathered, the hops are taken to a drying
room or oast. The oasts are still primitive, and Flanders has
been oustripped by England and Belgium in this respect.

1172

P. JEANCARD AND C. SATIE. **The Essences of Rosemary and their**
principle Characteristics. — (Les essences de Romarin et leurs
principales caractéristiques) *Revue Générale de Chimie pure et appliquée*, 13 année, T. XIV, n. 8, pp. 123-131, Paris, April 23, 1911.

France.
Austria.
Spain.
Algeria.
Tunis

The distillation of rosemary is carried on in France, Austria,
Spain and the north of Africa, in the following districts;
    1) France: Alpes-Maritimes, Basses Alpes, Var, Gard, Aude.
    2) Austria: the Dalmatian Islands: Lesina, Lissa, and Solta.

---

(1) See this *Bulletin*: Nov. 1910, p. 76 - Dec. 1910, p. 267, 269 - March
1911, n. 843.   (*Ed.*).

3) Spain: the provinces of Granada and Malaga.

4) Africa: Tunis and Algeria.

The essence known in trade as « Italian Rosemary » comes from Dalmatia.

According to the analytical data given in the paper, the variations in the characters of the pure essences are as follows.

Specific weight at 15° C. 0.900 to 0.920

Rotatory power: 0 to + 12°

Solubility at 15°, alcohol at 90° : 0.1 to 0.5.

Solubility at 15° C. alcohol at 85° : 0.5 to 0.1.

Index of saponification after acetylation: 35 to 60.

Total Borneol: 9.88 to 17.28

Rosemary essences are sometimes mixed with essence of sage. It is uncertain whether this mixture constitutes a fraud as both products have practically the same value on the market.

The sage and rosemary differ considerably in their organoleptic qualities, as well as in their constants. The following are the constants of sage essence:

Specific weight at 15° C. 0.925 to 0.930.

Rotatory power: + 10° to + 20°.

Solubility: alcohol at 80°, 1 to 2.

Solubility: alcohol at 75°, 1.5 to 5.

Solubility: alcohol at 70°, 8 to 12, (and 20)

Index of saponification, 30 to 40.

Index of saponification after acetylation, 70 to 90.

P. Dussert. **The Pruning of Vanilla at Mayotte.** (Le taille de la Vanille en usage à Mayotte) *L'Agriculture pratique des pays chauds*, N. 94.pp. 34-39, Paris Jan. 1911.   **1173**

In the vanilla orchards of Dapany (Mayotte), a special method   **Mayotte** of pruning has been applied to the vanilla plants, whose delicacy has always been a great difficulty. The object was to develop stem and branches. The treatment insures the following characteristics:

1. No fruit on the main stalk, which thus keeps all its strength for acting as a sap duct;

2. Fructification localised on the secondary branches, which are easily regulated as to number and length;

3. Suppression of the branches immediately after they have fructified.

The vanilla plant, when treated thus, if grown on flat ground, does not appear as usual in the form of a very long and bifurcated liane, but grows bushy, with numerous short stems.

The success of this method, lies in the fact that by the simple operation of bending, the branches which bear the fruit bcome secondary branches, and their removal, when the crop is gathered, does not interfere with the main stem. The fruit appears each year on secondary branches, which have not borne the previous season.

1174   HARMS. **Cultivation of the *Kerstingiella geocarpa* Harms. in Tropical Africa** (Ueber die Verbreitung der *Kerstingiella geocarpa* im Tropischen Afrika). — *Deutsche Kolonialzeitung*, N. 10, p. 160, Berlin, März 11, 1911.

Togo   The natives of Togo cultivate a bean, *Kerstingiella geocarpa*, which includes three varieties differing in the colour of the seed. The plant is analogous, if not identical, to that which grows in Dahomey, where it is called *Doi* (*Voandzeia Poissoni*, A. Clerc) (1). After flowering, the fruit of this Leguminosa works down into the soil, where it ripens.

The excellent qualities of this legume should lead to its cultivation in the German, French and English Colonies.

1175   **Electricity in Horticulture.** *Fruit, Flower, and Vegetable Trades' Journal.* London, April 15, 1911, p. 337.

Great
Britain:
England   At a meeting of the Farmers' Club held in London early in April, Prof. J. H. Priestley read a paper on « Electricity as a Fac or in Crop Production ».

The investigations carried out resemble those made by Mr. J. E. Newman and Sir Oliver Lodge. At Evesham on Mr. R. Bomfords' farm a network of electric wires was erected over several fields of wheat, while other fields where the same kinds of wheat were growing, were used to control the experiment. The electrified wheat gave a yield varying from 13 % for Webb's Red Standard to 39 % for Red Fife in excess of the yield of the un-electrified wheat.

---

(1) See this Bulletin, Nov. 1910, p. 79. According to Auguste Chevalier *C. R. de l'Acad. de Sciences*. Tome 151, N. 26, p. 1374. Paris, 27 Dec. 1910. *Kerstingiella geocarpa* Harms is identical with *Voandzeia Poissoni* and as Dr. Harms had studied this plant 18 months earlier, the name he has given should be adopted and *Voandzeia Poissoni* considered as a synonym. Neither of the two names is entered in the *Index Kewensis* nor in its supplements up to 1905.   (*Ed.*).

In these experiments the tension was transformed by a dynamo to 100 000 volts, the wires carrying only 0.10 amperes. Mr. Priestley also dealt with the application of electric light in greenhouses for stimulating plant growth (1).

The Trade in Vegetables and Early Fruits in the United States (Le Commerce des légumes et des Primeurs aux Etats-Unis). — *Bull. de l'Office du Gouv. Général de l'Algerie*, N. 8, p. 119, Paris, 15 Avril, 1911.

1176

It is a notable fact that vegetables import trade into the United States is continually increasing. Green peas and beans are imported from the following countries: Austria, France, Germany, Italy, the United Kingdom, Canada and Mexico.

United States

Asparagus is more generally sold in tins; very little arrives in the fresh state. The Argenteuil asparagus is particularly appreciated. In years when the home crop is poor, potatoes are imported in very large quantities, and the New York market may become of considerable interest to European exporters. The chief exporting countries are: England, Canada and the Bermudas. In addition to the different vegetables mentioned above, a large quantity of other vegetables is imported from Europe in tins: namely, carrots, celery, spinach, lettuce, turnips, sorrel, artichokes, cauliflowers, tomatoes, etc.

The early fruits can only be imported in small quantities.

Market Garden Cultivation at Dakar, Senegal (La culture maraîchère à Dakar, Sénégal). — *La Quinzaine Coloniale*, N. 7, p. 245, Paris, 10 Avril, 1911.

1177

Mr. W. Ponty has been encouraging the development of market gardening at Dakar, not only for local consumption, but also with the object of provisioning ships. The results obtained are excellent, and Dakar produces vegetables that are not inferior to those of France.

French West Africa: Senegal

---

(1) Compare with: T. A. PRIESTLEY, *Electro-Culture, Overhead Electrica Discharges and Plant Growth*, abstracted in the publication of the Intelligence Office of the Intern. Inst. of Agriculture, *The Science and Practice of Farming during 1910 in Great Britain as seen through the Scientific and Agricultural Press*, Rome, 1910, p. 225. (*Ed.*).

1178   **The Cultivation of Onions, near Naples.** (La coltivazione delle cipolle nella regione Vesuviana). — *La Rivista Agraria*, No. 2 e 3. p. 34, Napoli, genn. 15 e 22, 1911.

Italy:
Naples

Summer onions are grown near Naples, in market gardens, the spring varieties being a field-crop often grown in rotation with maize or hemp. The onions grown in clay soil contain a high percentage of essential oils. They are either sown on the spot or transplanted from a nursery.

Generally speaking, the *white* onions are summer, the *coloured* ones spring, varieties. The best Neapolitan varieties are: the *Barletta Onion*, the *Nocera*, the *Naples* and the *Bajano*. The most appreciated is the *Rocca Onion*.

Onions require a soil rich in potash. Near Vesuvius, the natural richness of the volcanic soils in potash, makes a potash fertiliser unnecessary.

The production is as follows in the province of Naples:

Kitchen garden onions: from 80 to 100 quintals per hectare.

Field onions: from 100 to 250 quintals per hectare.

The production is poorer in the kitchen gardens, because the onions are gathered before they are fully grown, in order that they may be put on the market more rapidly.

1179   GRANATO. **The Cultivation of Onions at St. Paul, Brazil.** (A cultura da cebola em S. Paulo). — *Boletim de Agricultura*, N. 11, p. 981, Sao Paulo, 1910.

Brazil:
St. Paul

The cultivation of onions was introduced into the State of S. Paul some time ago: the early white, the Italian white, the Egyptian and Madeira onions, and the Covent Garden variety have been tried with excellent results.

As Brazil imports about 500 000 kg. of onions from Portugal and Italy every year, it is clearly in her interest to encourage this cultivation on her own territory.

1180   H. SACHS. **Cultivation Experiments with Various Varieties of Peas.** (Die Erbsen-Anbauversuche im Jahre 1910). *Mitteilungen der Deutschen Landwirtschafts-Gesellschaft*, XXVI J., Stück 14, pp. 175-176, Berlin, April 1, 1911.

Germany

This is a description of the results of some experiments which were made in 1910 in continuation of those begun for the first time in 1909. These were carried out in five different localities, on plots of 2 ares and in two on plots of 1 are and 1.5 are respectively. The five following varieties were used, being given in order of ripening : *Express, Ueberreich, Monopol, Schnabel, Canning.*

	Production per hectare	
	Total Crop kg.	Maximum crop per plot kg.
Schnabel (improved)	6 632. 5	11 335
Express	5 319 —	12 050
Monopol	4 452. 5	10 050
Ueberreich	4 160. 5	8 135
Canning	4 078 —	7 200

The yield in seeds was as follows:

Schnabel	maximum	72. 5 kg.,	average	61 — kg.
Express	»	63. 6 »	»	45 — »
Monopol	»	63 — »	»	36. 5 »
Canning	»	48 — »	»	41. 5 »
Ueberreich	»	39. 6 »	»	29. 1 »

The results of the two years' experiments lead to the conclusion that the trial varieties are perfectly adapted both for cultivation in fields, and for preserving ; but low-growing kinds are the best, the use of props being costly.

E. V. WILCOX. **The Management of Pineapple Soils.** *Hawaii Agric. Exp. Station, Honolulu-Press*, Bulletin N. 29, 10 pages. .

1181

Hawaii

The cultivation of pineapples in Hawaii has greatly developed during the past fifteen years, a large part of the pineapple crop being grown on the upland plains of Oahu, principally in the Wahiawa and adjacent districts.

The pineapple soils of Oahu may be divided into two classes as regards colour, viz., black and red soils. In a preliminary report (*Hawaii Sta. Press* Bull No. 23) the peculiarities of the black manganiferous soils were emphasized ; in the present bulletin the management of the red soils is considered.

The practical results of the writer's investigations are summarized as follows :

The continued cultivation of pineapples on the same land (which contains large percentages of finely divided ferric hydrate and small amounts of humus) has already brought about conditions unfavourable to the growth of the crop. The use of fertilizers, such as lime, and manure have not restored this soil to its original productivity

The physical condition of the soil becomes affected and great exhaustion results.

While only a slight change has taken place in the humus, the clay has become deflocculated, thus reducing the size of the pores in the soil and effectually hindering drainage. This condition is brought about by working the soil when it is wet. In some instances, however, it has been caused by beating rains, accompanied by floods. In such puddled soils proper aeration is impossible and bad physical, biological and chemical conditions prevail.

The best remedy is prevention; these soils, as all clay soils, should not be cultivated when wet, for damage is sure to result. Sunshine and air aided by thorough tillage when the soil is in proper moisture conditions will help to restore fertility. The best possible drainage should be provided by introducing ditches at short distances apart. Manure, especially if accompaned with ample aeration, will tend to make the soil more porous and, thus, aid drainage. Lastly the continued cultivation of pineapples should give way to crop rotation.

1182   **The Fruit and Vegetable Trade on the North East Coast of England in 1910**. (Le commerce des Fruits et des Légumes sur la côte Nord-Est anglaise en 1910). — *Feuille d'Informations du Ministère de l'Agriculture*, N. 16, Paris, 18 Avril, 1911.

Great Britain: England

The North-east coast of England offers an extremely important market for the fruits and vegetables which England is obliged to get from abroad to the extent of three quarters of her consumption. Hull is the most importaut market on this coast, Newcastle coming a long way behind. The geographical situation of the former lends itself admirably to the fruit trade, and the port possesses some special conveniences. Since 1907 the trade in fruit and vegetables at Hull has risen to about 25 million francs (£ 1.000.000).

Oranges arrive in large quantities from all the exporting countries. The importation of bananas from the Antilles and the Canary Islands has been continually increasing since the ship services have been improved. The Canaries send bananas, tomatoes and potatoes every fortnight.

The importation of oranges and lemons from Italy is decreasing. Spain furnishes the largest quantity of fruit directly, and Belgium the largest quantity of vegetables.

The total importation in 1910 was as follows :

Apples and Pears . . . .   4 198 tons
Cherries. . . . .   —
Bilberries . . . .   80 564 packages (1)
Currants . . . .   16 362   »
Grapes . . . .   29 026   »
Melons . . . .   18 151   »
Oranges and Lemons . . . . .   161 036 boxes
Plums . . . .   38 636 packages
Bananas . . . .   1 090 tons
Carrots and Turnips . . . . .   1 544   »
Onions . . . .   8 628   »
Potatoes . . . .   10 850   »
Tomatoes . . . .   18 969 packages
Cabbages . . . .   5 517   »
Various vegetables . . . . . .   10 670   »

HORNE. (Brit. Consul) **Raisin Production in the Liao-Tung Peninsula.** — *The Board of Trade Journal.* N. 736, p. 40. London, Jan. 5, 1911.

·1183

Japanese Empire : Liao-Tung

A successful experiment in the production of raisins has been made by the Agricultural Experimental Station at Dairen, (Dalny). It is estimated that, fresh grapes costing 4-4 ½ sen (2) per lb., dry raisins would cost 13 ½-15 sen per lb. and that the wholesale price of the raisins would be 20-25 sen per lb.

J. L. VIDAL. **The Period for Pruning the Vine with Regard to the Reserve Function of the Root.** (L'époque de la taille de la Vigne, en considération de la racine, organe de réserve). *Revue de Viticulture,* N. 897, pp. 219-222, Paris, Feb. 23, 1911.

1184

France

The question of the most favourable period for pruning the vine is a very complicated one, and the various opinions expressed lead to the most contradictory conclusions; Mr. Vidal briefly reviews what has been said on this point, from the oldest writers to those of the present day, and deduces the following facts :

1) The pruning may be done, provided it be suspended during the periods of greatest cold, from the ordinary falling of the leaves

---

(1) From 20 to 25 packages are necessary to make a ton, according to the nature of the merchandise.   (*Ed.*).

(2) 100 sen = 1 yen = 2.55 frcs.   (*Ed.*).

until the vine begins to bleed, and may even be done as late as the bourgeoning, without much risk.

2) Too early or too late pruning weakens the plant, and delays the appearance of the bourgeons; and the earlier, or later, the pruning, the worse the mischief.

3) From the fall of the leaves to the beginning of the bleeding, the pruning has the effect of delaying the bourgeoning and the later the pruning the later the opening of the buds.

4) The southern writers prefer the pruning to follow the very cold period, while those on the shores of the ocean prefer the pruning to precede the cold.

5) There is no absolute certainty in regard to the efficacy of late pruning against frost.

6) Late prunings with a previous « espoudassage » (1), are less weakening.

7) The loss of sap consequent on late prunings is only slightly prejudicial.

8) Autumn pruning is advised for enfeebled vines, which then give finer fruit.

9) Late pruning lessens the dropping, and in certain cases increases, in others, decreases the production. A sufficiently early pruning has the same effect on the fructification and on the vigour as late pruning.

1185 **The Experimental Pruning and Manuring of Olive Trees at Spoleto in Italy.** (L'oliveto dimostrativo dell'Oleificio Sperimentale di Spoleto). — *Il R. Oleificio Sperimentale dalla Calabria all'Umbria. Attività, Esperienze, Ricerche, Studi,* Tip. dell'Umbria Spoleto, 1911.

Italy:
Umbria

The cultivation system adopted in the Olive plantation of the Spoleto Experimental Station is as follows. The grove is divided into two parts, on which the biennal pruning is carried out, alternating with a winter cutting of branches, which is in reality only a reduced pruning. Fertilisers are distributed as follows: in the portion that is pruned in the ordinary way: 1 kg. of superphosphate and 0.500 kg. of chloride of potassium are given

---

(1) In the Department of Hérault, the first part of a pruning, which is done in two parts, is called " espoudassage ". The operation is called " fiançailles " in Charentes and in Yonne, " curage en pied ". (*Ed.*).

per plant. In the year when the pruning is carried out, some superphosphates and from 25 to 40 kg. of farm manure or sheep manure is spread over half the portion, a green vegetable manure being worked into the other half. In this way, an exclusively mineral manure is supplied during the period when the ordinary pruning causes the cutting off of the larger amount of branches from the plant, so that the relation between the branch and root systems is not altered ; on the other hand, stimulating organic and nitrogenous fertilisers are given after the light winter pruning.

Investigations have been begun on the effects of the addition of manure in autumn and in spring and on the treatment against *Cycloconium* by a summer spraying, or by two sprayings in spring and summer, with Bordeaux mixture and with a mixture containing copper sulphate, iron sulphate and lime.

The effects on olive trees of cyanamide on a calcareous soil have been studied. The experiment was made on 36 trees, to which doses of cyanamide of 0.750 kg., 1 kg., 1.50 kg. and 2 kg. were given with other manure. The fertiliser was put down in April, and in August some leaves were observed to be scorched at the tip; this scorched appearance was greater where the larger amount of cyanamide had been given. In November many of the leaves fell, but the addition of stable manure appeared to lessen these effects. In the following April, the olive trees which had received large doses of cyanamide bore very few leaves and the young shoots were weak and stunted. The olive trees which served as control vegetated regularly.

These experiments show that calcium cyanamide in larger doses than 1 kg. per olive tree, in rocky calcareous soils, may be harmful.

MOREAU. **Olive Cultivation in the Matmata in Tunis.** (La culture de l'olivier aux Matmata). — *Bulletin Régence de Tunis*, N. 55, Tunis, 1910.

1186

Tunis :
Matmata

The number of olive trees in the region of the Matmata, at present 60 000 at least, is increasing yearly in the most satisfactory manner. The plantations are entirely carried out by the natives ; there is not a single European estate in the territory.

The pruning of young olive trees is begun at five years, and some very fine results might be expected from the regeneration of old olive trees, which has given such excellent results in the North of Tunis.

The method of extracting the oil in this region has not varied for centuries.

1187   **Apple Cultivation in Nova Scotia.** (Culture de la Pomme en Nouvelle' Ecosse). — *Rapport du Commissaire de l'industrie laitière et de la réfrigération.* Année terminée le 31 mars 1910, pp. XI 159. (137-139) Ottawa, 1910.

Canada:
Nova Scotia

The apple occupies almost exclusively the attention of fruit growers in Nova Scotia. The apple industry is almost entirely limited to three counties: Annapolis, Kings and Hants. From Digby to Falmouth, in the valley of the Annapolis and Cornwallis rivers as well as in the valley of the Gaspereaux and Avon, the apple crop is practically the only paying crop. The specialisation in this industry has perhaps reached a dangerous point. As many of the large tree growers keep little or no cattle, the provision of farm manure is not sufficient for their orchards.

The varieties most cultivated in Nova Scotia are: Baldwin, Northern Spy, and Gavenstein. The latter is losing its popularity, however, because the tree appears to be subject to crown rot.

During the season 1909-1910 there were at least 70 warehouses for the apple industry in the Annapolis and Cornwallis valleys.

1188   A. G. TURNEY. **Apple Growing in New Brunswick.** — *The O. A. C· Review.* Vol. XXIII, N. 6, March, 1911, pp. 287-290. Guelph, Ont. Canada.

Canada:
New
Brunswick

After reviewing the condition of the apple growing industry in various provinces of Canada, the writer refers to the adaptability of extensive sections of New Brunswick for orcharding, in which all the standard Canadian grown apple varieties can be produced profitably. The claim is made that highly coloured varieties, such as Duchess, Dudley, Alexander, Wealthy, Fameuse and Mc. Intosh Red can be grown to perfection. The best apple lands of the province are said to be in the lower St. John Valley, between St. John and Fredericktown.

1189   **Almond Cultivation and Trade in Sardinia.** (Culture et commerce des Amandes en Sardaigne). — *Feuille d'Informations du Ministère d'Agriculture,* N. 15, Paris, 11 Avril, 1911.

Italy:
Sardinia

The rise in prices and the very remunerative speculations which have been made during recent years in the commerce of almonds have caused a very noticeable tendency towards the extension of almond cultivation in Sardinia. Numbers of farmers have substituted almond groves for their vineyards affected by phylloxera. The day is probably not far distant when the Sardinian almond will compete in quantity and quality with the product of countries most renowned for almond production. The Sardinian almonds are of two species : the almond of the plains is flat, broad and thick, while that of the hills is small and rounded. Both sweet and bitter almonds are grown in Sardinia : the latter going mainly to Germany.

The present Sardinian almond production of an average season is about 10 000 quintals.

The Exportation of Almonds and Dates from Persia in 1909-1910.   1190
(L'exportation des Amandes et des Dattes de Perse en 1909-1910).
— *Bulletin de l'Office du Gouv. Général de l'Algérie*, No. 8. p. 119, Paris, 15 Avril, 1911.

The exportation of Persian almonds from the port of Bender-   Persia
Bauchir in 1909-1910 was higher than at any time in the course of the past three years, the falling off in the production of Southern Europe and America having increased the demand for this commodity.

$$1907\text{-}1908 \ldots \ldots \quad 529 \text{ tons.}$$
$$1908\text{-}1909 \ldots \ldots \quad 410 \text{ „}$$
$$1909\text{-}1910 \ldots \ldots \quad 627 \text{ „}$$

Of which 25 tons went to the United States.
„   342   „   „   „ India.
„   201   „   „   „ the United Kingdom.
„   51   „   „   „ Germany.

The almond crop at Ispahan and Schiraz was exceptionally good.

In 1909-1910, 288 tons of dates were exported from Bender-Bauchir, 264 tons of which went to India, while in 1908-1909 the total exportation was 294 tons, 292 going to India.

TSCHIRCH and RAVASINI. **The Wild Fig and its Relation to the**   1191
Capri-fig and the Cultivated Fig. — *C. R. de l'Ac. des Sciences*, T. 152, No. 13. pp. 885-888. Paris, 27 Mars 1911.

The wild fig of Italy and the Capri-fig were long thought to be   Italy
identical. A whole year's examination of more than 20 000 inflorescences from all the forms of fig-tree growing throughout Italy has given results that lead to an entirely different conclusion.

Far from being identical with the Capri-fig, the wild fig of Italy is a veritable prototype; it is an excellent and very constant type, diclinous, monoecious, which has continued to exist far from any other fig cultivation in some little islands of vegetation in Upper Italy, and may be reproduced from seeds of the cultivated fig-tree if the inflorenscences of the latter are visited by the *Blastophaga* (Diptera). This species of fig is called *Ficus Carica* (L.) Tschirch and Ravasini, and is characterised by three generations of fruit which succeed one another on the same tree.

The Capri-fig and the cultivated fig are cultural varieties, which cannot be multiplied by seed, but only by layering or grafting. The Capri-fig (*Ficus Carica*, α *Caprificus*, Tschirch and Ravasini) has three generations of uneatable fruits with male flowers or galls, while the cultivated fig (*Ficus Carica* β *domestica* Tschirch and Ravasini) produces three generations of eatable fruit (*Fichi-fiori, Pedagnuoli, Cimaruoli*, as they are called in Italian) which contain only female flowers.

In the wild fig the pollination is done by the *Blastophaga*, which, in its biological cycle, passes from the gall flower contained in the " *manune* " fruit to the male flowers of the " *profichi* " and the female flowers of the " *fichi* ". In the female cultivated fig pollination does not take place except by caprification, or else accidentally (without caprification) by the Blastophagae.

Caprification, which consists in suspending the male fruit (*pro-fichi*) of the caprifig, or wild fig in the cultivated fig trees, is necessary for all kinds of figs which are to be dried and exported; caprified figs are the only ones which can be preserved.

On the other hand, there are species of fig trees which have been differentiated for thousands of years, and produce without caprification or fecundation, sweet figs, which have no seeds and cannot be preserved. These are the " table figs "; the ripening of which is purely carpological and is similar to that of seedless fruit.

1192   DUCOUSSO. **The Mulberry Tree in Syria.** (Le Mûrier en Syrie). — *Bulletin des Soies et des Soieries*, No. 1765, p. 4, Lyon, 4 Mars 1911.

Ottoman Empire: Syria

The kind of mulberry which is found most extensively in Syria and Lebanon is the " Dwarf mulberry of Japan ", formerly called Cyprus or Cabroussi Mulberry.

This tree, which does not produce any fruit, gives two crops of leaves each year. Sandy soils are better for its cultivation than clay soils. The leaf of the wild stock, which is thinner and more tender than the leaf of the grafted mulberry, is given to the silkworm as soon as it is hatched, as well as at the beginning of each moulting period. It is for this reason that most mulberry plantations include a few plants of the wild stock. But the peasant of Lebanon, who has given up the cultivation of the vine and the olive tree for that of the mulberry, now prefers the orange tree on the plains and tobacco on the hills. Thus, in 1910, while many mulberry plantations have been cleared off the plain to make way for orange groves, not a single new plantation of the mulberry appears to have been made.

There are very few diseases in Syria which are likely to put the mulberry crop in danger, and in 1910 not a single tree was attacked.

Development of the Banana Industry in the Canary Islands. — 1193
The Tropical Agriculturist. p. 221-222, Colombo, March, 1911.

Of the many species which have long been known in the Canaries, the banana that has survived for the special purpose of trade with Europe is the Chinese banana (*Musa Cavendishii*), the least tropical and therefore the most suitable for cold climates. Its cultivation is now at the height of prosperity, and good irrigated land near the coast commands the almost fabulous rent of £40 per English acre. The part of the Canary Islands where most of the bananas are cultivated is the well-known valley of Orotava, owing to the comparatively abundant and never failing supply of water, which no doubt filters down from the high and extensive plateau of the Canadas, nearly 7000 feet high, surrounding the peak of Teneriffe, which is over 12 000 ft.

**Spain :
Canary Isles**

During the winter months there are abundant rains and snow, and the water gradually percolates to the region of the coast, where it is tapped by long, horizontal tunnels. It is then carried along an aqueduct for a great distance to irrigate the land lying below. Irrigation in this country increases enormously the value of land and the great profits made from the cultivation of bananas are unequalled by any other crop.

K. YOSHIMURA. Contribution to the Study of the Banana. (Beiträge 1194
zur Kenntniss der Banane). — *Zeitsch. für Untersuchung der Nahrungs und Genussmittel*, Berlin, 1 April 1911.

Mr Yoshimura's investigations regarded :
1) The chemical processes during the ripening of the banana ;
2) Enzyme-action in the banana ;

Japan.

3) The sugars of ripe bananas.

Some green bananas were gathered on November 3rd, and successively analysed at three different periods. The results were as follows:

	I Control analysis Nov. 9	II Analysis Nov. 16	III Analysis Nov. 23	IV Analysis Nov. 30
	%	%	%	%
Water	70.14	70.31	71.47	70.72
		In 100 parts of dry matter		
Tannin	1.75	1.71	1.71	1.67
Starch	68.16	47.51	24.40	14.48
Reducing sugar ⎰ Calcu-lated as ⎱	0	5.54	13.47	19.83
Saccharose . ⎱ inverted ⎰	0	14.92	28.60	30.12
Total sugar . ⎰ sugar ⎱	0	20.46	42.07	49.95
Inverted sugar: Saccharose = 1.	—	2.69	2.12	1.52

The tannin content remains practically invariable during the ripening process, which would suggest that it has no part in maturation. The transformation of starch into sugar takes place very rapidly: 20 % of the total sugar is obtained at the end of the first week, 42 % at the end of the second week and 50 % at the end of the third. The ratio between saccharose and reducing sugar gradually decreases during the ripening period, which shows that the sugar produced at the beginning is transformed into reducing sugar under the action of an enzyme.

The heating of unripe bananas to 110-120° C. gave the following results:

		In the dry matter	
	Unripe control bananas	At the end of 2 weeks	
		Non-heated	Heated to 110-120° C.
	%	%	%
Starch	68 160	24 400	47 080
Reducing sugar ⎰ Calcul-lated as ⎱	—	13 470	traces
Saccharose . . ⎱ inverted ⎰	—	28 605	—
Total Sugar. . ⎰ sugar ⎱	—	42 075	—

It is evident that the transformation of the starch into sugar is based on an action of the enzyme diastase, and the decrease of starch in the heated bananas is probably due to a corresponding formation of dextrine. The water extract of ripe bananas, submitted to autolysis at 50° C. for one hour, and the same extract boiled gave the following results:

	In 100 parts of fresh matter	
	Boiled	Autolysed at 50° C.
Reducing sugar) as inverted (	2.70 %	8.85 %
Total sugar . .) sugar)	8.41 %	8.88 %

Which shows that the saccharose has been transformed into reducing sugar by an invertase active at 50° C.

Some pieces of the same banana, half ripe, analysed immediately after a slow drying at 50-60° C., gave the following results:

	Reducing sugar (as inverted sugar)	Saccharose	Reducing sugar : saccharose = 1
Direct analysis.	4.50 %	9.75 %	2.155
Analysis after slow drying.	6.42 %	4.87 %	0.758

The slow drying favoured the action of the invertase and it is in this way that the oscillations which occur in the relation between the reducing sugar and the saccharose may be explained.

Some further investigations on the sugars found in ripe bananas led to the conclusion that bananas do not originally contain any other sugar than saccharose.

W. Burns. **The " Pairi '' Mango.** — *The Agricultural Journal of India.* Vol. VI, Part. I. Calcutta, January, 1911.

1195

British India

In the Bombay markets the mango most in demand is the « Alphonse ». This variety has been distributed to most quarters of India, to the West Indies, to America, and to Australia. Next to this variety a less known variety called the « Pairi » has a large production and sale. The size of both varieties is fairly constant. The taste of the « Pairi » fruit is delicious, and slightly more piquant than that of the Alphonse; but it does not keep well. This fact and its different flavour make it a cheaper mango than the Alphonse. The Pairi mango tree has a most vigorous spreading habit of growth. This character makes it an excellent stock for a composite grafted mango giving a vigorous stem. Two sub-varieties of the Pairi mango are known: the *Moti Pairi* and the *Kagdi Pairi*, so called on account of its thin and shining skin. The fruit is said to have firmer flesh and to be superior in flavour to the ordinary Pairi. (1)

(1) *Mangifera indica* has very many varieties, of which more than 500 are cultivated. See G. Watts, *Dictionary of the Economic Products of India :* London, 1891, vol. V. p. 149. (*Ed.*).

Forestry.

1196 **Plans for Eastern Forest Reserves in the United States.** — *American Agriculturist.* New York, April 1, 1911.

United
States

The United States Department of Agriculture announces preliminary plans for the proposed Appalachian and White Mountains forest reserves under the recently enacted Weeks law.

The States which have already passed Acts enabling the national Government to acquire land for the preservation of the navigability of streams are : Maine, New-Hampshire, Maryland, Virginia, West Virginia, North Carolina, Tennessee, South Carolina, and Georgia.

The first lands to be examined for purchase will be in the Appalachian and White Mountains. The lands acquired by the Government will be held as national forests. They will be protected from fire ; and the growth of the timber will be improved as much as possible. The lands will not be game preserves, but will continue to be open to the public for hunting and fishing, in accordance with the laws of the State in which they are situated. The areas within which purchase of land is desired are set forth in detail in the circular of the Forest Service.

1197 JENTSCH. **Kamerun Forests and the Utilisation of Tropical Forests.**
(Der Urwald Kameruns, Folgerungen aus den auf der Expedition 1908-09 gewonnenen Erfahrungen in Bezug auf den Zustand und die Nutzbarmachung des Waldes). — *Beihefte zum Tropenpflanzer*, B. XII, N. ½, pp. 199 +pl. V + 11, Berlin, März 1911.

Kamerun

The forest area in the German Kamerun, the composition of which is not well defined, may be estimated at 6 000 000 hectares.

The present publication explains the principles of the valuation and utilisation of these forests; which principles may eventually serve also for other forests in the tropics.

Twelve experimental plots were selected distinguishing primary virgin forest, secondary virgin forest and secondary forest. The plots, of about 0.5 hectare each, were in their turn subdivided in

6 classes, according to the size of the trunk at the height of a man's chest, from 7 to 60 cm. in diameter.

The average data obtained were the following:

Primary virgin forest; 63 species of trees; trunks per hectare 536; woody mass of more than 7 cm. in diameter 794 m². Wood of the trunk exceeding 60 cm. at the height of a man's chest, 322 m².

Secondary virgin forest: 95 species of trees; trunks per hectare 597; woody mass exceeding 7 cm. in diameter 426 m². Wood of trunk exceeding 60 cm. at the height of a man's chest, 207 m².

Secondary forest: the forest is formed of almost pure *Musanga Smithii.* Trunks per hectare 593; woody mass exceeding 7 cm. in diameter 270 m².

Mr. Jentsch strongly recommends selection felling, for which an annual growth of from 3 ⅓ to 4.4 % might be taken as a basis which corresponds, in absolute figures, to from 19 to 33 m² per hectare, or an average of 26 m² per hectare.

As to the utilisation, after the selection felling, the following number of trunks remain: in the primary forest 93.5 % on an average; in the secondary forest 97.5 %, or an average altogether of 94 ²/₃ %. The products are divided as follows in the cutting:

Primary forest: timber 62 m²; residue 228 m²; total 390 m² per hectare. Percentage of useful wood 42.

Secondary forest: timber 103 m²; residue 99 m²; total per hectare 202 m². Percentage of useful wood 55.

Collective average: timber 146 m²; residue 193 m²; total per hectare 339 m². Percentage of useful wood 43.

But as round wood is dealt with and account must be taken of defects, a further reduction of 33 % must be made, and the definite results would be:

Total quantity felled per hectare 339 m²; timber 97 m²; residue 242 m²; useful percentage 29.

In order to utilise afterwards a considerable proportion of the residues, which are ²/₃ or ³/₄ of the whole cutting, Mr. Jentsch suggests that dry distillation should be adopted, the products of which are in such demand.

The secondary products of the tropical forests under examination are, in addition to rubber, " rotang ", as the Spanish cane for manufacturing small pieces of furniture is called, the resins, barks and tannic extracts, and palm oil.

Three important supplements to Mr. Jentsch's report give the determinations of diameter, the nomenclature, and the botanical and technological descriptions of the timber of Kamerun.

1198   M. LEGA. **The Woods near the Lake of Mahabar.** — (In Dan-
kalia ed in Abissinia). *Bollettino della Società Geografica Italiana,*
N. 4, pp. 444-475, Roma, Aprile, 1911.

Abyssinia   The Lake of Mahabar lies in the region of Vorro-Callo, at an
altitude of 2500 m. above sea level ; it has no outlet. The natives
say that there are no fish living in its waters. Beyond the lake
there is a plain watered by small canals of a rudimentary construction. Over this plain, a ruinous deforestation is carried on, in order
to extend plough cultivation. The forests are retreating towards the
tops of the mountains ; and if their complete destruction is still retarded the delay is due to their extreme density.

These forests are almost entirely composed of the Abyssinian
Juniper (*Juniperus procera*). These are very tall trees which easily
grow to a height of 30 metres. They give fine timber.

1199   E. A. SMYTHIES. **Some Aspects of Fire Protection in Chir Forests,**
***Pinus longifolia,* in India.** *The Indian Forester,* vol. XXXVII,
No. 182, pp. 54-62, Allahabad, Jan. and Feb. 1911.

British India   Mr. Smythies considers three classes of Chir (*Pinus longifolia*)
forest, according as they are protected against fire for 35 years or
15 years, or are burnt annually. A comparison between the three
classes brings out several points of extreme interest :

1) After the year of burning, fire protection gives an extraordinary and universal stimulus to regeneration ;

2) Successful regeneration is possible under the most favourable conditions without fire protection ;

3) Long continued fire protection has always an adverse
effect on regeneration ;

4) Burning does not cause any damage to anything above the
seedling and young plant stage. Accidental fires, on the other hand,
sometimes kill the tallest trees ;

5) In the typical forests of *Pinus longifolia*, fire protection is
useful as far as regeneration is concerned, but only when the conditions are favourable, and it is not always necessary ;

6) When fire protection commences, regeneration takes place
practically everywhere ;

7) With the contrary method, regeneration is not required
everywhere at once, but should be restricted to the regeneration
areas and to blanks ;

8) There is only one way to do this : namely to protect the regeneration areas, and to burn the remainder. Blanks whether protected or not, would fill up, provided the conditions are not unfavourable ;

9) When an area has been successfully regenerated, it should be carefully burnt early in the year, when fires are not intense, and thereafter fire protection abandoned ;

10) It is possible that long continued fire protection causes the power of the forest to deteriorate.

Fire protection would certainly be advantageous under the following conditions ;

11) In all regeneration areas ;

12) In all areas where the protection of the soil is of paramount importance. Undoubtedly, the thick layer of grass and needles obtained in fire protected forests gives more efficient protection to the surface soil than the more scanty covering of burnt areas ;

13) In all plantations ;

14) In certain special cases where the crop has become so thin and scattered that it is advisable to have a complete regeneration even in the areas which are not in regular regeneration coupe.

15) In precipitous areas under the selection system.

Mr. Smythies dwells on the differences between European and Indian forests.

R. H. CAMPBELL. **Forest Fires and Railways in Canada.** — *Bulletin* No. 16 *Forestry Branch, Dept. of Interior*, Ottawa, Canada, pp. 8.   **1200**

Mr. Campbell observes that the proximity to a forest of a railway either in construction or operation increases the danger of fire. This, he says, is partly due to causes connected with the railway itself, and partly due to the crowds of land-seekers, prospectors, freighters, tramps and other irresponsible people, who follow it. The record of each year's conflagrations shows that the « iron road » is one of the chief occasions of forest fires. The question is treated by Mr. Campbell under the following heads : Fires arising from Railway Construction, Fires arising from clearing the way, Locomotive Equipment, Damages and Penalties. It is suggested that the Railways Act might well be amended, and the penalties be increased enough to make them serve as a deterrent and indemnify as far as possible the landowners.   **Canada**

1201   J. S. JONES. **Characteristic Northwest Timber-Soils in the United States.** — *The Journal of Industrial and Engineering Chemistry,* Vol. III, No. 4, pp. 246-247. Easton, Pa., April, 1911.

United States: North West

Among experts, an opinion seems to be prevalent that pine forest soils, as a class, are poor in the essential elements of plant nutrition. The analyses given indicate however very clearly that extensive areas of typical pine forest soils of the Northwest United States are well supplied with all the mineral elements required for plant growth, and are all exceptionally rich in phosphoric acid. As a rule, they are slightly acid in reaction; although substantial amounts of calcium are present, the application of finely crushed limestone is known to be of decided advantage in bringing them into a good state of cultivation.

1202   R. FALCI. **The Manna Ash** *(Fraxinus)* **Species and Varieties in Sicily.** — (Il frassino da manna in Sicilia). *Bollettino del R. Orto Botanico e Giardino Coloniale,* Palermo, Anno IX, N. 4, pp. 145-168.

Italy: Sicil /

This is a small monograph on the manna *Fraxinus* from the scientific and cultural point of view. The varieties of ash cultivated in Sicily for the production of manna are numerous, and each of them has a special local name. They are multiplied by grafting, and belong to the *Ornus* type.

The varieties of the *Fraxinaster* type are preferred in the territory of Castelbuono, such are *Fraxinus excelsior, oxyphylla,* and *australis,* which supply the manna at an earlier date and allow the harvest to be finished before the autumn rains, which are earlier at Castelbuono than in the other districts where this tree is cultivated.

Of the varieties of *Fraxinus Ornus,* those belonging to the sub-species *rotundifolia* are considered the best manna producers, although it is the varieties belonging to the sub-species *angustifolia* which are generally cultivated at Cinisi and Capaci.

According to old statements which now have been verified by the writer, the production of manna ceases when fructification begins; for this reason the varieties which flower without fructifying are preferred and are multiplied by grafting. At Castelbuono four cultivated varieties of the *Ornus* type are considered non-fructiferous: *Ugliataru, Marcuzza, Quarrato* and *Misciuso*; and six varieties of the *Fraxinaster* type: *Bianco, Niurru, Russu, Tardiu, Ziriddu, Dinarieddu.*

The enumeration of 32 varieties cultivated at Cin si and Castel-buono is given, with their description and an appreciation from the point of view of yield in manna. The great number of the varieties, well specified by their morphological characters as well as by their yield, show the importance of this cultivation, which could be improved by selection and hybridisation.

F. B. KNAPP. **The Pruning of White Pine.** — *American Forestry,*   1203
V. XVII, N. 4, pp. 204-205. Washington, April 1911.

There is a widespread theory among both American and Ger-man foresters that live branches must not be cut from evergreens. The experiments by Mr. Morton, begun in 1891, and later inve-stigations by Mr. Knapp, Director of the Eric Forest School, show that the contrary, at least with reference to the white pine, may be maintained. Not only the pruning of evergreen trees can be successfully done, but it should form the basis for the treatment of woods in many places. Every system of forestry has its own method, and must make some sacrifice in order to attain its end. United
States

The aim of this system is to secure a fair quantity of large, clean, high-grade timber. with a short rotation. To accomplish this, special attention must be paid to a small number of selected trees from the beginning. In the first stage of growth one must obtain by pruning and thinning a tall slender tree with clean bole of moderate length; and then get a rapid diameter growth by keeping the remaining branches alive and enlarging the head to its full capacity.

During the first two years the proper amount of protection, light, air, and soil are maintained and a single leader secured for each selected tree, and its neighbours are made subservient to it. When from 4 to 8 ft. high, the pruning of live branches is begun, leaving the head about one-third of the height of the tree. This pruning of live branches and the protection from competitors is continued through the first period of growth. Not over two whorls are taken off in any year. At the end of this time the result is a tree with a slender bole, no dead or sickly branches and a small but well developed head, closely surrounded though not crowded by more stocky trees. A typical tree with an 18 ft. bole would be 27 ft. high with 9 ft. spread of crown, a diameter of 4 in. breast high and between 2 and 3 in. just below the first branch.

Then begins the second and final stage of growth. The trees have been chosen far enough apart so that they will not interfere with each other, no more pruning is done, the last small wounds heal quickly. and from that time all the wood formed in the bole is clean. Through the ever increasing space occupied by the tree and the comparatively short stem, a good diameter growth is maintained to the end of the rotation and a large valuable log is obtained.

The Eric system may be used in combination with several of the older forms, but the most promising treatment seems to be the three-story one. It may be applied in plantations, in areas where pine is mixed with coppice and to especially good advantage on the many abandoned fields that are coming up by natural reproduction with a scattered growth of pine. The intermediate stages must vary with the condition of the tract when work is begun, but a fully stocked wood ready for the final cutting of the upper story under a sixty-year rotation will consist of three ages: forty trees, sixty years old ready to cut and occupying about eighty per cent of the space; forty moderate sized trees; and a greater number of small ones, the selected forty of which are just completing their first period of growth and require an insignificant amount of space. The nurse trees which have been retained, increase the crown cover and prevent the stand from becoming too open underneath. The spring after cutting the upper story, a dozen or more transplants are set out in each opening, and in twenty years another crop is ready to harvest.

1204   L. M. ELLIS. *Pinus divaricata or Banksiana*, the Jack Pine, in Western Ontario.— *Forestry Quarterly*, V. IX, No. 1, pp. 1-14 + 3 figs. Cambridge, Mass., March, 1911.

Canada: Western Ontario

Although Jack Pine owing to its frugality, hardiness and fecundity, grows on a wide range of soils, it nevertheless demands for its best development fairly deep sandy glacial till, such as is found on up-land gently rising ground where the drainage is good, and the moisture not far beneath the surface.

It grows still vigorously where hard wood, such as birch and aspen, no longer thrive, where successive fires burning off the loam and humus have created conditions unfavourable for their growth.

A mechanical analysis of typical pine soils shows that Jack Pine prefers naturally the coarser soils, although not necessarily confined to them:

SPECIES	Fine gravel 2.0 to 1 m.m.	Coarse sand 1 to 0.5 m.m.	Medium sand .5 to .25 m.m.	Fine sand .25 to .1 m.m.	Silt .05 to .006 m.m.	Clay .006 m.m.
White Pine (*P. Strobus*)	1.3 %	6.8 %	7.2 %	22.0 %	29.1 %	7.6 %
Red Pine (*P. Resinosa*)	.4 %	3.7 %	12.0 %	62.4 %	6.7 %	2.8 %
Jack Pine (*P. Banksiana*)	2.5 %	34.2 %	39.9 %	13.9 %	4.1 %	3.7 %

Jack pine at all ages is most intolerant of shade.

With the optimum amount of light, cones appear at the early age of ten years, but in close stands they do not appear until 5 to 10 years later. Where the soil is deep and loamy, and other conditions are favourable, seed production is delayed, but the increased quality of the seed balances the later fruiting. The period of maximum seed production lies between the ages of 40 and 90 years.

The germinating power of Jack Pine seed is high, 60 % to 75 %. The facility of reproduction after fires, and the inability of reproduction under mature stands, means that *Jack Pine forests can in Nature only be secured by fire.*

Jack Pine is one of the most hardy trees in America. The annual growth after the establishment of the root system is from 1 to 1.5 ft.; this rate holds fairly uniform for about 40 years, after which it steadily decreases, falling to an imperceptible amount at 100 years. Height of growth is a very good indication of soil conditions, for while on fertile soils the mature tree reaches 80 to 86 ft. on poor, wet, cold soils a mature height growth of 60 ft. is very good; the greatest growth seems between the ages of 10 and 20 years. During early youth, because of the density of the stand, the growth goes into height, but once the competition for light is lessened, volume and diameter growth become more prominent. From the 40th to the 70th year the progress is uniform at nearly 1.5 in. per decade. Then it slowly declines and at about 90 years the diameter accretion is practically at a standstill. For a 15 inch. diameter breast-high at 90 years the yield is greatest, amounting in all to 5.4 ties; this suggests that a rotation based on value increment should not exceed 90 years.

1205

BADER. **Cultivation Experiments with Osiers.** (Kulturversuche auf den Versuchsfeldern der K. Moorkulturanstalt, C. Moorkulturstation Moos, b. Gartenbauversuche, C. Dauerkulturen, 3. Korbweiden). *Landw. Jahrbuch für Bayern*, 1 J., N. 3, s. 253-254, München, 1911.

**Germany:
Bavaria**

These are the results of two plantations of osiers in a peaty soil manured with 50 kg. of phosphorus pentoxide and 60 kg. of potash, in the form of Thomas slag and kainit.

Varieties	Crop per acre: cwts.	Crop per are kg.	Height Inches	Height cm.
Salix viminalis purpurea .	134	167	86	220
» » *regalis* . . .	151	189	54½	140
» » *cinnamonea* .	66	83	39-58½	100-150
» *rubra angustifolia* . .	52	65	47-51	120-130
» *amygdalina fusca* . .	70	88	31-58½	80-150
» » *viridis* . .	56	70	19½-43	50-110
» *purpurea* Schultze . .	87-120	109-150	39-70	100-180
» » *emendata* . .	36	45	23½-47	60-120
» *uralensis*	84	105	58½-74	150-190
» *helix*	99	124	62½-70	160-180
» *fragilis trianda*	80-95	100-118.9	51-70	130-180
» *viminalis dasyclados* .	34-45	42-56	21-35	54-90
» *dasyclados*	88	110.5	60½	155
» *americana*	102	128	64	165

1206

S. SIRENA. **Vegetable fibre from the Dwarf- Palm, or Chamaerops humilis.** *Boll. del R. Orto Botanico e Giardino coloniale*, Palermo, Anno IX. N. 4, pp. 180-181.

**Italy:
Sicily
Sardinia**

Chamaerops humilis is a palm which grows wild in Sicily, and could be cultivated and thus supply an industry contributing to improve the economic conditions of the population.

The geographical area of the Dwarf.- Palm extends along the shores of the Mediterranean ; it is common in Northern Africa, from Tripolitania to Morocco, and in the South of Spain as far as Catalonia; it grows on the Riviera, in Sardinia, in some parts of Dalmatia, Albania, at Zante, Corfu, etc.

Chamaerops humilis is easily propagated by seeds and by shoots. The young leaves (*curina*) are submitted to a process which makes them white and elastic, so that they may be used in the manufacture of ropes, baskets, hats, mats, brooms, etc. The older leaves are used for the manufacture of vegetable fibre (*crine vegetale*) and brooms.

The vegetable fibre industry, which does not exist in Sicily, could be greatly developed there.

Mr. Sirena calculates that from one hectare planted with Chamaerops Palm it may be possible to gather leaves sufficient to produce about 31 800 kg. of vegetable fibre, which at the price of 10 to 15 fr. (8/-12/) per 100 kg. would represent a gross income of 3180 to 4770 fr. per hectare. The crop of adult leaves is only made every three years, and, considering that the cultivation, harvest and preparation expenses are paid by the young leaves, it may be considered that the annual income from a hectare would be from 1060 to 1590 fr. (£ 42-8-0 - £ 63-12-0). This income would be all the more appreciated because coming from poor soils, unadapted for other crops (1).

F. A. LEETE. **Forest Railways for the Extraction of Timber in Burma. Double-rail and Mono-Rail.** *The Indian Forester*, vol. XXXVII, No. 182, pp. 34-54 + pl. 2, Allahabad, Jan. and Feb. 1911.

1207

A full and detailed comparison between narrow gauge double line railway and the Shrewsbury mono-rail is not yet possible as the latter is still in the experimental stage. The only experiment made so far has been with animal traction of single cars. As soon as the system has been well introduced, it is safe to assume that a locomotive to ride astride the rail will not be long in making its appearance. It will then be possible to form trains and to simplify designs of the cars themselves.

British India:
Burma

There are certainly some places where the two systems will compete with each other, but the writer is of the opinion that, in many other places, either the one or the other system will have the advantage. The double-rail will prevail over the mono-rail under its present form for long ascents. Also where there is considerable traffic it is likely to be preferred; but for long descents, or on the level, the mono-rail certainly has the advantage.

---

(1) In Sardinia the inner part of the stem of the « palmizzo » *Chamaerops humilis* is used as food; it is eaten in a similar way to fennel.

The vegetable fibre from this Palm comes chiefly from Algeria; about 70 000 quintals are imported annually from Algeria into Italy, at a price of 9 to 12 frs the quintal (100 kg.).

V. VILLAVECCHIA, *Dizionario di Merceologia*, Roma, 1911, vol. I, p. 7/9
(*Crine vegetale*   (*Ed*).

1208

Mauritius

Tanning substances in Mauritius. (Matières tannantes de l'île Maurice). *La Quinzaine Coloniale*, N. 5, p. 161, Paris, 10 Mars 1911. (1).

Apart from the Filao (*Casuarina Equisetifolia*), the Mangrove tree and the Guava tree, the other barks which might be used in tanning are generally poor and valueless. The Mangroves of Mauritius are not so rich as those of Madagascar and the Seychelles, because they are not deprived by scraping of the outer rhytidome (outer dried part) ; this could be easily accomplished.

1209

French Indo China

G. VERNET. **Length and Frequency of the Incisions on Hevea** (2). (De la longueur à donner aux incisions de saignées et de fréquence des traitements dans l'Hevea). *Journal d'Agriculture tropicale*, No. 117,pp. 73-77, Paris, Mars, 1911.

At present the length and frequency of incisions on Hevea for rubber sap are not regulated in any way. The planters have no clear ideas as to the best method of tapping.

Some experiments have been instituted at the Kuala Lumpur Station with the object of determining the comparative value of the methods most in favour in the Malay Peninsula ; but some time must pass before any practical conclusion can be drawn.

The physiological studies undertaken by Mr. Vernet at Suoi-Giao have shown that there is no proportion between the yield and the capacity of the cortical tissue, nor between the yield and the surface of bark utilised. Rubber is a product of the physiological activity of the plant and as it serves in part for nutrition, only that which is superfluous ought to be taken.

It has been proved that the more extended the incisions the more rapid is the coagulation of the latex in the cups ; while frequency of tapping decreases the proportion of rubber in the latex.

The writer's hypothesis is that two conditions regulate the rapidity of coagulation in the latex : 1) a long incision cuts through a larger number of cells, whose content in coagulating substances makes the coagulation of the latex more rapid, the coagulation being proportional to the percentage of rubber. 2) When the trees are tapped daily, these coagulating substances are regularly leached out, their proportion in the latex decreases, and coagulation is less rapid.

This hypothesis is in agreement with the results of experience, whence the conclusion may be drawn that too much space should not be left between the tappings.

---

(1) Mangrove = *Mangifera indica ;* Guava tree = *Psidium guayava L.* Cp. this Bulletin March 1911. No. 871.
(2) Cp. this Bulletin March, 1911, No. 884.

Rubber and Gutta Percha in the German Colonies in 1909-1910.
(Official Colonial Report) (Kautschuk und Gutta-Percha in den
Deutschen Kolonien, 1909-1910). *Gummi-Zeitung*, N. 24,
p. 881, 17 März, Berlin, 1911.

1210

The year 1909-1910 marked a general increâse in the agricultural produce of the German Colonies, especially in the rubber and
gutta-percha industry.

German
Colonies

German East Africa : The total exportation of agricultural products from this Colony rose to 13 million marks, 7 of which represent
produce obtained by the natives. The plantations of Manihot
covered 16 212 hectares last year, comprising 14 425 526 trees, as
against 12 853 hectares and 12 661 166 trees in the previous year.
Some new plantations of *Kikxia* (1) and *Castilloa* have also been made
(about 70 hectares). The amount of liana rubber exported was
256 tons, worth 1 650 000 marks. The construction of railways, and
some rigorous regulations in regard to the reserve of liana woods will
have a great and beneficent influence on future exportation. There
is a great future in store for the region of Moschi, where, near Kilima-
Njaro, 1200 hectares have already been planted in rubber.

Kamerun : The rubber produced by the natives amounted to
1 517 000 kg., valued at 7 551 000 marks, or an increase in production and value of nearly two thirds over the preceding year. The
increase is particularly remarkable in the zones bordering on the
French and Spanish possessions. The *Kikxia* comes first; then the
lianas. The total area of rubber plantations is 4048 hectares, double
that of the previous year. In many plantations cacao is combined
with rubber.

Togo : At Togo, rubber cultivation comes after that of the
palm and maize, both of which are extensively grown. This explains
the decrease in export, although the value has increased in consequence
of the increase in price.

The *Manihot, Ficus, Kikxia* and *Hevea* are cultivated on about
160 hectares. The total production, which was only 150 000 kg.
of raw rubber, was imported into Germany.

Rubber is not grown at all in German South West Africa.

German New Guinea : In the Bismark archipelago, in the Salomon
Islands and in Wilhelm's Land an area comprising 2254 hectares
in all, is cultivated in *Ficus, Kikxia, Manihot, Castilloa* and *Hevea*.
To encourage the cultivation of rubber, Botanical Gardens have

(1) Synonym of *Funtumia elastica.* Cp. *Index Kewensis.*   (*Ed.*).

been instituted at Rabaul. The primeval forests of the island contain some gutta-percha trees which the natives have begun to utilise. In the Carolines, the Mariannes and Marshall Islands the cultivation is not progressing. The entire production was exported into Germany ; it was 6616 kg. in all, worth 45 746 marks.

Samoa : The *Hevea* is mainly cultivated in this island, where there are 430 369 plants. There are also more than 36 000 plants of *Castilloa alba* and a number of *Ficus* which serve mainly as windbreaks.

There has been no production so far. The number of rubber plants was increased by 62 000 *Hevea* last year.

1211   M. Paris. **The Rubber Plantations in Indo-China.** (Les plantations de Caoutchouc dans l'Indo-Chine). — *Bulletin de l'Office Colonial;* N. 39, pp. 65-79, Melun, Mars, 1911,

French Indo-China   Indo-China is the first of the French Colonies where important results have been obtained from rubber plantations. This Colony also possesses numerous species growing wild and supplying excellent qualities of rubber (1).

The exportation of rubber for the whole of Indo-China was 31 863 kg., in 1909, representing a value of 207 048 fr., and nearly the whole amount was obtained from tapping wild species.

In Cochin China the wild species are practically not turned to account ; but the efforts of the planters have been mainly concentrated in this colony, most satisfactory results having been obtained, on the cultivation of *Hevea Brasiliensis.*

The Chamber of Commerce of Saigon expects that from 1911 to 1920, about 400 000 trees will be planted every year.

The production of rubber at Cambodia has remained in the initial stage. Rubber is one of the principal exports from Laos, but no attempts have been made so far with plantation rubber.

No increase in the production of rubber from lianas is to be expected in Annam, where the number of planters who undertake this cultivation is still very limited. Experiments show that the cultivation of the *Hevea* is not to be recommended, except in the South of Annam.

The greater part of the rubber exported from Tonking is supplied by the tapping of lianas, the chief of which are the following:
> *Bousigonia Tonkinensis* (rosy rubber) ;
> *Xylinabaria Reynaudi* (abundant latex) ;

---

(1) See this Bulletin Nov. 1910, p. 111 and Dec. 1910, p. 298. (*Ed,*).

Xylinabaria sp. (very elastic rubber) ;
Ecdysanthera micrantha ;
Parabarium Tournieri ;
Melodinus Tournieri ;
Aganosma harmandiana ;
Rhynhodia fragrans ;
Only one tree, *Bleekrodea Tonkinensis* (1) gives a product of a
very appreciable market value. No definite result has yet been
obtained in Tonking from the cultivation of the species introduced.

The cultivation of the *Hevea* alone has given definite and encouraging results in Indo-China at the present time. But it seems
that this species should be limited to Cochin-China and South Annam. *Ficus elastica* might give interesting results in the northern
provinces.

As for the native species, measures should be taken to preserve
the natural plantations from complete destruction.

The Rubber Production in Portuguese East Africa. — *Journal of
the Royal Society of Arts.* N. 3044, London, March 24, 1911,
p. 491.

1212

From Laurenço Marques, at the extreme south, to Ibo, at the
northern extremity of Portuguese East Africa, *Landolphia* of various
species grows in profusion. This plant is extensively exploited from
Inhambane, Beira, Qualimane, Moma, Angoche, and Ibo, from the
last three through the town and island of Mozambique. South of the
Zambezi the *Landolphia* is a vine, sometimes of great length, and,
when permitted, it attains the thickness of a man's arm. This vine
Landolphia Kirkii, is considered rubber-bearing when it reaches half
an inch in diameter, and is tapped by a series of long cuts. The
flow is more abundant at the end of the rainy season, and owing to
the great difficulty of getting at the vines, whose habitat is in
the forests, they are tapped but once a year, and then bled for all
there is in them. This rapidly reduces the output of a forest, and,

Portuguese
East Africa :
Mozambique

---

(1) *Bleekrodea Tonkinensis* occurs sporadically over nearly the whole of
Tonking, with the exception of the Delta, but there are also numerous close
groves of it. Its habit of growth is similar to that of the birch-tree and it
varies in height, from 12 to 20 m. Its root nodosities, which form actual
water reservoirs, permit of its supporting long periods of drought.
   Cf. EBERHARDT and DUBARD, *L'Arbre à Caoutchouc du Tonkin*, Paris
Challamel ed. 1910.   (*Ed.*),

where supervision of the natives is impossible, the percentage of vines utterly destroyed yearly is very great.

Outside the territory covered by the Mozambique and Buzi companies, the collection of rubber, whether south or north of the Zambezi, is entirely in the hands of natives who collect and sell it to the Indians at the coast.

The best rooty rubber is that coming from the Matadane range, which lies between Moma and the Cocola river on the south, and Talalane and the Larde River on the north. Inferior qualities are gathered farther north, and their principal final exit is at Mozambique, the capital of the district. All Mozambique rooty rubber (and it must be remembered that the name applies only to rubber gathered north of the Zambezi) is marketed in a crude state, containing bark and rubber in almost equal quantities. Owing to the fact that most rooty Mozambique rubber comes from unpacified regions, to which white people have not had access, little was known as to the species of *Landolphia* growing in the district, and it was generally supposed that it was the same as that worked by tapping south of the Zambezi. Recently, however, the American Consul succeeded in crossing the Matadane country, and it was observed that while the plant bearing the rubber is a *Landolphia*, it is very different from the species known south of the Zambezi. The Matadane *Landolphia* has an extensive root system, running near the surface, out of proportion to the plant itself. The latex, which is rich in quantity and of very good quality, is found in the bark of the roots. The installation of simple machinery for cleaning out the bark and eliminating the damaging boiling process will bring Matadane rubber into favour in the market.

Besides the *Landolphia*, an indigenous rubber-bearing tree, *Mascarenhasia elastica*, has been discovered. (1) It yields rubber of good quality, but it is difficult to tap on account of the fluted formation of the trunk; and, as it requires fifteen years to mature, it would be of little value as a plantation tree.

The only plantation tree which has been largely exploited in the province of Mozambique is the *Ceara*, of which over 10 000 trees exist, mostly in small plantations. Up to the end of 1909, these trees had proved a failure and were mostly abandoned; but the visit of an expert on rubber in March 1910, has brought back confidence in the *Ceara* tree, and preparations are under way for extensive and systematic planting. The *Ceara* does well throughout a vast extent of the province, and reaches the tapping stage at the end of three years.

---

(1) Cp. this Bulletin, March 1911, No. 883.

H. JUMELLE AND PERRIER DE LA BATHIE. **The Rubber Plants of**   1213
the South and West of Madagascar. (Les plantes à Caoutchouc de l'Ouest et du Sud de Madagascar) L'*Agriculture pratique
des pays chauds*, IIe année, N. 96, pp. 117-194, Paris, Mars, 1911.

After a detailed description of the flora of West and South Ma-   **Madagascar**
dagascar, the following information is given respecting the utilisation of the different rubber plants of the country :

The « vaheabato » of the natives is a *Landolphia* of a new species,
which is confined to the massif of the Isalo. It forms an underwood
which is utilised only by the Bara of the neighbourhood, who pound
the bark of the stems and roots.

Landolphia sphaerocarpa is common in the basins of the Mangoky
and Onilahy.

A *Mascarenhasia* from the Isalo plateau appears to be a new
species which has the appearance and habit of *M. lanceolata* of Ma-
nongarivo. But the *Mascarenhasia* par excellence of the West,
M. lisianthiflora, the « guidronosy » of the Bara, is utilised in the
same way as the « vaheabato » with the difference, however, that very
often the roots only are used.

The rubber of the « guidronosy », prepared by the Bara, is in
small thin blackish-red slabs, 7 to 10 cm. square. It is very tough and
elastic, but deteriorates easily, perhaps on account of the defective
way in which it is prepared.

Cryptostegia madagascariensis and *C. grandiflora* are the « lom-
biri » of the natives ; they are very little used as rubber plants, the
latex being employed chiefly as a poison.

Marsdenia verrucosa, or « bokabe » is much more generally employed. A plant furnishes from 20 to 40 follicles, each of which gives an
average of 60 centigrams of rubber. A little before they are quite
ripe, the fruit, of which there is an almost smooth variety in the
West, is gathered and taken to the village, where the women
and children cut off the two ends, one after the other, placing
them on a sieve, through which the latex runs into a receptacle. The
« bokabe » rubber, which is at first tough and of good appearance,
rapidly becomes pitchy.

The « vahimainty » or « langalora » is *Secamonopsis madasca-
riensis*, a species of a new genus created by the writers and belonging
to the Asclepiadeae. It is a liane with numerous grayish stems
from one to four cm. in diameter. The rubber is not very tough
except in the large stems and in the nearly ripe fruit.

The natives use the fruit in the same way as that of the
« bokabe ». Each follicle will give as much as 75 cgr. of good rubber,

and as there are from 100 to 500 of them on each plant, the yield is from 75 to 400 gr. per stock.

The « kompitso » is *Gonocrypta Grevei*, a liane or bush according to whether it finds a support or not.   The climbing form is not very productive, and the shrub form is useless.

Euphorbia Intisy, the present habitat of which is in the extreme south of the island only, is becoming gradually rarer. This is the more to be regretted because it is the only southern plant which has a real economic value.   Its disappearance is due to the treatment of the natives, who are not satisfied with cutting the trunk without the least care, but also tap the root tubers to which the plant owes its resistance.

1214   **Apparatus for Measuring Rubber Trees.** (Appareil pour mesurer les arbres à caoutchouc). *Journ. d'Agric. tropicale*, No. 117, pp. 94-95, Paris, 31 Mars, 1911.

Ceylon   Mr. Burgess published in the *India Rubber Journal* the description of an apparatus which he has invented for measuring rubber plants.   It consists of a piece of wood, longer by 15 cm., than the height at which the trees are to be measured. At right angles to this piece of wood and at the measuring height is fixed a strap a little longer than the greatest presumed circumference of the trees.

This strap passes to the left, only a short length of from 12 to 15 cm. (4.6 in to 5.8 in) being left at the right. This short portion is about a centimeter in width, the remainder of the strap being 3 or 4 centimeters (1.1 or 1.5 in) wide, while there is a hole at the end through which a punch can be passed. The inner side of the strap is left rough, the outer part being smooth.

The piece of wood is placed vertically to the tree and the strap passed round the latter, passing again to the right through a cut made in the short end.   The strap must previously be covered along its entire length with a slip of paper, fastened down with glue. The native who is in charge fastens the strap firmly, and when it is well arranged on the tree, he pierces the paper through the hole in the strap with the above mentioned punch. Then he passes to another tree.   At the end of his round the paper is punctured with holes, which can easily be counted. By their number and arrangement they give the number of trees measured during the day and their circumference.

Fraud is rendered impossible by the circumstance that, amongst a large number of trees, there is a regular progression of trees with a considerably increasing diameter, and then an equally regular decreasing one.

It is easy to count up to 150 holes per inch along the length of the strap, and not more than 2 % of the holes will overlap one another. Mr. Burgess uses 4 of these instruments, with which 174 000 measurements have been made up to the present.

CH. RIVIÈRE. **Slip and Graft Experiments with the Rubber Ficus**   1215
(Expériences sur le bouturage et le greffage du Ficus à Caoutchouc). *Journ. d'Agric. Tropicale*, No. 117, p. 91, Paris, March, 1911.

Propagation by layers above ground is a common practice   Java.
with *Ficus elastica* in Java, where the natural tendency of the   Algeria
tree to shoot forth adventitious roots on the trunk and branches is turned to advantage. This peculiarity has been utilised by Mr. C. Rivière in the Experimental Garden at Algiers to make slips of very large branches and so obtain trees in a short space of time.

If a slip can be obtained with adventitious roots at its base, the slip quickly becomes a tree that can be tapped at an early date.

But it is not often that a mature *Ficus* has many branches which are sufficiently straight and capable of furnishing slips of large growth and with adventitious roots at the base. Mr. Rivière, having observed some cases of the natural union of above-ground roots with the lower branches, has succeeded in applying grafting by approach of roots to branches; and has thus been able to provide the slips he had selected with an artificially produced root system.

The grafting in the open air of strong stocks, and especially of one species on itself, gives sure results.

M. K. BAMBER and R. H. LOCK. **Ceylon Experiments on the Effect**   1216
of Different Intervals between Successive Tappings in Para
Rubber *(Hevea Brasiliensis)*. *Circulars and Agricultural Journal of the Royal Botanic Gardens*, Vol. V, N. 9. Ceylon. September, 1910.

The experiments described in this Circular were designed for the   Ceylon
purpose of ascertaining what differences, if any, exist in the quantity, composition, and properties of rubber latex drawn by tappings carried out at different intervals of time. The experiments were made on trees upwards of twenty years of age, which had not previously been tapped with any regularity, and which were beginning to show obvious signs of the ill-effects of close planting.

The following conclusions were reached :

The wound-response, although clearly recognizable, is not nearly so marked as in the case of Parkin's experiments (1).

The greatest increase in the yield of dry rubber was in no case much more than 100 per cent. Taking the first 40 tappings of each series, there is no sensible difference in yield which can be ascribed to the length of the interval between successive tappings. The yield from trees tapped daily and from trees tapped weekly is practically identical for the same number of tappings, both absolutely and in proportion to the area of bark tapped.

During the first few tappings the rate of fall in the percentage of rubber contained in the latex is more or less inversely proportional to the length of the interval between successive tappings, the fall being more rapid as the tappings succeed each other at shorter intervals. Sooner or later a nearly constant percentage composition of the latex is arrived at. This final percentage is lower in the case of trees tapped at longer intervals.

As might be expected from the less concentrated condition of the latex, the proportion of scrap rubber obtained is lower in the case of more frequent tappings.

Mature trees tapped daily for eighteen months continue to afford a profitable yield of rubber. After over 7 lbs of rubber per tree had been obtained in this period, the average amount at the 440th tapping was at the rate of 4 lbs of dry rubber per tree annually. The general appearance of the trees at this time was quite healthy and they showed no signs of having suffered from the severe tapping which they had undergone.

Frequent tappings are therefore to be recommended from a practical point of view as far as mere yield is concerned, but the removal of bark is of course proportionally more rapid. On the quarter system of tapping this is of less importance, and it still remains to be determined whether it would not pay better to tap daily during certain months and rest the trees, or only tap at two or more days interval during the months when the flow is less. The experiments described are still in progress and in presenting their final report, Messrs. Bamber and Lock hope also to make a detailed comparison between yield and rainfall at different seasons of the year.

(1) Parkin, on tapping 4 trees in 1899, at Peradeniya, found an increase of over 600 per cent at the end of 14 tappings made at intervals varying from 3 to 7 days (average interval 5 to 6 days).

C. C. **The Heveas of French West Africa.** (A propos des Heveas de l'Afrique Occidentale Française). *L'Agriculture pratique des pays chauds*, IIe année, N. 96, p. 249, Paris, Mars 1911.

1217

Mr. Yves Henry, Director of Agriculture in French West Africa, has informed the authorities at the Colonial Garden that the examination at Kew of some samples of Hevea from the garden of Ebute Meta (Lagos) which were sent under the names of *Hevea brasiliensis* and *H.Spruceana*, has shown that the first is correctly named and that the second belongs to another form of *H. brasiliensis*. This form has hitherto been known as *H. Spruceana* or « Medeiros » Hevea This latter botanical name ought therefore to be suppressed, since *H. Spruceana* is only an interesting variety of *H. brasiliensis*.

French
West Africa

P. J. S. CRAMER. **The Cultivation of the Hevea.** La culture de l'Hévéa). — *Manuel du Planteur*, 1 vol. Ill. pp. 132, Amsterdam, Paris, 1911.

1218

This work, which has been translated into French by Prof. E. de Wildeman, deals theoretically and practically with the cultivation of the Hevea.

Malay
Archipelago

The manual is in three parts, and describes 1) the establishment of the plantation : preparation of the soil, canals and drainage, cultivation of young Heveas, position of plants, etc. ; 2) maintenance of the plantations : care of the soil, catch crops, growth, pollarding and pruning, diseases and pests ; 3) tapping : the practice of tapping, instruments, housing of the produce, preparation of the rubber. There are 40 illustrations, and the book is arranged to serve as a planters' manual.

Funtumia Elastica at **Martinique.** (La *Funtumia elastica* à la Martinique). (*La Quinzaine Coloniale*, N. 7, p. 241, Paris, 10 April 1911.

1219

In the cultivation trials with rubber trees at Martinique, *Hevea* and *Castilloa* have not given good results. *Funtumia elastica*, on the other hand, was very satisfactory.

Martinique

There are 60 000 plants in the nurseries of the Colony gardens. The Chief of the Agricultural Department advises the direct sowing in forests, which would form one of the best kinds of reforesting.

1220   **Rubber Plants on the West Coast of Mexico.** (Kautschukbäume
an der Westküste von Mexico). *Gummi- Zeitung*, N. 25, s. 427,
Berlin, 24 März 1911.

Mexico:
Sinaloa,
Tepic

There has been a mistaken impression that certain rubber plants
called « Palo Amarillo » which give a very small quantity of rubber,
abound on the Pacific coast of Mexico ; but it is, on the contrary, the
« Palo Colorado», also called « Chilte », which is to be found there, and
it gives a plentiful supply of an excellent rubber.   An analysis of its
latex has given 37 % of dry rubber.   At Sinaloa and Tepic, 20 tons
were collected in two months.

Another tree, similar to this, from which it differs only in
colour — the « Copalillo » — grows in the valleys, whereas the « Palo
Colorado » grows on the mountains.   The latex of « Copalillo » gives
52 % of dry rubber.

These plants grow in large numbers in the wild state at Sinaloa
and Tepic.

1221   **A New Rubber Plant.** (Nueva planta que produce Hule). *El Hacendado Mexicano*, vol. 9, p. 116, Mexico, 10 Marzo 1911.

Mexico:
Sinaloa

The plant known under the name of *Clavel de España*, which
abounds in the district of Rosario and in a large part of the State of
Sinaloa, is being specially studied at present, because its latex produces
a rubber of the first quality.

This plant is particularly plentiful on the mountains of the Al-
cadia ·of Matatan.   The Government of Sinaloa has exhibited at
the Prefectures some rubber obtained from the latex of the *Clavel*,
and it is hoped in Mexico to obtain as satisfactory results from this
plant as from the *Guayule*.

1222   **The Muliya Rubber Tree of Rhodesia.** — *The Rhodesia Agricultural
Journal*. Salisbury, February, 1911.

Rhodesia

Two samples described as rubber were received from the Administration of North-Western Rhodesia under the native name of
Muliya.   Specimens of the tree from which the rubber was obtained were also forwarded for determination, and on examination
in the Botanical Laboratory, the Muliya tree proved to be identical with the so-called Rhodesian rubber tree « M'toa Ungamama-
sane » *(Gouioma Kamassi)* order *Asclepiadaceae.*

The M'toa tree is widely distributed throughout Southern Rhodesia, and enquiry is sometimes made as to whether the latex

might not be of some commercial value. The Imperial Institute, South Kensington, London, has drawn up the following report.

Muliya Rubber, N. 1

	In material as received	Composition of dry material
Moisture	25.5 %	—
Caoutchouc	21.9 »	29.4 %
Resin	46.2 »	60.7 »
Proteids	1.9 »	2.6 »
Insoluble matter	5.5 »	7.3 »
Ash	1.0 »	1.3 »

The material described in the above table as *caoutchouc* was left after extracting the resins with acetone ; it consisted of a blackish, slightly sticky, rubber-like substance, which was fairly tenacious but possessed little elasticity. Material of this type would have very little, if any, commercial value.

Ai Camphor Production in Burma. (Kampfergewinnung in Birmannia). — *Osterreichische Monatschrift für den Orient*, Wien, Feb. 1911.

1223

The production of Ngai-or Ai-Camphor is continually progressing in Upper Burma. The plants of *Blumea Balsamifera*, which are very numerous in the woods of this region, are mainly utilised for the production of camphor and the oil of camphor. The natives do not concern themselves with camphor, however, except when they have nothing better to do.

Burma

O. SPERBER. **The « Chicle » Gum and its Production.** (Das Chiclegummi und dessen Gewinnung). — *Der Tropenpflanzer*, 15 J., N. 4, pp. 220-223 fig. 1, Berlin, April, 1911.

1224

The « Chicle » gum was introduced into the United States in 1876, where it is very largely consumed at the present day ; it is used in the preparation of chewing gum.

« Chicle » gum is extracted from the thick juice of the « Chiclezapote » tree (*Achras Sapota*, Linn.), which is rich in sweet matters.

United States
Mexico
Central America

This plant is a native of Mexico and Central America ; there are important plantations of it in the States of the South of Mexico. It grows to a height of from 13 to 17 m. (from 42 to 55 ft) with a diameter of from 87 (34 in) to 115 cm. (45 in); a tree of these dimensions produces from 13.5 to 16 kg. (or 29.7 lb to 35 lb) of « Chicle » gum per year.

The wood of the tree is a fine redbrown ; it is adapted to diffe-rent purposes and is easily mistaken for mahogany.

The fruit, which is called « Sapodilla » is very much appreciated, but it has almost completely disappeared from the Mexican markets, because the collection of the sap interferes with the production of the fruit.

The sap is collected all through the year, with the exception of the 3 or 4 rainy months; it is obtained by means of incisions made at the fork.   It is fluid and milky as it comes from the tree, and is afterwards condensed by heating in boilers, and exported.

A good « Chiclero » will produce from 225 to 270 kg. (or 495.lbs to 594 lbs.) of « Chicle » gum, of the value of from 34 to 37.50 fr. (or £ 1.7.2½ to £ 1.10). The sale price per « quintal » of 45 kg. varies from 125 to 137.50 fr. (or £ 5 to £ 5-10s), while the cost price is about 50 fr.

Most of the gum is exported to Canada, where it is dried, in which operation it loses 50 % of its weight.   It can be sent into the United States more profitably after being prepared in this way, because it has to pay a high customs duty there.

The importation into the United States, which was only 416 000 kg. (or 915 200 lbs) in 1885, with a value of 768 000 fr. (£ 30 720) had risen to 2 352 000 kg. (or 5 174 400 lbs) in 1909, worth 10 431 000 fr. (£ 417 240).

Since there is such a large and increasing consumption of this gum, the cultivation of the « Chiclezapote » has to be considered. The trees are planted at intervals of 3 m. 30, which gives 1000 trees per hectare (404 to the acre) ; it is calculated that a tree of from 8 to 10 years, of a diameter from 30 to 38 cm., (or 11 in, to 14 in.) will produce on an average from 2.27 to 2.7 kg of gum., or from 5 lbs to 6 lbs.

The most suitable soils for this cultivation are good, deep, calcar-eous clay soils, for which the price has risen from 15 to 75 fr. per hectare.   The rainfall required is about 2250 mm.

It is expected that this cultivation will give rise to a speculation movement, similar to that which occurred recently in the case of the rubber plantations in Mexico.

Live stock Breeding. — Aviculture. — Beekeeping. Silk-Production — Animal Industries.

The Control of Bovine Tuberculosis. Report of International Commission; *Department of Agriculture*, Ottawa, Canada, pp. 29.

1225

This pamphlet constitutes the first report of the International Commission on Bovine Tuberculosis, appointed by the American Veterinary Medical Association at its annual meeting in 1909, to study the problem of tuberculosis among cattle and to report upon reasonable and practicable methods or systems to be recommended to officials and live stock owners for eradicating the disease. The conclusions reached are presented with a view of crystallizing public opinion and so clearing the way for legislative action. Resolutions that are to be presented to the American Veterinary Medical Association have the following titles : Dissemination, Tuberculin Test, Evidence from Tuberculin Test, Compulsory Notification, Localization after slaughter, Disposal of Tuberculous Animals, Prevention, Control of Tuberculin Test, Education, Publicity, Legislation, Sanitation, Immunization, Animal Tuberculosis and Public Health.

Canada

Five appendices give the reports of the committees on education and legislation, localization of tuberculosis, dissemination, disposal of tuberculous animals and the plan adopted by the Commission for dealing with tuberculous animals,

E. B. HART, E. V. Mc COLLUM, AND J. G. FULLER. **Studies on the Nutrition of Animals.** (Twenty-fifth and Twenty-sixth Annual Reports of the Agric. Exper. Station of the University of Wisconsin) — *The Rôle of Inorganic Phosphorus in the Nutrition of Animals.* Research Bulletins. 8vo, pp. VII + 52 + 228. No. 1. (p. 1-40) Madison, 1910.

1226 (1)

The problem was to determine whether inorganic phosphates, such as di- and tri-calcium phosphates, could take the place of organic forms of phosphorus in a ration for growing swine.

In the experiments 5 lots of pigs were used. Lot 1 received the basal ration (rice, wheat-gluten and bran from which the

United States: Wisconsin

_____

(1) Numbur 1226 and 1227 in the French Bulletin for April 1911.

phytin had been removed by washing). Lots 2 and 3 received the basal ration and in addition different amounts (40 and 20 gr. per pig daily) of precipitated calcium phosphate (consisting of 70 % di-calcium phosphate and 30 % tri-calcium phosphate). Lot 4 received a ration composed of rice, wheat gluten and whole bran. Lot 5 was fed a standard ration for growing pigs, consisting of corn, oats, wheat middlings and oil meal.

The results may be summarized as follows :

1) On the standard ration extremely low in phosphorus, pigs made as large gains (up to 75 or 100 pounds, when starting at weights of from 40 to 50 pounds) as animals receiving an abundance of this element. After reaching this point, loss of weight began, followed by collapse.

2) Animals fed on a low phosphorus ration, supplemented with inorganic phosphates, made as vigorous a development as others receiving their phosphorus supply wholly in organic form.

3) Precipitated calcium phosphates gave no better results than did floats, a crude tri-calcium phosphate.

4) Phytin, as a supply of phosphorus, gave no better results than the inorganic phosphates.

5) Animals on the low phosphorus ration maintain the proportion of calcium and phosphorus (in the principal organs and tissues) constant and comparable to that of normally fed pigs.

6) The percentage of ash in the skeleton of pigs on the depleted phosphorus ration was reduced to nearly one-half that of pigs receiving a normal ration, or a ration poor in phosphorus but supplemented by an inorganic phosphate.

7) This marked reduction, together with the ability of the animal to build up a skeleton very rich in calcium phosphate when an abundance of the latter is supplied in organic forms, strongly points to a synthetic power possessed by the animal, which enables it to convert inorganic forms of phosphorus into organic forms.

8) When the animals were starving for want of phosphorus, they drew this element from the skeleton, but removed calcium and phosphorus in the proportions found in the tri-calcium phosphate.

9) The daily phosphorus supply for a 50 pound (22 ½ kg.) growing pig should be at least 3 grams. A supply of 4 to 5 grams is probably a safer quantity.

E. B. Hart, E. V. Mc Collum and G. C. Humphrey. **The Ash Constituents of Wheat Bran in the Metabolism of Herbivora.** — *Twenty-fifth and Twenty-sixth Annual Reports of the Agricultural Station of the University of Wisconsin.* Research Bulletin No. 5, p. 173-188.

1228

In a previous publication (1) it has been shown that wheat bran contains phytic acid in combination with potassium, magnesium and calcium.

United States: Wisconsin

This investigation was undertaken to study further the action of the components of the phytin complex when administered separately as salts, their channels of excretion and general relation to the phenomena of constipation and diuresis, with the consequent effect on milk secretion.

The principal conclusions arrived at may be summarized as follows :

1. When calcium or phosphorus were deficient in quantity in the food, the skeletal tissues appeared to be ready sources of supply. The average quantities of calcium oxide and phosphorus pentoxide metabolized and excreted daily by the experimental cow (a vigorous pedigree Holstein), during periods of deficient supply, were respectively·50 and 60 grams.

2. Variations within wide limits in the form and quantity of supply of potassium, magnesium or phosphorus, did not influence the percentage content of these elements in the milk.

3. With the cow experimented upon there was no appreciable fluctuation in the percentage of organic constituents in the milk relative to the supply of phytin.

4. Marked diuresis was produced by the quantity of phytin supplied. A high potassium and magnesium intake as sulphate and chloride produced an effect similar to that of potassium alone when supplied as chloride. This would indicate that the high potassium intake accompanying the whole bran ration was responsible for this phenomenon.

5. The channel of excretion of phosphorus, calcium and magnesium especially and a part of the potassium, when supplied in wheat bran, is by way of the gut.

_____

(1) *Jour. Amer. Chem. Soc.*, 1904, 31 : 564.

1229

P. WAUTERS. **The Feeding of Animals in Regard to the Increase of the Fatty Matters in Milk** (Peut on augmenter la teneur du lait en matières grasses par l'alimentation des animaux?). — *Laiterie et élevage*, Louvain, 15 Fév., 1911, N. 4, pp. 29-31, 1 Mars, 1911. N. 5, pp. 35-37.

**Belgium.
France**

There is no question relating to the production and composition of milk which has been more discussed than that of the effect of feeding on its fat content. Contrary to the opinion generally held by farmers and dairymen, experiments show that diet has but very little influence on the composition of the milk. This is the conclusion reached after 20 years' regular examination of the milk from each of the nine cows belonging to Mr. Wauters and kept on special diet; and it is confirmed by all the literature on the subject. It may be said that the varying proportions of the fat content of milk are much more a question of breed or individual than of feeding.

Recently in France, the practice called *le mouillage au ventre* (1), or over feeding milch cows with sloppy foods has been condemned as a frandulent practice, which contributes to deterioration of the quality of the milk. It is hoped that experiments will be made on a large scale, in various countries and for a sufficiently long time, in order to verify exactly the influence of diet on the fat content of milk.

1230

F. G. HING. **Select and Breed for Baby-Beef Type.** — *American Agriculturist*. New York, February 18, 1911.

**United
States:
Indiana**

The best method of disposing of the vast amount of roughage (2) produced on the farm is causing more thought than any other problem that now confronts the feeder. Since to raise a steer from birth to two years of age on high-priced land is undoubtedly an economic waste, the only solution is to make the cattle fat while young.

Calves can be fattened at $ 1.35 per hundred-weight (1 cwt. = 50.8 kgr.) cheaper than yearlings and $ 1.65 cheaper than two-year-olds.

(1) This practice consists in giving milch cows a watery diet, the object being to stimulate the production of a larger amount of milk, which is then supposed to contain less fat.   (*Ed*).

(2) *Roughage:* any rough material, as straw for bedding animals, a term locally used in the U. S. (*Standard Dict.* Ed. K. FUNK. London, 1910. (*Ed.*).

The subject of baby beef, which means the selling of cattle at the age of 12 to 25 months and weighing 800 to 1200 lbs (360 to 540 kgr.) has been discussed and recommended very strongly, but the professional feeder continues to buy older cattle and get them off his hands in one season. But it is the breeder, and. not the professional feeder who must put the production of baby-beef on a firm and permanent basis.

The trials of age made at Purdue (Indiana) have given the following figures :

Effect of Age on Cost and Rate of Gain.

	Calves	Yearlings	Two-year-olds
Length of feeding-period . . .	270 days	200 days	180 days
Initial weight	479.9 lbs.	820 lbs.	1033.4 lbs.
Final weight	1010.8 »	1265 »	1484 »
Total gain	513.9 »	445 »	450.6 »
Average daily gain	1.89 »	2.23 »	2.50 »
Cost per 100 lbs. gain	$ 7.74	$ 9.09	$ 9.37

In the above table, maize is reckoned at 50 cents per bushel, cotton seed meal at $ 28 per ton, clover hay at $ 8 per ton, and maize silage at $ 2.50 per ton.

The calves that were used in the comparison of ages noted above, were of a very high-grade Hereford breed and they required 270 days to finish, while the two-years-olds, of rather plain breeding but mature, became fat in 180 days. As long as cattle can be secured which will fatten in six months with practical certainty, the feeder will not use young cattle which take three months longer to fatten and offer no certainty as to whether they will finish uniformly or even get fat at all. Last fall, hundreds of range-bred calves were shipped into the maize belt at a cost of from $ 25 to $ 30 per head.

Before baby beef production becomes a general . practice cows that are poor producers must be eliminated. A cow that will not produce a calf capable of being made into a fat marketable animal by the time it reaches the age of 15 to 18 months, and at the same time produce enough milk to help it reach its early development, must be eliminated and be replaced by a cow that will. One of the principal objections to raising one's own cattle on a farm is the necessity of keeping high-priced land in pasture to support the cows. With modern silage methods it is possible to keep a breeding cow for the six winter months on the product of three fourths of an acre of land, while the summer pasture would require about one and a hal to two acres of the same kind of land.

Thirty-five pounds of maize silage and five pounds of clover hay daily will not only maintain a cow at the same weight but will keep her in good condition and let her furnish enough milk to grow the calf into excellent baby-beef. By extending the use. of silage into the summer, as many dairymen have done, it is possible to reduce greatly the area required for pasture; and by using silage the entire year, to keep one cow a year on the silage and clover produced on 1 ½ acres of land. Many dairymen have found it possible to produce enough roughage on one acre to keep a cow a year.

When, by the use of silage during the entire year, and only a small amount of pasture, a $ 25 calf is produced on 1 ½ acres, baby-beef production must come to be popular and will make for a permanent live stock industry (1).

1231   A. CHIESI. **Margarine added to Milk for Fattening Calves.** (Il latte margarinato nell'ingrassamento dei vitelli). — L'*Industria lattiera e zootecnica*, anno IX, N° 9, pp. 121-122, Reggio Emilia, 15 Aprile 1911.

Italy: Emilia   The use of margarine as a cream substitute in skimmed milk appears to give good results in the fattening of calves. The following data are from an experiment made by Mr. Chiesi; margarine was used at 3 % by weight, i. e. about 5 $^1/_{202}$ par gallon.

INCREASE OF WEIGHT IN SIMMENTHAL CALVES.

Date of commencement of experiment	Sex	Age	Initial weight	Duration of feeding	Weight at end of experiment	Total increase in weight	Daily increase in weight
		Days	kg.	Days	kg.	kg.	kg.
February 8	m	37	86	12	95	9	0.750
» »	m	36	65	23	89	24	1.043
» »	m	36	65	52	123	58	1.115
» »	f	14	52	54	89	37	0.685
» »	m	7	43	54	95	52	0.963
March 11	m	14	66	26	86	20	0.776
March 29	f	21	54	8	65	11	1.375

(1) Compare with K. J. J. MACKENZIE. *Baby Beef. The Journal of the Board of Agriculture*, London, June 1910, XVII, p. 177, abstracted in the publication of the Intelligence Office of the International Institute of Agriculture: *The Science and Practice of Farming during 1910 in Great Britain*, page 524.   (*Ed.*).

Average increase per calf per day, 0.957 kg. (= 2 lbs. 1 3/4 oz).
Milk given per kg. of increase, 10.440 litres (= 1.04 gall. per
lb. increase).

ECONOMIC RESULTS.

Expenditure and Returns	Debit	Credit
	Frcs.	Frcs.
Whole milk given 4.32 qs. at 13 fr.	56.16	—
Oleomargarine 66.20 kg. at 1.50 fr.	99.30	—
Total increase of weight, at the average price of 1.60 fr. per kg., 211 kg.	—	337.60
Total.	Fr. 155.46	Fr. 337.60
Net profit	Fr. 182.14	—
Balance	Fr. 337.60	—

Skimmed milk supplied, 22.1 qs. (= 488 galls).
Price realized for the skimmed milk, 8.27 fr. per quintal
(= 1/6 per gall). (1).

A. GOUIN and P. ANDOUARD. **Raising Calves on Skimmed Milk**   **1282**
with Cassava Meal. (Elevage des veaux à la farine de Manioc).
— *Journal d'Agriculture pratique*, N. 11, pp. 332-355. Paris,
16 mars, 1911.

Messrs Gouin and Andouard have tried substituting cassava   **France**
meal for potato starch in the raising of calves on skimmed milk
and starch. The meal is much cheaper, and while its content in
nutritive substances is equal to that of potato starch, it has been
found on trial to be much easier of digestion. The cassava should
be steeped in tepid water for a certain time.

Cooking does not coagulate it as it does starch, but softens it
and allows it be be easily mixed with milk: 60 gr. of cassava may
be used to each litre of skimmed milk. The calves must be fed for
a week on pure cows' milk before being put on this diet.

This artificial feeding is not as good as with whole milk,
because a litre of skimmed milk with the addition of 60 gr. of
cassava is equal to only $^3/_4$ of a litre of pure milk. Calves for
slaughter which are fed in this new way are a little lacking in fat,

---

(1) This is the price realised for the skimmed milk in the veal produced
taking no account of labour and other expenses·   (*Ed.*).

and they fetch 5 centimes per kg. live weight less than the naturally fed calves. The artificial feeding, however, has no disadvantages for breeding.

The system has its advantages in both cases. A calf of 50 kg. must consume 500 litres of pure milk in order to attain a weight of 90 kg. The butter value of these 500 litres is 50 fr. The price of 30 kg. of cassava, added to 500 litres of skimmed milk is 9 fr. The difference between these two prices, that is, 41 fr., divided into the total weight of 90 kg., is 45 centimes per kg.; and as the depreciation in the sale is only 5 centimes per kg., there is still a gain of 40 centimes per kg. in the case of the artificial feeding.

1288 A. D. EMMETT & E. C. CAROLL. **Protein in Animal Nutrition. A Study of the Physical Constants of Fats from Swine.** Proceedings of the American Society of Biological Chemistry. — *The Journal of Biological Chemistry.* Vol. IX. No. 2, pp. XXIII-XXV. Baltimore (Hd.) April, 1911,

United
States

Berkshire pigs of known pedigree and age were fed on different amounts of a highly nitrogenous blood-meal. In conjunction with this a basal feed of ground maize was used. Further, crude calcium phosphate was so fed that all the animals got approximately the same amount of phosphorus in the ration. Nine pigs were used, divided into three lots of three. Lot I was on the low protein plane; Lot II, on the medium, or balanced plane; and Lot III on the high plane.

At the slaughter test it was found:

1. If pedigree, age and type of the animals are not considered in comparing the data, the different amounts of protein feed have no apparent influence on the physical constants of the fats. Individual temperament of the animals may be a factor as great as that of feed, or greater.

2. If litter mates be compared, the differences in the physical constants due to feed are very slight. Here, however, the matter of individuality again may be the controlling factor.

3, If the data from the various samples be compared with respect to the kind of fats, they show that the values for the iodine number and melting point of the back fat are quite different from those of the leaf and composite samples of fat.

4. Comparing all samples of fat (in respect to both the protein-feed and the kind of fat and without regard to pedigree, age, and type of the animal, or to individuality), the specific gravity, saponification number, the insoluble acids and the index of refraction appear to be practically constant in each case.

P. CHAVAN. **New Estimate of Fodder Values.** (Nouvelle estimation   **1234**
de la valeur des fourrages). — *La Terre Vaudoise*, 3ᵉ année.
No. 16, pp. 167-169, Lausanne, April 22, 1911.

Mr. Chavan sums up the advantages of Kellner's new method   **Switzerland**
of estimating feeds, based on the « starch value » and the « digestible protein » (1).

Basing his conclusions on this method, he has calculated the
value of some food stuffs which are on the market, and tabulates
as follows the figures, as far as the present market price in Switzerland is concerned :

	Market Price per 100 kg. Fr. (2)	Estimated Value per 100 kg. Fr.	Difference
Wheat	22 —	17.81	— 4.19
Rye	20 —	17.80	— 2.20
Oats	19.25	14.95	— 4.35
Barley	21.—	16.94	— 4.06
Maize	19 —	20.12	+ 1.12
Bran	16 —	11.01	— 4.99
Potatoes	14 —	4.57	— 9.43
Straw	7.50	1.31	— 6.19
Rice flour	15 —	16.89	+ 1.89
Feeding meal	22 —	18.40	— 3.60
Hay	7.50	5 —	— 2.50
Husked groundnut oil-cake	18.50	22.50	+ 3.70
Ditto, 2nd quality	17 —	21,26	+ 4.26
White sesame oil-cake	16 —	19.78	+ 3.78
Poppy oil-cake	15.50	18.02	+ 2.52
Coprah »	15.25	19.26	+ 4.41
Linseed »	25 —	19.41	— 5.59

(1) See KELLNER. *Die Ernährung der landw. Nutzthiere.*   (*Ed.*)
(2) 100 kg. = 220 lbs; 1 fr. = 10 a.

These few figures show the advantages of oil-cake over other feeding-stuffs; their value is much above the market price. Maize and rice flour are also very cheap ; while barley, oats, hay and fodder meal are fairly dear. On the other hand, it is evident that price is not the only thing to be considered in choosing rations. There are a number of other points to be borne in mind : the volume of the ration, the relation between the quantity of hay and that of other foods, the nature and age of the stock, their state of health etc. But these data may be taken into consideration to a certain extent in the choice of commercial feeds.

1235   L. VUAFLART. **The Toxic Qualities of Colza Oil Cakes** (Sur la Toxicité des tourteaux de Colza). — *Journal d'Agriculture pratique*, No. 12, pp. 364-366, Paris, 23 Mars, 1911.

France   The seeds of Cruciferae, such as black mustard (*Brassica nigra*), charlock (*Sinapis arvensis*), the Colzas, etc., may in the presence of water, produce irritating compounds resulting from the action of a soluble ferment, myrosine, on a glucoside, myronate of potash. These compounds are formed of isosulphocyanate of allyl more or less mixed with sulphide of allyl. They remain in the oil-cake, and may cause injury to cattle. Mr. Vuaflart has endeavoured to estimate the amount in the various oil-cakes. Black mustard, the exotic Colzas, Yamba (*Eruca sativa*), are recognised as unsuitable for food. The native Colza, which is frequently used, gives rise at times to mischief, of which the exact cause is not yet known; Mr. Moussu is of opinion that, in certain cases, more of the toxic substance is produced in the stomach than in the laboratory experiments.

It is recommended that not more than from 2 to 3 kg. (4 to 6 lbs) of colza cake should be given to a fattening ox. Care should be taken not to let this fodder get damp ; it should be boiled or have boiling water poured over it. Moisture, in fact, causes the formation of the deleterious compound, while treatment with boiling water stops its development, the active enzyme being decomposed by boiling.

Estimating the amount of the toxic substance it may be seen which oil-cakes are to be considersd poisonous. Such cakes should either be rejected, or boiled before use ; while cakes which contain little, of the acrid substances should be given sparingly and only to a few animals at first.

I. H. SKINNER and W. A. COCHEL. **Steer Feeding. Influence of Age on the Economy and Profit of Feeding Calves, Yearlings and Two-year-olds.** — *Purdue University Agricultural Experiment Station*, Bull. No. 146, pp. 599-608, Lafayette Indiana, June 1910.

1236

At the Agricultural Experiment Station of Purdue University, experiments carried out on the influence of age on the economy and profit from feeding calves, yearlings and two-year-olds led to the following conclusions:

United States

1) The initial cost per hundred pounds weight of calves is greater than that of older cattle.

2) The length of time necessary for finishing steers decreases as their age increases.

3) The rate of gain and the cost of gain increase with the increased age of the cattle.

4) The amount of rough fodder and concentrated food consumed increases with the increased age of the cattle.

5) The amount of extra food necessary for finishing cattle of equal condition decreases as their age increases.

6) The difference in total quantity of feed necessary for finishing cattle of different ages and fed to the same marketable finish is negligeable.

7) The average margin required between buying and selling prices to prevent loss was $ 1.60 (1) per hundred pounds on calves, $1.71 on yearlings and $ 1.55 on two-year-olds; the margins secured on a stationary market were $ 2.02 on calves, $ 2.22 on yearlings and $ 2.09 on two-year-olds, resulting in a profit of 42 cents per hundred pounds on calves, 51 cents on yearlings, and 54 cents on two-yearolds.

8) The increase in live weight necessary to make calves prime was 103 %; yearlings, 54 % and two-year-olds, 43.0 % of their initial weights at the beginning of the feeding period.

9) At a uniform price for feeds, the difference in cost of gains between calves and yearlings was $ 1.35; between yearlings and two-year-olds, 28 cents per hundred pounds.

10) The experienced farmer who *feeds* cattle should handle older cattle in preference to calves; while the farmer who *produces* and *finishes* his own cattle may find calves preferable.

(1) $ 1 = 4 sh.

1237

Algeria

MARÉS, **The Present State of Stock Raising in Algeria, and its Future** (L'Elevage en Algérie, son état actuel, son avenir). — *Bulletin Agricole de l'Algérie et de la Tunisie*, N. 5, pp. 101-116, Alger-Mustapha, 1er Mars, 1911.

In Algiers in 1907 there were :

Sheep	8 799 000
Oxen.	1 078 000
Goats.	3 959 000
Dromedaries	201 000
Pigs	96 000

The dromedaries are entirely in the hands of the natives of the south (1).

The pigs are raised exclusively by Europeans, and the supply is less than the demand. Tunis annually exports 3000 pigs into Algeria.

There are a few cross-bred Algerian goats which mature early and are very easy to fatten, but are poor milkers ; they are the descendants of Angoras imported at Mondjebour. The dairymen keep some herds of goats of Spanish origin outside the towns in the district of Oran. In the districts of Algiers and Constantine the goats are of Maltese origin. The indigenous goats belong almost exclusively to the natives. There is very little exportation of goats from Algiers.

There are three distinct groups of sheep. The breed of the oases is of very little value for meat, and of even less use for wool. The Barbary sheep are mainly found in Tunis, and are of very little interest. The contrary is the case with the Berbers ; two principal divisions must be recognized amongst the numerous varieties of these sheep ; that of the East or Chellala, and that of the West or Tiaret.

The Chellala has a white head and is often hornless ; its wool is short and thick ; it is tall, and gives from 18 to 22 kg. of meat. The Tiaret is thicker-set than the preceding, shorter in the legs, and is considered thriftier and hardier. Its wool is very similar to that of the Merino. The Algerian breeder has no means at present of judging of the superiority of one cross over another. The Agricultural Associations would do well to procure some stud animals and start experimental herds.

In Algeria, cattle raising is both stationary and nomadic. In the Tell, the animals are put under shelter at night ; but this is never done on the borders of the Tell and on the plateaus.

_____

(1) In 1908 there were in Algeria 236 168 horses, 187 714 mules, 271 794 asses, 204 715 camels, 1 092 202 cattle, 9 632 177 sheep, 4 199 096 goats, and 1 092 302 pigs. Wool-clip in 1908, 410 255 cwts. *The Statesman's Yearbook* for 1911, p. 797. (*Ed.*).

The exports are increasing. From 987 000 head of cattle exported in 1890, the number has risen· to 1 246 000 head in 1910. The numbers of the Algerian herds, on the contrary, remain stationary.

Among the measures which are likely to develop sheep-raising are the arranging of watering places, the opening of wooded lands for pasture during dry seasons, the restoration of the perennial pasturages of the south by stopping access to them during years of abundance, and lastly, the prohibition to export ewes for a certain number of months in summer and autumn.

The Algerians have two breeds of oxen, the Gulema and the Moroccan. The Gulema are excellent animals for slaughter; said to be regular miniature Shorthorns. The average weight of the oxen is 250 kg.' and they are very thrifty. The Moroccan breed, which is a little heavier, and taller than the Gulema, is very similar to the Spanish breed, with which it is frequently crossed in the district of Oran.

The Algerian cattle are inferior to what they were fifteen years ago. The present herds number somewhat less than 1 100 000 head. Algeria receives yearly from 4000 to 5000 head from foreign countries.

In order to improve the Algerian cattle breed, it should be crossed with the Zebu. The hybrid Zebu is immune from summer diseases ; it is hardy, drinks little, and is satisfied with dry and rough food, fattening even on stubble ; it matures earlier than the native breed, which has a finer skin and lighter frame ; it is more agile and quicker, and of a better build than its parents.

W. J. RUTHERFORD. **Classification for Horses.** — *Bulletin* No. 2. *University of Saskatchewan, College of Agriculture,* Saskatoon, Saskatchewan, Canada, pp. 47, illustrated.

1238

Canada: Saskatchewan

This Bulletin has been prepared to assist in bringing about a fuller and perhaps better understanding amongst horsemen as to the proper classification of horses for exhibition and sale. The requirements of a choice horse are described under the headings : Conformation, Type, Constitution, Quality, Disposition, Carriage and Action, Manners, Soundness, Age, Color, Sex and Condition.

Descriptions are given of horses of the following classes : Draft, Agricultural, Farm Chunks (1), Carriage Horses, Road Horses, Saddle Horses and General Purpose Horses. Photo-engravings are shown of typical specimens of each of the classes described.

---

(1) Chunk, figuratively a small and thick-set beast.   (*Ed.*).

1239   H. R. Smith. **Economical Beef Production**. — *The Farmer's Advocate*. Vol. XLVI No. 95. p. 222, Feb. 9, 1911. London, Ontario.

United
States:
Nebraska

The Nebraska Experiment Station has just issued Bulletin 116 which includes the results of several experiments in cattle-feeding. Part I deals with food stuffs as affecting economy of production, while Part II concerns the individual gaining capacity of animals representing different types.

In two experiments, a comparison was made of wheat, bran, linseed meal, and cotton-seed meal as protein supplements. The principal part of the ration was composed, in the first experiment, of a mixture of whole Indian corn and meadow hay, and in the second of whole Indian corn and green corn.

It was found that linseed meal is more nutritious than cotton meal, at equal weights, while bran has only half the nutritive value. The best results were obtained where lucerne hay was used as part of the fodder to furnish the desired amount of protein. The cost of the lucerne hay was 13 dollars per ton, and of the cotton meal 30 dollars per ton.

In a third experiment, cold-pressed cotton-seed cake was substituted for the cotton-seed meal, and the results were favourable for the cotton-seed cake, though the profits were higher with lucerne, 6.87 dollars per head with the former and 8.16 dollars with the latter. The quality of the meat produced ou the several rations was in favour of the lucerne as compared with the commercial protein foods.

Three experiments were made to determine the most profitable proportion of Indian corn to lucerne.

When Indian corn is worth from 35 to 50 cents per bushel, and lucerne not more than 7 dollars per ton, approximately half a feed of Indian corn — 10-12 lbs — will produce more profitable gains, if a good quality of lucerne is liberally given; in fact all will be consumed. This presupposes the steers being in fair condition, and a few weeks extra being given, in order to attain the desired finish.

In the last two experiments, individual records were kept in groups of 6 steers each, in order to study the build and quality of the animals from the point of view of profit, and very careful measurements were made of the animals used.

It was found that depth of body and size of middle girth were the chief factors determining the daily gains.

A difference in gains of not less than six-tenths of a pound per day, was found in all groups, the steers of a given group being fed alike.

Almost without exception, the largest gainers were large and roomy in the region of the paunch, and, usually, also large in heart-girth.

These experiments prove that there is great variation in the fattening capacity of cattle, and it is hoped that by following up this work, some conclusions may be arrived at as to the relation of external conformation to gaining capacity, in order that the most economical types may be selected.

E. Iwanoff. **A New Breed of Cattle** (Fertilité des hybrides de *Bison americanus* and *Bison europaeus*). — *C. R. de la Société de Biologie*, T. LXX, N. 14, pp, 584-586, Paris, 14 Avril, 1911,   **1240**

Some experiments in hybridization which have been carried out in Mr. Falz-Fein's Zoological Park, give hope of the creation of a new, stable, and fertile breed of cattle from the half-blood hybrid *Bison americanus* × *Bos taurus*, which is strong and capable of working faster and with less fatigue than the ordinary pack-ox of the Oukraïna breed.   **Russia**

But still more certain results appear to have been obtained by Mr. Iwanoff, of the veterinary laboratory of the Ministry of the Interior at St. Petersburg, in Mr. Falz-Fein's Park, by the hybridization of the *Bison americanus* with *Bison europaeus*. Both sexes of these hybrids are fertile and some further hybrids have already been obtained by crossing them with one of the parent species. These hybrids do not appear so far to have been obtained in any other place. The close consanguinity of the two species is certain, and the fertility of both sexes of their half-bred hybrids is only a further proof of this consanguinity. But the geographical distribution and the anatomical peculiarities of *B. americanus* and *B. europaeus* do not allow of their being considered as two varieties of the same species. The question is one therefore of a very rare case of half-bred hybrid mammals of which both sexes are equally fertile.

Van Andenaerd. **The English Leicester.** (Le mouton anglais Leicester). — *Journal des Sociétés Agricoles du Brabant et du Hainaut*, N. 7, p. 85. Bruxelles, Feb. 11, 1911.   **1241**

The English Leicester is one of the oldest and purest breeds of long-wooled sheep in the whole world. It is the point of departure for three other breeds; the Lincoln, the Border Leicester   **Great Britain. New Zealand**

and the Romney Marsh. The Leicester is thick-set and well made. It is particularly suitable for crossing with the Merino breed. Its improvement has been directed towards the quality of the meat and the wool rather than form.

In New Zealand, the Leicester is a particular favourite for crossing with all breeds of sheep. From the point of view of wool. the latter variety does not produce such a heavy fleece as the Lincoln, but it has the same glossiness and general characteristics.

The Leicester breed occupies a special position as far as the colour of the face and ears is concerned ; the original black colour sometimes recurs around the eyes and in the ear spots (1).

1242

DEVÉDEIX. **Training Farm for Elephants in the Belgian Congo. Their Utilisation in Agriculture.** (Ferme de dressage d'Eléphants au Congo Belge. Leur utilisation en Agriculture). — *Journal d'Agriculture pratique*, No. 12, p. 369, Paris. 23 Mars, 1911.

Belgian Congo

There is a training farm for elephants in the Belgian Congo, containing about fifty of these animals, which are used for agricultural purposes. The training of elephants is likely to be of great service in Africa, where all other domestic animals are decimated by the Tsetse fly. By making use of the elephant, it has been possible to plough vast tracts of land which were hitherto unproductive, and which are now cultivated in cassava and rice, products which are invaluable in the country. It is impossible to set up a farm without domestic animals, and the elephant surpasses all others in strength, longevity and intelligence.

It is to be hoped that this species, which is tending to disappear in tropical Africa, may also be employed in the French Congo for agricultural purposes, as it already is in India.

1243

Dairying in Switzerland. (L'Industrie laitière en Suisse). — *Laiterie et Elevage* (*d'après le Recueil consulaire* 1911). Tome 152, livraison III, 6e année, No. 7, Louvain, Avril 1, 1911.

Switzerland

Thanks to the importance of cattle-raising in Swiss agriculture, this country has suffered less than others from the rainy season of 1910.

---

(1) For information on the Leicester breed and on the other British sheep, see ROBERT WALLACE, *British Breeds of Sheep*, published by the Board of Agriculture and Fisheries, in *Breeds of Live Stock*, London, 1910.

See also the publication of the Intelligence Office in the International Institute of Agriculture: *The Science and Practice of Farming during 1910 in Great Britain*, p. 479. (*Ed.*).

Nearly three quarters of the agricultural land, properly so-called, is under forage crops; in the cantons of St. Gall and Appenzell the proportion is as much as 90 %. There are altogether 1 100 000 hectares (2.717.000 acres) of Alpine grazing land.

Since the development in the lowland country of the industry of products connected with cattle-raising, there is a tendency to fatten cattle in connection whith dairying, since the utilisation of mountain pasture land has been increased by the installation of aerial cables, by means of which the hay, enclosed in nets, is sent down into the valleys.

Whereas in 1829 Switzerland had no more than 750 000 head of cattle at grass, there are now 1 500 000. But on account of the deficient market for dairy produce the farmers are at present specialising in the raising of pedigree cattle.

It is calculated that a cow in Switzerland averages 2 650 litres (588 gals.) of milk per year. The milk production is thus 20 million hectolitres (444 million gals.) representing an average value of 33? million francs (£13 320 000). Of these 20 million hectolitres half is consumed as milk, 7 millions are used in the manufacture of cheese and butter and the remainder in preparing milk flour (*farine lactée*) and milk chocolate.

The following table gives the production of all the branches of Swiss dairying since 1897, in thousands of francs (1):

	Yearly Average Value		Annual Value 1907	Annual Value 1908
	1897-1901	1902-1906		
Fresh milk & cream	496	1 042	1 839	2 159
Fresh butter	231	68	92	48
Condensed milk	23 101	30 246	31 445	27 103
Cheese . . . . , .	41 101	44 406	54 183	54 128
Milk Sugar	35	3	13	1
Dried Milk Flour.	2 529	2 464	2 784	2 536
Total . . .	67 493	78 229	90 356	85 974 .

Butter is the only dairy-product which is not exported; on the contrary, it is imported, to the value of 10 million frs. (£400 000)

(1) 25.25 frcs. = £1; 1000 frcs. = 40 £.   (*Ed*).

yearly. There is however a big exportation of the other dairy products.

Switzerland is obliged to get a part of her cattle for slaughter from abroad. During the last three years, she has imported the following cattle for this purpose :

	1907 head	1908 head	1909 head
Oxen	46 320	45 524	47 366
Pigs.	90 325	55 170	50 932
Sheep	115 420	115 682	118 140

Since 1886, the number of pigs in Switzerland has doubled, and is now a little more than half a million head, which is not nearly sufficient for the demand.

In 1906 there were 360 000 goats in Switzerland, representing a total value of about 10 million francs (£400 000) (1).

1244   CH. CLÉMENT. **Cost in Belgium and in Prussia of the Transport of Milk** (L'Amelioration du transport des produits lactés). — *Laiterie et Elevage*, 6e année, No. 8, pp. 57-60, Louvain, Avril 15, 1911.

Belgium.
Germany :
Prussia

This study on the improvement in the transport of dairy produce from the point of view of rapidity and price begins with a comparison between the Prussian and Belgian tariffs.

A consignment of 210 kg., (2) or 480 bottles of 125 gr. in pigeon-hole boxes, sent by goods train to a distance of 50 km., costs 3.40 fr. in Belgium, including the return of the boxes with the empty bottles, while the same in Prussia costs 1.50 fr. A consignment of 258 kg., or 128 bottles of 1 litre, sent under the same conditions and also including the return of the boxes, costs 3.60 fr. in Belgium, and 2.25 fr. in Prussia. The freightage is raised at the rate of 0.007 fr. per bottle of 125 grams in Belgium, and 0.004 fr. in Prussia ; 0.03 fr. per litre bottle in Belgium and 0.019 fr. in Prussia.

It must be remembered that, like milk in cans, the milk in pigeon-hole boxes is sent by passenger train in Prussia, or by fast

---

(1) In 1906 (last census) there were in Switzerland 135 372 horses, 1 498 144 cattle, 209 997 sheep, 548 970 pigs, 362 117 goats *The Statesman's Yearbook for 1911*, p. 1260.   (*Ed.*).

(2) 1 kg. = 2.2 lbs; 1 gram = 15.43 grains Troy; 1 km. = 0.621 mile; 1 fr. = 10 d.   (*Ed.*).

goods trains, which offers a great advantage for this kind of merchandise.

An inquiry of the same kind in other countries, which the writer proposes to make, will be very useful; because the question of supplying the great centres with pure and wholesome milk at the general market price, is a very important one.

BORDAS and TOUPLAIN. **Organic and Inorganic Phosphorus in Milk.** 1245
(Phosphore organique et Phosphore minéral dans le lait). — *C.-R. de l'Acad. des Sciences*, T. 152, N. 13, pp. 899-900. Paris, 27 Mars, 1911.

The phosphoric acid contained in the ash of milk represents France
the whole phosphorus content inorganic and organic which it is interesting to differentiate and estimate separately exactly.

Mr. Bordas has been studying since 1903 the variations in the lecithine contained in milk after creaming, pasteurisation, etc. The information which we possess as to the phosphoric constituents of albuminoids is very inexact.

By oxidising the organic matter by means of nitric acid and potassium permanganate, to estimate the organic phosphorus contained in the coagulum (butter-casein), figures are obtained which, added to those yielded by the determination of the phosphates in the lactoserum, give a total result equivalent to the amount of phosphates found in the ash of the entire milk.

We thus possess a simple means of estimating the quantity of phosphorus both in organic and in mineral compounds, completing the estimation of the total phosphorus by adding that contained in the lactoserum and in the coagulum.

E. FLEURENT and LUCIEN LEVI. **On the Estimation of Phosphorus** 1246
in Milk. (Sur le dosage du phosphore dans le lait). — *C. R. de l'Acad des Sciences*, Tome 152, N. 15, p. 1015, Paris, 10 Avril, 1911.

The writers, speaking of Messrs. Bordas and Touplain's prea- France
ceding note on the estimation of organic [and [mineral phosphorus in milk, point out that, if from their point of view, it may be admitted that the loss in phosphorus (0.065 gr. of P_2O_5 per litre) during the combustion of the organic matters in milk might be neglected (although it attains 3.90 % of the total phosphorus) the question

is not the same if this loss be considered in relation to the organic phosphorus, since this amounts to 21.30 % of the quantity determined by the above-mentioned investigators.

1247   A. FUNARO and L. MUSANTE. **Ewe's Milk in the Adulteration of Cows' Milk**. (Il latte di pecora nelle falsificazioni del latte di vacca). — *Atti dell'Accademia dei Georgofili* di Firenze, 1911.

Italy: This note deals with an adulteration which is practised generally
Tuscany   at Leghorn, where large quantities of ewe's milk arriving daily from Pisa, Lucca and Grosseto, instead of being used in the manufacture of "pecorino" cheese, serve to make up the deficiency in fat of skimmed cows' milk. Thus detection of the sale of skimmed milk is rendered difficult. By this fraud watered or skimmed milk may be sold with a profit, amounting even to 2.50 fr. per 100 litres. It is therefore necessary to find a rapid means of discovering the adulteration (1).

Messrs. Fleurent and Levi confine themselves to the determination of the density of the serum ; which, in pure milks even when they are very different from one another, varies within very narrow limits. Now this particular adulteration, although it brings the fat contents up to normal, disturbs the proportion of salts in the serum, decreasing its density. The determination of the density of the serum may easily be carried out in less than two hours.

Adding ewe's milk to cow's milk is of interest also from the hygienic point of view, because the digestibility and composition of ewe's milk is different from that of cow's milk.

1248   A. OLIVA. **Cost of Working Parmesan Cheese or „*Grana Cheese*",
by Steam**. (La lavorazione del Grana a vapore). — *L'Avvenire agricolo*, anno XIX, N. 3, pp. 106-111, Parma, 31 Marzo, 1911.

Italy   The standard manufacture of the Grana Parmesan cheese of Reggio and Lodi has been carried out up to the present by heating the milk directly on a wood fire.

---

(1) The mixture of milks of different animals constitutes true frauds, as for the production of certain cheeses; thus ewe's milk, which ought to be used alone in the manufacture of Roquefort cheese, is sometimes mixed with goats' or cows' milk.

See VILLIERS, COLLIN and FAVOLLE *Aliments lactés et aliments gras.* — Paris, 1911.   *(Ed.).*

But in consequence of the high price of wood and the improvements which have been made in the machines for steam heating, the latter system has now been introduced into the many cheese dairies of Parma, Reggio and Modena.

Mr. Oliva estimates the installation cost (for 2 boilers and a 4 HP motor) at 5575 fr. (£223) and the cost of transforming the direct heating machines into steam heaters at about 4000 fr. (£160). The annual expenditure for steam manufacture is as follows:

Interest on installation capital . . . . 250 fr. (£10)
Depreciation (calculated for twelve years) · . . . . 400 » (£16)
Fuel (100 qs. at 4.50 per q.) . . . . 450 » (£18)
Repairs and lubricants . . . . 100 » (£ 4)

Total expenditure . 1200 fr. (£48)

The expenditure for the manufacture over wood fires is as follows:

Hiring of two boilers . . . . 100 fr. (£ 4)
Wood, about 500 qs. . . . . 1300 » (£52)

Total expenditure . 1400 fr. (£56)

The difference in cost between the two methods is slight; but the steam installation can also be used for churning, giving a larger yield of butter of more even grain than hand labour. From 3 to 4 % of butter can also be obtained from the whey; in a cheese factory which works 3500 quintals of milk yearly, this gives about 12 quintals of butter in the year. With butter at 250 fr. (£10) the quintal, there is thus a surplus yield of 3000 fr. (£120) per year.

In order that the steam manufacture of the Grana may be economical two, or better, three forms should be worked simultaneously every day.

G. FASCETTI, **Study of " Bitto '' Cheese of Lombardy**. (Studi sul formaggio " Bitto "). — *Rivista scientifica del latte*, anno I, p. 1-12, Reggio Emilia, Marzo, 1911.

1249

" Bitto " cheese takes its name from the valley of the Bitto, a tributary of the Adda. It is made in two types: the fat type

Italy:
Lombardy

which is similar to the Battelmatt (1), and the Sbrinz type (2),
which is made with partially creamed milk.

The annual production of this cheese, which is manufactured
in the hills, is about 3000 quintals, half of which is of the Sbrinz
type, and it is all brought to the market of Brinzi, where traders
from Bergamo and Como go to make their purchases.

The cheeses which are freshest and have some holes are consumed immediately, while the others are allowed to ripen for a year
or two.

The travelling lecturer and the agricultural cooperative associations of Sondrio and Morbegno have started cooperative stores,
thus creating an important market for the cheese.

The original " Bitto" cheese is made of whole cow's milk, with
about a fifth of goats' milk added to it.   The weight of each cheese
varies between 15 and 30 kg.. the average being 20 kg. ; the cheeses
from 30 to 50 cm. in diameter, and the colour of the paste is something like that of Emmenthal.

The paste inside is smooth and brilliant and contains small
holes of a diameter of from 2 to 3 mm., which are very regularly
distributed.   The cheese when two years old is harder and has a
stronger flavour, and the holes are filled with a dense liquid which
has a pleasant taste.

A hectolitre of milk gives 12 kg. of fat or 9 kg. of semi-fat
cheese, and 3 kg. of butter.   " Ricotta " is made from the whey.

The analysis of four samples of " Bitto " cheese has given the
following average percentages:

> Water 31.78
> Fatty matters. 33.59
> Casein 28.81
> Ash. 4.83

A peculiarity of the manufacture of " Bitto " cheese is that
the milk is heated up to 40° C. for coagulation. The following
are other technological data of this manufacture:

---

(1) « Battelmatt » a fat, soft cheese, with holes like Gruyère, is made in
Switzerland and in the Vorarlberg: each cheese weighs from 20 to 25 kg.
(1 kg. = 2.2 lbs) and the usual dimensions are, height from 8 to 10 cm., diameter 50 to 60 cm. (1 cm. = 0.39 inch). Cf. BESANA, *Caseificio*, Torino, 1908. (*Ed.*).

(2) « Sbrinz », which is better known under the name of Spalen cheese,
is made in Switzerland in the Cantons of Unterwald, Uri, Lucerne, Zug, etc.
It is a semi-fat cheese weighing from 10 to 30 kg., of similar dimensions to
Gruyère, and similar to it also in technique. Cf *op. cit.*   (*Ed.*).

Coagulation temperature, 41° C.
Liquid rennet % cc. 11.
Breaking up of the curd and duration of coagulation, 30 min.
Duration of cooking. 31 minutes.
Cooking temperature, 44° C.
Duration of stirring (*Spinatura*) away from the fire, 7 minutes.
Resting of cheese in boiler, 18 minutes.
Pressure, 2 kg. per kilogram of cheese.
Yield, 11.70 %
Loss in weight after two months, 14.60 %.

Roquefort Cheese Produced in Corsica. (Formaggio di Roquefort   1250
prodotto in Corsica). — *Bollettino del Ministero di Agric., Ind.
e Comm.*,Series E., Fasc. 2, p. 96, Roma, Jan. 16, 1911.

Some French manufacturers of Roquefort cheese set up dairy   **France:**
farms in Corsica six years ago, where they have been making Ro-   **Corsica**
quefort cheese with success.

The milk used in this manufacture should not be sour; it
should scale 17° by the lactometer, and the temperature of the
premises should be 20° C. The milk is steam heated to 30°; the
liquid rennet is added, the whole stirred, and the whey strained off.

The curds are then cut into pieces, weighing half a kilogram
(1.1 lb.) and put into iron moulds after being covered with a blue
powder, prepared from mouldy unleavened rye bread. The cheese
should be allowed to drain for 5 days, after which it is put into
a cold cellar; it is salted only once. It is pierced in several places
with an iron wire, in order to aerate and let the wa ter run out.

The satisfactory results obtained in Corsica, show that Roquefort cheese could be produced in Sardinia and in the Roman Cam-
pagna. The secret of the manufacture has nothing to do with the
caverns of Roquefort (in which the original cheese is prepared), but
is simply due to the cold storage and the use of rye-bread mould,
which can be prepared everywhere.

The Use of Cold Storage Meat in the French Army. (L'emploi de   1251
la viande frigorifiée dans l'armée en France). — *Revue général
du froid*, No. 23. pp. 188-198, Paris, Avril, 1911.

There was an interesting discussion in the French Chamber of   **France**
Deputies on March 14th, 1911, on the use of cold storage meat in
the French army and the organisation of the necessary services.

Frozen and cold-stored meat should be given to the soldiers even in times of peace, in order that the persons who have to attend to the work of preserving the meat may learn how to preserve all its qualities.

The discussion is published *in extenso* in *Revue gen. du Froid.*

1252

The Petaluma Poultry Industry in California — *The Illustrated Poultry Record.* Vol. III, No. 7. p. 312. London, April. 1911.

United
States:
California

Petaluma, in Sonoma County, California, is one of the greatest egg centres of the world. The city, of 7 000 inhabitants, is situated about 40 miles (64 kms.) north of San Francisco, and is about 20 or 30 miles inland. It is connected with San Francisco by water and rail and its transportation facilities have been an important factor in the development of the industry.

Petaluma, Santa Rosa, Healdsburg, Cloverdale and other smaller towns in Sonoma County supply San Francisco with about half its annual supply of eggs. Petaluma alone sent out, in 1910, 7 159 481 dozen eggs and 120 018 dozen fowls.

The following figures give the exports from Petaluma from 1903 to 1909. To obtain the total production, to these figures should be added the number of eggs used for hatching and the eggs and other poultry produce used for home consumption:

Year	Eggs Doz.	Poultry Doz.
1903	3 407 333	32 535
1904	3 493 321	32 286
1905	3 837 061	39 392
1906	4 334 321	39 938
1907	4 422 968	39 392
1908	5 312 804	83 136
1909	7 159 481	120 018

Recent organisation among the producers and a system adopted for grading eggs has given encouragement to more careful methods. A Cooperative Egg Exchange has been established. The producers deliver their eggs to the Exchange, where they are graded. But only a portion of the produce of Petaluma is handled through the Exchange. The average price for all eggs, in 1909, was 27 ³/₄ cents (or 1s 1 ¼d) per dozen.

The Transylvanian Naked Neck Fowl. — *The Illustrated Poultry Record*, Vol. III, N⁰. 7, pp. 302-303. London, April, 1911.

1253

There are in South Eastern Europe two breeds of poultry with very distinctive peculiarities. These are the so - called Danubian Goose, with its long, abundant posterior feathers and the Transylvanian Naked Neck Fowl. The last breed is to be met with in Austria, Hungary, Servia, Bulgaria, Roumania and Bessarabia. It is further stated that there are Naked Neck fowls in Madagascar.

Austria
Hungary.
Servia
Bulgaria
Russia

Probably the breed originated in Central Asia and thence passed into Europe and by Persia or India to Madagascar.

The appearance of the birds is very peculiar. In size they are medium (4 to 6 lbs, or 2 to 3 kgs), with longish neck and legs, giving a somewhat stilty look, as the thighs are small. The body is round and well developed, flat and muscular in front, with large, strong wings. The cock's tail is full and carried almost horizontally. The head is neat, and the comb single. The head and neck for four or more inches (ten or more centimetres) downwards are naked except for a full, clear-cut band of soft feathers a little above the shoulders; the head and flesh thus left uncovered are bright red. As a rule, the best specimens are pure white in plumage ; a few coloured Naked-Necks are seen, mainly reddish brown.

The peasants of the countries named prefer this breed to all others; the Naked Neck Fouls are so hardy and vigorous. They are very and active during the greater part of the year find all their own food.

Silk Production in Bengal. (La Sériculture au Bengale).— *Bulletin des Soies et des Soieries*, N. 1772. pp. 5-6. Paris-Lyon, 22 Avril, 1911.

1254

The exportation of silk from Bengal showed the following figures during the last four years :

British
India:
Bengal

1907	288 544 kg. =	5 680 cwt.
1908	255 882 » =	5 228 »
1909	204 579 » =	4 224 »
1910	398 678 » =	7 848 »

The marked increase in 1910 is due to the efforts made by the Agricultural Department of Bengal for the promotion of silk-worm rearing.

The Committee appointed consists of the Director of Agriculture, the Collector of Murshidabad and four persons from the first silk houses in the country.

There are now 18 silk production stations in Bengal. The experiments carried out have demonstrated that it is possible to avoid the silkworm disease known under the name of « pébrine », which has largely contributed to the depression of the silkworm industry in Bengal.

The total product of the sale of silkworm eggs in 1909-1910 has risen to 6 566 rupees, or 692 rupees more than in the previons season.

The experiments which have been carried out at Berhampore with some Italian mulberry trees, as well as those at Calcutta for the preservation of silkworm eggs and cocoons by cold storage, have been very successful.

A school has been opened for the children of the silkworm breeders employed at the Berhampore silk-culture station.

1255   D. E. LANTZ. **Raising Deer and other Large Game Animals in the United States.** — *U. S. Dept. of Agric.-Biological Survey Bull.* No. 36, pp. 7-39. Washington, Dec. 31, 1911.

United States

The raising of indigenous or imported mammals, which are allowed to live in a wild state, is opening a new field for breeding experiment in the United States, while it also offers an advantageous investment for capital.

The preservation of species which are disappearing, as *Hippotragus leucophoeus*, their use, the skin industry and the game trade make the solution of this problem of interest. *Cervus canadensis* (Rocky Mountain Elk) and *Odocoileus virginianus* (Virginia Deer) may, as shown by the first experiments, be raised successfully as well as cheaply in all climates and in the most different places.

About seven years ago, the Otzinachson Rod-and-Gun Club introduced 90 deer into a park of 4000 acres and today the herd comprises 2000 head.

There are more than 250 000 000 acres of land in the United States which are not suitable for cultivation and cannot be used as pasturage for horses, cattle or sheep. This vast region, which is completely unproductive for the moment, might be profitably utilized for the production of game.

1256   KUHNERT. **Fertilisers for Fish Ponds.** (Teichdüngungsversuche). — *Mitteilungen der Deutschen Landwirtschafts-Gesellschaf* XXVI J., S. 14, pp. 173-175, Berlin. April 1, 1911.

Germany

Mr. Kuhnert recommends the use of fertilisers for fish ponds. Comparative experiments should be the following:

Pond No. 1: not treated.

Pond No. 2 : 5 to 6 kg. of bàsic slag or superphosphates, 2 to 3 kg. of potassic salts at .40 % or 6 to 8 kg. of Kainit per *are*.

Pond No. 3 : as No. 2, and in addition, 2 to 4 kg. of nitrate of soda per *are*.

The basic slag and the potassic salts may be spread over the bottom [of the pond, or thrown in to the water during the winter; the superphosphates should always be applied before the water is put into the pond, while the nitrate of soda should be divided into 3 or 4 parts and put into the water during the first warm days of spring, from the end of April to the middle of May.

The experiments made by the writer in 1910, continuating others of previous years, with carp and tench, have confirmed the great utility of phosphatic and potassic fertilisers which increase the produce by more than a third. It is therefore obvious that the Chili nitrate fertiliser would increase the production still more, so that, after deducting the cost of the nitrate, there would be a net profit of from 24 to 84 frcs per hectare from the additional fish.

Mr. Kuhnert also recommends that experiments be made with calcium and stable mauures.

P. Pyrlas. **The Resinous Wines of Greece**. (Les vins résinés de Grèce). *Progrès Agricole et Viticole*, N. 11, pp. 321-326, Montpellier, 12 Mars, 1911.

1257

Two kinds of wine are manufactured in Greece for common consumption ; the ordinary wines, part of which are exported, and the *resinous* wines, entirely for home consumption. The latter are made by the fermentation of the must, to which pine tree resin has been added. A very long time ago, the Greeks discovered that the addition of resin to the must acts as a preventive to various diseases, and resinous wines are still preferred by them.

Greece

The principal stocks used to make the resinous white wines at Athens are : the *Savatianno* and the *Rhoditis*. Immediately after the vintage, the grapes are pressed and the must is sent to the cellar of the wine merchant, who adds resin in the proportion of 4 to 5 kg. per hectolitre or more. The resin is first worked up with a small quantity of must to ensure its better distribution. During fermentation the resin floats on the surface, but when the carbonic acid stops coming off, the density of the liquid having lessened, the greater part of the resin is precipitated to the bottom. A sort of slow separation then takes place, the oily part of the resin floating to the surface and forming a protec-

tive layer which prevents the passage of the air. This oil of turpentine becomes resinised under the action of the oxygen of the
air, and in this state is precipitated to the bottom of the cask;
but it is continually renewed at the top. A very small quantity
of turpentine is dissolved in the wine, which acquires a strongly
resinous taste. Before being put on sale, the wine is kept until
all the resin is precipitated.

The wine is not racked, and is left on the lees until it is put
on sale; the merchants are of opinion that racking destroys the
freshness of the wine and prevents it from keeping so well. In
spring, the wines often become sour (*tourne*); ropy (viscid) (*graisse*)
or suffer from pushing (*pousse*) (Germ. *das Treiben*). If they are
protected from the air when racked, all these diseases may be prevented. Resinous wines become affected with damp-spot (*piqûre*,
Germ. *Moderflecken*) when the protective layer of oil is insufficient,
and the mannite disease (*la casse*) is also produced at times; the
latter should be treated with citric acid.

Resinous wine should be very dry and contain from 12° to 13°
of alcohol. The acidity expressed in sulphuric acid per litre
should oscillate between 4 and 4.50 gr. These wines are deficient
in tannin. The consumer requires the following qualities: 1) perfect
clearness; 2) colour clear amber yellow; 3) *very pronounced* taste
of resin; 4) freshness and even a slight carbonic taste; 4) neither
too insipid, nor too acid, nor too alcoholic (13° at the maximum).

These wines cannot be left to get old; they become bitter,
and turn red in colour on account of the incessant oxidation of
the turpentine. Amongst the principal resinous wines of Greece are
the following: those of Athens, Salamina, Ægina, Megara, the Island
of Euboea, Patras, Nauplia and Tripolitza. The resinous wines
promote digestion, and are diuretic and stimulating; they should
be highly esteemed amongst table wines.

1258　**Sugar and Alcohol Regulations for Madeira Wines.** (O Regimen
de Assucar e do Alcool na Ilha da Madeira) — *A Vinha Por-
tugueza*, N. 3, p. 93. Lisboa Março, 1911.

Portugal
Madeira　　　A Decree has been issued by the Portuguese Government with
regard to sugar and alcohol in Madeira.

Foreign molasses may now be imported into the island when
the local production of sugar cane is not sufficient for the needs
of the Madeira wine manufacturers.

At the same time the cultivation of the cane is restricted to the best soils and the danger of the continuous cultivation of one crop thus avoided.

The Decree also sets aside a certain capital for the protection, development and improvement of the Madeira wine industry.

O. PRANDI AND E. CIVETTA. **Manganese in Wine.** (Il manganese nel vino). — *Le Stazioni Sperimentali Agrarie Italiane.* Vol. XLIV, E. I., pp. 58-65, Modena, 1911.

1259

The analysis of 24 samples of Piedmontese wines of different quality has given a minimum of 0.53 gr. of manganese per litre, and a maximum of 1:65: average 0.82. Generally speaking, the finest wines. those which have the most delicate bouquet when they are old, such as the *Nebbioli,* and especially the *Barolo,* and *Barbaresco,* are the richest in manganese. A *Nebbiolo* of 1883 was an exception to this rule; it had completely lost its colouring matter, and had an abundant sediment.

Italy:
Piedmont

L. MOREAU and E. VINET. **Method of Eliminating Arsenate of Lead from the Vintage.** (Comment s'elimine l'arséniate de plomb apporté par le vendange). — *C. R. de l'Acad. des Sciences,* T. 152, N. 16, pp. 1057-1060. Paris, 8 April 1911.

1260

As only a small quantity of arsenate of lead is introduced by gathering grapes from vines which have been treated before flowering and as nearly all of this is eliminated during the pressing and wine-making operations, very slight traces, at the most. should be found in these wines as a rule. In practice, these traces, when they exist, are more often than not similar to those found in wines made from vines which have never received arsenical treatment. Under these conditions, it would seem that the wine made from vines which have been treated before flowering may be consumed without danger.

It might be quite another matter if the vines were treated late after the flowering.

The elimination of arsenate of lead should be carried out especially during the pressing, because this substance would otherwise be retained in the residuum, since it is found exclusively on the stalks, to which it adheres more readily than to the fruit.

France

1261   A. Mertens. **The Preservation of Hops when Removed from Cold Storage.** (La conservation du Houblon après sa sortie du frigorifère). — *La Bière et les boissons fermentées.* 20ᵉ année, N. 3, pp. 26-28. Paris, March, 1911.

Belgium

Hops are now stored in bundles weighing 150 kg., but the present monthly consumption in the French high fermentation (1) breweries is little more than 100 kg. ; and it is also customary to use several kinds simultaneously. The result is, that after the hops come out of cold storage they are sometimes left exposed in the barns of the brewery for a very long time.

Mr. Mertens, of Louvain, wishing to discover in what way they might be preserved, took several specimens which had been kept in cold storage in different places and for periods varying from 10 to 22 months. The antiseptic power of the different hops was very variable, but the curve graphically representing the antiseptic power of the duration of preservation after they came out of the cold store, was constant under the trial conditions. The antiseptic power may fall to 30 % of its initial strength in less than a month.

The brewer should use hops which have been cold stored, as soon as possible after they come out of storage ; he should keep them under the best conditions, that is to say, in a cool, dry place and preferably in the dark.

Hops which are to be used in average or small high-fermentation breweries, should be made up in packages weighing 50 kg. at most, and the consignments to the brewery should be made in proportion to the needs.

1262   E. Kaiser. **Researches on the Juice of Beer Yeast** (Recherches sur le suc de la levure de bière) *C. R. de l'Académie des Sciences,* T. 152, N. 14, pp. 975-977, Paris, 3 Avril 1911.

France

Whilst studying Mr. Lebedeff's convenient methods (2) for procuring the active juice of yeast, Mr. Kaiser found that the state of

---

(1) The fermentation of beerwort is performed by two different methods, namely, " high " and " low " fermentation. High fermentation wort is made at a relatively high temperature, which varies from 12º C. to 20º C. Low fermentation, on the contrary, generally takes place at a temperature of from 6º to 7º. In the first case, the fermentation is finished in from two to five days, while in the second it lasts from 8 to 15 days.

See E. Boullanger, *Industries agricoles de fermentation,* Paris, 1903.

(2) These consisted of extracting the zymase by maceration. See No. 398 of the Bulletin of February 1911.   (*Ed*).

the yeast, the method of drying, the proportion of water added to it, and especially the temperature at which the maceration is carried out are of great importance. Repeated microscopical observation has shown how this juice may easily be preserved at the ordinary temperature even without the addition of antiseptics.

The study made of the influence of the temperature, the nature of the sugar and the concentration of the juice, shows that the substance obtained by Lebedeff is very similar to Buchner's zymase.

The Dried Yeast Industry. (Die Hefe-Station der Brauerei. Anregungen für die Brauereimaschinen-Austellung auf der Oktobertagung 1911). — *Tageszeitung für Brauerei*, IX J., N. 83, pp. 415-416, Berlin, April 1911.

1263

The investigations made by the Experimental Institute and School of Brewery at Berlin into the utilisation of the surplus yeast produced by the breweries have been brought to a conclusion. The results may be summed up as follows:

Germany

1) The technical basis of the desiccation of yeast is now established; the German mechanical industry is in a position to supply the breweries with good, remunerative desiccating apparatus, of various constructions.

2) Desiccated yeast which is not deprived of its bitterness (fodder yeast) is affirmed to be a food of the first quality for fattening numerous species of animals.

3) Desiccated yeast deprived of its bitterness (alimentary yeast) has been recommended as a suitable, savoury and very digestible food for man.

4) The necessary expenditure for taking away the bitterness is very small, and there is an average yield of 80 and even 90 %.

5) Beer yeast may be usefully employed in the preparation of the simple products of the biscuit factory.

An outlet being assured for fodder, alimentary and baker's yeast, it is to the interest of the brewers to collect the whole of the yeast that they produce.

For the completion of its studies on this subject, the Experimental Brewery Institute has decided to instal a special Section at the Brewery Machine Exhibition which is to be held in October of this year, on the occasion of the Berlin Congress. This Section which will be called the Brewers' Yeast Station, will exhibit all the devices and apparatus for the improvement of the production and utilisation of yeast.

The following is the plan of the exhibits:

I. EXTRACTION OF THE YEAST FROM THE FERMENTATION VATS.

1) Dredges for collecting and taking away the yeast from the fermentation vats.

2) Pumps for transporting the yeast from the fermentation to the washing receptacles.

II. WASHING OF THE YEAST.

1) Sieves for separating the impurities and membranous clots; agitators and rinsers: applications of motors.

2) Apparatus for washing, and depositing and for removing the bitterness.

III. YEAST REFRIGERATORS.

Vats and barrels for preserving the yeast, ice and salt-mixture refrigerators.

IV. EXTRACTION OF THE YEAST FROM THE WASHING WATERS.

1) Centrifugal separators for the complete separation of the yeast from the washing water.

2) Yeast presses;
   a) hand; b) hydraulic; c) steam. Sacks, press cloths, etc.

V. MACHINES FOR CUTTING UP THE YEAST
AND FORMING THE COMPRESSED YEAST INTO PIECES OF A FIXED WEIGHT AS BAKERS' YEAST.

VI. DRYING INSTALLATIONS.

1) Apparatus for transporting the moist or compressed yeast to the drying chambers, such as pumps, bands and spirals.

2) Drying chambers.
   a) steam, drums or flat, with direct steam or evaporation, with and without vacuum; b) air; α) drying by direct fire with a device for heating the air; β) by injector with a device for the spraying of the fresh yeast by the injection of air and drying of the " yeast mist " by hot air.

VII. COLLECTION, TRANSPORT AND STORAGE OF THE DRIED YEAST.

1) Ventilators for the yeast drying chambers for the collection of the yeast dust,

2) Apparatus for transporting the yeast to the warehouse. Elevators, bands, spirals, pneumatics.

3) Warehouses, pits for preserving the dried yeast.

A part of this material serves, not only for the treatment of the surplus yeast produced, but also for the production of the yeast itself which makes it indispensable to have culture barrels, barrels for the production of the yeast, and mixture and aeration apparatus.

The exhibition will be of great importance to the beer industry, and supplies a real need.

Sugar Production in Spain. (Produción de azucares) *España Económica y Financiera*, Madrid, Enero 28, 1911.

1264

Spain

According to the information published by the General Direction of the Spanish Customs the sugar factories of Spain have done good business in the half year July 1st to Dec. 31, 1910.

The following are the figures of the raw material used by the factories and their output of sugar during the working years 1909 and 1910 :

	1909	1910
Raw material	Kg. 545 536 200	Kg. 419 883 087
Sugar product	» 58 463 582	» 44 285 178

This statement shows that in 1910 there was a decrease of 125 653 113 kg. in raw material and of 14 178 404 kg. in sugar on the preceding year.

LAURENT. **The Present State of the Starch Industry.** (L'état actuel de la féculerie industrielle) *Revue générale de Chimie pure et appliquée*, Tome, XIV, N. 6. pp. 105-116.

1265

France

Although the French starch production in the Department of the Oise alone reaches nearly 5 million kg. yearly, there were only some simple didactic treatises and not a single modern monograph on the starch industry in the French language, constituting an original critical work. This industry, which is in the hands of small cultivators, half farmers and half industrials, is one of the most backward in the country.

This brief monograph is written with the object of describing the starch industry as it should be. By a comparative examination of the different crops, the methods of extraction and purification of the starch and the working of the by - products, it leads to the conclusion that French starch-making might be improved to the point of being able to compete with the products obtained elsewhere; this would require better cultivation of potatoes and the creation of well equipped central works with a properly qualified staff. The article is illustrated by numerous figures.

1266   **Preserved Olives, and the Countries where they are prepared.** (Les conserves d'Olives et leur pays de production). *Bulletin de la Direction de l'Agriculture, etc. Régence de Tunis*, N. 57, pp. 492-505, 4e trimestre, 1910.

Mediter-
ranean
Countries.
California

Up to a very few years ago, the preserving of green and black olives was an industry confined to European Countries bordering on the Mediterranean.

At the present day, Africa and America have begun to produce this article, and the olives which they send to the market have a great reputation.

France. The Departments of the South of France produce a very large number of varieties for preserving both in the green and black stage. The following are preferred: *Verdale, Lucques, Picholine* and *Amellaou*.

The French production fluctuates from year to year; it reaches about 600 000 kg., without counting home consumption.

Algeria. The green olives are sliced with reeds, and preserved in brine or vinegar spiced in various ways.

The black olives are salted and consumed during 6 or 8 months of the year.

Kabylia, where the first factories for olive preserving were set up, is now rivalled by the Department of Oran where the proprietors of the olive groves are mostly European.

The average production of olives in Algeria is about 2 000 000 kg. The most remarkable varieties are: *Bounchok, Zéradj, Aberkan, Téfah, Hamma* and *Bréa*.

Tunis. It seems likely that there will be a certain number of factories for preserving olives in Tunis when the transport service is better. The varieties to be recommended here are: *Barouni, Besbassi, Zarazi Ressassi, Marsaline,* etc.

Greece. Greece does a considerable trade in preserved olives, for which the Prefectures of Magnesia and Phocis (Pelion and Parnassus in Doris)are especially famous. The preserved black olives of Thessaly are called Pelion olives.

The olives of Kalamata are celebrated.

The cultivation of olive trees with large fruit is made for the most part on the Pelion group which overlooks the town of Volo. In 1907 the export amounted to 5 533 827 kg., and more than half the olives exported are bought by America, Egypt and Turkey.

Turkey. Preserved olives are largely used in the food of the Turks, especially amongst the country people and soldiers.

European and Asiatic Turkey produce an average of 100 000 tons of preserved olives and in Brussa alone the production is 60 % of this total.

This industry is mainly in the villages on the shores of the Sea of Marmora, the islands of the Egean sea and Tripolitania. The most valued varieties are called : *Tchelebi, Zeituni de Sélé and Zeituni de Trigli*.

About a quarter of the production is exported, that is, about 25 000 tons, to Russia, Bulgaria, Roumania and Servia.

Spain. Spain has a world-wide reputation for her preserved green olives, and those of Seville, the *de la Reine* the *Zorzatenas*, etc., are particularly esteemed. Andalousia furnishes the largest supply and the trade is concentrated in Seville. The total production is 175 000 quintals.

Portugal. Portugal exports mostly bottled olives for the Anglo-Saxon countries and for Brazil. The *Cordovil* and the *Judiaga*, which weighs as much as 14 gr., are the most celebrated.

Italy. Italy holds a certain rank in the production of preserved olives, although her exportation is limited to the *Lucca* and *St. Francis* varieties, from the district of Ascoli. In the Southern provinces, the following olives are cultivated ; *Crossa, Concia, Andria, Santo Agostino, Passola, Arcolana, Rotondella* and *di Spagna*. The *Nocillara* is renowned in Sicily.

In good years the Italian production of preserved olives is estimated at 35 000 quintals.

California. During the past twenty years the preserved olive industry has made considerable progress in California. The varieties prepared are known under the names of *Mission* and *Manzanilla*.

The production in 1906 was already about 1 000 000 bottles of 1 litre. The county of San Diego is likely, by its situation, to become a very important centre for the industry, as well as the county of San Joachim, where there are already three important factories.

1267   **The Preservation of Olive Pomace in Tunis.** (La conservation des
Grignons d'Olives en Tunis). — *Buletin de la Direction de l'Agriculture, etc., Régence de Tunis*, N. 57, pp. 476-487, 4ᵉ trimestre, 1910.

Tunis   Olive pomace, kept in heaps in the open air, becomes considerably altered; the oil taken from it turns very acid, and there is
also a very considerable loss of fatty matters.

The method of preservation which has given the best results
is that of keeping this residue submerged in a weak solution of
sulphate of copper.

The method of dry preservation most recommended is in ensilage, with tight packing, and then the removal by vertical cutting. The object to be attained is to keep the substance moist,
and entirely protected from air and sun.

If the pomace becomes dry, it should be watered when it is
piled in heaps. The preservation would be greatly furthered by
the injection of carbon disulphide into the interior of the mass after
the silos have been made.

The lining of the silo requires some time, and the watering of the layers of skins, little by little as they are stacked up,
with a 1 or 2 % solution of formic aldehyde, would certainly help
the preservation, while the better quality of the resulting product
would, to a great extent, compensate for the additional expense.
The residue ought always to be inspected before use, because if it
has become mouldy, it may be a serious danger to the cattle.

1268   **A New Transatlantic Steamer with Cold Storage Plant.** (Un nou-
veau transatlantique à installations frigorifiques). — *La Revue
Générale du Froid*, 3ᵉ année, tome III, N. 4. pp. 174-177,
Paris, April 1911.

France   On March 19th last the Messageries Maritimes Company
launched a new large packet boat, the " Paul Lecat ". This ship is of
interest on account of its cold storage installations, the main object
of which is the preservation by cold of all the commodities consumed on board; but an auxiliary storeroom is reserved for the
transport of merchandise.

The total space set apart for cold storage is more than 300 cub.
metres and is subdivided as follows:

    3 chambers for meat, a thawing chamber and a butchery;

    2 chambers for vegetables;

    1 chamber for fish and game, with two large cupboards an-
nexed for thawing;

1 chamber for butter and cheese ;
1 chamber for fruit ;
1 ice-house with the apparatus for ice making, giving 300 kg. of transparent ice daily ;
1 cellar for wine where the temperature is from 10 to 12° C.

The arrangement of the cold storage chambers is described on a plan inserted in the text of the article. They are all abaft the engine bulkhead on the third deck. The meat chambers are kept cold by means of circulation of cold air and radiation from pipes of brine placed inside the chambers. The others are kept cold by the circulation of brine.

The two carbonic acid compressors have each a power of about 40,000 frigories for a sea water temperature of 30° C.. and a brine temperature of —15° C,

The Use of Cold Stored Meat in the French Army. — See No 1251 of this Bulletin.

1269
France

Agricultural Engineering and Farm Machinery and Implements.

C. A. OLCOCK. **Sanitary Cow Stalls and their Construction.** *The Maritime Farmer, Sussex, New Brunswick, Canada.* Vol. 16, No. 12, March 21, 1911, pp. 375-377.

1270

With the aid of numerous photo engravings and line drawings, the writer describes four different styles of unpatented stalls for cows that have been found satisfactory when put into practical operation during the past few years.

Canada :
New
Brunswick

The features aimed at in these stalls are comfort of the animals, sanitation and cleanliness in regard to milk supply. Bills of material, with cost of construction for these several stalls are given.

1271   B. COVENTRY. **The Bamboo Wattle Silo.** *The Agric. Jour. of India.*
Vol. VI. Part. 1, pp. 20-27. Calcutta, Jan. 1911.

India   Round silos having been found successful in America, and the
demand for silage increasing in Pusa (India), it seemed well to
devise a silo having the proper shape and dimensions, but constructed with inexpensive materials, which would provide the Agricultural and Military Departments with a cheap means of storing
fodder, and would also meet the requirements of cultivators.

The silo was made of bamboo wattle covered over with a
plastering of mud, it had a light roof of thatch; the size was 24 ft.
by 18 ft. diameter, and the gross capacity 6 096 cubic ft. Windows were let into the wattle at intervals of 6 ft., and the top
window was cut in the roof and provided with a weather-roof. A
brick foundation is necessary to prevent rotting at the base.

The cost of construction is small, but varies with circumstances
from Rs 50 to Rs 200 (£ 3.7s. to £ 13.6s,).

The material is placed in the silo either by coolies, or by means
of an elevator.

The best crops for siloing are maize and sorghum.

1272   **The Zehetmayr Cylinder Harrow.** (Die Zehetmayrsche Walzenegge)
Deutsche landw. Presse, N. 21. s. 246. Berlin, 15 März 1911.

Germany   In Germany and Austria, the Zehetmayr cylinder harrow has
given very good results. This harrow serves not only for cultivation
in rows, for which it was especially constructed, but also for ordinary crops. Its strength and simplicity allow of its being used by
any of the peasants. It may be used for harrowing wheat in
spring.

It is composed of three rectangular steel or iron frames,
arranged in a triangle, one in front of the others. Several toothed
cylinders turn in each frame, and, rolling over the soil, harrow,
level and press it. An ordinary harrow may be fixed on behind
if necessary.

1273   GASPARI. **The Milking Machine in Belgium.** (La machine à traire
en Belgique). — *Journal des Sociétés Agricoles du Brabant et du
Hainaut*, N. 4, pp. 42-43. Bruxelles, 21 Janvier, 1911.

Belgium   The use of the first milking machine marks a new era for milk
production in Belgium. It is of the Wallace type, and has been
bought by a farmer at Kain-les-Tournai. The cows do not mind

the machine, and are perfectly quiet during milking; this takes about the same time as milking by hand, while the execution is greatly superior. The milk is absolutely clean, the cow is not inconvenienced, and the teat cannot be injured.

The introduction of this machine makes possible the production of an absolutely pure milk. It may be predicted that the cost of the machine-milked product will not be greater than of that milked by hand.

The Alfa Dalen Milking Machine. (La machine à traire Alfa-Dalen). — *Journal des Sociétés du Brabant et du Hainaut*, N. 11, p. 141. Bruxelles, March 11, 1911.

1274

In the course of the past year, the Alfa-Dalen milking machine. was used in some interesting experiments at the Zootechnical Institute of the University of Louvain.

Belgium

The authors of the experiments came to the following conclusions :

The Alfa-Dalen milking machine marks a great progress in machine milking. Experimentally it is satisfactory. It presents great advantages, epecially the obtaining of a much purer milk than is possible by hand, and the milking is equal, no matter how many cows are treated ; it also saves a great deal of labour.

The Testing of Separators. (La verification des Ecrémeuses). — *La Laiterie Belge*, Série 1911, N. 1, pp. 1-7.

1275

In choosing a separator attention should be paid principally to the perfection of the separating, all other considerations being left until it is a question of choosing between several machines which have the same separating capacity.

Belgium

When comparing two separators one of which leaves 0.1 % of fat while the other leaves 0.25 %, it will be found that there will be an annual loss of 5589 fr. in a dairy treating 3000 litres (660 gals), of milk daily.

It is not sufficient, either, to test the machine at the time it is bought; periodical tests should be made to make sure that it is continuing to do good work.

The best way of ascertaining this is to measure the fat left by the apparatus in the skimmed milk. This estimation should be made by dissolving out the fat ; the cost of an analysis by a good chemist is worth while, as by this means the separator can be adjusted to do its most profitable work.

The defect in the separating once verified, care must be taken to make sure that it is not due to causes outside the apparatus, such as: resistance of the milk to separating, too high temperature, insufficient number of revolutions, irregularity of movement, too rapid delivery, etc.

1276   **New Receptable for Wine and Similar Liquids.** (Behälter für Wein und ähnliche Flüssigkeiten). — *Die Deutsche Essigindustrie*, XV J., N. 14, pp. 105-106, Lübeck, April 7, 1911.

Hungary   This is the description of a new receptacle which was patented under the number 240356, on December 21st, 1910, by the firm of Joseph Frish & Sohn, of Tapolcza.

The specification states that the bottom, lateral walls and, sometimes, the anterior and posterior walls of this receptacle are of reinforced concrete, the remainder being made of wooden staves which are solidly joined to the concrete, so that the air may enter the receptacles through the pores of the wood.

1277   **Müller's New Sack Lifter.** — *The Implement and Machinery Review*, London, February 1, 1911.

Great Britain: Scotland   Messrs. A. Müller & C⁰ of West North Street, Aberdeen, have constructed a new sack lifter which should be of much assistance to grain and flour merchants, millers and farmers and would considerably lighten the labour of loading, besides conducting that operation economically. The full sack is placed either by hand or with the help of a sack barrow, on to the stationary platform of the lifter. By pulling down the lever with the hands, the sack is lifted to any height which enables it to be easily removed on a man's shoulders.

The appliance can also be converted into a sack barrow. It is estimated that a saving of some 50 % in labour can be obtained, and the apparatus permits of the rapid handling of material.

PLANT DISEASES
NOXIOUS INSECTS AND OTHER PESTS.

Phytopathological and Entomological Stations.

F. GUITEL. **The Entomological Station of the Rennes Faculty of Science since its Foundation** (La Station entomologique de la Faculté des Sciences de Rennes, depuis sa fondation). — *C. R. du Congrès des Sociétés savantes en* 1909 (*Sciences*), pp. 257-262, Paris, 1910.

1278

Until 1904, France had only three official laboratories for entomological work, which were:

France

1) The Paris Entomological Station dependent on the Ministry of Agriculture, with headquarters at the Agricultural Institute. It was founded in 1894 and is under the direction of M. Paul Marchal.

2) The Entomological Laboratory of the Montpellier Agricultural School, which is directed by M. Valéry Mayet. This laboratory studies especially the insect pests of vines and olive trees.

3) The Regional Laboratory of Agricultural Entomology, Rouen, founded and directed by M. Paul Noel.

These three establishments do good service but they are too few in number for a large country like France, and, moreover are either too specialised, or too little known to the public. To overcome these difficulties the Rennes Entomological Station was founded. It was annexed to the Zoological Laboratory of the Faculty of Sciences by a decision of the Council of Rennes dated April 22, 1904.

From its foundation to December 31, 1908, this station has supplied gratis no fewer than 2587 notices.

Since 1910 the Station has been in a position to take up experimental work, having removed to new premises, which comprise:

1) A workshop for the construction and repair of breeding apparatus;

2) A laboratory and office combined for the use of the Director of the Station⁻;

3) A museum, containing collections of insect pests and specimens of the damage caused by them, as well as a collection of apparatus for destroying them.

4) Two basements for winter cultures.

5) A large kitchen garden, about 16 *ares* (1600 sq. metres) in area, forming a good field for experiments.

6) A greenhouse for a large number of cultivations.

7) A cement tank for the biological study of aquatic insects.

Amongst the gifts sent to the Station may be mentioned the splendid collection of Lepidoptera as well as a complete set of his works presented by Mr. Charles Oberthür. And it is due to the liberality of Mr. René Oberthür that in the Station there is a young entomologist capable of assisting, and if necessary, replacing the technical Sub-Director.

The example set by Rennes is beginning to be followed, for the Universities of Lille and Nancy have hastened to organise services for giving information as to the best means of destroying insects.

Non-parasitic Diseases of Plants and their Control.

1279   O. Schreiner. **Organic Substances which are injurious to Plants**. (Symptoms shown by Plants under the influence of different Toxic Compounds). *Proceedings of the American Society of Biological Chemists. — The Journal of Biological Chemistry*, Vol. IV, No. 2, pp. XIII-XIV (VIII-XL). Baltimore, Ma. April. 1911.

United States   Some experiment made on the modifications caused in the growth of wheat stalks by differents organic substances, show that toxins have a specific effect in changing certain definite and characteristic functions of plants.

For example, when plants are treated with coumarine, the leaves become stunted, broad and distorted.

Vanilline considerably arrests the growth of roots.

Quinine has a contrary effect to coumarine on plants; the growth is stronger and straighter, while the leaves are thin and narrow.

These varied effects of toxic compounds are entirely neutralised by different fertilisers; the effects of coumarine by phosphates, vanilline by nitrates and quinine by potassium salts.

While the plants are under the action of these toxic substances they absorb these salts in different ways, thus showing that the poisons influence the entire metabolism.

Some previous studies on plants and toxic compounds had been made, but they failed to show that the plants were affected in any special manner by the different poisons. The idea has been put forward that plants, like animals, show characteristic symptoms with specific poisons, that is to say there is a plant pharmacology just as there is an animal one.

Since it is a fact that substances can cause changes in certain definite characteristics of plants, such as distorsions, changing of metabolism, etc., the natural conclusion arises that dangerous organic substances contained in the soil or in the plants themselves, may be the direct or indirect cause of some little known physiological maladies.

P. Passy. **Treatment of Fruit Trees** (Traitement d'arbres fruitiers).   **1280**
— *Revue Horticole*, 83e année, N. 6, p. 129-131, Paris, 16 mars 1911

After describing the appearance of a chlorotic plant, Mr. Passy   **France**
remarks on the analogy between the chlorosis of trees and the anaemia of human beings; and as iron is used in anaemia, so it has also been used in chlorosis (1).

In certain cases, the results obtained by this treatment were favourable, but they were rather irregular and always transient.

Nevertheless, in consequence of the improvement obtained, it was concluded that the iron was assimilated by the plant and was directly useful to it. But analysis shows that chlorotic plants sometimes have more iron than the others, and that those treated with sulphate of iron may have less than non-treated ones.

---

(1) The old experiments of Eusèbe Gris had shown the correlation between iron and the formation of chlorophyll. He proved that a chlorotic leaf of maize or of any other plant when washed with iron sulphate, recovers its green colour by the local formation of chlorophyll. These experiments led to the use of ferrous sulphate as a remedy for the chlorosis of the vine. See E. Gris, *De l'action des composés ferrugineux sur la végétation*, 1843, and 1844; and W. Pfeffer, *Pflanzenphysiologie*, Leipzig, 1897, I, Th. 421. (*Ed.*).

The chlorotic leaves and shoots have less total solid matter than the healthy ones, and this want of dry matter chiefly affects the carbon and the nitrogen. The content in ash, on the other hand, is above normal; these ashes are principally charged with silica, while the proportions of potassium and of phosphoric acid are too small.

Now, chlorophyll, a nitrogenous substance, is lacking in chlorotic plants, and in consequence of this they cannot carry out their chlorophyllian functions, in other words, their content in carbohydrates is very small, whilst by respiration they lose the normal amount of carbon, and consequently become more and more impoverished.

Chlorosis is therefore the result of bad nutrition, in which certain elements are too abundant and others too scarce.

If there is no doubt as to the action of iron salts and particularly of iron sulphate, yet the manner of its action is not understood; moreover, this action is so uncertain that it is better to try to modifiy the nature of the soil according to the plants.

For some time, however, experiments have been made with iron sulphate in a dry state introduced into the body of the tree. The method is to bore a hole through the tree with an auger whose diameter is one tenth of the trunk's, until the pith is reached, then to fill up the hole with sulphate of iron to the inner edge of the bark and plug with grafting wax.

This treatment, recommended by Dr. Mokrzecki, should be done as a rule in May. Up to the present, the results are satisfactory.

1281   A. HOLLICK. **Factory Smoke.** (A maple tree fungus). — *Proceed. Staten Isl. Assoc. Arts and Sci.*, 2 (1909). No. 4, p. 190; Abst. Experiment Station Record, vol. XXIV, no. 4, p. 342. Washington, 1911.

United
States:
New York

The writer calls attention to the death of the *Acer saccharinum* along the southern side of Staten Island, New York. This tree is killed by the smoke from the factories which makes the leaves and branches fall off. In the wounds thus formed, an infection is developed, especially that of the *Pyropolyporus igniarius* which completes the destruction of the trees.

Parasitic Diseases of Plants.
Parasitism. — Bacteria and Fungi as Parasites and Saprophytes. — Remedies.

P. VOGLINO. **The Fungous Parasites of Some Plants observed round Turin in 1910.**(I funghi parassiti delle piante osservati nella provincia di Torino e regioni vicine nel 1910). Estr. dagli *Annali della R. Acc. di Agric. di Torino*, Vol. LIII, p. 38. Torino, 1911.

On the fungi which attack the crops in the province of Turin and the neighbouring regions, M. Voglino declares that in 1910, a very wet year, the conditions were favourable to the development and propagation of parasitic diseases.

He names more particularly the following amongst these: The «gummosis» on the trunk of the peach tree; *Bremia Lactucae* Reg. on *Dimorphotheca aurantiaca*, a nornamental plant; *Sclerotinia Libertiana* Fuck. on *Scorzonera, Helianthus, Daucus Carota, Brassica, Solanum*; the perithecial form of *Sphaerotheca pannosa* Lév. on the branches of the peach tree; *Rosellinia radiciperda* M. on the trunk of the apple tree; *Gibellina cerealis* Pass. on wheat; *Macrosporium parasiticum* Thüm. on onions; *Nectria ditissima* Tul., very injurious to the apple tree; *Gibberella moricola* (De Not.) Sacc., injurious to young mulberry trees; *Gloeosporium fructigenum* Berk. on the fruit of the pear tree; *Scolecotrichum melophthorum* Prill. and Dell. very injurious to pumpkins, and two new forms: *Botrytis parasitica* Cav. f. *Armeriae* on the flower tops of the *Armeria magellensis* cultivated in the alpine Garden «La Chanousia» in the Little St. Bernard and *Ramularia Doronyci* Vogl. on *Doronycum scorpioides* and *Doronycum Olonum* cultivated also in «La Chanousia».

HITIER. **Vine Diseases and the Vintage Decrease in France** (Causes of the Decrease in 1910) (Les maladies de la Vigne et la diminution de la production vinicole en France en 1910 (Causes de la diminution de la récolte des vins en 1910). *Bulletin de la Société d'Encouragement pour l'industrie Nationale*, année 1910, 1er. sem., tome 115, N. 3, pp. 403-404. Paris, mars 1911.

M. Prosper Gervais gives the following reasons for the vintage decrease in 1910; at first, there was a series of spring frosts; then, suddenly, repeated attacks of mildew just before blossoming; and lastly formidable and constantly increasing invasions of Cochylis and Eudemis.

The chief causes of these troubles were the excessive damp of spring and summer, which encouraged all kinds of cryptogamic diseases, as well as the most destructive insects.

The attacks of mildew had never been so repeated, so frequent, and so serious. Favoured by an exceptional temperature and by incessant rain, they did not give the vine-dresser time to look for them, nor the chance of defending himself. The germs multiplied so rapidly, and were so widely disseminated that all the organs of the vine (leaves, branches, shoots, fruit) were attacked, and mostly destroyed in the majority of cases; the treatment with copper salts hitherto recommended appeared to be so inadequate that their efficiency has been called in question in various quarters.

This fear is happily unfounded; it has been proved that, if in some exceptional cases, the severity of the cryptogamic attacks baffles all foresight and calculation, they can nearly always be successfully controlled by repeated preventive treatments.

It is quite otherwise with the struggle against certain insects, such as the Cochylis and the Eudemis, because up to the present the whole system of treatment is faulty.

For the first time the South has felt the attacks of the Cochylis to such a degree, that M. Prosper Gervais speaks of certain estates where, owing to the ravages of these insects, nearly three quarters of the vintage was ruined, and of others where the destruction was almost complete.

1284   R. SARCIN. — **Mechanical Determination of the Resistance of Cereals to Diseases and to the Attacks of Insects.** (Determination méchanique de la résistance des céréales aux maladies et aux attaques des Insectes). *La Défense Agricole et Orticole*, 8ᵉ année, n. 334, pp. 230-231. Amiens, 9 avril 1911.

Austria :   It is known that cultivated plants vary in their resistance to
Bohemia   diseases and to insect attacks. Dr Stranak of Prague has shown that the inroads of either stand in close relation to the anatomy of each plant. As a matter of fact, healthy ones have a thicker and more compact cellular formation of the cortical layer, and so are less open to the causes of the evil. The differences in this formation have been determined by means of an apparatus, which tests them mechanically by imitating in its action the work of the enemies of the plants.

Here are some of the figures collected by him in 1910:

	Resistance to piercing expressed in grammes.	Thickness of the cortical layer. μ.	Thickness of the external membrane of the epidermal cells. μ.	Percentage of stalks attacked by the larva of *Chlorops laeniopus* (Gout Fly).
Old Bohemian Wheat. .	260	1.3	4 to 8	0
Ruska Wheat.	220	1.0	3 to 5.5	5
Bordeaux Wheat.	125.	0.8	2 to 3	50
Square Head.	120	0.6	1.6 to 3	50
Fratusitz Wheat.	90	0.6	1	80
Podbiellzy Wheat	36	0.5	1	90

It is clear from this table that the plants' susceptibility to the *Chlorops* stands in inverse ratio to the hardness of the haulms and their anatomical structure.

VERMOREL and E. DANTONY, **The Fungicidal Spraying Mixtures.** 1285
(Sur les bouillies anticryptogamiques mouillantes). *Comptes-rendus Hebdomadaires des Séances de l'Académie des Sciences*, Tome 152, No. 14, pp. 972-974, Paris, Avril 3, 1911.

Messrs. Vermorel and E. Dantony have made a number of France
experiments with the object of finding some fungicides with strong wetting power obtained from the sodium oleate in soap.

Last year they recommended the use of mixtures containing silver soaps with an excess of soluble alkaline soap. The wetting power of the cupric mixtures may also be increased by the addition of soap.

In a preliminary series of experiments the writers prepared some Burgundy mixtures from the following solutions:

1) 2 kgs. of copper sulphate dissolved in 50 litres of water (5lbs to 11 gals);

2) 2 kgs. of commercial sodium carbonate dissolved in 50 litres of water.

The sodium carbonate used was of such purity that the excesses of alkali was 400 grs. per hectolitre (4 °/oo).

Mixture A. — If the solution of sodium carbonate is poured all at once into the copper sulphate, a precipitate is formed (without the liberation of carbon dioxide) which reacts on the excess of sodium carbonate and then on the copper salt, so that the mixture thus prepared finally contains insoluble copper hydrocarbonate and soluble copper bicarbonate.

Mixture B. — If, on the other hand, the sodium carbonate is poured slowly, carbon dioxide is liberated and the mixture thus prepared contains insoluble copper hydrocarbonate and sodium carbonate in excess.

If 1000 grs. (2.2lbs) of white soap containing no alkaline carbonates but a high percentage of oleate is added to mixture *A*, the superficial tension of the liquid is such that 5 cc. furnish 85 drops (drop-bottle giving 66 drops of distilled water). This superficial tension does not change on standing.

Now, it is sufficient to add only 100 grs. (3.502) of the same soap to mixture *B*, In order to obtain the same superficial tension. But the superficial tension of the mixture *B* changes in time ; it gives only 83 drops at the end of three hours.

The mixture *B* with 1000 grs. of soap gives 151 as soon as it prepared ; 139, twenty minutes after ; 100, six hours after ; and so on, tending towards the limit 85 of mixture *A*.

We see therefore :

1) That the same wetting power can be obtained with quantities of soap of 100 grs. or 1000 grs. per hectolitre according to the rapidity with wich the sodium carbonate is added.

2) That, notwithstanding 1000 grs. of soap per hectolitre, mixture *A* has practically no wetting power while mixture *B* is much better.

3) That great attention must be paid to the decrease of the wetting power. Mixture *B* containing the 1000 grs. of soap` wets the bunches of grapes as soon as prepared, but twenty minutes later does not wet them at all..

1286 STORMER. **Rust in Seed Corn: the Remedy.** (Die Beizung der Saatgetreides gegen Flugbrand). *Mitteilungen der Landwirtschaftskammer für das Herzogtum Gotha*, N. 5, S, 33. Gotha, März 11 1911.

Germany:
Gotha

The « rust » on spring wheat and barley cannot be prevented by treating the grain with Bordeaux mixture. But treatment with warm water or boiling steam is effective ; the latter method however requires special apparatus.

Spring wheat must be soaked in warm water at 30º C. (86º F.) for five or six hours, and barley in warm water at 25º C. (77º F.) for the same length of time. The grain put loosely into sacks so that it can swell freely, is plunged into the barrels containing the water.

At the end of five hours, the swollen grain is put for a few minutes into water at 50º C. (122º F.), then it is spread out to cool and dry on the floors of chambers where the temperature is 30º C. (86º F.),

A. DESFLASSIEUX. **Zinc arsenate.** (*L'Arseniate de Zinc*). — *Progrès*   **1287**
Agricole et Viticole, No 12, pp. 358-359. Montpellier, Mars 19, 1911.

Amongst the arsenical compounds used in viticulture, lead arse-   **France**
nate is the most recommended on account of the addition of the
poisonous properties of lead to those of arsenic.
But this salt is dangerous to handle and it may cause some
serious accidents by lead poisoning. The writer thinks it could be
replaced by zinc arsenate, the salts of which are less poisonous and
have, otherwise, various advantages. Zinc arsenate is lighter than
the lead salt; it does not precipitate in the cupric mixtures, even
if used in excess. Zinc, like the heavy metals, silver, lead, copper, etc., also has an anticryptogamic action which might strengthen
the treatment against mildew.

Tha formula recommended for trial is the following:

Anhydrous sodium arsenate . . . . grs. 200 (7.oz.)
Commercial zinc sulphate . . . . » 475 (1lb. 1.oz)

It is mixed with the cupric mixtures so as to make 100 litres
22 gals.) in all.

MARCILLE. **On the Action of Sulphur used to Control Oïdium**   **1288**
(Sur le mode d'action des soufres utilisés pour combattre l'Oï-
dium). — *Comptes-Rendus de l'Academie des Sciences*, T. 152,
N⁰. 12, pp. 780-783. Paris, Mars 20, 1911.

The object of Mr. Marcelle's researches at Tunis was to de-   **France:**
termine the manner in which sulphur acts as a fungicide. The spon-   **Tunis**
taneous volatilisation of sulphur is of very small importance; its
spontaneous oxidation could not, according to the writer, produce
a quantity of sulphur dioxide capable of exercising any toxic power.
The quantity of sulphuric acid produced spontaneously through the
action of damp, light and the renewal of the air is very small, and
its efficacy is at least disputable.

In his opinion, the sulphur acts on the oïdium only through
the sulphuric acid that it contains already formed, especially when
it is in the insoluble state of carbon disulphide. This hypothesis
explains, just as well as the results obtained by Mach (1), the fact

---

(1) This writer found sulphur dioxide in quantity proportional to the
surrounding temperature of the air in some vineyards which had been treated
with sulphur.
See VIALA, *Les Maladies de la Vigne*, p. 42, 1893.   (*Ed.*).

that the sulphur destroys the oïdium *in situ,* inasmuch as the sulphuric acid can be reduced to sulphurous acid by the action of the organic matter. The same hypothesis takes into account the specially efficacious action of extra sublimated sulphur which contains considerable quantities of sulphuric acid.

For the farmer, the practical result of these researches would be the saving of expense, by the commercial preparation of sublimated sulphur containing more sulphuric acid than that at present supplied.

1289   **The control of the *Cycloconium.*** See No. 1185 of this Bulletin.

Parasitic Diseases of various Plants
and means of Prevention and Cure (1).

1290   EM. MIÉGE. **Vegetable and Animal Parasites of Buckwheat (Fagopyrum).** (Recherches sur les principales espèces de *Fagopyrum* (Sarrasin). — *Imprimerie des Arts et Manufactures,* 426 pp., 1 pl. (Chapter IV: Pathologie, pp. 413-417, fig. 152-153), Rennes, 1910.

France: Mr. Miège remarks that all works 'on agriculture are unani-
Brittany   mous in declaring that buckwheat (*Fagopyrum*) has neither enemies nor diseases (2). This assertion, however, must be regarded as at least exaggerated. As a matter of fact, if the crop has practically never been seriously damaged by vegetable or animal parasites, it is none the less true that the plant is not free from their attacks.

Amongst the vegetable parasites, Prillieux notes the presence on the leaves of *Phytophthora omnivora,* and Saccardo mentions 7. fungus parasites of *Fagopyrum esculentum : Ascochyta Fagopyri, Botrytis vulgaris, Depazea polygonicola, Didymella Fagopyri, Humaria Patouillardi, Puccinia Fagopyri, Ramularia curvala.*

---

(1) The plants are put in the same order as in the first part of this Bulletin.

(2) For a list of diseases and pests of buckwheat, see: O. KIRCHNER - C. NEPPI, *Le malattie ed i guasti delle piante agrarie coltivate,* Torino. 1901; p. 94.

In 1908, the writer found on some crops of gray buckwheat (1) in the neighbourhood of Rennes, numerous evidences of the attacks of *Ramularia curvala*.

In 1910, in the experiment fields of the National School of Agriculture at Rennes he found two new diseases of *Fagopyrum* caused by a *Peronospora* (which appeared to be very similar to the *P. Polygoni*) and by a *Heterosporium*. A *Cladosporium* and a *Botrytis* were often associated with these two cryptogams.

These diseases appeared in the first days of July, and spread very rapidly. They mainly attacked *Fagopyrum emarginatum* and *F. esculentum* while *F. tartaricum* and *F. stenocarpa* suffered very little.

The damage was greatest and most extensive on clayey soils. Under these conditions, the plants are often puny and more or less stunted, with small and frequently deformed leaves. The least harm was done those growing in sand. The actual death of any plant was, however, very rare.

On July 10th, these diseases appeared on some young seedlings of various buckwheats, situated at a short distance from the fields which had been previously infected, and their dissemination was very rapid. They seemed to be localised on the leaves, and on the organs already diseased were found traces of *Cladosporium* and *Botrytis*, the appearance of which seems to be consequent on that of the cryptogams *Peronospora* and *Heterosporium*.

At a later date, the writer found the same diseases on some buckwheat crops in other localities.

Amongst the animal parasites, a Nemathelminth (*Tylenchus devastatrix*), was found on the stems of *Fagopyrum esculentum*. It caused very serious damage in certain years, and had already been observed on buckwheat.

During the summer of 1907, it was found in abundance in many crops of *Fagopyrum* in the district of Fougères (Ille-et-Vilaine) and especially where buckwheat had succeeded clover, carrots or turnips.

T. PETCH. **Root Diseases of Tea.** *Circulars and Agricultural Journal of the Royal Botanic Gardens, Ceylon*, vol. 5, No. 11, pp. 95-144, Colombo. Oct. 1910.   **1291**

In 1903 the Royal Botanic Gardens of Ceylon sent out a circular on the root disease of the tea plant (*Rosellinia*), and since   **Ceylon**

---

(1) A variety of *Fagopyrum esculentum*.   (*Ed.*).

then it has been found that the facts mentioned relate to several root diseases, five of which have been extensively studied. These diseases, in order of importance, are caused by: *Ustulina zonata* Lév; *Hymenochaete noxia* Berk. ; *Poria hypolateritia* Berk. ; *Botryodiplodia Theobromae* Pat.; *Rosellinia bothrina* B. and Br.

The distinguishing marks of these five diseases are given below. They may be divided into two classes: in the first the mycelium is visible on the exterior of the root, while in the second the root is perfectly clean.

I. External Mycelium present on the Root :

a) Tawny brown mycelium, cementing stones and sand to the root in a thick crust: *Hymenochaete noxia*.

b) red and white mycelium, in solid patches and strands adhering closely to the roots: *Poria hypolateritia*.

c) mycelium at first cobwebby and gray, afterwards forming black strands on the roots, and white stars between the wood and cortex: *Rosellinia bothrina*.

II. No External Mycelium :

a) Mycelium running between the wood and the cortex in white fan-shaped patches : *Ustulina zonata*.

b) No mycelium visible between the wood and the cortex; at the end of some days the root is covered with a black powder : *Botryodiplodia Theobromae*.

I. *Hymenochaete noxia*. This is in fact an omnivorous disease which attacks the *Hevea*, Cacao, Tea, Dapap, *Castilloa*, Cotton Cavaronica, Coca, *Cinnamomum*, *Cassia*, etc. in Ceylon.

In other countries it has been found on the bread-fruit trees and *Albizzia stipulata* in addition to the other species which have been mentioned, and specimens found on the *Funtumia* have recently been received from the Gold Coast.

When attacked by this disease, the roots of the tea-plant become incrusted with a mass of sand, earth, and small stones to a thickness of 3 or 4 mm.; the crust extends up the stem for 2 or 3 inches.

Later on, the wood acquires a honey-comb structure. The fructification is rare. The mycelium spreads from the dead bush to others, therefore dead bushes should be dug up and burnt, and it is advisable to fork in quicklime over the affected spots.

II. *Poria hypolateritia*. This disease is one of new clearings and is more prevalent on old *chena* land than on land which was virgin jungle. It has attacked newly-planted fields in the Kandy, Kegalla and Kelani Valley districts and also in the southern Province.

The bushes attacked are from 2 to 3 years old. Their roots are covered by a compact mycelium, red externally ; black patches also occur.

When the malady has existed a long time, the wood becomes soft and gelatinous. The wood of a young root is little affected.

The spores of the fungus are produced within tubes, which are short and form a soft layer seated on a red solid substratum in the form of a plate.

III. *Rosellinia bothrina.*

This is the least common tea root disease. Its most remarkable feature is the 'extraordinary spread of the mycelium, which can travel three or four yards in a week; it advances in the top two or three inches of the soil, and when it reaches a tea-bush, goes down the root for a distance of about a foot. While the underground mycelium is killing the root, that at the surface forms a sheet round the stem; it is first purple-gray, and then black. The sheet extends to about 6 in. above the soil.

The fungus has at least two forms of fructification - a conidial and a perithecial stage ; the latter occurs on every tea-bush attacked.

The perithecia are produced after the plant has been dead a long time.

The disease is conveyed by means of spores, and the ground is permeated by mycelium.

The bushes should be scorched and then dug up and burnt, quicklime forked into the bare soil, and scattered in the trenches. Infected patches must not be replanted within 18 months.

IV. *Ustulina zonata* Lév. This is the commonest tea root disease in Ceylon, and is in great measure preventible, as it usually spreads to the tea-bushes from old Grevillea and Albizzia stumps.

The Grevillea trees should be felled in such a way as to leave the « stump » a foot below ground, and a trench should be dug round the stumps of old Albizzias, cutting through all the lateral roots ; young plants can be uprooted.

Ustulina zonata is one of the most protean of fungi, but as a rule, the mycelium forms fan-shaped white patches overlying the wood, which often blend into a sheet. It has two kinds of spores, one produced in asci, and the other at the apices of stalks.

V. *Botryodiplodia theobromae.*

The most usual feature of this complaint is the death of apparently healthy bushes after pruning.

It is chiefly a low-country disease, though cases have occurred at an elevation of 2000 ft.

The mycelium runs within the cells of the wood and bark ; it produces blackish-brown discolouration.

The fructifications are minute, black, spherical bodies imbedded in the bark and invisible from the exterior, the spores are oval and divided across the middle.

The two main sources of the infection of tea bushes are buried prunings and dead Albizzias.

The dead tea-plants should be up-rooted and burnt with the help of kerosene, and the affected soil forked over with quick-lime.

1292   L. D. LARSEN. **Diseases of the Pineapple.** — *Pathological and Physiological Series.* Bulletin No. 10. Report of Work of the Experiment Station of the Hawaiian Sugar Planters' Association. 8⁰, p. 70, Honolulu, Hawaii, Dec. 1910.

Hawaii   *Thielaviopsis paradoxa* (1) is the most widely spread and destructive fungus connected with the pathology of the pineapple. It is the cause of three diseases : the Soft Rot of the fruit, the Base Rot of the cuttings, and the Leaf Spot. It is also largely responsible for the decay which occurs in the roots.

The following preventive measures have all been used with success : Cut the fruits leaving long stems and a portion of the bractea, use straw as packing material, wrap the fruit in paper and fumigate with gaseous formaline.

Brown Rot. At Hawaii, there is one, perhaps several, species of *Fusarium* which may cause this disease, characterised by brown discolorations in the tissue of the fruit. The infection occurs mainly, if not exclusively, when the pineapple begins to ripen. Stockdale reports that a species of *Penicillium* causes trouble of the same kind in the West Indies ; in Queensland a similar disease, due to a *Penicillium*, attacks the smooth Cayenne variety while the Prickly

---

(1) *Synonyms.* The name which has been commouly adopted for this fungus is : *Thielaviopsis ethaceticus.* It was used for the first time by F. A. F. G. Went in 1893 in connection with the Pine-apple disease of the sugar-cane in Java.

In 1904 Dr. Von Höhnel drew attention to the fact that the fungus called *Thielaviopsis ethaceticus* by Went in 1893 had been described by de Seynes in 1886 under the name of *Sporoschima paradoxa* and by Saccardo in 1892 as *Chalara paradoxa.* Von Höhnel considering that a special genus would represent the position of this fungus better that the genera *Sporoschima* or *Chalara* adopted the name *Thielaviopsis* first given by Went to the genus, keeping *paradoxa* as the name of the species, and called the fungus *Thielaviopsis paradoxa* (De Seynes) V. Höhnel.

variety is attacked by a species of Monilia accompanied by an Acarus.

Ripe Rot. This disease is produced only when the fruit is perfectly ripe. Therefore it is only dangerous when the pineapples are carelessly gathered. The experiments made by. Mr. Larsen show that *Thielaviopsis* is capable of living and penetrating some distance into the soil. An increase of organic matter leads to a more rapid growth of the fungus. The experiments also show that the pineapple and sugar cane *Thielaviopsis* are specifically the same.

The following are the diseases which attack the pineapple in Hawaii :

The *Thielaviopsis* Fruit Rot or Soft Rot. It may attack the fruit in the fields or in the large preserving factories, but generally appears in the packed fruit during transport. The fungus *Thielaviopsis paradoxa* is alone responsible for this disease. It is capable of penetrating to the interior of the pineapple, even if the surface of the latter be sound, provided the weather is damp enough, and it attacks the green and ripe fruit indiscriminately.

There are at least two other organisms besides the *Thielaviopsis* which cause forms of rot in the pineapple that are quite distinct from the disease produced by the *Thielaviopsis*.

Certain insects, by puncturing the surface of the fruit, distribute the spores of the fungus from place to place. The « mealy bug » (*Pseudococcus Bromeliae*), the « fruit beetle » (*Carpophilus humeralis*), certain « vinegar flies » (*Drosophila ampelophila* and others) and a grasshopper (*Xyphidium varipenne*), are the most important of these insects.

Sun Scald or *Sun Burn.* This is a disease caused directly by the solar rays on the pine-apples, which have been planted in such a way that one side is constantly exposed to their action. The flavour and texture of the inside being also affected. It occurs frequently in Hawaii, and has also been found at Porto Rico and in some other pineapple growing countries and may be prevented by sheltering the fruit.

Base Rot of Cutting. Characterised by the rot which attacks the plants as soon as they are planted. It begins by the decay of the lowest leaves and the underground parts ; later on it spreads to the central leaves, which ordinarily remain green after the roots and the lower leaves are completely decayed. The fungus *Thielaviopsis paradoxa* is the cause of this disease. W. V. Tower found it at Porto Rico in 1906.

Heart Rot. This is characterised by the rotting of the heart of the plant, including the tender tissue at the base of the most recently formed leaves. Very often the plants attacked give one or more off-shoots, which grow into sound plants.

The Pineapple Leaf Spot.. The *Thielaviopsis* attacks the leaves through the wounds made by insects (the commonest of these is a grasshopper, *Xyphidium varipenne* Swezey) and by the serrated edges of neighbouring leaves. It causes large discolorations or spots which often spread over the entire leaf, and kill it. Although the harm done to each tree is comparatively small, the total damage is considerable. It is probable that the Leaf Spot found at Porto Rico is identical with that at Hawaii.

Wilt. The wilting of the pineapple is generally considered to be its most serious disease. The most characteristic symptom is a loss of rigidity in part of the leaf, which gradually droops and decays. There is very little known at present as to the cause of this malady. It is generally believed that it is like the decay of the cotton plant, and is caused by a fungus which penetrates the roots and develops in the main stem of the plant. The disease is known in all parts of the world where the pineapple grows.

Tangle Root. After wilting, Tangle Root is the disease most frequently found in the pineapple. The leaves turn yellow, beginning at the tip, and gradually this colour spreads all over the plant, which then begins to wither and dry up. The growth of leaves at the base of the plant and a poor soil are generally the cause of the stunted growth of the lateral roots. The remedy is to attend to the cultivation and to clear away the plants affected.

Parasitic Root Fungi. *Thielaviopsis paradoxa, Trichoderma lignorum* and a species of *Fusarium* are the fungi which appear most frequently in the root cultures of decayed pineapples. The *Tielaviopsis*, however, is the only one that completely destroys the roots, which it does in an exceedingly short time, if injected into the tissue.

Nematode Root Galls. Heterodera radicicola, which attacks a large variety of crops in nearly every part of the world, also forms galls on the youngest roots of the pineapple. The following remedies have been tried : the use of snare-plants (a mustard *Brassica Rapa rapifera* Wetzg., and the common garden nightshade *Solanum nigrum* were used) ; the application of chemical substances to the soil, which is of little value, however, from a practical point of view ; tilling and harrowing the ground during a long period of drought, which gives good results when the atmospheric conditions are suitable. Sterilisation by steam is a very efficacious method, but unhappily cannot be employed in fields.

Manganese Yellow. This disease is characterised by the yellow appearance of the plant. The fruit, when there is any, is very poor in quality and size. The presence of large quantities of manganese in the soil is in all probability the cause of the malady.

Diseases unknown at Hawaii. These are the *Long Leaf* disease, found at Porto Rico and characterised by the fact that the leaves grow long and slender and remain fixed to the base, the *Sanding*, caused by the sand, which is carried along by the wind and fills up the fruit bud of newly planted trees, and the *Bitter Heart* (in Florida), the chief signs of which are that the heart seems saturaeed with water and the fruit turns bitter.

Septoria Viciae **West.** — See No. 454 in this *Bulletin.*   **1293**

R. LAUBERT and M. SCHWARTZ. **Diseases and Enemies of the Rose**   **1294**
Tree. (Rosenkrankheiten und Rosenfeinde). — *Eine Anleitung, die Krankheiten und Feinde der Rosen zu erkennen und zu bekämpfen*), pp. VI + 59, I Taf. Jena, G. Fischer, 1910.

The object of this monograph is to provide a guide for recogn-   **Germany**
ising and controlling the chief vegetable and animal parasites of the rose tree.

In the first part of the work, which has been executed by Mr. Laubert, the following diseases will be found:

1) *Phragmidium subcorticium* (Schrank) Winter (Rose-rust).
2) *Sphaerotheca pannosa* (Wallr.) Lév. (Rose-mildew);
3) *Actinonema Rosae* (Lib.) Fr. (Rose leaf-blotch);

These three fungi damage the leaves of the rose tree.

After these come:

4) *Coniothyrium Wernsdorffiae* Laub., which attacks the bark of the branches and twigs of the rose tree;

5) the disease which completely kills the plant and is known in Germany under the name of " La France-Krankheit ", because it was discovered on the " La France " variety; certain writers attribute it to physiological causes, for instance, to a degeneration of the variety, or even to traumatic or cultivation reasons; Mr. Laubert considers it is due to the presence on the roots of the plants attacked of *Roesleria pallida* (Pers.) Sacc. (= *R. hypogaea*, *Coniocybe nivea*);

6) The blackening of the peduncles (" Schwarzwerden der Rosenstiele ") caused by a special form of *Botrytis;*

7) The Rose-tree Rot, caused by *Botrytis cinerea;*

8) *Peronospora sparsa* Berk. (False mildew);

9) Canker of the rose-tree, which seems due primarily to the damage caused to the branches by frost.

In the second part of this publication, Mr. Schwartz enumerates the diseases caused to the rose-tree by animal parasites, and mentions the different means of controlling them; there are four categories as follows:

I. Damage to floral buds, flowers and fruit, caused by the larvae or adult insects of:

Phyllopertha horticola L. (" Buckwheat Beetle ') ; *Hybernia defoliaria* L. (" Mottled Umber Moth) ; *Cheimatobia brumata* L. (" Winter Moth ") ; *Ardis plana* (Klg.) Knw. (" Saw fly") ; *Anthonomus Rubi* Herbst (" Raspberry Anthonomus ") ; *Clinodiplosis rosiperda* Rübs. ; *Cetonia aurata* L. (" Green Rose Chafer ") ; *Forficula auricularia* L. (" Common Earwig ") ; *Grapholitha roseticolana* Z.

II. Anomalies and damage to the leaves caused by the larvae or adults of *Melolontha vulgaris* L. ("Common Cockchafer); *M. Hippocastani* Fb. (" Horse-Chestnut cockchafer ") ; *Phyllopertha horticola* L. (" Buckwheat Beetle "); *Lymantria dispar* L. (" Schwammspinner "); *Euproctis chrysorrhoea* L. (" Brown-Tail Moth"); *Malacosoma neustria* L. (" Lackey Moth ") ; *Orgyia antiqua* L. (" Common Vapourer Moth ") ; *Hybernia defoliaria* L. (" Mottled Umber Moth") ; *Cheimatobia brumata* L. (" Winter Moth"); numerous " Sawflies ' such as *Emphytus cinctus* L., *E. viennensis* Schrank, *E. rufocinctus* Retz, *Cladius pectinicornis* Fours., *Hylotoma Rosae* L., *H. pagana* Panz.. *Eriocampoides aethiops* Fabr. ; several " Rose-leaf miners " such as *Nepticula anomalella* Goeze, *N. centifoliella* Z., *N. angulifasciella* St. ; *Coleophora gryphipennella* Bouché ; *Tortrix Bergmanniana* L. ; *Grapholitha tripunctana* F. ; *G. cynosbana* F. ; *Teras forskaleana* L. ; *Blennocampa pusilla* Klg. ; *Lyda inanita* de Vill. ; *Dichelomyia Rosarum* Hardy ; *Rhodites Rosae* Gir. (" Gall-wasp of Rose ") ; *Monophadnus elongatulus* (Klg.) Knw. (" Saw fly ") ; *Siphonophora Rosae* Réaumur (" Rose Aphis ") ; *Typhlocyba Rosae* L. ; *Tetranychus telarius* L. (" Red Spider of the Hop ").

III. Damage to branches and large shoots. produced by three " weevils " ; *Rhynchites conicus* Illig., *Rh. minutus* Gyll., *Rh. pauxillus* Germ.; *Anthonomus Rubi* Herbst ("Raspberry Anthonomus"); two " Bürstkornwespen " : *Hylotoma Rosae* L. and *H. pagana* Panz.; *Ardis bipunctata* Klg. (" sawfly") ; *Monophadnus elongatulus* (Klg.) Knw. (" sawfly ") ; *Emphytus cinctus* L. ; *Orthotylus nassatus* Fabr. ; *Siphonophora Rosae* Réaumur (" Rose Aphis ") ; *Aulacaspis (Diaspis) Rosae* Bouché (" Rose Scale ") ; *Clinodiplosis oculiperda* Rübs.

IV. General decay of the plant, in consequence of the destruction of the root by the larvae of *Melolontha vulgaris* L.; *M. Hippocastani* Fb.; *Phyllopertha horticola* L.; Elaterides ("Skip-jacks"); Tipulides ("Crane-Flies"); *Bibio hortulanus* L. ("Fever-Fly").

P. NOEL. **The *Gnomonia* of the Cherry Tree.** (La *Gnomonia* des Cerisiers). — *Bulletin du Laboratoire régional d'Entomologie agricole*, Deuxième trimestre de 1911, (Avril - Mai - Juin) pp. 9-10, Rouen, 1911.

1295

In the Department of the Eure and especially in the neighbouring Communes of the Seine, Saint-Pierre-du-Rouvray, Gaillon, Vernon, etc., the cherry trees are affected with *Gnomonia erythrostoma* (1).

France: Eure

Mr. Noel gives the results of some experiments made by Mr. Boudehan, President of the Horticultural Society of Gaillon, who has made a special study of cryptogamic diseases.

The following treatments were used:

1) Removal of dry leaves;

2) Two light sprayings with Bordeaux mixture from the beginning of the vegetative period.

The results were as follows:

1) Removal of dry leaves only: The trees treated in this way had magnificent foliage, and the fructification was good. Those attended to in October were better than the ones left until March and April,

2) Sprayings only: The disease seemed to decrease somewhat. The trees put forth shoots and produced sound fruit, but the results were not so good as those obtained by plucking off the dry leaves.

3) Plucking off leaves and sprayings. Very good results especially on the trees which had not been diseased for more than two or three years, and a noticeable improvement in those much affected.

The disease is very contagious, and care should be taken to attend to all the trees in a district.

Those which are well manured and freed from caterpillars are better able to fight against the malady.

Mr. Boudehan found that considerable havoc had been caused by the fungus in the Lower Seine, Sologne, Périgueux and the South of France as well as in the plains of Gaillon.

---

(1) See this Bulletin for March 1911, n. 1025.

1296   N. PATOUILLARD. **The Root disease of Cocoa Nut Palms. Disagreements of Writers in Regard to the Fungus Which Causes the Disease: *Botryodiplodia*, *Fomes* or others? The only Treatment is to Pull Up the Roots.** (La maladie des racines du Cocotier. Divergences des Auteurs sur le champignon, cause de la maladie : Botryodiplodia, Fomes ou autres? Le seul traitement est l'arrachage). — *Journal d'Agriculture Tropicale*, IIᵉ année, No. 117, pp. 65-66, Paris, Mars 31, 1911.

Ceylon:
Antilles, etc.

One of the most serious diseases which threaten the cocoa plantations is the " root" disease " (1).

This trouble appears to exist in all countries where the cultivation of the cocoa tree is of an extensive character; in British Antilles, Java, the Philippines, Ceylon, India, East Africa, etc.

The trees are attacked here and there throughout the plantations, sometimes singly, sometimes in little groups. The outer leaves begin to turn yellow, then they wither and curve outwards until they hang vertically to the stalk; the other leaves quickly suffer the same alteration, while those in the centre decrease in number and size, and finally wither. The tree does not produce any fruit, because the floral branches are destroyed.

The " root disease " is by common accord attributed to a fungus which attacks this organ directly.

In the Antilles, Stockdale found on the roots a brownish mycelium without fructification, and he considers the receptacles of a Botryodiplodia which developed on the petiole of the diseased leaves to be the fructification of the root fungus.

This supposition is not supported by any proof, according to Mr. Patouillard, and it is probable that the fungus of the petioles is nothing but a saprophyte.

Butler observed a similar mycelium at Travancore ; the parasitic roots, placed in a culture medium in the laboratory, developed the pycnidia of a *Botryodiplodia* which is still specifically undetermined.

More recently, Petch found in Ceylon that the roots of dying trees contained a mycelium ; when these roots are put under observation, they are seen to develop a series of fungi, the last of which is also a *Botryodiplodia* ; it is evident that this fungus is here also a saprophyte.

On the other hand, Petch saw the filaments of a white mycelium in the vessels of the base of the trunks, which, on culture,

---

(1) See this Bulletin for Dec. 1910, p. 368.

bore the fructiferous receptacles of a higher Hymenomycete, *Fomes lucidus*. He regards this *Fomes* as the actual cause of the " root disease " of the cocoa tree in Ceylon.

It is clear there is no certainty as to what fungus is the dangerous host of the roots. The only important fact which appears to stand out from observations made in the various localities, is the discovery of parasitic mycelium in the tissues of the roots.

It is practically impossible to apply fungicides without risk of killing the tree as well as its host. The use of manures can do no more than prolong the life of the tree for a little while. The only thing to be done is to uproot the diseased plant and burn the underground parts and the base of the trunk, and also to clear the ground of the woody debris which lies rotting there as a rule.

No new plantations must be made in the places where trees have died from this malady.

Fr. BUBÀK. **A New Disease of the Mulberry.** (Eine neue Krankheit der Maulbeerbäume) (II Mitteilung). — *Berichte der deutschen botanischen Gesellschaft*, Bd XXIX, Heft 2, s. 70-74, 1 Abbild. im Text. Berlin, 30 März 1911.   **1297**

Mr. Bubàk found a Sphaeropsidean on some branches of *Morus alba* gathered by Mr. P. Tankoff at Vraca (North Bulgaria), which had developed on the old stromata of *Thyrostroma Kosaroffii* (Briosi) Bubàk.   **Bulgaria**

Basing his decision on the study of this Sphaeropsidean, the discoverer has created the new genus *Dothiorellina* and the new species *D. Tankoffii*.

E. CUIF. **The Oak Oidium. Effect of the Application of Sulphur in Nurseries.** (L'Oidium du Chêne. Action du soufrage en pépinière). — *Revue des Eaux et Forêts*, Tome 50, N. 9, pp. 270-272, 1 fig. Paris, 1er Mai, 1911.   **1298**

Since the " *blanc du chêne* " was observed for the first time in forest of Amance (Meurthe-et-Moselle) towards the end of the spring of 1908, every attempt has been made by the application of sulphur to save the plants in the nursery called the *Etang de Brin* from being attacked by the fungus. About 40 000 five-year-old oaks are taken from this nursery every year.   **France**

The first year's treatment, however, was not successful, being applied too late.

In 1909, on June 2nd and 3rd, before the appearance of the disease, some naphthalin-sulphur was spread in all the beds,of the nursery where the oaks were growing, the method followed being that of alternate rows, one of which was sulphured, the other serving as control. The operation was twice repeated, at the end of July and in the middle of August.

The first treatment was in 1910; all the oaks in the nursery were treated with flowers of sulphur at three different periods, at the end of May and the beginning of July and August. The malady did not appear in the nursery, although its ravages continued on the seedling and young growth of neighbouring plantations.

In 1910 a sulphuriser (Soufreuse) was used instead of the gardeners' bellows, (Soufflet du jardinier). In a nursery of two-to five-year-old plants 5 cm. apart and placed in rows 15 cm. apart, the qnantity of sulphur used averaged 1 kg. per are for each treatment. Flowers of sulphur cost from 0.20 to 0.25 fr. per kg. and the entire cost of a treatment for 1 are, including labour and depreciation may therefore be estimated at 1 fr.

The disease may reappear on the trees planted in the forest, but the attacks will be less severe the trees being more isolated and taller.

1299   G. BRIOSI and R. FARNETI. **The " Ink Disease " of Chestnuts.**
(La Moria dei Castagni (" Mal dell' inchiostro "). Osservazioni critiche ad una Nota dei signori Griffon e Maublanc). — *Atti dell'Istituto botanico dell'Università di Pavia*, Ser. II, vol. XV, pp. 43-51. Milano, 1911.

Italy   In an article entitled *Sur une maladie des perches de châtaigniers* (1) (On a disease of the chestnut coppices), Messrs Griffon and Maublanc declare that the malady described by Briosi and Farneti (2) is identical with that observed in France in the nurseries of Limousin.

The investigations mentioned in the above article, were confined to coppices, although, as the Italian writers have shown, the full-grown chestnuts in forests are equally attacked by this disease, which kills them.

Both sets of investigators found characteristic cankers on the branches of the diseased trees, a mycelium ramifies in the bark,

---

(1) See No. 332 of the January *Bulletin*, 1911.
(2) See No. 635 of the February *Bulletin*, 1911.

while fructifications, in the form of a *Coryneum* and a *Melanconis*, occur upon the surface.

The Italian scientists point out that the three forms of fungus which they have found on the chestnuts affected with the " ink disease ", and which they have named *Coryneum perniciosum, Fusicoccum perniciosum* and *Melanconis perniciosa*, should be considered as distinct from *Melanconis modonia* Tul. and its conidian and pycnidian forms.

Pyropolyporus ignarius Injurious to the Sugar Maple. — See No. 1281 of this *Bulletin*.

1800

W. RANSOM. **Dry Rot in Timber.** — *Surveyor*, 38, (1910), No. 892, pp. 643-644 *Abst. Experiments Station Record*, Vol. XXV, No. 4, p. 353, Washington, 1911.

1801

This disease, which appears to be on the increase (1), seems to be favoured by moderate heat, by damp and by lack of ventilation ; the fungus *Merulius lacrymans* almost exclusively attacks wood felled in the sap. Thoroughly seasoned timber, placed in well-ventilated conditions, is not attacked as a rule. Phenol, creosote, and carbolineum are good preservatives.

United States

Causes of the Decreased Vintage in France, in 1910. See No. 1283 of this Bulletin.

1802

---

(1) The abstract does not state where. (*Ed.*).

Phanerogamic Parasites and Weeds. — Their Control.

1303 ADVISSE-DESRUISSEAUX. **Influence Exercised by some Plants on the Vanilla Tree** (De l'influence exercée par quelques plantes sur le vanillier — *L'Agriculture pratique des pays chauds*, 10e année, N. 88, pp, 33-42, 5 figs., 1910. *La Quinzaine Coloniale*, 15e année, No. 5, p. 162, Paris, 10 Mars 1911. (Summary by Mr. Em. Perrot).

Java
Ceylon
Mayotte

Certain woody or herbaceous plants, when they grow in the neighbourhood of the vanilla tree, have a very injurious influence on the latter, while others, under the same conditions are useful to it and are therefore sought after by planters.

Injurious plants: Jack bread-fruit tree (*Artocarpus integrifolia*) "Affouches" (*Ficus cinerea, F, lucens, F. rubra, F. terebrata*), *F. mauritiana, F. sororia, F. elastica*, the bread-fruit tree (*Artocarpus incisa*) and the Rimier (*A. nucifera*).

The vanilla does not feel the influence of the supporting tree until its adventitious roots are in contact with the living tissue of the latter. The injurious influence is attributed to the sap, or rather to the latex, of these plants.

Useful plants. — The best known of these are herbaceous: several species of *Oxalis* and *Hydrocotyle asiatica*. They have a double role; the maintenance of a constant moisture which prevents any direct action on the roots of the vanilla, and the formation of a favourable humus.

Bananas are also useful on account of the shade which they afford, but they must not be too numerous or they exhaust the soil.

1304 E. RABATÉ. **Destruction of Runch by Sulphuric Acid** (Destruction des Ravenelles par l'acide sulfurique). — *Journal d'Agriculture pratique*, n. 13. pp. 407-409, Paris, 30 Mars 1911.

France

For a long time the only way of destroying runch (1) was harrowing. Copper sulphate was then used with success, and at present the practice of using sulphuric acid for the destruction of weeds

---

(1) The runch, or wild radish (*Raphanus Raphanistrum* L.) is one of the Cruciferae. It is a weed on sandy, loamy and humous soils in France. Cf. D. ZOLLA, *Dictionnaire d'Agriculture*, p. 658, Paris 1904).

in wheat has become very widespread in Lot-et-Garonne. The spraying with acidulated water is done between February 1st and March 15th, when the wheat has five or six leaves. Experience soon shows what strength to use. With 5 parts of acid at 60 or 66° Baumé in 100 parts of water, two or three out of the six leaves on the wheat are immune; the runch plants are scorched, but the vetch („vesces") and vetchling („gesses") may escape. With 10 parts of sulphuric acid per 100 parts of water, all the leaves of the wheat are scorched but the stalk escapes, and the plant picks up in eight or ten days. With this streangth wild oats, dogs-tooth grass (*Cynodon Dactylon*) and cardoon grow again. With eight parts of acid the result is much the same, and this is the strength most frequently employed.

It is as well, however, to make some preliminary experiments on small plots. Sulphuric acid has a powerful effect on all the soil constituents, with the result of increased fertility. The acid solution attacks the spraying apparatus, if made of copper ; lead-covered sheetiron should be used.

It is estimated that 10 hectolitres of liquid per hectare (90 galls. per acre) are necessary, that is, at 8 %, 80 litres (about 7 galls.) of sulphuric acid; at 60 or 66° B., this is equal to 130 to 140 kg. (about 300 lbs.) of acid. The cost price at 11 or 12 fr. the 100 kg,, is from 15 to 17 fr. If manual labour be taken into consideration, the total cost per hectare would be from 35 to 40 fr.

The Destruction of Stinging Nettles. *The Journal of the Board of Agriculture*, vol. XVII, N. 72, pp. 986-988, London, March 1911.   **1305**

Great Britain
Germany

   The large stinging nettle (*Urtica dioica*) and the small stinging nettle (*U.urens*) are equally injurious in field and garden.

   The best way of controlling *Urtica dioica* in arable land is to pull it up and burn it, and afterwards to plough deep and hoe frequently.

   In meadows, the nettles may be pulled up by hand and burnt, if they are only to be found on very small areas. They may also be covered with large sheets of tarred paper, which should be pegged into the ground and kept down with heavy stones; on the spots which are thus deprived of light, vegetation is destroyed. The places treated in these two ways must all be resown.

   In the case of large or small areas, nettles may be killed by regularly cutting the shoots as soon as they appear in spring. This is done when the new shoots are from 6 to 12 ins. in height.

The extermination of the weed may be hastened by the use of a solution of salt (5 ½ lbs. per rod, or for larger areas 6 cwt. per acre) after the cutting of the shoots in spring.

Some experiments made in Germany in 1909 with the object of destroying stinging nettles on large areas showed that the young shoots are destroyed in spring by a spraying with a 15% solution of Kainit (it is very probable that the action of Kainit is chiefly due to the common salt which it contains).

The small nettle (*Urtica urens*) is successfully controlled, wherever it appears in arable land, by thorough and regular weedings, which prevent it from being reproduced for one or two years.

1806   **Destruction of Thistles.** (Field Expts. in Staffs and Salop and at Harper Adams Agric. Coll.; Joint Rept. 1909). *The Journal of the Board of Agriculture*, London, March, 1911, p. 1019.

Great Britain   In 1996 and 1908 some dressings of salt and copper sulphate were found to have little effect on thistles (*Cnicus* spp.), and this treatment was therefore given up in 1909, and the plants cut. By checking the growth of the thistles above ground in the early summer, the development of the underground stem is hindered and the plant is not able to spread so freely. The second growth is not so strong, and the seed-producing stems are less luxuriant. Second cutting, in July, weakens the plant, the growth of which is further checked by the third cutting.

If the same treatment is carried out in the second year, very few thistles are left and at the end of the third year there are practically none.

Insects and Other Injurious Invertebrates
Their Biology and Control.

FRED. V. THEOBALD. **Report on Economic Zoology for the Year Ending April 1st, 1909.** — *The Journal of the South-Eastern Agricultural College,* Wye Kent, No. 18, pp. 443 (108-195. London and Ashford, Kent, 1909.

1807

ANIMALS INJURIOUS TO FRUIT TREES AND BUSHES.

The Raspberry Weevil (*Otiorhynchus picipes*) has been observed on cherry trees at Oakhampton, Stourport. The parasite is well known in this locality, where it is called the Cherry Bug. It damages the buds, foliage and fruit.

Great Britain: England

This insect also attacks pear grafts in Kent, the bark being some times completely stripped off.

The Raspberry Beetle (*Byturus tomentosus*) attacks the Loganberry (1). It causes great damage in Kent and Worcestershire, and to some extent in Somersetshire. It is well known that this insect cuts off the flowers of raspberries; but it is a worse foe to the loganberry, it eats passages around the perianth and the stamens of the open flower, and thus the blossom is killed. Sprayings with arsenical washes are useless. This insect also devours the flowers of the apple tree.

The Apple Blossom Weevil (*Anthonomus pomorum* Linn.) was again very plentiful in Worcestershire, Cambridgeshire and Kent. The life-history of this insect is well known, but no effective method for its control has been found.

Leaf Weevils (*Phyllobius* spp.) on Fruit Trees. Different species of *Phyllobius* sometimes cause serious damage to the fruit trees, destroying the buds and flowers and devouring the leaves. On the other hand, these insects are sometimes found in large numbers on a tree without doing any apparent harm. These beetles may be caught on grease bands, as, hatching from the ground, they first crawl up the tree-trunks.

---

(1) The Loganberry is a remarkable hybrid reproduced at Santa Cruz, California, by the accidental crossing of the Aughinbaugh blackberry with the Old Antwerp raspberry. Cf. BAILEY, *Cyclopedia of Am. Hortic.* (*Ed.*).

The Apple Sawfly (*Hoplocampa testudinea* Klug) persists in districts where it has previously been reported. Quite young fruit showed the perforations, mealy sinuous tunnelling, and brown discoloration due to the larvae.

The Slugworm (*Eriocampa limacina* De Geer) was observed on pear and cherry trees. Generally speaking, it appears late in the year, and consequently does but little damage; but sometimes it occurs in large numbers in August, and then, by destroying the foliage, it prevents the wood from ripening sufficiently. Spraying with arsenate or hellebore, or dusting with lime by means of a sulphurator will soon destroy them.

The Plum Sawfly (*Hoplocampa fulvicornis* Klug) has undoubtedly increased very much during the last three years. It is probable that it is indigenous in several districts, since it is to be found even in wild plums. From this source an orchard may soon become invaded. Drastic measures are therefore necessary. All the fruit which is affected, should at once be destroyed and the ground dressed with " Vaporite ".

Wood Leopard Moth (*Zeuzera pyrina* Linn.). The larvae of this moth were found at Mereworth tunnelling into apple-trees; in Norfolk it attacked cherry trees, and in Huntingdon, pear trees. This insect is never abundant, but a few do so much harm that they are readily noticed. The branches attacked should be cut right back and the larvae found in them destroyed.

The Garden Swift (*Hepialus lupulinus* Linn.). The larvae of the above were unusually abundant in the winter of 1908. In Kent and Worcester they attacked, not only the roots of strawberries, but of all kinds of garden plants. Mint is one of their favourite foods. When these caterpillars attack the strawberry-plants they devour the fibrous roots, and tunnel into the rhizomes, thus killing the plant.

A parasite of the *Hepialus*, *Cordiceps entomorrhyza*, was observed in two cases.

The Vapourer Moth (*Orgyia antiqua* Linn.). The ova of this moth were sent for identification from Chart Sutton, Taunton, Sevenoaks, Northampton and Exeter. The insect is found on fruit trees, but is often very harmful to rose trees. It occurs occasionally on hops, and in 1908 it even attacked peach trees. It was introduced into the United States with some rose trees imported from France. It does not cause much damage to fruit trees in Great Britain.

The Magpie Moth (*Abraxas grossulariata* Linn.). This is very general over Great Britain, but it does not cause much damage as a rule.

The Green Pug Moth (*Chloroclystis rectangulata* Linn.) was observed at Longfield, Sevenoaks, Worcester and near Exeter. The larvae eat into the buds and flowers of apple and pear trees, devour the tender tips of shoots and foliage and spin the trusses of blossom together. An early spraying of arsenate of lead or of nicotine wash will rapidly destroy these caterpillars.

Tortrix larvae (*T. ribeana* and *T. pruniana*). These were observed on apple and plum trees.

The Vine Tortrix (*Tortrix reliquana* Hb.). The larvae were found under the bark of an indoor vine in December, which shows that this insect hibernates in the larval state.

Plum Fruit Moth (*Opadia funebrana* Fr.). During the summer of 1908, serious damage was caused by this insect in certain parts of Great Britain, and also it seems, on the Continent. In Germany a very useful paper banding was used which is also efficacious for trapping *Carpocapsa pomonella*, etc. The paper is double, the under half being deeper than the upper, and between is placed a layer of fluted paper; the larvae creep up into the latter and hibernate there. The bands should be removed and burnt in April.

Cherry Tree Borer (*Semasia Woeberiana* Schiff). This pest is still reported from the Sittingbourne area of Kent and has now been traced to beyond Maidstone.

Raspberry Shoot Borer (*Lampronia rubiella* Bjerk). This is the cause of serious damage in Somersetshire. Smearing the canes with soft soap at the beginning of March catches the larvae and seems the best plan for checking the pest.

Pith Moths (*Blastodacna hellerella*, etc.). This appeared in several localities in 1908. The method already recommended, which consists of pruning the blistered shoots where the larvae winter, has been found efficacious.

The Pear Midge. (*Diplosis pyrivora* Riley). Appeared at Rodmersham, Bourne near Faversham, and again at Reigate and Hereford.

Cecidomyia Larvae in mummy plums. Some mummified Czar plums were examined, which contained small red larvae, these proved to be larval *Cecidomyidae* belonging to a group which has, as yet, not been worked out or named. It is known that these larvae feed on fungi; especially mildews and moulds, but from their small size, they are very little good.

Black Flies (*Bibionidae*). There are several common species, the most common being perhaps *Bibio hortulanus*; they do little harm themselves, but their larvae destroy the roots of strawberries, hops and most garden plants.

Leater Jackets (larvae of *Tipula oleracea*) in Loganberries. These new pests to a valuable fruit are likely to be of occasional occurrence and the soil should be cleared of them before planting. « Vaporite » and « Fumite » are valuable remedies.

Apple Sucker (*Psylla Mali* Schmid). In Worcestershire and Kent good results have been obtained with washings of lime and salt.

The Currant Root Louse (*Schizoneura Ulmi* or *S. fodiens*) has been observed at Longfield. As Barsacq's studies have shown, Buckton's *Schizoneura fodiens* is only an alternate generation of *Schizoneura Ulmi*.

The Green Fly (*Aphis Grossulariae* Kaltenbach) of the gooseberry and currant probably occurs widely over the country. It has been confused with *Rhopalosiphum Ribis*, but is quite distinct from it. It causes the top skoots to become dwarfed and the leaves to curl up.

Wooly Aphis (1). Fumigations with hydrocyanic acid are very efficacious for the control of this insect.

Mussel Scale (2). Good results have always been obtained in Kent and Worcester in the [control of Mytilaspis with Woburn Winter wash of paraffin and caustic soda.

The Nut Bud Mite (*Eriophyes Avellanae* Nalepa) was observed in several localities. It is generally believed that it is the same as the Big Bud Mite of the currant, but it is quite a distinct species, for several attempts to infect currants with it have been unsuccessful.

Plum Leaf Blister Mite (*Eriophyes phloeocoptes* Nalepa). Observed in Kent.

Pear Leaf Blister Mite (*Eriophyes Piri* Scheut). This appeared in large numbers in different localities in 1908. The treatment which keeps it most in check is that of winter sprayings with lime, salt, caustic soda or sulphur, followed by an early spring dressing of paraffin emulsion and this may also be used in the autumn, after the fruit has been gathered.

MAMMALS.

Damage to Fruit Trees by Voles (3). Both the Bank Vole (*Erotomys glareolus*) and the Field Vole (*Microtus agrestis*) weill attack the

---

(1) *Schizoneura lanigera* (Board of Agriculture Leaflet, 37). (*Ed.*).

(2) *Mytilaspis pomorum* Bouché (Board of Agriculture, Leaflet 107). [*Ed.*]

(3) Short-Tailed Field Vole = *Microtus agrestis* (formerly called *Arvicola agrestis*); Water vole or water rat = *Microtus amphibius;* Bank vole = *Erotomys glareolus*, Cf. *Voles and their Enemies*, Board of Agriculture, Leaflet 6.

bark of fruit trees above ground but the damage done below the surface is due to the Field Vole. This rodent is common in England, Wales and Scotland (with the exception of Lewis), but is unknown in Ireland. It is the most injurious species to the farmer and forester, and it may prove so to the horticulturist and fruit-grower. Vole plagues have been numerous in Great Britain; such as those of 1580, 1813-14, 1874 to 1876. Destruction on a large scale is very difficult. Excellent results have been obtained with Virus, but sometimes it proved useless; injection of carbon disulphide into their tunnels is efficacious, but expensive.

GENERAL.

Grease banding of Fruit Trees (1). Nicotine experiments. The proportions of nicotine used were: *a*) 1 $^1/_5$ oz of 98 % nicotine; *b*) 1 oz of 98 % nicotine and *c*) ½ oz of 98 % nicotine per 10 gallons of water both plain, and a similar series vith ½ lb. soft soap in addition.

The test was applied in the open, upon the larvae of the winter moth (*Cheimatobia brumata*) and of the Gooseberry Sawfly (*Nematus Ribesii*) adult Rose-grubs (*Tortrix* sp.); Ivy Red Spider (*Bryobia pretiosa*); *Psylla Mali;* Apple Aphides (*Aphis Pomi*); Plum Aphides (*Aphis Pruni*); Currant Aphides (*Rhopalosiphum Ribis*); Turnip Flea (*Haltica nemorum*); Mussel-Scale (*Mytilaspis pomorum*); *Thrips* sp. and Cuckoo-spit. In every case the nicotine was much more efficacious when mixed with soft soap. The general results showed that for certain adult insects, such as the *Psylla, Thrips,* Cuckoo-Spit (*Euacanthus interruptus*) and the young larvae, the nicotine is fatal, as it is also for certain Aphides. Its effect on mature caterpillars is very doubtful and on Flea-Beetles (*Halticae*) and Celery-Fly it proved quite useless.

ANIMALS INJURIOUS TO CORN CROPS.

"*Tulip Root*" in Oats and other eel-worm attacks. The condition which is called "*Tulip Root*" or "*Segging*" of the oat plant is entirely due to *Tylenchus devastatrix* Kuhn. This pest has caused serious damage in Devon, Dorset, Somerset, Wiltshire, Herefordshire,

---

(1) The general results of these experiments are published in the *Journal of the Board of Agriculture*, Vol. XVII, N. 7, p. 542. See also, p. 173 of the *Bulletin* of Nov. 1910. (*Ed.*)

Middlesex, Kent, Surrey, Hampshire, Sussex, Suffolk, Yorkshire and Monmouthshire. In certain cases the "*Tulip Root*" was accompanied by an attack of *Oscinis frit.* The appearance of attacked oats is very marked. The whole plant is stunted, the leaves assume an unhealthy appearance, and the edges of the blades become crinkled and wavy. The lower parts of the stems swell above ground and assume a bulb-like appearance. Later, the plants turn brown and die.

In addition to oats, *Tylenchus devastatrix* also destroys wheat, rye, onions, potatoes, clover, buckwheat, hyacinths and other bulbs, as well as many wild plants: grasses, teazles and *Polygonum.* It is also found on the roots of hops and of plants in pots, as well as on the stalks of the wallflower (*Cheiranthus Cheiri*).

Tylenchus devastatrix as a potato parasite, is well known in South Africa, Tasmania, New Zealand, etc.; it has been found near London and in Kent.

Heterodera Schachtii on wheat. *Heterodera Schachtii* is well known on wheat on the Continent ; two more cases have been reported from England since the one mentioned in the previous year's report.

ANIMALS INJURIOUS TO GRASS LANDS.

Heather Beetle (*Lochmaea suturalis* Thoms.). Observed in the peninsula of Wirral.

Chafer Larvae (*Melolonthidae*). The larvae of *Rhizotrogus solstitialis* are very plentiful in the south of England. The Garden Chafer *Phyllopertha horticola* is common in Wales.

ANIMALS INJURIOUS TO ROOT CROPS.

The *Mangold Fly* (*Pegomyia Betae* Curtis). The flies deposit their eggs on the leaves of mangolds and beets. The first generation causes very little damage, but the later ones are very injurious, devouring the leaves. The larvae which tunnel into the cotyledons do not survive, while those which attack the first young leaves mature. It is generally stated that there are two generations in the year; but in 1908 there were three.

ANIMALS INJURIOUS TO PULSE.

Bean Beetles (*Bruchus rufimanus* and *B. flavimanus*). The *Bruchidae* rarely do any damage in England, because infected seed is, as a rule, not sent ont. There was, however, one exception at Greenhithe.

ANIMALS INJURIOUS TO HOPS.

Fever Flies (*Bibionidae*). Considerable injury has been caused in several localities by the larvae of *Bibio hortulanus* and *Bibio marci*.

The hops were also damaged by *Diplosis humuli*, *Ptinus fur* and *Tylenchus devastatrix*.

ANIMALS INJURIOUS TO VEGETABLES.

The *Large Cabbage White Butterfly* (*Pieris Brassicae* Linn.). In 1908 the larvae did considerable damage in parts of East Anglia and elsewhere.

These caterpillars are much preyed upon by parasites of which one of the chief is *Microgaster glomeratus* Linn; others are: *Pimpla instigator* Fab., *Pteromatus Brassicae* Curtis, *P. partiae* Linn. and *Polynema gracilis* Nees.

Some *Bibio* larvae were observed on rhubarb at Hereford: *Celery Fly* (*Acidia Heraclei* Linn.) at Orpington; *Celery Stem Fly-* (*Piophila Apii* Westwood) at Westerham and Ely; *Cabbage Root Maggot* (*Phorbia Brassicae* Bouché) at Newark, and in Cornwall, Suffolk and Kent.

Asparagus Beetle (*Crioceris Asparagi* Linn.). It is generally considered in England that this insect does but little damage to the asparagus, since it only attacks the leaves, but in North America it is a much more serious enemy, because it devours the young shoots as soon as they appear above the ground.

Aphis Carotae has done damage to carrots at Chelmsford and Wye.

MUSHROOM FOES: *Aphodius fimetarius* and a *Podurid*.

ANIMAL PESTS OF FLOWERS.

The larvae of *Otiorhynchus picipes* destroyed the *Echevinas;* rose trees were attacked by *Blennocampa pusilla* Klug., which curls up the leaves, by *Emphytus cinctus*, which damages the leaves and buds, and by ants (*Formicidae*), which latter were very numerous in 1908.

Several experiments were made with various substances and the following were found to be the most efficacious against ants: injections of disulphide of carbon, waste acetylene refuse, boiling water, and " Vaporite ".

Rose trees were also attacked by *Otiorhynchus picipes* and *Typhlocyba Rosae* Linn. Eel worms were found attacking pot-plants and fern-fronds.

ANIMAL PESTS OF FOREST TREES.

Considerable havoc was caused by: *Cryptorhynchus lapathi* Linn., *Chermes Pini* Kalt., and *Cryptococcus Fagi* Barens.

ANIMALS WHICH ARE INJURIOUS TO MAN.

A complete list is given of the British *Culicidae*, as that included in Verral's list of British Diptera is now out of date.

1808   O. GEMMERIG. **Do Bees Injure Grapes ?** (Ist die Biene ein Schädling des Weinbaues?) — *Deutsche Landwirtschaftliche Presse*, N. 19, S. 219, Berlin, 8. März 1911.

Germany   It is sometimes stated that bees do damage to grapes.

The following conclusions have been arrived at by a German farmer who has made observations on bees for several years:

1) Bees never attack uninjured grapes, but suck the juice from those already damaged by wasps or other creatures.

2) When a bee finds a damaged grape it sucks away all the juice, thus preventing its spoiling the sound fruit.

3) The presence of bees near a vineyard keeps away wasps.

1809   **Insect and Fungoid Pests.** — *Nature.* No. 2 161, vol. 86, pp. 161-162. London, March 30th., 1911.

United States South Africa   A recent bulletin by Mr. H. E. Burke states that the flatheaded borers (*Agrilus*) cause damage amongst forest trees to the extent of 100 000 000 dollars yearly in the United States alone. Methods of treatment are now known and much of the damage can be prevented.

The San José scale (*Aspidiotus perniciosus*) may be destroyed, according to L. A. Quintance, with petroleum or kerosene washes or with lime and sulphur washes.

« Brown rot » (*Sclerotinia fructigena*) and Plum curculio (*Conotrachelus nenuphar*) are very injurious to peaches and plums respectively, but can be kept in check by a lime-sulphur wash containing lead arsenate.

The clover-root curculio (*Sitones hispidulus*), is not a common pest. It is destroyed by a number of birds, and in the larval stage is attacked by a fungus.

The common Colorado ant (*Formica cinereorufibarbis*), protects the aphis of the melon. It is said that it is not an uncommon sight to see the ants hard at work killing and carrying away the larvae of the Syrphides which destroy the aphides. Some adult Lady-birds *Hippodamia convergens*, the nabid bug, *Reduviolus ferus* and a species of Chrysopa, were also carried away by the ants. The most simple method of extermination seems to be watering the nests with a weak solution of cyanide of potassium.

In a recent number of the « Agricultural Journal of the Cape of Good Hope », Messrs. Law and Manning discuss the extermination of ticks on the veld.

Of the three methods used: periodical dipping and spraying of the hosts, grass burning, and isolating the affected areas for a period long enough to cause the ticks to die through the absence of their hosts, dipping or spraying seems to be the best, but the other two are also effective.

Another article describes the ostrich wire-worm (*Strongylus Douglasii*), a worm which is found in the proventriculus of the ostrich; the treatment usually adopted is that of giving the bird a strong dose of carbolic acid, insufficient of course to kill it. The treatment is not satisfactory, however, and others are discussed, but none can be depended on as certain.

G. LÜSTNER. **Solenobia triquetrella Zell in Germany, an Insect Resembling the Vine Cochylis.** (Ein Doppelgänger des Heu- und Sauerwurms, der dreieckige Sackträger, *Solenobia triquetrella* Zell.) *Weinbau und Weinhandel*, 29 Jahrg., N. 16, S. 187-188, Mainz, 22 April, 1911.   **1310**

During this winter, in many parts of Germany, an insect was   **Germany** seen which resembled Cochylis so much as to be easily mistaken for it. This was *Solenobia triquetrella* Zell., called in Germany « dreieckige Sackträger », on account of the triangular form of its cocoon.

It is not possible to affirm yet whether this insect should be counted amongst vine pests. According to Mr. Lüstner, it is not very likely to be harmful, as *Solenobia* feeds on dead animal and vegetable substances.

1311   **List of Plants Attacked by** *Diaspis pentagona.* (Elenco di Comuni ai quali fu imposta la cura dei gelsi infetti dalla *Diaspis pentagona*, fino al 31 dicembre 1910). — *Bollettino del Ministero di Agricoltura, Industria e Commercio*, anno X, vol. II, serie B, fasc. 10, pp. 297-310. Roma, 11 Marzo 1911.

Italy   The following plants which have been recognised as subject to infection by *Diaspis pentagona* have been added to the list made by those Communes of Italy, which have been intrusted by the Ministry of Agriculture with the care of mulberry trees affected by that disease:

Nettle-tree (*Celtis australis* L.).
Berberis stenophylla Hance.
Caryopteris Mastacanthus Schau.
Catalpa (*Bignonia Catalpa* L.).
Newjersey Tea (*Ceanothus americanus* L.).
Bittersweet-Nightshade (*Solanum Dulcamara* L.).
Runner beans and their varieties (*Phaseolus vulgaris*).
Ash (*Fraxinus excelsior* L.).
Spindle tree (*Evonymus europaeus* L.).
Mulberry and its varieties (*Morus alba* L., *M. nigra* L.).
Paper-Mulberry (*Broussonetia papyrifera* Went.).
Jasmine (*Jasminum officinale* L.).
Kentucky Coffee (*Gymnocladus dioica* C. Koch).
Gleditschia ferox Desf. and Honey Locust tree (*G. triacanthos* L.).
Horse Chestnut (*Aesculus Hippocastanum* L.).
Kerria japonica D. C.
Cherry laurel of Trebizond (*Prunus Laurocerasus* L.).
Hop (*Humulus Lupulus* L.).
Almond (*Amygdalus communis* L.).
Mahonia (*Berberis Aquifolium* Pursch.).
Walnut (*Juglans regia* L.).
Nettle (*Urtica dioica* L.).
Paulownia imperialis L.
Pelargonium sp.
Peach and its varieties (*Amygdalus Persica* L.).
Lombardy or Italian poplar (*Populus pyramidalis* Salisb. = *P. italica* Duroi).
Pueraria (*Pachyrhizus*) *Thumbergiana* Benth.
Red currant and its varieties (*Ribes rubrum* L.).
Willow (*Salix* sp.).
Common sage (*Salvia officinalis* L.).
Choisya ternata H. B. and K.

Lilac (*Syringa vulgaris* L.).
Sophora japonica L.
Spiraea japonica L. = *S. Fortunei* Planch.
Trachelospermum (Rhyncospermum) jasminoides Lem.
Ribes Uva-crispa L.
Virginian Creeper (*Ampelopsis quinquefolia* Michx.).
Vine (*Vitis vinifera* L.).
Cucurbita sp.

L. MARTELLI. **The new Coccus of Citrus Fruits, *Chrysomphalus* 1312 *dictyospermi* var. *pinnulifera* Mask. and its natural Enemies.** (La nuova Cocciniglia degli Agrumi, *Chrysomphalus dictyospermi* var. *pinnulifera* Mask. (volg. «bianca rossa»), — *Conferenza tenuta al Comizio Agrario Circondariale in Acireale il* 15 *gennaio* 1911, pp. 1-13.

Chrysomphalus dictyospermi var. *pinnulifera* Mask. (1), is a scale **Italy:** which does much harm to the citrus fruits in Sicily, where it was **Sicily** recently introduced and is known under the name of « bianca rossa ». Mr. Martelli states, amongst other things, that some experiments are being made to find a natural method of controlling this insect.

Hithertho, only one possible parasite has been seen hovering around the citrus fruit plantations infected by the *Chrysomphalus*. It appears be a species of *Aphelinus*.

To this insect must be added two native Coleoptera, *Chilocorus bipustulatus* and *Exochomus 4-pustulatus*. But as these are indigenous and have parasites in their turn, their utility in the control of the Chrysomphalus is limited.

In consequence the Royal Station of Acireale for the Cultivation of Cirrus and other fruits introduced a new Coccida, *Rhizobius lophantae*, in March-April, 1910; it appears already to have become acclimatised.

This parasite, which is very active against *Diaspis pentagona*, is native to Australia, whence it has come to us by South Africa (Cape of Good Hope). It is an ardent hunter of other diaspides, and consenquently of *Chrysomphalus*.

In addition to the *Rhizobius*, the Royal Station will introduce other parasites of Chrysomphalus from the tropica regions of Asia.

---

(1) Seen No 688 in the February *Bulletin*, 1911.

Mention is made of the probable introduction into Sicily of another scale which is fatal to the citrus fruits, *Aonidiella Au-rantii* Mask., which has already made its appearance in Italy, where the introduction is feared of *Aspidiotus perniciosus* Comst., which has done so murch harm in America to fruit trees.

At the conclusion of the article the various plants which the *Chrysomphalus* attacks are enumerated. They are the following: Evonymus japonicus, Hedera, Camellia japonica, Deutzia cre-nata, Ficus Carica, Cocos australis, Crataegus glabra, Ligustrum vul-gare, Gardenia grandiflora, Kentia Belmoreana, Cycas revoluta, Chamaedorea elatior, Latania borbonica, Araucaria sp., Myrtus communis, Aucuba japonica, Magnolia sp., Rose trees, etc.

1313
Bohemia

R. Sarcin. **Mechanical Determination of the Resistance of Cereals to the Attacks of Insects.** (Détermination mécanique de la résistence des céréales aux maladies et aux attaques des in-sectes). See no. 1284 of this Bulletin.

1314

Insecticide Competition at Valencia. (Concours d'insecticides à Va-lence). — *La Petite Revue Agricole et Horticole*, 17e année, N. 392, p. 78, Antibes, 9 Avril, 1911.

Spain

An international competition for insecticides is to be held in the province of Valencia (Spain) for the control of *Chrysomphalus dictyospermi, Mytilaspis flavescens, Parlatoria Ziziphi* and *Dacty-lopius Citri*, parasites which attack the orange and lemon trees.

Hydrocyanic acid is not included in the insecticides which are to be tried, because a Special Commission is at present making experiments in fumigations with this gas in various provinces and especially in Valencia.

1315

Ch. Bernard. **Observations On the Tea Plant in Java.** — *Bull. Dept. Agr. Indes néerlandaises*, N. 60, 1910. *La Quinzaine Coloniale*, 15e année, N. 5, pp. 162-163, Paris, 10 Mars, 1911.

Java

In consequence of some experiments made at Buitenzorg in the course of 1910, it has been found that it is better to burn the twigs of the tea plant after pruning than to bury them at the foot of the bushes. Acari, and especially the orange Acarus (*Brevipalpus obovatus*), are not killed by burying and reinfect the plantations.

Treatment on a large scale with insecticides does not seem pos-sible, and the only thing which has given favourable results has been the improvement ·of the cultivation conditions, so that the plant is itself in a better condition for resisting attack.

·A certain number of Acari affect the tea plant also indirectly, such as the *Phytoptus*, which causes galls on the leaves of *Indigofera galegoides*, a leguminous plant much used for green manure.

J. CAPUS and J. FEYTAUD. **The Invasions of Eudemis and Cochylis in the Gironde in 1910.   Studies on the Use of Insecticides.** (Les invasions d'Eudémis et de Cochylis dans le Gironde en 1910. Recherches sur les traitements insecticides). — *Revue de Viticulture*, Paris, 27 Avril, 1911.

1316

France: Gironde

The experiments of 1910, confirm those previously made by the writers in so far as the. determination of the favourable moment for the application of insecticides in spring and summer is concerned. This has been found to be when the eggs are laid, and precedes the invasion by several days.   In years when the generations are hatched at especially long intervals, as in 1910, it is still possible to destroy a given generation with a single treatment, but under these conditions, the determination of the opportune moment is more difficult than in those years when the hatching of all the moths takes place within a brief period.

The repetition of a treatment after some days, which is useless as far as Eudemis is concerned, may sometimes be successful in the case of Cochylis, on account of the eggs being hatched at longer intervals.

Arsenic is not necessary·; nicotine in a cupric mixture is a most efficacious remedy against both pests.   Chloride of barium may be substituted for the nicotine, and added to sulphate of copper mixtures. ·

Soap, which has been so much recommended by German experimenters, cannot replace nicotine, nor can it even increase its effect in preventive applications.   The stripping of the leaves assists the summer treatments, and increases their efficacy.

Messrs. Capus and Feytaud recommend the *application of a nicotine cupric mixture.*

a) Formula: to one hectolitre of neutral or basic Bordeaux Mixture with 2 % of copper sulphate, add 133 gr. of pure·nicotine, that is, 1 ⅓ litre of tobacco juice at 10 %.

b) Number of treatments: two yearly, or one against the first and one against the second generation, under ordinary conditions. When the appearances of the moths occur at long intervals owing to the year or the climate, it will sometimes be advantageous to repeat each of these treatments.

c) Time: the moment when the moths are most plentiful. (Generally at the end of May and June in the Gironde).

d) Apparatus: a knap-sack sprayer which leaves free the hand that is not holding the tube. For the exclusive treatment of the bunches a stop-jet is preferable.

e) Preliminary precautions: expose the bunches, if necessary, by thinning the leaves or shoots.

f) Spraying: examine the bunches well and spray then thoroughly. Pass along both sides of the row, so that none shall be overlooked.

1317   R. W. Jack. **Resin Wash for Scale Insects on Citrus trees.** *The Rhodesia Agricultural Journal*, pp. 416-422 Salisbury, February, 1911.

Rhodesia   The use of resin wash as a remedy for scale insects on citrus trees has already passed the experimental stage and is being adopted in ordinary practice by the planters in California.

The formula used is as follows:

Resin 18 lbs (8.15 kg.)

Caustic soda (70%) 5 lbs (2,26 kg.)

Fish oil 2 ½ pints (1.16 litre)

Water 100 gallons (454 litres).

Modified formula, omitting the fish oil:

Resin 40 lbs (18.12 kg.)

Caustic soda (70%) 5 lbs (2,26 kg).

Water 100 gallons (454 litres)

These formulae, which have been recommended in the United States as the best, have been tried in South Africa.

It has been found that no useful modifications can be made in the Californian formula, and that is it really efficacious if care is taken to apply the mixture hot.

The formula without the fish oil was found efficacious, when applied hot, against soft scales; but it was less effective than that with the fish oil (weight of resin being equal) for red and other hard scales

The standard formula recommended for use in Cape Colony is as follows :

Resin 24 lbs (10.87 kg.) ;

Caustic soda (98 %) 5 lbs (2.26 kg.) ;

Fish oil 2 bottles (1,50 litre) ;

Water 100 gallons (454 litres) ;

This mixture is prepared as follows :

First crush the resin, then pour 15 gallons or more of water into the cooking pot, stir in the soda and oil, and bring to the boil.

Then gradually stir in the powdered resin never letting any settle,and boil for 10 or 15 minutes after it is all dissolved ; the solution should be the colour of strong coffee.

Less than three quarters of an hour is sufficient for this preparation provided that the resin is well crushed and is not allowed to settle ; if it gets into a mass, the operation may take 3 hours. Some more water, either hot or cold, should then be added very gradually if the mixture foams up strongly, and when the whole has boiled sufficiently, the quantity of water should be at once increased to 25 gallons.

This mixture may be preserved indefinitely, but care should be taken to prevent a deposit ; if this should occur, it must be boiled again. The hot or cold water can be added at any moment,

---

Insects Injurious to Special Crops.

MAGEN. **An Insect Pest of Rice in Cochin China.** (*Bull. écon. de l'Indochine*, n. 82). *La Quinzaine Coloniale*, 15ᵉ année, n. 5, p. 163, Paris, 10 Mars, 1911.

1318

A Hemipteron (of the group of the Geocorinae) is causing considerable damage to the rice in Cochin China.

French Indo China : Cochin China

The rice which has been attacked is easily recognised by its yellow colour and the fact that the leaves lose their turgescence. During the growing period, the insects crowd together at the base of the stalk, at the etiolated part. Between the stems, groups of about 50 eggs are found forming hexagonal plates 5 mm. in diameter.

The adult, in the normal condition, inhabits the forest, but towards the month of September the female seeks for a favourable place to lay her eggs, and descends upon the rice fields.

For the protection of the latter in the western provinces of Cochin China, where there are forests, it is absolutely necessary that the rice fields shonld be sloped in such a way as to keep the height of the water at about 20 cm, above the crown of the plants. The plants mnst be irrigated in proportion as they grow, so that it is impossible for the female insect to lay her eggs upon them.

1819   D. T. FULLAWAY. **Insects attacking the Sweet Potato at Hawaii.** —
Hawaii Agric. Exper. Station Bulletin, No. 22, 8°, pp. 31. Honolulu, 1911.

Hawaii   Although the sweet potato is not cultivated on large areas at
Hawaii, the total crop is large and is very commonly used as an
article of food.   A list is given of the insects which attack it and
a description of their life-cycle, habits, natural enemies, means of
control, etc.

Elateridae. Out of 35 or more species of indigenous or introduced cutworms and army worms (Elateridae) only 8 are common
at Hawaii and damage the crops.   These are: *Cirphis unipuncta,
Agrotis ypsilon, A. crinigera, Feltia dislocata, Lycophotia margaritosa,
Spodoptera mauritia, S. exigua, Caradrina reclusa.* The others are
more or less confined to the mountains and kept in check by pararites.

The invasions of Elateridae occur more frequently in the cold,
damp winter months than at any other period of the year.   The
Their natural enemies are numerous and fairly efficient.   The
Tachinids, *Frontina archippivora* and *Chaetogaedia monticola, Ichneumon Koebeli,* and birds are particularly useful.

The Sweet Potato Sphinx. The larvae of the Sphinx moth (*Pro-
toparce Convolvuli*) feeds on the various species of Ipomaea.   It is
said that it attacks the sweet potato in the United States, the
West Indies, the Madeira and Canary Islands, Australia and India.
In Hawaii it often destroys the wild Ipomaea, completely stripping
it of its leaves, and sometimes attacks the sweet potatoes.   The
species is kept in check by a Hymenopteron, *Pentarthron semi-
fuscatum* Perkin, which acts as a parasite on the eggs. Dr. Perkins
mentions that the larvae are also destroyed at their earliest stage
by parasites probably *Echthromorpha* and Tachnid flies.

The Leaf Miners. The genus Bedellia (Tineidae) is represented
at Hawaii by 7 species, the larvae of which are leaf miners.   *Bedellia
somnulentella* and *B. minor* mine the leaves of Ipomaea, *B, oplis-
meniella* those of a grass *Oplismenus compositus,* and *B. boehmeriella*
attacks the leaves of *Boehmeria stipularis.*   The leaf miner which
usually attacks the potato in the environs of Honolulu is, according
to Bask, *B. Orchilella* which is not known outside the Hawaiian
Islands. *B. minor* is found in Florida aud Hawaii. B. sommulen-
tella has a wide distribution.   The leaf miners are kept well in
check by the Chalcid *Omphale metallicus,* which is a parasite of the
larvae, and by another Eulophid (*Pediobius*).

The Sweet Potato Stem Borer (*Omphisa anastomosalis*) is not
a native insect, but was probably introduced recently from China.

It is indigenous to the Indo-Malay region. It was observed for the first time at Hawaii in 1900, since when it has been continually on the increase, and promises to become a serious scourge if not kept in check by its natural enemies, The damage is caused by the larva or caterpillar, which bores through the stems of the plants, these fade, and finally die. An Ichneumon fly *Pristomerus* sp. has been bred from the larva, but it is not known to what extent it is a parasite.

The Sweet Potato Leaf Roller (*Phlyctaenia despecta*) was only recently observed on this plant, although it is common in the mountains, on the wild species of the genus Ipomaea. It is an indigenous insect. The larvae of P. despecta roll up the leaves, living on the under surface. The moth is sometimes very injurious to *Batatas edulis*, but is generally kept in check by parasites. Mr. Fullaway has bred *Limnerium Blackburni*, a parasite of the larvae, and Dr. Perkins has bred *Chelonus Blackburni* and *Chalcis obscurata*. A common wasp of the genus *Odynerus* (*O. nigripenus*) has been seen collecting the caterpillars.

The Tortricid Leaf Roller (*Amorbia emigratella*), which contorts and rolls the leaves, is not an indigenous insect, but was introduced into Hawaii, where it has been known since 1900. It is also found in Mexico and at Porto Rico, aud was probably brought to Hawaii from those countries. It has developed very rapidly, and the large number of food plants that it attacks makes it a serious pest. The larvae roll the leaves of many species of plants and are often so numerous as to defoliate trees.

This insect has been found on the citrus trees, cotton plant, avocado, guava tree, rose tree, passion flower, tomato, papaya tree, cacao tree, as well as on the sweet potato and various indigenous plants in the mountains. It has *Chalcis obscurata* for parasite.

Unfortunately the egg parasite *Trichogramma* sp., which contributes more than anything else to keep this class of pest in check, is incapable of penetrating the thick covering of the eggs of the *Amorbia*.

Weevils. There are two weevils which attack the tubers of the sweet potato at Hawaii. The smaller one is the insect mentioned in the fauna under the name of *Hyperamropha squamosa* Blackburn. It is now thought that it is the common West Indian form *Cryptorhynchus Batatae* Waterhouse. This is the commoner of the two in Hawaii, but is not generally prevalent. The larger of the weevils is *Cylas formicarius;* it is a native probably of Cochinchina, but is now very extensively found in the Tropics. It is not very common at Hawaii. It attacks *Ipomaea pes-caprae* as well as *Batatas edulis*.

Less important foes. There are some minor pests of the sweet potato. *Nesosydne ipomoeicola* and *Aloha ipomoeae* are two common leaf-hoppers on this plant. *Plusia chalcites* sometimes attacks the foliage. A mealy bug (undetermined species of *Pseudoccus*), and a scale-insect (*Saisettia* sp.) are commonly met with, and the Japanese beetle (*Adoretus tenuimaculatus*) sometimes attacks it and skeletonizes the leaves.

The leaf hoppers are much parasitized by *Anagrus, Stylops* and *Echthrodelphax,* and are not of much importance.

Plusia is not very dangerous, and has tachnid flies for parasites. The Coccidae are unimportant, and the Japanese beetle seldom does any harm.

Useful insects. The wasps of the genus *Odynerus* prey on caterpillars of medium sized Lepidoptera and carry them off to their nests to feed their young. The most common species is probably *O. nigripennis.* The Polistes wasps act in the same way. Certain predacious bugs (*Oechalia grisea, Zelus renardii* and *Reduviolus Blackburni*) are active on the sweet potato.

Methods of control. On account of the numerous caterpillars which eat the leaves of *Batatas edulis*, the latter should be sprayed 4 to 5 times a year with an arsenical preparation. Arsenate of lead is recommended as the most useful and the least likely to burn the leaves.

In the case of a serious infestation, sweet potato growing should be given up for a certain time.

Another sweet potato pest is described in the *Rhodesia Agricultural Journal* (vol. 8, No. 3, pp. 438-440, Salisbury; February 1911), It is said that the Tortoise Beetle (Cassidinae) has been much more plentiful this season (1910-1911) than all the other insects which attack the potato in Rhodesia, and has caused great damage in several places.

In addition to *Batatas edulis* the insect has also attacked the creeping *Ipomaea*, and has been found in large numbers on the leaves of the melon. This pest could be easily controlled by sprayings of arsenate of lead. One lb arsenate of lead in 20 gallons of water is sufficient to kill these insects.

W. W. FROGGART. **The French - Bean Fy**. (*Agromyza Phaseoli* Co-   1820
quillet). — *Agricultural Gazetze of New South Wales*, vol. XXII,
Part 2, pp. 151-154. Sydney, February 1911.

No market gardener of New South Wales had ever remarked   **New**
this disease of the French bean until it appeared in the district of   **South Waels**
Gosford in the spring of 1898. Last year, 1910, it not only reap-
peared as a serious pest but spread over a much larger area than
in the preceding years. The insect is apparently an indigenous species, and it is very remarkable to see how local it is in its range;
starting about Kincumber, it reaches only to the district of Gosford
around Erina and Wamberal. It is known to gardeners in the larva
and chrysalis states.

The adult is a small short, broad black fly, which measures
only 1-5 mm. in length. It attacks the main stem of the bean from
the surface of the soil to a height of about two or three inches.
The eggs are deposited in cracks, or beneath the epidermis of the
plant. When numerous, the flies also attack and injure the petioles; they puncture the upper surface of the leaf at the junction
with the petiole, and sometimes the larvae burrow tunnels down
the latter.

Remedies. Growers find that the flies may be controlled in good
growing weather by banking up the plants before the insects make
their appearance. No spraying or wash seems to have any effect
on the flies, and as the larvae do not feed on the surface of the
plant, but in the tissues, no poisonous spray upon the foliage would
injure them. It is a case for clean cultivation. All infested plants
should be removed and burnt, as soon as the beans are gathered.

E. MIÉGE. **Vegetable and Animal Parasites of Buckwheat** (*Fago-*   1821
pyrum). — See No. 1290 of this Bulletin.

G. MARTELLI. *Pieris Brassicae* L., and *P. Rapae* L., **Parasites of**   1822
***Capparis rupestris* Sm**. — (La *Pieris Brassicae* and *P. Rapae* L.,
parasite del *Capparis rupestris* Sm. *Mem. Classe Scienze, R. Accad.
Zelanti*, vol. VIII, pp. 4, Acireale, 1910). *Rivista di Patologia
vegetale*, anno IV, n. 19-22, p. 309, Pavia, March 15, 1911

The larvae of *Pieris Brassicae* and *P. Rapae*, according to obser-   **Italy :**
vations made at Acireale, Sicily, appear to attack the caper-bush   **Sicily**
and devour its leaves as well as those of the cabbage.

The butterflies of these two kinds of *Pieris* deposit their eggs
on the cultivated cabbage, and also on the caper-bush, on which

they fulfil their complete biological cycle. For this reason, *P. Bras-*
sicae and *P. Rapae* should be considered as habitual, and not merely occasional, parasites of *Capparis rupestris.*

1324   L, LAUBERT and M. SCHWARTZ. **Diseases and Enemies of the Rose.**
          See No. 1294 of this Bulletin.

1328   **Causes of the decreased Vintage in France in 1910.** See No. 1283
          of this Bulletin.

1325   P. R. JONES and J. R. HORTON. **The Orange Thrips. A Report of**
          Progress for the Years 1909-1910. — *U. S. Dept. of Agr. Bu-*
          reau of Entomology, Bulletin N. 99, Part I, 8°, pp. 16 + Pla-
          tes III, Washington, March 6, 1911.

United   The orange thrips (*Euthrips citri* Moulton) is a small orange
States :   yellow insect of the order Thysanoptera which curls and distorts
California
and Arizona   the leaves and scars the fruit in the valley of San Joaqin in Cali-
                fornia — the orange belt of South California — and the Salt River
                valley in Arizona.
                    The havoc caused by this insect, which was first noticed 15 or
                16 years ago, has considerably increased with the development of
                the citrus fruits industry, and has recently assumed serious economic
                importance.
                    The orange thrips is probably native to North America. Its natu-
                ral habitat is probably the Sierra Nevada foot-hills or the adjoin'ng
                plains of the southern San Joaqin valley. It was thonght that
                the thrips attacked only citrus trees but entomologists have disco-
                vered it on other host plants.
                    The following citrus fruits are attacked; *Citrus Aurantium* var.
                sinensis; Citrus nobilis; Citrus decumana; Citrus medica var. *Limon;*
                Citrus medica var. *acida;* and *Citrus japonica.*
                    The following miscellanons plants fall victims : *Punica Granatum,*
                Vitis vinilera, Schinus molle, Pyrus communis, Prunus Armeniaca,
                Prunus Persica, Prunus domestica, Salix sp., *Rumex* sp., *Portulaca*
                oleracea, Olea europea, Rubus idaeus, Rosa sp., and *Solanum* sp.
                    Injury to citrus trees and fruit is caused directly by the feeding
                of both adults and larvae upon the surface of the parts attacked.
                They consume the young fruit, the nearly mature fruit, and the new
                tender foliage.

The orange thrips has numerous generations every year; its life cycle is about 20 days, and it is found on the trees from March to November.

The thrips may be destroyed with four sprayings of a solution of lime-sulphur solution combined with an extract of commercial tobacco, which should be applied when the insects are fairly numerous. Three applications must be made in spring to protect the fruit and spring buds, and the fourth in the autumn to lessen the injury to the autumn growth of the trees. From 2 to 8 gallons of this combination spray should be used per tree, and the spraying should be done very thoroughly and at high pressure, because only those thrips which are hit by the solution are killed.

Some spraying experiments have shown that three thorough applications at the proper times have resulted in from 20 to 60 % more " fancy " fruit in the sprayed than in the unsprayed blocks. The following are other thrips which attack the orange tree: *Euthrips occidentalis* Pergande, which is only found at times and rarely does serious damage, and *Euthrips Tritici* Fitch, which sometimes infests the orange trees in the north central portion of California.

S. A. ROHWER. **The Genotypes of the Sawflies and Woodwasps of the Superfamily Tenthredinoidea.** — *U. S, Dept. of Agr., Bureau of Entomology. Technical Papers on Miscellaneous Forest Insects, Technical Series*, No. 20, Part II, p, 69-109, Washington, March 4, 1911.   1826

The Sawfly and Woodwasp belong to the superfamily of Tenthredinoidea of the order of Hymenoptera, and are amongst the most important enemies of forest trees in North America. The real sawfly, in the larval stage destroys the leaves of conifers and other trees; the larchsawfly, which lives on the foliage of this tree in Europe and North America is extremely destructive. The woodwasp in the larva state burrows holes in dying and dead standing and fallen trees, causing a rapid deterioration of the timber. In addition to a large number of species which belong to the United States, there are several other very destructive species which have come from other countries. The knowledge of these insects, from the scientific and economic points of view, is very limited, especially as far as the North American species are concerned.   North America

Mr. Rohwer has been nominated by the Bureau of Entomology of the United States Department of Agriculture to study the Sawfly.

The present paper contains part of the results of his preliminary work andgives an alphabetical list of the generic names used in the super-families of the Tenthredinoidea and Siricoidea with their type species and the synonyms of certain genera.

It also gives the summary of the work of William H. Ashmead on the Tenthredinoidea.

Mr. Rohwers' future papers will be in the form oi monographs dealing with special groups.

1827   L. M. ELLIS. **Some notes on Jack Pine, *Pinus divaricata*, in Western Ontario.** *Forestry Quarterly*, vol. IX, N.1, pp. 1-14. — Cambridge, Mass., March, 1911.

Canada   The sound trees of the *Pinus Banksiana* or *P. divaricata*, are practically exempt from insects. In the rare cases where sapling trees have been wounded, a resinous excrescence has been noted, on which a chrysalis, presumably *Retina Comstockiana* was developing.

The trees which are damaged by fire, on the contrary, are attacked by insects of the genus *Monohammus* and *Pissodes Strobi*, to such an extent, that in two seasons the wood became useless for lumber, and could only be used for making sleepers.

1828   **The Destruction of Field Mice.** (La destruction des Mulots et Campagnols). — *Le Cultivateur Français*, 5e année, N°. 7, p. 7, Lyon, Feb. 18, 1911.

France   In order to destroy field mice (1) the Agricultural Station at Blois recommends the use of baryta bread (wheat flour with the addition of carbonate of baryta and coloured with colcothar), which the rodents eat readily. One to three pieces should be placed in each of the holes which are frequented, and the opening then filled up with a stone. Holes in slopes should be treated with especial care, as well as those in hedges and along the edges of roads, where the rodents prefer to congregate. The best time for the treatment is when the animals have most difficulty in finding food, viz from November 1st to March 20th, whenever the earth is not covered with snow. A kilogram of bread is sufficient for a hectare. Care must be taken to keep the bread out of the way of useful animals, because the poison is very strong and dangerous even to man.

---

(1) See Nos. 361. 362, 363 of this *Bulletin* for Jan. 1911.

J. Surcouf. **Stinging and Bloodsucking Insects which trasmit Diseases.** (Les insectes piqueurs et suceurs de sang transmetteurs des maladies). — *L'Agriculture pratique des pays chauds*, 11e année, N.º 96, pp. 244-248. 1 fig., Paris, March, 1911.

1329

The results of investigations on puncturing Diptera in the environs of Hué (Annam).

Indo-China: Annam

This study is of eminently practical interest, because Annam is a region where the « Surra » (1) makes great ravages as an endemic disease. From 1904 to 1909, Mr. Bauche verified the death of fifty horses, buffaloes and dogs from this cause in Hué alone.

The stinging flies : Taons, *Chrysops, Stomoxys*, appear at the end of the rains, during the fine weather of March.

A large number of specimens have been sent to the Colonial Laboratory of the Natural History Museum at Paris, but the nnmber of the species is very small, and there is only one species of Taon (represented by 283 specimens, 277 of which are females and 6 males), and described by the writer as new under the name of *Tabanus annamiticus* - and one species of *Chrysops, C. dispar* Fabricius (= *C. impar* Rondani, *C. ligatus* Walker, *C. lunatus* Gray, *C· terminalis* Walker). This species, represented by 34 specimens, was already known in Southern Asia, the Philippine Islands, Hong-Kong and the Indian Archipelago, but had never before been observed in Annam.

These investigations, if carried out systematically, might result in a typical collection at the Colonial Laboratory of the Museum of stinging and blood-sucking insects found in the Colonies. These collections would be of the greatest use in colonisation, becanse the insects which transmit microbes could be studied and destroyed with certainty.

---

(1) Epidemic disease of domestic animals dne to the first pathogenic trypanosome known, *Trypanosoma Evansi* Steel, discovered by Evansen in 1880 in India. Cf. M. Neveu-Lemaire. *Précis de Parasitologie humaine*, 4e edit. p. 256, Paris, 1908. (*Ed.*)

1880   R. A. BLACK. **Hemlock (*Conium maculatum*) Proclaimed a Weed.** —
The Agricultural Gazette of Tasmania, vol. XIX, N. 2, pp. 72-
73, Tasmania, Feb. 1911.

Tasmania   Under Section 6 of the Local Government Act, 1906 (6 Ed. VII,
N. 31), of December 20th, 1910, the hemlock was proclaimed an
injurious weed in the territory of Table Cape ; since then the decree
has been extended to the whole of Tasmania.
        It is incumbent now upon all Municipal Councils to take mea-
sures for the destruction of the weed. Section 3 of the Californian
Thistle Act, 1883 (47 Vict., N. 17), as read with subsection 12 of
section 130 of the local Government Act., 1906, provides that all
holders of lands in Tasmania in which the hemlock is found to be
growing must cut it down in order to prevent it from blossoming
or be liable to a penalty not exceeding £ 20.

International Institute of Agriculture

BULLETIN OF THE BUREAU OF

AGRICULTURAL INTELLIGENCE AND

OF PLANT-DISEASES ❧ ❧ ❧ ❧ ❧

2nd YEAR - NUMBER 5

MAY 1911

ROME, 1911 — PRINTED AT THE INSTITUTE'S PRINTING OFFICE

CONTENTS

LIVE STOCK BREEDING. — AVICULTURE.
BEEKEEPING. — SILK PRODUCTION. — FISHERIES AND GAME.
ANIMAL INDUSTRIES.

AGRICULTURAL INDUSTRIES.

AGRICULTURAL ENGINEERING

PLANT DISEASES
NOXIOUS INSECTS AND OTHER PESTS.

THE INTERNATIONAL INSTITUTE OF AGRICULTURE

The International Institute of Agriculture was established under the International Treaty of June 7th, 1905, which was ratified by 40 Governments. Eight other Governments have since adhered to the Institute.

It is a Government Institution in which each Country is represented by delegates. The Institute is composed of a General Assembly and a Permanent Committee.

The Institute, confining its operations within an international sphere, shall:

a) Collect, study, and publish as promptly as possible statistical, technical, or economic information concerning farming, vegetable and animal products, the commerce in agricultural products, and the prices prevailing in the various markets;

b) Communicate to parties interested, also as promptly as possible, the above information;

c) Indicate the wages paid for farm work;

d) Make known the new diseases of vegetables which may appear in any part of the world, showing the territories infected, the progress of the diseases, and, if possible, the remedies which are effective;

e) Study questions concerning agricultural co-operation, insurance, and credit in all their aspects; collect and publish information which might be useful in the various countries for the organisation of works connected with agricultural co-operation, insurance and credit;

f) Submit to the approval of the Governments, if there is occasion for it, measures for the protection of the common interests of farmers and for the improvement of their conditions, after having utilized all the necessary sources of information, such as the wishes expressed by international or other agricultural congresses or by congresses of sciences applied to agriculture, or agricultural societies, academies, learned bodies, etc.

The Institute publishes: *a*) a Bulletin of Agricultural Statistics; *b*) a Bulletin of Agricultural Intelligence and Diseases of

Plants; c) a Bulletin of Economic and Social Intelligence; d) a Bulletin Bibliographique hebdomadaire (published every Saturday) It has also published a volume on " The Organization of Agricultural S atistical Services in the Several Countries ", and a volume on " Statistics of Cultivated Areas and of Vegetable and Animal Production in the Adhering Countries " (an Inventory drawn up from documents published by Governments), and " Studies upon the present condition of Agricultural Association in certain countries ".

Officers of the Institute
and List of the Delegates to the Permanent Committee.

President: Marquess RAFFAELE CAPPELLI, *Delegate of Italy*
Vice-President : M. LOUIS-DOP, *Delegate of France.*
General Secretary: Prof. PASQUALE JANNACCONE.

Delegates of the adhering States to the Permanent Committee.

	States adhering to the Institute	Groups in which adhering States are classified	Names and Rank of the Delegates
1	Germany . . .	I	Dr. T. MUELLER, Privy Councillor.
2	Argentine Rep. .	I	His Excell. E. PORTELA, Minister Plenipotentiary of the Argentine Rep. to H. M. the King of Italy.
3	Austria	I	Chev. V. DE POZZI, Government Councillor.
4	Hungary	I	E. DE MIKLÓS DE MIKLOSVÁR, Secretary of State for Agriculture. Member of the House of Magnates.
5	Belgium	IV	O. BOLLE.
6	Brazil	I	A. FIALHO, Ex-Deputy; Ex-President of the National Agricultural Society.
7	Bulgaria	III	D. RIZOFF, Minister Plenipotentiary of Bulgaria to H. M. the King of Italy,
8	Chile	I	S. ALDUNATE BASCUÑAN, Minister Plenipotentiary of Chile to H. M. the King of Italy.
9	China	I	His Excell. OUTSONGLIEN, Minister Plenipotentiary of China to H. M. the King of Italy.
10	Costa-Rica . . .	V	R. MONTEALEGRE, Minister Plenipotentiary of Costa-Rica to H. M. the King of Italy.
11	Cuba	V	C. M. DE CESPEDES y QUESADA, Minister Plenipotentiary of Cuba to H. M. the King of Italy.

	States adhering to the Institute	Groups in which the adhering States are classified	Names and Rank of the Delegates
12	Denmark	IV	H. H. KONOW, Secretary to the Danish Legation to the Italian Government.
13	Ottoman Empire	I	Dr. MEHMED DJÉMIL BEY.
14	Egypt	II	B. CHIMIRRI, Delegate of Eritrea and Italian Somaliland.
15	Ecuador	V	LOUIS-DOP, Delegate of France.
16	Spain.	I	ENRIQUE RODRIGUEZ DE CELIS, Agronomic Engineer.
17	United States . .	I	DAVID LUBIN.
18	Ethiopia	V	Prof. G. CUBONI, Director of the Station of Vegetable Pathology of Rome.
19	France	I	LOUIS-DOP, Vice-President of the Institute.
20	Algeria	V	LOUIS-DOP, Delegate of France.
21	Tunis	V	LOUIS-DOP, Delegate of France.
22	Great Britain & Ireland	I	H. G. DERING Counsellor to the British Embassy to the Italian Government.
23	Australia	IV	. . . .
24	Canada	II	H. G. DERING, Delegate of Great Britain and Ireland.
25	British India . .	II	H. G. DERING, Delegate of Great Britain and Ireland.
26	New Zealand . .	IV	H. G. DERING, Delegate of Great Britain and Ireland.
27	Mauritius . . .	V	H. G. DERING. Delegate of Great Britain and Ireland.
28	Greece	IV	A. CARAPANOS, Chargé d'affaires of Greece to the Italian Government.
29	Italy	I	Marquess R. CAPPELLI, Vice-President of the Chamber of Deputies, President of the Istitute.
30	Eritrea and Italian Somaliland	IV	B. CHIMIRRI, Member of Parliament.

States adhering to the Institute	Groups in which the adhering States are classified	Names and Rank of the Delegates
31	Japan	I	NAOTSI MARUMO, First Secretary to the Imperial Japanese Embassy to the Italian Government.
32	Luxemburg . . .	V	O. BOLLE, Delegate of Belgium.
33	Mexico	II	G. A. ESTEVA, Minister Plenipotentiary of Mexico to H. M. the King of Italy.
34	Montenegro . . .	V	G. VOLPI, Director General of the Monopolies of the Kingdom.
35	Nicaragua. . . .	V	V. E. BIANCHI, Consul General of Nicaragua at Rome.
36	Norway.	IV	Dr. A. FJELSTAD, Landowner.
37	Holland	IV	H. DE WEEDE, Minister Plenipotentiary of Holland to H. M. the King of Italy.
38	Peru	V	Dr. M. M. MESONES.
39	Persia	IV	A. DEL GALLO, Marquess of ROCCAGIOVINE.
40	Portugal	IV	LUIZ FILIPPE DE CASTRO, Professor of the Institute of Agriculture at Lisbon.
41	Roumania. . . .	I	G. C. NANO, Minister Plenipotentiary of Roumania to H. M. the King of Italy.
42	Russia	I	His Ex. G. ZABIELLO, Conseller of State, Consul General of Russia in Rome.
43	Salvador	V	A. BALLO, Acting Consul General of Salvador at Genoa.
44	San Marino . . .	V	His Excell. L. LUZZATTI, Minister of State of the Kingdom of Italy.
45	Servia	III	B. I. SOUBOTITCH, Secretary to the Servian Legation to the Italian Government.
46	Sweden	IV	G. V. T. DE STRÅLE, Councillor to the Swedish Legation to the Italian Government.
47	Switzerland . . .	IV	J. B. PIODA, Minister Plenipotentiary of Switzerland to H. M. the King of Italy.
48	Uruguay	V	REQUENA BERMUDEZ, Chargé d'affaires of Uruguay to the Italian Government.

AGRICULTURAL INTELLIGENCE

NB. The Intelligence contained in the present Bulletin has been taken exclusively from the books, periodicals, bulletins, and other publications which have reached the Library of the International Institute of Agriculture in Rome during the month of May 1911.

The Bureau assumes no responsibility with regard to the opinions and the results of experiments outlined in the Bulletin.

The Editor's notes are marked (Ed.).

AGRICULTURAL INTELLIGENCE

Development of Agriculture in Different Countries — Scientific Institutions — Education in Agriculture and Forestry — Experimentation — Congresses — Rural Economy.

MARVAND. **Agriculture in Corsica.** — *Revue Economique Internationale*,   **1331**
Vol. II, N. I, pp. 105-134. Bruxelles, Avril, 1911.

The destruction of chestnut woods and of forests generally is
ruinous to Corsica and to the regulation of its water-courses.

It would be to the advantage of the island if sheep and cattle   **France:**
were raised rather than goats. For this purpose natural or arti-   **Corsica**
ficial meadows should be extended and irrigation improved.

Potatoes could be grown to advantage in the mountain districts
and might even be exported. Tobacco and sugar-beets can be profitably grown, and more especially early vegetables for exportation.

The methods of preparing oil and wine require improving and
the formation of co-operative associations would greatly benefit
these industries. The cultivation of the olive, which flourishes in
all parts of the island and covers already 13'000 hectares (32 110
acres), and fruit trees, could also be extended.

The drawbacks in the way of agricultural progress in Corsica
are the excessive subdivision of the land, the want of roads, and
the scarcity of capital and labour.

Agricultural and Horticultural Improvements in Holland. — *Bul-*   **1332**
letin mensuel de l'Office de Renseignements Agricoles, N. 3,
pp. 315-316. Paris, Mars, 1911.

The compulsory inspection of pork exported from Holland has
made it much in demand in England.   **Holland**

The cultivation of sugar beets in Holland is extending every year, and the results obtained in 1910 are all the more satisfactory as the yield in sugar has been excellent (1).

Horticulture is of great importance in the Netherlands and is gaining ground daily.

Market gardening, favoured by the great fertility and moisture of the soil and by the number of canals which run through the cultivated land, not only supplies enough vegetables to meet the home demand but the produce is exported on a large scale. Production is greatest in the provinces of South and North Holland.

Orchards are even more important than market gardens. A large trade is done in apples, pears, cherries, plums, gooseberries, currants and raspberries.

Table grapes are grown a few miles west of the Hague in glass-houses covering an area of 300 000 sq. metres (74 acres) ; the annual yield is estimated at 1 000 000 kgs. (2 204 000 lbs.), and the grapes, more especially the " Frankenthal. " " Gros Colman, " and " Black Alicante " varieties are, placed on the market in great quantities from the end of May to November.

·   The nursery gardens, which are generally surrounded by navigable canals supplying an excellent means of transportation, are very prosperous.

30 % of the total area under nursery gardens is in the province of South Holland. America, Germany and England are the principal customers of the Boskoop nurseries. America buys rose trees, rhododendrons, azaleas, peonies, conifer saplings, box shrubs, Japanese maple-trees, lilacs. Germany and England purchase rose trees, rhododendrons, azaleas, lilacs, conifers, *Prunus*, yews, box, *Aucuba*, etc. France and Belgium buy shrubs, plants in pots hydrangeas, azaleas, Japanese maples, etc.

Floriculture prospers in almost all the villages and towns of Holland. Aalsmeer, in the province of South Holland, is one of the most important centres of this business.

---

(1) The areas under sugar-beet in Holland were 32 970 hectares in 1907, 33 399 in 1908. and 34 104 hectares in 1909. The average yield in 1909 was 272 metric quintals per hectare.

The Dutch export of bulbs. shrubs and trees was valued in 1908 at 12 621 000 gulden ; in 1909 at 14 849 771 gulden. The exportation of vegetables in these two years was respectively 60 600 000 and 51 000 000 gulden (1 gulden, or guilder = 1 shilling 8 d.; that is 12 gulden = 1£). *The States-man's Yearbook for* 1911, p. 1041.   (*Ed*.).

Agricultural Development in Bourgas, Bulgaria. — *Feuille d'Informations du Ministère de l'Agriculture*, N. 14, Paris, 4 Avril, 1911.

1833

The use of agricultural machinery and implements in the district of Bourgas increases every year. Agricultural machinery is bought from Germany, England and the United States.

Cultivated forage crops are increasing in acreage as the result of the free distribution of alfalfa and other grass seeds by the Government. About 10 000 kgs. (10 tons.) of such seeds were distributed in 1910.

Bulgaria

With a few exceptions in Messemoria, Sozopolis, and Bourgas, phylloxera is destroying the old vineyards everywhere. The Government encourages the restocking of the vineyards with American vines.

Sericulture is progressing to some extent and finds excellent climatic conditions in the department of Bourgas, but mulberry-trees are not sufficient for an extensive development in silk-production.

The breed of cattle is deteriorating as no serious steps have been taken to improve it. Yet live-stock is one of the principal resources of Bulgaria. The latest statistics show that the department of Bourgas has:

Horses	30 112
Mules.	636
Donkeys	11 755
Cattle	111 223
Buffaloes	45 646
Sheep.	1 092 710
Goats.	160 899
Pigs	39 986
Poultry	450 159 (1)

(1) The returns for live-stock for the whole of Bulgaria in Dec. 1905, were

Horses	155 917
Mules.	11 947
Donkeys	124 080
Cattle	1 695 533
Buffaloes	476 872
Sheep.	8 130 997
Goats.	1 384 116
Pigs	465 333
Poultry.	6 408 252

See: *Statistique des superficies cultivées, de la production végétale. et du bétail dans les Pays adhérents. Essai d'inventaire d'après les documents publiés par les Etats.* Institut International d'Agriculture. Rome 1910.   (Ed.)

1334   W. Ewald. **Agricultural Development in the Russian Empire.** (Generalbericht über die wirtschaftliche Entwickelung Russlands). *Export*, N. 15, pp. 267-269. Wien, 13 April, 1911.

Russian
Empire:
Siberia.
Turkestan.
Crimea.
Ferghana.

The first attempts at raising sugar beet in the steppes of Barabin in Siberia have proved so satisfactory that a sugar refinery has already been opened there.

The Congress of Russian Farmers at Kiew passed resolutions favouring the extended use of chemical fertilisers on Russian farms, and calling for special railway tariffs for the transportation of such fertilisers.

Fruit farming has developed to such an extent in Turkestan that express trains are being run a distance of 5000 kilometers to Riga to encourage its exportation. Turkestan exports about 300 million kgs of apples, pears, plums, walnuts, etc., worth in Europe about 187 million francs. Turkestan is also raising now about 50 million francs worth of cotton, all this for the benefit of a population not exceding 6 million inhabitants.

The fruit-farmers in Crimea, who export over 50 million francs worth of fruit to Russia and England, are now organizing a cold storage warehouse modelled on that of Chateaurenard in France.

The great peat bogs near St. Petersburg will soon be worked first for the peat which has commercial value, and then with a view to raising suitable crops in these districts.

The vast territory which stretches between the Amur and Ussuri rivers will slowly be opened up for cultivation. It is rich in cedar, pine, and fir forests, of which some 400 000 sq. kilometers belong to the State. They are already being exploited to meet the requirements of the railways. In five years time the yield of Russian forests has more than doubled and many saw mills have been opened.

There is a splendid future for flax growers, in spite of the tendency in Western Europe to limit the acreage under this crop. Large areas are cultivated with flax in the North without interfering with cereal production. Flax gives work to the peasantry during the winter months in preparing and transporting the products of this crop.

Large sums have been provided for engineering works to stop the sands from encroaching on the fertile black soil lands of the South East.

Siberia is now exporting tinned mutton to England.

Mongolia exports beef to Russia, for the army, at 0.125 francs per pound, each soldier receiving 3/4 of a pound per day.

Cold-storage warehouses are being built in Astrakhan to store the fish which is there obtained in quantities: from 250 to 350 million kilos a year are fished, that is to say five times the yield of the German North Sea fisheries.

: The cotton crop will certainly have tripled in a short time in Ferghana. Great interest is taken in this crop and the yield per hectare is twice that obtained in America. Ferghana alone can supply the needs of the whole Russian Empire and still have cotton to export, such is the excellence of the soil and climate.

Agriculture, Live-Stock. Game and Fisheries in Southern Russia.
Agriculture. Elevage, Chasse et Pêche dans la Russie Méridionale
— *Recueil Consulaire du Royaume de Belgique*, Vol 153, Ière livraison, pp. 1-46. Bruxelles 1911.

1835

The agrarian reforms, by improving the methods of farming and by enlarging the area under cultivation, will increase the yield and thus improve the general economic status of Russia.

Southern Russia exports large quantities of cereals, which are shipped from the ports of Azov and the Black Sea. Farming in these districts has assumed an industrial and commercial character. The exportation of Russian cereals is increasing on the whole, though not in proportion to the increased production, which is absorbed by the home market, where the demand is constantly growing wth the growth of industrial life.

Russia

The principal measures now un der consideration for improving the trade in cereals are the inspection of exports, the development of credit and the building of large elevators.

As a general rule, stock-breeding is much neglected in Southern Russia. The Government is, however, taking an interest in this question, and provides the « moujiks » with pedigree breeding-stock and tries to stimulate competition by organising district and local shows. Besides keeping choice breeding stock in dépôt in the several districts where stud-books are also kept, the Government tries to encourage progress by agricultural education. The curriculum in the training colleges comprises a complete course of study in stock-breeding, book-keeping, veterinary medicine, and dairying. These colleges are provided with a farm where stock-breeding is carried on by the pupils themselves, who thus have a really practical training.

Both native and imported breeds of sheep are raised in Russia. The imported breeds are the Rambouillet merinos, usually large sized, with fleece of medium fineness. ; They are mostly in Southern Russia. The native breeds which are numerous, and very widely spread, are the following: Romanovskaia, from Ekaterinoslav; Tsigano, from Bessarabia ; Karakul, from Kéchétilowskaia and Sokolskaia in the Gove rnment of Poltawa; Tchoujka from Bessarabia, and the Valak breed.

Pig-breeding is carried on mostly in southern Russia, but not yet to any great extent. There is a promising future before it as pork and hogs' bristles are in demand for exportation.

Poultry farming prospers and a large and increasing trade is done in poultry and eggs, which are exported.

Game is plentiful in many parts of Russia. Quails abound in southern Russia, where hares, wolves, and wild boars are also common.

Nearly 100 million francs (£4 000 000) worth of fish is obtained annually from the rivers of Russia. The great sturgeon, common sturgeon, carp. bream, smelt, shad, sterlet of the Don, herring, and a variety of other fish, are found in the South.

1336

Moricz (Austrian Consul.) **The Agricultural Development of the Hinterland of Trebizond.** — *Berichte der K. u. K. Oster-Ung. Konsularämter, Europa-Turkei-Trapezunt,* Jahr 1910, pp. 1-36, Wien.

Ottoman Empire

The cereals raised in the hinterland of Trebizond supply local needs for from two to eight months, according to the year. Wheat, barley and maize are raised. Haricot beans are good and plentiful ; about 33 000 quintals are exported. Hazels are grown extensively, and from 20 to 25 million kgs. of hazel nuts are obtained annually. Tobacco is excellent and the acreage under this crop is extensive ; in 1909, 309 000 kgs of Tobacco were grown in the neighborhood of Trebizond. and 1 575 710 kgs near Platana. Fruit farming is pretty well developed near Trebizond, Laristan and Gümülschane; the best pears and apples are grown near the last named place ; the pears of Gümülschane are sold at Smyrna and Constantinople. As many as 25 000 quintals of fruit are sometimes exported. Eggs are produced in large quantities and 12 000 boxes are yearly shipped to Marseilles. About 100 000 sheep are sent each year to Constantinople; and cattle and goats and their bye-products (hides and mohair) are also exported.

1337

Smits. (Belgian Consul). **Agriculture in British India.** L'Agriculture dans l'Inde Britannique. — *Revue générale Agronomique,* N. 3, p. 106-116. Bruxelles, Mars, 1911.

British India

The soil, seasons, local conditions and usages of agriculture vary to an extraordinary extent in India.

The plough is the principal and often the only agricultural implement, and, except at Madras, Bombay, and the Central Provinces, the share is always made of wood. Cultivators and drills are only in general use in the Deccan (1).

Irrigation is absolutely necessary in India. Lakes, ponds, reservoirs, and canals have been excavated and carefully kept up since remote antiquity. The English have now taken this work over, improving and extending it. There are 41 340 miles of irrigation canals, and in 1908 25 million acres of land were irrigated (2).

The principal drawback to agriculture in India is the scarcity of manures, as the country is relatively poor in mineral fertilisers (3).

The principal crops are rice, wheat, millet, oil-seeds, sugar cane, cotton, jute, tobacco, opium, pepper, tea, coffee, indigo, cinchona, vegetables and fruits (4).

---

(1) " I cannot help suspecting that the system of shallow ploughing, as practised by the Native, and his aversion to ploughs that turn over a broad slice and form a wide furrow, may have something to do with the retention of moisture, and that the effect of deep ploughing would too generally be to lose the very moisture the cultivator so treasures. " JOHN A. VOELCKER. *Report on the Improvement of Indian Agriculture.* Second Edition. Calcutta, 1897, p. 43. (*Ed.*).

(2) Irrigation Works, for which capital accounts are kept, paid 7.79 % in 1908-09 on their capital outlay. The estimated value of the crops irrigated by such Works in 1908-1909 was 61 ½ crores of rupees. (One crore is equivalent to 100 lacs of rupees. equivalent to £666 666. The total irrigated area in British India, in 1909, was 23 349 459 acres. *The Statesman's Yearbook for 1911,* p. 139. (*Ed.*).

(3) Bones are practically the only source of supply of phosphates to the soil. Small quantities of apatite and phosphatic nodules were found by Dr Warth and Mr Parsons at Mussorie (N. W. P.) in 1884, and by Dr Warth in the Eocene of the Eastern Salt Range. Coprolites have been discovered in spots in East Berar and the Upper Godaveri District in Hyderabad, but nowhere in anything like sufficient quantity to be profitably worked. Fish manure, which may be considered partly a phosphatic manure, is prepared in parts along the sea-coast, such as Mangalore (Mysore) and is transported inland within certain distances, being used almost entirely by the coffee planters of Coorg and Mysore. J. VOELCKER, loc. cit., p. 113. (*Ed.*).

(4) The following is the total acreage under the chief crops in British India in 1908-1909:

Rice	75 800 536
Wheat	21 198 764
Other Cereals and Pulse	102 837 820
Sugar Cane	2 254 067
Tea	520 487
Cotton	12 958 974
Oil-Seeds	14 105 598
Indigo	286 354
Tobacco	953 712

Besides cotton, other fibres occupied 3 558 171 acres, of which 2 835 454 grew jute. Coffee plantations 52 780 acres in Madras, 44 316 acres in Coorg. The total area cropped in 1908-09 was 246 189 000 acres, the net area cropped being 218 039 793 acres. *The Statesman's Yearbook for 1911,* p. 137. (*Ed.*).

Rice is the staple food of the people ; more than half of the area under rice is in the province of Bengal. In 1908-09 the Indian rice crop amounted to 19 945 490 tons. In the same year 1 512 000 tons were exported.

Wheat grows in the cold season ; the area under wheat is mostly in the Punjab and frontier states, the United Provinces, the Central Provinces, Berar, Bombay, and Bengal. Bearded wheat is the most common Indian variety ; farmers prefer it because it does not shed its grain so soon as other varieties and therefore can stand longer after ripening. About 19 million acres are under wheat.

Some 25 million acres are under millet, and about 1 ¼ million under tobacco.

Opium is grown in some of the native states, especially Indore, Gwalior, Bhopal, Udaipur. For some years past this crop has been greatly reduced in Behar and Benares.

Three fourths of the area under cotton is in the Presidencies of Bombay and Madras, the Central Provinces, Berar, and the Punjab. The best varieties of cotton can only be grown in soil which retains its moisture for a long time or where the rainy season is of long duration. This is noticeably the case with Broach and Dharwar cotton.

Pepper is one of the most ancient exports of India. It grows wild in the forests of Malabar and Travancore, and is cultivated on a large scale by native and European planters in Southern India.

The acreage under jute is estimated at 300 000 acres and this product has held for some years past the first place in Indian exports. The qualities most in demand are obtained from plants grown in hilly districts ; the low lands produce coarser fibre.

Tea plantations cover more than 625 000 acres in Bengal, Assam and Burma. Tea grows at altitudes of from 550 to 11 500 feet. The different varieties grown in India are : Chinese, native Assam, Manipur or Burmese, Naga and Cachar.

Coffee plantations are mostly in the States of Mysore, Coorg, Travancore and the mountains of Nilgiri and Shevaroy in the Madras Presidency. Coffee grows at altitudes of 2,300 to 5,500 feet. The average yield per acre is from 270 to 360 lbs.

Cinchona is a generic term applied to trees producing quinine, quinaquina, cinchonine, and cinchonidine. Darjeeling and the Nilgiri Hills are the centres whence these products are obtained. The area of these plantations is decreasing, and does not now exceed 4 000 acres. The plantations at Nilgiri yield two kinds of bark, red and yellow.

The Central Provinces, Bengal, the United Provinces and Bombay produce linseed.

Sesame grows in Bengal, the Central Provinces, Burma, Madras, the United Provinces, and Bombay.

Colza is principally grown in the Punjab, the United Provinces, and Bengal.

Pea-nuts are grown in Southern India and Burma.

The Hindoos raise indigo. Recently both Natal and Guatemala indigo have been introduced into India. The indigo plantations are in Bengal, Madras, the United Provinces and the Punjab.

The most important fruit is the Mango which in good seasons is the staple food of the poor of Northern India for several weeks.

The Indian forests cover some 12 ½ million acres. The most common timber trees are teak, sal, deodar, ebony, Sandal wood, *Ficus elastica*, *soundari* (building timber), pine, fir, oak, beech, aspen, date palm, fig and bamboo.

H. RUSSIER & H. BRENIER. **Resources of Farm and Forest in French Indo-China.** (L'Indochine française). — In 8°. pp. 356 + 4 cartes. Paris, Colin, 1911.

1838

This book consists of an introduction (history of the explorations in Indo-China and bibliography) and four parts : geographical description ; population ; economic resources ; political and administrative organization. Here only that part which deals with the resources of farm and forest is summarised.

French
Indo-China

Forests. The great variety of species of timber trees and the inadequate means of communication make the exploitation of the forests of Indo-China a difficult matter. The following table shows the volume of rough timber produced in the several States of the French Indo-Chinese Customs Union in 1908 :

	Timber c. meters	Wood fuel c. meters	Free deliveries c. meters	Total c. meters
Cochinchina	91 309	207 975	7 825	307 109
Cambodia	100 669	133 561	44 789	279 019
Tonkin	39 570	213 589	4 054	257 213
Annam.	48 172	66 564	501	115 237
Totals	279 720	621 689	57 169	958 578

The following table shows the commercial importance of the forest products which are exported :

Products	Average for 1902-1906	1907	1908		
India-rubber (liana) . .	510 tons (value 3 336 000 francs)	212 tons	36.9 tons		
Badiaa or Star-anis (1)	40 »	53 »	29.9 »		
Cinnamon..	330 »	300.5 »	210.6 »		
Cardamom	250 »	255.9 »	412.5 »	» worth frcs.	1 252 000
Benzoin	33 »	70 »	30.6 »	»	91 900
Stick-lac	390 »	501.4 »	524 »	»	1 048 000
Gamboge	27 »	43 «	35 186 »	»	87 900
Cunau (Dye plant)	. 5635 »	4651 »	3898 »	»	584 000
Rattan	.1800 »	2245 » (worth frcs. 561 000)	875 »	»	218 000

Star-anis grows only 'n the district of Langson.

Cinnamon is plentiful in Annam (Thanh-hoa, Quang-nam, | Quang-ngai).

Cardamom from the Cardamom Mountains (Krevanh mountains) in Cambodia is scarce but highly valued ; the so-called wild carda-mom of Boloven and of Upper Tonkin is much less valuable.

Benzoin comes mostly from Hua-panh.

The lacquer-tree proper is found in Cochinchina and Cambodia, but is still commoner in Tonkin, especially in the Phu-tho region. This tree besides the lacquer gum produces a green vegetable tallow which is highly prized. Stick-lac is produced by the secretions of certain insects which live by preference on the *Cajanus indicus.* Gamboge is a speciality of Cambodia and of Laos in Siam.

Oleaginous trees, which are only just beginning to be made use of, are plentiful in Indo-China. The «*Abrasin*» and the «*Ban-ooulier*», or walnut of the Moluccas, are found in Tonkin and in North Annam, the *Bancoulier* is also found in Cochinchina. *Gar-cinia tonkinensis* grows in the basins of the Black River and the Clear River; *Camellia drupifera* in Tanh-hoa. The Chinese tallow-tree (*Stellingia sebifera*), the leaves of which can be used to feed the *con cuoc,* or wild silk-worm, from which Florentine horse-hair (*crin de Florence*) is made, grows in Tonkin and North Annam ;

---

(1) Star-anis has been known in Europe under the names *Anis de la Chine, de la Sibérie, Foeniculum sinense, Badian.* The latter name, from the Arabic *Bádyan* (Fennel) has been long used. This name *Badian* was first used by Picere Domet, the author of *Histoire géneral des drogues,* in 1694. E. Gıɪ,-DEMEISTER u. Fr. HOFFMANN, *Die Actherischen Oele.* Berlin, 1899, p. 457.

(*Ed.*).

Calophyllum Inophyllum of the Guttifereae or gum-bearing family, is found in Cochinchina and Cambodia.

A saponiferous tree, *Sapindus Mukorossi*, grows in Tonkin and Annam.

The Indo-chinese flora is also rich in Dipterocarpeae, yielding resins and oleo-resins, and mangroves, from which tannins and dyes are obtained. *Cus-cus* or Vetiver, Lemon-grass and *Ylang-ylang* are plants from which perfumes are distilled (1). Indo China produces also rushes for matting, medicinal plants, etc.

Crops. Indochina is the second rice growing country of the world, the first being Burma.

From 3 to 3 3/4 million acres are under rice in Cochinchina; from 2 to 2 1/4 million in Tonkin; 1 3/4 million acres, or 4.5 % of the total area, in Cambodia.

Rice is generally transplanted; it is only sown broadcast in certain districts (for instance in South Annam), or in the case of certain varieties. There is one crop in the year in Cambodia, Cochinchina, and South Annam (January to February); two in Tonkin, North Annam and Central Annam. A good average yield is 16 to 20 cwt. per acre.

The cultivation of maize is spreading throughout Indochina. The exports of this cereal rose from 107 tons in 1904 to 92,000 tons in 1909.

Pulse, sweet potatoes, yams, taro, manioc, and arrowroot are raised all over the country, but more especially in Tonkin and North Annam; sweet potatoes and manioc, more especially this latter, are staple crops from which tapioca is made. An excellent kind of maccaroni, is prepared from a small green haricot, the *dau-*

---

(1) Cus-cus, or Vetiver is a perennial Grass: *Andropogon muricatus* Retz The leaves of this Grass have no smell, but the roots give a special strong myrrh-like odour. This plant is common on the Coromandel Coast, in Mysore, in Bengal and in Burma; it grows in Reunion, Mauritius and the Philippines, and also in the West Indies, in Porto-rico and Jamaica, and in Brazil.

Lemongrass is *Andropogon citratus* D. C., its essence being much prized by the natives of India as a protection agaiust cholera. Lemongrass is cultivated on a large scale on the Malabar coast, in Travancore. The essence of Lemongrass is also produced at Singapore, Ceylon, in S. Thomé and in Brazil at Porto Alegre.

Trivandrum in Travancore is the chief market for Lemongrass essence; the exportation from the Malabar-coast was in 1897 3000 boxes, each box containing 12 flasks, altogether with 7 1/2 kgr. of essence. E. GILDEMESTER u. FR. HOFFMANN: *Die Aetherischen Oele.* 1899, pp. 367,371.   (*Ed.*).

xanh. The pepper tree is cultivated in Cochinchina (Hatien), and more especially in Cambodia (Kampot).

Tea plantations are successful in Annam (Ha-tinh, Quang-nam) and in Tonkin (Phu-tho, Ninh-binh, and Bac-giang).

Excellent coffee could also be grown in Tonkin (Provinces of Ninh-binh and Hannam) were it not for the Borer parasite (I).

Sugar-cane grows throughout the country, but is most common in Annam (Quang-nam, Quang-ngai, and Phu-yen), in Cambodia, and in Eastern Cochinchina.

Lastly we must mention betel, areca-nut (Cochinchina and Central Annam), and tobacco which is grown in Tonkin (Provinces of Hai-duong, Kien-an, Thai-binh), in Central Annam (region of Cau-lo), in Eastern Cochinchina, and in Cambodia.

The principal fibre-plants of Indochina are cotton, ramie, jute, kapok, and mulberry-trees, and the more important oleaginous plants are the cocoa-nut tree, sesame, earth-nut, castor-oil plant, etc.

The chief agricultural districts are the valley of the Mekong in Cambodia and the Province of Tanh-hoa for cotton ; the basin of the Black River, North Annam (region of Phuqui, in Nhgé-an), Laos (to the north-east of Khong), and Cochinchina (province of Baria) for ramie ; the Tonkin delta and Central Annam (Binh-dinh) for mulberries ; Cochinchina (along the Mé-Kong), Cambodia (shores of the Gulf of Siam), South Annam and Central Annam for the Cocoa-nut palm ; Cambodia, Eastern Cochinchina, South Annam and Tonkin for sesame ; Cochinchina and Annam for pea-nuts ; Tonkin for the castor-oil plant, more especially the provinces of Son-tay, Phuc-yen, and Bac-giang.

Hevea gum trees grow readily in the red soil of Eastern Cochinchina where the number of trees now planted (1910) is estimated at 1 000 000.

Stock-Breeding. The principal live-stock in Indo-China are buffaloes, oxen, horses, pigs, and poultry.

---

(1) Borer-*Xylotrechus quadrupes.* This insect punctures the stalks of the coffee-plant, penetrating right to the pith, and destroying the central ti - sues of the plant. Plantations exposed to the full sun are more readily attacked by these Borers. This insect does much damage in Coorg and Wynaae (India), and in lower Cochinchina. Almost all the stalks of the *Coffea arabica* at Saigon are attacked by this pest, the *C. liberica* would seem to be immune. (E. RAOUL & E. DAROLLE, *Culture du Caféier,* p. 30-31, Paris, Chal. lamel, 1897). See also H. MAXWELL-LEFROY, *Indian Insect Life,* p. 374. Calcutta and London, 1909.   (*Ed.*)

Oxen (*Bos taurus*) and zebus (*Bos indicus*) work in the rice fields ; in Eastern Cochinchina and Cambodia they are used more for draught. The « Stieng ox », a special Cambodian breed, produces trotting animals.

The provinces of Yen-bay and Bac-kan in Tonkin are noted for their breeds of oxen as also the districts of Vinh, Tanh-hoa, Lang-bian, Phu-yen and Binh-thuan in Annam, and Cambodia.

The elephant is bred at Laos and in Cambodia.

Unfortunately severe epizootic diseases, which are of frequent occurrence, hinder the stock-breeding industry throughout the colony. A special zootechnical service which is well developed in Tonkin does its best to ward off and counteract these diseases.

Sheep do not do well in Indo-China, owing to the excessive moisture of the climate. But in spite of this a Malay breed, known as the Kelantan, has done well at the agricultural station of Yen-Dinh, in Tanh-hoa.

The silk-worms of Indo-China produce 5 or 6 broods a year ; they have small cocoons (1 100 to 1 200 to the kilogram as compared to 400 to 450 in the case of the fine annual French breeds), and from 22 to 23 kgr. of cocoons are required for 1 kgr. of silk; but the breed is robust and the silk has a beautiful sheen.

Stations for silk-growing have been opened at Phu-lang-thuong (Tonkin), Hué, Tau-Chau (Cochinchina) and Pnom-penh.

Hunting and Fishing. Hunters and trappers obtain valuable spoils such as elephants' tusks, rhinoceros horns, tiger skins, aigrettes, marabou feathers, etc.

After rice, fish is the staple food of the natives, and comes next to rice in importance as an export. From 11 to 12 million francs worth per annum is exported.

PAILLARD. (French Consul). **Agriculture in Korea.** *Rapports Commerciaux des Agents Diplomatiques et Consulaires de France.* N. 943, pp. 1-12. Paris, 1911.

1889

For the past two years agriculture has improved in Korea continuously as the result of the encouragement given it by the Japanese authorities. Agricultural development has, however, to struggle against serious drawbacks, the chief of which are ascribed to the excessive number of large land-owners who take no personal interest in improving their lands. Korean farms yield only one harvest a year; but by alternating the crops and improving the methods of irrigation and manuring two crops could be obtained in the year.

Japanese Empire: Korea

The chief Korean exports are pulse grains such as miso, soya, etc.

The cotton crop, of which great hopes had been entertained, was very unsatisfactory in 1910. Presumably this check was fortuitous and this crop may be expected to give the results hoped for in the future. Mokpo in Southern Korea, is the chief market for cotton.

The possibilities of growing sugar beets continue to attract the attention of Japanese capitalists, but so far no progress has been made in this direction beyond a few experiments. In one district alone, Wang-ju, there are said to be 60 000 hectares of land suited to this crop.

Ginseng, which for many years was one of the principal resources of Korea, has undergone a further set back. It is not thought that this crop can regain its former importance for two or three years.

From Fusan to the district north of Pyeng-yang there is a stretch of barren hilly and mountainous land ; the Japanese authorities are doing their best to reclaim it, and considerable sums are spent each year on reafforestation. By the exercise of care and skill it is hoped that more prosperous conditions will prevail in a few years' time and that Korea may no longer need to import building timber, which now figures for a sum of 1 680 000 yen (a yen = 2.60 frcs) in the official statistics (1).

1340

P. CLERGET. **Production and Trade in the Philippines.** — *La Géographie*, XXIII, N. 4, pp. 286-287. Paris, 15 Avril 1911.

Philippine Islands

The Philippines are now the greatest producers of copra (⅓ of the world's crop) ; three fifths of the copra exported, valued at 22 507 000 frcs, is shipped to France where it is in great demand for the manufacture of vegetable butter (*végétaline, cocose*), which has become an important article in Marseilles.

The climate of these islands is particularly favourable to the cocoanut tree and the high prices obtaining encourage the planters.

---

(1) Korea is a purely agricultural country; the cultivated area is about 4 500 000 acres, but the methods of cultivation are of a backward and primitive type, and the means of communication few and difficult, though improvement is gradually being made in this respect. In the south, rice, wheat, beans and grains of all kinds are grown, besides tobacco and cotton; in the north the chief crops are barley, millet and oats. 2200 acres are under cotton, the value of the cotton produced in 1909 being about 74 000 £. The principal exports were in 1909: rice, 5 530 557 yen; (soy) beans 3 513 753 yen: cowhides 815 210 yen; cattle 426 249 yen. *The Statesman's Yearbook for 1911*, p. 996.   (*Ed.*).

The output of Manila hemp has increased and the prices it fetches fluctuate as it competes with other textile fibres such as sisal and New Zealand hemp.

Almost the entire crop of Manila hemp (1) (1 278 548 bales) is exported to the United States and England.

Now that the United States has opened its markets duty free to exports from the Philippines, the sugar industry has revived and farming in all its branches will doubtless develop.

The irrigation committee, formed in June 1908, has planned improvements to be made in the canals now existing and proposes to extend them to other districts. These plans deal with an area of 129 000 hectares (319 000 acres) and entail an expenditure of 13 and a half million francs. (£ 540 000). Several experiment stations and model farms have been opened with a view to encouraging scientific farming.

The finest tobacco is grown in the valley of the Cagayan, where small farms prevail. There are no fewer than 49 861 farmers in this district on an area of 25 thousand hectares (61 750 acres); in 1909 they harvested 18 million kgs (18 000 tons) of tobacco.

Attempts at forming rubber plantations have been unsuccessful. 10 355 000 hectares (25 577 000 acres), are occupied by forests which are only now beginning to be exploited (2).

Agricultural Development in the Dutch East Indies. — *La Quinzaine Coloniale*, N. 6, p. 201. Paris, 25 Mars, 1911.

1341

The experiments made for some years past at the Government station of Tjiepetir in farming gutta-percha are now yielding results not only in the shape of gutta, but also caoutchouc and coca.

Dutch
East Indies

---

(1) See n⁰ 114, Bull. for Jan. 1911.

(2) 15 883 577 dollars worth of Manila hemp was exported from the Philippines and 6 657 740 dollars worth of copra during the business year, closing on June 30, 1909. In the year 1910, the export of Manila hemp was worth 17 404 922 dollars, and that of copra 9 153 951 dollars. The tobacco exported in 1910 was valued at 1 619 744 dollars and the Manila cigars at 2 973 630 dollars. The sugar export for 1910 is valued at 7 040 690 dollars. The wide forests of valuable timber, gum and dye woods are under the supervision of the Forest Bureau, which frames plans and rules for their protection and working. The Islands are divided into 14 forest districts, each containing a number of forest stations (55 in all), in charge of foresters, rangers, or inspectors. Each forest contains native trees of many species, which are officially classified in four groups, according to their commercial value. *The Statesmans' Yearbook for* 1910, p. 556; and *for* 1911, p. 557.   (*Ed.*).

At present the gutta is still extracted solely from the leaves which are obtained by pruning.

The Government has opened an experimental field for the cultivation of *Hevea* at Langsar, but the plantations only cover 500 *bouws* (877 acres) as the Government rightly deems it unwise to experiment on a large scale. It must be noted that *Coffea robusta*, which does very well there, has not been cultivated, on the ground that the cost of up-keep is too high to allow of a profit.

It would seem that excellent cotton could be grown in the east of the archipelago. Experiments have been made in paper manufacture, and samples were to be seen at the Brussels exhibition made from various material : rice straw, sugar-cane, bamboos, « alang-alang », *Albizzia moluccana*, agave fibre waste, maize straw.

It is interesting to remember that three varieties of coffee were examined by an expert of Soerabaja in November 1909, and were found of good quality and sold. They are « quillou », « excelsa », and « robusta ».

1842   MUIRHEAD COLLINS. **The Agricultural Development Dry-Farming and the Future of Australia.** — *Journal of the Royal Society of Arts.* N. 3047, pp. 541-554. London, April 14, 1911.

In Australia with increasing knowledge, improved methods of farming and with irrigation, the evil effects of drought steadily diminish. So it is with land classed as desert. It may be said that, as science advances, the desert recedes.

Australia

The possibilities, however, of Australia, as regards rainfall and production, can at once be realised by a consideration of the following facts: Land with an annual rainfall in excess of 18 inches, provided the soil is of good quality, has been considered for some time suitable for farming settlements. It is computed that Australia has not less than 529 000 000 acres of such land, that s, more than the areas of France, Germany and Spain together.

Recently, a conference was held at Adelaide to consider the question of dry farming. Expert officials from all parts of the Commonwealth attended. It was pointed out that many millions of acres of agricultural land, of which the rainfall varied from 10 to 16 inches per annum, were awaiting development.

The Minister of Agriculture said that South Australia alone had 30 000 000 acres, and that last season 55 per cent of the wheat produced in that State came from land having less than 16 inches rainfall. It can be seen from this what a revolution is being effected by dry farming (1).

Australia is a land unrivalled in the production of wool. Australian farmers have made increasing efforts towards the development of their flocks. When pure merino rams were first introduced into Australia from Spain, they averaged about 3 ½ lbs. of wool. To-day the stud merino ram yields over 40 lbs, and the average for a million of flock sheep is nearly 8 lbs. at each shearing.

As a wheat producer, Australia is in its infancy. The production of wheat for last year was 89 735 000 bushels, of which 28 943 000 centals was exported. The area at present under wheat represents probably one-twentieth of the lands of Australia fitted to produce crops under existing conditions of cultivation, and probably only one-fortieth of the area in which wheat could be grown under scientific methods of dry-farming.

Australia has splendid areas of land available for irrigation. It is often said that her rivers are relatively insignificant, but still it has been unmistakably shown that if their waters are properly conserved and distributed over the soil, instead of being allowed to run to the sea, they will become a most important factor in Australian national wealth.

The purpose of irrigation will be to increase the output on the lands already settled, and the indefinite expansion inland of the areas suitable for farming. A remarkable feature of the inland country is its sweetness. Hundreds of miles from the coast, the soil in good years is thickly coated with a great crop of natural grasses and herbages which are nutritious right down to the ground. This ample territory of light rainfall is always ready with its prolific response to moisture. Give it water, and it will grow almost anything.

---

(1) "Australia, larger than the continental United States, is vitally interested in dry-farming, for one-third of its vast area is under a rainfall of less than 10 inches, and another third is under a rainfall of between 10 and 20 inches. Two-thirds of the area of Australia, if reclaimed at all, must be reclaimed by dry-farming. The realisation of this condition has led several Australians to visit the United States for the purpose of learning the methods employed in dry-farming. The reports on dry-farming in America by Surveyor-General Strawbridge and Senator J. H. Mc Coll have done much to initiate a vigorous propaganda in behalf of dry-farming on Australia." JOHN A. WIDTSOE, Dry-Farming, New York, 1911, p. 393.   (Ed.).

Round some of the artesian wells of the interior beautiful
oases of native grasses and edible shrubs, of lucerne, cereals, and
many varieties of fruits are found. In the State of Victoria, which,
although by no means the least favoured by rainfall, has pioneered
irrigation in Australia, we find that already £ 3 500 000 have been
spent on the construction of irrigation works during the last
twenty-five years, utilizing over 1 000 000 acres for irrigation, and
giving a stock and domestic water-supply over 6 000 000 acres.

It is anticipated that the present rush of settlers will speedily
exhaust the irrigated land available in Victoria, and therefore it is
a satisfaction to know that an even bigger scheme is in progress on
the other side of the Murray, in New South Wales.

In this State a great dam, with a water-holding capacity
nearly as great as that the famous Assuan Dam, is being constructed across the Murrumbidgee River at Barrenjack.

South Australia is also initiating works on a big scale. It is
safe to say that for many years to come Australia will be duplica-
ting these schemes and making large areas of land available for the
stranger from over the sea.

1343   AERY and MONROE N. WORK. **Tuskegee Institute and the Agricul-
tural Development of the Negro in tke United States and
Africa.** — *The Southern Workman.* February, 1911. Hampton,
Virginia, pp. 73-87.

Every year since 1891 Tuskegee Institute has conducted a Negro
farmers' conference for the benefit not only of those who are interested in the production of cotton, corn, garden truck, cattle,
United   pork, poultry, eggs and other marketable goods, but also of those
States.   who are concerned with the establishment of better schools and
West-Africa more attractive homes. Dr. Washington, a Negro, has never failed
to present to his people the possibilities of winning from the soil
through skill and perseverance, a comfortable and profitable living
and of climbing, shoulder to shoulder with the Southern white man,
to a higher round of civilization.

From many states and from many walks of life more than
two thousand men and women, members of the white and the
black races, came gladly to Tuskegee to learn what is being done
in the South to improve farming and rural life. Dr. Washington
said that the old farming methods are passing away and that the
rural negroes will have to rely more and more upon themselves to
provide food, implements, seeds, fertilizers and other necessary goods
for the production of their cotton and garden crops.

In 1908, an agricultural school was started at Akubo in Gambia. In the Gold Coast Colony agricultural education has been more successful. One evidence of the deep interest that the natives are taking in agriculture is that the corner stone of the S. B. Thomas Agricultural College was laid at Maleang in Sierra Leone in 1909.

Agricultural shows or fairs are being used extensively throughout Negro Africa to stimulate and instruct the natives. They are having a farreaching effect on the development of the country. Agricultural demonstration has been carried on in West Africa for several years, and to facilitate this work numerous experiment stations, or botanic gardens, have been established. Seeds and plants are here grown for distribution and the stations themselves serve as model farms. On the Gold Coast, natives who have received agricultural education are used to a large extent as demonstration agents. In 1908 one of these native workers from the Ashantee agricultural department travelled through the various parts of that country and lectured on the cultivation and preparation of cocoa and rubber.

This summary of African agriculture shows that there is much promise and great possibilities in the developpement of both the natives and the continent on which they live. There is but little doubt that by the end of the present century Africa will have taken its place as one of the world's greatest producers and exporters of agricultural products. Already — through the introduction of modern agricultural methods — the wealth of the people is being very greatly increased and their condition very much improved.

Modern agriculture, as it is now being introduced into Negro Africa, is proving to be one of the chief factors in the redemption of the Dark Continent.

CH. F. BARRETT. **Agricultural Education and Development in Oklahoma.** *Farm and Ranch.* Dallas, Texas, March 18th, 1911.

1344

The six district agricultural colleges of Oklahoma were created by the first and second legislatures and are maintained wholly at the State expense, and in addition to the State experiment stations attached to these schools the State has provided for 69 demonstration farms of 40 acres each which are worked directly under the supervision and control of the State Board of Agriculture.

United States: Oklahoma

These colleges and schools, experiment stations and demonstration farms are closely connected with the Country Farmer's Institute system and comprise in their entirety the Oklahoma method of dealing with the subject of practical education for the agricultural masses.

Each of the State's agricultural institutions issues an annual report and the Agricultural College publishes a paper « The New Education ». In addition to these publications, the State Experiment Station publishes numerous bulletins and reports. Plant breeding, fertilization, cultivation tests, soil surveys, seed analyses, live stock breeding experiments, feeding tests, etc. embrace a few of the important subjects to which their attention has been directed These publications are furnished free to members of the Farmers' Institute (1).

1345   H. A. BALLON.   **Report on Agriculture in Florida.**   *West Indian Bulletin*, Vol. XI, No. 3, Imp. Agr. Dep. — Barbados.

United States: Florida. British West Indies

Visiting the Florida State University and Experiment Station the writer was impressed by the remarkable progress made in the improvement of the quality and yield of maize. The average yield in the State was about 12 to 13 bushels per acre. Now crops of 100 bushels per acre are often produced under careful treatement and the record yield was very much greater.

In Bulletin No. 100 of the Florida Experiment Station the following figures are given,

Yield of maize in Florida:

1908. . . . . . . 4 351 000 bushels, at the rate of 10.5 bushels per acre
1909. . . . . . . 8 379 000   »   »   »   » 12.6   »   »   »

Value of principal crops in Florida :

Oranges . . . . $ 4 221 000
Cotton (Sea Island and Upland) . . . .   »   3 653 080
Maize . . . .   »   3 409 000

These figures show that maize is a crop of considerable value in Florida, in spite of the fact that the average yield for the whole State is lower than that at which the crop gives a profit.

_____

(1) In Oklahoma, the Agricultural and Mechanical College, founded in 1891 had, in 1909, 38 professors and 651 students; while the coloured Agricultural and Normal University, with 13 instructors, has 360 students.

Oklahoma is mainly agricultural: The yield of Maize in 1909 was 101 150 000 bushels; of wheat 15 680 000 bushels; of oats 15 950 000 bushels. Other products are potatoes, hay, sorghum, fruits and cotton. The cotton crop for 1909 on 1 767 000 acres amounted to 573 786 bales. Flax is also widely grown. The western part is devoted to stock-breeding. In 1910 the stock comprised 355 000 milch cows, and 1 637 000 other cattle; 1 302 000 hogs, 108 000 sheep, 804 000 horses and 191 000 mules. There are few manufacturing industries, flour and grist-milling, cotton ginning, the manufacture of cotton-seed oil and oil-cake being the more important. *The Statesman's Yearbook for 1911,* p. 503.   (Ed.).

The figures relating to yield and general improvement are of special interest when compared with the conditions existing in certain of the West Indian islands, where large amounts of maize are imported, and where it is planted as a catch crop, or one of minor importance. Good maize can be raised in these Islands and with the proper methods of improvement by selection and of drying and storing, this crop might easily become of much greater consequence than it is at present.

Great activity is also shown in Florida in the development of the cultivation of small fruits and vegetables for the northern market. Certain districts raise particular crops such as strawberries, tomatoes, cucumbers, musk melons, water melons, pine-apples, and Irish potatoes, some of which are coming into serious competition with the greenhouse and field crops of the North (1).

Agricultural Development in Salvador. *Questions Diplomatiques et Coloniales,* N. 339, p. 407-413. Paris, 1 Avril 1911.

1846

There is very little unproductive land in Salvador, which thus contrasts with its sister republics where vast areas are still uncultivated. Even the slopes of the Santa Ana, San Salvador, San Miguel and San Vincent volcanoes are covered with coffee plantations almost to their summits.

Salvador

The *Myroxylon peruiferum,* from which is obtained the balsam improperly known as Peruvian balsam, used in the preparation of

---

(1) In 1900, only about 12.6 % of the area of Florida was under cultivation, but a considerable area is being reclaimed. The chief products are pine-apples and oranges, the former fruit being grown almost nowhere else in the United States. Other crops are tobacco, 3 195 000 lbs in 1909; rice, 25 000 bushels in 1909; besides maize, oats, peas and pea-nuts. In 1909 the cotton area was 237 000 acres and the yield 62 930 bales. Forests of valuable timber cover three-fourths of the State, and large quantities of pitch-pine are exported as well as oak-timber for ship-building. Tar, turpentine and rosin are prepared in increasing quantities. From Pensacola, tar, resin and turpentine are exported to the value of over 500 000 £ sterling annually. The tobacco industries are prosperous, and Key West and Tampa compete with Cuba in the manufacture of fine cigars. In 1905, the output of spirits of turpentine was 12 872 869 gallons and of resin 1 445 902 barrels. Phosphate rock is an important mineral product of Florida, but little of it is used in the manufacture of fertilisers, wich consist largely of cotton-seed meal. *The Statesman's Yearbook for 1911.*   (*Ed.*).

perfumes, grows only in Salvador. It was for a long time the exclusive monopoly of the native Indians. (1)

Salvador is preeminently an agricultural country ; the land is much sub-divided, and there are very many small farmers owning only one or two *manzanas*. (A *manzana* = 6989 sq. metres or 8317 sq. yds.). These farmers are active and industrious and raise maize, haricot beans, and tobacco for the local markets.

The large landowners prefer to devote their attention to coffee, sugar cane, and indigo plantations, or else they breed live-stock.

The Government opened an agricultural training college in 1907, under the management of a French agricultural engineer.

There is no market for the tropical fruits of Salvador owing to the difficulties in the way of rapid transit to the United States, for Salvador has no outlet on the Atlantic.

Exportation of Coffee: value in gold dollars (a gold dollar =4 s.)

	1902	1903	1904
Germany	407 000	528 000	885 000
United States . . .	448 000	750 000	988 000
France	1 231 000	1 693 000	1 999 000
Great Britain . . .	339 000	505 000	747 000
Italy	470 000	515 000	681 000

This table shows that the agricultural exports of Salvador are increasing from year to year, and that the chief trade of the country is with France.

---

(1) According to Baillon, *Myroxylon peruiferum* is a variety of *Toluifera peruiferum*; this and *T. Balsamum* he considers the only species of *Toluifera;* but Peruvian balsam he thinks is extracted from a variety of *Toluifera Balsamum*, which is indistinguishable from that which supplies balsam of Tolu. Peruvian balsam is known by that name because it used to be shipped to Europe from the port of Callao in Peru. It gives rise to important colonies in Salvador and the exploitation of the Miroxylon forests is a real industry there. Over 120,000 kgs (264 000 lbs) of this product are exported.

DUJARDIN, BEAUMETZ & EGASSE. *Les plantes médicinales*, Paris, 1889 ; and JACOB DE CARDEMOY, *Les plantes à Gommes et à Résines*, Paris, 1911.

(*Ed.*)

The balsam exported from Salvador in the first six months of 1910 was worth 39 187 silver dollars. The export of coffee in the same period was worth 4 541 446 silver dollars, and that of indigo 107 936 silver dollars. (The *Dollar* of 100 *centavos*, has a nominal value of 4 s., its real value is about 19 *d*). *The Statesman's Yearbook* for 1911. p. 1197.   (*Ed.*)

SAPPER. **The Economic Status and Agricultural Progress of the   1847
Lesser Antilles.** (Die wirtschaftlichen Verhältnisse der Kleinen
Antillen). — *Mitteilungen aus Justus Perthes' Geographischer
Anstalt,* März Heft, s. 125. Gotha, 1911.

The British group of the Lesser Antilles passed through a period of economic and agricultural depression as a result of the abolition of slavery, and many Englishmen who had settled there returned to the United Kingdom. This depression was most marked
in the Virgin Islands and at Antigua.

The British Colonial Government has, however, recently started a splendid work of reorganization, both from a financial and
an agricultural stand-point. To the Agricultural Service is due
credit for reviving the prosperity of the sugar-cane plantations
by granting subsidies, organising exhibitions, by agricultural training, etc. At the same time it has improved the sugar refining
industry. The sugar-cane plantations were restricted to the most
favourable districts; auxiliary crops were introduced and those already existing were improved. To this end attention was paid to
the cocoa-nut groves of Trinidad, Grenada, St. Lucia, St. Vincent, and Dominica, cotton plantations were started at St. Vincent, in the Grenadines, at Montserrat and in the Virgin islands;
lemon-groves at Montserrat, Dominica, and Trinidad; and bananas, pineapples and onions were grown at Grenada. Thanks to
these Government measures, all the British islands of the Lesser
Antilles and especially St. Vincent have made real agricultural progress.

The climate of the Dutch Lesser Antilles is inferior to that of
the British possessions; they are subject to severe drought which
also affects the Dutch group of the Windward Islands. Yet, in spite
of this, the efforts of the Dutch colonial government have improved
the economic and agricultural status of these islands.

The islands of Curaçao and Bonaire produce phosphates, and
sisal grass is grown there. Cotton plantations are extending in
St. Martin, and the straw hat industry is compensating Curaçao
for the decline in its liquor trade. A school has been opened at
Saba for training workmen in the making of straw hats; and in
1906 the exports were worth 831 000 francs (£. 33 240), as against
293 000 frcs (£. 11 720) in 1904.

The value of the agricultural exports from the Dutch WestIndies
rose to 2 177 693 frcs. (£. 87107) in 1906 as against 593 754 frcs
(£. 23749) in 1901. Experiments are now being made with sisal-
grass plantations at St. Eustache.

Marginal note: I esser Antilles: Leeward Islands. Windward Islands. Dutch West Indies Danish West Indies. Guadeloupe, etc.

St. Thomas, St. John and St. Croix, of the Danish group of the Lesser Antilles offer a splendid field for agricultural enterprise.

The French group of the Lesser Antilles: Guadeloupe, Marie-Galante, Les Saintes, Désirade, Martinique, St. Barthèlemy, are most exposed to danger from volcanic eruptions and from hurricanes, and their progress is variable, nevertheless the cacao and coffee plantations are paying. It is much to be desired that the Government should introduce agricultural training and modern improvements in the cultivation of the sugar-cane and the manufacture of sugar (1).

1848 JANSSEN (Belgian Consul at Montevideo). **Agriculture in Uruguay.** — Recueil consulaire. Ministère des Affaires Étrangères du Royaume de Belgique, Vol. 153, N. 2, pp. 61-72, Bruxelles, 1911.

The climate of Uruguay is temperate, and quite similar to that of the South of France. It rains on an average 60 days a year.

Uruguay Of the rivers which flow through Uruguay, the Rio Negro, an affluent of the Uruguay, waters a vast stretch of country and along its banks are situated the most fertile fields in the country. There are 1901 schools and one university in Uruguay, frequented respectively in 1908 by 99 025 school children (9.75 % of the population) and by 600 students.

Some 600 000 hectares (1 482 000 acres) or 3.15 % of the total area of the Republic, are under cultivation (2). The average

---

(1) In Guadéloupe the chief cultures are: sugar cane, grown on 26 000 hectares, employing 35 000 persons; coffee, on 6 000 hectares, employing 18 000 persons; cacao, 2540 hectares; manioc, 6 926 hectares. The forests, covering 71 256 hectares, of the mountainous district, are interspersed with valuable timber, which is little worked. *The Statesman's Yearbook* for 1911, p. 819.

(2) To these must be added 14 800 000 ha. or 36 556 000 acres of grazing land in 1910. For 1909 the areas of the chief crops in Uruguay were: wheat 276 787 hectares; linseed, 18 341; oats, 6 891; barley 3 487; millet, 141. In 1909, 233 910 metric tons of wheat were produced, and 169 464 tons of maize. In 1908 the live stock of Uruguay consisted of 9 000 000 head of cattle, 1 000 000 horses, 26 000 000 sheep, 60 000 mules, 40 000 goats, and 120 000 pigs. In 1907 breeding stock was introduced from Europe and Argentina to the extent of 540 cattle, 2 282 sheep and 181 horses. *The Statesman's Yearbook for 1911*, p. 1316.   .(*Ed.*).

yield of the land is reckoned as follows: one hectare yields 740 kgs (per acre, 11 bushels of 60 lbs.) of wheat, 742 kgs. (11 bush.) of flax, and 641 kgs. (9 ½ bush.) of maize. The department of Minas which is more fertile than the others, has yielded 1000 kgs. (15 bush. per acre) of wheat per hectare and 980 kgs. (14 ½ bush.) of maize.

During recent years the cultivation of the vine has acquired importance (1); most of the stocks have been imported from the South of France. and now 20 million litres (4 400 000 gallons) of wine are made annually.

Live-stock is one of the main riches of the country ; a census taken on the farms in 1909 returned the number of head of live-stock at 28 million, or nearly 150 per sq. km. (388 per sq. mile). Of these 63 % were sheep and 31 % oxen and cows. There are 19 cold storage warehouses in Uruguay where from 600 to 650 thousand animals are slaughtered annually. The Liebig Co. slaughtered from 1903 to 1907, 765 455 animals valued at 15 935 301 piastres, or 79 676 505 frs. (£3 187 060).

Agricultural Development in Algeria. (L'Office de l'Algérie en 1910). *Bulletin de l'Office du Gouvernement Général de l'Algérie*, (Supplement au N. 5). — Paris. 1911.

1849

The Algerian Office (*Office de l'Algérie*) continues to play a useful part in the economic development of the Colony.

Frequent enquiries are made as to the terms on which free grants of land are made, their size, the position of the centres, and the date of settlement. 800 papers on the subject were distributed during the year; and in 1910, 245 requests for grants were made, mostly by farmers from Central and Southern France.

Algeria

Of these 245 requests, 135 have already been forwarded to Algiers with all formalities complete. On the other hand the Government, in deciding on the requests sent in during previous years, notified in 1910 through the Office that 11 grants and 120 refusals had been made.

The Algerian Government has organized public sales (*vente à bureau ouvert*) for the purchase of lands. The regular advertising which has been carried on since 1905, by posting up in French post-offices

---

(1) More especially in the Departments of Montevideo, Canelones, Salto, and Colonia. Tobacco and olive trees are also cultivated. (*Statesman's Year-Book, 1910*).   (*Ed.*).

notices of the six first sales, has called attention to them, and the
seventh sale has caused inquiries to be made ever since the beginning
of 1910, from all parts of France.

During the same year the Office, besides giving daily information on the organisation of commerce, on the customs' tariffs of
the several countries, on the cost of carriage abroad, on the Algerian customs' régime and the *modus operandi* of the maritime *octroi*
— has been consulted on all the branches and details of Algerian
agriculture.

1910 was a prosperous year in the developement of Algerian
trade. Business done with France amounted to 825 334 000 frs.
(£33 013 360) showing an increase of 193 463 000 frs (£7,738,520) as
compared with 1909,

The following table shows the exports on which this increase
was realised :

Products	1909	1910
Cereals	2 344 807 qls. (1)	3 402 483 qls.
Wine	6 047 282 hl. (2)	6 963 174 hl.
Sheep (head)	1 057 597	1 235 262
Fruits	459 875 qls.	536 080 qls.
Potatoes	125 815 »	199 303 »
Olive oil	15 697 »	79 846 »
Vegetables	183 688 »	234 938 ɾ
Leaf tobacco	23 962 »	39 344 ɔ
Cattle (head)	18 626	23 933
Alcoholised grape juice .	76 486 hl.	79 049 hl.
Raw hides	30 388 qls.	32 543 qls.

The trade between Algeria and other French Colonies and
foreign countries amounted to 175,755,000 frs. (£7,030,200) an increase of 23,660,000 (£946,400) on 1909, which was almost entirely
due to exports.

Details are given on the trade of Algeria with several countries.

1850   O. MANETTI. **Agriculture in Italian Somaliland.** (L' Agricoltura
nella Somalia Italiana). — *L'Agricoltura coloniale,* Anno V. N. 3,
pp. 112-125. Florence, 1911.

**Italian
Somaliland**

An extract from the Report of the Governor of Benadir, Mr.
de Martino, and from the agricultural supplement to this Report
by Dr. R. Onor.

(1) 1 Quintal = 100 Kilo = 220.548 lbs.
(2) 1 Hectolitre = 22.01 gallons, or 2.75 bushels.

The flora of Southern Italian Somaliland is of a uniform character. Outside the luxuriant forests which grow along the banks of the Yuba, from Yiumbo to Bardera, the vegetation of the great plains of Benadir consists of brushwood formed of a monotonous growth of stunted shrubs, with a few baobabs, palms and acacias.

The leaves of the *dum* palm (*Hyphaene*), which is common, are used by the natives for tent making; but the tree does not grow in such quantities as to admit of employing it further. The fruit might perhaps make a good cattle feed, but the stones could hardly rival the American *corozo* as material for buttons. Acacias and *dobère* trees yield fine compact timber; the bark of the baobab provides fibre for rope. *Sansevieria Schimperi* of which the fibre is greatly prized, grows in abundance. Leguminosae and Burseraceae supply resins and gums. The bark of some of the leguminous plants also contains valuable tanning material which is used in the Colony, where the trade in hides prospers.

There are 885 000 cattle and 297 300 camels in Italian Somaliland and the rich and plentiful grazing lands would allow of further development in this direction. A cow is worth twice as much as an ox, especially if she has a good supply of milk. A good Somaliland cow which has just calved, gives as much as ten litres (2.2 galls.) of milk a day.

An ox of 400 kgs. (880 lbs) yields about 200 kgs (440 lbs) of meat, and is worth 20 thalers, or from 40 to 45 frs (from £ 1, 12s. to £ 1, 16s.) (1) so that, deducting the value of the hide, meat is seen to be worth from 0.20 frs to 0.30 frs. per kg. ($1^{\underline{d}}$ to $1\ \frac{1}{2}^{\underline{d}}$ per lb) Meat might be advantageously exported from Benadir to Italy, but the live-stock of Benadir require protection against disease and raids.

The natives raise maize, doura, wheat, sesame, and manioc, with haricot beans and water melons as intermediary crops. Cotton, flax, pea-nuts, sesame, doura, wheat, maize, taff, dagonna, bultuc, are crops that might well be extended in Somaliland (2).

Good results could be obtained with rubber manihots, sisal grass (*Agave sisalana*) and the cocoa-nut tree.

---

(1) The thaler of Maria Theresa is worth about 2.25 frcs.
(2) See this Bull. April, 1911, N° 1146.

1351   ELEONOR L. BURNS. **Farm Women Congress in Connection with the Sixth International Dry Farming Congress.** *The Dry Farming Congress Bulletin,* vol. IV, no. 6. — Colorado Springs Colo. March 1st 1911.

There will be held in Colorado Springs in connection with the sessions of the International Dry Farming Congress (1), the week

United States: Colorado

of October 16th 1911 one of the most important conventions that has been held in the West of the United States.

It is reserved to Colorado Springs to call the first Congress of farm women, and to secure the great benefits to be derived from this gathering. Not from the West alone but from the East comes the cry for « better farming » for the men and « better and more attractive home life » for the women. From all indications this meeting will be a milestone in the progress of American womanhood.

1352   **Resolutions passed by the Union of the Agricultural Experiment Stations of Austria.** (*Beschlüsse des ausserordentlichen Vollversammlung des Verbandes der landwirtschaftlichen Versuchsstationen in Oesterreich abgehalten am 3, 4 u. 5 April,* 1911, *im Sitzungssaale der k. k. landwirtschaftlich-chemischen Versuchsstation zu Wien*). Zeitschrift fur das landw. Versuchswesen in Oësterreich, XIV. J., H. 4, s. 722-741. — Wien, April 1911,

Austria

The General Assembly of the Union of Agricultural Experiment Stations of Austria, held in April 1911, decided :

1. To adopt the rules laid down by the *Codex alimentarius Austriacus* even in the case of those researches which are not contemplated by the Pure Food Act.

_____

(1) At the fifth International Dry Farming Congress held at Spokane Washington . Oct. 3rd to 6th, 1910, this organization had 10 500 members and membership representation in 15 foreign countries; 10 of which had delegates present at the meeting. The officers of the International Dry Farming Congress for 1911 are:

Dr. J. K. Worst, President (North Dakota Agricultural College, Fargo, N. D.). Three Honorary Vice-Presidents and Three American Vice-Presidents for the International Divisions for the British Empire, Brazil, Chile, France, Germany, Hungary, Mexico, Russia and Turkey.

A Board of International Corresponding Secretaries, a Board of Governors, an Executive Committee of 19 Members, and an Executive Secretary Treasurer, Mr. John T. Burns, residing at Colorado Springs, Colo. The *Dry Farming Congress Bulletin*, No. 23, Vol. III of December 1, 1910 contains all the names of the officers and « The Constitution » as revised at the Fifth Congress at Spokane. Wash. Oct. 4 1910.   (*Ed.*).

2. To approve the publication of the *Codex alimentarius Austriacus*, and to solicit the publication of those volumes which have not yet appeared.

3. To instruct the President's bureau to come to the necessary understanding with the principal associations interested, in the adoption of a uniform method for analysing manures and forage; and to submit to the next General Assembly those amendments and additions which the associations may propose.

4. To declare that those Stations which have not joined the Union shall not be considered qualified to make test analyses and give expert opinions.

5. To insist on the compilation of statistics of Austrian wines.

A. Borzì. **The Colonial Garden at Palermo and its Work.** — (*Il giardino coloniale di Palermo e la sua attività*). 1 br. p. 13, Palermo, 1911.

1858

The Colonial Garden, annexed to the Botanical Gardens of Palermo, was only opened four years ago; it has already issued a catalogue of 900 species grown in the garden, which are of economic importance to the colonies. Some of the more important results obtained are here summarised.

Italy: Sicily

The rubber plants best suited to the Sicilian climate are *Ficus elastica*, *Mascarenhasia arborescens*, *Cryptostegia grandiflora*, which have been quite acclimatised to Palermo, and *Parthenium argentatum*, or rubber tree of Guayule, Mexico, which has been grown for some years past and the cultivation of which can be recommended.

Encouraging results have been obtained with some gum and resinous plants such as several acacias, *Cinnamomum Camphora*, *Eucalyptus globulus* and *E. viminalis*, *Pistacia Lentiscus*, etc.

Eighty different kinds of cotton have been experimented with, and Sicilian cotton has already fetched a good price on the Milan Exchange (1). Sisal grass (*Agave sisalana*) does well and can be recommended for Sicily. The tannin plants which have given the best results are acacias (2) and *Eucalyptus diversicolor* or karri (3).

---

(1) See N. 449 in this *Bull*. February, 1911.   (*Ed.*).

(2) See N. 499 in this *Bull*. February, 1911.   (*Ed.*).

(3) Karri comes from Australia and belongs to the family of the *Myrtaceae*, genus *Eucalyptus*. It grows rapidly, often rising to a height of 60 or 80 metres (200 to 260 ft.), and sometimes much more. It grows exclusively in Western Australia with the Jarrah (*Eucalyptus marginata*), and oc-

Experiments and studies are being made with indigo, coffee, hard woods, medicinal plants, etc. The results obtained so far at Palermo are satisfactory and justify hopes that the Colonial Garden will succeed in introducing into Southern Europe several valuable colonial products.

1354

P. HILLMANN, **Agricultural Geography in Higher Education** (Die land-wirtschaftliche Erdkunde als Gegenstand des Hochschulunter-richts). — *Fühlings landwirtsch. Zeitung* 60 Jahrgang, Heft 9, pp. 289-297, Stuttgart, 1 Mai, 1911.

Germany

The importance of agricultural and economical Geography is pointed out, especially in the preparation of students intending to settle in tropical and sub-tropical countries. The article dwells on some of the chief divisions of the subject, illustrating the climate, the nature of the prevailing soils, the Flora, the native agriculture and the different economical features of each country. Ethnogaphical studies are considered of special importance, regarding the economical capabilities of different races.

1355

A. HENRY. **A Panoramic Agricultural Map of Belgium**. (La carte panoramique agricole de la Belgique). — 11 pages. Louvain, 1911.

Belgium

This map was awarded a first class diploma at the Brussels Exhibition, and M. Henry, intends publishing it for the use of schools (1).

M. Henry had been struck by the fact that maps showing the relative intensity of different branches of cultivation gave no idea of their relative importance. Such a comparison can only be made by juxtaposition and this is difficult and unsatisfactory as the tints of the colours used have not been graded according to scale.

In 1905 Mr. Golescu, Director of the Agricultural Statistical Service of Roumania, represented the several products graphically,

---

cupies about 485 000 hectares (1 200 000 acres) of forest land, or ¹/₂₀ of the total area under forests. The principal centres of this timber are on the banks of the rivers Warren, Shannon, Doully, Walpole, Gardner, Denmark and Karridale. Karri wood is much used for road-paving, J. BEAUVERIE, *Le Bois*, pp. 999-1003. Paris, 1905.   (*Ed.*).

(1) See also the map " A Bird's eye view of English Agriculture " by James S. Macdonald. Fry's Magazine, London, May 1910, p. 127.   (*Ed.*).

on a scale commensurate to their importance in each province, and also inserted the actual figures; but the large number of figures overloaded the map.

M. Henry's map divides Belgium into cultivated, wooded, and waste lands. The forests are subdivided into those composed of deciduous trees and those consisting of conifers. The arable land is divided as in the statistical reports : cereals and grain crops, pulse, industrial crops, forage crops. The more important members in each group are represented separately. To each of these divisions and subdivisions is allotted the proportionate area which it actually covers; the areas under one crop have had to be grouped together and placed in those districts where it attains its maximum intensity.

Where the number of animals on the cultivated land is heaviest, the number on 100 hectares (247 acres) is given.

Whilst small holdings are the rule in Belgium (68 %), there are many large and medium-sized estates. The chief character of these are their farm buildings, of which a certain number of types peculiar to the different districts are shown.

The mode of tillage, whether by hand, by animals, or by machinery, depends on the size of the farm. This aspect of rural economy is represented by graphic illustrations of the work of man, animal (dog, ox, horse, single or in teams), and machinery.

The map measures 5 metres × 4 metres (16 ½ ft × 13 ft), and has the appearance of a picture.

The forests of the Ardennes, the grazing lands and oat fields of Condroz, the wheat fields and beet crops of the alluvial districts, the rye of the sandy lands, the meadows of Flanders, the pine woods and wastes of Campine, the fertile lands of Hesbaye, the alluvial plains of the Meuse, the pastures of 'Herve, are all represented.

Teaching Canning and Preserving Food-stuffs at Naples. *Rivista*   1356
tecnica coloniale di scienze applicate, ɪ Anno N. 5, pp. 76-77. —
Napoli, ɪ Maggio 1911.

Dr. G. Onofrio, is giving, at the Agricultural Training School
of Naples, a pratical course on the industry of tinned and preser-   Italy
ved foods.

A. E. BARTHE. **Agricultural Training in the Republic of S. Domingo.**   1357
Revista de Agricultura, An. VI, N. 12, Marzo, 1911.

Dr. Barthe, Director General of Agriculture, publishes a letter   Santo
from the Secretary of State for Agriculture in Santo Domingo,   Domingo

Rafael Diaz, announcing for the end of March the opening of a
« Theoretical and Practical School of Agricultural Experimentation ».   This school will confer a diploma of « *Capataz agricola* »
after a two years' course of study, and a diploma of « *perito agricola* » after three years.

After setting forth the program, Dr. Barthe gives some additional explanations and remarks, insisting on the special importance
of developing the different branches of agricultural education in
Santo Domingo, where agriculture is the chief source of welfare (1).

1358

The Principles of Plant Breeding. *Mark Lane Express Agricultura
Journal.* — London, April 10th, 1911.

After a lapse of more than half a century the Royal Agricultural
Society of England has revived the practice of lectures being delivered at the Society's house.   The first of the new series was by
**Great
Britain:
England**
Prof. Biffen of Cambridge University, who dealt with « The Principles of Plant Breeding».   Prof. Biffen said that the improvement
of stock and plants by breeding for the qualities desired had in
the past ten or twelve years been pursued on more definite lines
through the adoption of the Mendelian principle.   The advantage
of this method was that it shortened the time required to evolve
and fix types.   The application of Mendel's laws to the breeding
of live stock was only yet in the indefinite stages, but with wheat
and certain other plants it was passing from the experimental to

---

(1) The area of Santo Domingo is estimated at 18 045 English square
miles. Of the total area about 15 500 square miles is cultivable.   Sugar-
growing is a flourishing industry; shipments in 1909, 155 642 109 lbs., to the
value of 3 304 931 dollars, being an increase of 16 235 593 lbs. and 212 502 dollars
over these of 1908.   Cocoa was exported in 1909 to the extent of 32 672 671 lbs.
valued at 2 759 191 lbs., The export of tobacco leaf in 1909 amounted to
24 822 461 lbs., value 1 239 486 dollars.   The cotton export for 1909 was
1 542 284 lbs., valued at 128 202 dollars.   Coffee exports are increasing.   Experiments are being made in cotton-growing.   The cultivation of rice is being
undertaken by a concessionaire, who has obtained an exclusive right for the
purpose.   Some attention has recently been given to cattle raising and dairy
produce. Large sugar plantations and factories are at work in the south and
west of the Republic.

.   Santo Domingo is rich in timber, including mahogany, satin-wood, logwood, cedar, iron-wood, sabina and other woods; transport facilities however
are wanting.   Phosphates and guano are among the mineral products of Santo
Domingo of interest to agriculture.

The Statesman's Year-Book for 1911, p. 1200.   (*Ed.*).

a state of established routine. The lecturer exhibited on the screen specimen wheats to illustrate the inconsistencies and reversions which take place in breeding for new types and delay progress. In spite of the uncertainties and disappointments, however, he said encouraging success had been met with in raising new varieties, and the Mendelian theory promised to lead to important economic developments, not only as regarded wheat, but the breeding of plants generally and of farm animals (1).

H. W. MUMFORD. **Live Stock or Grain Farming in Illinois.** — *The Farmers' Review.* Chicago, March 25, 1911.

1859

Inquiry throughout Illinois shows a wide spread tendency to give up live stock because : 1. High prices of feeds have made grain farming more profitable for brief periods ; 2. Many stockmen have moved to cheap Western lands ; 3. The great difficulty of getting tenants who have succeeded with live stock ; 4. The extensive talk of a simple system of grain farming, which when properly carried out has permanent agriculture in view; 5. General failure to appreciate the value of farm manure.

United
States:
Illinois

Farmers have frequently been seized with panic with regard to live stock, and yet it has survived. If there ever was a time when farmers were warranted in largely discontinuing live stock that time has passed.

Exclusive grain farming is not likely to be as profitable as live stock, until maize, clover hay, alfalfa and other foods used largely to produce meat, come into more general use for human food. These crops, the most natural and profitable in Illinois, are suited primarily to live stock and will be so used. If live stock is forced out of Illinois, land may be forced to produce crops which are primarily suited for human food but not those best adapted to Illinois soils and climate. In Germany, France, Denmark, Holland, Italy and the British Isles there is a tendency with but few exceptions for live stock per capita to increase. A distinct shortage stimulates prices,

---

(1) A. B. BRUCE « Mendelism and its Application to Stock-breeding » *The Journal of the Board of Agriculture.* Vol. XVII no. 4. p. 284. July 1910. Abstract in : *Science and Practice of Farming during 1910 in Great Britain.* 1. vol. International Institute of agriculture. December 1910.

It is in Denmark that for the first time the difficulties of this problem as set forth by the recent discoveries of Hugo de Vries have been dealt with.

See on this subject, an article by K. A. WIETH-KNUDSEN : « The laws of Heredity and of Breeding from the economical point of view in Agriculture» in the « Nationalökonomisk Tidskrift » Copenhagen 1903.   (*Ed.*).

a distinct advance in prices stimulates production and there is no likelihood that live stock production will be overdone as the area that can be devoted exclusively to it is rapidly disappearing, while the meat-eating population is increasing more rapidly than live stock production.

Intelligent systems of live stock husbandry are the most profitable under conditions likely to prevail for many years.

A system of permanent agriculture by exclusive grain growing has been worked out and because of its simplicity is being widely adopted and exploited, but unfortunately there is a marked tendency to adopt this system on farms naturally better adapted to live stock and where it is entirely practicable.

There are several systems of live-stock husbandry which are even more profitable than the system of grain farming and equally permanent; and what the State has done to exploit a system of grain farming should now be done in a larger way in establishing and exploiting systems of live stock husbandry, which would retain as much as possible of the fertility removed in cropping.

Agriculture. — Agricultural Physics, Chemistry and Botany.

1360

Prussic Acid in Plants. (L'acide cyanhydrique dans les plantes). — *Bull. Sem. Schimmel et Cie.*, pp. 158-161. Miltitz, près Leipzig, Avril 1911.

Mr Greshof has studied at Kew a large number of plants, many of which contain prussic acid, benzoic aldehyde or methyl salicylate. The following plants contain prussic acid :

Alectryon excelsum, Gaertn., *Anacyclus officinarum*, Hayne, *A.*

Great Britain. Germany. Brazil. Belgium, etc.

pedunculatus, Pers., *Andrachne colchica*, Fisch., *Anthemis aetnensis*, Schouw., *A. altissima*, L., *A. arvensis*, L., *A. austriaca*, Jacq., *A. Blancheana*, Boiss., *A.chia*, L., *A. Cota*, L., *A. Cupaniana*, Pod., *A. elbuensis* (?), *A. montana*, L., *A. rigescens*, Willd., *Canella alba*, Murn., *Cercocarpus parvifolius*, Nutt., *Choisya ternata*, H. B. and K., *Clematis Fremonti*, Wats., *C. integrifolia*, L., *C. lanuginosa*, Lindl., *C. orientalis*, L., *C. pseudoflammula*, Schmalt., *Cornus foliosa*, Franch., *Cortaderia conspicua*, *C. Kermesiana*, *Cystopteris alpina*, *C. bulbifera*, Bernh., *C. fragilis*, Bernh., *Davallia brasiliensis*, H. K., *D. elegans*, S. W., *D. hirta*, Kaulf., *D. majuscula*, Lowe, *D. pentaphylla*, Bl., *D. strigosa*, S. W., *Dimorphotheca Ecklonis*, D. C., *Dionaea muscipula*, L., *Drimis Winteri*, Forst., *D. aromatica*, *Drosera binata*, Labill., *D. rotundifolia*,

L., *Hydrangea Hortensia, H. Lindleyana, H. Thunbergii, Isopyrum fumarioides, Jamesia americana, Kageneckia angustifolia, K. oblonga, Lucuma deliciosa, L., L. mammosa, L. multiflora, Macadamia ternifolia, Oxytropis lapponica, Paliurus australis, Peraphyllum ramosissimum, Platanus, Potentilla davurica, Protea cynaroides, Securinega ramiflora, Stipa capillata, S. Lessingiana, Umbellularia californica.*

According to E. Fickenday, the organs of the stalk of *Ophiocaulon cissampeloides,* Hook. f. (*Passifloraceae*), a common liana in the virgin forests of Tropical Africa, contain from 0.064 to 0.092 % of free prussic acid. The negroes use this plant in fishing.

Eriobotrya japonica, Lindl., (*Rosaceae*) has been studied by Mr. Peckolt ; it is called the *Canada plum* in Brazil, where it yields abundantly. The fresh kernels give on distillation 0.016 % of prussic acid. The flowers yield an essential oil (1).

In a paper on the formation of prussic acid in plants, Mr. A. Jorissen alludes to the hypothesis of Treub that prussic acid may be produced in the vegetable organism as a result of the assimilation of nitric acid. This supposition is supported by the researches of Seyewetz and Pizat, who have observed that a great number of organic compounds form prussic acid on oxidation by nitric acid. In this case nitrous acid plays an important part, for with the addition of urea, which destroys nitrous acid, no prussic acid is produced. These experiments were carried out at a somewhat high temperature; but Mr. Jorissen has observed that some substances in plants produce prussic acid through nitric acid at low temperatures ; for instance, morphine, brucine, and especially vanilline. In all these experiments the addition of urea prevents the formation of prussic acid; the addition of asparagin does not prevent it.

CURTIUS and H. FRANZEN. **An Aldehyde in Green Leaves.** (Une aldéhyde des feuilles vertes). — *Bull. Sem. Schimmel & Co.,* p. 158. Miltitz, près Leipzig, Avril, 1911.

1361

Germany.

M. Reinke showed, in 1881, that green leaves contain reducing compounds that are rendered volatile by a current of steam ; he

---

(1) For researches on the seeds of *Mespilus (Eriobotrya) japonica,* Japanese Medlar, now so common as a fruit tree in Italy and in Southern Europe generally, see MARCO SOAVE, *I glucosidi cianogenetici delle piante e la utilizzazione dell'azoto delle riserve.* Annali di Botanica, di R. PIROTTA, vol. V, fasc. 1. Roma, 1907. M. Soave was the first to investigate the evolution of prussic acid during the germination of bitter almonds, in 1899.

For a recent comprehensive study on Prussic acid in Plants, see GIUSEPPE GOLA, *L'Acido Cianidrico e i Glucosidi Cianogetici nel Regno Vegetale.* Supplemento Annuale all'Enciclopedia di Chimica, diretto da ICILIO GUARESCHI, Vol. XXIII, Torino, 1907. (*Ed.*).

considered them to be aldehydes without being able to isolate them (1). MM. Curtius and Franzen, continuing these researches, distilled hornbeam leaves in a current of steam. To the distillate an alcoholic solution of benzhydrazide was added, a hydrazone being formed, with melting point at 167° C. From this hydrazone an aldehyde can be separated, having the formula $C_5 H_9 CHO$, which, on oxidation by silver oxide, produces α and β hexylenic acid. This aldehyde therefore may be considered as the α β hexylenic aldehyde, of the formula $CH_3 \cdot CH_2 \cdot CH_2 \cdot CH : CH \cdot CHO$.

This aldehyde has been prepared from leaves of hornbeam, chestnut, vine, imperial fern, black alder, maple, oak, lupin, clover, copper beech, raspberry, hazel and walnut. The leaves of the horse chestnut and the lime produce a slightly soluble hydrazone, with melting point between 234° and 238° C. It appears evident that hexylenic aldehyde is connected with the production of glucose, playing an important part in the transformations which take place in the living plant.

1362   G. Bertrand and M. Javillier. **Influence of Zinc and Manganese on the Mineral Constituents of** *Aspergillus niger.* (Influence du zinc et du manganèse sur la composition minérale de l'*Aspergillus niger*). *C. R. de l'Acad. des Sciences*, T. 152, N. 20, pp. 1337-1340. — Paris, 15 Mai, 1911.

The writers have observed by experiments with *Aspergillus* that manganese accumulates in this mould in higher proportions when associated with zinc than when alone. This applies also to cases when the mould grows on natural substrata containing only traces of manganese and of zinc.

France

These two catalytic elements not only act reciprocally upon each other, but generally influence mineral assimilation in *Aspergillus*. It is probable that the catalysing action of small quantities of zinc and manganese may be observed in other elements; and that these actions, verified in the case of *Aspergillus niger*, may apply also to higher vegetable organisms.

(1) See also the researches of A. Mori, in 1882, and the more recent ones (since 1899) of Gino Pollacci, at the Botanical Institute of the University of Pavia.   (*Ed.*).

JULIUS STOKLASA. **Physiological Importance of Manganese and of Aluminium in the Vegetable Cell.** (De l'importance physiologique du manganèse et de l'aluminium dans la cellule végétale). *C. R. de l'Acad. des Sciences*, T. 152, N. 20, pp. 1340-1342. — Paris, 15 Mai, 1911.

1363

Professor Stoklasa has studied the influence of aluminium and of manganese on vegetable growth, employing three modes of culture: in aqueous solutions, in pots, in field plots.

Both in aqueous solutions ₐand in pot cultures it was observed that the presence of $\frac{1}{100}$ of the atomic weight of manganese or of aluminium expressed in grams, dissolved in 1 litre of the nutritive solution, is capable of inducing an evident increase of vegetable growth.

Austria : Bohemia

The original nutritive solution used by Stoklasa contained in 1 litre: potassium sulphate, 1 gram; crystallized magnesium chloride, gram 0.5; sodium nitrate, gram 0.5; ferrous sulphate, gram 0.01; calcium silicate, gram 0.5.

A greater effect on vegetation is obtained when aluminium or manganese is used in the proportion of $\frac{1}{2000}$ of the atomic weight expressed in grams.

The plants experimented upon were *Triticum vulgare, Secale cereale, Avena sativa, Hordeum distichum, Polygonum Fagopyrum*.

It is interesting to note that all plants which contain a certain quantity of manganese always contain aluminium also, for instance: *Lycopodium*, tea, Bohemian hops, *Abies excelsa, Pinus sylvestris, Armeria maritima, Crenothrix ochracea, C. manganifera*, etc.

The physiological experiments of Stoklasa show that leaves contain larger quantities of aluminium and manganese than any other organ.

Both aluminium and manganese have a special function in the processes of assimilation and of transformation in the plant; it is possible, as the experiments seem to point out, that these elements play an important part in chlorophyllian assimilation, or photosynthesis.

It may be added that recent experiments have shown that hops only prosper when they contain manganese and aluminium. The best varieties of hops always contain a larger proportion of manganese and of aluminium than inferior varieties.

J. POUGNET. **Action of the Ultra Violet Rays on Green Vanilla Pods.** (Action des rayons ultra-violets sur les gousses vertes de vanille). — *C. R. de l'Acad. des Sciences*, T. 152, N. 18, pp. 1184-1186. Paris, 1er mai, 1911.

1364

In continuing his researches on those plants of which the perfume is latent, the writer experimented on the action of the ultra-

France

violet rays on green vanilla pods, which have no perfume when fresh.

The pods were exposed to the rays produced by a mercury vapour quartz lamp, acting under the influence of an electric current of 110 volts and 4 ampères. A control pod, exposed at the same time, but protected by a glass screen, exhaled no scent. When the burner was placed at a distance of 10 to 30 cm. (3.9 in to 11.8 in) the scent from perfectly green pods was perceptible in from 2 to 6 hours ; from pods showing a little yellow, in 1 to 4 hours; and from pods showing a good deal of ₊yellow, in 20 to 45 minutes. On their surfaces a very few small drops of colourless liquid exuded, but no crystallisation of vanilline was observed.

The pod turns first brown and then gradually black and wrinkled, and for about 3 months remains soft keeping its original size. It then dries (the riper it was, the more rapidly) and after 5 months it is reduced to a quarter of its original volume.

In a second series of experiments, the fresh fruit was made to absorb through its stalk, a solution of chloride of manganese (Mn Cl$_2$) at a dilution of $\frac{1}{1000}$. In the presence of manganese in the plant-tissues, the time of exposure necessary for producing the perfume was reduced by one quarter, the perfume obtained being stronger than in the untreated pods.

M. Pougnet recalls the experiments of Heckel who failed to produce any perfume from quite green vanilla pods, when experimenting with anæsthetics (ether, chloroform) which in this connection have perhaps an action somewhat analogous to that of ultra-violet rays.

In conclusion : 1. Ultra-violet rays induce the exhalation of perfume from fresh vanilla pods, even when completely green; 2. Salts of manganese hasten and intensify this action.

1365   J. POUGNET. **Action of Ultra-Violet Rays on Plants containing Coumarin.** (L'action des rayons ultra-violets sur les plantes à coumarine). — *Bull. Sem. Schimmel et Co.*, p. 157. Miltitz, près Leipzig. Avril, 1911.

M. Pougnet has studied the action of the ultra violet rays on plants containing coumarin and on those whose perfume is due to decomposition of glucosides. He used a quartz mercury Nagelschmidt lamp (110 volts, 4 ampères) and experimented on *Melilotus officinalis* Lam., *Anthoxanthum odoratum* L., *Asperula odorata* L. and *Herniaria glabra*, L. These all give off coumarin under the ultra-violet rays, *Herniaria glabra* requiring the longest exposure. Immediately after exposure, M. Pougnet made sections of the plants and observed that the protoplasm was detached from the membrane and partly shrivelled up. (1).

He also exposed to the rays watercress, horse-radish, red radish and cherry-laurel leaves. After a short exposure they all gave out their characteristic odour, which is a proof of the decomposition of their glucosides. Under the microscope the cells present the same appearance as in the plants containing coumarin mentioned above. The ferments were not altered ; in the red radishes M. Pougnet found myrosine, and in the laurel leaves emulsine.

E. HECKEL. **Effect of Cold and of Anaesthetics on the Leaves of Angraecum fragrans.** (Les effets du froid et des anesthésiques sur les feuilles de l'*Anagraecum fragrans*). — *Bull. Sem. Schimmel & Cie.*, p. 157. Miltitz, près Leipzig, avril, 1911.

1366

M. Heckel studied the effects of cold and of anaesthetics on the leaves of *Angraecum fragrans*, Thou. (Faham) and on ripe vanilla beans (2). He thinks that hydrolysing and oxidising ferments are probably destroyed by cold. He observed, further, that the elimination of water plays no part in the formation of vanilline or of piperonal. It is only in ripe vanilla pods that the ferments can set free coniferylic alcohol, vanilline or piperonal ; for when unripe fruits are exposed to the action of anasthetics they remain green and without perfume.

France

---

(1) Coumarin exists in considerable quantity in Tonka-beans (*Coumaruma odorata* or *Dypteryx odorata*, being found in small white crystals between the seed coating and the kernel. It is also found in woodruff (*Asperula odorata*), in *Melilotus officinalis.*, in the flowers of Sweet-scented vernal grass (*Anthoxanthum odoratum*), in the leaves of Faham, an orchidaceous plant (*Angraecum fragrans*), in the leaves of *Orchis fusca*, and in the dried leaves of *Liastris odoratissima*, a composite plant growing in the southern parts of North America. H. WATTS, *A. Dict. of Chemistry*. London 1882. vol II, p. 93.

(*Ed.*).

(2) See this *Bulletin* Jan. 1911, no. 41.

Cp. with the researches by PUGNET, this *Bulletin*, Abstr. no. 1364, May 1911.

1367   L. CAILLETET. **Organic Matter in the Nutrition of some Ferns.** (Sur l'origine du carbone assimilé par les plantes). — *C. R. de l'Acad. des Sciences*, T. 152, N. 19, pp. 1215-1217. Paris, 8 mai, 1911.

It is generally admitted that green plants decompose the carbon dioxide of the air, fixing the carbon they require. In three series of experiments in one of the temperate green-houses in the Jardin des Plantes, in Paris, M. Cailletet has shown that *Adiantum* ferns, planted in soil without organic manure, watered with pure water to which phosphate, ammonium nitrate and potash are added, and placed in a dim light, grow for a short time and then die. The control *Adiantum* placed in the same conditions, but in (unsterilized) soil formed of organic mould and heath soil, developed well.

According to the author this shows that ferns draw their carbon from the organic substances in the soil, as do certain fungi, which grow in complete darkness on decomposing animal and vegetable matter.

MM. Mazé, Molliard and others have shown that plants can absorb various carbo-hydrates through their roots, and doubtless also humic compounds from the soil.

It appears that the ferns studied by M. Cailletet, although they are green plants, draw their carbon either from the carbon dioxide of the air, or from organic matter in the soil, or from both together, according to the conditions of light.

France

1368   J. DE RUFZ DE LAVISON. **Contribution to a Theory on the Mineral Nutrition of Vascular Plants based on Root Structure.** (Essai sur une théorie de la nutrition minérale des plantes vasculaires basée sur la structure de la racine). — *Rev. gén. de Botanique*, Tome XXIII, No. 269, pp. 177-211, 2 fig. Paris, 15 Mai, 1911.

Experimental and anatomical studies on the mineral nutrition of vascular plants in connection with their root-structure have shown:

1) That salts which cannot penetrate the protoplasm remain in the suberised tissues of the root endoderm. In order to penetrate further into the plant they must be transformed, perhaps assimilated.

France

2) Those salts which pass through the protoplasm, undergo, on penetrating the plant, a sort of filtration in the endoderm. The degree of filtration depends: *a*) on the nature of the plant; *b*) on the salt; *c*) on the condition of the protoplasm and of the endoderm.

The writer observes that these questions have still to be studied under many different aspects before a complete theory can be formulated of the absorption of mineral substances by plants.

H. B. Derr. **A New Awnless Barley** (Science n. ser. 32, No. 823) **1369**
E. S. R. Washington. April 5, 1911.

A true beardless or awnless barley has been produced by selection among hybrids resulting from the crossing of Tennessee Winter and a white six-rowed barley (*Hordeum vulgare*) with Black Arabian, a two-rowed variety (*H. distichum*).

In the third generation, a form occurred in which the awns on the median spikelets were from 3 to 4 in. long. while grains with short awns appeared in some lateral spikelets. The short-awned rudimentary grains produced heads like those from which they originated, except that on one plant most of the lateral spikelets contained perfect short-awned kernels. From these short-awned kernels a plant was secured which contained heads upon which all of the spikelets were fertile, the heads being 6 rowed with large plump grains without awns. Of the several hundred heads produced in 1910, 99 per cent were of the awnless type.

United
States

The progressive reduction of the awns and a persistence of the awnless condition for two seasons lead the writer to believe that the type is fixed. He proposes the name « hooded » barley for that which was formerly called « beardless » and the restriction of the term beardless to the new hybrid.

F. T. Shutt. **Influence of Heredity in Mangels.** — *Experimental Farms,* **1370**
Report of the Chemist, p. 210. Ottawa, 1910. (App. to the Rep. of the Min. of Agr.).

In order to learn to what degree characters of composition in Mangels may be attributed to heredity, two well known and distinct varieties were selected ten years ago: Gates Post and Giant Yellow Globe, varieties which at that time appeared to represent the extremes of composition in this class of roots.

Canada

Without a single exception, the Gates Post has shown itself the superior variety, both in respect to dry matter and in sugar. The fact that these varieties have maintained, practically, their relative positions for ten consecutive seasons goes far towards establishing the contention that heredity plays an important part in determining the composition of roots.

1871   P. BECQUEREL. **Does Traumatic Action Produce Permanent New Vegetable Forms?** (Par la méthode des traumatismes, peut-on obtenir des formes végétales véritablement nouvelles?). — *C. R. de l'Acad. des Sciences*, T. 152, N. 20, pp. 1319-1322. Paris, 15 Mai, 1911.

France

On analysing his own results with the *Zinnia* (1), and those of Mr. Blaringhem with maize, Mr. Becquerel considers that the new characters induced by traumatic action in poly-hybrid plants are all either atavic or simply malformations. They are characters which have appeared sporadically during several thousands of years. Mr. Becquerel agrees with Messrs. Ettingshausen and Krasan in thinking that traumatic action is only interesting for the study of evolution in so far as the throwing back to ancestral forms admits of the reconstruction of the life-history of plants.

1872   L. BLARINGHEM. **Production of a New Form of Maize by Traumatic Action.** (Production par traumatisme d'une forme nouvelle de Maïs à feuilles crispées). — *C. R. de l'Acad. des Sciences*, T. 152, N. 17, pp. 1109-1111. Paris, 24 avril, 1911.

France

Starting with seed from an abnormal panicle, obtained after section in 1904, the writer observed in 1905 a plant with two stems, one of which terminated in an abnormal panicle bearing about a score of small female spikelets at the base of the shoots covered later on by male spikelets.

This stem bore at one side a well developed female ear, but having singularly deformed bracts, folded and crumpled like the leaves of curled kale.

This anomaly is hereditary, and during ten years, among hundreds of rows of maize, the writer found it only in plants descended from the original abnormal ear. Plants which show this abnormal structure in a very high degree should not be used for seed, as their descendants either die early or are sterile. Reproduction is obtained through intermediate types, in which the abnormality is only slightly developed.

(1) PAUL BECQUEREL, *Variations du « Zinnia elegans » sous l'action des traumatismes.* C. R. de l'Acad. des Sciences, 13 décembre, 1909.

L. DANIEL. **Multiple Grafts of Anthemis.** (Les greffes multiples d'Anthemis). — *Revue horticole*, 83ᵉ année, N. 10, pp. 233-236. Paris, 16 Mai, 1911.

Mr. Daniel made experiments with multiple grafts (1) on herbaceous or semi-ligneous plants, especially on Compositae.

The variations obtained, whether from heterophyte (2) or homophyte grafts lead him to think that the hypothesis of the autonomy of the stock and of the graft must give way to that of variation, to which M. Daniel's earliest researches led him to incline.

L. DANIEL. **Biometric Researches on a Graft Hybrid of the Pear and the Quince.** (Recherches biométriques sur un hybride de greffe entre Poirier et Cognassier). *C. R. de l'Acad. des Sciences*, T. 152, N. 18, pp. 1186-1188. Paris, 1 Mai, 1911.

A biometric study of hybrids formed by grafting the pear on the quince, and cutting off the graft immediately above its junction with the stock (*bourrelet*). When the graft begins to grow the quince characters predominate; later on those of the pear appear. The determining character is the serration of the leaves of the graft hybrid compared with those of its parent tree, because the leaves of the quince are entire. The study of 1034 leaves showed the graft in question to be a hybrid, with characters more or less intermediate between those of the parent stock and the parent graft.

A. TRUELLE. **Size of Fruit in Relation to Germination of Pips; Experiments of S. U. Pickering at Woburn.** (Le volume des fruits influe-t-il sur la germination des pépins?) — *Revue Horticole*, 83ᵉ année, N. 10, pp. 224-225. Paris, 16 Mai, 1911.

The only real test of seed is not size or colour, but its germinative powers alone.

1873

France

1874

France

1875

Great
Britain

---

(1) When one stock bears many grafts, or when one graft is nourished by several stocks, the process is called multiple grafting. See L. DANIEL, Nouvelle classification des greffes et des procédés du greffage. *Revue bretonne de Botanique*, 1910.   (*Ed.*).

(2) Heterophyte multiple grafts are defined by the writer as cases in which scions from plants of different genera or species are attached to the same stock; homophyte multiple grafts as those in which all the grafts are of the same species.

Mr. Spencer U. Pickering, at the experimental fruit farm at Woburn, near Bedford in England, has endeavoured to estimate the influence that size of fruit, and the number of pips contained in the loculaments may have upon the seeds. The experiments were carried out, during three years, upon the pips of a Crab apple, of the *White Admirable* cooking apple, and of the *Marie Louise* pear. The following table shows the percentage of sound pips:

	1897		1898		
	Large fruit	Small fruit	Large fruit	Average fruit	Small fruit
Crab apples	97 %	95 %	88 %	79 %	69 %
White Admirable apples	80 %	82 %	88 %	71 %	71 %
Marie Louise pears	63 %	57 %	20 %	27 %	23 %
Averages . . .	80 %	78 %	65 %	59 %	·54 %

The difference is barely perceptible between the sound seeds of large or small fruit.

The seeds were sown, under identical conditions, in January. The number of seeds varied, with the size of the fruit, between 83 and 300. The following figures show the results:

Germinative power. — 1. Total germinative power, without regard to size:

Crab apples . . . . from 6 to 25 %
White Admirable apples . . . » 23 » 76 %
Marie Louise pears. . . . . . » 7 » 19 %

2. Taking account of size:

	Small fruit	Large fruit
Crab apples	12 to 25 %	6 to 25 %
White Admirable	24 » 68 %	23 » 76 %
Marie Louise pears	13 » 18 %	7 » 19 %

3. Total average:

Large fruit . . . . 21 to 46 %
Small fruit . . . . 19 » 38 %

Resistance of Seedlings. — The average percentage of seedlings that survived in the above conditions was about the same for large fruit (15 %) as for small (16 %).

Germination of pips from loculaments containing one, or two seeds. — For the three varieties examined, the total percentages were:

From compartments with 1 seed oniy, 40 %
»   »   » 2 seeds,   30 %

The number of surviving seedlings of the first series was 21 %; of the second, 23 %.

Notwithstanding great variation in the results, which makes it impossible to form a theory as yet, they seem on the whole favourable to large fruit.

A. Müntz and E. Lainé. **Purification of Sewage by the Soil or by**   **1876**
Bacterial Beds. (Les phénomènes d'épuration des eaux d'égout par le sol et par les lits bactériens). — *C. R. de l'Acad. des Sciences*, T. 152, N. 19, pp. 1204-1208. Paris, 8 Mai, 1911.

Whether sewage is spread on the fields, or filtered through artificial bacterial beds, the process of purification is considered to   **France** be the same, except that it is intensified in the bacterial beds where the surface is restricted.

The chief if not the only purifying action has been attributed to the nitrification properly so called, of the nitrogenous matters which are the principal source of infection.

The writers have already shown (*C. R.* t. 152, p. 822) that in bacterial beds the chief purifying action is due to direct combustion phenomena, produced by the common micro-organisms that destroy organic matter. By new experiments on the nitrogen transformations in sewage in fields, they have shown that the two methods of purification differ considerably.

In the soil, nitrification greatly predominates and the action on the nitrogen compounds of the common organisms that destroy organic matter is very slight.

During 6 ½ months, 1206.52 litres of sewage were added to 535.47 kg. of soil in a vat, bringing a total of 67.388 grams of nitrogen. The drainage water drawn off was 1217.03 litres, and contained 50.8384 grams of nitrogen. At the end of the experiment the soil was analysed; the following table shows the balance of nitrogen:

Original Nitrogen content:		Nitrogen found:	
Of the soil	gr. 664.362	In the soil	gr. 670.182
Of the sewage	» 67.388	In the drainage water	» 50.838
Of the rain-water	» 0.298		
Total	gr. 732.048	Total	gr. 721.020

Here was an evident loss of 11.028 grams of nitrogen, too much to be experimental error. In the control vat, to which no sewage was added, there was neither gain nor loss of nitrogen, which shows that it is not the nitrogen of the soil, but that of the sewage, which is dispersed as gas during the watering.

If it is considered that the nitrogen dispersed as gas by bacterial beds is 60 %, and that lost during spreading on the field is only 16.36 °, it will be admitted that the soil is a far superior nitrifying medium to artificial bacterial beds.

1877   C. Gerber.   **Influence of Certain Mineral Compounds on the Action of Diastase upon Starch.** (Action de divers composés mineraux sur la saccharification de l'empois d'amidon par les ferments amylolytiques). — C. R. hebd. de la Soc. de Biologie. T. LXX, N. 16, p. 724-730. Paris, 12 mai, 1911.

A. Chromium compounds.

France   1. *Salts containing chromium as basic oxide.   Chromic salts*, added up to a certain amount, are accelerators, their action being favourably influenced by a slight acidity ; beyond this limit, their action becomes retarding or preventive, this being due to the alteration and subsequent destruction of the diastase. The same result is in fact obtained by putting chromium salts either in starch paste before adding pure diastase, or in pure diastase before adding starch paste, although in the latter case the final content of chromium salts in the mixture is much less than in the former. The inhibitive amount is weaker in the case of the diastase from the fig than in the diastase from *Broussonetia*.

Chromous salts. These being unstable when in solution have not been experimented upon.

2. *Salts of alkali metals containing Chromium as acid oxide.*

Chromic acid acts in a similar manner to chromates, with the difference that the inhibitive dose is far weaker.

Bichromates, in small and average quantities act as accelerators ; but in large amounts they retard diastasic action. Small amounts of *neutral chromates* are inactive ; large ones retard.

The retarding action in the case of bi-chromates and neutral chromates is not due to an alteration of the diastase, but to a special condition unfavourable to its activity.

B. Magnesium, Manganese, Iron and Aluminium Compounds.

1. *Magnesium salts.*   Are inert in small and average amounts, if added in large proportion, they retard, and may even inhibit the

action. As in the case of the alkaline chromates, the retarding and inhibitive property is not due to the decomposition of the diastase. The diastase from *Broussonetia* proves more sensitive to these actions than that from the fig.

2. *Manganous salts.* Like Magnesium salts, added in small and average amounts, they accelerate, in large they retard.

3. *Ferrous salts.* In all cases they retard diastase action, being inhibitive in strong doses.

4. *Ferric and aluminium salts.* Added up to a certain amount, they accelerate; beyond this they retard and eventually inhibit. The acceleration is due to the slight acidity imparted to the starch paste by the small doses of these salts ; an excess of this acidity decomposes and destroys the diastase.

C. Alums.

The action of alums upon diastase has been successively investigated by Kjeldahl, Effront, Ebstein, Schultze, Litner, etc. but without sufficiently explaining the action. Of the two compounds that constitute the alums, the *sesquioxide sulphate* is acid to litmus, acting therefore, when present in small amounts, as an accelerator to diastasic action, gradually retarding and inhibiting it as the quantity increased. On the other hand, small and average amounts of the other constituent of alums, the *protoxide sulphate*, which is neutral, are inactive on diastase, while larger amounts are only slightly retarding. The alums therefore act upon diastasic saccharification in a similar way to the protoxide sulphates, accelerating when present in very small proportions, retarding when added in average amounts and inhibiting when these increase ; but the intensity of this action varies greatly with the composition of the alum. The accelerating action of small amounts of alums is due chiefly to the slight acidity they impart to the starch. On the other hand, the retarding and inhibitive action is due to the alteration of the diastase.

A. Guillemard. **Culture of Anaerobic Bacteria in Free Air, in Presence of Ferrous Sulphate.** (Culture des bactéries anaérobies à l'air libre en présence de fer). — *C. R. hebd. de la Soc. de Biologie*, T. LXX, N. 16, p. 685. Paris. 12 mai 1911.   1878

The writers' object was to add to the culture media a substance which, combining with oxygen, should form a complex ion which   France would not react upon the cellular membrane, which is affected by free oxygen. He experimented with the following solution :

Water . . . . 1000 cm³
Peptone Chapoteau . . . . .   20 grams
Glucose   10   „
Citrate of ammonium . . .   6   „
Crystallised ferrous sulphate 3   „
(Slightly alkalised whith ammonia).

Tubes simply plugged with cotton wool and containing 8 to 10 cubic centimetres of this mixture, sterilised, showed, 15 to 20 hours after inoculation an abundant development of anaerobic bacteria. The experiments were repeated with only one tenth of the ferrous sulphate, *i. e.* 0.3 grams $\%_0$, and gave almost identical results, but the nutritive solution must be used soon after preparation to avoid having an excess of oxygen in proportion to the toxic element; the iron must also be united to an organic substance such as citric acid, otherwise there is precipitation of ferrous oxide in a neutral or alkaline medium.

1879   E. KAYSER. **On Yeast Extract.** (Sur le suc de levure de bière). — *C. R. de l'Acad. des Sciences,* T. 152, N. 19, pp. 1279-1280. Paris, 8 mai, 1911.

France   W. Kayser has studied the stimulating action of manganese salts on alcoholic fermentation by yeast extract, obtained by the Lebedeff process (1). His experiments showed that the stimulating action of phosphate and nitrate of manganese is comparable to that of the same salts of potassium. The condition of the yeast at the time of desiccation has great importance, as has also the temperature of maceration. Portions of the same yeast, kept for different lengths of time, give, after desiccation and maceration, extracts of very varying activity.

The kind of yeast is also important; this point, like many others in the preparation of Lebedeff's extract, has still to be explained. A new method has, however, been devised by Lebedeff for the study of microbic secretions.

---

(1) See this *Bulletin* Feb. 1911, No. 398.   (*Ed.*)

N. L. Söhngen. **Fat-splitting by Bacteria** (Proc. Akad. Wetensch. Amsterdam, 1911, 19,667-680). — *The Journal of the Chemica Society*, Abs ii 319, London, April 1911.

1380

Numerous bacteria exist which separate fats anaerobically, oxidise them aerobically and denitrify nitrates and nitrites when present, all these processes being due to the secretion of lipase by microbes. Several fat-splitting organisms produce two lipases; α-lipase which acts both in acid and alkaline solutions and β-lipase which is formed in acid media but only becomes active after neutralisation.

Netherlands

The bacteria thrive well when supplied with fat as the exclusive form of carbon and with ammonium chloride as source of nitrogen. The injurious effect of fat-splitting organisms on the quality of dairy products is chiefly due, in addition to their lipolytic properties, to the production of bitter and odoriferous substances from proteins and casein.

Agricultural Metereology in France. (La Météorologie agricole en France). — *Journ. d'Agric. Pratique*, 75 année, T. 1, N. 16, p. 488. Paris, 20 avril, 1911.

1381

On the 11th of December 1910, the French Chamber of Deputies passed the following resolution : " The Chamber invites the Minister of Agriculture to develop meteorological research, already encouraged by the Department of Agricultural Hydraulics; and to study, with regard to the budget for 1912, the means necessary for organising an agricultural meteorological service ",

France

The Minister of Agriculture accordingly appointed a Commission of 64 members, presided by M. Violle, to study the question. (1).

J. F. Voorhees. **Relation of Temperature and Rainfall to Crop Systems and Production.** — *Bulletin of the Agr. Exp. Sta. of the University of Tennessee*, No 91, pp. 1-23, Knoxville, Tenn. January, 1911,

1382

The climatic data used in this Bulletin, containing 16 charts, were obtained wholly from the published records of the U. S. Weather Bureau, during a period of forty years.

United States: Tennessee

(1) See the Report presented by M. Louis-Dop, French Delegate, Vice-President of the Permanent Committee of the International Institute of Agriculture to the Permanent Committee, on question N. 6 of the programme of the General Assembly of 1911, concerning Agricultural Meteorology. (*Ed.*).

For the most effective and economical application of the results obtained by the different experiment stations, to the needs of
the farmer, a knowledge of the climate is necessary; and this Bulletin is intended to show that now there is no necessity for the Connecticut farmer to spend time experimenting with different systems
of cropping in order to learn which is best suited to the climatic
conditions of this State.

From the standpoint of climatic conditions, there is no good
reason why Tennessee or the states furthest south of Tennessee should
not be among the best corn - growing states. The summers are as warm
as in the valleys of the Ohio, Missouri and upper Mississipi rivers; the
growing season is longer, the summer rainfall is more abundant and
the winter rainfall, with its opportunity for moisture conservation,
is far greater. The fact then is that the yield of maize per acre in
Tennessee is small, not because of climatic conditions, but in spite
of them. Neither is the soil responsible for the deficiency, for many
farmers scattered over all parts of the State have produced crops
of maize that can not be exceeded anywhere. The trouble is that
most of the farmers have not adapted farming methods to the climate and soil conditions of the State. What is needed is a system
of farm management and a rotation of crops that will utilise the
abundant heat and moisture that the land receives.

A system must be followed that will increase the humus content of the soil and a rotation that will keep the ground covered
in winter as well as in summer. The double-cropping system, as
practiced at the Tennessee Experiment Station, and to a greater or
less extent by the most successful farmers of the State, is well adapted for this purpose and should be used on all arable lands.

Experience has shown that two crops may be grown where the
average growing season is as long as 200 days. The winter is about
one-fourth of the year in Tennessee; and during the greater number
of winter days such crops as wheat, barley, oats and rye among the
cereals and winter legumes will grow and, by their growth, protect
the soil from washing. By deep-tilling these crops into the land, at
least one year in three, the moisture holding capacity of the soil is
so greatly improved that much of the rainfall, amounting in Tennessee to 48 inches a year, is saved to the crops for use during
drought periods.

The following rotations are based on these important facts and
any of them will result in soil improvement and increased crop
production when mineral fertilizers are properly used in them.

A. — *Four - year Rotations.*

I. — 1st year — Corn or cotton, with wheat or rye sown in at last cultivation.

2d year — Soy beans for hay.

3d year — Winter wheat.

4th year — Clover and grass.

II. — 1st year — Wheat or barley or winter oats top-dressed in winter, followed by soy beans sown last of June for hay.

2d year — Wheat.

3d year — Clover and grass for hay.

4th year — Pasture.

III. — 1st year — Winter barley or winter oats top-dressed in winter for grain followed by soy beans for hay.

2d year — Wheat and vetch (sown previous fall) ploughed under. Ground fallowed until August then sown to red clover without a nurse crop.

3d year. — Clover for hay. Ploughed after first cutting and sown to soy beans for hay.

4th year — Wheat and vetch, sown after bean crop. Turned under followed by maize or cotton.

IV. — (For rich land only). 1st year — Barley, wheat or winter oats ploughed immediately after harvest fallowed until August, then sown to crimson clover and turnips. Turnips off in the fall.

2d year — Crimson clover turned under in May. Land fallowed until July then planted to Irish potatoes.

3d year — Wheat and vetch (following potatoes) for hay, followed by red clover sown without nurse crop in August.

4th year — Red clover for hay followed by soy beans for hay.

For Tobacco.

V. — 1st year — Tobacco ; wheat or rye sown at last cultivation.

2d year — Soy beans for hay.

3d year — Winter wheat.

4th year — Red clover

VI. — 1st year — Tobacco.

2d year — Wheat.

3d year — Clover.

4th year — Pasture to be fall - ploughed.

B. *Three - year Rotations.*

I. — 1st year — Maize and peas.

2d year — Winter oats sown previous fall, followed by soy beans for hay·

3d year — Wheat or rye sown previous fall, turned under for cotton sown at last cultivation to rye.

II. — 1st year — Winter oats and wheat; seeded in spring to Japan clover (1) pasture.

2d year — Japan clover hay or pasture.

3d year — Wheat or rye sown previous fall turned under for cotton or maize.

III. (For rich land). — 1st year — Winter wheat, barley or oats. Land ploughed immediately after harvest, fallowed to August then sown to crimson clover and turnips. Turnips off in the fall.

2d year Crimson clover turned under. Ground fallowed until August then sown to red clover without nurse crop.

3d year — Clover for hay. Land ploughed after first crop and sown to soy beans for hay.

For Sweet Potatoes.

IV. — 1st year — Maize with cowpeas. Hogged off and sown to wheat and vetch.

2d year — Wheat and vetch turned under in April; sweet potatoes.

3d year — Winter oats and vetch (sown previous fall to be turned under next spring before planting maize.

C. — Two Year Dairy Rotation-Two crops a year.

1st year — Barley, wheat or winter oats top dressed with manure followed by soy beans for hay.

2d year — Wheat and vetch, or winter oats and vetch followed by maize and peas or sorghum and peas for silage.

D. Five year Rotation.

1st year — Maize and peas hogged off.

2d year — Wheat and vetch (sown previous fall) turned under followed by soy beans, off for hay or hogged off with maize.

3d year — Oats or wheat, (sown previous fall) seeded to Japan clover in spring. Japan clover, pasture or hay if heavily seeded.

4th year — Oats for hay, sown previous fall on Japan clover, disc-drilled without ploughing followed by Japan clover hay.

5th year — Wheat or rye sown on Japan clover previous fall, turned under, followed by cotton, cotton seeded to wheat or rye at last cultivation, to be turned under for maize and peas the next spring.

1383   S. T. PARKINSON. **The Influence of the Soil on Plant Growth**. — *The Journal of the South-Eastern Agricultural College, Wye, Kent*. No 19. 1910, pp. 426 (258-261). London and Ashford, Kent.

It is a universally accepted fact that the nature of the soil or
Great   subsoil is of the greatest importance in determining what sort of
Britain

---

(1) Japan clover, *Lespedeza striata*, indigenous to China and Japan; now extensively cultivated south of the Ohio. L. H. BAILEY. *Cycloped. of Americ. Horticulture*. New York, 1906.

growth a plant makes, but it is not generally realized how pronounced the influence is.

As a demostration it was decided to grow specimens of the same kind of plant side by side on subsoils of different character

The results were as follows: The general growth of the plants upon loam was very satisfactory.

On peat, the plants were larger and heavier than those grown on any of the other plots except on the loam, but the roots and especially those of a fleshy nature, such as the carrot and chicory, were badly « fanged ». « Fanging » seems to have been due to the acid nature of the peat and not to mechanical resistance offered to growth by the stiff soil. It is curious to notice how the shape of the carrot is entirely altered, and instead of being long and tapering has become short and stumpy, so that it might easily be mistaken for an entirely different variety.

On Gault clay, « fanging » occurred again in carrots, but the « fangs » were fewer and larger than was the case in the peat and they penetrated well into the clay. Possibly the close, stiff texture of the soil hinders growth of the main root and the food passing down the root is captured by lateral buds which form new root branches which otherwise would not grow out.

On sand the size and general appearance of the plants indicates an all-round deficiency of plant food.

On chalk the starved condition of the plants was indicated by their minute size.

The average weight (in grams) of the carrot and chicory plant grown on each plot was as follows:

	Carrots (first year)				Chicory	
	Whole plant	Root	Whole plant (air-dried)	Root (air-dried)	Whole plant	Root
Loam	758	512	100	56	506	313
Peat	117	83	15	8.5	96.5	26
Gault	125	96.5	20	15	47	17
Sand	45	34	6	4	3.75	1.5
Chalk	10	6.75	1.25	1	4	1.5

1884

A. PETIT. **On the Fixation of Phosphoric Acid by Organic Matter in the Soil.** (Sur la fixation de l'acide phosphorique par la matière organique du sol). — *C. R. de l'Acad. des Sciences*, Tome 152, No. 20, pp. 1317-1319. Paris, 15 mai, 1911.

France

These experiments were made to discover whether the organic matter in soils does really help to fix phosphorus by combining with phosphoric acid.

To a solution of phosphoric acid, of known strength, were added, in one case forest soil, in the other organic matter taken from a certain quantity of market garden soil; the fixation of phosphorus was in both cases so slight as to be negligible. The garden soil used in a preceding experiment, when an appreciable amount of phosphorus had been fixed, owed this property to the action of mineral salts, especially salts of calcium, iron and aluminium.

1885

W. W. BURR. **Storing Moisture in the Soil.** — *Bulletin of the Agricultural Experiment Station of Nebraska*, V. XXII, A. IV, pp. 9-11, figs. 4 + Ch. XIII + tab. X. Introduction by W. P. Snyder. Lincoln, Nebraska 1910.

United States: Nebraska

Results of an investigation made at the Experimental Substation, North Platte, Nebraska, aiming to show the effect of tillage on the water in the soil and the use of water by growing plants.

1. Land which is under thorough cultivation absorbs water much more freely than land not under cultivation, or which is covered with grass or for any reason has a hard surface.

2. Land under thorough cultivation loses but little water from below the first foot (30 cm.) by surface evaporation, so long as the mulch is kept in good condition.

3. A growing crop uses water from the land in proportion to the growth of dry matter in the crop.

4. Land under summer tillage or thorough cultivation from May 1 to September 1 on the Sub-station Farm has accumulated from 5.5 to 7 inches (140 to 179 mm.) more water in the first 6 feet (m. 1.820) of soil than similar land growing a crop. The water so stored has been equal to from 40 to 50 per cent. of the rainfall for the same period. The moisture content on summer tilled land increases below the 6 feet area and is apparent to a depth of at least 10 feet (m. 3. 040).

5. Water stored in the subsoil to a depth of at least 6 feet is available for the use of farm crops, and alfalfa is able to draw water much deeper.

6. Abundance of water in the subsoil is a great protection to the crop against drought. Moisture in the surface soil, while it may favor the immediate growth of the plant, does not protect it against drought. The protection of the crop against drought is in almost exact proportion to the total available soil water within the reach of the crop.

7. Grass crops (alfalfa and brome grass) dry the subsoil to such an extent that the first crop following grass is wholly dependent on the season's rainfall for its moisture supply.

8. A rainfall of from a quarter to a half-inch (mm. 6.3-12.7) may have a decidedly beneficial effect upon a growing crop and is of great assistance in securing a good stand at seeding time. Such a rainfall has little or no effect in increasing the water in the lower soil, unless the surface is already moist from previous rains. Less than a half-inch (mm. 12.7) of rain falling on a dry soil mulch does not wet the soil below the mulch and is soon evaporated by the sun and wind.

F. T. SHUTT. **Influence of Soil Moisture on the Composition of Wheat.** — See No. 1399.

1886
Canada

FRANK ADAMS. **Second Progress Report of Cooperative Irrigation Investigations in California.** — *U. S. Department of Agriculture Office of Experiment Stations.* Circular 108, Pp. 39. Washington, March 10, 1911.

1887

Experiments on the Water Requirements of crops:

Alfalfa. — Experiments with alfalfa at Davis in 1910 gave an increase in yield with the increased water applied up to 30 inches (762 mm.); above that amount the increase was not in proportion to the water applied.

United
States:
California

On non-irrigated plats six cuttings in a year gave 4.08 tons per acre (102.4 metric quintals per ha.) of hay; on plats which received 30 in. (762 mm.) of water six cuttings gave 8.09 tons per acre (203 q. per ha).

Barley. — Two irrigations with a total depth of 5.2 in. (132 cm.); yield: 2.23 tons per acre (55.8 q. per ha.) of hay and 1840 pounds (20.6 q. per ha.) of grain per acre, an increase in grain over the unirrigated plat of 58.5 %.

Wheat and Barley. — In the vicinity of Tulare the best results with wheat and barley will be obtained by the use of 18 to 24 in. (48 to 60 cm.) of irrigation water An average depth of 2 feet (about 60 cm.) will about represent the amount applied to grain crops in the cooler climates.

Egyptian corn. — Irrigation by the furrow method. — A single irrigation on June 24, of 3.75 inches (95 mm.), gave a yield of unthrashed heads 90 per cent. greater than the unirrigated plat. A single irrigation, on July 15, of 3.10 in. (79 mm.) gave 117 per cent increase in yield. Two irrigations on June 24 and July 13, total depth as in former case; increased yield 174 per cent.

Indian corn. — No water: 7.15 tons per acre (179.5 metric quintals per ha.), green fodder. A depth of 3.3 in. (83.8 mm.) in one irrigation: increased yield 23.2 per cent. Two irrigations: total depth 5.3 in. (134.5 mm.): increased yield 30.7 per cent. 8 in. (203.2 mm.), in three irrigations: increase 47.1 per cent.

Vineyards. — As a rule, vineyards are not irrigated in California. On the few irrigated vineyards, the average depth applied is 5.2 in. (131.0 mm.) water with one irrigation and 10.3 in. (262 mm.) with two irrigations.

Citrus fruit. — The average for Riverside is 2.03 feet (616,9 mm.) for Porteville 1.40 feet (426.7 mm. and for Pomona 0.81 foot 246.9 mm.). It may be added that the average annual rainfall at Riverside is 0.83 foot (253 mm.), at Porteville 0.70 foot (213 mm.), and at Pomona 1.65 feet (503 mm.)

Present State of Irrigation Development in California. — Eliminating projects still in the promotion stage, a conservative estimate places at 750,000 acres (303,450 ha.) the area for which construction to provide irrigation water is now under way. Of this area, about one-third is in Southern California and the remainder north of Techachapi.

The aqueduct being built to supply water to Los Angeles will also provide irrigation for the Southern coastal region. Increase in pumping plants is under way, notably round Corona, Chino, Pomona, Whittier, Cavina, Anaheim, Fullerton, Riverside, and San Jacinto Valley in Southern California; and in the foothill sections of Kern, Fresno and Tulare counties, north of Techachapi. One of the largest pumping irrigation systems in the West is now in operation in San Joaquin Country.

Irrigation works are now under way in Sacramento Valley and at Orland where 14 000 acres (5664 ha.) will be irrigated.

An approved project provides for the reclamation and irrigation of 27 000 acres (10.924 ha.) of Klamath Marsh, and about an equal area of Tule Lake.

Another project, not yet approved, provides for the irrigation of 10 400 acres (4108 ha.) in California south and west of Clear Lake reservoir

Irrigation Works in Cuba. — *The Board of Trade Journal*, No 754, p. 275. London, May 11, 1911.   1388

A Bill has been introduced into the Cuban Senate providing for the grant of a 60 years concession for the construction and working of irrigation works throughout Cuba, of an initial cost of 25 000 000 dollars (about 125 000 000 frs.). By the Bill, the Government are to guarantee 5 per cent. interest on the capital, and the concessionary company is to levy taxes on the land irrigated. The Government may take over the works at the end of 30 years. A technical commission is to be appointed to prepare the scheme for the works.   Cuba

A. D. HALL. **Mustard and Rape versus Leguminous Green Manures. Rothamsted Experimental Station.** — *The Journal of the Board of Agriculture.* London, March, 1911.   1889

In the experiments in green manuring made at the Royal Agricultural Society's Farm at Woburn, Dr. Voelcker always obtained better results with wheat grown after mustard than · after vetches, both crops having been ploughed in.   Great Britain

The experiments at Woburn have been repeated until no possible doubt of their validity can be left; on the average, the yield of grain after mustard has been 50 % higher than after vetches. When the Woburn results were first manifest, similar plots were started at Rothamsted in order to see if the results obtained on the light dry land at Woburn would hold for the heavier and moister soil that prevails at Rothamsted. The following table gives the results for the two crops of wheat, of 1907 and 1910, both grown on the plots on which rape, crimson clover, vetches, and mustard were sown and ploughed in at the end of the summer in 1904, 1905, and 1906 and again in 1908 and 1909.

Yield of Wheat per acre after Green Manuring.
Little Hoos Field, Rothamsted.

	Previous Green Crop	Dressed Grain	Dressed Grain	Offal Grain	Total Grain	Straw
		Bushels	Lbs.	Lbs.	Lbs.	Cwt.
1907	Mustard	29.9	1923	96	2019	22.5
1907	Rape	21.3	1376	75	1451	29.6
1907	Crimson clover . . .	32.5	2096	294	2390	36.1
1907	Vetches	39.7	2542	210	2752	39.4
1910	Mustard	19.6	1247	34	1281	15.3
1910	Rape	20.8	1327	37	1364	16.3
1910	Crimson clover . . .	30.8	1926	85	2011	27.0
1910	Vetches	34.4	2144	127	2271	34.7

The superiority of the wheat after the leguminous crops of crimson clover, and particularly of vetches, is beyond any possible limit of experimental error.

The following determinations of the percentages of nitrogen in the grain and straw would indicate that the superiority in the yield of the plots on which the vetches and crimson clover had been grown was due to the greater amount of nitrogen there available in the soil; but the general superiority of these plots over the wheat elsewhere must be set down to the better condition of the soil brought about by the accumulation of organic matter.

Quality of Wheat grown after Green Manuring.

Previous Green Crop	Weight per bushel	Nitrogen in grain	Nitrogen in Straw	Ratio of Grain to Straw	Ratio of Offal to Dressed Grain
	Lb.	%	%	%	%
1907 Mustard	64.3	2.065	0.276	59.9	5.0
1907 Rape	64.7	2.088	0.267	56.5	5.4
1907 Crimson clover . . .	64.5	2.217	0.320	58.0	14.0
1907 Vetches	64.0	2.386	0.441	61.3	8.2
1910 Mustard	63.5	1.849	0.3162	74.8	2.7
1910 Rape	63.8	1.852	0.3054	74.6	2.8
1910 Crimson clover . . .	62.7	1.888	0.3756	66.4	4.4
1910 Vetches	62.4	1.953	0.3595	58.4	5.9

The grain and particularly the straw of the wheat grown after vetches and crimson clover are much richer in nitrogen than the corresponding grain and straw following the non-leguminous crops, pointing to a greater amount of nitrogen in the soil available for the former crops. Until the experiments have been repeated for a somewhat longer period it will be impossible to determine with any accuracy whether there has been any accumulation of nitrogen in the soil of the plots growing mustard and rape, though these crops are themselves incapable of fixing any nitrogen. Although it has been possible in the laboratory to raise the proportion of nitrogen in the soil by merely adding organic matter containing no nitrogen, and thus giving the Azotobacter material to work upon and derive the energy necessary to bring the nitrogen into combination, the evidence that this process goes on in the field is still very scanty.

Dr Voelcker commenting upon the different results at Woburn has indicated that there the question is probably one of water supply ; though the vetch crop does contain about twice as much nitrogen as the mustard which is turned in, it seems to leave the land in a drier and more open condition and this on the light Woburn soil seems more to affect the crop than the extra nitrogen.

It would, however, be unsafe to conclude that either the amount of nitrogen brought in by the two crops or the effect upon the physical conditions of water supply of the soil are the only factors concerned. Some practical men have found that vetches are always followed by a good crop of wheat, while others hold that the result is invariably poor. It is interesting to find that this divergence of opinion is illustrated so distinctly by the contradictory results at Rothamsted and Woburn. From the practical point of view the Rothamsted results would seem to show that on strong land the farmer will do better to sow vetches or crimson clover for green manuring than one of the non-leguminous crops.

E. MAINE. **Eichornea crassipes, and other Aquatic Plants as Green Manure in Indo-China and other Tropical Countries.** (Plantes aquatiques comme engrais vert en Indo-Chine et autres pays tropicaux). — *Journ. d'Agric. Tropicale*, XI année N. 118, pp. 108-110. Paris, 30 avril, 1911.   1390

The " Luc Binhs " of Indo-China which would appear, according to the Editor of the *Journal d'Agriculture Tropicale*, to be identical with *Eichornea crassipes*, are disastrous in tropical rivers. *Eichornea crassipes* abounds in many rivers of the Amazon basin, choking their passage and rendering navigation impossible. Dr Willis considers this planta threatened danger to the rice fields of Ceylon.   Indo-China-Senegal

In Indo-China it has invaded all the rivers and even ponds, forming a thick sheet and thus preventing navigation and killing the fish.

An analysis made in the Laboratory at Saigon shows that the plant might be used as manure:

Nitrogen	1.28	%
Phosphoric acid	0.31	„
Potash	4.66	„
Lime	3.16	„
Magnesia	0.59	„

Mr Maine considers that an analysis of the " Tambalayes ' of Senegal (1), for the destruction of which special grants had to be

---

(1) According to the *Journal d'Agriculture Tropicale* the Tambalayes include different species growing together, among which *Pistia stratiotes* predominates.   (*Ed.*)

made, might show them to be suitable when fresh and moist, together with the molluscs, minute fish, insects etc. which live among
them, for manuring the siliceous soils of Senegal.

1391   **Analyses of Sea-Weeds.** (Analyses de varechs). — *L'Engrais* 26.
année. N. 11. p. 297. Lille, 17 Mars 1911.

Great
Britain :
Cornwall

Three varieties of seaweed, collected at Padstow on the nor-
thern coast of Cornwall, were analysed by Mr W. H. Barlow in the
Cooper Laboratory at Watford (England).
The following are the results, calculated on dry substance.

	Fucus nodosus	Fucus serratus	Fucus versiculosus
Organic matter	73.99	76.97	71.35
Ash	26.01	23.03	28.65
Nitrogen	1.78	2.88	2.29
Potash	4.47	5.00	6.29
Phosphoric acid	0.29	0.55	0.45

The total alkalis found in the ash of the three varieties examined
was nearly uniform, as the following table shows :

	Soda	Potash	Total alkali
F. nodosus	23.19	17.19	40.38
F. serratus	17.76	21.69	39.45
F. vesiculosus . . .	18.72	21.94	40.66

1392   H. WOLTERECK. **On Production of Ammonia from Peat** (Sur la production de l'ammoniaque et l'économie de l'azote de tourbe). —
C. R. de l'Acad. des Sciences, T. 152, N. 19, pp. 1245-1247, Paris,
8 mai, 1911.

The writer has made some new experiments on the action of
a mixture of air and steam at 450° C. on peat, which confirm the

France   results of his preceding experiments. They show that the production
of ammonia is greater than could be accounted for by the nitrogen
content of the dry peat. · · · · · · · · ·
As some have thought this to be due to the action of the
steam alone, and not to atmospheric nitrogen, M. Woltereck made a
series of experiments first on peat treated only with steam and then
on the residues, which after the formation of ammonia and after
determining the nitrogen content, he treated with mingled air and
steam.

The experiments were in three series:

In A, the peat was treated with steam alone at 450° C.
In B, the residues of A were treated with mingled air and steam at 450° C.
In C, the peat was treated with mingled air and steam at 450° C.

Each experiment lasted 6 hours; the evolution of gas was finished within 3 hours and in series A, the formation of ammonia was completed after 5 hours.

The results showed decisively that the treatment of peat by steam alone produces only $\frac{1}{3}$ of the ammonia produced under the same conditions by mingled steam and air. And the amount of nitrogen lost by the action of steam corresponds very nearly to that of the nitrogen regained in the form of ammonia.

The treatment of the residues, in series B, gave a perceptible increase of nitrogen. The following are the details of the analyses of 100 grams of peat treated with mingled air and steam at 450° C.:

Moisture . . . . grams 61.5
Dry matter . . . .   »   38.5
Residue (ash) . . . .   »   4.2
Charred matter . . . .   »   34.3
Total nitrogen . . . .   »   1.6709
Nitrogen obtained, calculated as ammonia (NH_3)   »   1.7150 = 102.63 %(1)
Nitrogen in residue . . . .   »   0.000
Acetic acid . . . .   »   0.8593 = 2.31 %

An unexpected result was the complete absence of acetic acid in series A, the control experiment C having given 2.31 %.

BRIT. CONS.. HEWETT. **The Nitrate Industry in Antofagasta**. *Diplomatic and Consular Reports*. No. 4633 - P. 1-10. London, April, 1911.

1893

The present condition of the Nitrate Industry at Antofagasta, may be considered as satisfactory and its prospects exceptionally good, as the demand for nitrate of soda is steadily increasing year by year. Propaganda is carried on by the producers in the chief countries of the world for making known the advantages of nitrate

Chile
Antofagasta

_____

(1) Of total nitrogen.   (*Ed.*).

as a fertiliser. Experimental farms are installed in some countries.
where the marvellous results to be obtained are practically demonstrated. In 1909 a total sum of £.88 400 was expended, of which
the Chilian Government contributed £.40 000. The steady increase
in the yearly consumption throughout the world is shown in the
figures for the last five years which appear below.

In the Province of Antofagasta there are 62 *oficinas* or nitrate
works, of which 43 are at present working and 19 are closed.

NITRATE EXPORTED FROM ANTOFAGASTA.

	1909	1910
Spanish quintals of 100 lbs	24 039 896	27 338 340

CONSUMPTION OF NITRATE OF SODA.

	1906	1907	1908	1909	1910
Europe	28 552 200	28 643 970	31 637 070	33 523 560	37 863 375
United States . . .	8 149 851	8 110 411	7 096 498	9 372 358	13 047 340
Sundry Markets . .	908 843	1 043 020	1 153 921	1 582 819	386 074
Spanish quintals of 100 lbs.	37 610 894	37 797 401	39 887 489	44 478 737	51 296 789 (1)

1394   D. N. PRIANISCHNIKOV, W. P. KOTSCHETKOV and W. J. SAZANOV.
Utilisation of Russian Phosphorites. (O Khimiceskoi Perera-
botkie nascik Fosforitov). — *Is viestiïa Moskovskago Selskokho-
siaistvennago Instituta,* 1911. (*Annals of the Agricultural Institute of Moscow*), G. XVII, Kn. I, pp. 1-93. Moskova, 1911.

Russia   The use of chemical fertilisers in Russia is limited to the Western Governments, the cost of transport becoming gradually prohibi-
tive towards Eastern Russia.

---

(1) In 1905, the number of work-people employed in Chile in the nitrate
of soda workings was 30 600.

The total exports of nitrate and of iodine (obtained with the nitrate) in
recent years is stated as follows:

Years	Nitrate metric tons	Iodine metric tons	Years	Nitrate metric tons	Iodine metric tons
1900	1 465 935	318	1907	1 649 623	289
1905	1 668 976	564	1908	2 033 612	330
1906	1 766 805	351	1909	2 309 141	—

In 1909, the Chilian export of nitrate was valued at 15 815 262 £., and
that of iodine at 517 888 £.

The nitrate imported from Chile into the United Kingdom was valued
in 1908 at 1 359 895 £., and in 1909 at 845 991 £.

The Statesman's Yearbook for 1911, p. 683.   [*Ed.*].

A special Commission undertook in 1909 the examination of the rich beds of phosphorites in Central and Eastern Russia, and of the deposits of pyrites in the Urals, with a view to preparing double superphosphates, as, with the exception of those of Kasan and Kostroma, most of the Russian phosphorites are too full of impurities to make simple superphosphates.

The composition of the phosphorites examined is the following. Carolina phosphates are added for comparison:

	Phosphorites of Kostroma. %	Phosphorites of Kasan. %	Carolina Phosphates. %
Phosphorus pentoxide, $P_2 O_5$	·27.19	26.45	27.64
Carbon dioxide, CO_2	5.97	5.83	4.53
Sulphur trioxide, SO_3	0.46	1.15	0.57
Lime, Ca O	42.82	42.01	42.94
Magnesia, Mg O	0.76	0.15	0.61
Manganese oxide, Mn O	2.14	2.12	—
Iron pyrites, Fe S_2	1.05	undetermined	—
Ferric oxide, $Fe_2 O_3$	3.75	3.31	2.00
Alumina, $Al_2 O_3$	0.46	0.89	2.64
Fluorine	2.60	1.83	3.43
Moisture	0.57	1.66	1.15
Loss on ignition	6.89	10.90	7.70
Part insoluble in acids	5.75	3.87	7.79

In transforming these Russian phosphates into superphosphates it was found that for 2 kg. of powdered phosphates, the quantity of sulphuric acid at 52.1° B. to be used was from 1 400 to 1 500 cc.

The writers have made researches on the influence of temperature upon the solution of the phosphoric acid contained in the mineral phosphates, and on the structure of the superphosphates produced.

In order to obtain from these phosphates a product containing phosphates soluble in ammonium citrate the Wiborg process was applied, consisting in calcination of the phosphate with soda.

The following results were obtained with the phosphates of Kasan:

	Total $P_2 O_5$ %	$P_2 O_5$ soluble in ammonium citrate %	Ratio between citrate-soluble and total $P_2 O_5$ %
1 part of phosphate and ½ part of soda	22.00	21.72	98.70
	27.72	21.54	99.17
1 part of phosphate and ¼ of soda	24.79	18.02	72.69
	—	19.23	77.57

	P2 O5 %	soluble in ammonium citrate %	citrate soluble and total P2 O5 %
1 part of phosphate and 1/2 of soda	21.82	21.57	98.85
1 part of phosphate and 1/4 of soda	25.75	19.10	74.17

The products thus obtained contain the phosphorus pentoxide under a perfectly assimilable form, as has been shown by cultures in pots and in the open ground.

It is intended to continue these experiments on a large scale.

1895 **New Zealand Phosphates** (Les phosphates de la Nouve'le Zélande). — *L'Engrais*, N. 18, p. 495, Paris, 5 mai, 1911.

New Zealand Extensive phosphate beds have been discovered in New Zealand. The Ewing Society (Ltd.) has been formed for their extraction and calcination on a commercial scale. After calcination, the rock is crushed and treated with acid for its transformation into super-phosphate. It has been found satisfactory as a fertiliser, and the industry is expected to develop, so that New Zealand may soon export, instead of importing, phosphatic fertilisers.

1896 BARON de FECHTIG. **Dry Farming Experiments in Hungary in 1909-1910**. (Essais culturaux en Hongrie d'après la méthode Campbell (Dry Farming) pendant l'année d'exploitation 1909-1910). — *Communication de M. E. de Miklós de Miklósvar, Délégué de la Hongrie à l'Institut International d'Agriculture.*

Hungary M. de Fechtig has drawn up a concluding report on the dry farming experiments carried out on his property. They are the more interesting in that the year 1909-1910 was exceptionally damp, a condition unfavourable to dry farming methods. Having proved the value of the system, M. de Fechtig hopes to modify the Campbell system by adapting it to the meteorological and cultural conditions of his part of Hungary.

M. de Fechtig insists especially on the fundamental rule in dry farming: *break up and keep open as much as possible the surface of the ground.* Below this upper loosened stratum and above the lower stratum, never reached by the plough-share, there must be a certain depth of soil well cultivated, but compressed, which retains the moisture of both strata.

M. de Fechtig gives the following rules for the application of the Campbell systems.

a) *Each ploughing must be preceded by disking.*

b) *Stubbles must be disked after ploughing and immediately harrowed.*

c) *All ploughed land must be harrowed immediately.*

d) *All ploughed and harrowed soil should be immediately compressed by a packer.*

e) *The fields should be ploughed before the frost sets in.*

This last ru e is difficult to follow, although indispensable, in countries like Hungary where draught animals are scarce.

f) *Spring ploughing should be avoided.* (The experiments of M. de Kerpely have shown the value of this rule) (1).

g) *Winter and spring cultures should be cultivated with the harrow.*

These general principles must be adapted to soil, climate and economic conditions, and require in the farmer knowledge of the conditions of his land.

M. de Fechtig gives a few examples of variations to the rules given, which may be found necessary.

Maize fields, although well cultivated during the summer, have sometimes been completely dried up by the beginning of autumn, because the vigorous growth of the maize has absorbed nearly all the moisture in the soil.

When the maize was gathered the stubble was disked twice ; but the soil was so hard that the disk only affected from 2 to 3 inches of the surface. Here it was impossible to apply the rule that " disking should be immediately followed by ploughing "; for even if it had been possible to plough, no seed could have been sown, because of the hard clods. The method had to be adapted to the conditions, and wheat was sown in the shallow cultivated surface. The wheat germinated in autumn, throve under harrowing in spring and notwithstanding unusual drought yielded 13.3 quintals per *arpent cadastral* (0.5665 hectare), i.e 35 bush. per acre.

---

(1) See the Report presented by G. de Miklós de Miklósvar, Delegate for Hungary to the Permanent Committee of the International Institute of Agriculture on question N. 9 in the programme of the General Assembly of 1911, regarding the Campbell dry-farming system.   (*Ed.*).

The nature of the soil may also modify the methods to be followed. Strong clay soils containing a high proportion of soluble salts (the Hungarian *szikes földek*), even when cultivated in autumn, cannot be sown with wheat in spring because they absorb so much moisture in winter that in spring they are dry on the surface and wet in the subsoil. These soils can only be sown very late, when much of their moisture has evaporated. Winter cultures are suitable for these soils, after the application of dry farming methods during summer.

M. de Fechtig, after four years' experience, considers that even in a wet season dry farming methods would not give a lower yield than other methods, and he draws attention to another advantage of the system. Damp years generally have short periods of excessive drought which may prove disastrous, as was the case in 1909-1910. The heat was so extreme that the leaves of the maize rolled up, and beet stopped growing, except where dry farming methods had been adopted.

The following comparative table shows the results obtained by the Baron de Fechtig with dry farming methods, and the average crops obtained in Hungary.

	Average yield per acre on M. de Fechtig's property		Average in the Kingdom
	1909	1910	1910
Winter Wheat (bushels of 60 lbs.)	48	29	20
Winter Rye (bushels of 54 lbs.)	24	34	20
Spring Barley (bushels of 55 lbs.)	69	21	17
Maize, hand cult. (bushels of 60 lbs.)	47	65	30
Maize, horse cult. (bushels of 60 lbs.).	79	93	30
Oats (bushels of 42 lbs.)	78	43	21
Mangolds (tons)	37 ½	47	12

1897   **Culture Systems in the United States** (Les systèmes de culture aux Etats Unis). — *Journ. des Sociétés Agricoles du Brabant et du Hainault*, N. 20, p. 251. Bruxelles, 13 Mai, 1911.

United States   During the last 60 years a vast area of land has been brought under cultivation in the United States. At first the virgin soil yielded good crops with little expense; and as the land in the older States became exhausted, the tendency was to move further west in search of new virgin soils, so that the area that will still yield under a constant repetition of the same crop is now very much reduced. This extensive exhaustion of the soil makes it urgently necessary to adopt the systems of rotation familiar in the old countries.

The prices and the rents of farms have gone up. The exhausting system of continual culture without putting anything into the land seems to have gone on upon rented farms without any of those measures of control considered necessary elsewhere. The leases are short, so that the farmer, uncertain of reaping any future benefit, has no interest in keeping up the fertility of the soil, and exhausts it by the same methods employed when it was first brought under cultivation.

The U. S. Department of Agriculture now endeavours to diffuse among farmers a knowledge of the principles of soil-fertility.

In the first place the keeping of more cattle on the farms is recommended; and, where possible, that leases should be longer. When the tenant is unable to buy sufficient head of cattle, it is even suggested that the owner should supply them.

The Department further recommends the culture of leguminous plants, systematic rotations, an increased use of fertilisers, improvement of seed, cultivation of forage crops for the cattle, etc. Such changes take time and will necessitate more capital and more labour, but there can be no doubt of their ultimate success

J. M. B. Connor. **Northern Grain Experimental Fields in Victoria:** **Federation Wheat the best variety.** — *The Journal of the Department of Agriculture of Victoria*, Vol. IX, Part 3. Melbourne, 10th March, 1911.

1398

This report deals with the results of the sixth year's field trials carried out upon the experimental plots to be conducted for seven years under agreement with the Department of Agriculture of Victoria throughout the northern wheat areas. One of the principal objects of these experimental plots is to endeavour to ascertain by practical demonstration on the farmer's own land, the advantages to be gained to the particular district by the introduction of new varieties of wheats and other cereals likely to yield greater returns per acre.

Australia:
Victoria

The experimental fields at present being worked under the supervision of the Field Branch of the Department of Agriculture, comprise a total area of 531 acres as against 335 acres last year.

The wheat fields are carried out under arrangements which admit of cropping over seven consecutive years and are devoted chiefly to variety seed tests, fertilizer tests, quantity seed tests, and rotative courses.

The forage fields comprise cereals, millet, rape, roots, maize, soy-beans, tick beans, tares and peas. The experiments in connexion with development of poor lands are concerned chiefly with the improvement of the light sandy soils in the southern parts of the State and the clay lands in the northern areas.

The owner of each seven-year experimental field of 10 acres has undertaken to conduct continuous experiments over that time. The agreement terminates this coming season. The seed and manure are provided free by the Department, whose Field Officers sow the crops and supervise the harvesting operations. The farmer conducting the experiments receives a cash payment of £. 15 per year and two-thirds of the resultant crops, besides having the right to graze the area, which has been securely fenced by the Department. The results of this year's experiments were the following :

Throughout the State the Federation variety of wheat still takes first place as a grain yielder with the splendid average of 24.13 bushels per acre.

This variety is followed by College Purple Straw, 21.47 bushels and Yandilla King with 21.03 bushels.

The average yield for all varieties is 19.22 bushels per acre, as compared with 18.40 on the same fields last year and 14.62 for the preceding year. In the seed test plots, where Federation wheat was sown in varying quantities per acre, the 65 lbs. per acre gave the best general average namely 19.87 bushels per acre, but in the Mallee districts the 80 lbs. per acre gave the best results by 1.60 bushels per acre.

Among the oats, Garton's Stout White stands out first with 33.29 bushels per acre and at Goorambat gave the splendid yield of 49.44 bushels. This variety is closely followed by Algerian with an average of 32.24 bushels, whilst Tasmanian Giant takes third place with 30.58 bushels.

These particular varieties of oats, together with Western Wolth's Rye grass, were introduced into the plots for the purpose of demonstrating that suitable fodder plants can be profitably grown in the northern areas as a stand-by for live stock grazed on the farm.

Field Crops. — Industrial Crops. — Horticulture. Arboriculture.

F. T. SHUTT. **The Composition of the Grain as Influenced by the Soil Moisture.** — *Experimental Farms, Report of the Chemist, Wheat,* pp. 193-194. Ottawa, 1910. (App. to the Rep. of the Min. of Agric.).

1899

A series of experiments on irrigated and non-irrigated land in 1908, showed that Red Fife on the former contained 2.67 per cent. less protein than that on the drier soil; similarly with Kharkow a difference in protein-content of approximately 1.0 per cent. was obtained.

Canada

The repetition of this work during 1909 has afforded results of still more marked character :

Red Fife Wheat	Protein p. c.
Parent seed grown on non-irrigated land, 1908 . . .	13 97
» » » » irrigated	11.74
» » » » non-irrigated land	16.63

One irrigation only was made, on July 10, the moisture being respectively :

Date	Soils Irrigated	Non-irrigated
	%	%
July 16, 1909	9.62	8.50
August 1, 1909	8.19	6.20
» 25, 1909	8.16	5.99

Perhaps it is only right to state that the higher protein-content wheat, while the more valuable for mixing with soft wheats, may not necessarily yield the better flour for bread making; and, further, the yield of wheat is, as a rule, considerably higher on irrigated than on non-irrigated areas.

E. G. MONTGOMERY. **Oats. Variety Tests. Rate of Sowing. Cultivation.** R. Agri Exper. Station of Nebraska, V. XXII, A. III pp. 15 + fg. 1 + tab. XI. Lincoln, Nebraska, U. S. A.; 1910'

1400

Results of seven seasons of experimenting with oats :

1. The same treatment does not ensure the same results each year.

2. In years of much more than normal rainfall, positive damage is done by cultivating either oats or wheat.

United States: Nebraska

3. When there is sufficient moisture to mature a heavy crop of grain, it is certainly unwise to destroy plants with harrow or pulverizer.

On the other hand, when precipitation before seeding has been meagre, and dry weather follows, cultivation of grain results well.

4. Early varieties of oats have given an average of 14 bushels per acre (12.6 hectol. per hectare) greater yield during the past five or six years than late varieties.

5. The early varieties used have been rather small-grained and dark in colour.

6. Eight pecks per acre (1.8 hl. per ha.) has given the best results with drilled oats; and ten pecks per acre (2.25 hl. per ha.) when the oats were sown broadcast.

7. Cultivation of drilled oats has given an increased yield of 4.8 bushels per acre (4.3 hl. per ha.), while cultivation of broadcast oats has given decreased yield.

1401   EM. MIÈGE. **Buckwheat Varieties.** (Recherches sur les principales espèces de *Fagopyrum* — Sarrasin). — 1 vol. pp. 426 illust. Paris, 1910.

France

The culture of buckwheat (*Fagopyrum*) all over the world covers a surface of about 3 620 000 hectares (8 941 400 acres); the total value of the annual yield is about 430 000 000 frs. (£. 17 200 000), Notwithstanding the importance of this plant, this is perhaps the first comprehensive study on the subject.

The writer begins with the morphology of four principal types of *Fagopyrum*, characterised respectively by the following measurements:

$$
\begin{aligned}
\textit{Fagopyrum esculentum} & \ldots \ldots \text{ mm.: } 4 \quad \times 2.5 \\
\textit{F. tataricum} & \ldots \ldots \ldots \text{ » } : 3.75 \times 2.75 \\
\textit{F. stenocarpa} & \ldots \ldots \ldots \text{ » } : 4 \quad \times 2.5 \\
\textit{F. emarginatum} & \ldots \ldots \ldots \text{ » » } 4 \quad \times 3.25
\end{aligned}
$$

The following table gives the weights of 1000 grains of each kind:

		= grams (1)	
	Gray	= grams (1)	16.9
	German	= »	16.1
	American	= »	24.0
Fagopyrum esculentum	Russian	= »	15.9
	Japanese summer	= »	24.0
	Japanese autumn	= »	20.9
Fagopyrum tataricum		»	13.95
F. stenocarpa		»	13.6
F. emarginatum		»	17.6

(1) gram = 15.43 grains Troy.

The American and Japanese buckwheats have not only the largest and heaviest grains but also a smaller proportion of husk. . The composition of the grain does not differ much in the four kinds; it is very rich in non-nitrogenous substances, which average 63.3 %; nitrogenous substances form about 10 %, fatty matter about 2.25 % and mineral substances about 3 %. It constitutes therefore a complete and very nourishing food.

The grain of *Fagopyrum* can be used for seed immediately after harvesting: after the second, or at most the third, year it loses its germinating power, though not its value as food. As a general rule, the larger and heavier the grain, the greater its agricultural value.

Buckwheat requires a soil-moisture of 15 to 25 %, and a humous or sandy soil without much lime. It germinates fairly well at a depth of 16 to 18 cm. (6¼ to 7 inches) but develops best at ½ to 5 cm. ($^1/_5$ to 2 ins).

A normal crop of buckwheat takes out of the soil about 117 kg. (257.4 lbs.) of lime, 68 kg. (149.6 lbs.) of nitrogen, 87 kg. (191.4 lbs.) of potash, and 43 kg. (94.6 lbs.) of phosphoric acid, and these elements should be supplied in a rapidly assimilable form (2).

The development of the root system, the rapidity of vegetation and the intensity of transpiration indicate the need of a deep and careful cultivation, more than is generally thought necessary.

Experiments in selection show that buckwheat lends itself to be much improved.

F. J. ALWAY. **The Importance of the Inoculation of Alfalfa on Nebraska Upland Soils**. — *Twenty-third Annual Report of the Agricultural Experiment Station of Nebraska*, Appendix, pp. 3-20. Lincoln, Nebraska, U. S. A., 1910.

1402

Observations have been made in various parts of Nebraska during the past eight years on the importance of the inoculation of alfalfa.

United
States :
Nebraska

(2) « According to recent researches on the composition of the grain and stalks of buckwheat, an abundant crop contains about 40 kg. of nitrogen, 20 kg. of phosphoric acid, and 60 kg. of potash. 100 to 200 kg. of superphosphate and 100 kg. of potassium chloride, harrowed in before sowing, suffice for the needs of the plant ». BARRAL et SAGNIER. *Dict. d'Agriculture*. T. IV, p. 570. Paris, 1892.

See also (for calculations according to the analyses of BOUSSINGAULT and E. WOLFF) M. MARRO *Coltiv. delle piante erbacee*, 3ª ed. p. 316. Roma, 1909. For a good crop of Buckweat one may calculate 66.4 kg. of nitrogen, 26 kg. of lime, 18.9 kg. of phosphoric acid, 21 kg. of potash and sodium.   (*Ed.*).

Alfalfa sown on fields subject to occasional inundation, or on upland fields receiving storm waters from well-established alfalfa fields, may be expected to show complete inoculation from the first. On upland fields receiving no run-off from old fields there may be expected to be found a considerable number of inoculated plants. These may be identified both by their color and vigor and more surely by the examination for nodules on their roots. On upland fields on which alfalfa has been grown before in very recent years, or on which manure from alfalfa-fed animals has been scattered, complete inoculation may be expected. On farms in which there are already fields of alfalfa, the newly-sown fields have several sources of more or less complete inoculation : the wash from the old fields, the carrying of the inoculated soil by farm implements, and the droppings from the alfalfa-fed farm animals pasturing or working in the field. For this reason, other things being equal, a farmer already having alfalfa is more likely to get a good stand than his neighbour who has not. Some upland fields will, without any attention to their inoculation, give satisfactory stands; but others will give very thin and unsatisfactory stands, even when the preparation of the seed bed has been properly carried out and the weather conditions have been favorable. Everyone sowing alfalfa on Nebraska upland should either provide for its inoculation at the time of sowing the seed, by dressing the field with inoculating soil or with manure from alfalfa-fed animals; or, after the plants have been growing long enough to show that they are not inoculated, by dressing it with the inoculating soil. In the latter case, this soil, which usually can be found in some part of the newly sown field or obtained from some adjacent old alfalfa field or from roadside patches of sweet clover (1) should be scattered over the field just before rain.

1403   W. R. DUNSTAN. **Cotton Culture Throughout the World.** (La culture du coton dans le monde). — *Revue Economique Internationale*, Vol. II, No. 1, pp. 14-30, Bruxelles, Avril, 1911.

World Production   The superior quality of raw cotton required for European manufacture comes almost entirely from the sub-tropical regions of the United States and of Egypt, especially from the United States, the

---

(1) *Melilotus alba* called also Bokhara clover, is grown somewhat as a forage plant; cattle come to like it. It is an excellent bee plant. L. H. BAILEY Cyclop. of Americ. Horticulture. New-York, London, 1906,

Egyptian qualities being reserved for finer and dearer products. The ravages of the boll-weevil have led to a diminution of the export from the United States; the weevil has already invaded a large part of the cotton area, and will probably invade it all. The researches of the U. S. Department of Agriculture have shown that the cotton weevil is less destructive in dry regions; and that early varieties of cotton are much less liable to attack, as they mature before the weevil develops. Efforts are therefore now directed to a more careful choice of soil and to the introduction of early varieties, so as to reduce to a minimum the damage caused by this pest.

As it will be some time before these measures can affect the export of cotton from the United States, the cultivation of cotton in other regions should be increased; for not only is there scarcity of cotton but the price is likely to rise, and cannot in any way be controlled by European buyers.

In Egypt there is a distinct diminution of the yield per acre and also of the quality, due to unscientific cultivation. The Egyptian Government is about to organise a technical service, so as to remedy the deficiency without delay.

The possibility of cultivating cotton in the Sudan on a large scale depends on obtaining the water supply without prejudice to the needs of Egypt; there are good hopes of being able to overcome all the difficulties.

India is one of the great cotton producing countries, but Indian cotton is mostly coarse and the fibre is short. The immense extent of good agricultural soil, the excellent climate, the aptitude of the native labourers, the improving financial prospects — all point to India as the future source of raw cotton — at least for British industries.

In Algeria and Tunis cotton culture is increasing under favourable conditions.

An American variety of cotton might be grown on the plains of Cilicia. Other parts of Asia Minor, some of the Islands of the Levant, and parts of the Syrian coast, are all suitable for cotton growing. Mesopotamia, when the irrigation project has been carried out, will offer a vast region for the culture of cotton and of cereals.

In China a great deal of coarse cotton is grown and is used in the country; but the cultivation will probably extend in China.

Vast regions of Western Africa are suitable for cotton growing, and in many places the natives are disposed to make plantations. It grows well in Southern Nigeria, Togoland and Dahomey; it seems that a good American type might be grown in Western Africa, suitable for European manufacture. Northern Nigeria, traversed by a great

river and with abundant rains might become the foremost cotton-
producing country in the world.

Cotton does well in German and in British East Africa and in
Uganda.

In Peru, Mexico and Chile a good but rather coarse sort is grown;
there seems little probability of improvement in quality or increase
of production in South America.

The British, and in some degree the French, West Indies produce
a good deal of cotton, especially of the Georgia long fibre or Sea
Island type.

1404   E. De Wildeman. **Utilization of the Cotton Plant and Improvement in its Culture.** (Usages du Coton et amélioration de la
culture du Cotonnier dans le monde). — *Revue Economique Internationale*, Vol. II. N. 1, pp. 5-14. Bruxelles, Avril 1911.

Cotton is the most important industrial plant in the world; cotton oil is used for food and for industrial purposes (1).

Belgium   The whole of the seed is turned to account; fibre, oil, and residues
of extraction. In their green state, the stalk and leaves can be used
as forage, a fact of great importance in many regions where cotton is grown. The dry stalk furnishes an excellent raw material for
making paper.

The intensive culture of cotton does not pay unless carried on
with the best methods. National and international Associations have
been formed for this purpose. Seed should always be chosen from the
region where it is to be sown and where it is already acclimatised.
Direct introduction may give good results but often leads to disappointment. Degeneration of seed is more rapid in tropical countries
than in North America.

Even in the most favourable conditions the greatest care must
be used in the choice and control of the seed. Hybridization is often
necessary, but it is best to obtain first a good, constant native type.
Great attention must be paid to the offspring of hybrids, as a mixture
of seed may have a bad effect on future crops. The choice of variety
must depend not only on the yield, but on the quality of the fibre
and the requirements of the market.

As cotton cultivation and cotton industries are likely to develop
all over the world, technical and economical knowledge of the subject ought to be far more generally diffused.

---

(1) See this *Bulletin* March, 1911, n. 949.   (*Ed.*).

It is principally for want of knowledge that this cultivation and industry does not develop better in many regions: knowledge of proper cultural methods, of the right varieties, and of the way to prepare and to sell the fibre.

Cotton Cultivation extending in California. — *California Cultivator.* Los Angeles, April 20, 1911.

1405

Experiments in cotton culture made for some years in the Im perial Valley in California created but little general interest. Now it is estimated that not less than 50 000 acres will be planted next season.

Experiments have been made with various kinds of seed. All that has been raised commercially has been short staple Upland cotton, most of it being of the varieties known as Sim's Improved and Mebane Triumph. Several growers are experimenting with Egyptian Cotton. Enough has been raised to show that it can be made commercially profitable, but up to date, the rich soil and abundant water have produced very large stalks, sometimes reaching to a height of eight or nine feet without a corresponding amount of fruit. This no doubt can be remedied by a proper selection of seed and with less frequent irrigations. This cotton having a much longer length of staple sells for about thirty cents a pound on the market, when ordinary short staple brings only about half that. The crop is being marketed on the Pacific Coast, the Oakland Cotton Mills taking a portion and Japanese buyers the remainder.

United States: California

The labor question seems to have solved itself between American pickers and an occasional Mexican or Indian. A few colored pickers have been induced to come from Southern localities, but their help has not been found necessary.

A. Dumazet. **Cotton in Algeria** (Le Cotonnier en Algérie). — *Journ d'Agriculture pratique*, 75ᵉ année, N. 21, pp. 651-653. Paris 23 Mai, 1911.

1406

Cotton cultivation, which was in 1900 considered impossible in Algeria, has attained some importance within the last two or three years. In 1907, cotton was grown on 75 hectares (185 acres) and yielded 98 000 kg. (215 600 lbs.); in 1909, 400 hectares (1000 acres) were under cotton. In 1910, in the departments of Algiers and Constantine alone, 444 and 127 hectares (1097 acres and 314 acres) respectively were cultivated with cotton.

Algeria

The yield is much greater on irrigated than on dry soils, but the cost is greater. Near Philippeville, where there is no irriga-·ion, the expenditure per hectare is from 250 to 300 frs (£. 4 — £. 4. 16s. per acre). On the outskirts of the Cheliff region where 411 hectares (1015 acres) are under cotton, irrigation brings the expense up to 500 frs. the hectare, (£. 8 per acre) but the result is more certain.

Cotton on unirrigated land may yield 1 000 kg. per hectare (900 lbs. per acre); on irrigated land, 1 200 kg. (1070 lbs.). Near Blida as much as 1 700 kg. (1520 lbs.) have been obtained, equal to a gross revenue of 1 500 fr. per hectare (£. 24.6s. per acre) for an expenditure of less than 500 fr. (£. 8 per acre).

1407

F. MAIN. **Cotton *versus* Sugar cane in Louisiana.** (Coton contre Canne à sucre en Louisiane) — *Journ. d'Agriculture tropicale*, XI année, No. 118, pp. 104-106. Paris, 30 Avril 1911.

United States: Louisiana

The great damage done by the Cotton Boll-Weevil is making Louisiana planters consider the question of growing sugar-cane instead of cotton. A good cotton crop may yield 350 lbs. of picked cotton per acre, representing a value of $ 35 per acre (about 440 francs. per hectare). A good crop of cane is about 25 000 kg. (55 000 lbs) per acre, worth $ 100 per acre (1250 fr. per hectare). The drawback is that the cost of transport amounts to 50 times that of cotton per acre. There would however always be a gross return of $ 80.75 per acre (1000 fr. per hectare), which is far more than cotton would ever bring in, and sugar is considered a very sure crop. The work also has to be done in season when labour is least difficult to obtain.

A recent number of the *Louisiana Planter* announced that a number of lots of 50 acres each were being offered to farmers emigrating from districts devastated by the cotton weevil.

It should however be noted: that the price of sugar is subject to far greater fluctuations than cotton ; and that sacchariferous plants are not restricted to special climates or species. The commercial preparation of sugar demands, moreover, a much more costly plant than is required for picking and pressing cotton.

1408

BRIT. CONS. WILEMAN. **Manila Hemp in the Philippines.** — *The Board of Trade Journal*, no. 653, p. 252. London, May 4, 1911.

Philippines

During the last few years, the production of Manila hemp in the Philippines has been steadily increasing. The production in 1909 was some 1 280 000 bales, and last year about 1 340 000 bales, and it is expected that it will this year reach 1 400 000 bales, or possibly more. The price of hemp in the islands has fallen considerably in recent years, but the tendency is still for the production to increase, as the natives have to produce more hemp in order to obtain a living income. Machinery plays practically no part in the production of hemp in the Philippines, as no practicable machine for cleaning the fibre has yet been invented, although attempts have been made from time to time to introduce machines. The reason is that no machine has been invented sufficiently 'light and portable to go into the hemp country (1).

Useful Fibres in Cuba. *The Board of Trade Journal*, No. 754   **1409**
p. 300. — London, May 11th 1911.

According to the Cuban Department of Agriculture, there are a number of useful fibres in Cuba. The bark of the *Majaqua* tree furnishes a long and strong fibre, used in making ropes. The *guana*, a product from the interior bark of the tree of that name, comes in several layers, and is so strong and fine that it resembles woven silk. The *corojo* fibre, of great strength and very white, is used locally for making fancy bridles and girths ; experiments are being made with a view to make it serve as a support for the rubber in motor-car tires. Jute does well in Cuba, but until recently no attempt has been made to develop the industry, the possibilities of which are now under consideration. Henequen, planted only in the past few years, grows abundantly ; it is used for various purposes. Other fibres are those from the Jarey palm (*Sanseveria Quisaso*) and Ramie.

Cuba

Sugar Production in Spain. (Die Spanische Zuckerindustrie). — *Das*   **1410**
Handels-museum, N. 14, p. 215. Wien, 6 April, 1911.

Spain produces both cane sugar and beet sugar. The production of beet sugar is four times that of cane sugar. Beetroots occupy about 27 500 hectares (68 000 acres) in Spain: 9000 (22200 acres) in the pro-

Spain

---

(1) The exportation of Manila Hemp from the Philippines was valued in 1910 (fiscal year ending June 30, 1910) at 17 404 922 dollars. It is by far the most valuable of Philippine exports. *The Statesman's Yearbook for 1911*, p. 558. Cp. this Bulletin, Dec. 1910, p. 191; Abstr, No. 114, Jan. 1911; Abstr. N. 454, Febr. 1911. (*Ed.*).

vince of Saragossa, 8000 (19800 acres) in Andalusia, of which 5000 (12350 acres) are in Granada, and the rest in Malaga, Castille, and Navarre. The total production has attained 715 000 tons, or 26 tons per hectare (10½ tons per acre). There are 51 sugar factories, of which 14 are in Granada, 9 in Saragossa, and 4 in Malaga. The sugar produced is about 12.9% of the weight of the beets. In 1910, 86147 tons of beet sugar were produced.

Sugar cane is cultivated exclusively in the provinces of Granada Malaga, and Almeria, on a total area of 6500 hectares (16 000 acres). Cane industry employs 23 factories and 13 mills. In 1910, 251 000 tons of cane were used, yielding 21 670 tons of sugar, or 8.63%.

1411   CH. S. KNIGHT. **The Beet Sugar Industry in Nevada.** — *Agr. Exp. Sta. University of Nevada.* Bulletin, N. 75. Reno, Nevada, March, 1911.

United States: Nevada

This report is intended to give brief and practical suggestions to the sugar beet growers and other farmers who are interested in the culture of the crop. Special attention is given to the cultural methods and to irrigation.

The sugar beet factory at Fallon Nevada has been under construction since August 1, 1910, and will be in working order in time for the 1911 crop.

The factory is to have a beet slicing capacity of 500 tons in 24 hours. It will be able to handle about 75 000 tons a season, which would mean 150 days operation, starting the 1st of September and finishing the 1st of February.

During the first season, the factory is planning to handle only about 50 000 tons of beets which will produce about 14 million pounds of sugar at an expense of about three and one fourth cents a pound. The factory will pay for the beets $ 4.50 a ton for 15 per cent, 30 cents a ton more for every per cent above 15 per cent, and 25 cents less per ton for every per cent below 15 per cent. On December 15, 1910, contracts had been signed up for about 2000 acres of beets to be grown during the season of 1911, but it is expected that this acreage will increase to about 5000 acres.

The average yield per acre for this crop in the irrigated States, is ten or twelve tons per acre; but for successful growers of sugar beets the average yield per acre is approximately seventeen tons. Yields as high as thirty-six tons per acre have been noted and from twenty to twenty-five tons are not unusual.

From figures gathered throughout the irrigated sugar beet dis-
tr'ct the following items of average cost are given which do not
include original levelling of the land, interest and depreciation on
farm implements, or fertilizing, nor is the interest on the original
investment considered.

COST AND PROFIT FROM GROWING SUGAR BEETS.

17 tons of beets at $ 5 flat rate. . . .		$ 85.00
Ploughing land 10 to 12 inches deep . .	$ 3.00	
Harrowing, levelling, cultivating and pre-		
paring seed bed	» 2.00	
Drilling in seed	» 0.50	
20 pounds seed.	» 2.00	
Cultivating 5 times . . . , ...	» 2.00	
Furrowing twice	» 1.00	
Irrigating three times, labor	» 3.00	
Thinning, hoeing and topping contract .	» 20.00	
Ploughing out	» 2.00	
Hauling at 50 cents per ton (17 ton crop)	» 8.50	
Water charge for maintenance of canals	» 0.75	
Total cost of raising . . .		$ 44.75
Profit per acre.		$ 40.25

In California the hand-labor item is usually less but the cost
of water for irrigation is higher, so that the total is about the same.
Generally speaking, an 8 ton or a 10 ton crop will just about pay
the expense of growing, while anything above that yield will be
profitable, and as the tonnage increases, the greater the returns in
proportion.

On smaller fields, the grower and his family very often do all,
or the greater part, of the work themselves, so that they earn good
wages besides the profit from a good yield. Where beet land is
rented for cash, $ 8 to $ 15 per acre is charged, which includes
water rights, while for share rent, one fourth of the crop is the
usual rate. The total cost of raising beets in Nevada will probably
not exceed $ 35 per acre, since considerable cheap labor can be
obtained from the Indians of the different reservations who have
proved themselves very efficient in this class of work.

The sugar-beets grown at Reno in 1910, by the Exp. Station,
on a clay loam soil, contained from 17.95 to 21.47 % of sugar.

Sugar-Cane in Natal. (Zuckerernte und Industrie in Natal). —
Deutsches Kolonialblatt, N. 6, Berlin, 15 März, 1911.

1412

About 60 000 acres are at present under sugar-cane in Natal.
The yield is about 80 000 tons, supplying 30 mills and one large

Union of
South Africa:
Natal

refinery. A second large and very modern refinery is being built. Natal furnishes 80 % of the sugar consumed in British South Africa; the other 20 % comes from Mauritius. The production of sugar is developing fast and will soon be more than enough even for the increasing local consumption. (1).

1413   **The Sugar-Palm of the East Indies.** *Journal of the Royal Society of Arts*, No. 3048, pp. 567-569. — London, April 21st 1911.

Duch East
Indies

The Sugar-Palm (*Arenga saccharifera*) grows abundantly in all the Dutch East India islands, and provides the natives not only with a fermented beverage termed *saqueiro* but with sugar, cordage for the rigging of boats (*prams*) and material for calking them, and brooms for sweeping. The palm is called *pokko gamutu* by the Malays, and plenty of the trees are always found in the neighbourhood of the villages. It is the stalk of the male inflorescence only which is tapped for the sap. As the cluster is very heavy and also contains a cavity filled with *saqueiro*, the stalk is generally supported by a stout prop. The palms produce fruit more or less throughout the year. Of recent years Europeans have felled and burned off much *Arenga saccharifera* to make room for rubber, cocoanut and other plantations.

Ceram is, at the present time, almost the only island in the Dutch Indies which is practically untouched, and already forests are here being cleared for growing cocoa-nut trees.

1414   OLSSON-SEFFER. *Sesamum indicum* **and its Occurence in Mexico**. — *The Tropical Agriculturist*, pp. 205-206. Colombo, March 1911.

Mexico

The oil of commerce obtained from the Sesame seed is a product of an annual herb known in India as *Gingili*, Japan *Goma*, China *Mua* and in Mexico as *Ajonjoli*. Some progress has been made with the cultivation of sesame in Mexico. Last year about five million pounds were shipped from the Balsas Valley region in Mexico, between San Miguel and the Pacific Coast. The climatic and soil conditions of Mexico seem peculiarly favourable to the growth of oil seeds. Sesame will grow in almost any soil except in very heavy clay or low damp places. It thrives best in light sandy loam sheltered from the prevailing winds.

---

(1) In 1907-08, the area under sugar in Natal was 14 627 acres, with a yield of 71 664 700 lbs. In 1908-09, the area rose to 24 512 acres with a yield of 173 580 000 lbs. *The Statesman's Yearbook for 1911* p. 212.   (*Ed.*).

One of the advantages of the culture of this plant consists in quick return of products. When the farmer in Mexico knows that he can grow and manufacture on his own farm an oil which can be used largely for household purposes and feeding pigs, cattle, and poultry, he will greatly regret that he has not before noticed this herb and cultivated it.

A. FAUCHÈRE. **Cacao Varieties in Madagascar. Proportionate Weight of Beans and Pods.** (Sur le rendement en graines, comparativement au poids des cabosses, dans quelques variétés de Cacaoyer). — *Journal d'Agric. Tropicale*, IIe année, N. 118, pp. 106-107. Paris, 30 Avril, 1911.

1415

The following data were furnished to the *Journal d'Agriculture Tropicale* by the Station of Tamatave in Madagascar, where there are specimens of all the West Indian varieties of cacao. The question of cacao varieties is of special interest to experts in Java and Trinidad.

Madagascar

The cacao pods were chosen on the trees in such a way as to represent an average.

VARIETY	Average weight of pod. grams	Weight of fresh beans, extracted from 100 kg. of fruit Kgr.
1) — Long, yellow, curved and very pointed pod; slightly constricted near the stalk — « Criollo de Trinidad » ; — « Caracas vrai de Surinam ».	756	19.6
2) — Very long, yellow, barely pointed pod, slightly constricted near stalk, skin slightly wrinkled — « Caracas de Surinam ».	724	25.6
3) — Smooth, short, red pod, — « Amelonado de Trinidad ».	625	19.7
4) — Smooth, short, yellow pod, ribbed slightly. — « Porcelaine de Surinam ».	645	23.4
5) — Pod like No. 4.	656	24.0
6) — Red pod, in shape like No. 1.	528	15.9
7) — Very small, smooth, yellow pod, ·ribbed slightly. — « Calabacillo du Venezuela ».	293	26.7
8) — Pod like No. 7.	358	29.7
9) — Small, ribbed pod, — « Calabacillo ».	310	34.1

1416   L. DECOUX. **Tobacco in Belgium.** (Le tabac en Belgique). — *Progrès agricole belge*, 8ᵉ année, N. 21. Jodoigne, 20 mai, 1911.

The cultivation of tobacco is likely to spread in Belgium wherever the labour of ˉthe family is sufficient for average or small undertakings.

Belgium

The Havana tobacco cultivated in Belgium contains an average of 2.68 % of nicotine ; the native tobacco, 3.66 %. The success with which tobacco is grown in the region of the Semais, in Southern Belgium, where the soil is very poor, confirms the results of the experiments of Messrs. Girard and Rousseau in France. In the poorest soils, as long as they were deep and permeable, splendid crops of tobacco were grown with the help of chemical fertilisers.

The varieties cultivated in the neighbourhood of Jodoigne are the following : *Havana*, with large leaves 50 cm. long, which become very light when dry ; *Petit Grammont*, with shorter, thicker leaves, with marked ribs, yielding a strong tobacco ; *Obourg*, with leaves of a deeper colour, the secondary ribs of which are ramified.

The Havana yields 6 kg. per 100 plants ; the other two varieties 7 kg. The seed is sown in beds early in March.

1417   **Tobacco Cultivation in Northern Albania.** (Tabak-bau in Nord Albanien). — *Oesterr.-Monatschrift für d. Orient.* Wien, Februar, 1911.

Ottoman Empire: Albania

For the first time in many years Albania has exported tobacco to Samos. This exportation has been facilitated by the lowering of the exportation dues, which will tend to stimulate the growing of tobacco in the plain of Scutari.

1418   SAMSON. (Brit. Cons). **Tobacco Production in Xanthi and Gumuljina Districts in Thracia.** — *The Board of Trade Journal*, No. 753, p. 250. London, May 4, 1911.

Ottoman Empire: Thracia

The production of tobacco in the districts of Xanthi, Gumuljina, Cheh Djouma, Daridere and Ahi Chelebi for the year 1910 may be reckoned at 4 000 000 kilogs ; or about 25 per cent. larger than an average crop. This increase causes a considerable demand for manual labour. The consequent rise in the cost of which acted to the detriment of the growers, who have therefore agreed to sow some 40 per cent. less acreage in 1911 than that sown in 1910. The proportion of « Maxouls » (superior quality) and «Sirapastals» (inferior quality) may be taken as 25 per cent. and 75 per cent. respectively of the crop.

There has been a large demand for light-coloured mild tobaccos of «Sirapastals» quality, which is usually purchased for the British and German markets.

Sowings for 1911 have taken place throughout the Xanthi and Gumuljina (Gumurdzina) districts under favourable climatic conditions.

Tobacco in Martinique. (La culture du tabac à la Martinique). —   1419
La Quinzaine Coloniale, N. 8, p. 285. Paris, 25 avril, 1911.

Tobacco growing is increasing in Martinique. The Government makes efforts to encourage the industry in its early stage, and there   **Martinique** seems every propability of its complete success.

R. CATELANI. **On the Use of Lignite in Drying the Kentucky type**   1420 **of Tobacco.** (Sull'impiego della lignite nella cura mista dei tabacchi di tipo Kentucky). — *Boll. tecn. della coltivaz. dei tabacchi*, Anno X, N. 2, pp. 90-102. Scafati, Marzo-Aprile, 1911.

, Experiments have been made in Italy on the use of lignite in drying tobaccos of the Kentucky type in hot air.

These experiments were carried out with a stove of the usual type, placed outside the drying houses, the roofs of which are con-   **Italy** structed so as to allow the escape of more or less moisture, regulated at will.

The drying was done leaf by leaf and by plants in two drying houses. The stove heated with wood was lighted first, and when the leaves were completely brown, then the stove with lignite. Meanwhile, in a third house, the lignite stove was lighted 17 hours after the wood stove, and the leaves turned brown under the simultaneous action of both stoves ; afterwards the leaves and ribs were dried with the lignite stove only.

The results showed that the mixed heating has economical advantages ; that it is better to let the moisture evaporate slowly through the roof than by opening occasionally the doors and windows, as is done in Valdichiana, in Italy.

The product obtained by mixed heating leaves perhaps something to be desired as to uniformity of colour, which is deeper in the plants than in the separate leaves. The system makes no difference in the gloss and elasticity of the leaves, and the flavour, perfume and combustibility are much superior.

1421

A. DONNINI. **Packing of Tobacco** (Confezionamento delle balle di tabacco). — *Boll. tecn. della coltivaz. dei tabacchi*, An. X, N. 2, p. 103, Scafati, Marzo-Aprile, 1911.

Tobacco is generally packed by compressing the leaves between thin boards, fastened with cord, and wrapping the package in canvas when it leaves the press. At the Station of Borgo San Sepolcro, in Italy, a new system has been adopted, with distinct saving of time and expense.

Italy: Tuscany

The package leaves the press already wrapped in canvas. The canvass for wrapping three sides of the package is placed on the lower face of the press, and on the upper that for the other three sides; when sufficiently pressed, the long sides of the canvas can be sewn together, so that very little more has to be done when the package leaves the press.

1422

H. BLIN. **Tobacco Oil** (Huile de Tabac). — *La Nature*, 39ᵉ année, N. 1980, Suppl. p. 181. Paris, 6 mai 1911.

In 1848 an Englishman observed that tobacco seed contains an oil of superior quality and easy to extract. A recent number of the *Farmer's Magazine* gives a method for its extraction. The oil is quite limpid and has greater drying properties than any of the oils commonly used, which would render it very valuable for varnishes and adds another interest to the cultivation of tobacco (1).

Great Britain

1423

ENGELBRECHTEN. **Tamarinds in Adamaua, Kamerun.** (Verwendung der Tamarindenfrucht bei den Eingeborenen von Adamaua). — *Deutsches Kolonialblatt*, N. 7, s. 287. Berlin, 1. April, 1911.

The cultivation of tamarinds is spreading in the centre and north of Adamaua; the climate of these regions, situated at an average of 700 ft. above sea level, suits the tamarind tree (2).

Kamerun

---

(1) Tobacco seed, under a simple pressure yields readily 36 % of a greenish, scentless oil, density 0.923 at 15° C. solidifying at — 25° C. and drying rapidly. (HENRY WATTS, *A Dictionary of Chemistry*, Vol. V, p. 851, London, 1883).   (*Ed.*).

(2) Tamarind (*Tamarindus indica* L.; LEGUMINOSAE) is cultivated all over the tropics for its pods, wich yield a sweet juicy pulp; these are also preserved in various forms. See BAILEY, *Encycl. Amer. Hort.*   (*Ed.*).

In some districts the natives collect silk-worms off these trees. To prepare tamarind juice, the fruit is cut into very small pieces, which are then boiled with the addition of water and sugar.

Cultivation of Caraway in Holland (La Culture du Carvi en Hollande). — *Bull. scientifique et industriel Roure-Bertraud fils*, 3ᵉ Série, n. 3, pp. 54-57. Grasse, avril 1911.

1424

It is not generally known how much the cultivation of caraway has spread in Holland (1). *Carum Carvi* is a biennial umbelliferous plant: in Holland it is sown, as an under-crop, with other crops such as peas, mustard, poppy or spinach. Sown broadcast, about 10 kg. of seed per hectare (9 lbs. per acre) are required; but sown with a drill, in rows from 35 to 50 cm. (14 to 20 inches) apart, 8 kg. (7 lbs) are enough. Care must be taken with the drill not to sow too deeply, as they will then develop slowly, or possibly not at all. It must be kept clean of weeds especially from darnel. When the other crop has been harvested, the young caraway crop is cleaned by passing a cultivator between the rows; in spring it is lightly harrowed when the young plants begin to develop. The weeding only ceases when the plants are in flower. The flowering lasts about three weeks, and the formation of the seed another three weeks. It is generally then cut or mown, about the end of June, set up in sheaves, and then thrashed with a flail. The yield varies between 1000 and 2000 kg. per hectare. The area under caraway in Holland in 1880 was 1,600 hectares (4000 acres); in 1909 7,000 hectares, (17 300 acres) in which year the total production was 8 587 000 kg. (8 400 tons).

Holland

Production of Vanilla in the Islands of the Indian Ocean. (Vanillen Produktion auf den Inseln des Indischen Ozeans). — *Deutsches Kolonialblatt*, N. 6, s. 241. Berlin, 15. März, 1911.

1425

The production of Vanilla is increasing in the French islands in the Indian Ocean, but not in those belonging to Great Britain (Seychelles). The total production of the islands in the Indian Ocean is more than 200 tons. Madagascar, Réunion, the Comoros and the Seychelles produce together more than half of the total world-pro-

Madagascar, Seychelles, etc.

(1) See p. 78 of this *Bulletin* for Nov. 1910.   (*Ed.*).

duction. Mexico and Tahiti, where the rest of the vanilla is produced, seldom put on the market more than 140 and 100 tons respectively of vanilla (1).

1426   G. VOLKENS. **Perfume Plants of Togo** (Les plantes utiles du Togo).
— *Bull. Sem.*, Schimmel et Cie. pp. 141-143, Miltitz, près Leipzig,
Avril, 1911.

In an article on Togo (*Notizblatt des Kgl. bot. Gartens u. Museums zu Berlin-Dahlem*, 22 Append., No. 30, 30. Nov. 1910, p. 70
et seq.) Mr. Volkens gives the following list of plants containing
Togo   volatile oils, or having perfumed flowers:
Andropogon Schoenanthus, Flück. et Hamb. non L. Culture experiments are being made in Togo with this plant which furnishes
the essence of palmarosa.
Cyperus longus, L. (*Cyperaceae*). The tubercles on the rhizomes
of this plant contain an essential oil that has a slight scent of
violets.
The Curcuma root (*Curcuma longa*, L. *Zingiberaceae*) is cultivated
everywhere in Togo, as is also ginger.
Opilia celtidifolia Endl. ex Weelp (2), (*Opilaceae*), called by the
natives " Njemidro " or " Yubeno " is a liana of the steppe; its
flowers have an agreeable scent of carnations.
Ximenia americana, L. (*Oleaceae*), called by the negroes " Marka ";
Schweinfurth recommended the use of these flowers in perfumery;
they have a strong scent of orange.
Moringa oleifera, Lam. (*Moringaceae*), called by the natives
" Jevoti " " Baganluá " " Bagäléan " or " Mágarua Masér ". A tree
growing to 6 metres, native of India ; its seeds yield oil of béhen,
and the roots are used in the same way as horseradish.
Byrsocarpus (Rourea) coccineus, Sch. and Th. (*Connaraceae*).
A shrub growing to about 1 metre, called by the natives " Hesre "
or " Ssamala "; its flowers have a very remarkable scent of violets,
which should make it a valuable plant for perfumery.

---

(1) In 1909, the export of vanilla from Madagascar was valued at 47 630 £.
In Mayotte the cultivation of vanilla has superseded that of the sugar-cane.
Réunion exported in 1909 about 39 ½ tons of vanilla.
    From the Seychelles the export of vanilla in 1909 was valued at 13 356 £.
The Statesman's Yearbook for 1911, p. 188, 804, 806, 807.   (*Ed.*).
    (2) *O. amentacea*, Roxb.; v. *Ind. Kew.*, 1895.   (*Ed.*).

Acacia Farnesiana, Willd. (*Leguminosae*). Planted on the coast and sometimes in the interior.

Daniella thurifera J. J. Benn. (*Leguminosae*). Grows to 20 or 30 metres, very common in the plains, and furnishes a scented resin. According to Kersting, this resin is used in the same way as incense. The secretion of the resin is caused by the boring of certain insects, which make galleries in the trunk an inch in diameter and ramifying in all directions. The resin collects in these galleries and exudes at their openings. The natives collect the resin and tear off the dead bark, beneath which is found the wood more or less decayed and impregnated with resin. In northern Nigeria a wood-oil used in pharmacy is extracted from the *Daniella thurifera* and exported.

Cyanothyrsus (*Leguminosae*). One species of this genus, called by the natives " Olifi " or " Olüifi ", secretes a resin.

Hannoa undulata, Planch. (*Simarubaceae*). An essential oil can be extracted from the flowers.

Lecaniodiscus cupanioides, Planch. (*Sapindaceae*), called by the natives " Awetjé " " Kességplé " or " Yèletimlé ", a tree growing in the forests on the mountains or along the coast. Its flowers have a remarkably agreable perfume. In certain parts of Africa, but not in the Togo, aromatic waters are distilled from the flowers.

Butyrospermum Parkii (G. Don) Kotschy (*Sapotaceae*). A butter tree. Its flowers have a scent of honey.

Jasminum gardeniodorum, Gilg. (*Oleaceae*). This plant, which is almost constantly in flower, might perhaps be useful in perfumery.

Lippia adoënsis, Hochst. (*Verbenaceae*), a shrub called by the negroes " Nyöna " or " Fasan ", found everywhere; its leaves have a smell of peppermint.

European Markets for Fresh Fruit and Vegetables. (Marché européen des légumes et fruits frais). — *L'Agriculture commerciale*, N. 9, p. 213. Paris, 14 mai, 1910.

1427

Germany and Great Britain have by far the largest importation of fresh vegetables, respectively 209 000 and 94 000 tons. Switzerland comes next, with 47 000 ; then Austria-Hungary, with 37 000 ; Belgium, with 28 000; France, with 25 000. Holland at the same time exported 150 000 tons ; France and Algeria, 72 000 ; Austria-Hungary, 71 000 (*transit*); Italy, 47 000 ; Spain, 12 000, and Denmark, 12 000 tons.

Europe

Germany and Great Britain have also the largest importation of fresh fruit: but while German importation continues regularly to increase, British importation has diminished; this is due to the appearance o bananas on British markets.

The following figures give the annual averages for the principal fruit- exporting countries and their proportion of the total export: France, 108 500 tons, (34 %); Austria-Hungary, 82 000, (26 %); Italy, 73 901 (23 %); Spain, 15 900 (5 %).

1428   F. FAREY. **Strawberry Growing in Vaucluse, France.** (La culture du fraisier en Vaucluse). — *Revue Horticole*, Paris, 1er Mai, 1911.

France:
Vaucluse

During the last fifteen years strawberry growing has made great progress in Vaucluse, principally in the neighbourhood of Carpentras, Pernes, and Monteux, in consequence of the efforts of the Agricultural Association of Carpentras to find markets for strawberries in Paris and in England.

In Vaucluse strawberries are generally grown in the open, on pebbly ferruginous soils of Alpine diluvium which abound round Carpentras.

Now that these lands have been irrigated and adapted to strawberry culture, they sell at from 6000 to 7000 fr. the hectare (£ 96 to £ 112 per acre). The permeability of these soils suits the strawberry; for they soon warm in spring, which hastens ripening, and they drain so rapidly after rain or watering that the strawberries are not liable to decay.

In making a strawberry bed, which should last some years, 26 to 39 tons of farm manure per hectare (10 to 16 tons per acre) must be given. In the following years commercial fertilisers are generally applied, principally oil cake or *chrysalides* (silk cocoon refuse) together with some ferrous sulphate to prevent chlorosis, which sometimes appears on calcareous soils, especially after too abundant watering. In spring it is well to complete this manuring by the following mixture:

Oil-cake . . . . . . per *éminée* (7.7 ares)	100 kg.;	per acre 10 cwt.
Sodium nitrate	20 »	2 »
Superphosphate 16-18 % soluble $P_2 O_5$) . .	50 »	5 -
Potassium sulphate (48-51 % $K_2 O$)	20 »	2 •
Ferrous sulphate	10 »	1 »

Strawberries manured in this way resist disease and require little care: it is enough to keep them hoed and watered, and particularly to thoroughly remove the runners, which exhaust the plants and spoil the crop.

As earliness is the first commercial 'quality for strawberries, they are forced in spring by means of shelters.

The first year the crop is not large, but the strawberries are early and fine. The second year gives the finest crop; and, the third year it diminishes. In first-rate culture, strawberry beds are only kept three years.

A great number of varieties have been tried in Vaucluse, of which ten have been found to answer the requirements of culture, transport etc. These ten ripen from the end of April to the middle of June; the following are the more important (in order of ripening):

1. *Reine des hâtives*, good sized fruit, long shaped, fine deep red; good flavour; not very prolific.

2. *Milner*, a comparatively new variety with large fruit, early and prolific; recommended.

3. *Héricart de Thury*, an old variety, hardy and prolific; begins to be superseded by *Reine des hâtives*.

4. *Noble*, a large, fine fruit of excellent quality, with the seeds deeply sunk, suitable for exportation to England; a strong, prolific plant, ripening rapidly.

5. *Paxton*, long-shaped, brilliant red fruit, exported to England; very prolific and bears all the summer.

6. *Sovereign*, large delicate fruit, unsuitable for carriage; very prolific, and ripening gradually; requires shelter from wind on account of the length of the stalks.

7. *Victoria*, large and round, fine flavour, late; hardy; does well on middling soils.

Strawberries produce from 4 000 to 10 000 kg. the hectare (1 ½ to 4 tons per acre); well cultivated, they average about 8 000 kg. (3 tons). The price falls rapidly as the season advances, and varies between 300 and 20 fr. the 100 kg. (£. 6 to 8s. per cwt.); 40 frs. (16 s.) may be taken as an average, so that the gross yield of a hectare is between 1 600 and 4 000 frs (£ 25 to £ 64 per acre).

The expenses are considerable: interest on the initial capital of 6 000 to 7 000 frs. the hectare; taxes, watering, shelter, manure, cultivation (women, at 2.50 frs. a day), gathering (women, at 3 frs. a day), sorting and packing.

The total expenses may be calculated at between 1 000 and 2 500 frs. per hectare (£ 16 to £ 40 per acre), so that the profit varies between 600 and 2 000 fr. the hectare (£ 10 to £ 32 per acre); on an average it is 1 000 frs. (£ 16 per acre).

1429   **Pineapples in Cochin China and Cambodia.** (La .culture des Ananas en Cochinchine et au Cambodge). — *La Quinzaine Coloniale*, N. 6, p. 210. Paris, 25 Mars, 1911,

French
Indo-China

Pineapples grow in most parts of Cochin China, but they are cultivated principally in the eastern regions where the soil, formed largely of sand and gravel, and covered in many parts with forest, is very favourable to them. From the southern extremity of the province of Thudaumot as far as Phu-Tho in the north, there is a series of pineapple gardens covering not less than 2 000 to 2 500 hectares (5 000 to 6 000 acres).

These plantations are made in the middle of the woods. The chief centres are: Lai-Thien, Bienhoa, Thudaumot and Thu-Duc. This industry does not develop in Cambodia, although the pineapples there are as good as those of Cochin China.

There are only a few plantations in the province of Kampot, where pineapples do extremely well.

1430   **Importation of Fruit and Vegetables in Denmark and Modes of Packing.** (Commerce des fruits, des primeurs et des fruits secs au Danemark). — *L'Agriculture commerciale*, N. 6, p. 129. Paris, 26 Mars, 1911.

Denmark

Dry fruits have a good sale in Denmark, especially nuts and almonds. The consumption of nuts is valued at 1 100 000 fr. and of almonds at between 300 000 and 400 000 fr. They are imported chiefly from France, and also from Spain and Italy. The best qualities of sweet almonds, shelled, sell in Copenhagen at about 4.20 fr. the kg.; bitter almonds, at 4.50 fr. Walnuts and chestnuts are imported in sacks.

Black grapes are imported in small boxes lined with cotton wool, containing about 2 ½ kg.; 4 or 6 boxes are packed in one hamper, in straw, hay or shavings, and the hamper is sewn down with canvas. White grapes, which are less delicate, are packed in tubs containing about 20 kg., in cork chips.

Apricots and peaches are packed in boxes containing a single layer of 12 fruits, each wrapped in tissue paper; four boxes are packed in one hamper.

Cherries are generally packed in boxes, not more than 10 cm. deep, as. they spoil if. too many are packed together.

The comparative failure of the early vegetables imported is attributed to the mistake of sending them in shut boxes, so that

they remained several days without air, losing all their freshness.
For the future they will be sent in baskets which permit the circulation of air (1).

BARRET. **Future of the Raisin Industry.** (Possibilité de l'industrie   **1431**
des raisins secs en France). — *L'Agriculture Commerciale*, N. 9,
pp. 211-212. Paris, 14 mai, 1911.

Wherever fruit trees can be easily grown in France, the fruit
drying industry may be carried on. There is no reason why this   **France.**
industry should not develop.   **Spain.**
The drying of grapes was long exclusively a Spanish industry,   **California**
carried on principally at Malaga, more renowned for its raisins than
even for its wine. The grapes are dried in the sun with great and
minute care (2).
Grapes are dried in California on the same principles, but with
much less care than in Spain.
The annual value of the raisins exported by Spain and California all over the world exceeds 5 000 000 fr.

Production of Grapes in Australia. (La production des raisins en   **1432**
Australie). — *Feuille d'Informations du Ministère de l'Agriculture*, N. 20. Paris, 23 Mai, 1911.

The following figures show the rate of increase in the production of grapes in Australia for the year 1909-10 :

Australia

	(In quintals of 100 kg.).	
	1908-09	1909-10
New South Wales.	1 435	1 482
Victoria.	81 465	108 452
South Australia	52 456	63 860

(1) Compare with, G. BELLETTRE, *Fruit Packing for England of French
Products*, in *The Science and Practice of Farming during 1910 in Great Britain*, p. 303, published by the International Institute of Agriculture.
(2) See this *Bulletin*, March, 1911, N. 852.   (*Ed.*).

Queensland produced only 12 quintals in 1909, and none, apparently, in 1910. The increase for the whole of Australia was 38 426 quintals, or in the proportion of 28.1 %. (1).

1438   N. GARCIA DE LOS SALMONES. **Vine Stocks for Dry Calcareous Soils.**
(Les porte-greffes les plus appropriés aux terrains calcaires et secs). — *Le Progrès agricole et viticole*, 28ᵉ année, N. 20, pp. 613-632. Montpellier, 14 mai, 1911.

A report presented at the International Agricultural Congress at Madrid, May 5th, 1911, from which the following conclusions may be drawn:

1. The pure forms of the *Berlandieri* are not generally adapted for the reconstitution of vineyards on dry calcareous soils, on account of their slowness of growth and difficulty in taking root, which form a great drawback in hot regions; nor have the pure
Spain. *Berlandieri* any special advantages over their hybrids for replan-
France. tation on these soils in the more northern climates of the vine.
Italy
2. The pure forms of the varieties *cordifolia*, *cinerea* and *candicans*, which at the time of the importation of the *Berlandieri* were advertised as stocks adapted for calcareous soils, have no value for vineyard reconstitution on these soils.

3. In reconstituting vineyards on limestone soils it is absolutely necessary to cultivate the soil to a good depth, and to choose the varieties carefully with regard to local conditions.

4. On soils of this nature, in the northeen regions of vine-culture it is absolutely necessary to use ready grafted nursery vines; and in the south either rooted or grafted plants, when reconstituting with *Berlandieri* and its hybrids.

5. It is especially necessary, for these soils, to choose hardy vines that show a good resistance to phylloxera and develop rapidly,

---

(1) In New South Wales, the area under vines was 8 251 acres in 1909, with a production of 736 262 gallons of wine, 29 953 gallons of brandy, and 3 150 tons of table-fruit. In 1910, the acreage under vines was 8 330 acres, with a production of 808 870 gallons of wine, 26 439 gallons of brandy and 4 181 tons of table fruit.

In Victoria, in 1908-09, there were 24 430 acres under vines, with a yield of 1 437 106 gallons of wine. In 1909-10, the area was 22 768 acres, with a yield of 991 941 gall. of wine.

In South Australia the vine-acreage was 20 353 acres in 1909, with a production of 2 569 797 gallons of wiue, of which 1 045 678 gallons were exported.

· *The Statesman's Yearbook* for 1911.   (*Ed.*).

The less resistant and hardy the vine, the greater its need of manure and of careful culture.

Organic manures and fertilisers containing phosphoric acid and potash should be given periodically. During the first years ferrous sulphate should be applied round the vines, or sprayed upon them.

6. Direct hybrids of *Berlandieri* and *Rupestris Ganzin* with *viniferas*, and of others with the strong American *viniferas* (1202 *Couderc*, *Aramon rupestris N.* 1, etc.), are at present the type most resistant to lime and drought.

These observations show what advantages might be derived from *special international services for Viticulture*, and the organization of experimental fields for the special study of management, resistance to phylloxera, adaptation, and individual affinity and selection.

7. Viticultural nations should communicate to one another the results of experimentation, suggestions for improvements, and the qualification of the more interesting hybrids in each country (1).

HUGUES. **Comparative Study of Grapes from Frosted and Sound Vines.** (Etude comparative de raisins provenant de vignes gelées et non gelées). — *Annales des Falsifications*, IVe année, N. 30, pp. 175-177. Paris-Genève, Avril, 1911.

1434

The data in the following tables are from a vineyard planted with *Aramon*, in the neighbourhood of Nimes, which had suffered from the frost (*gelée noire*) of April 1, 1910:

France

	Frosted Vines	Sound Vines
Yield of grapes, per hectare . . . . Kg.	4 500	15 000
Weight of stalks (*rafles*) per 100 kg. gathered . »	3.42	3.55
» of berries » » . . . . »	96.58	96.25
Total acidity of must calc. as $H_2 SO_4$ per litre. Gr.	8.20	9.50
Total reducing sugar, as glucose per litre . »	160.90	120.00
Ratio glucose: levulose of must . . . . . . »	1.10	1.16

(1) For observations and experiments on the hybrids of American vines, see this *Bulletin* for Nov. 1910, p. 84; and Jan. 1911, Nos. 161 and 342; and Feb. 1911, No. 480.   (*Ed.*).

A study of this table would lead to the inference that wine from vines that had suffered frost is of a normal chemical composition. This is also shown by the following table:

WINE-CONSTITUENTS	Wines from frosted vines	Wines from sound vines
Alcohol, in vol. %	9.4	7
Dry extract, at 100 °C., per litre	gr. 25.30	gr. 24.50
Total acidity, calculated as sulphuric acid.	» 5.80	» 7.80
Volatile acidity, » » » »	» 1.30	» 1.40
Reducing sugar, calc. as glucose	» 1.10	» 1.05
Gypsum calc. in the equiv. potassium sulph.	less than 1 gram	less than 1 gram
Total alcohol + fixed acidity	gr. 13.90	gr. 13 60
Ratio alcohol : extract.	» 2.9	» 2.6

1485

Rossati. **Lemon Culture and Industry in Italy.** (La culture et l'industrie des citrons en Italie). — *Bull. de l'Office du Gouvern. Gén. de l'Algérie*, No. 9, pp. 133-134. Paris, 1er Mai, 1911.

Italy:
Sicily.
Calabria

Sicily is the great centre of lemon cultivation in the Kingdom of Italy. Of the total 8 ½ million lemon trees 7 millions are in Sicily. This number is 15 times that of the lemon trees in California. A well managed lemon tree will yield in Sicily from 800 to 1200 lemons (1).

The crop in Sicily and Calabria in 1907 was of 6 900 000 000 lemons. In Italy lemons are a more paying crop than oranges.

---

(1) According to Mr. Arnao, a lemon tree in Sicily will produce normally, in its 14th year, 650 lemons. Arnao, *La coltivazione degli agrumi*, Palermo, 1899, pp. 123, 396. According to Alfonso, a lemon tree, in very favourable conditions, may produce 800 fruits.

P. Cuppari, in calculating the production of a lemon-orchard at Messina, put 490 trees (*piantoni*) to the hectare, with a total production per hectare of 490 000 lemons. Pietro Cuppari, *Manuale dell'Agricoltore*, Firenze, 1870, pp. 146, 151. Cuppari, in 1870, calculated that one hectare of lemon orchard gave a net income of 2778 frcs.   (*Ed.*).

The lemon groves in Sicily extend from the coast into the valleys of the interior and on the hill-sides, up to 450 metres (1475 ft.)

Lemons are gathered in autumn. There is also a variety called *Verdelli*, which is gathered in summer; they are obtained by stopping irrigation in June and July, forcing the trees with rapidly acting fertilisers, and resuming an abundant irrigation as soon as the blossom appears.

Lemons are exported in boxes of oak (*cerro*) the wood being imported from the United States. There are generally from 300 to 360 lemons in a box. Italian lemons are remarkable for their good keeping qualities, richness in essential oil, high degree of concentration of the juice, and the high percentage of citric acid. Imperfect, overripe or malformed lemons are not exported; they are used in the manufacture of essences, of citrate of lime, of concentrated lemon juice (*agro cotto*) and other products.

About a third of the produce is consumed in the country, a third is exported and a third is used in the manufacture of citrate of lime, and lemon essence. The citrate is obtained from the juice, the essence from the rind of the fruit.

The total value of the lemons and their industrial products amounted, in 1908, to about 43 million francs (£ 1 720 000).

E. REBOUL. **Lemon Culture in Martinique.** (La culture et l'industrie du citron à la Martinique). *L'Agricult. des Pays chauds.* — IIᵉ année, N. 97, pp. 337-340. Paris, Avril, 1911.

1436

The cultivation of the lemon (*Citrus Medica* var. *acida*) has entered on the experimental stage in Martinique; 21 808 lemon-tree saplings were sold during 1910 by the Experimental Stations, some planters having planted 10 or 12 hectares.

Martinique is well suited to the cultivation of the lemon, which grows wild there, producing juicy and fragrant fruit; green and yellow kinds both occur The lemon tree grows on poor, shallow soil; it is hardy and is attacked by few parasites. It only requires to be protected from high winds, and does not need shade trees; from 500 to 850 trees can be planted per hectare, according to the richness of the soil. At five years old the lemon tree is in full bearing, when from 200 to 250 barrels of lemons are obtained per hectare. A barrel contains from 1400 to 1500 lemons, yielding from 35 to 60 litres of raw juice, or about three litres of concentrated juice; this is worth from 180 to 200 frcs per hectolitre.

Martinique

It is advisable to export the raw juice, or better still to make citrate of lime which is prepared by a very simple process.

The gross receipts from a lemon-grove vary from 1400 to 1800 frcs per hectare, of which from 700 to 1000 frcs are net profit.

Whilst waiting for the lemon-groves to bear, which they only do to an appreciable extent after the 4th or 5th year, the soil can be utilised for vegetable crops, sugar cane, and cotton.

1437

S. F. MORSE. **A New Table Fruit: the Papaya.** *The Country Gentle-man.* — 81st year. Vol. LXXVI, N⁰ 3041, Albany, N. Y. May 11, 1911.

In the tropics of North and South America grows the fruit called the Papaya (1). The papaya bids fair to become a popular table-fruit. It is like a melon in shape, but often weighs as much as 20 lbs.; the flesh is pink or yellow and in the centre are small black seeds. The flavor is delightfully refreshing and people become extremely fond of the papaya when they have once learned to like it.

Tropical America: Mexico, etc.

Because of its peptonic qualities, the papaya is popular with those afflicted with dyspepsia. So strong are the digestive powers of this fruit that the natives of the regions where it grows put pieces of tough meat between two halves, in order that it may be made tender and somewhat predigested.

The papaya is a dioecious biennal plant, growing from seed and producing fruit at nine months to a year old; it continues to bloom and bear fruit throughout the succeeding year and then dies. The culture is simple. Seeds are planted, in hills or checks eight feet apart. After the seeds sprout, the plants are gradually thinned down to one healthy stalk per hill; this stalk may grow from four to twenty feet in height. Clean culture is practised, and the melons are harvested as they ripen. A light well-drained soil is best suited to the papaya; farm - manure or a dressing of 800 to 1500 lbs of a 4-8-10 high grade fertiliser is necessary in soils that have been cropped for five or more years. Irrigation, or at least 75 inches annual rainfall, and plenty of heat all the year round are essential.

With few exceptions the papaya has only been cultivated in a few localities. Even in the city of Mexico, 12 hours ride from the papaya country, this fruit fetches from 15 to 50 cents apiece.

_____

(1) The fruit of *Carica Papaya L.* (*Caricaceae*); tree similar to the palm in shape, which grows in Florida and British India.

It keeps well and can stand shipping and when once known should become a favourite.

By seed selection it will be possible to produce papayas of a uniform superior flavour and smaller size, more adapted to general consumption.

Forestry.

R. Zon. **The Forest Resources of the World.** — *U. S. Dep. Agr. Forest Service Bul.* 83, pp. 91. E. S. R. Washington. April 5, 1911.

1438

This Bulletin presents a statistical study of the forest resources of the principal timber-producing countries of the world with special reference to the influence of foreign resources upon the forest products and future supply in the United States. The topics discussed for each country are as follows: Forest area, distribution of the forests throughout the country, composition and character of the forests, annual consumption, cutting, growth per acre and wood prices.

World Production

Except for slight modifications, the subject matter is similar to that presented in the writer's report to the National Conservation Commission on foreign Sources of Timber Supply.

Russian Forests. (Les Forêts en Russie). — *Recueil Consulaire du Royaume de Belgique.* Tome 153. Première livraison, p. 24-27. Bruxelles, 1911.

1439

Forests are one of the natural resources of the Russian Empire which have not yet been adequately utilised. Indeed, the immense forest wealth of Siberia has as yet not even been properly inventoried.

The total area under forests in Russia in Europe is 201 598 000 hectares (about 780 000 sq. m.), of which 173 610 000 hectares (about 670 000 sq. m.) are in Russia proper, 20 435 000 hectares (79 000 sq. m.) in Finland, and 7 553 000 hectares (29 000 sq. m.) in the Caucasus.

Russian Empire

The Crown forests, which cover 115 695 000 hectares (about 450 000 sq. m.) in Russia alone, are administered by the Ministry of Agriculture and Crown Lands (1).

---

(1) " Of the total area of the Russian Empire under forest, oniy that of European Russia proper, the Kingdom of Poland, and the Caucasus can be estimated with some degree of certitude. In European Russia forests

In several provinces there are Forest Preservation Committees presided over by the Governors. There are several forestry associations formed for the purpose of diffusing knowledge on forestry. Most of the timber obtained from the Russian forests is now used by local industries, but the possibilities for exportation are of yet greater importance.

The principal kinds of trees are pine, fir, oak, birch, alder, aspen, lime, ash, and hornbeam. These species are rarely found growing in groups of one kind only.

The forests of the Caucasus are noted for the more valuable species (the silver fir, *Abies pectinata*, the Caucasian palm-tree, and the walnut).

The variety of species would allow of a very important trade in rough timber. Meantime it has given rise to flourishing home industries such as saw mills and wood work, the extraction of resins, and the manufacture of wood pulp. No fewer than 1428 big factories are engaged on this work.

1440   A. FIORI. **Eritrean Trees.** *L'Agricoltura coloniale* Anno V, No. 3, pp 81-100. Firenze, Marzo, 1911.

Eritrea   This section of Mr. Fiori's work includes the enumeration of plants belonging to the genera *Albizzia, Acacia, Dicrostachys*, and *Eulada*. The writer calls attention to *Albizzia amara*, the timber of which is suited for cabinet making, to *A. anthelmintica*, the bark

---

cover a territory of 474 millions of acres; in Finland. 50.5 millions; in Poland 6.7 millions in the Caucasus 18.7 millions, reaching a total for the regions named of 550 millions of acres, 39 % of the total area. In the two Ural mountain provinces, forests cover 70 % of total area; in the two northern provinces 68 %; in Finland, 63 %; in the four lake provinces 57 %.

The State forests of the Empire are distributed as follows (Jan. 1er 1908):

	Total area acres	Area in exploitation acres
European Russia	286 023 315	228 949 445
Caucasus	13 418 328	8 450 771
Asiatic Russia (excl. of Amur reg.) .	361 945 497	192 640 912
Total	961 387 130	430 041 128
Amur region . . .	288 742 000	—

In 1908, the State forests of the Empire had a revenue of 61 712 000 roubles, the expenses being 19 054 000, and the net profit 42 658 000 roubles ". *The States man's Yearbook for* 1911, p. 1171.   (*Ed.*).

of which is said to contain an alkaloid of great value as taenifuge to *A. lophantha* Benth., of Australia, which latter is valuable with a view to raising *Ceroplastes* (Scale-insects) for their wax.

The *Acacia* family is the most important of the flowering trees of Eritrea, especially in the valleys and plains, whilst the wild olive-tree is in the ascendant on hills and table-lands. Several important products are obtained from the acacia: wood-fuel and charcoal, timber for building and carpentry; fibrous bark for ropes, gum (*A. Senegal, Seyal* etc.) ; ·tannic substances (bark of *A. etbaica*, 6.33 % tannin) ; and fodder (*A. spirocarpa, flava, Seyal, Senegal*).

The genus *Dichrostachys* Wight and Arn. is represented by the species *Dichrostachys nutans*, Benth., the wood of which is well suited for manufacturing implements, duplicate parts in machinery, etc., the blossom of this Acacia is highly decorative.

A. VISART. & J. T' SERSTEVENS. **Forest Fires: Their Causes, Damage,** 1441
Remedies. Report by the Special Commission of the Belgian
Superior Council of Forestry. (Incendies de Forèts. Causes,
Dégâts, Remèdes. Rapport de la· Commission speciale du Con-
seil supérieur des fôrests). — *Bulletin de la Société Centrale Fo-
restière de Belgique.* 18ᵉ a., 3ᵉ-4ᵉ Livr. pp. 153-167 et 229-240,
Bruxelles, Mars et Avril, 1911.

A late dry spring, severe cold at night retarding vegetation, and violent east winds, greatly favored forest fires in Belgium du- Belgium
ring the spring of 1910.

As a result the Minister of Agriculture requested the Superior Council on Forestry to examine the question. The following are replies to enquiries addressed to landowners and foresters.

1. *What are the most frequent causes, other than railways, of forest fires ?*

In order of importance, the replies are the following:

a) Carelessness of foot passengers, who generally take paths through woods overgrown with bracken and heather, and strewn with dry foliage.

b) Carelssness of woodmen, farm hands and shepherds.

c) Carelessness of workmen engaged in preparing ashes, cutting and burning turf, preparing the soil for planting trees, etc.

d) Carelesness of children.

e) Incendiarism.

f) Lastly, but very rarely, lightning.

2. *What precautions have so far given the best results?*

a) Notices put up on the outskirts of woods and forests reminding Art. 67 of the Forest Code:

« It is forbidden to carry or to light fires in woods or forests, or at a distance of 100 meters from the same, under penalty of a fine of from 10 to 100 frcs »;

b) The establishment a regular system of clearings in the woods to stop the spread of fires.

c) Carefully planned clearings in clumps of resinous trees.

d) Observation posts, where help can be obtained, on heights near or in the woods

3. *What should be done to complete these precautions or increase their efficacy?*

a) Stricter enforcement of the Forest Laws and the improvement of the same.

b) Special teaching in schools should be useful as a preventive.

4, *What are the best means for extinguishing forest fires?*

a) The means which seem likely to give the best results are the establishment of a regular system of clearings in the woods to stop the spread of fires; The use of such clearings is two-fold :

1. Such cuttings made amidst the clumps of trees and carefully cleared of all inflammable matter, often suffice by themselves to limit the fire.

2. In case of very bad fires. which by attacking the trunks are likely to extend beyond the clearings, they have the great advantage of making it possible to use counterfires which are the last resource in desperate cases.

b) Another valuable precaution is that of keeping the roads, especially the by-paths very clean.

c) Owners of property along the bordering on such roads should clear the ground for a width of at least 5 meters of all inflammable matter and should lop off the lower branches from plantations of resinous trees.

d) This would be much easier and less costly to do if the owners were to plant by the roads screens of thick foliaged trees such as beeches.

e) As a precaution against the trunks of trees taking fire it is most desirable that a strip from 8 to 13 meters wide be cleared of heath, bracken, and all inflammable matter round pine and fir plantations : and that the lower branches of resinous trees be lopped off.

f) These measures could be encouraged by awards which insurance companies would find it to their advantage to offer owners.

g) Finally, it is desiderable that:

1, all works to be carried out in the neighborhood of danger spots be reserved for the dry season so that a staff of well-equipped men may be ready at the first alarm;

2, observation posts should be installed;

3, foresters should be instructed to make more rounds and to keep a sharp look out during dangerous periods.

5. *Are fires caused by railway engines due to cinders or coals falling from the fire-box or to sparks from the funnel? Which are the more frequent?*

Fires are caused both by sparks and by cinders.

Fires in woods' bordering on the State railways are generally caused by sparks, and in those bordering on local lines by coals or cinders. In hilly country sparks are generally sent off in going up hill, cinders and coals fall out in going down hill.

6. *What is the maximum distance from the railway line at which fires have been caused by sparks?*

Forty meters is the maximum distance ever noted, and only in very exceptional cases.

7. *Do fires break out as frequently on both sides of the line and along all its sections?*

When the cause of fire is the fall of coals or cinders it makes no difference on which side of the rail they may fall; when sparks are the cause fire only occurs on the side against which dry winds are blowing. Fires break out more easily along some sections of the railway than others.

8. *What steps should be taken to prevent danger from sparks, coals and cinders?*

To diminish danger from sparks the ditches along the railway lines should be cleared out as early as February, and the number of plates, and more especially of wire screens, 8×8 mm., should be increased. Stokers and firemen should be instructed not to clear out the fire-box when running through country where there is danger of fire.

9. *What precautions should be taken to prevent fires from engines and to minimise the loss incurred?*

There is only one valid precaution: to clear a protective belt, from 20 to 40 meters wide, on the side of the line against which dry winds blow, and in those sections where there is danger.

Conclusions of the Belgian Council of Forestry:

1. Request that the Minister of Agriculture and Public Works publish a leaflet on forest fires for wide and general distribution.

2. Amendment of Art. 167 of the Belgian Forestry Law as follows :

« It is forbidden to carry or to light fires or to smoke in woods or forests, heathlands or moors, and at a distance of 100 meters from the same, from March to October inclusive, under penalty of a fine of from 10 to 100 frs.

« Permission can however be obtained to set fire to heath-lands or moors for farm or forest works, on condition that at least 48 hours notice be given to the burgomaster of the Commune and to the Foresters who must be informed of the precautions taken.

« Labourers working in woods and on heath-lands are authorised, as an exception, to light fires to cook their food if they conform to the rules laid down by the foresters on the estates on which they are working ».

3. Draw the attention of the road surveyors and the Communal authorities to the advisability of clearing some paths of under-wood, heather, bracken, etc., which in the neighbourhood of woods and in frequented parts is often a cause of danger from fire.

4. In view of the heavy damage caused by fires kindled by locomotives, the State and local railway authorities should be requested :

a) to frequently remind their stokers and firemen of the precautions they should take;

b) to fit the engines of the district railway services running through exposed country with wire spark screens 5×8 mm., and to redouble all the preventive measures against fire.

c) to consider whether it would not be advisable, in view of the heavy damages paid by the railway companies under this heading, for them to purchase a strip of land from 20 to 40 meters wide, in dangerous and very exposed localities, and to establish on said strip, clearings to prevent fires, or to grow thereon farm crops, or to subject these strips of land to preventive burning.

1442　　**Grafting Chestnut on Oak.** (Greffe du Châtaignier sur le Chêne). — *Révue horticole*, 83ᵉ Année, N. 10, pp. 219-220. Paris, 16 Mai, 1911.

France　　For some years Mr. Binon of Tigy, (Loiret), has been trying to reconstitute chestnut groves by grafting the chestnut on the oak. Having observed that failure is due to the disparity in the date at which the two trees start vegetating in the spring, he now uses in his experiments early varieties of English or pedunculate oaks, grafting on a level with the soil. The young chestnut scions still in the green or herbaceous stage, are grafted on one year old oak-stocks.

CHARLES RABOT. **The Shrinkage of the Area under Scotch Pine in the Swedish Mountains.** (Le recul du Pin sylvestre dans les montagnes de la Suède), — *La Géographie*, Bull. de la Société de Géographie; XXIII, No. 4, pp. 270-276. Paris, 15 Avril, 1911.

1443

Since the post-glacial age the lowering of the altitude at which Scotch pine grows in Sweden can probably be safely estimated at from 150 to 250 metres (500 to 800 ft). When *Pinus silvestris* had attained its maximum extension it occupied the whole of the zone now held by the birch and probably exceeded it. Indeed the upper limit of the birch zone now shown on modern maps coincides with the limit reached by the Scotch pine at a recent period. The zone occupied by birch has also receded, but so far only a small number of sub-fossil specimens have been found above the zone it now occupies; nevertheless the researches made by Mr. Sélim Berger and Mr. Axel Gavelin afford proofs of this. This regression cannot be ascribed to the influence of man, as the Swedish peasants find more timber than they require in the valleys near their homes, and do not send their cattle to pasture on the mountains. The lower altitude at which the pine now grows must be ascribed to climatic changes, or, more precisely, to a lower summer temperature. According to Mr. Axel Gavelin the hardier spruce has been unaffected.

Sweden

M. RODIER. **The Extraction of Resin from the Aleppo Pine in Algeria.** (Résinage du Pin d'Alep en Algérie). — *Revue de Chimie industrielle*. Tome XXII No. 257, pp. 137-141. Paris, Mai, 1911.

1444

The Aleppo pine grows wild in Algeria; the pine-forests worked for resin cover an area of nearly 100 000 hectares (247 000 acres). There is a dense growth of a million and a half trees on this area,, but large openings caused by forest fires, occupy more than half the space.

The forests are fairly well kept and for the past five years or so have been actively worked. There are many roads, paths and cuttings, though far fewer than in similar woods in France. The

Algeria

underwood consists of ever-green oaks, lentiscus, and halfa ; the latter gains ground as one approaches the table-land, and the under-wood in the forests to the south of Daya consists exclusively of halfa. The amount of resin obtained depends on several conditions: the altitude, age of the trees, density of the plantation, situation, and nature of the soil. Hence it is difficult to estimate beforehand the probable yield of the woods when carefully worked.

The labourers are Kabyles, Spaniards, and especially Frenchmen from the Landes. The extraction, distillation and treatment of the resin is done on the French system. The yield in essence varies according to the agglomerations (*amasses*) from which it is obtained. Whilst the three first lots yield 25 % of essence, only 17 % is obtained from the later lots, and from 15 to 16 % from the *barras* (1). The quality of the resin obtained from the latter agglomeration is also inferior. The percentage of impurities contained in the gum varies from 5 to 8 % of water, wood, etc. The workmen are en-couraged by rewards to obtain the resin as pure as possible.

After laying the resin out on trays it is put into barrels made of native wood, and exported in casks of 400 kgs. (880 lbs.).

1445   PAULGRAVE ELLMORE AND O' REY. **Osier and Willow Cultivation in Great Britain.** — *The Journal of the Board of Agriculture,* vol. XVIII, no. 1, p. 12-18. London, April 1911.

That the basket-makers of the United Kingdom are increasingly dependent on imported supplies of raw material is evident from the Annual Statement of the Trade of the United Kingdom for 1909, which shows that the importation of willows and rods for basket-making were as follows in 1909.

Great
Britain
and
Ireland

Germany . . . . (2)	£	26 308
Netherlands	»	10 975
Belgium . . , ...	»	10 643
Other foreign countries	»	15 129
British possessions	»	13 746
	£	76 801

(1) The resin collected in pots is the gum proper (*gemme*). That portion which solidifies on the trunk (*quarre*) and which is easily removed by hand, and therefore nearly pure, is called " *galipot* "; lastly the part which adheres to the wood and cannot be easily detached is called " *barras* " See: BARRAL et SAGNIER; *Dict. d'Agric.*, under " *Gemme* ".   (*Ed.*).

(2) (£. = Fr. 25.25).

There is no apparent reason why home cultivators should not meet the whole demands of the home market, and supply also the requirements of colonial consumers, who are now served direct by Continental growers.

The botanical species known as *Salix triandra* embraces many of the choicest fine-top varieties. *Salix purpurea* is a bitter species, which rabbits and cattle will seldom touch unless under great stress of hunger. These, and several hybrids, will do best under damp and moderately heavy soil conditions. Other varieties, chiefly those of the *Salix viminalis* species — the true osier — will thrive under much drier conditions.

If the best financial results are to be achieved, a good quality of ground is imperative. The plot, too, should be easily accessible, so as to save the expense of long carting journeys in winter and the land should also be in the highest state of fertility and kept quite free from weeds.

Spirits of Turpentine - Consumption - Extraction in the Landes (France), in British India, and in Sakhalin. (Essence de térébenthine - Consommation - Extraction dans les Landes (France), dans l'Inde Britannique, et à l'Ile de Sakhaline). — *Bulletin Semestriel de la Maison Schimmel et Cie.*, pp. 190 (108-112). Miltitz près Leipzig, Avril, 1911.

1446

The United States Consul has drawn up some reports on the consumption of spirits of turpentine (turpentine) and its substitutes. These show that in 1909 England imported this product from the following countries, in the given quantities:

France.
British
India.
Japan, etc.

	Amount Cwt. (1)	Value Dollars (2)
United States	479 484	2 979 875
Russia	77 382	224 585
France	31 084	150 117
Germany	2 290	6 399
Other Countries	2 640	26 634
	592 880	3 387 610

Many substitutes are used in England costing from a few cents up to 24 cents less than real turpentine. These substitutes

(1) A dollar = 49.3 pence.   (*Ed.*).

are generally sold direct to painters and oil-colour-men, who do not declare the percentage of substitutes contained in the turpentine with which their colours are mixed.

The trade in substitutes is active whenever the price of turpentine exceeds 2.60 frs. (50 cent.). Information from Liverpool states that many turpentine distillers there prepare substitutes also.

In 1909 Switzerland imported from the following countries 3 064 200 lbs. (2 003 192 kg.) of turpentine.

	Lbs.	Kil.
France	1 518 000	687 654
Spain	1 515 000	686 295
United States	13 660	618 598
Belgium	8 150	6 392
Germany.	5 950	2 695
Italy.	2 400	1 087
England	600	272
Austria-Hungary	440	199
	3 064 200	2 003 192

The average price on the Swiss frontier was 15.63 $ per 220.45 lbs. (81.16 fr. per quintal).

The high price fetched by spirits of turpentine at Johannesburg (Transvaal) has led to a large demand for substitutes.

The mode of extracting spirits of turpentine and resin in the Landes is explained by Mr. Vèzes in a pamphlet published at Bordeaux by the laboratory of chemistry applied to the resin trade.

The pamphlet is entitled *La récolte et le traitement de la gemme du Pin maritime* (Bordeaux. 1910). The writer describes an apparatus invented by Castet for continuous distillation, in which the temperature never exceeds 140° C. In this apparatus the vapours, previously cooled at low pressure, pass into a second refrigerator at a pressure of two atmospheres, which causes rapid condensation.

A method of extracting turpentine, which is recommended by Mr. Schkateloff, consists of filtering the resin at 100° C. and then letting it cool. The sylvic acid then precipitates in crystals. These are squeezed and the turpentine extracted from the liquid thus obtained. Sylvic acid obtained by compression, to which a small quantity of turpentine is added, produces an excellent quality of resin.

The high price fetched by essence of turpentine has induced the Indian Government to again study the native mode of extracting thi substance from *Pinus longifolia*, which is very rich in essential oil.

Experiments will shortly be made at Kangra (British India) (1) and in other parts so as to ascertain the most favorable time of year and the mode of collecting the resin, the yield per tree, the influence of tapping on the life of the tree, the distillation of the spirits, etc.

The 50 000 gallons of essence hitherto produced are used for home consumption. This quantity is thought to be a mimimum yield as the raw material is very abundant.

The slow flow of the resin of *Pinus longifolia* is perhaps due to its composition which is very different from that of ordinary turpentine, from which it is dist'nguished by its much higher content of sylvic acid. As a result it lacks the oxygenising and drying qualities so valuable in other kinds of turpentine which contain little else but pinic acid (pinène).

The preliminary experiments made by the Japanese Government with a view to the production of turpentine in the Japanese portion of Sakhalin, have given excellent results, and the production of essence of turpentine is about to be undertaken on a large scale. Turpentine is extracted from *Larix dahurica* Turcz. known in Sakhalin by the name of « Rakuyoscho ».

Production and Exportation of Camphor in China. (Kampferausfuhr und Produktion in China). — *Das Handels Museum*, N. 13, S. 202. Wien, 30 März, 1911.

1447

The exports of raw camphor from China amounted:

in 1907 to 25 789 pikuls (1 pikul = 60.341 kgs or 132.75 lbs)
» 1908 » 18 072 »
» 1909 » 9 759 »

China

This decline is chiefly due to the low price of camphor, which offers no stimulus to production or trade. Moreover the distillation of camphor is prevented in South China by brigandage, which hardly exists in Central China.

In Central China, more especially in the Province of Sz-chwan, vast regions could be utilised for the production of camphor. If prices were to rise, the supply would be abundant and the product would be of a superior and uniform quality as the result of rational systems of distillation.

---

(1) For further information on the extraction of turpentine from *Pinus longifolia* in British India, (United Provinces) and on its chemical properties and commercial value see: " Bulletin of the Imperial Institute ", vol 4, p. 215, 1906; *ibid.*, vol. 9, pp. 8-10, 1911.   (*Ed.*).

1448   **The Production of Rubber in Zanzibar.** (Der Kautschukhandel San-
sibars im Jahre 1909). — *Gummi-Zeitung*, N. 25. Berlin,
24 März, 1911.

Zanzibar

The production of rubber in Zanzibar and Pemba is still in the
initial stage. The forests of Pemba contain many *Landolphia Kirkii*
plants, of which 3000 lbs. of rubber are exported annually. Since 1908
the Government has planted 120 000 *Ceara* trees and about 3 000
Hevea trees. There are, moreover, some hundreds of plants of
Glaziovia on private estates, both in Zanzibar and Pemba.
Mascarenhasia elastica (1) is also found in Pemba.

1449   **The Cultivation of « Guayule » Rubber in Mexico.** (Schätzung
Guayule-Ausbeuten in Mexico). — *Gummi-Zeitung*, N. 26, s. 960.
Berlin, 31. März, 1911.

Mexico

The rubber output of Mexico, which did not exceed 200 000 kgs.
(440 000 lbs) in 1906, can now be estimated at 11 000 000 kgs.
(24 200 000 lbs) all of which is exported to the United States. This
enormous increase is entirely due to « Guayüle », *Partenium argentatum*, which yields all the rubber exported by Mexico, with the
exception of some 300000 kgs. (660 000 lbs) obtained annually from
a few other plants.

1450   G. VERNET. **At What Angle Should Incisions be Made in Rubber
Plants ?** (Quelle est la pente à donner aux incisions de la sai-
gnée ?). — *Journal d'Agriculture Tropicale*, XIᵉ année, N. 118,
pp. 100-103. Paris, 30 Avril, 1911.

French
Indo-China

The writer continues his articles on the tapping of rubber
plants (2). He prefers incisions at an angle of 45°, for herring bone
tapping, though he admits that puncturing along spiral ducts would
be more in conformity with the ideas set forth in his studies, and
in this case the inclination of the collecting incision should be 60°
to 70°.

---

(1) See this Bull March 1911, No. 883.
(2) See this Bull. March 1911, No. 884, and April 1911 No. 1209, (*Ed.*).

A. Cayla. **Starting Coagulation in the Latex of " Ficus elastica ".** 1451
(Un progrès dans la coagulation mécanique du latex de " Ficus
elastica "). — *Journ. d'Agric. Tropicale.* II. année, No. 118,
p. 125. Paris, 30 Avril, 1911.

Mr Weijs calls attention to the fact that the coagulation of
watery latex has been greatly facilitated on a Javanese farm by
" priming " (*amorçant*) the coagulation.   For this purpose a small   **Duch East**
quantity of the denser latex, about a quart, is taken each day from   **Indies:**
the stock collected.   This is rapidly coagulated by twirling it round   **Java**
with a wooden spatula.   When once this coagulum has been ob-
tained even very diluted latex will coagulate much more rapidly
by pouring it into the same recipient than it would by beating it.
The first nucleus of rubber has « primed » (*amorcé*) or started coagulation.

A Rubber Substitute from Soya Bean Oil. — *The Tropical Agricul-*   1452
turist, p. 280. Colombo, March, 1911.

Now that soya beans have come to the forefront, two Germans
have seen in the oil extracted from them a means for the manufacture of a rubber substitute.   They prepare the substance by   **Germany**
mixing soya bean oil with about half its weight of nitric acid, when
an emulsion is produced.

This is heated to approximately the boiling point of water; a
reaction then takes place, a frothy mass being produced of homogeneous consistency, which is washed with cold water and treated
with a 5 per cent. solution of ammonia until dissolved.   After neutralisation with a dilute acid and more washing, the water is
pressed out, and the mass heated to a temperature half as high
again as that of boiling water.   The result of all these operations
is a tough elastic substance, more or less like rubber, and which
can be vulcanised.

F. Fournet. **The Truffle and its Place in Agriculture.** (Le Truffe   1453
et son rôle en agriculture). *Le Sud-Est.* Bulletin du Conseil dép.
d'Agr. de l'Isère, pp. 165-170. Grenoble, 15 Avril, 1911.

Truffles are gathered in 50 Departments of France.   Thirty-two   **France:**
of these Departments produce or could produce melanospora, that   **(South-East)**
is to say truffles of real commercial value.   Nine million frcs.

(£ 360 000) wort of truffles are sold annually in France, of which five millions (£ 200 000) go to the single department of Lot, where they are divided between a few cantons only.

Eolithic and lithographic limestone is the favorite soil of the truffle; it also grows in steep marly and chalky slopes, from which rate water drains off quickly. Light gravelly and marlstone soils of the Neocomian age also produce fine quality truffles. The following analysis by Mr Chatin of the French Institut shows the constituents which go to make an excellent soil for truffles.

Truffle-growing soil at Souillac (Lot).

Nitrogen	0.08	%
Organic, non-nitrogenous, matter	10.10	,,
Phosphoric acid	0.20	,,
Sulphuric acid	2.00	,,
Lime	13.00	,,
Magnesia	0.40	,,
Potash	1.00	,,
Soda	0.15	,,
Iron peroxide and alumina	15.12	,,
Silica	45.20	,,
Carbon dioxide and loss	12.75	,,
Oxide of manganese	traces	

A truffle ground can generally be prepared at a small cost on soil of the right kind, which as a rule is worth little. All that has to be done is to dig trenches 25 cms. (9.75 in) deep. 1 m. (3 ¼ ft) wide, and 6 meters (19.5 ft) apart, in which are planted young truffle-breeding oaks 3 ms. (9.84 ft) apart; 542 such trees can be planted per hectare (220 per acre); according to the writer the cost does not exceed 250 frs per hectare (£ 4 per acre), including the cost of up-keep of the truffle-ground during the first years., which is estimated at 80 frs (£ 3.4s.). After the fourth year the plantation calls for no special care. The truffle-bearing mycelium begins to develop in the fourth year, forming in the sixth year those burned-up patches, well known to truffle-growers, which announce the appearance of the first truffles. From the sixth to the tenth year the crop will be very uncertain, depending more especially on the nature of the soil; but from the tenth to the twentieth year one can count on an average yield of from 700 to 1200 frs. per annum. (£ 11 to £ 19 per acre). These figures have been exceeded, as much as 3 000 frs per hectare (£ 48 per acre) being often realised.

A still cheaper way of forming a truffle ground is by planting truffle-bearing oaks between the rows of vines in a vine- |

yard. By this method the vine can be fully utilised, and all interruption in the productivity of the soil is avoided; it is much in favor in the Departments of Lot and Corrèze. Whichever method is selected, success chiefly depends on the choice of the oaks, and the writer considers that acorn-bearing trees are always the best.

Growers should select trees with very fibrous roots and reject those in which the tap-root is highly developed and rootlets scarce. These qualities are excellent for ensuring fine, vigorous trees, but they are most unfavorable to the production of truffles, as the mycelium, from which the truffle grows, only forms on the dried up sections of the rootlets which spread in shallow soil.

This accounts for the fact that the most productive trees are often the most unhealthy and stunted, partly because they grow under conditions unfavorable to their development, and partly because, by suppressing the tap-root, the most important portion of their root system has been done away with.

Besides the melanospore (*Tuber melanosporum*) and the *brumal* (*Tuber brumale*) there are several secondary varieties of some value. (*Tuber aestivum, Tuber excavatum*, etc.) (1).

Live Stock Breeding. — Aviculture. — Beekeeping.
Silk Production. — Animal Industries.

RAILLET, MOUSSU, HENRY. **Enquiries into the Treatment of Liver-Fluke, or Distomatosis in Sheep.** (Recherches sur le traitement de la distomatose du Mouton). — *C. R. de l'Acad. des Sciences*, T. 152, N. 17, pp. 1125-1127. Paris, 27 avril 1910. **1454**

At the urgent request of the French Ministry of Agriculture, the writers have tried to find a means of destroying *Distoma hepatica* (2) (liver-fluke) a parasite which occurs in the bile-duct and has caused serious losses among the live-stock.

---

(1) See ORESTE MATTIROLO, *I tartufi. Come si coltivano in Francia. Perchè non si coltivano e come si potrebbero coltivare in Italia*. Annali della R. Accademia di Torino. Vol. LII. 1909.

See also this Bulletin, December 1910, pp. 334-335, and this Bulletin January 1911, No. 197. (*Ed.*).

(2) Large fluke-worms, *Fasciola hepatica* L.; small fluke-worms, *Dicrocoelium lanceatum*, Stiles and Hassal, seu *dendriticum*, Rud. (*Ed.*).

Their experiments show that good results are obtained with only one medicine, ethereal extract of the male fern. It seems to take effect only on large liver-flukes. Four doses of at least 5 gr. (1 gram = 15.43 grains Troy) seem needed to ensure success.

The use of this medicine, which is well known as a taenifuge, is at the same time valuable in treating other parasitic diseases, more especially gastro-intestinal strongylosis.

1455   V. A. MOORE. **Some Methods Employed in Northern Europe to Control Bovine Tuberculosis.** *Amer. Vet. Rev.,* 38, N° 1. *E.S.R.* Washngton, April 1911.

The methods employed for the control of bovine tuberculosis in Denmark, England, Germany and Holland are briefly reported. The so-called Bang method, practised in Denmark, was found to be quite as effective in small as in large herds. The method is generally **Denmark.** considered by cattle owners in Denmark to be entirely satisfactory **Great** and if carefully applied to give the desired results. The increased **Britain.** profit accruing to those who have sound herds is tending to bring **Germany.** more and more farmers to apply the method. **Holland**

In Germany the system which for the time is receiving most attention is that proposed by Ostertag. This consists in eliminating by slaughter all clinical cases of tuberculosis, removing the calves promptly after birth from their dams and keeping them separated for some months, after which they may be placed with the other cattle.

Although there is no country where the feeling is stronger that bovine tuberculosis is of great sanitary significance than Great Britain, there seems to be no other where so little direct effort has been put forth to eliminate this disease. In Holland, at present, only cattle belonging to breeders are killed and compensated for by the government.

The lesson from the experience in Denmark is that in order to keep herds free from tuberculosis, the owner must be educated in the nature of the disease and that until he is thus educated there is little hope of securing herds permanently free from this disease.

1456   VICTOR A. NORGAARD. **Blackleg, Its Nature, Cause and Prevention.** *U. S. Department of Agriculture. Bureau of Animal Industry.* — Circular 31 (Third Revision), p. 23. Washington, March 4, 1911.

United In 1850, Rayer and Davaine discovered the Anthrax bacillus in **States** the blood of sheep which had died from anthrax; but although a number of scientists verified this discovery, they did not recognize the bacillus as the cause of the disease. In 1877 Pasteur demonstrated that the bacillus was the one essential for the appearance of the disease; and in 1879 it was proved by Arloing, Cornevin, and Thomas, that symptomatic anthrax, or blackleg, is caused by an entirely different organism and consequently is a distinct disease from Anthrax. The following year the same Authors demonstrated that the disease could be produced in susceptible animals by inoculation, and that immunity may be produced by introducing the bacillus into the circulatory systems of such animals under certain favorable circumstances This discovery was the beginning of a series of experiments which finally led to the introduction of preventive vaccination by hypodermic injections of blackleg virus.

There are but few countries in the world where blackleg or symptomatic anthrax does not prevail to some extent. In the United States, with the exception of the Southern, Atlantic and the Eastern Gulf States there are but few districts where the disease has not been observed.

Experiments were begun in the Pathological Laboratory of the Bureau of Animal Industry, in 1896, for the purpose of preparing a blackleg vaccine which by a single inoculation would produce practical immunity and still be sufficiently attenuated to cause only a minimum amount of loss at the time of inoculation. All the various suggested methods were tried, and it was finally decided to adopt Arloing's principle, with Kitt's modification. As the vaccine produced gave uniformly good results, doses of it were sent to stockmen, in order to have them tested in practice on their cattle. The effect of the vaccine in preventing outbreaks of the disease and in immediately abating outbreaks already in progress has been highly satisfactory. More than 15 500 000 doses have been sent out during this period.

W. THOMSON. **The Influence of Atmospheric Pressure and Humidity on Animal Metabolism.** Manchester Literary and Philosophical Society, March 21 — *Nature*. London, April 27, 1911.   1457

In a previous paper it was stated by Mr. Thomson that the percentage of carbonic acid gas contained in the air exhaled from the lungs was greater when the air is dry and the atmospheric pressure low than under the opposite conditions. The experiments recorded in the present paper were made upon the exhaled air from three men and one boy, and upon guinea pigs and mice, and the results of all show that, as a rule, when the barometer fell, the percentage of car-

Great
Britain

bon dioxide in the exhaled air rose, and when the barometer rose
the percentage of carbon dioxide fell. As the air became more moist,
the percentage of carbon dioxide fell and it rose when the air became
drier. There was a lower percentage of carbon dioxide in the exhaled
air when the weather was warm than when cold.

1458   J. B. MARTIN. **Whey as a Food for pigs.** (L'Utilisation du Sérum
du Lait pour l'alimentation des Porcs). — *L'Industrie Laitière*,
36. année. No 18, pp. 295-296. Paris, 30 avril, 1911.

France

The whey collected from the vats at a temperature of 40° to
45° C. remains warm enough to be given to the pigs during the
day without reheating. The pigs experimented upon were two
months old.

A lot of pigs were fed on pure whey for 63 days and sold at
an average weight of 45 kilos (99 lbs).

A second lot of 5 pigs fed on pure whey for another two
months, with the addition of rice flour, weighed when sold 530
kilos, (1166 lbs) or 109 kgs. each (233 lbs).

A third lot fed in the dairy stye weighed 105 kgs. (231 lbs)
each at the end of 5 months.

The pigs took the whey greedily and did not seem to suffer
either from scouring or constipation. No death occurred, whereas
when they were fed with skimmed milk the death rate was from
2 to 3 %. Their meat was found to be of good quality.

Thus pigs can be advantageously fed on whey, until the time
comes for fattening them, when farinaceous foods or potatoes
should be added to their diet.

1459   E. POHER. **Oil Cakes as a Feed for Live-stock.** (Les tourteaux dans
l'alimentation du bétail). — *Journal d'Agriculture pratique,*
75e année, N. 20, p. 619. Paris, 18 Mai, 1911.

France

Shelled earth-nut cake is five times as rich in nitrogenous matter
as ordinary hay; it is suited to pigs, sheep, cattle and horses.
It imparts no flavour to milk or meat. This cake is rather heating,
owing to its high nitrogenous content; and it is advisable to counteract this tendency by the use of watery foods (roots etc.).

Decorticated cotton-cake, which contains two and half times
as much nitrogenous matter as hay, is admirably suited for milch
cows and fatting stock.

The author advises the following average daily rations for farm stock:

	Husked pea nuts	Oil Cakes Decorticated cotton-seed
Cattle	6 ½-9 lbs.	4 ½ lbs.
Sheep	1 »	10 ozs.
Pigs	2 »	1 ½ lbs.
Horses	1 »	10 ozs.

Oil-cakes should be gradually added to the rations of live-stock so that the animals may grow accustomed to them. They should be stopped, in the case of stock being fattened for market, a few weeks before selling, so that the surface fat may harden. This adds to the market value of the animals.

Live-stock in Argentina. — *The Journal of the Board of Agriculture.*   **1460**
Vol. XVIII, N. 1, pp. 76-77. London, April 1911.

According to the Argentine Agricultural Census the total number of cattle in the Republic in 1908 was 29 116 625. The total number of bulls of ascertained breed was returned at 368 888, breeding cows   **Argentina** at 927 279. Classified according to breed (whether pedigree, pure cross-bred, or half-bred) these cattle are distributed as follows:

Shorthorn	7 385 880
Hereford.	553 555
Aberdeen Angus . . . , .	125 829
Red Polled	1 702
Jersey	2 076
Flemish	2 844
Swiss	2 401
Dutch	21 164
Unclassifed	471 652
	8 567 193

The number of horses in the Republic is given as 7 531 376; of these 49 000 are pure bred, 1 693 637 half-bred, and 5 788 739 native. The chief breeds of pure and half bred horses are Percherons with 254 357 head; Clydesdales 225 643; Normandy 69 434; and Hackneys 47 736.

Since the last census was taken (1895) there has been a decrease in the number of sheep of 7 167 808 head. This is to be attributed to the growth of agriculture in the provinces of Buenos Ayres,

Santa Fè, and Cordova.   The number of sheep in 1908 was 67,211 754, of which 34 621 578 are classified by breeds as follows:

Rambouillet	8 961 267
Negrete or black-face.	388 938
Lincoln.	18 307 216
Southdown.	300 209
Shropshire	304 950
Leicester	90 488
Other breeds not specified	6 268 510

The total number of swine is stated to be 1 403 591; of these 34 462 were pure-bred, 589 126 half-bred, and the rest native. The numbers of those of English breeds were as follows: Berkshire 69 491; Leicester 21 129; and Yorkshire 62 455.

During the four years, 1905-8, the sheep-breeding industry alone contributed the sum of £500 000 to English breeders for the purchase of pure bred stock. It may also be mentioned that of 16 156 head of pedigree cattle imported into Argentina from 1880 to 1907, 14 624 came from the United Kingdom, while of 71 488 pedigree sheep imported during the same period 65 724 came from the United Kingdom.

It is calculated that the average annual consumption of live stock in the Republic amounts to 2 700 000 cattle, 5 500 000 sheep, and 150 000 pigs. Of these about 922 000 cattle, 3 289 000 sheep and 6 000 pigs pass through the freezing factories annually for purposes of exportation.

The first establishment for preserving meat was founded in 1883; by 1906 the number of freezing etc. factories had risen to 26. In this year the export of chilled and frozen beef amounted to 148 000 tons, and of frozen sheep and lambs to 70 000 tons (1).

1461   **Trade in Horses in Hungary.** (Commerce des chevaux en Hongrie). — *L'Agriculture commerciale*, N. 4, p. 81. Paris, 26 Février, 1911.

Hungary

The census of horses in Hungary in 1909 returned 1 876 018 head as against 1 859 856 in 1908, exclusive of Croatia and Slavonia.

---

(1) In 1909, there were in Argentina eight freezing establishments, 278 creameries, 18 butter factories, 68 cheese-making establishments, and 37 mixed factories. In 1908, 3 550 tons of butter, 43 977 tons of tallow, 175 538 of wool were exported. The exports in 1910 of animals and their products was valued in Argentina at £ 22 764 413. *The Statesman's Yearbook for 1911*, p. 578. (*Ed.*).

The number exported has risen to 58 868 as against 47 688. Their market value in 1909 amounted to 31 ½ million crowns. Italy was the greatest purchaser of Hungarian draught-horses, and an increasing number were exported also to Roumania, France and Turkey. The exports to Germany have however declined.

The exports of army mounts rose from 6 115 to 8 225. Turkey purchased 2 800, Italy 1 143, and Roumania 2 980.

It should be noted that the exports of colts under two years of age have declined during this same period — 1909 and 1908 — falling from 1 560 to 1 340, most of which were purchased by Austria.

The Breeding of Thoroughbred Horses in South-Africa. — *Live Stock Journal*, N. 1935, p. 467. London, May 5, 1911.

1462

The breeding of thoroughbred horses is gaining a strong foothold in South Africa. The foundation stock comes from England, and it is said that animals touched in the wind improve in that climate, while their offspring do not wheeze at all. The aim of the breeders is to develop the most likely colts for racing. The bulk of the colts, however, will be sold for army remounts. It is claimed that the soil and climate favour the development of unusual bone and substance, so that the strength required for Army purposes is easily attained.

South African Union

MARRE. **Racka, Tsigaia and Frisian Sheep in Hungary.** (La race des brebis de Frise en Hongrie). — *Bulletin mensuel de l'Office de Renseignements Agricoles*, N. 3, pp. 283-293. Paris, 1911.

1463

The *Racka* breed, which is found more especially in the mountains of Upper Hungary, and the *Tsigaja* breed, which is the favourite in Transylvania, are the two breeds of milch sheep of Hungary. Elsewhere, and notably in the plains, they have been ousted by breeds noted for their wool and meat, such as the Merinos of Rambouillet, the Dishley-Merinos, etc.

Hungary

In the Carpathian mountains the flocks' of the *Racka* breed are kept by shepherds known as *batchos*. The *Racka* sheep of the Upper Tatra is small but well proportioned ; its live weight rarely exceeds 30 kgs. Its wool is long and harsh with a large proportion of stiff hairs (*jarre*). The cheese prepared from its milk is sold under the name of *Liptò* or Carpathian cheese. In some parts of the County of Liptò a cheese known as *ostyapcka* is made.

At the Agricultural College of Kassa a flock of Frisian sheep are kept for breeding purposes. The following table shows the average weights of ewes at Kassa:

Thoroughbred Frisians . . . . 125 lbs or 57 Kgs
       »   » Rackas . . . . 86 » » 39 »
       »   » Tsigajas . . . . . . 88 » » 40 »
Cross-bred Prisian-Rackas . . . . . 153 » » 69 »
       » Frisian-Tsigajas . . . . . 139 » » 63 »

The yield of milk increases by 30 % in the cross-breds. At the College of Kecksemet, in the great plain of Alföld, the influence of the infusion of Frisian stock has made itself felt in an increase in the milk, in fertility, and in weight of meat. At Kecksemet the thorough-bred Rackas give an average of 15 gallons (70 litres) of milk; the cross-breds from 21 to 25 gallons (96 to 112 litres). The wool of the cross-bred sheep is much finer; " Trappist " cheese is made from their milk.

1464   **Sheep-Breeding in Canada.** — *Bulletin mensuel de l'Office de Renseignements Agricoles.* N. 3, pp. 397-398. Paris, Mars 1911.

There has been a marked decrease in the number of sheep in Canada: in 1879 they numbered 3 155 509, in 1909 only 2 705 390 (1). At the same time the officers and inspectors of the Ministry of **Canada**   Agriculture are carrying on an active campaign, showing that the soil and climate of Canada are highly suitable for sheep-breeding, and that farmers would find it very profitable.

The Government has recently appointed a Commission to enquire into the causes of the general indifference in Canada regarding sheep-breeding, and to suggest the best measures for its encouragement.

1465   **The Dairy Industry in Hungary.** — *Bulletin mensuel de l'Office de Renseignements Agricoles.* N. 3, pp. 313-315. Paris, Mars 1911.

The Dairy Industry has not been able to attain an adequate de-**Hungary**   velopment in Hungary, owing to the persistent predominance of extensive cereal-culture. It is only within the last fourteen years that the output has been considerable.

---

(1) In 1910, the sheep in Canada numbered 2 598 470. *The Statesman's Yearbook for 1911,* p. 247.   (*Ed.*).

The chief product is butter, 200 000 quintaals (about 20 000 tons). Cheese-making is very backward; the cheeses produced are mostly of foreign types; Gruyère, Emmenthal, Trappiste, and Romadour; the chief indigenous cheeses' are Pusztadöri, Ovar, and Carpathian.

The production of curds is of some importance, amounting to nearly 900 quintals (90 tons) in 1908.

Besides cow's milk, there are also ewe's and buffalo's milk in Hungary. Ewe's milk is used for various cheeses, of which the chief are Transylvanian, Ostyepka, Parenyica, Kaskaval, and Lipto or Carpathian - the last a white cheese. Buffalo milk is almost entirely consumed fresh.

The total agricultural production of Hungary may be estimated at 4 milliards of francs (160 millions £.) ; of this, dairying gives only 7 %. With a view to continually increasing this important branch of national wealth, the Government has allotted about 2 million francs (£. 80 000) a year for its encouragement.

In 1907, there were already 651 cooperative dairies ; seven of these also included cheese-making, and two the preparation of ewe's milk cheese. The central butter-factories are under permanent State control.

The Dairy Industry in California. (L'Industrie laitière en Californie)   **1466**
(d'après le rapport de M. F. Wodon, consul de Belgique à
San Francisco). — *L'Industrie laitière belge*, 10ᵉ année, n. 4,
p. 31. Verviers, 6 mai 1911.

The development of the dairy industry in California proceeds
side by side with the progress of irrigation. The out-put of butter   United
has increased, that of cheese has remained stationary, but cheese   States:
is now made in 24 counties. Humboldt county to the north of   California
the State, on the Pacific coast, is the chief butter producing centre.
Cheese is chiefly produced in the three counties of Monterey, Santa
Clara and Sacramento, which alone supply one third of the total
out-put.

Nevertheless, large quantities of butter and cheese are still
imported from the Eastern States and from abroad, and it is only
by the further development of irrigation that imports can be done
away with.

At present the value of the dairy products of California is
estimated at 27 million dollars (1),

(1) In January 1910 there were in California 452 000 milch cows and
1 120 000 other cattle. *The Statesman's Yearbook for* 1911, p. 411. (*Ed.*).

1467 J. B. Lindsey. **The Cost of Producing Market Milk at the Massachusetts Experiment Station** *E. S. R.* Washington, March 1911

United
States:
Massa-
chusetts

The average yield per cow for the 7 cows, which were grades and pure bred Jerseys, was 5874.4 lbs (kg. 2661); the food cost per cow was $78.19 (fr. 402.67) and the cost of a quart (l. 0.946) of milk 3 cents (fr. 0.155). In 1908 the yield per cow in case of 9 cows was 5639.5 lbs (2564 qts) (kg 2546) the food cost per cow $ 82.21 and the food cost per quart (l. 0.946) of milk 3.3 cents (fr 0.17).

If other items of cost are added, it is believed that the total cost of producing milk satisfactory in sanitary quality and containing from 4 to 5 per cent of butter fat will usually be found to amount to from 4 to 5 cts per quart (fr 0.206 to 0.256 per quart = l. 0.946). Milk produced under more than average sanitary conditions or certified milk will naturally cost considerably more than the figures presented in these estimates.

1468 A. Blaclesseanu **Sanitary Inspection of Milk and its By-products at Constantza (Rumania).** (Le contrôle sanitaire du lait et de ses dérivés à Constanza, Roumanie). — *L'Industrie Laitière*, 36e année, n. 21, pp, 349-351. Paris, 21 mai, 1911.

Rumania

Milk is sold at Constantza by hawkers who carry it about the town, sometimes loaded on horses, sometimes on carts, and sometimes on their own backs.

This milk — cow's milk, buffalo's milk and ewe's milk — comes from the small holdings in the neighborhood of the town where the hawkers go twice a day to fetch it.

These hawkers had taken to adulterating the milk, and had succeeded in raising its price to 50 and 60 centimes a litre (about 5d a quart) an exhorbitant price in Rumania. The milk was, moreover, sold under very unclean conditions.

In 1908 the Constantza municipality reorganized the sanitary service, and now the milk is pure and cheap after enforcing the following rules :

All milk cans must be fitted with a hermetically closed lid and with a tap at the bottom of the can and the milk must be drawn off by this tap. Before placing the milk on sale the hawkers have to take it to the Municipal laboratory where it is examined, then the lid of the milk-can is sealed and the tap alone can be opened.

When the laboratory tests are satisfactory a certificate is handed to the hawker, of which the following is an example :

VETERINARY SERVICE OF THE CITY OF CONSTANTZA

Milk Inspection Certificate

(Name, surname and domicile of milk-vendor)

MORNING MILK		AFTERNOON MILK	
No. of cans	4	No. of cans	8
Organoleptic test	good	Organoleptic test	good
Density	0.31	Density	0.31
Reaction	negative	Reaction	negative
Butter content	4 %	Butter content	4 %

The animals are milked morning and evening, and the milk is inspected twice a day.

The Government meets the expenses of the laboratory. In summer from 400 to 500 cans per day are inspected, in winter only 150. The laboratory also makes analyses of the bye-products of milk : butter, cream, « yaourt », cheese.

A municipal decree has fixed the maximum price of milk at 30 centimes in summer, 40 centimes in winter.

During the three years in which this inspection has been organized, adulteration has almost disappeared.

Methods of Sampling Milk (Les meilleures méthodes de prélévement des échantillons de lait). — *Laiterie et Elevage*, 6ᵉ année, nos. 9, and 10, pp. 65-66, and 75-78. Louvain, 1 and 15 Mai 1911.   1469

An official enquiry made in June-July 1910, in England, has led to a comparison of the different ways in which samples of milk for analysis are taken.

Experiments were made with the « dipper » spoon, and with the « plunger », which is a metal disk with eight holes bored in it, the milk being stirred before either was used.

Great
Britain:
England

Samples were also taken with a dropping-tube, slowly introduced into the milk and touching the bottom of the jug, the milk
having first been well stirred.

Besides these, five other samples were taken with a « dipper »
from milk which had not been stirred. These experiments led to
the following conclusions:

a) Samples taken with a dropping-tube (pipette) do not give
a correct idea of the milk, as the milk thus obtained from a jug
whose sides are not parallel, is not representative of the layer of
cream and the layer of milk as contained in the jug.

b) The use of the « dipper » does not always. ensure an
adequately uniform mixture. To obtain satisfactory results by this
means the dipper should reach to the bottom of the jug, stirring
the milk from the bottom upwards.

c) Samples obtained with the « plunger » disk are much the
same as the above. If the milk be stirred for a longer time the
results would be quite the same.

d) By decanting, a uniform mixture is obtained.

1470   N. L. Söhngen. **Bacterial Separation of Fats, and Dairy Produce.**
(See No. 1380 of this *Bulletin*).

1471   Riccardo Sanfelici. **Enquiries into the Watering of Milk.** (Inter-
pretazione dei risultati analitici nella ricerca dell'annacquamento
del Latte). — *Rivista scientifica del Latte*, anno I; Fasc. I,
pp. 13-25. Reggio Emilia, Marzo, 1911.

In analysing milk to detect watering the following points must
be carefully considered :

1. The density at 15⁰ C.

Italy   2. The cryoscopic index.

3. The extract, minus the butter, or dry non-fatty extract.
4. The density of the serum at 15⁰.
5. The refractive index of the serum.
6. The proportion of mineral matter in the serum.

Particulary important is the determination of the physical properties of the serum, for its composition is almost uniform, whatever be the breed, the period of lactation, the age of the animal,
the quantity of milk produced, and the food.

Refractometer observations of the serum cannot be depended
upon when milk has been watered with solutions having the same

·degree of refraction. When care is taken to observe strictly uni-
·form methods in preparing the serum, its density is a safe test.

Milk may be condemned as watered when the density of its
·serum, as determined by Quevenne's lactometer at 15°, is less
·than 1.0259.

The ash of the serum varies from a minimum of 0.50 %
to a maximum of 0.56 %; most samples fluctuating between 0.50 %
and 0.53 %. M. Sanfelici considers this value as a « saline constant »,
by the help of which the smallest additions of water can be detected.
Any milk the serum of which is found to have an ash content
lower than 0.50 % may be considered watered.

Dr. O. LAXA. **The Catalase Test in Milk.** (Le dosage de la catalase).   **1472**
(Communication de l'Institut lactologique de l'Impériale et Royale
Ecole polytechnique tchèque à Prague). — *Révue générale du
Lait,* Vol. VIII, No. 22. Bruxelles, Mai 10, 1911 (1).

The Catalase Test plays now an important part in the test-
ing of milk, since it has been found that catalytic action is   **Austria:**
·stronger not only in adulterated milk and in colostrum, but also in   **Bohemia**
the milk of diseased cows than it is in that of healthy cows.

Most of the methods of determining the catalytic action of milk
·are founded on the amount of oxygen given off by hydrogen peroxide.
Hitherto the best known tests were those of Funke, Burri-Staub,
and König, but they were too elaborate and expensive. The writer
proposes a new method, for which he uses a glass tube, of which
one of the ends terminates in a small aperture, and the other in
·a tap. The tube can contain 20 cubic centimeters of liquid and
is graduated in tenths of cb-cm.

Before testing, about 15 cc. of milk and 5 cc. of hydrogen
peroxide solution are measured off, and then mixed; the small
aperture of the tube is then immersed in the liquid, the tap is
opened, and the liquid is drawn up by suction until the tube is
filled with the mixture, to a level above the tap. The tap is then
·closed, the apparatus is put into a glass and left standing.

---

(1) Catalases are oxidising enzyms, characterised by their power of de-
·composing solutions of hydrogen peroxide, with evolution of free oxygen.
·Catalases are widely distributed in vegetable and animal tissues. See H. M.
VERNON, *Inter-cellular Enzymes,* London, J. Murray, 1908, p. 127.   (*Ed.*).

In a few minutes oxygen begins to be given off and accumulates under the tap, whilst a corresponding quantity of milk flows out of the tube by the lower aperture, into the glass placed beneath it. After some time the volume of oxygen evolved can be read off on the graduated tube. If the milk is very active a larger quantity of milk flows out of the apparatus, and the readings become less exact. Should there be froth on the surface of the milk the meniscus can easily be unified by gently tapping the tube, while the lower aperture of the tube is kept stopped with a finger.

1473

BORDAS & TOUPLAIN. **The Original Acidity of Milk.** (Sur l'acidité originelle du lait). — *C. R. de l'Acad. des Sciences*, t. 152, N. 19, pp. 1274-1276. Paris, 8 Mai, 1911.

The writers have tested separately, with phenolphthalein, the acidity of the serum of milk; of the coagulum (butter casein) containing insoluble salts; of the casein and insoluble salts; and, of **France** the pure casein. They conclude that the degree of acidity of free casein contained in milk corresponds to that of the milk itself.

Experiments also showed that no free lactic or citric acid, or salts with an acid reaction are found in fresh milk. This point may be valuable in testing for watering.

The acidity of milk is increased by the casein separating from caseinate of lime, and by monocalcic phosphate formed by the action of lactic acid on the bicalcic phosphate present in milk.

1474

Butter Production and Trade in Ireland. (La production et le commerce du beurre en Irlande). (D'après le rapport de M. Velten, consul de France à Dublin). — *L'Industrie Laitière*, 36ᵉ Année, N. 20, pp. 334-335. Paris, 14 Mai, 1911.

United Kingdom: Ireland

After cattle, butter is the most important of Irish exports. The Irish trade in butter can be estimated to average £ 4 000 000 a year (1).

The British market absorbs almost all the butter exported from Ireland, besides some £ 24 000 000 worth of foreign and colonial butter. After Denmark, Ireland is the largest exporter of butter to

---

(1) See No. 910 of the *Bulletin* for March, 1911.

England. For the last four years Irish exports have however declined
continuously:

Year	Tons.	Francs
1906	43 045	107 085 000
1907	41 718	100 226 000
1908	38 349	100 650 090
1909	37 700	90 627 000

or a decline of 16 458 000 francs in four years.

The decline in the quantity of Irish butter exported is due
mainly to permanent causes, of which the most important is the
irregularity of the Irish output, which is practically restricted to the
six summer months; and to the competition of Danish butters which
arrive with such regularity that they hold the markets in winter,
and Irish Creameries are compelled to import Danish butter to supply
local demand.

Besides this, Danish butter is very carefully made, and dealers
are unanimously of the opinion that uniform appearance, taste and
colour, from week to week, are an essential condition of success on
the British market.

It may seem strange that such a country as Ireland, which
annually exports to England about 40 000 tons of butter averaging,
4 million pounds sterling in value, is unable to meet its own home
demand, and has to import annually from abroad, chiefly from
Denmark, from 3 000 to 3 200 tons of butter, at a cost of £ 380 000.

Production and Exportation of Russian Butter. (Production et
exportation du beurre russe). — *Feuille d'informations du Ministère de l'Agriculture*, N. 13. Paris, 28 Mars 1911.   **1475**

Butter now occupies the second place in the foreign export
trade of Russia (1).

Of all the butter-making countries Russia made the greatest   **Russian
progress in 1909; then come France, Sweden and New Zealand, whilst   Empire**
the output of other countries remained nearly stationary or sensibly
declined, as is the case in Holland, Austria, and the United States.
In 1909 Russia exported 3 456 000 poods of butter (1 pood = 36 lbs.)
as against 3 111 000 poods in 1908.

---

(1) Statistical returns for 1907, 1908 and 1909 show that dairy products
occupy the 4th and 5th place in the list of the more important exports.
See *Statesman's Yearbook*, 1910, p. 1174 and 1911, p. 1176.   (*Ed.*).

Russian butter is sold chiefly to England, Germany and Denmark, and comes mostly from Siberia, where this industry is ever
gaining in importance. The producers show a marked tendency to
form co-operative associations and to deal direct with the purchasers.

1476   **French Cheeses imported into the United States.** (Les principaux
fromages français importés aux Etats Unis). — *L'Agriculture·
Commerciale*, N. 6, p. 130. Paris, 26 Mars, 1911.

The principal French cheeses imported into the United States
are Camembert and Roquefort. The amount imported has increased
ten-fold since 1900. The constant increase of population, and the
United   evident favour they enjoy with the public, justifies the hope that·
States.   demand for these cheeses will continue to grow. Brie, Coulommiers·
France   and Pont l'Evèque are less in demand, and are hardly known
outside New York, Boston, Philadelphia and Chicago. Experts·
however consider that the market for these cheeses could easily be
enlarged. Port-Salut has been almost completely ousted by a
Canadian imitation, very inferior in quality to the French original.

1477   BARRIER. **The Hygiene of Slaughter-houses.** (L'Hygiène des Abat-
toirs). — *Office international d'Hygiène publique, Bull. mensuel,*
Tome III, fasc. 3, pp. 451-467, Mars, 1911.

A report on the special and general conditions on which licenses should be granted to private slaughter-houses has been submitted by Mr. Barrier to the Council of Hygiene and Public Health
France   of the Department of the Seine. The report dwells on the necessity
of requiring all private slaughter-houses, to give the same guarantees·
as those which are obligatory as public slaughter-houses. An important point is the minimum area which applicants should be required
to provide.

The slaughter-houses attached to butcher's shops fall into three·
main classes: those that are used by the butcher only for his·
own business ; those that supply meat· markets, and those in which
the butcher slaughters a large number of animals for outsiders. In
the first case the area of the slaughter-house per customer should
not be less than 0.35 sq. m., (3.77 sq. feet) in the second case·
0.26 sq. m. (2.8 sq. ft.) and in the third case 0.22 sq. m.·
(2.37 sq. ft.). These figures show that the owners of slaughter-

houses whilst finding it advantageous to increase their business, at the same time try to conceal its importance.

The slaughter-houses attached to pork-butcher's shops can also be distinguished, according to Mr. Martel, into three classes: those of little importance, which require a space of 0.088 sqm. (0.95 sq. ft,) per inhabitant; those of twice this importance, which should have 0.073 sq. m. (0.79 sq. ft.) per inhabitant; and lastly the large slaughterhouses requiring 0.05 sq. m. (0.54 sq. ft.) in the case of those slaughtering from 50 000 to 200 000 kgs. (110 000 to 440 000 lbs.) and of 0.02 sq. m. (0.21 sq. ft.) for those slaughtering more than 200 000 kgs. (440 000 lbs.) of meat per year.

This report, the conclusions of which have been accepted by the Paris authorities, summarises in 29 articles the general conditions on which licences should be granted for private slaughter-houses. The rules regulating the arrangement, construction and installation of those sections which are not the stables, sheep-pens and slaughter-room for butcher's meat, and the pig-styes, curing rooms (*brûloir*) and hanging-rooms for pork, are identical with those in force for public slaughter-houses.

MAUREL & ARMAND. **Formation of Albumose in Sausage-meats.** 1478
(Formation de substances albuminosiques dans les charcuteries).
— *C. R. de la Soc. de Biologie*, Tome LXX, N. 16, pp. 709-711.
Paris, Mai 12, 1911.

Messrs Maurel and Armand had already shown that sausage-meat and other preparations of pork almost always contain staphylococci, colibacilli, and the *Bacillus mesentricus vulgatus*. As two of these microbes liquify the gelatine of which these preparations contain a large proportion, and as this liquefaction may produce peptonisation, they have now tried to discover what quantity of these substances — gelatine and albumose — was contained in freshly made sausage-meat and what quantity in sausage-meat preparations of more or less long standing. **France**

Experiments were made on pork pies and two on saveloys (*cervelat*) with concordant results. As long as the preparation is fresh, the quantity of gelatine plus the albumoses (precipitated by alcohol) increases considerably (nearly 33 % more than the initial amount); but as soon as it begins to be tainted, this percentage diminishes. The method employed did not allow the gelatine to be separated from the albumoses.

The following conclusions were arrived at:

1) Sausage-meat, even when fresh, contains a certain proportion of albumose which increases gradually as the meat gets older, whereas the gelatine, from the mere fact of its liquefaction, cannot but diminish.

2) Some of this albumose is probably the product of the gelatine, which however cannot *alone* account for the increased quantity of this precipitate; it therefore follows that the other albuminoids must contribute to it.

3) This transformation is apparently due to microbes, especially to those which liquefy gelatine.

4) The decrease in the proportion of albumose due to tainting, coincides with a more advanced stage of mineralization, perhaps in the direction of the formation of ammonia compounds.

5) Some of these albumose products may be poisonous, which would account for cases of poisoning by sausage-meats.

6) It appears that the Staphylococcus is introduced by the hands of those engaged in preparing the pork; therefore the formation of albumose could be avoided by greater care in the preparation of the meat, which should be rendered aseptic by heat, and by proper storage.

1479   **The Wool Problem in Australia: Methods of Cross breeding.** (La Question lainière en Australie: Méthodes de croisement). — *Bull. de l'Office du Gouvt. Gén. de l'Algérie*, N. 10, pp. 148-159. Paris, 15 Mai, 1911.

The quality of Australian wool is generally estimated by the number of « counts ». The higher the number of « counts » the

Australia finer the wool, both in the actual diameter of the fibre and proportionately to its length.

A small sheep can never produce so much low priced coarse wool as to give the same profit as a larger sheep with finer wool. It is therefore essential that a cross-bred animal taking more after the long-woolled sheep than the merinos in the quality of its fleece, should be large; otherwise there would be no advantage in the cross breeding.

The good qualities of the large, long-woolled sheep should, by judicious crossing, be uniformly blended with those of the smaller merinos whose wool is finer and thicker.

The Australian long-woolled sheep which can be crossed with the Merinos so as to produce wool-bearing hybrids are the Lincoln, the Cotswold, the Leicester, the Border Leicester, the Romney Marsh, ond the Cheviot.

Of these different breeds those best suited to crossing with the merinos are the Lincoln, the Leicester, and the Border Leicester. The crossbred Lincoln-Merino is the favourite with Australian breeders.

These hybrids can again be crossed successfully, producing quick-growing very profitable breeds for the butcher.

Poultry Farming in Russia. *The Illustrated Poultry Record.* — Vol. III, N. 8, p. 351. London, May 1911.   **1480**

Poultry-farming has made the greatest progress in the more thickly populated parts of Russia and the export of eggs has increased from 1686 millions valued at £ 3 023 000 (76 330 750 frs.) in 1909, to 2845 millions worth £ 6 566 000 (165 791 500 francs), in 1909. The increase in value is far greater than in quantity, and it is ascribed rather to the improved quality of the produce than to the general rise in food prices, though doubtless the latter is partly responsible.   **Russian Empire**

Besides eggs, there is a considerable export of dead fowls, the value of which rose from £ 834 000 (21 058 500 frs.) to £ 1 500 000 (38 102 250 francs).

In addition, feathers and down, of the value of £ 190 000, are exported, so that the value of all poultry products amounts to £ 8 265 831 as against £ 3 857 009. In spite of the increasing export and of the rising prices of poultry products, the consumption within the country increases, not only among well-to-do customers, but also among the producing peasant farmers themselves.

In many places it is thought possible that, as the land is more and more subdivided into small holdings, poultry - farming may supersede the cattle industry.

MONSEU. **The Xograph, an Instrument for Egg-Testing.** (Le Xograph, instrument pour examiner les œufs). — *Chasse et Pêche,* N. 32, pp. 752-753. Bruxelles, 6 mai 1011.   **1481**

The Xograph is an instrument by which fertilized and unfertilized eggs can be distinguished when newly laid. It is also said to be able to determine the sex of the embryo; *if this be the case,* it will be of great use in poultry-rearing and in raising fancy   **United States. Switzerland** breeds. The farmer, who breeds for the table, will set eggs which contain male embryos, while, when fowls are required for sitting, those eggs which will produce hens will be incubated. The unfertilised eggs can be discarded at once.

Very conclusive results have already been obtained with regard to determining unfertilized eggs, only 6 or 7 in 100 having been found on incubation to have been incorrectly tested.

This apparatus has been exported from America to Geneva, where its is now on sale.

1482   **Ostrich Farming in Sardinia.** — *Bollettino del Ministero d'Agricoltura, Industria e Commercio*. An. X, Vol. II, Série A, fasc. 4, pp. 101-102. Rome, 28 Gennaio 1911.

Italy:
Sardinia

An ostrich farm has been started at S. Maria Navarese, Lotzorai, by Mr, G. Meloni. The eight ostriches, of which six are females, were purchased from the Hamburg Zoological Gardens.

The ostrich farm was enlarged by the addition of four male birds in 1910. The farm occupies sandy soil, by the sea shore, and the climate is sub-tropical.

The birds are fed on two rations of lucerne, cabbage, and other chopped-up leaves, and a ration of maize, bran, or other similar forage.

Mr. Meloni has obtained beautiful brown and black feathers but few white ones; he hopes, however, to obtain these latter by preventing the ostriches from sitting on their eggs, as it seems that the feathers darken during this process. For this purpose an incubator will be used on the farm.

Mr. Meloni has purchased 25 hectares (61.75 acres) of land, near the sea, and not far from the station of Arbatax, where he purposes opening another ostrich farm surrounded by fields. On these he will raise maize, beans, lucerne and vegetables, so as to ensure food for a large number of ostriches, either kept in pens or left free (1).

By further purchases and by the use of the incubator M. Meloni hopes to have some hundreds of ostriches in a few years time and to be able to supply specimens to zoological gardens and museums and supply the Italian market with black and white ostrich feathers.

---

(1) Green, dry, and chopped lucerne is particularly favorable to the growth of ostriches; it increases the fertility of the females. See *Ostrich breeding in California*. See No 928 in this Bulletin. March, 1911.   (*Ed.*).

A new Ostrich Farm in South Tunis. (Une nouvelle autrucherie   1483
dans le Sud-Tunisien). — *Révue Tunisienne de l'Institut de*
Carthage. XVIII année, N. 85. Janvier, 1911.

A company has been formed which has opened an ostrich farm   **Tunis**
at Bazma, near Kebili, to the south of Tabaga. Forty ostriches
have been imported from Egypt, and there is every reason to believe
that this undertaking will be successful.

G. CARLE. **Ostrich Farming in Madagascar.** (L'élévage de l'autruche   1484
à Madagascar). — *Journal d'Agriculture pratique*, 75e année,
N. 17. Paris, 27 Avril, 1911.

Ostrich farming in Madagascar dates back to 1902, and   **Madagascar**
it is now about to enter on the profit-making stage. All methods
of natural and artificial incubation were tried with various results.
The problem of artificial incubation appears to be successfully solved
by conforming to the following rules:

1. The incubator must be placed in a well-ventilated room,
free from draughts which might affect the lamp.

2. During the first fortnight the temperature must be kept
at 37.5° C.; and then gradually lowered to 36° C. towards the end
of the period of incubation.

3. The eggs must be left undisturbed in the incubator during
the first two days.

4. After that, the eggs must be turned over morning and
evening, and left lying in the open air for a quarter of an hour
each morning at first, and for half an hour towards the close of the
period of incubation.

5. The egg-shell must be cracked on the 40th day, to facilitate the hatching of the chick.

As a rule the chicks are not hatched before the 42nd day, but
this is not always the case. To wait till then before cracking the
shell entails risks which can be avoided by doing so on the 40th day.

During the hot season hatching is sometimes premature, occurring on the 38th and even on the 36th day.

In 1909, 925 eggs · were laid in the ostrich farm by 11 pairs
aged 3 years, and by some 12 pairs then in their third year.

24 % of the fertilized eggs hatched out.

The valuation in January 1910 was as follows:

30 pairs of breeding birds (valued at 1 000 frs. = £ 40) = 30 000 frs. = £ 1 200
7 adult males at 350 frs. . . . . = 2 450 » = » 98
1 adult female at 350 frs. . . . . = 350 » = » 14
7 young birds from 13 to 18 months, valued at 250 frs. = 1 750 » = » 70
22 chicks from 3 to 5 months, valued at 150 frs. . . = 3 300 » = » 132
20 chicks aged 3 months, valued at 100 frs. . . . . = 2 000 » = ». 80

39 850 » = » 1 594

or in round numbers 40 000 frs; 116 birds had already been sold.
The sale of the feathers yielded in :

1906 a net sum of . . . . .   5 410 frs. = £ 216.8 s. —
1907 - »   . . . . . 1 103 » = » 44.2 s. 2 d.
1908   »   . . . . . 3 691 » = » 147.12 s. 9 d.
1909   »   . . . . . 5 498 » = » 219.19 s. 2 d.

The ostrich farm at Tuléar will put on sale 150 birds this year. Ostrich farming is therefore now a paying business.

The Governor General has already experimented with an ostrich farm at Majunga and success seems ensured (1). This will make it possible to develop ostrich farming on a large scale in Madagascar, and the feathers will become one of the staple exports of this great island.

1485   MAY. **The Autumn Rearing of Silk-worms in Japan** — (Les éle- vages d'automne des Vers à Soi en Europe). — *Bulletin des soies et des soieries*, N. 1768. Lyon, 25 mars, 1911.

The summer, especially the autumn, rearing of silk-worms has acquired great importance in Japan of late years, and this largely accounts for the almost automatic increase in the output of Japanese silk. (2).

Japan.
France.
Italy

---

(1) See this *Bulletin*, p. 133, November, 1910.
(2) The export of silk products was valued as follows. in yen:

	1908	1909
Raw silk	108 609 052	124 243 339
Silk waste	7 872 465	6 928 707
Silk manufactures.	34 428 839	26 169 295

The three silk crops of Japan are obtained from eggs of the same year, the hatching of which is retarded by suitable winter storage. There is no need for cold storage stations. The Japanese store the eggs in grottos or caves, at a temperature not exceeding 6° or 8° C. When a suitable spot on the side of a mountain has been found for winter storage, a small store-house is built there for the eggs, protected from the sun by a double roof. Experience has taught the Japanese that the end of February or the beginning of March is the best time to place the eggs in these grottos, for the inside and outside temperature is then pretty much the same. At present some 120 grottos or caves are utilised for the winter storage of eggs.

Similar storage houses could easily be arranged in France and Italy, in localities where there are no cold storage stations, either in the Cevennes or on the Alps and Apennines.

DELONCA. **The New Tendencies of the Silk Industry in France.**   **1486**
(Orientation nouvelle de l'Industrie Séricole en France). — *Le Moniteur des Soies*, N. 2636, p. 4. Lyon, 6 Mai, 1911.

The breeds of silk-worms of the Alps, the Pyrenees and the Var are those which are now raised in the Cévénnes, Dauphiné, and the Rhone valley, and which yield the wonderful cocoons of the Cévennes, and the less valuable products of the Rhone valley, and of the Isère.   **France: South-East**

The uniform quality produced throughout great silk-breeding regions proves the preponderating influence of climate on the quality of the cocoons. So great is this influence that at the end of one season the imported breeds lose some of their distinguishing characters and acquire new ones.

The production of cocoons, measured in Kwans (1 Kwan = 8.28 lbs avoird). and of raw silk, also weighed in Kwans, was as follows in Japan:

Year	Cocoons	Raw Silk
1905	2 723 333	2 606 124
1906	2 970 727	2 917 509
1907	3 456 967	3 236 692
1908	3 530 171	3 512 242
1909	3 625 227	—

In 1908, woven silk goods, in Japan, were valued at 94 799 152 yeu, aud those of mixed silk and cotton, at 21 632 156 yen. *The Statesman's Yearbook* for 1911, p. 989.   (*Ed.*).

Yet better results will be obtained when the silk-growers realise the need of getting their cocoons more uniform and of placing on the market only two distinct types: first, slender cocoons rather under the average in size, but well covered and heavy for the Isère, the north of the Drôme, and Ardèche; and, secondly, fine average cocoons for the other silk-growing districts. Purchasers will then be able, in spite of differences in the eggs, to obtain almost uniform cocoons, each district producing thus a regular type.

1487   COLESCO. **Sériculture in Rumania.** (La Sériculture en Roumanie). — *Le Moniteur des Soies.* N. 2537, p. 6. Lyon, 13 Mai 1911.

The returns of the General Statistical Service of Bukarest supply the following particulars on the production of silk in Rumania in 1910 :

Rumania

Communes growing cocoons : 1523.

Number of silk-breeders; 35 176.

Quantity of silk eggs incubated; 198.55 kgs. or 7 942 ounces (1).

Cocoons gathered : 215 120 kgs.

Yield of cocoons per ounce of eggs: 27.07 kgs.

Number of mulberry trees planted in Rumania: 405 068.

1488   LÉPICE (French Consul). **The Silk Industry in Yunnan.** (L'industrie de la Soie dans le Yunnan). — *Bulletin de soies et de soieries,* M. 1776, pp. 3-4. Lyon, 20 Mai 1911.

For some years past the provincial authorities of Yunnan have made efforts to encourage the silk industry in this province, and their efforts will no doubt soon be crowned with success. A school

China.
Yunnan

of sericulture has been opened at Yunnanfu, which is attended by 500 pupils from different parts of the province.

An exhibition recently organized by the local authorities at Yunnanfu enabled European traders to become acquainted with some excellent silks there on view.

The cultivation of the mulberry is encouraged throughout the province, and excellent results are obtained. The silk-worms used in Yunnan come from Cheh-Kiang (2).

---

(1) Ounce = 25 grams.

(2) " Silk-culture in China is not in a prosperous condition. Still 27 % of the world's supply of raw silk is from China, the most serious rivals being Japan with 28 % and Italy 25 % " *The Statesmans Ycarbook* for 1911, p. 697.

(*Ed.*)

Production of Honey in Holland and its Importation in 1910.   1489
(Production et importation du miel aux Pay Bas en 1910). —
Feuille d'Informations du Ministère de l'Agriculture, N. 20. Paris,
23 Mai 1911.

Holland produced a large quantity of honey in 1910, more
especially in the heather growing districts. Denatured sugar has   Holland
been used with success as food for bees, as much as 200 700 kgs.
(441 540 lbs.) being employed for this purpose.   Yet the honey
trade is still far from prosperous, and there is an urgent demand
that matters should be remedied.

Germany provides a large market for Dutch honey; in 1910 the
exports to that country amounted to 72 000 kgs. (158 400 lbs.),
as against 8 000 (17 600 lbs.) in 1909, and 43 000 (94 600 lbs.) in
1908 out of a total production of 78 000 kgs. (171 600 lbs.) in 1910,
28 000 kgs. (61 600 lbs.) in 1909, and 58 000 (127 600 lbs.) in 1908.

943 000 kgs. (2 074 600 lbs.) of honey were imported into Holland from the United States, 308 000 (677 600 lbs.) from France,
156 000 (343 200 lbs.) from Germany, and 113,000 (248 600 lbs.)
from Belgium.

WILHELM MATTHES. **The "Nosema" Disease of Bees.** (La Maladie   1490
" Nosema " des Abeilles). (Extrait de la *Deutsche Illustr. Bienen-
zeitung*). — *L'Apiculteur*, 55e année, No. 5, pp. 194-196. Paris,
Mai 1911.

The germ of this disease was discovered by Zander, who named
it *Nosema Apis.*

The spores of the *Nosema Apis* are spread by the diseased   Germany
bees in the hives and their vicinity (drinking troughs, etc.).   Bees
in search of water, alighting on the damp earth, or on the stalks and
leaves of plants, take up the parasite, which then makes its way in
to their intestines, where it lodges, multiplies, and destroys the cells;
for it is more especially a cell-parasite. The intestine becomes milky
white. The infected bees fly out into the open, and die after a
short time. This disease is easily detected in the spring, when the
young brood is not yet numerous.

There is no remedy for Nosema. All that can be done is
to remove the tainted honey, collect and burn the dead bees,
carefully disinfect the hives, dig up the surrounding soil and turn
it over, and remove any drinking vessels near. As a rule all troughs
visited by bees and containing stagnant water are dangerous. It is
very difficult, if not impossible, to stop the spread of contagion.

1491 · **Opossum Farming in Australia and utilising Eucalyptus trees.**
Journal of the Royal Society of Arts, N. 3049, p. 593. London,
April 28 1911.

Australia

On account of the recent rising market for opossum skins in
Australia, much attention is now being given to the possibility of
breeding opossums for their fur, in timbered parts of Australian
farms.   It is apparent that the future demands for Australian opossum skins can only be met by carefully breeding these animals commercially.   Every eucalyptus tree on Australian farms can be made
productive by providing food for opossums.   For every good-sized
gum or eucalyptus tree the income of the farm might be increased
by about two shillings.   A proportion of one male to three or four
females would be recommended, and a simple method of keeping
stock would be to place a number of small boxes, large enough to
hold one opossum, in an accessible position in the trees.   The opossums would use these to sleep in during the daytime, when it is their
habit to sleep; and the boxes would make it convenient to catch
and examine them.

The cultivation of maize and of the chief fodder crops is also
recommended in order to increase the opossum-carrying capacity
of the farm and to enable these animals to reach maturity more
quickly.

Their chief food however, consists of eucalyptus leaves, which
are naturally very abundant in Australia, the native home of the
eucalyptus tree.

1492   A. H. CLARK. **A list of the Birds of the Island of St. Lucia.** —
West Indian Bulletin, Imp. Agr. Dep. Vol. XI N. 3. Barbados.

West Indies:
St. Lucia

The list of the birds recorded from St. Lucia together with
remarks on the protection of the native species prepared by
Mr. A. H. Clark, of the Smithsonian Institution, Washington, is
reproduced in the West Indian Bulletin, in view of the general
interest that it bears in relation to the West Indies. The protection
of the birds and the classes of birds to be protected are discussed.
Dealing with the problem of the introduction of foreign birds, Mr.
Clark says: « The introduction of foreign birds should be strictly prohibited ; but if it be allowed, it should be only permitted upon the
recommendation of an authoritative society, such as the British Orni-
thologists'Union or the Zoological Society ».

« Far more harm than good has resulted from the indiscriminate introduction of birds and animals into new localities, and new experiments along this line should be firmly discouraged. Usually, the introduction of a bird into a new region is unsuccessful, the stock quickly dying out. Many instances of this are found in the ornithological history of Barbados and St. Vincent ; but sometimes it is far too successful and the interloper becomes a perfect nuisance, if not an actual pest.

« Every new element introduced into a fauna necessitates a readjustment of the constituent elements of that fauna... A new balance must be struck. Under normal faunal conditions, the native species collectively consume the entire available supply of food as rapidly as it is produced; the addition of a vigorous exotic species deprives a certain proportion of the original endemic species of their food supply and consequently they gradually disappear, their disappearance being often hastened by hostility on the part of the intruder ».

«The history of the introduction of birds into new localities shows that, economically, it has very rarely been a success ; and scientifically, the disturbance of the faunal conditions in an exceptionally interesting island — conditions duplicated nowhere else in the world — is greatly to be deplored ».

Fresh-Water Fish in Tonking. (La pêche en eaux douces au Tonkin). — *La Quinzaine Coloniale*, N. 9, p. 308. Paris, 10 Mai, 1911.

1493

In the rivers of Tonking, fishermen catch not only various Fish, Mollusks and Crustaceans, but also Batrachians and Insects. In fact, natives quite frequently fish for a species of gigantic water bug. Among the fauna of these waters, are found, strange to say, marine forms become adopted to fresh water: Crustaceans and Fish such as Soles and Skates which may be found as far as Viétry. Fishing is carried on by means of fishing rods, bow nets, gigantic square fish nets, sweep nets and finally by traps so varied, so complicated and so specialized that no European words can describe them.

French
Indo-China:
Tonking

Salmon-Fishing in Siberia. — *Journal of the Royal Society of Arts* N. 3048, p. 571. London, April 21, 1911.

1494

The most important industry of Nicolawsk is fishing. About twelve years ago the business was of little importance, and its mar-

. Siberia

vellous growth dates from that time. In 1909 the catch in the
Amur River and in the vicinity of Sakhalin Island, amounted to
90 million pounds, an increase of 18 million pounds over 1908.

There are three varieties of salmon at these fisheries, Gorbusha,
summer-salmon and autumn-salmon, the most valuable being the last
named. The amount of caviar obtained from 1000 Gorbusha salmon
is 90 lbs. from the same number of summer salmon 126 lbs., and from
1000 autumn salmon 144 lbs. There are two refrigerating plants near
Nicolaevsk and large quantities of fish have been frozen. About
two-thirds of the annual catch of salmon is shipped for Japan. The
remainder is smoked or salted for Siberia and Russia.

Fishing in the Amur Province is in the hands of the Cossacks,who
own the lands along the river fronts.

1495   **The Transport of Fish Spawn.** (Le Transport du frai de Poisson).
Revue Scientifique, 49ᵉ année, Iᵉʳ sem., N. 17, p. 535. — Paris,
29 Avril, 1911.

The systematic exchange of fish spawn, with the view of experimenting in acclimatization, is much practised in the United
States, as the Fish Breeding Stations are often situated at great

United States   distances from one another.

In order to preserve unimpaired the vitality of the eggs,
they are placed in specially constructed boxes, which allow a constant, and fairly low temperature to be maintained.

The spawn (either rolled up in muslin or not) is packed in
moss and placed in light crates (usually of deal) piled one on
the other.

A receptacle filled with ice and usually not in contact with
the pile of boxes, prevents any rise of temperature, and the whole
is enveloped in a thick layer of non-conducting substance.

Cases are thus made which vary in size according to the
amount of spawn which is to be transported. There are types
adapted for winter use and also for travelling in summer, either
in cold storage compartments, or otherwise.

Two kinds are especially interesting, those used for very long
journeys, such as from Europe to Argentina. One is the Argentine case, of which the external dimensions are 100 × 60 × 75 cm,
and the other the German-Chile case, which was improved in
1907-1908 by M. A. Tulian, of the Pisciculture Department of
Argentina.

The German-Chile case was originally devised in 1876 by M. Ch. Tellier, at the request of the Paris Society for Acclimatisation, for the purpose of conveying fish spawn into France from Argentina. The loss on the journey was only 5 %.

Agricultural Industries.

MOREAU et VINET. **Jerez or Sherry Wines.** (La viticulture et les vins de Jerez. Espagne). *Revue de Viticulture*, n. 907, p. 509-513. — Paris, 4 mai, 1911.

1496

In Jerez, there are firms which have existed for 180 years and which can supply wines dating from the year of their establishment.

The real Jerez (or Sherry)wines have an exquisite bouquet and and are from grapes grown in the neighbourhood of the town, on calcareous slopes where the amount of calcium carbonate in the soil is 50 or even 70 %. After the phylloxera crisis, only a part of the old Jerez vineyard was replanted.

Spain:
Andalusia

In the *Albarizas* the soil is dry, calcareous or marly, eminently suited to the vine, and produces the *Palomino*, an early white variety of grape from which is made the typical Sherry.

The *Palomino* vine is subjected to a special kind of mixed pruning with the object of improving the quality of the fruit at the cost of reducing the yield, which amounts on an average to 40-50 hectolitres per hectare In Jerez, as in nearly all Spanish vineyards, no poles are used, but the vine is supported by a small wooden fork. The vine is allowed to bear ample foliage in order to check evaporation, the leafy branches cover the soil and protect it from the sun's rays. (1)

Besides *Palomino, Mantuo de Pilas, Castellano* and *Perruno* are vines also cultivated, at Jerez; they are however later varieties than *Palomino* and more suitable to sandy soils. *Tintilla* is a vine that

---

(1) The amount of transpiration depends on the quantity and surface of the foliage. Ample foliage may check the direct evaporation from the soil, but must favour transpiration. causing a great loss of moisture from the soil. (*Ed.*).

flourishes on dark coloured soils and produces a red wine of the Burgundy type.

The grapes are gathered gradually as they reach maturity. They are placed on esparto mats which are spread on a beaten level surface (*almijar*) in the sun. The exposure to the sun lasts from 6 to 8 hours and may be prolonged in order to obtain a higher degree of concentration in the sap. The peculiar bouquet of Jerez wine is attributed to this drying of the grapes before pressing out the must.

The first must is trodden out by foot (the workers being shod in special shoes for the purpose) then the residue is slightly pressed and the resulting product, *yema*, is added to the « first wine » and it is this mixture alone which is used for Jerez wine.

The pomace is then put in to a Mabille presser, and the juice obtained is used for the second quality wines which are usually distilled.

1497   J. LABORDE. **The Characteristics of Rose-coloured Wines and of White Wines made from Black Grapes.** (Caractérisation des Vins rosés et des Vins blancs de Raisins rouges). — *Annales des Falsifications*, IV Année, N. 30, pp. 177-182. Paris-Genève, Avril 1911.

France   Rose-coloured wines and the brownish and amber wines derived from them, rank commercially with ordinary red wines and those white ones which are made from black grapes.

Being prepared from different varieties of grapes, and by different processes, these rose-coloured wines are very variable in their composition. Their quality cannot be determined by ordinary analysis. M. Laborde is of opinion that some light may be thrown on the subject by investigating the tannin costituents, found in all wines. He has determined the total weight of these substances and studied the proportions of their component parts, the colouring matter and the oenotannin.

Rose-coloured wines are made by four processes.

1) Fermenting only those grapes which on ripening have a rosy, or more or less distinctly grayish-blue colour. This method is little practised, as such grapes are usually consumed locally.

2) By the rapid fermentation of entirely black grapes. The process is limited to one day at the most, hence the name 24 hours', or one night wines. This method is also little used.

3) By pressing black grapes, separating the more or less coloured must from the residue and fermenting the former. Most of the rose-coloured wines of commerce are thus made.

4) By the decoloration of red wines. This is an illegal proceeding, but it is well that the fraud should be exposed. The analyses of red wines, of 24 hours' wines, and of rose-coloured wines, all made from grapes of the same quality coming from Aramon and Carignan vines, show that rose-coloured wines are much inferior in tannin substances to red ones, the proportion of colouring matter to oenotannin is always above unity, and varies in inverse proportion to the total content of tannin substances.

In red wines this proportion rarely reaches unity, and should also be very low in wines from brownish grapes which have been submitted to a long fermentatiou.

Rose-coloured wines, which have been made by the partial decoloration of red wines, are easily detected, as the proportion of colouring matter to oenotannin and also the tannin content are decreased.

White wines which are made from dark grapes, are easily distinguished from those made from white grapes, for the addition to the former of a little cold hydrochloric acid produces a slight rose reaction. This rose colour, which does not occur if the wine has been discoloured with bone-black either before or after fermentation, can be brought about by hydrochloric acid at 120° C. This reagent has no effect upon white wines from white grapes, but reddens white wines which have been made from decolorized red wines.

Sulphur Dioxide in Wine-making in France. (Emploi de l'acide sulfureux dans la vinification). — *Conseil supérieur d'Hygiène publique en France.* J. Ogier et Richaud. Rapporteurs. Annales des Falsifications, 4ᵉ Année, N. 30, pp. 197-214. Paris-Genève, Agrll 1911.

1498

The French Minister of the Interior laid before the Council of Hygiene a letter from the Minister of Agriculture regarding a modification of the Decree of Sept 3rd 1907 on the use of Sulphur dioxide in wine-making (1).

France

The Ministerial letter is published *in extenso* and a résumé given of the opinions of different physiologists from a medical standpoint,

---

(1) See this Bulletin Nov. 1911. Page 139.

after which the technical side is considered. According to data collected by the Bordeaux Commission, and embodied in Mr. Gautrélets' report a man can take 650 mg. of sulphur dioxide daily, without any unfavourable symptoms resulting.

If however a known quantity of the sulphur dioxide, which in solution forms sulphurous acid, is added to wine, it is impossible to be sure how much of the acid will remain free, and what amount will enter into combination ; for the composition of musts varies greatly according to the climatic conditions which prevailed while the grapes were ripening.

Though free sulphurous acid hinders excessive alcoholic fermentation, and checks harmful secondary fermentations, the amount used should be limited by strict scientific rules.

Therefore it was determined by the French Council of Hygiene that:

1) A new law should be passed in France, limiting the amount of free and combined sulphur deoxide in wines.

2) The maximum amount of free sulphur dioxide per litre may be raised to 100 milligr; and that of combined sulphur dioxide to 350 milligr. that is to say, a total content of 450 milligr., 10 % being tolerated.

1499

L. MATHIEU. **Detection of Copper in Wine.** — *Bulletin de la Société des Viticulteurs de France et d'Ampélographie.* 23ᵉ année, N. 4, pp. 87-88. Paris, avril, 1911.

France

Salts of copper can be detected by a certain acid, bitter taste, followed by a sweetish sensation, when the amount does not exceed 7 or 8 mgms. per litre (1); when it is more than 12 mgms. the nausea which is a distinct symptom of copper poisoning supervenes.

As a rule, salts of copper in small quantities, when present in the vat or press, are precipitated in the form of an insoluble sulphide, by means of the sulphuretted hydrogen produced by the reducing action of the yeast. But sometimes it happens that this precipitation does not take place, and then the soluble copper salts remain in the wine.

A very simple way of detecting copper in wine consists in dipping a well polished perfectly clean knitting-needle in a glass of

---

(1) 1 milligramme = 0.0154 grain Troy.
1 gram = 15.432 grains Troy.

the wine to be tested. At the end of half an hour or an hour, if the wine contains copper, the needle is covered with a film of bright red copper. An hour's immersion of the needle will detect a quantity as small as 5 mgms. per litre. The deposit becomes more visible if the wine be concentred by evaporation, or slightly warmed.

The same method may be used to detect copper in cognac, only the latter must first be made very acid by adding 1 gm. of tartaric acid, or a spoonful of vinegar, to every 100 cub. cm.

There is no need of exaggerating the danger caused by traces of copper salts in wine and cognac. Many substances like coffee and chocolate contain minute quantities of salts of copper, and these are perfectly tolerated ; while if the amount be rather large, vomiting is induced, and they are consequently rejected.

Cold Storage and Apple Cider. (L'emploi du froid dans la preparation du cidre). *Le Cidre et le Poiré*, 23e année, no. 1, p. 11. — Paris, Mai, 1911.   **1500**

Experiments have been made by the Bureau of Chemistry of the United States Department of Agriculture to ascertain whether the cold storage of apple juice might be of practical use in the cider industry. The juice of sound apples, cooled down to 0° C., immediately after leaving the press, and kept at this temperature, remained·from 36 to 57 days without any perceptible fermentation; and 90 to 119 days elapsed before any sourness could be detected.   **United States**

There was no loss of quality in the cider prepared from such juice, and the flavour was, if anything, improved.

Alcohol from the Tuna Cactus in New Mexico. *Pure Products*, vol. VII, No. 4, p. 220. — New York, April, 1911.   **1501**

The Agricultural Station of New Mexico has investigated the sugar content of the Cactus known by the common name of   **United States: New Mexico**

Long ago it has been ascertained that copper accumulates in the system; it would therefore not be all ejected by vomiting.

It may be observed that the danger of introducing undue quantities of copper into the human system increases nowadays with the increased application of copper salts in combating diseases in plants. Copper has been found sometimes in preserved vegetables, to which copper salts are fraudulently added to mantain the appearance of a fresh green colour. The increasing dangers from copper poisoning call for great severity in regard to food and beverages that are found to contain copper salts.   (*Ed.*).

Tuna (1). The fruit of the cactus on Aug. 17th showed a content of 6.8 % sugar. Analyses made after a few days showed that the percentage of sugar was gradually increasing, until a month later it amounted to 11.92 %. At the same time the acidity decreased from 0.28 % on Aug. 17th to 0.04 % on Sept. 17th. Tuna fruits may therefore be useful for preserving, for distilling spirits, etc.

1502   P. DE MORAES. **Alcohol from Coffee Pulp.** (Alcool de Café). *Chacaras e Quintaes*, vol. III, No. 4, pp. 40-41. — Rio de Janeiro, Abril 1911.

Analyses have proved that 1 000 kilos (2 200 lbs.) of dry coffee pulp contain about 24 % of Carbohydrates which, theoretically, can be converted into 134 litres of absolute alcohol. The actual amount obtained is, however, from 5 to 6 % less, which gives 127 litres for every 1 000 kilos (2 200 lbs) of dry pulp.

Brazil

The process consists firstly in boiling the product, or otherwise drying and over heating it at a temperature of 110° C, for 15 or 20 minutes (to destroy all ferments which hinder proper fermentation) and after cooling to add the yeast or ferments which promote the right alcoholic fermentation.

1 000 kilos (2 200 lbs) of dry coffee pulp correspond to 1 250 kilos (2 750 lbs) of commercial coffee, which are worth about 1 800 fr. (£. 72).

If the price of a litre of alcohol is estimated at 30 centimes (3^d) (a very low figure) the return obtained from coffee products by this means is 10 % more than from maize.

Other pulps, like that of *Henequem*, more resistent to fermentation than the pulps of coffee berries, have been successfully prepared for the distilling by the process here described. The yeasts usefal in these fermentations are specially prepared and preserved (2).

---

(1) Tuna, *Opuntia horrida*, grows in the West Indies and in Mexico. Of all the species of *Opuntiae* it is probably the one most cultivated. From the earliest days of Spanish sovereignty Tuna has been cultivated in the S. E. of the United States, in the Antilles and in Mexico.   (*Ed.*).

(2) See N° 946 in this Bulletin. N° 3. March 1911.

Loss in Weight of Stored Flour. *Modern Miller*, p. 12. — St.   **1503**
Louis, Mo., April 15, 1911.

Experiments have been made at the Kansas State Agricu
tural College to determine the change of weight to which flour may
be subject when stored.

Twenty-seven sacks piled as closely together as possible, in   **United**
three layers of nine sacks each, were stored in an airy room, which,   **States:**
during the winter, was heated to ordinary room temperature. The   **Kansas**
sacks were kept in the same positions in the pile throughout the
test, but no difference due to position was detected. The sacks were
stored on a double floor, and were protected from mice by hardware
cloth of one-fourth-inch mesh.

The average weights including the sack, were:

	lbs.		Kgs.
11 Aug. 1909	48.19	or	21.90
11 Sept. »	48.05		21.84
11 Oct. »	47.90		21.77
17 Nov. »	47.73		21.69
11 Jan. 1910.	47.65		21.65
11 March. »	47.55		21.61
11 April »	47.40		21.54
13 May »	47.43		21.55
14 June »	47.55		21.61
10 Aug. »	47.67		21.66

A Bedouin Bread. *American Grocer*, vol. LXXXV, No. 17, p. 11. —   **1504**
New York. April 26, 1911.

In Arabia a bread is prepared from a small plant called *samh*,
which grows wild on the desert plateau. The Arabs pull it by hand,
flail out the seed pods, throw them into water holes, of the size   **Ottoman**
of a bath tub, and tramp them for a few minutes. When the   **Empire:**
water opens the pods, the seeds fall to the bottom and the hulls,   **Arabia**
which float, are skimmed off.

The seeds are dried, sifted through fine sieves to take out
as much of the sand grit as possible, and ground in basalt hand-
mills. The bread made therefrom is baked on a convex sheet
iron over a manure fire, or on flat stones in a dome-shaped clay
oven. It is black and gritty, but is improved by putting sugar
or juniper molasses in the flour.

1505

A. E. Collens. **Quantitative Experiments on drying Unripe Bananas.** — Department of Agriculture, Trinidad, Bulletin. Vol. X, N. 67, pp. 79-80 Trinidad, January - March 1911.

Trinidad

Experiments to ascertain the weight of saleable dry slices from fully developed, but unripe bananas, showed 12:4 to 14.3 per cent.

If then 100 lbs, of bananas are taken, only 12 lbs. of dried material will be obtained, which at 3 cents per lb. will realise 36 cents. Two fair sized bunches of bananas will weigh about 100 lbs.; and each bunch would only realise 18 cents when converted into dried material. It follows that at a price in London of £ 14 a ton, the drying of bananas is not a promising industry, so long as green bananas can be shipped and sold at £ 11 or £ 12 per ton.

The preserved ripe bananas at £ 20 to £ 23 a ton offer more promise of success.

1506

Utilisation of Banana Flour in San Domingo. (Verwendung von Bananenmehl in der Dominikanischen Republik). *Deutsches Kolonialblatt*, N. 6, p. 245. — Berlin, 15. März 1911.

West Indies: San Domingo

The consumption of banana flour is steadily increasing in San Domingo. The fruit is gathered green, peeled and cut into slices and then placed in the sun for three days, in order to dry it thoroughly. Then it is ground and yields an excellent fine yellow meal. Cooked in milk, it is eaten as a soup, and it is also made into bread.

About ten bananas are required to furnish a pound of flour.

1507

Ed. Neckel. **The Servian Giant Maize as an Important Constituent of Paper Pulp.** *Bulletin des Séances de la Société Nationale d'Agriculture de France*, Tome LXXI, n. 4, pp. 317-322. — Paris, Avril 1911.

France

The Servian giant maize is noted for the height and thickness of its stalks, which in the South of France reach from 10 ft. to 13 ft. (3 or 4 metres). They bear three or four conical female spikelets, from 7.80 to 9.75 inches (20 to 25 cm.) in length, larger at their base than at the top, and covered with big grains, yellow or reddish in colour. In Provence these original characters are usually preserved in the plant, although in some plantations stalks of only 6 ½ ft. (2 metres) and spikelets varying from 3.90 to 4.68 inches (10 to 12 cm.) are to be seen.

Attempts have been made in the United States to use stalks of ordinary maize in the manufacture of paper pulp (1); but although the paper obtained was of excellent quality, it was found that only from 20 to 30 % of the material could be utilised, an amount insufficient for commercial success.

The unusual size and toughness of the Servian maize stalks led Mr. Heckel to carry out further experiments at the Paper Manufactory School of Grenoble. In the laboratory the yield of cellulose was 51 %, which means not more than 40 % in practice. The stalks contained 6 % of ash. The paper produced was very sliff and fairly resistant, ruptaring at 4526 m. (4936 yds.) lengthwise, and 3021 m. (3296 yds.) crosswise. Weight per square yard 4.25 oz· or per square metre 118 grammes.

It forms a good packing paper and might be sold at the rate of 16 s. to 24 s. per 210 lbs. (20 to 30 frs. per 100 kilos). For making paper of fine quality, the Servian maize pulp must be mixed with other pulps because the yellowish tinge of the former cannot be entirely removed. There is one great drawback to this pulp; the fact that however short the refining process may be, it becomes thereby very greasy, and sticks firmly to the presses, occasioning much trouble and loss. As however, on the whole, the Servian maize may be usefully employed in the paper industry, Mr. Heckel recommends its being introduced in the Isère Department as well as in those bordering on the Garonne, where there are many paper mills.

Indian industries: Wood Pulp and Sardine Oil. *Journal of the Royal Society of Arts*, No. 3049. Vol. LIX. — London, April. 28th, 1911.

1508

According to the Director-General of Commercial Intelligence at Calcutta, one of the most important industries of the country, that of wood pulp, is showing marked signs of progress. Eight paper-mills are in operation, whilst others are approaching completion.

British India

The value of the output for 1909 amounted to £. 516 666, or 12 916 650 frs. the highest on record.

---

(1) See this *Bulletin*, Dec. 1910: p. 332.   (*Ed.*).

A new industry appears to be on the eve of development, oil of good quality having been produced in considerable quantities from boiled sardines, on the west coast of Madras. This oil is said to contain a large amount of fish tallow (stearine) (1).

1509   **The Inspection of Silk Fabrics in Japan.** (Inspection des Tissus de soie au Japon). — *Bulletin des Soies et des Soieries*, N. 1768. Lyon, 25 Mars 1911.

Japan

The Corporation of Yokohama silk merchants have presented to the Diet a petition requesting the establishment in that city of a Bureau for the inspection of silk fabrics. Further, the Department of Agriculture and Commerce has provided for the next fiscal year, 30 000 yen more than usual for the inspection of the *Habutai* which will be carried out with the utmost rigour. The Department also hopes to obtain a uniform standard of quality.

1510   A. GUISELIN. **Cold in the Manufacture of Artificial Camphor.** — (Emploi du froid dans l'industrie du Camphre artificiel). *Bull. Sem. de la Maison Schimmel et Cie*, pp. 190 (112-118). Miltitz près Leipzig, Avril 1911.

In 1910, M. Guiselin presented to the International Congress of Low Temperatures his work upon the use of cold in the manufacture of camphor. If 100 kilos (220 lbs) of turpentine (pinene) are converted in one hour into chloride of bornyl, (chlorhydrate of pinene) 119 000 calories are liberated, and in order to obtain the temperature necessary for the reaction ($+ 15°$ C.) refrigerators are required to absorb this heat.

At the above temperature, the yield of bornyl chloride is 100 to 110 % of the turpentine used, while if the refrigeration were dispensed with, it would amount to 35 % at the most.

1511   **Milk Transport in Cold Storage Cars in Argentina.** *L'Agriculture Commerciale*, N° 7, p. 156, Paris, 9 Avril, 1911.

Argentina

The Minister of Public Works in the Argentine has appointed a Commission to study the best means of transporting milk to Buenos-Ayres. A suitable type of cold storage car, fitted with complete hygienic apparatus is wanted.

---

(1) The residue of this extraction could be used in agriculture either as a fertiliser or as food for cattle and poultry.   (*Ed.*).

Agricultural Engineering and Farm
Machinery and Implements.

A. GUISSET. **Saving of Labour effected by the Use of Machines.**   **1512**
(La réduction de la main d'œuvre résultant de l'emploi des machines). — *Revue Générale Agronomique*, 20ᵉ ann., n⁰ 3 et 4, pp. 129-134 et 184-188. Bruxelles, Mars et Avril, 1911.

The writer first discusses rural depopulation in Belgium, and the question of " back to the land ", particularly as bearing on the use of agricultural machines.

He then examines the saving effected by the use of machines over hand-labour (considering *only* the men employed) on a farm   **Belgium**
of 150 acres, comprising wheat 25, oats 25, roots 35, potatoes 7 ½, flax 7 ½, green crops (various) 5, clover 7 ½, meadow 12 ½, pasture 25.

The machines include:— binder, mower, horse-rake, tedder, horse-hoe, drill, manure-distributor, oil-engine, thrashing-machine, chaff-cutter, root-slicer, cake-breaker, oat-crusher, and milking-machine.

Manure-distributor and drill. No saving of manual labour as compared with broad-casting.

Horse-hoe. In roots does over 6 acres a day, 10 times as much as a labourer. Saving on the 35 acres: 50 man-days. In cereals 5 acres a day, by hand one eighth acre. Saving (45 acres hoed) 350 man-days.

Flax-weeding. Time saved by use of machine (5 acres) 50 man-days.

Mowing and making hay. Mowing with machine, 4 man-days for the 20 acres of clover and meadow; scything 32 man-days. Saving 28.

Hay-making with hand-labour, 4 man-days per acre; with machine about 1 ¼ man-days. Saving (12 ½ acres of meadow) 35 days.

Harvesting. Reaping (with sickle) and tying, nearly 3 man-days per acre; binder 2 men, 5 acres per day. Saving 120 man-days.

Thrashing. Crop of 55 tons from the 50 acres. Thrashing by flail 560 man-days, by thrashing-machine and engine 140 man-days (60 of these by women), saving 420 man-days.

Indoor farm work. Estimated by the writer in a previous paper at 35 man-days of 10 hours for a farm of 150 acres. Includes milk separating, churning, corn-crushing, root-slicing, chaff-cutting, pumping, liquid-manure pumping, cake-breaking, root-cleaning.

Milking-Machine. A Wallace machine to milk two cows at once does 16 cows per hour, i. e. twice as many as a man. Saving 1 ½ hr. per day or 55 man-days per year.

The total saving comes to about 1150 man-days per year.

1513   AUSTED and HEWETT (British Consuls). **Agricultural Machinery and Irrigation in Chile.** *The Board of Trade Journal,* N. 750. London, April 13 1911, p. 72-73.

Chile:
Coquimbo

In the district of Coquimbo, there is an increasing need of agricultural machinery, to supplement an ever decreasing supply of farm labourers. Although the aggregate quantity of machines of late imported is still insignificant, yet a beginning has been made, and one sees implements of European and of United States make more frequently than heretofore.

The Central Government contemplates undertaking irrigation works which, when completed, will be managed by the Department of Public Works. There exist extensive tracts of land suitable for culture but which are at present sterile for want of irrigating canals : the tillage of these tracts should help to meet the demand in the province of Coquimbo for an increased food supply.

In the province of Atacama, in the vicinity of Copiapo, a scheme for irrigation on a considerable scale has been approved and is likely to be commenced shortly.

1514   P. DE MAILLARD. **Potato-Drill.** (Planteuse de Pommes de Terre). *Journal d'Agriculture pratique,* 75ᵉ année. Tome I, N. 16, p. 496. Paris, 20 Avril 1911.

Germany

This potato-planter, constructed by Messrs. Flammger Zudse and Co. of Dresden, resembles a drill with a fore-carriage. It carries a receptacle in which are placed the seed potatoes which are round and graded mechanically by passing through riddles 40 millimetres in diameter (1.56 inch). A chain, with cups, set in motion by the back wheels, traverses the bottom of the receptacle, picks up the potatoes singly, and empties them into a tube which descends within 0.10 m. (4 inches) of the bottom of the furrow.

The furrow is cut by a two winged plough-share similar to that of a double mould-board plough, and is closed by means of two discs placed behind ; it is preferable to use oxen walking at a ploughing pace rather than horses to draw the machine.

This potato-drill plants two rows m. 0.60 (2 feet) apart, at a time, and drops the potatoes m. 0.30 (1 ft.) apart in the rows.

Two men with a team of three or four oxen can plant 150 ares (3.8 acres) per day.

Motor Hoeing Machine. (Bineuse automobile) *La Nature*, 39ᵉ année, N. 1982 suppl. p. 195, Paris, 20 May, 1911.

1515

This hoe belongs to the machines with automatically moving blades. The forward motion imparts to the blades the horizontal motion, while the vertical one is regulated by a special arrangement. The hoeing machine is m. 1.40 (55 in) long. m. 0.80 high (31 in) and can by altered in width according to the distance between the rows of the crop. It consists of a horizontal frame supported by three wheels, those in front are the driving-wheels, the one at the back is free, and serves to steer the machine. the engine is 3 to 4 H. P; it is cooled by means of a fan ventilator. The pinion of the driving-shaft is attached by means of an eccentric wheel to the bar carrying the blades, and the former performs an alternate oscillating movement round its axis, thus causing the blades to ascend and descend regularly.

France

By a special contrivance. this motive power can be converted into a propelling power or can be detached so that the blades are fixed.

The steering of the machine is the only point which requires the attention of the worker.

The hoeing-machine can, thanks to a specially arranged crank controlling a vertical screw, hoe either lightly, or to the depth of several inches.

One hectare (2½) acres) with a frame only 60 cm. (2 ft.) wide can be hoed in 6 or 8 hours.

J. REZEK. R. von LIELIENBERG and L. RICHTER. **Trial of Weed Extirpator**. (Prüfung einer Unkrautjätmaschine der Maschinenfabrik K. and R. Jezek in Blansko). — *Wiener Landw. Ztg.* 61 J. N. 35.S 408-409, fig. 5. Wien 3 Mai, 1911.

1516

An account of the trial at the Vienna Station for Agricultural Machinery of a weed extirpator constructed by the Firm of K. and R. Jezek of Blansko.

Austria

The machine is efficient, practical, and durable, one strong draught animal is generally sufficient to work it, except in the case of ground which is unusually infested with weeds. The extirpator accomplishes a very satisfactory amount of work, owing to the careful construction of the automatic arrangement for cleaning the combs.

1517   ENG. BUGNON. **Vallotton Auto-mower and Agricultural Motor.** (Auto-faucheuse et moteur agricole Vallotton). — *La Terre Vaudoise,* 3e année, N. 20, pp. 199-201. Lausanne, 20 Mai 1911.

Switzerland

M. Vallotton mechanical-engineer at Geneva has succeeded in affixing a mowing-blade to a petroleum motor which latter is able, either alternatively or simultaneously, to propel automatically the whole machine and set in motion the knife. One of the driving-wheels can be instantly thrown ont of gear, this allows the machine while in motion, to make evolutions and turn on the spot. The knife is released automatically. These mowing machines must be of five H. P. but more powerful ones are made also. The cylinder is kept cool by means of a rotatory pump affixed to the motor. The water for cooling traverses a radiator provided with a powerful ventilator, which obviates the necessity of renewing it during operations.

By the removal of the mowing apparatus the machine can be converted into a traction engine, or an agricultural engine suitable for threshing, chaff-cutting, root-slicing, dairy purposes, etc.

PLANT DISEASES
NOXIOUS INSECTS AND OTHER PESTS.

INTELLIGENCE

Phytopathological and Entomological Stations.

Phytopathological Station in Médoc, France. — *Bulletin de la* **1518**
Société d'études et de vulgarisation de la Biologie agricole,
10me *année,* N. 2, p, 71. Bordeaux. Avril 1911.

A syndicate for the prevention of cryptogamic diseases and
of insect pests has been formed in Médoc with the view of pro- **France:**
viding a service of information, resembling thal which has already **Médoc**
existed for 10 years at Cadillac. The observatory is under the
direction of M. Léonard. Information will be given to the vine-
growers of the district of Lesparre respecting anticryptogamic treatments, and preventive measures against *Cochylis* and *Eudemis*.

A. v. JACZEWSKI. **Plant Pathology in Russia.** Ocerk Sostoianiia i Ras- **1519**
vitiia Fitopatologhii v Rossii). — *Buiro po Mikologhii i Fitopa-*
thologhii Ucenago Komitata, pp, 1-18. St. Peterburg, 1911.

The study of cryptogamic diseases and their prevention has
hitherto not been sufficiently carried out in Russia. **Russia**
In 1907, in the Kakhetie vineyards alone, a [loss of 38 %, representing about 500 000 roubles, was due to cryptoganic diseases.
In certain districts of Central Russia, the apple and pear " rot "

destroys every year a good half of the crop. At Gseatsko, in the government of Smolensk, flax cultivation, otherwise so profitable, has been made impossible for several years by the *Fusarium Lini*. In 1860 an interesting monograph on *Puccinia Helianthi* was published by Woronin.

In 1880 the Boards appointed for combating the phylloxera began to make themselves felt ; but it was only in 1901 that systematic accurate researches were started on a well-organised basis. A central phytopathological Station was then established :

1) To determine the diseases and to reply to enquiries by farmers.

2) To explain the means of combating cryptogamic diseases.

3) To test the efficiency of the remedies in use, and if possible, discover better ones.

4) To study plant diseases, and make cultivation experiments.

5) To instruct farmers, by opening a public phytopatological Museum, distributing leaflets, pamphlets etc.

6) To publish phytopathological research work.

Thanks to this Institute, the knowledge of cryptogamic diseases, in Russia and the organisation of preventive measures has been greatly extended. Among its periodical publications, the *Annuaires* are specially useful. They give an idea of the distribution of the diseases so far determined throughout Russia, the numerous correspondents in each district supplying valuable information.

In 1907 the Minister of Agriculture established a Mycological and Phytopathological Department divided into the following three sections.

I. *Correspondence Section :*

1) To determine the parasitic fungi and saprophytes found in the infected plants sent by Societies or private enquirers.

2) To suggest efficient remedies.

II. *Scientific Section :*

1) To publish a Mycological Flora of Russia.

2) To study plant diseases in general, and those of cultivated plants in particular.

3) To draw up the life histories of parasitic fungi.

4) To try to discover new remedies for cryptogamic diseases.

5) To publish the scientific work of the Department.

6) To give public lectures, periodical courses, and pamphlets.

7) To provide a Mycological Herbarium and a Phytopathological Museum.

8) To make an annual report of the proceedings of the Despartment.

III. *Acclimatization Section.*

a) To collect information bearing on disease-resisting species of plants, contributing to their introduction and diffusion throughout Russia.

The Department has a good special library. The Mycological Herbarium is one of the best in Europe, and the Museum is constantly being enriched by a large number of interesting and rare specimens.

Although Russia was very late in taking up the study of Phytopathology, she has nevertheless gone very far in a short time. The service of correspondents is so well arranged that the infected zones are clearly marked out, and due warning is always given of the appearance of new diseases. This allows measures to be taken in time for their suppression or control. The activity of this section of the Ministry is also shown by the number of scientific papers it publishes.

Among the chief *desiderata* for the future are :

1) The institution of a Mycological Laboratory in every agricultural experimental station.

2) The appointment of special teachers and inspectors to deliver practical lectures on plant diseases.

Station of Plant Pathology in Costa Rica. — *Bulletin of the Pan American Union.* P. 785, Washington, April, 1911.   **1520**

The President of Costa Rica has authorized the establishment in San José of a Station of Plant Pathology, under the direction of the Technical Bureau for Agricultural Experiments.

The station will contain a garden for the work of plant and fruit tree propagation and improvement; it will study plant life in all its relations to agriculture ; investigate the diseases of native crops and carry on field tests and demonstrations regarding the   **Costa Rica**

control and prevention of these diseases. Special bulletins will be
issued (1).

1521   H. U. LEFROY. **Fourth Annual Report of the Committee of Control
    of the South African Central Locust Bureau (Cape Town).** —
    The Agricultural Journal of India, vol. VI, Part. I. Calcutta,
    January, 1911. See also *Nature*, London, April 6, 1911.

The Central Locust Bureau of South Africa was formed in 1906
to collate reports from the various Colonies of South Africa regarding

**S. African
Union.
German
S. W. Africa.
Portuguese
E. Africa**

locusts, mainly their occurrence and movements, in order that, over
the whole area, measures against them could be correlated and the
best methods of procedure should be widely known. The British
colonies contribute to the cost as do also German South West Africa
and Portuguese East Africa. Every month the Bureau issues maps
showing the occurrence of locusts over the whole area; and these
are, at the end of the year, united to form this report.

It is probable that the work of the Board will devolve upon
the Department of Agriculture of the Union Government.

Practically the sole remedy used is the application of a strong
solution of arsenic with sugar to the vegetation the locusts are
about to eat. This method has been tried in India and abandoned
on account of its supposed danger.

Yet here is another year's experience under very similar conditions in South Africa, and the successful use of the method is
reported. Locusts in India are very different from those of South
Africa and the poisoned bait method could scarcely be used there;
but it is as well to realise that over large areas of land a solution
containing twelve times as much arsenic as in an ordinary spray
for crops is freely used.

The 1909 campaign cost the Government a sum approximating
4000 £.; even so it is impossible to estimate its worth to the
country, either directly or indirectly; but the editor thinks the

---

(1) The principal agricultural products of Costa Rica are coffee and bananas. In 1909, 66 000 acres were devoted to the cultivation of coffee; 81 400
acres to bananas; 24 200 acres to the sugar-cane; 63 800 acres to maize. There
is a brisk banana trade with New Orleans, Mobile, New York and Boston,
and also between Limon and Bristol and Manchester. Other exports are cocoa,
rubber, cedar, mahogany, fustic and other woods. New rubber plantations
are proving productive. Maize, sugar, rice and potatoes are commonly cultivated. *The Statesman's Yearbook* for 1911, p. 719.   (*Ed.*).

saving effected by the campaign may be safely set down as at least a hundredfold. First of all there is the direct benefit which accrues from the saving of the crops, and second the destruction of vast armies of locusts which will materially lessen if not entirely prevent the recurrence of swarms during the succeeding season.

In comparing the 1909 visitation with that of previous years it is stated that it was probably the most severe one which has been experienced since 1893, as altogether no fewer than 15306 swarms were accounted for and tabulated in the monthly returns. These do not, however, take into account the numerous swarms destroyed by the Railway Department or in those districts where there was no locust officer.

The term « swarm » is of exceedingly vague significance, and it is quite impossible to estimate the average size of those which were destroyed. But these may be said to have varied in size from those covering a few square rods to others of such magnitude that they covered hundreds of acres.

One of the most interesting chapters in this report is that which deals with locust-eating birds, the species referred to being the white stork (*Ciconia alba*) though other members of the pelargi are evidently included, and small pratincoles (*Limicolae*). It is stated that these birds practically cleared the country of the swarms of locusts that had escaped being poisoned and that they are the leading factors in the natural control of these pests.

Non Parasitic Diseases of Plants and their Control.

W. Sabachnikov. **The Effect of Tar Vapours upon Vegetation** (1).   **1522**
Vliianiie Dëgtiarnekh Isparenii na Rastitel nost urna l Boslieni Rastenii. — *Journal of Plant Diseases*, 5 G. N. 1-2, pp. 1-7, St Petersburg, 1911.

Recent researches have shown that various causes, viz anaesthetics, freezing, ultra-violet rays, wounding, drought, certain salts etc.,   **Russia** bring about coloration phenomena in green plants which are termed

---

(1) See page 353 of this Bulletin for Dec. 1910. No 281 of Bulletin for Jan. 1911, and No 592 of Bulletin for Feb. 1911.

II

blackening (*noircissement*) and which are often accompanied by the setting free, outside the plant, of volatile compounds, as Hydrocyanic Acid gas. Amongst the causes may be reckoned the vapours which are given off at ordinary temperature by tar.

These penetrate into the vegetable cells and through killing the protoplasm by plasmolytic rupture of the plasmic membrane, bring about the liberation of certain substances in a gaseous state.

This is due to the fact that on the death of the protoplasm, cellular compounds, which were confined within the living plant, are now set free.

Once in contact with one another they react chemically (generally by a diastasic action) and produce new compounds, of which some (often coloured) remain within the cells, while others pass outside the plant.

1528   G. Kranzlin. "**Leaf-Curl**'' **in the Cotton Plant**. (Beitrag zur Kenntniss der Kräuselhrankheit des Baumwolle. *Der Pflanzer*, Jahrg. VI, N. 9-12. Amani. Ostafrika 1910). — *Rivista di Patologia vegetale*, anno IV, n. 19-21, p. 318. Pavia, 15 marzo 1911.

German East Africa   Towards the end of 1909, there broke out, first in Impanganya and afterwards throughout the whole of German East Africa, a serious disease of the cotton plant. The first symptom of this malady was the intenser green colour of certain parts of the plantations, for which no cause could be discovered on examining the plant, although the position of the leaves was different. Later, the leaves became discoloured and curled up, commencing with those situated near the centre of the plant and finally the disease spread to the young portions of the stem and branches. In the affected parts, different species of fungi (*Alternaria macrospora* Zimm, (*Uredo Gossypii* Lagh) were found, together with Aphides and other insects, but apparently the disease was not due to their presence, nor to the exclusive effect of the climate. Probably it was caused by a too vigorous and rapid growth of the plant.

The choice of resistant species is recommended and of such as are thoroughly acclimatized to the districts where they are cultivated.

Parasitic Diseases of Plants. — Generalities.
Parasitisim. — Bacteria and Fungi as Parasites
and Saprophytes. — Control.

F. L. STEVENS and J. G. HALL. **Diseases of Economic Plants.** — *The* 1524
Macmillan Co., pp. X-513. New York, 1910 ; Reviewed in *Nature*,
N. 2168, Vol. 86, pp. 376-377. London, 18 May, 1911.

This book is intended: (1) for those students who wish to recognise and treat plant diseases, without studying their causes
deeply; (2) for those who desire to study the etiology and causes of
these maladies. Descriptions are given of the prominent characteristics of the most destructive diseases of fruit and vegetables cultivated in the United States, as well as information regarding the
latest methods of prevention or cure. All the best bulletins of the
numerous State Agricultural Experimental Stations and of the U. S.
Department of Agriculture have been examined for facts ; the authors have had the help also of various specialists in reading over
the proofs of certain parts, *e. g.* Dr Erwin F. Smith has thus
assisted with the bacterial diseases, Dr. L. R. Jones with potato
diseases, and so forth. Descriptions are given of the various life-
stages of the species of fungi causing plant diseases ; these are accompanied by practical advice as to the methods to be employed
against each stage by the grower. Directions are given for the
making and application of fungicides, and also useful information
on the subject of spraying machinery.

Practical details are given of the disinfection of seeds by the
use of formaldehyde gas and the various methods of soil disinfection
are discussed. It is pointed out that the presence in land of the
causal germ of the wilts of melon, cowpea, cotton and tobacco or
of onion « smut », cabbage « black rot » etc., may result in a depreciation of 50 per cent or more in the market value of the land.
In dealing with many of the diseases of cereals, pea, bean, lettuce,
celery, potato, carnation, violet, asparagus, grape, strawberry, and
other fruits, the authors are not content with merely stating that
" resistant " varieties or " strains " should be grown, but in all

United
States

cases mention the names of such " resistant " varieties obtainable
on the market.

Throughout the book we·find instances given of fungous diseases
of different crops which have become epidemic in various districts
in the State and have caused serious money losses; on the other hand
we have detailed evidence given showing that such losses may often
be avoided by careful and thorough spraying with the right fungicide at the right time. The annual loss caused by potato « blight »
in the United States is estimated at 36 000 000 dollars (186 480 000
francs) ; that caused by wheat « rust » 67 000 000 dollars (347 060 000
francs). Turning to horticultural crops, we are told that the violet
« leaf-spot » caused, in 1900, a loss, of 200 000 dollars (1 036 000
francs) ; the celery « leaf-spot » is stated to have caused a loss,·in
California, in 1908, of 1950 car-loads, and a money loss of 550 000
dollars (2 849 000 francs).

Account is given of the gradual invasion of the States since·
1896 by the asparagus « rust » ; it is now known in every State
where asparagus is grown. " In some States the invasion of this
disease has almost, if not quite, prohibited commercial asparagus-
growing. The Palmetto varieties are quite resistant, and offer a
.solution of the rust problem in some localities. "

Of the « American gooseberry mildew·» (which has, since its
introduction into Europe, about 1900, now spread over the whole
of Ireland and England) it is said: " This disease has quite prohibited
the cultivation of the finer sorts of English gooseberries in America,
and is a grave menace to the culture of gooseberries in Europe ".

One or two points of purely scientific interest may be noted.
The statement is made that the « pea mildew » (*Erysiphe polygoni*),
hibernates in seed derived from affected pods, and that the celery
« leaf-spot » (*Septoria petroselini*, var. *Apii*), is probably carried by
the seed of celery. The mistake is made of identifying the mildew on cucumber, cantaloupes, and muskmelons with *Erysiphe polygoni*
although Reed's interesting work on the specialization of parasitism
shown by this mildew—which this mycologist correctly referred to
E. Cichoracearum—was recently published in the States. The book
is very well illustrated.

1525   P. VOGLINO. **Diseases of Plants in Italy. Report on the Work of
the Phytopathological Station of Turin in 1910.** Relazione sui
lavori compiuti dall'Osservatorio consorziale di Fitopatologia
nell'anno 1910, pp. 21. Torino, 1910.

Italy: The Phytopathological Station at Turin has been supplied with
Piedmont information by 500 observers, and so has been able to keep in

touch with the appearance and spread of various diseases in the province of Turin, and also to advise as to treatment. In 1910 the staff examined 1511 specimens, sent out 2405 letters, paid 816 visits, and held 88 meetings.

This Report gives the chief diseases identified and the remedies used ; the descriptions of the animal and vegetable parasites are given in the Bulletins of the Station published at the end of every month.

The Report is divided into two parts, the first dealing with diseases of trees (vine, fruit-trees, ornamental trees and forest trees), the second with diseases of field crops (cereals, grassland plants, field crops, vegetables, and ornamental plants).

Amongst the most severely attacked crops come vine, apple, pear, tomato, and French beans.

Particular attention should be given to the results obtained against vine mildew (*Plasmopara*) with sprayings of sulphate of ammonia at 120-150 gr, per 100 l. ($1\,^1/_5$ to $1\,^1/_2$ lbs. per 100 gallons)·

Good results were also obtained at Novaretto (Susa) against both mildew (*Plasmopara*) and powdery mildew (*Uncinula*, «*Oidium*») with home-made lime-sulphur mixture : 700 gr. of lime and 2 kg. of very fine sulphur were boiled gently in iron vessels in $12\,^1/_2$ litres of water ; the liquid so obtained was made up with water to 50 litres, and $^1/_2$ kg. of dissolved sulphate of copper was added. (This is at the rate of $5\,^1/_2$ lbs. of lime and 16 lbs. of sulphur in 10 galls.; diluted to 40 galls. with 4 lbs. of sulphate of copper added). The mixture must be used directly it is made, and the spraying machines must be thoroughly washed out afterwards.

Near Aosta experiments were made with washes for *Cochylis ambiguella* and *Eudemis botrana* ; good results were obtained with chloride of barium mixed with dextrine or starch-paste, with arsenate of lead, with tobacco-juice, and with quassia — 1 kg. extract in 50 litres of hot water (2 lbs. in 10 gallons).

Sphaerotheca pannosa, the mildew of apple and peach, was succesfully controlled by « 4 % » lime-sulphur and by repeated sulphurings.

F. BUBÀK. **Diseases of Plants in Bohemia in 1910.** (Bericht über die Tätigkeit der Station für Pflanzenkrankheit und Pflanzenschutz an der k. landw. Akademie in Tábor (Böhmen) im Jahre 1910). — *Zeitschrift für das landw. Versuchswesen in Oesterreich*, XIV J., H. 4, pp. 700-705. Wien, April 1911.

1526

An enumeration of the Plant-diseases studied in 1910 at the Station of Plant-Pathology of the Agricultural Academy of Tábor (Bohemia).

Austria:
Bohemia

Throughout Bohemia cereals suffered specially from *Chlorops taeniopus* ; in several places, as near Rakonitz, oats were. attacked by *Oscinis Frit*. Barley was attacked by *Bibio hortulanus*; wheat by *Zabrus gibbus*, *Cecidomyia destructor*, *C. cerealis*, and *C. equestris*. *Thrips cerealium* and *Siphonophora cerealis* were observed frequently on all cereals. About Beneschau, *Lema cyanella* larvae caused serious damage to wheat; elsewhere, as near Tábor, only slight damage was observed, caused by *Calandra granaria*, *Tribolium ferrugineum*, and *Tinea granella*.

The chief fungi on cereals were : *Tilletia Tritici* and *Ustilago Tritici* on wheat ; *Ustilago Hordei* on barley, and *Urocystis occulta* on rye ; there was also quite an epidemic of *Tilletia secalis* on rye in Bohemia. The rusts were : *Puccinia glumarum* and *P. dispersa* on rye ; *P. graminis* and *P. triticina* on wheat ; *P. simplex* on barley, and *P. Lolii* on oats. *Cladosporium graminum* caused serious damage to wheat and barley in a number of places. The spring barley in particular was attacked and destroyed by *Fusarium nivale*. A species of *Septoria*, perhaps new, from Russia, spread on barley and wheat, destroying them.

Sugar Beet was attacked by *Melolontha vulgaris*, *Silpha atrata*, *Cassida nebulosa*, and *Heterodera Schachtii*. On seed-plants *Sclerotinia Semen* appeared ; and on the one-year beets *Rhizoctonia violacea*. An interesting outbreak at Ibrochow-Teinitz was that of *Cercospora beticola*, which did much damage.

On potatoes appeared « blackleg » (Schwarzbeinigke t) (1), a bacterial disease, and the leaf curl disease ; these diseases spread. every year in Bohemia, particularly in dry seasons. *Phytophthora infestans* caused much damage.

The most serious insect attack was that of *Chlorita flavescens*. Hops were also attacked by this *Chlorita* in var ous places, and also by *Aphis (Phorodon) Humuli*, *Tetranychus telarius*, *Otiorrhynchus Ligustici*, *Cnephasia Wahlbomiana*, and *Caloceris fulvomaculatus* ; also by *Sphaerotheca Humuli*.

Vines were severely attacked by *Plasmopara viticola*, *Lecanium Vitis*, *Phytoptus vitis*, and *Conchylis uvana*.

Vetches, .French beans, and green peas, particularly the last-named, were badly damaged by *Sitones lineatus ; Sclerotinia Trifoliorum* did a good deal of damage to clover.

---

(1) This disease, also known as « Stengelfäule », is attributed by Sorauer to his *Fusarium pestis*. Cf. P. SORAUER, *Handbuch der Pflanzenkrankheiten*,. III Auflage, II Bd., p. 469. Berlin, 1908.   (*Ed.*).

Species of *Aphis, Thrips* and *Tetranychus* appeared frequently on marrows ; and damage was caused by bacteria, *Botrytis cinerea* and *Erysiphe Cichoracearum.*

The larvae of *Ceutorhynchus macula alba* were frequently noticed attacking poppies, for instance near Beraum.

Near Pribram and Tábor flax was much damaged by a species of *Thrips.*

On cabbages *Plasmodiophora Brassicae* and *Ceutorhynchus sulcicollis* were observed ; these two and also *Aphis Brassicae* attacked kohl-rabi. On carrots larvae of Elaterids were found. In some places celery was damaged by *Hypudaeus amphibius.*

Turning to fruit-trees, apples were attacked by *Pieris Crataegi, Coleophora hemerobiella, Simaethis pariana, Mytilaspis pomorum, Sphaerotheca pannosa, Monilia fructigena* and *Fusicladium dendriticum* ; pears by *Anthonomus Piri, Phytoptus Piri* and *Fusicladium pirinum* ; egriot cherries by *Eriophyies similis* and *Polystigmina rubra* ; sweet cherries by *Argyresthia ephipella, Lyonetia Clerckella,* and *Monilia fructigena.*

The roots of pinks were damaged by Elaterid larvae ; those of Cyclamens by *Heterodera radicicola.* Dahlias were attacked by *Apion dichroum,* Wistarias by *Thrips,* Begonia roots by *Heterodera,* Begonia leaves by *Aphelenchus olesistus* and *Fumago vagans.*

Among forest-trees, *Tilia parvifolia* was attacked by *Eriophyies Tiliae* and *Gloeosporium Tiliae* var. *petiolicolum;* conifers by *Chermes* spp. ; pines by *Tetranychus ununguis* and *Lecanium hemicryphum.* Near Lounowitz the death of young branches of *Abies excelsa* was found to be due to *Botrytis cinerea. Hartigiella Laricis* occurred on larch.

A. v. JACZEWSKI. **Report for 1909 on Diseases of Cultivated and Wild Plants in Russia.** (Exegodnik Swiedenii o Boliesnakh i Povrexdeniakh Kulturnik i Dicorastusteikh Polesnikh Rastenii). — *Biuro po Mikologiii Fitopatologhi Ucenago Comiteta,* V. G., St. Peterburg, 1910.

1527

Special importance is given to the damage done by *Tilletia Tritici* and *Sclerotinia Libertiana* Fckl.; to the latter the death of young cereals in early spring is attributed.

Russia

Among the diseases of industrial crops and vegetables may be mentioned : *Plasmodiophora Brassicae* Wor., *Phytophthora infestans* D. B., *Phoma Betae* Frank, *Uromyces Betae* Kuhn.

In the section dealing with diseases of fruit-trees the writer goes into considerable detail on numerous fungicides and their value and also on the injection of certain nutritive substances into the trunks. Among the most general diseases are mentioned *Fusicladium dendriticum* Fckl., *Monila fructigena* Pers., *M. cinerea* Bon., *Exoascus bullatus* Fckl., *E. deformans* Fckl., etc.

Notice is taken of : *Sphaerotheca mors-uvae* Berk. et Curt., *Marsonia Potentillae* Desm. on strawberries, *Oidium dubium*, and *Lophodermium pinastri* Chev. causing considerable damage to the leaves of young pines.

The work is well illustrated.

1528

I. B. POLE EVANS. **The Cereal Rusts of South Africa.** (South African Cereal Rusts, with Observations on the Problem of Breeding Rust-Resistant Wheats). — *The Journal of Agricultural Science.* Vol. IV, part I. pp. 95-104. Cambridge, May 1911.

The rusts at present known in South Africa are :

British South Africa

Puccinia Graminis Pers. on wheat, barley, oats, and rye.
P. triticina Eriks. on wheat.
P. coronifera Klebahn on oats.
P. dispersa Eriks. on oats.

The black rust (*Puccinia graminis*) is certainly the most serious one ; it produces uredospores throughout the year, and is particularly bad in periods of drought.

The writer describes the results of a great many experiments made with a view to obtaining resistant wheats. He used Biffen's method. His resistant varieties were " Bobs Rust Proof " and " White Egyptian ", the susceptible ones " Wol-Koren " and " Holstovi ".

Eight plants of " Bobs Rust Proof " (resistant), eight plants of " Wol Koren " (susceptible), and eight plants of the hybrid from crossing these two, were simi ary infected with uredospores from the same source (" Klein Koren " wheat). After seven days a certain number of white spots were visible on the leaves of the resistant variety, while the leaves of the susceptible variety and the hybrid were covered with incipient pustules. Examination two days later showed 71, 595, and 638 pustules on the resistant, susceptible and hybrid varieties respectively.

A number of other cases have shown that hybrids are more susceptible than their parents; the writer thinks this may be explained by their greater luxuriance, offering more nourishment to the fungus. Further teleutospores, which are rare on the parents, form on hybrids.

Another interesting fact is that the spores produced on the hybrids possess unusual virulence, and can infect resistant varieties. This was shown by the following experiment: nine resistant plants (" Bobs ,,) were infected with spores from a susceptible variety, and nine others with spores from hybrids. Thirteen days afterwards the first lot showed no pustules while the second lot had 209.

These experiments prove that the virulence of the fungus is increased by its growing in the tissues of the hybrid (1); if this is generally true the problem of breeding rust-proof varieties becomes much more difficult.

M. SHIRAI and K. HARA. **Some New Parasitic Fungi of Japan.** 1529
The Botanical Magazine, Vol. XXV, N. 290, pp. 69-83, 1 plate. Tokyo, March, 1911.

A description of some new species of fungi examined in the Botanical Laboratory of the Agricultural College of the Imperial University at Komaba.

Asterula Chamaecyparisii and *Lophodermium Chamaecyparisii*   Japan
Shirai and Hara (on the leaves of living branches of *Chamaecyparis obtusa* S. and Z.).

Mycosphaerella Paulowniae (on leaves of *Paulownia tomentosa* (Thunb) H. Br.

M. Zingiberi (on the leaves of *Zingiber mioga* Rosc.).

M. Macleyae (on the leaves of *Macleya cordata* Br.)

Sphaerulina Aucubae (on the leaves of *Aucuba japonica* Thunb.).

Phaeosphaerella japonica (on the leaves of *Cercis Chinensis* Bge).

Leptosphaeria Cinnamomi (on the leaves of *Cinnamonum Camphora* Nees).

F. D. HEALD. **New Species of Texas Fungi.** *Micologia*, vol. III,   1530
N. 1, pp. 5-22. Lancaster, Pa. January, 1911.

The writers give a list of the new species of fungi which they have found in the neighbonrhood of San Antonio and Austin, Texas. The following may be mentioned: United
States:
Texas

(1) The writer does not actually state that he has found the hybrid-   Texas
grown rust capable of infecting resistant varieties other than the parent of
the hybrid.   (*Ed.*).

Phleospora multimacnlans on *Platanus occidentalis L.*, *Juglans nigra L.*, and *J. regia L.*; *Phyllosticta congesta* on *Prunus* sp.; *Septoria persuta* on *Sorghum halepense L.*; *Colletotrichum caulicolum* on *Phaseolus vulgaris L.*; *C. griseum* on *Euonymus japonicus* Thunb.; *Cilindosporium solitarium* on *Robinia Pseudacacia L.*; *C. tenuisporum* on *Ulmus crassifolia* Nutt.; *Cercospora adusta* on *Ligustrum californicum* Hort.; *C. aurantia* on *Citrus Aurantium L.*; *C. Capsici* on *Capsicum annuum L.*; *C. Chrysanthemi* on *Chrysanthemum* sp.; *C. Fici* on a form of *Ficus Carica L.*; *C. obscura* on *Cynara Scolymus L.*; *Clasterosporium diffusum* on *Hicoria Pecan* (March) Britton (1); *Exosporium concentricum* on *Euonymus japonicus* Thunb.

1531   E. NOFFRAY. **Sources of Infection of Clover Mildew, *Erisyphe communis*.** (Propagation du « Blanc des Trèfles » (*Erisyphe communis*) sur les plantes cultivées par l'infection des plantes spontanées). — *Journal d'Agriculture pratique*, n. 18, pp. 562-564. Paris, 4 mai, 1911.

France   In this article the author gives numerous cases in which attacks of clover mildew (*Erisyphe communis*) on clover leys and in gardens have been due to infection from fungi growing on wild plants in or near the fields.

This ubiquitous fungus has been found by the writer on over two hundred species of plants. These include viper's bugloss, wild bugloss, borage, mulleins, thistles, teasel, knotgrass, plantains, restharrow and red deadnettle.

Clover mildew is also to be found in permanent grass-land, but it does not do any appreciable damage to the leguminous forage-plants there. Its chief hosts are buttercups which are let grow too freely, comfrey, angelica, hogweed, dyer's greenweed, plantains, burnet saxifrage, and marsh thistle.

The preventive measures are :

1. Pull up and bury deeply all wild plants found diseased at any season of the year.

2. Keep a watch on clover-leys and directly any mildew appears cut out a patch a yard all round the diseased place.

3. Look out for weeds, and pull them up and remove them : a precaution when several centres of infection have been found. Indeed, the wild plants mentioned above should be reduced to a minimum, and, if possible, exterminated.

(1) *Carya olivaeformis* Nutt. *Index Kewensis.*   (*Ed.*).

In vegetable gardens the mildew may attack turnips. Red valerian, Michaelmas·daisies, larkspur, love-in-a-mist, etc. may become centres of infection and the most radical methods should be used in their destruction as burying, and sulphuring (*soufrages*).

G. WESTERDIJK. **Researches on Sclerotinia Libertiana.** (Untersuchungen über *Sclerotinia Libertiana* Fuckel als Pflanzenparasit). — *Mededeelingen zit het Phytopathologisch Laboratorium Willie Commelin Scholten*, II, pp. 5-26. Amsterdam, Maart 1911.

1582

In Holland *Sclerotinia Libertiana* Fuckel does considerable damage to lettuce, cumin, beans, and carrots; also some damage to clovers and mustard.

Holland

The fungus passes readily from one plant to another, and does not form biological races.

Under favourable conditions of growth it does not lose any of its parasitical properties when kept for a long time as a saprophyte. Infection is favoured by ruptures in the cortex of the host and by considerable atmospheric humidity.

Sclerotinia Libertania does not produce a conidial form. Ascospores may also be absent from the life-cycle, in which case the formation of fresh mycelium depends entirely on the sclerotia. On sclerotia obtained in artificial cultures apothecia never form.

W. B. BURGESS. **The Chemistry of Lime Sulphur Wash** (1). — *The Journal of the South-Eastern Agricultural College, Wye, Kent.* N. 19. pp. 61-69. London and Ashford, Kent, 1910.

1583

The following investigations were undertaken in order to discover: (1) the most satisfactory proportions of lime and sulphur for making the wash; (2) the chemical changes which the wash undergoes when exposed to the air under conditions similar to those which obtain when the wash is used as a summer spray.

Great Britain: England

Summary and conclusions.

Lime sulphur wash as a summer fungicide acts in two distinct ways.

_____

(1) See no. 688 of this Bulletin for Feb. 1911 and nos. 1000 and 1001 of the March 1911 number.

(1) As a contact spray, the polysulphides in the wash acting in a way similar to liver of sulphur.

(2) As a protective coating to the leaves, due to the thin layer of sulphur in a fine state of division deposited from the thiosulphates and polysulphides by decomposition. This sulphur would be much more efficient than flowers of sulphur for two reasons :

(a) It adheres very closely to leaves ; in fact it cannot be removed by the most drastic washing ; thus a very great drawback in the use of flowers of sulphur is overcome.

(b) Owing to its fine state of division, the deposited sulphur would oxidize more quickly than flowers of sulphur, and thus prove a more powerful fungicide, as its action probably depends on the formation of sulphur dioxide.

It is probable that the chief value of lime sulphur wash lies in its use as a means of applying free sulphur to leaves. As to the question of injury, the polysulphides are the most likely to damage the sprayed plant, as liver of sulphur, where used too strong, is known to cause severe leaf scorching. However, these compounds have been shown to be very rapidly decomposed, so their injurious action would not be very prolonged.

Little appears to be known about the action of thiosulphates on host-plants or fungi. Some preliminary trials with sodium thiosulphate on hop leaves showed that, even with 20 % solutions, only insignificant injury was done just at the tip of the leaves. This points to the fact that little injury is likely to come from this source

All possibility of harm would be removed by the first rain after spraying, as all soluble constituents of the wash would be washed off, leaving a layer of free sulphur with a little calcium sulphate or sulphite.

1534   **Lime Sulphur as a Fungicide** (1). — *U. S. Department of Agriculture. Farmer's Bulletin* 485. Experiment Station Work LXII. Pp. 24 (12-16), Washington, March, 17, 1911.

The standard fungicide is Bordeaux mixture, but this spray on
United
States
certain varieties of trees and under certain weather conditions often russets the fruits, or causes serious damage to the foliage, especially

---

(1) Compiled from: Delaware Sta. Bul. 85; Maryland Sta. Bul. 143; Michigan Sta. Bul. 49; Cornell Sta. Bul. 276; New York State Sta Bul. 320; Oregon Sta. Bul. 106; Pennsylvania Sta. Bul. 92; Tennessee Sta. Bul. 88; Virginia Sta. Bul. 188; U. S. Dept. Agr. Bur. Plant Indus. Buls. 155, 174; Circs.

when used during the summer. For this reason lime sulphur is often used as a substitute for Bordeaux mixture.

The self-boiled lime-sulphur mixture of Scott is made by using 8 pounds of fresh stone lime and 8 pounds of sulphur (either flowers or flour of sulphur) — to 50 American gallons of water (kg. 1.920 of lime, kg. 1.920 of sulphur, 1 hectolitre of water); this mixture is commonly called the " 8:8:50 mixture ". Or the strength may vary from 6:6:50 (kg. 1.44 lime, kg. 1.44 sulphur, 1 hectolitre water) to 10:10:50 (kg. 2,4 lime, kg. 2,4 sulphur, 1 hectolitre water), governed by the time of year the mixture is to be applied, the kind of fruit trees to be sprayed, and the fungus to be controlled. The mixture can best be prepared in rather large quantities, say enough for 200 gallons (756 litres) at a time, making the formula 32 pounds (14.5 kg.) of lime and 32 pounds (14,5 kg.) of sulphur to be cooked with a small quantity of water — 8 or 10 gallons (30 or 38 litres) — and then diluted to 200 gallons (756 litres).

The lime should be placed in a barrel and enough water poured on to almost cover it. As soon as the lime begins to slake, the sulphur should be added, after first running it through a sieve to take out the lumps. The mixture should be constantly stirred and more water added as needed to form a paste thick at first, and then gradually thin. The lime will supply enough heat to boil the mixture several minutes. When well slaked, water should be added to cool the mixture and prevent further cooking. It is then ready to be strained into the spray tank, diluted and applied. Care must be taken not to allow the boiling to proceed too far, as some of the sulphur will then go into solution, forming sulphides, which are injurious to the foliage. This mixture should be applied immediately after it is made, with a spraying outfit equipped with an agitator.

The home-boiled concentrated lime-sulphur solution, Cordley's, is prepared as follows : Sulphur 100 pounds (49.830 kg.); good stone

27, 54, 58; The Summer Use of Concentrated Lime Sulphur, by H. H. WHETZEL: Reprint from Proc. N. Y. State Fruit Growers Assoc., 9 (1910), pp. 31-44; Revue de Viticulture 33 (1910), No. 862, pp. 691-692; Journal of the Board of Agriculture [London], 17 (1910), No. 3, pp. 184-189; Fruit Grower, 20 (1909), No. 1, pp. 6-7.

Compare The Science and Practice of Farming during 1910 in Great Britain, International Institute of Agriculture, pp. 396-400 Rome, 1910: and E. S. SALMON's experiments, in this Bulletin, abstr. 1001, March, 1911. (Ed.).

lime 25 pounds (12.457 kg,). Slake the lime in a kettle, making a paste of the sulphur with a little water, add the sulphur paste to the slaked lime, and add water to make 60 gallons (227 litres). Boil 30 to 40 minutes. Allow to settle, and then pour off the clear, amber liquid, of which there should be approximatively 45 gallons (170 litres) scaling 30° by the Baumé hydrometer. This concentrated stock solution is then diluted to 1 : 11, 1 : 30 etc. according to the season of the year and the trees to be sprayed.

A third type of lime-sulphur sprays is given by the commercial lime-sulphur concentrated solutions, which must be diluted before using as fungicides.

Of the three types of lime-sulphur preparations, the so-called self-boiled lime-sulphur spray of Scott has probably been the most widely and thoroughly tested. W. M. Scott's experiments with this funcigide have included tests on « peach brown rot », « peach scab », « cherry leaf spot », « apple scab », « apple leaf spot », « sooty mould » « bitter rot » and « apple blotch » in many States and with various varieties of peaches and apples. The efficiency of the self-boiled mixture in controlling the « peach brown rot » and « peach scab » has been tested in Georgia, Arkansas, West Virginia, Delaware, Maryland, Tennessee, and Illinois; and in the majority of cases, has proved very successful, especially in Georgia, Arkansas, West Virginia and Illinois, where the peach trees were sprayed 3 to 4 times with an 8 : 8 : 50 solution (kg. 1.920 : 1 hl.), to which 2 pounds (479 gr. to 1 hl.) of solution of arsenate of lead was added when the curculio was bad.

In addition to controlling the brown rot and the scab without injury to the foliage, the fruit sprayed with the self boiled lime-sulphur was larger and more highly colored. However, there is some danger of staining the fruit if the mixture is applied within two or three weeks of the ripening period.

Very satisfactory results were obtained with this mixture in controlling the " cherry leaf spot " and leaf diseases in general of the peach and cherry. On varieties of apples subject to russeting and foliage injury from Bordeaux mixture, the self-boiled lime-sulphur preparation has proved a good substitute for controlling leaf spot, fruit spot, sooty fungus and for mild cases of scab infection, without injury to the fruit or foliage, but is of doubtful value in controlling apple blotch and bitter rot. 2 pounds of arsenate of lead added to every 50 gallons (479 grams of arsenate of lead added to every hectolitre) of the self-boiled mixture proved of value in controlling the codling moth and was entirely harmless to the apple foliage.

The self boiled lime-sulphur mixture seems, therefore, to be of value especially as a summer spray for the fungus diseases of the peach and cherry and for several diseases of the apple, and does not injure the foliage or fruit when properly prepared and applied. It has not proved efficient in the United States against black rot of the grape, although a modified self-boiled lime-sulphur mixture consisting of 2 pounds of sulphur, 1 pound of lime, and 2 pounds of copper sulphate, diluted to 1 and 1 $\frac{1}{2}$ per cent solutions, is reported by a French vineyardist as having given complete protection to his vineyard of 30 000 plants against the grape oïdium for the past 10 years. A somewhat similar spray has recently been tested by M. B. Waite, of the U. S. Department of Agriculture, on the apple with success against fungus diseases, but with some russeting and foliage injury to certain varieties.

The self-boiled lime-sulphur mixture has also been tested on tomatoes, cabbages, onions, strawberries, peas, celery, sweet potatoes, asparagus and cantaloups, chiefly to ascertain whether injurious effects would ensue. With the exception of the cantaloups, no damage was noted on the plants sprayed, and slight, if any, benefit was derived in the prevention or control of diseases.

The commercial lime-sulphur spray has proved very effective against peach leaf curl and apple scab, but fruit subject to bitter rot must be treated with a stronger fungicide.

In general, it would seem that the self boiled lime-sulphur mixture is the best for the peach; and either the commercial or the home-boiled solution for the apple. The home-boiled mixture has also been tested in England on the hop-mildew, gooseberry mildew and apple scab, where it was very efficacious in combating the hop-mildew, and is recommended for trial against powdery mildews and apple scab.

W. M. Scott and A. L. Quaintance. **Spraying Peaches for the Control of Brown-Rot, Scab, and Curculio.** — *U.S. Department of Agriculture. Farmers' Bulletin* 440. pp. 40. Washington. 27 March, 1911.

1585

" Brown-rot " 'is caused by *Sclerotinia fructigena* (Pers.), Schröt, which produces a so-called rot of the fruit and blight of the twigs in stone fruits and to a less extent in some of the pome fruits.

United States

" Peach scab " also known as " black spot " and " freckles ". and in some districts improperly called " mildew ", is caused by

Cladosporium carpophilum Thüm, which grows in the skin of the fruit, producing small, circular, dark-brown spots.

The " plum curculio " has many other common names such as " peach curculio ", " peach worm ", " fruit weevil ", " little Turk ", " curculio " etc. It is a native American insect and fed originally on wild plums and other wild fruits, especially *Crataegus*. The plum curculio is still confined to North America, ranging from Southern Canada south to Florida and Texas and west to about the onehundredth meridian. Practically all stone and pome fruits are used by the curculio for feeding and egg-laying purposes.

During 1909, spraying experiments aganist these pests were made at Fort Valley, Georgia, including the treatment of 1100 Elberta peach trees. The self-boiled lime-sulphur mixture (8:8:50 mixture *i. e.* 1.92 kg lime + 1.92 kg sulphur + 1 hectolitre water) plus 2 pounds of arsenate of lead (480 grams for 1 hl. of mixture) was used.

This combined treatment gave the following results. At picking time 95.5 per cent of the fruit on the sprayed block was free from brown-rot, 93.5 per cent free from scab, and 72.5 per cent free from curculio. On the unsprayed block, only 37 per cent of the fruit was free from brown-rot, 1 per cent free from scab, and 2.5 per cent free from curculio injury. In packing the fruit for market, it was found that the yield of saleable fruit on the sprayed block was 10 times as great as from the unsprayed block containing the same number of trees.

During the season of 1910, the same experiments were carried out as during 1909. As during 1910 neither the " brown-rot " nor the " plum curculio " was so abundant in Georgia as the previous, year the contrast between the sprayed and the unsprayed blocks was not so striking. Nevertheless, the very satisfactory results obtained fully substantiated the conclusions previously reached (1)· as to the value of spraying.

1536   V. VERMOREL and E. DANTONY. **Colloidal Copper-Soap Fungicide.** (Bouillie anticryptogamiqué au savon de cuivre colloïdal). — *C. R. de l'Acad. des Sciences.* t. 152, n. 19, pp. 1263-1265. Paris, 8 Mai, 1911.

France   After numerous attempts the writers have succeeded in obtaining copper soaps in a colloidal condition, and in concentrations suitable for agricultural purposes. From these copper soaps they have obtained a liquid fungicide which can be prepared as follows:

---

(1) See this Bulletin February 1911, Abs. 628.   (*Ed.*)

1) Dissolve 500 grams of sulphate of copper in 50 litres of water (5 lbs. in 50 galls. English) ;

2) Dissolve 2000 gr. (varying according to the purity) of soap free from alkali, in 50 litres of water (20 lbs. in 50 galls. English);

3) Contrary to what is usually done in similar mixtures, pour the copper solution into the soap.

Instead of the bulky and heavy precipitate of the ordinary copper soaps, this gives an opaque greenish-blue liquid, with a surface tension as low as that of simple alkaline soaps, and capable of wetting grapes as readily as would alcohol.

This formula is for rain-water. With water containing lime salts the soap must be increased; but in this case the lime soaps formed are not of the usual curdy nature, but are very incoherent, so that they would not block the nozzles.

More concentrated copper soaps can also be readily obtained in hot water, keeping the same proportions. On cooling, the copper soap, retained in the excess of alkaline soap, settles out. This solid dried and powdered, will dissolve in hot water, giving fresh colloidal solutions.

If the value of these colloidal mixtures should be confirmed on a large scale, the trade would be able to supply a product all ready for use. The results obtained by the writers with silver soaps, and those of MM. Lumière with colloidal silver, make it likely that colloidal copper soaps may become useful in vine-growing.

The soaps to be used for these mixtures are white soaps, as rich as possible in sodium oleate and containing no excess of sodium carbonate or alkaline hydrates.

Sodium stearate, which occurs in considerable quantity in almost all powdered soaps, makes the preparation of colloidal copper soaps difficult. In general, stearate ought to be excluded from all insecticides and fungicides containing soap ; according to the writers' experience, its presence considerably increases the surface tension and reduces the coefficient of solubility.

Copper Oxychloride as Fungicide, and Barium Chloride as Insecticide. (Oxychlorure de cuivre contre le « mildew » de la vigne et chlorure de baryum insecticide). *Bull. de la Soc. d'hort. et de vit. d'Eure-et-Loir.* — Chartres, Mars 1911.

1537

I. Treatments for mildew with Bordeaux mixture have the disadvantage of requiring considerable manipulation ; first, solution of the sulphate of copper, then precipitation with the lime. Again,

France

the amount of copper used is considerable, as the mixture uses 2 kg. of sulphate per hectolitre (2 lbs in 10 galls.), that is 12 million kg. (roughly 12 000 tons) for France, and at the same rate 42 millions kg. (41 000 ton.) for Europe; that is to say, 10 500 metric tons (10 300 Engl. tons) of metallic copper are withdrawn from industrial circulation.

M. Chuard proposes to replace the sulphate by the oxychloride, an insoluble substance which can easily be used in suspension. At ½ kg. per hl. (½ lb. in 10 galls.) it gives results at least as good as those with Bordeaux mixture containing 2 kg. of sulphate of copper. Like almost all chlorides, copper oxychloride in suspension has remarkable powers of adhesion.

The price of this oxychloride is about 3 ½ fr. per kilo; there is thus no saving in expense, but there would be considerable saving in labour.

II. M. Ac. Truelle speaks well of barium chloride to replace the more dangerous arsenates. Barium chloride is a white salt, very soluble in water; at 15° C. 1 litre will dissolve 435 gms. It costs 15 fr. per 100 kilos; it is used as a coloured adhesive liquid.

Several barium mixtures have been proposed, and all have given good results. The Russian entomologist Mokrzecki uses a mixture of 2 kg. of barium chloride with 215 gr. of carbonate of soda per 100 litr. (20 lbs. and 2 lbs. 5 ozs. per 100 galls.); it is the barium carbonate thus produced which sticks to the leaves. Mr. Barsacq adds starch at 1 ½ kg. per 100 l. (15 lbs. per 100 g.). Substances added to procure adhesiveness hinder the insecticidal action slightly,

Barium chloride has been found very effective against the weevil (charançon) of beets and against fruit tree caterpillars.

1538　　E. RABATÉ. **Tobacco Juice.** (Les jus de Tabacs à 20 grammes de nicotine par litre). *Revue de Viticulture*, 18ᵉ année, t. XXXV, n. 908, p. 552. — Paris, 11 mai 1911.

France　　M. Rabaté has experimented with tobacco juice containing 2 % of nicotine manufactured by the French government. He purposely used a strength (10 % by volume) greater than that required in practice; this juice, neutralized by milk of lime, produced no scorching of either flowers or leaves of cherries, peaches, plums, apples, or pears; even the young shoots of roses and vines were not injured.

Tobacco juice can be used in two ways:

1) Pour 7 or 8 litres of the 2 % juice into 100 litres of water and neutralize with milk of lime.

2) Pour 7 or 8 litres of the 2 % juice into a solution containing 2 kg. of sulphate of copper; neutralize with clear lime-water, and make up to 100 litres. (Equivalent to 7 or 8 galls. of tobacco juice, and 20 lbs. of sulphate of copper in 100 English gallons). This gives a Bordeaux mixture with nicotine. In this mixture the cupric precipitate is coloured greenish by the organic matter present and the liquid above is also green. The slight excess of lime decomposes the salts of nicotine, giving free nicotine, which, according to M. Schloesing junr., has more insecticidal value than the sulphate. On the other hand free nicotine is more volatile than nicotine sulphate, and its action is therefore probably less lasting. The Bordeaux-nicotine mixture is therefore a mixture for immediate use.

ED. ZACHAREWICZ. **The " Unica " Sulphurer.** (Une nouvelle soufreuse : la soufreuse « Unica »). — *Le Progrès agricole et viticole,* 28e année. N. 18, pp. 556-559, Montpellier, 30 avril 1911.

1539

This new type of sulphurer is small, easily managed, and at the same time as efficient as a large apparatus. The operator walks behind, and supports the machine by means of handles. The hopper contains not less than 30 kilos (66 lbs.) of sublimated sulphur or 35 (77 lbs.) of sulpho-steatite or cupric powders.

France

The sulphurer consists of a frame-work which bears two tubular shafts by means of diverging iron supports which permit of the shafts being held in a horizontal position above the tallest vine. This much facilitates the passage of the apparatus through the vineyard. The left wheel carries a toothed pinion, which by means of a chain, moves the pinion of the ventilator. The latter introduces air into the bottom of the hopper within which is a contrivance for grinding and sifting the sulphur and other powdery mixtures.

Parasitic Diseases of Various
Plants and Means of Prevention and Cure.

1540   H. R. FULTON. **An Anthrachnose of Red Clover caused by Gloeo-sporium caulivorum.** (*Science*, n. 802, p. 752, 1910). *Rivista di Patologia vegetale*, anno IV, nn. 18-21, pp. 295-296. — Pavia, 15 marzo 1911.

Mr. Fulton found a form of anthrachnose on the stems of red clover (*Trifolium pratense*). This form was characterised by the appearance of blackish sunken spots. The cause of the disease is **Great Britain** *Gloeosporium caulivorum*. The infection is propagated through small wounds, and is encouraged by damp.

Mr. Fulton reproduced the disease experimentally in the red clover by inoculation; but he did not succeed with the white clover (*Trifolium repens*) or with lucerne (*Medicago sativa*). For the control of this disease, the destruction of the plants affected is recommended, as well as shifting of the crops.

1541   R. OLSSON-SEFFER. **Sugar Cane Diseases in Mexico.** (Métodos para impédir las Enfermedades de la Caña de Azucar). *La Hacienda*, vol. VI, no. 7, pp. 210-211 ; 4 fig. — Buffalo, N. Y., April, 1911.

For the last thirty years sugar-canes in Mexico have suffered from numerous diseases. The varieties « Ribbon » and « Otahiti », **Mexico** the best grown, have become susceptible to these attacks, having largely lost the primitive vigour which made them immune.

The two most serious sugar-cane diseases, « Sereh » (1) and « Gummosis » (2), have not caused serious loss in Mexico.

---

(1) V. this *Bulletin* Dec. 1910; p. 400. The « Sereh » disease was first known in Java, where it caused serious loss. In the typical Sereh condition, the stock of the cane is composed of short stems with very short internodes; the shoots, particularly low down, develop so as to form a dense bush covered with a mass of leaves, somewhat resembling *Andropogon Schoenanthus*.

F. W. SOUTH. **Fungus Diseases of Ground Nuts in the West In-**   **1542**
dies. *West Indian Bulletin Vol. XI, N. 3 Impr. Agr. Dep.*
Barbados.

Three diseases of ground nuts have been observed in the West
Indies.

A rust fungus *Uredo arachidis*. This is of very general distribution, both on imported and local varieties throughout all the
islands. The amount of damage which it is capable of causing
appears to vary in different islands as does the success of the control measures employed.

A leaf spot fungus, *Cercospora personata*. This has been observed
at present in Dominica and Barbados only, and is not of serious
nature.

A root disease unidentified. This occurs in Barbados, Grenada,
Dominica, St Kitts and Nevis. Its host plants are numerous and
of a very general nature. It is an important fungus, difficult to
control.

Descriptions of the diseases and references are given.

**British
West Indies:
Barbados.
Dominica.
Grenada.
St. Kitts.
Nevis.**

E. INGLESE. **Tobacco-Fumago.** (La fumaggine del tobacco). *Bollet-*   **1543**
tino tecnico della coltivazione dei tabacchi, pubblicato per cura del
R. Istituto sperimentale in Scafati, N. 2, pp. 81-89, Scafati, 1911.

Fumago vagans Pers. has appeared at Milazzo in Sicily, in the
plantations where tobacco of a common quality is grown. Mr. Inglese
does not think that the « mielat » the sugary substratum necessary
for the growth and diffusion of *Fumago* is due to the secretions of
insects, for instance, aphides that are on the plant, but is due
to the pathological condition of the plants, suffering certain special
conditions of the environment; this sugary substance is then produced in consequence of this pathological condition.

**Italy:
Sicily**

Some believe that this disease (« Sereh » is its Javanese name) is of physiological origin; others consider it pathological and mention *Heterodera java-*
nica, Tylenchus Sacchari, Bacillus Sacchari, B. glangae, and *Hypocroea Sac-*
chari. Cf. NOEL DEER, *Cane Sugar,* pp. 145-147, Norman Rodger, Altrincham
(Manchester), 1911.   (*Ed.*).

(2) A disease characterised by exudations of gum from the exposed
surfaces of the plant. Cobb believes it to be related to the presence of a microorganism, *Bacillus vascularum (Pseudomonas vascularum,* Cobb). *Ibid.* p. 44·
                                                                       (*Ed.*).

The aphides do not cause the « mielat » to flow out in consequence of the punctures they make in the plants, but attack the
latter for the purpose of sucking the juice, thus greatly weakening
the plants. The nectar-like secretion flows out and spreads as a
result of the pathological condition of the plant.

Fumago prevents the normal physiological functions of the organs affected. In order to remedy this state of things, the general
condition of the plant must first be improved by means of stimulants
and rich nitrogenous manures. Nitrate of soda is particularly suitable,
especially if used when the tobacco gives manifest signs by its pale
colour of weakness and decline.

The tobacco plants should be watered in the evening, care being
taken not to overwater them; and the soil should never be trampled
on when wet. The soil should also be aerated frequently, and the
plants well topped, in order that they may not become too exhausted.

The aphis which attacks the tobacco plant is the *Aphis Sca-
biosae* Scloz. A remedy which is considered very efficacious is
tobacco juice at 2 or 3 %, mixed with black soap and 2 or 2 $^1/_2$ %
of water. An ordinary hose may be used to spray this mixture
on the under part of the leaves of tobacco plants infested with the
aphides.

1544 L. PAVARINO. **Bacteriosis of the Tomato: *Bacterium Briosii* n. sp.**
(Sulla batteriosi del pomodoro: *Bacterium Briosii* n. sp. *Atti
Ist. Bot. di Pavia*, Serie II, vol. XII, pp. 337-344, 1 tav., 1910)
Rivista di Patologia vegetale, anno IV, num. 19-21, p. 314. Pavia,
15 marzo, 1911.

Italy

A description of the bacteria which cause tomato-rot, the rot
generally appearing at the top of the fruit: a disease already
studied by Prillieux, who admitted the bacterial origin of the
disease, but did not determine the pathogenic microorganism.
Mr. Pavarino has identified this microorganism, which he considers
to be an autonomous species naming it *Bacterium Briosii* n. sp.

Bacterium Briosii sometimes attacks the leaves and stalks as
well as the fruit, causing the leaves to shrivel up and the newest
buds to become deformed; more or less lengthy spots of a brown
colour also appear on the full grown stalks.

B. Briosii is optionally aerobic, mobile, liquefying gelatine; forms
in broth a compact and persistent pellicle of denticulated colonies

of a yellow colour, and does not produce either indol or sulphuretted hydrogen, or any other odorous substances.

Mr. Pavarino has been able to reproduce the disease by inoculation in the fruit and in other organs of the tomato.

N. S. GIDDINGS. **The Bacterial Soft rot of Muskmelons, caused by** **1545**
Bacillus Melonis n. sp. — *Vermont Agric. Exper. Station, Bull.,*
N. 148, pp. 366-416, 14 figs., 1910. *Rivista d. Patologia vegetale.*
anno V, num. I, p. 11. Pavia, 1 Aprile 1911.

The muskmelon crops in Vermont were attacked in 1907 by a   United States:
bacterial disease, which caused a soft rot of the fruit and de-   Vermont
stroyed 25 % of the crop, from the beginning of September to the
end of the season.

The pathogenic agent is a new *Bacillus* which has been named
B. Melonis n. sp. The alteration begins in the lower part of the
fruit and spreads rapidly under the skin, causing a fruit to turn
black and finally to shrivel up and die.

The disease, which spreads very rapidly and destroys the fruit
within periods ranging from 3 to 10 days, according to the temperature, has been reproduced by inoculation. The temperature most
suitable for the development of this *Bacillus* is about 30° C., but
it can resist a temperature as high as 49° or 50° C.

M. TURCONI. **Withering of the Water-Melon (Cocomero) in Italy;**   **1546**
the Mycosphaerella citrullina (C. O. Sm.) Grossenb. on Plants
affected by the Disease. (L'Avvizzimento dei cocomeri in Italia
e la presenza della *Mycosphaerella citrullina* (C. O. Sm.) Grossenb. sulle piante colpite dal male). — *Rivista di Patologia vegetale*, Anno IV, N. 19-21, pp. 289-292. Pavia, 15 Marzo, 1911.

For the first time in Italy, Mr. Turconi has found numerous
perithecia belonging to the *Mycosphaerella citrullina* Grossenbacher   Italy:
(= *Sphaerella citrullina* C. O. Smith), which causes a species of   Parma
decay of the melon in America, on some plants of watermelon (*cocomero*) from Parma, suffering from *Fusarium niveum*, the cause of
the serious « water-melon decay » in both America and Italy.

On this same material from Parma, the writer also found the
pycnidian form of the fungus *Diplodina citrullina* Grossenbacher
(= *Ascochyta citrullina* C. O. Smith).

Washing of the plants with Bordeaux mixture is recommended for the control of the *Mycosphaerella*. As to the *Fusarium niveum*, a selection of the most resistant individuals must be locally made.

1547

E. O. Essig. **Wither Tip of Citrus trees:** *Colletotrichum gloeosporioides* **Penzig. Its History, Description, Distribution, Destructiveness and Control.** — *Pomona College Journ. of Econ. Botany*, Vol. I, N. 1, pp. 25-36, 8 figg., 1911. — *Rivista di Patologia vegetale*, Anno V, N. 1, pp. 20-21. Pavia, 1° aprile, 1911.

United States: (Florida). East Indies. Australia

This is the detailed description of *Colletotrichum gloeosporioides* Penzig., of the alterations which it produces in citrus trees, and the damage it does. This disease is very widespread in Florida, the East Indies, Australia, etc.; where, according to the organ of the plant which it attacks, it is known as « Wither-tip », « Leaf spot », « Tear stain » or « Lemon spot ».

The writer recommends that the disease be controlled by washings with Bordeaux mixture or with boiled lime-sulphur mixture; and by abundant pruning in December and January.

1548

Plum Trees killed by Eutypella Prunastri. — *The Gardener's Chronicle*, Vol. XLIX, N. 3674, p. 329. London, May 27, 1911.

Great Britain: Cambridgeshire

During recent years, young plum trees have been frequently killed by this fungus in Cambridgeshire, the Czar variety being particularly susceptible to attack.

Young plum trees, which on a casual examination in the autumn, appear to be healthy, may be found to be dead in the following spring, the fungus having girdled the bark of the main stem in the meantime. Such trees were infected by the fungus during the previous summer, but the death of the tree does not result until the following year. Older plum trees have not been attacked, nor have apple trees succumbed to the disease in this district. The pulp of the fruit which contains the spores becomes covered with small black pustules during the early summer. The spores are of two kinds, one of which does not develop until the second year after infection. Plum trees are most liable to attack when they have been planted too deeply, though in the case of Czar plums, which have been killed by the disease in Cambridgeshire this year, the trees had not been placed deeply in the soil.

Trees that have been killed by *Eutypella prunastri* should be burnt at once; and if plum trees are thus destroyed they should be replaced by apples.

E. Essed. **The " Panama Disease " of Bananas** (1). — *Annals of Botany*, vol. XXV, No. XCVIII,. pp 343-361, pl. XXIX. London & Oxford, April, 1911.

1549

This disease appeared in banana plantations in the State of Panama about five years ago. In one district the crops suffered severely, while twenty-five miles away the disease appeared, but not as an epidemic.

Panama

In Costa Rica its ravages have been confined to certain places; there are still about 60 000 acres of fine banana plantations where the disease is not prevalent and causes no real damage.

In neither of these States, however, has the disease been so disastrous as in Surinam where it appears on the one-year plants, and where a quarter to three quarters of the second and third year crops may be lost; there have even been plantations in which all the plants were destroyed. One of the most readily attacked varieties is « Gros Michel »; the varieties « Indian Banana » or « Wine-coloured Banana », « Silverskin », « Apple Banana », and « Horse Banana », the Dwarf, and some others known as « Plantains » (2) are more or less susceptible. The varieties « Ladies'-finger », « Congo Banana », and the ordinary ones are resistant.

The disease is seen by a withering of the edges of the leaves; a discoloration appears along the median dorsal line of the sheath; sometimes only the youngest leaves wither; at other times the oldest leaves show signs of dying, while the buds still continue to develop for a time: this constitutes the first stage. In the second stage growth stops, the leaves droop, and the whole plant looks as if it lacks moisture; then wrinkles appear on the blade and sheath of the leaves, which soon dry up; lastly, the stem falls right over.

The disease is caused by a previously undescribed fungus which the author proposes to call *Ustilaginoidella musaeperda*. In the rhizome of a diseased plant the fungus is found chiefly in the wood-vessels and adjoining tissue ; the vessels become discoloured and the

---

(1) Compare nos. 328 and 329 of this *Bulletin* Jan, 1911.   (*Ed.*).

(2) In countries where bananas are grown on a large scale, the innumerable varieties of *Musa paradisiaca* are divided into two main groups, eating and cooking; the first corresponds to the « bacove » of the Guiana natives, « sweet banana « or simply « banana » in English, and « camburi » or « platano guinea » in Spanish. The cooking banana is called « plantain » in English, and « platano arton » in Spanish. — Cf. E. de Wildeman, *Les plantes tropicales de grande culture*, tome I, p. 310. Bruxelles Paris, 1908.   (*Ed.*).

sap is absorbed by the fungus in them. The first change in the parenchyma is an unusual cloudiness of the protoplasm, apparently caused by an enzyme secreted by the fungus ; the brown discolouration and the slimy degeneration of the walls of the vessels must also be ascribed to an enzyme. Gradually the cell contents are absorbed and replaced by the cartilaginous sclerotium. Transverse sections of the leaf-blade show that the hyphae in the vessels send out branches at right angles to the walls; these end in the intercellular spaces among the sub-epidermal cells and produce oblong or irregular sclerotia. In the sheath special sclerotia are formed in the star-shaped parenchyma cells: the hyphae which enter these cells send branches into the rays, where they form sclerotia which give rise to little spores.

In the leaf-blade the fertile hyphae develop in or among the palisade parenchyma cells; some of them reach the inner walls of the outermost parenchyma layer, forming sclerotia which after remaining dormant for a time produce spores; the spores may remain in the sclerotium, or the pressure of the surrounding tissues may force them into the cells above; they become free after the leaf has decayed. The hyphae may also penetrate into the subepidermal layers, filling the cells with sclerotia; or they may emerge on the surface of the leaf as little brown gall-like swellings (*Mycocecidia*); sometimes they go back through the epidermis or through the stomata, or they ramify all over the surface of the leaf, producing numerous sickle-shaped conidia.

Micrococcus sulfureus and a form of *Bacterium fluorescens* were isolated from the diseased plants; but like bacteria in general they have nothing to do with this banana disease, as shown by inoculations. Further, inoculations prove that *Ustilaginoidella musaeperda* is the cause of the disease in Surinam. All efforts to find a remedy for this disease have so far been unsuccessful.

1550 E. ESSED. **The Surinam Disease of Bananas. A condition of Elephantiasis of the Banana caused by *Ustilaginoidella œdipigera*.** — *Annals of Botany*. Vol. XXV, No. XCVIII, pp. 363-365, pl. XXX. London & Oxford, April, 1911.

Dutch Guiana. Surinam. Colombia Besides the « Panama disease », described in the previous article, another disease has long been known, though never widespread, in the banana fields of Surinam and Colombia ; but it does not cause much apprehension among the planters.

The disease shows as a swelling, sometimes enormous, of the base of the stem ; this is why it is called « bigie footoe » or « ele-phantiasis ». The oldest leaves then begin to wither, owing to rup-ture of the tissue close to the stem ; these leaves hang on during the winter and do not look any different from the ordinary dead leaves ; but careful examination shows a number of little galls (*Mycocecidia*) on the sheaths and leaf-stalks, some of them projec-ting through the epidermis. The end of the shoot may go on growing for some time after the outer leaves are dead, but the young leaves are always poorly-developed and chlorotic. At this stage the upper part of the rhizome can be broken off clean by a slight pull.

Sections in the rhizome show that the fungus attacks first the outer and upper part of the parenchyma. The sloughing of the lower leaves is probably due to tension caused by the enormous quantities of hyphae making their way through the tissues to the outside of the leaf-sheaths ; and probably also to a slow disin-tegration caused by enzymes secreted by the fungus. As the fun-gus extends horizontally just below the bases of the outermost leaves, it is probable that this is the region of infection ; if it is only when the tissues at this point are young and thin that infec-tion can take place, the slow spread of the disease receives a ready explanation.

The writer has obtained from the diseased plants pure cultures of a fungus, and has named it *Ustilaginoidella oedipigera*.

The disease can be checked by sulphate of copper solution.

A. v. JACZEWSKI. **The Cryptogamic Diseases of Forest Trees and   1551
their Control.** (O Gribnekh Bolies niakh Liesnekh Porod i Mierakh Borbi s nimi) — *Bureau de Mycologie et de Phytopa-thologie.* St. Peterburg, 1911.

Mr. Jaczewski first deals with the bad condition of the forests in Russia, especially in comparison with the condition of German forests, and urges the necessity of developing Forest Phytopathology   **Russia** in Russia.

Several fungi attack the seeds of forest trees and at the sowing period, they sometimes mupltiply rapidly and spread to other seeds, preventing them from germinating. Amongst these fungi are *Scle-rotinia Betulae* Naw. of the Birch, *S. Alni* of the Alder and *S. pseu-dotuberosa* Rehm of the Oak.

The forests of the Government of Kostram have recently been seriously damaged by *Pucciniastrum Padi* Dietel, a heterœcions Uredinea, which passes the aecidial and conidial stages on the young cones of the Fir and forms uredospores and teleutospores on the leaves of the wild cherry (*Prunus Avium*).

Among fungi which injure young plants, *Lophodermium Pinastri* Chev., which attacks young Pine trees, must be placed in the first rank; and the following measures are recommended against it :

1) Have the nurseries at some distance from the forests, in order that the spores cannot be brought there too easily.

2) Keep the nurseries clean and in good condition, taking away and destroying immediately infected young plants.

3) Plant thogether Pines and Firs in the nurseries;

4) Nurseries should be preferably on a loamy soil ;

5) At the end of July or the beginning of August, give two applications of Bordeaux mixture, with an interval of 15 days between each application.

Great damage has been caused of late by *Fusarium Pini* R. Hartig, which produces root rot int he young trees. The following remedies are recommended :

1) Treat the seeds with a solution of formalin ;

2) Pull up and destroy infected young plants, and then disinfect the soil with formalin.

Serious damage is caused to full grown plants by *Polyporus omnivora*. Last year, *Polyporus betulinus* Fries did considerable damage to the Birches in the Government of Smolensk. *Polyporus annosus* Fr., *Rhizina undulata* Fr. and *Armillaria mellea* are also injurious.

1552   M. Turconi and L. Maffei. **Mycological and Phytopathological notes. I. *Cercospora Lumbricoides* sp. nov. on the Ash; and *Nectria Castilloae* sp. nov. on *Castilloa elastica* in Mexico. II. *Steganosporium Kosaroffii* sp. nov. on the Mulberry in Bulgaria.** (Note micologiche e fitopatologiche. I. *Cercospora Lumbricoides* n. sp. sul frassino; e *Nectria Castilloae* n. sp. sulla *Castilloa elastica* nel Messico. II. *Steganosporium Kosaroffii* n. sp. sul gelso in Bulgaria. *Atti dell'Istituto botanico di Pavia*, ser. II, vol. XII, pp. 329-336, 1 tav. 1910). — *Rivista di Patologia vegetale*, anno IV, N. 19-21, p. 306. Pavia, 15 marzo, 1911).

Mexico:
Bulgaria

Irregular spots were found on the leaves of the Ash, more clearly visible on the under than on the upper surface, which had been caused by a new species of Cercospora, named *C. lumbricoides*

·on account of the form of its conidia, which are very long, septate and surounded by appendices resembling small worms.

The branches of the *Castilloa* were sprinkled with small light-red warts, which are nothing but the perithecia of a new species of *Nectria* (*N. Castilloae*) the mycelium of which invades the· sub-·cutaneous tissues right to the pith.

A new Melanconia, *Steganosporium Kosaroffii*, is described in the second Note : it was studied on the branches of the Mulberry ·sent to the Laboratory at Pavia from Bulgaria.

Phanerogamous Parasites and Weeds. — Their Control.

D. LARIONOV. **The Possibility of the Diffusion of " Cuscuta ra-**   **1558**
cemosa'' Mart. in Russia. (O Voxmoxnosti Rasprostranieniia
V. Rossii Grosdevidnoi Poviliki *Cuscuta racemosa* Mart.). —
Khos iaistro (*Husbandry*) VI G. N° 10, pp, 297-300, Kiev-109ª
Marta, 1911.

Cuscuta racemosa Mart., American Dodder, imported into Europe with the seeds of fodder plants, has spread rapidly in Italy, Austria-Hungary and Prussian Silesia, whence it has passed into Russia. It   **Russia**
has appeared in the lucerne and clover fields of the Governments of Podolia and Volhynia, as well as in the district of Yekaterinoslav. The damage caused by this species of dodder is the same as that caused by *C. Epithymum* Murr., var. *Trifolii*. The seeds of *C. racemosa* are from 1.0 to 1.75 m/m long and from 0.9 to 1.50 m/m broad. The size of these dodder seeds renders it difficult to distin-guish them from the seeds of lucerne and red clover, which have the following dimensions:

Lucerne : 1.76 to 3 mm by 1.0 to 1.25 mm.

Red clover: 1.5 to 2.5 mm. by 1.25 to 1.5 mm.

Mr. Larionov insists on the necessity of keeping a severe control ·over the seeds from localities infected by *Cuscuta*, and recom-

mends farmers not to use any seeds but those which have been
examined and guaranteed (1).

1554
Tropical
Africa

Mistletoe on *Funtumia elastica* in Tropical Africa. — (See Abstr.
1599 of this *Bulletin*).

1555
Ceylon

**" Luc Binh " (*Eichornia crassipes*) as a Weed in Rice Fields in
Ceylon.** (See Abstr. 1390 of this *Bulletin*).

Insects and other Injurious Invertebrates. Their Biology and Control.

1556

H. A. BALLOU. **Citrus-tree Pests in Florida: Report on a Visit to
Florida.** *West Indian Bulletin.* Vol. XI; N. 3. Imp. Agr. Dep.
Barbados, pp. 172-182.

Florida
West Indies

This Report of the Entomologist on the Staff of the Imperial
Department of Agriculture of the West Indies deals particularly
with his special mission to Florida, the principal object of which
was the study of orange and grape cultivation with reference to
insect pests and their control by means of natural enemies.
The Citrus white fly (*Aleyrodes citri*) is the principal insect pest
of citrus trees in Florida. Two other species of white fly occur
which are of minor importance, the cloudy-wing white fly (*Aleyrodes Nubifera*) and *Aleyrodes Howardi*.

---

(1) The Intelligence Office and the Office of Plant Diseases of the International Institute of Agriculture have since 1909 drawn attention to the importance of a severe control on the trade of clover, lucerne or alfalfa and of
other leguminous seeds, with a view to preventing the spread of the different
kinds of dodder (*Cuscuta*). It was urged that the question should be submitted
to international consideration, the diffusion of dodder being greatly due to the
international trade of clover and leguminous forage seeds, a trade that is rapidly growing in importance.
See: *Institut International d'Agriculture. Services des Renseignements Agricoles et des Maladies des Plantes. Rapport de la II Division. Novembre 1909.*
Imprim. de la Chambre des Deputés, Rome, 1909.   (*Ed.*).

The purple scale (*Lepidosaphes Beckii*) and Glover's scale (*L. Gloveri*) and Florida red scale (*Chrysomphalus ficus*) also occur in Florida as citrus pests, generally of less importance than the white fly.

These insect pests are capable of being held in check, principally by means of beneficial fungi, of which nine species are found in the State. Six of these are known to occur on white fly; their names and dates of discovery are as follows:

Red fungus (*Aschersonia aleyrodis*, Webber) 1893.
Yellow fungus (*Aschersonia flavo-citrino*, P. Henn) 1893.
Brown fungus (*Aegeritis Webberi*, Fawcett) 1896.
Cinnamon (*Verticillium heterocladum*, Penzig) 1907.
White fringe fungus (*Microcera* sp.) 1907.
    ,,   ,,   ,,   (*Sporotrichum* sp.).
Red-headed fungus (*Sphaerostilbe coccophila*) 1903.

Also one on both white fly and scales, red-headed fungus (*Sphaerostilbe coccophila*); and two on scales, white-headed fungus (*Ophionectria coccicola*) and black fungus (*Myriangium Duriaei* Mont.) In years of abundant moisture the fungi assume naturally a varying degree of control of white fly and scale insect pests. In other seasons they may be established during short rainy periods by artificial means, of which the spore-spraying method is the most satisfactory. Even in favourable seasons, fungi may be assisted to assume control more quickly by artificial introduction. Some six to eight weeks may be gained in this way.

When, for any reason, the pests become so numerous that treatment is required at once, the trees may be sprayed with oily or soap mixtures, or fumigated, without injury to the fungi. (1) Hymenopterous parasites do not appear to exert any influence in the control of these pests.

The rust mite (*Phytophus oleivorus*) occurs in Florida as a pest of citrus trees but is held in efficient check by the regular use of sulphur, applied dry or in water.

Cover crops and mulches act as aids in increasing moisture and thus help to preserve conditions favourable for the growth of beneficial fungi. Nitrogenous fertilizers are used sparingly. Only shallow tillage is given after the roots of the plants in the citrus groves have taken possession of the soil.

In the West Indies conditions are different; scale insects are the principal pests of citrus crops, and their natural enemies include both fungi and parasitic insects. In Dominica, the fungi

---

(1) See below, no. 1562.   (*Ed.*).

are perhaps in largest abundance, and this is probably mostly due
to the greater moisture of the atmosphere in this island; while
in Montserrat the beneficial effect is probably more equally
divided between fungi and parasitic insects. In Florida the cover
crops of beggar weed (*Desmodium tortuosum*) and the natural growth
of grass and weeds are considered to be an aid to the maintenance
of the moist atmospheric conditions which are favourable to the
development of the fungi, although the humidity of the atmosphere
in Florida is very considerable without any such aid. In Montserrat, the use of Bengal beans (1) has been presumed to aid in the control of scale insects in a similar way, but it has not yet been proved that the use of this crop as a cover to lime trees increases
greatly the amount of scale-attacking fungus. About twenty years
ago these insects were the principal pests of citrus cultivations in
Florida; and the white fly, probably of more recent introduction
than the scale insects, has increased until it holds the position of
first importance in this regard.

It is not possible at this time to say whether experience in
the West Indies will be similar to that in Florida, but in this
connexion it is especially desirable that a careful investigation of
the species of white fly occurring in the West Indies should be
made, with notes on their distribution and food plants, in order
that records may be available; so that from time to time in the
future it may be possible to determine whether or not a decided
increase of this class of pest is occurring.

1557   GASTINE. **Geographical Distribution of the Mulberry Pest,** *Diaspis*
pentagona (Dispersion géographique de la *Diaspis pentagona*).
— *Bulletin mensel de l'Office de Renseignements Agricoles*, N. 4,
pp. 432-456. Paris, Avril 1911.

Years ago, this insect was observed by Mr. Targioni-Tozzetti,
formerly Director of the Station of Agricultural Entomology at Flo-
Italy. rence, as a parasite of the Mulberry tree, and described by him as
Japan a new species under the name of *Diaspis pentagona*. There is every
India, etc. reason to believe that it was imported with some mulberry plants
from Japan.

(1) *Mucuna pruriens* DC., Cowhage. — A lofty annual climber with large
papilionaceous flowers and velvety legumes not unlike those of a sweet pea.
It occurs commouly throughout the tropical regions of America.   (*Ed.*).

The following are the plants on which it has been observed in the various countries:

Italy (1). — Mulberry, Nettle-tree, or *Celtis australis*, Chestnut, Walnut, Ash, *Bignonia Catalpa*, Acacia, *Sophora Japonica*, Elm, Willow, Almond, Peach, Plum, Bay-laurel, Lilac (*Syringa vulgaris*) Jasmine, Currants and Gooseberries, *Evonymus europaeus*, Pumpkin, Beans, *Berberis stenophylla*, *Solanum Dulcamara*, *Kirria japonica*, Hop (*Humulus Lupulus*), Poplar, *Salvia officinalis*, *Spiraea japonica*, Vine, etc.

Japan. — Mulberry, Walnut, Elm, Peach, Plum, Cherry, Pear, Vine, *Paulownia imperialis*, *Sterculia platanifolia*, *Carica Papaya*, *Paeonia montana*, *Zanthoxylum piperitum*, *Diospyros Kaki*, *Elaeagnus macrophylla*, Bamboo.

India and Ceylon. — *Callicarpa lassata*, *Erythrina*, *Geranium*.

Martinique. — *Cyrcas circinnatis*, *Zamia mexicana*.

England. — *Calotropis procera*, *Prunus Pseudo-cerasus* and greenhouse plants.

United States. — Mulberry, Peach, Apricot, Plum, Pear, Cherry, Melon, *Acanthus*, *Hibiscus esculentus*, *Cycas media*, *Elaeagnus*.

Jamaica. — Cotton, *Pelargonium*, Vine, Peach, *Passiflora*, *Diospyros*, Jasmine, *Sedum*, Rose laurel, Pimento (*Capsicum*), *Guazuma ulmifolia*.

Cape Colony. — Mulberry, Peach, Apricot, Plum, Pear, Cherry, *Myoporum*, Jasmine, *Passiflora edulis*, *Polygala myrtifolia*, *Ipomea*, *Fuchsia*, *Pelargonium*.

Australia. — Peach, Pear, Melon, *Melia Azedarach*, *Solanum sodomoeuum*, *S. giganteum*, and *S. aculeatum*.

These lists include the principal fruit trees, a number of floral or ornamental species cultivated in gardens and parks, and many trees, among which are to be found some forest species; so that the Japanese Cochineal, passing from one to another of these plants, may be spread in all directions.

The trade in floral and horticultural plants is thus seen to be a cause of danger, on account of the possibility of a widespread diffusion of the *Diaspis*. Japan alone has sent this dangerous insect into all quarters of the globe by means of the various ornamental plants which she exports so extensively.

---

(1) For the list concerning Italy see Abstr. 1311, *Bulletin*, April, 1911.

1558

F. W. URICH. **Identification of the Sugar Cane Froghopper.** (1) — *Department of Agriculture*, Trinidad, Bulletin, Vol. X, N. 67, pp. 58-59. Trinidad, January-March, 1911.

There has always been some doubt as to the dentity of the Sugar Cane Froghopper. The insect was referred to the family *Cercopidae* by Mr. J. H. Hart. It was described as *Tomaspis postica*, Walker, by Hart, Collens and Barrett; as belonging to two species, viz: *Tomaspis postica*, Walk. and *Tomaspis postica*, var. Walk. by M. Heideman. Prof. E. Ball has now determined it as *Tomaspis varia* Fabr.

**Trinidad.
Mexico**

The true *Tomaspis postica* was taken on sugar cane in Mexico; but this species is quite different from the Trinidad Sugar Cane Froghopper.

The following is a list of the froghoppers recorded from Trinidad.

1. *Tomaspis varia* Fabr. Distribution: Trinidad, Tobago. Food plants: Grasses of several species and sugar cane. Adults are sometimes observed feeding on palms.

Very common in Trinidad, being found on sugar · as well as cacao estates all over the island.

2. *Tomaspis rubra* Linn. var. *sororia* Germ. (Christmas Bush Froghopper). Distribution: Trinidad, Demerara. Food plant: *Eupatorium odoratum*, Christmas bush. Not found on grass up to now.

3. *Tomaspis pubescens*, Fabr. (Black Froghopper). Distribution : Trinidad, Demerara. Food plants: Several species of grass growing in damp situations.

4. *Tomaspis* sp. near *tristis* Fabr. (Spotted Froghopper). Distribution: Trinidad.

1559

G. STEHLI. **The Black-veined White: Pieris** (Der Baumweissling). — *Landwirtschaftliche Umschau*, 3º Jahrgang, N. 21, pp. 511-512. Magdeburg, 26 Mai, 1911.

It is due to the excellent organisation of the phytopathological service and the activity of the farmers in Germany that the " Baumweissling " (*Pieris*) (2) does not accomplish so much harm in that country as in other parts of Europe.

Germany

The reddish coloured larvae which are hatched from the eggs laid by the female in large numbers up to the beginning of August,

---

(1) See below, no. 1584.   (*Ed.*).
(2) Or *Aporia Cratægi*; very rare in England.   (*Ed.*).

devour a great quantity of leaves, especially on the cherry, pear and plum trees.

These larvae pass the winter curled up in an envelope of leaves held together by a tangle of threads spun by them; they come out in early spring.

For the control of these insects, the "tents" should be collected and burnt towards the middle of autumn or in winter; or, if possible, the eggs, which are to be found in little golden yellow heaps on the upper part of the leaves, might be destroyed directly.

Influence of Liquid and Farm Yard Manure on Phylloxera and its Eggs (Die Einwirkung von Stalldünger und Jauche auf das Leben der Reblaus und ihre Eier). — *Deutsche landwirtschaftliche Presse*, XXXIII Jahrg., N. 32, p. 380. Berlin, 22 April 1911.

1560

MM. Moritz and Börner have been experimenting with phylloxera and its eggs treated with farm and liquid manure·

a) Action of liquid manure. Two ᵢexperiments were made with liquid manure; the first with fresh and the second with old liquid manure, the reaction of which was slightly alkaline. The phylloxera eggs were not dead after six hours immersion in the two manures; of the insects, a part died, a part were poisoned and the remainder continued alive.

Germany

The insects hatched from the eggs treated with the liquid manure were capable of infecting the plants. After 12 hours immersion, nearly all the insects died, but the eggs were still alive.

After 18 hours immersion, all the insects were dead, while the eggs, although still alive in many cases produced insects that were incapable of infection.

b) Action of farm manure. If the manure is well decomposed the insects and eggs continue to live as long as a month, and may be centres of infection. If the manure is fresh, on the other hand, the danger of infection does not last more than a week or two.

These experiments show that it is not advisable to use in healthy vineyards manure which has been taken from farms infected with phylloxera, especially very decomposed manure.

1561   F. D'HERELLE. **Bacterial Epizoon on Mexican Locusts** (Sur une épi-
zootie de nature bactérienne sévissant sur les Sautrelles au Mexique). — *C. R. de l'Acad. des Sciences*, t. 152, n. 21, pp. 1413-
1415. Paris, 22 Mai 1911.

At the beginning of 1910 the writer observed an epizoon infest-
ing the locusts (*Schistocerca pallens*) in Yucatan, Mexico.

Mexico: He found numerous coccobacilli in the contents of the intes-
Yucatan   tinal tubes of the dead locusts, and was able to isolate them and
to demonstrate their pathogenic role. M. d'Herelle did not find any
coccobacilli in the locusts caught whilst flying and belonging to
swarms amongst which the disease was not rife.

Out of a number of locusts from swarms suffering from
the epizoon, 25 were selected from amongst the most flourishing :
6 of these died from the infection within 3 days, the remainder
surviving. Out of these surviving 19, which were dissected after
being kept under observation for 8 days, 5 showed the specific coc
cobacillus in the intestinal contents, and did not appear to have
suffered at all. The number of locusts which become immune may
therefore be estimated at 20 or 25 %.

According to the information given to the writer by the planters of Yucatan, the number of locusts had so greatly diminished
by March, 1911, that it was estimated that the damage caused this
year would be very slight; and the infection was raging amongst
the swarms which remained.

The coccobacillus is not pathogenic for hens, guinea pigs and
rabbits.

M. D'Herelle thinks the Yucatan epizoon may be possibly useful in many countries in controlling locusts.

1562   E. W. BERGER. **White-fly *(Aleyrodes nubifera)* a Citrus Pest: Control in Florida.** *University of Florida.* Agr. Exp. Sta., Bull.
103, pp. 5-28, E. S. R., vol. XIV, no. 4, p. 355. — Washington, April, 5th, 1911.

The essential facts concerning white fly control, through the
United   use of fungi and by spraying, are here brought together in brief
States: form.
Florida
Experiments on the artificial spreading of fungi show that
there are definite advantages to be gained. It has been found that
the yellow fungus *Aschersonia flavo-citrina* thrives only on *Aleyrodes*

nubilera. White-fly pupae appear to be more or less immune to fungus attacks.

The operations and experiments of the past year indicate clearly that effective spraying can be done. Temperature as well as stage of development of the larvae is apparently a factor in successful spraying, since we would expect the solutions to be more penetrating when several degrees warmer. Thus only .91.3 per cent of the 1st to 3rd and 30 per cent of the fourth stage larvae, were killᵉd with « Gold-dust » with an initial temperature of 88° F (equiv. to 31° C) and a mean for 7 days of 74.5° (23°.6 C) while 99.5 per cent of the 2nd and 3rd and 89 per cent of the 4th and 5th stages larvae were killed when the initial temperature was 99° (37.2° C) and the mean for 7 days 80.8° (27.° C).

The results after June 15th on 4th stage larvae with the soap solutions were excellent, with an initial temperature of 98° (36°.6 C) and a mean of 83.1° (28°.3 C).

Directions are given for winter treatment, spring, summer and autumn spraying etc. It is stated that frost destroys directly but few, if any, of the larvae on leaves that remain uninjured.

The food plants of *Aleyrodes citri* are listed, and it is recommended that all useless and abandoned citrus trees be condemned and destroyed.

The Preservation of Aphis-eating Lady-Birds. A new Opening for Cold Treatment. (La conservation des Coccinelles aphidiphages. Une nouvelle application du froid). *Revue générale du froid*, 3ᵉ année, tome III, n. 3, pp. 232-234. — Paris, Mai, 1911.

1563

The Horticultural Commission of California has recently organised a service for the destruction of the aphids and plant-lice which do such havoc in the vineyards and orchards that form the wealth of that State. The best means for controlling these pests is the employment of Aphis-eating Coccinellidae, or Lady-birds.

United States: California

The varieties chosen for the purpose are those which pass the winter in a state of lethargy; these insects are collected by gangs of workmen who seek for them in the moss under the snow in the cañons of the Sierra Nevada; they are put into sacks and sent to the « California State Insectary », where they are preserved in this condition by cold storage, as long as desired. There is no need to feed them during that time.

Nearly every American insect can be preserved more or less well in cold storage. When the insects have reached a certain stage of development, their growth is arrested by cold and they are put into a condition similar to that of natural hibernation. The species imported to the United States arrive there in the cold storage chambers of steamers; this method of cold storage is chiefly applied to the Coccinellidae and the losses are very small. A native species, *Hippodamia convergens*, collects in large numbers on high mountains : the site of these colonies is marked out on special maps in the autumn, and in December and January between 2 and 3 tons of the insects are collected, and let loose in spring or summer, according to need, against the different species of plant-louse. The larger part of them is sent to the Imperial Valley, where melons are grown.

The insects are passed into the sacks through a sieve which is too fine to allow leaves, twigs and pebbles to enter. The colonies are generally found on the ground under the litter of leaves, pine needles, and moss. The insects, after being sifted, are put into a machine, which packs them into special wooden boxes at the rate of about 60 000 each; the boxes are covered with a trellis work, the interstices of which are carefully filled in with very dry and clean fibre. The boxes are then placed in ordinary cold storage chambers, the temperature of which is kept as nearly as possible at 4° C. The preservation of the insects depends largely on the renewal of the air and on its moisture, and it is advisable that there be a special chamber where the air is kept moist. Results as good, if not actually better, are obtained by freezing, by means of which the insects may be kept for as long as six months without being fed. The sole precaution necessary is that the sacks must be kept in a cold place from the time the insects are gathered until they are put in the cold storage. If exposed to heat even for a short time before being packed, they cannot be preserved for a week.

1564   ARTHUR M. LEA. **A Minute but Useful Ladybird Beetle.** *The Agricultural Gazette of Tasmania*, vol. XIX, no. 2, p. 65. — Tasmania, February 1911.

Australia

In dry summer months the red spider (*Tetranychus telarius*), red mite (*Bryobia pratensis*) and other mites often become very troublesome, and seriously injure the leaves of many fruit trees, vegetables, and garden plants.

On examining affected leaves, there may often be seen feeding on the mites a ladybird, *Scymnus vagans*. The adult will eat many

red spiders or red mites in a day; but its larvae are even more voracious, as each larva before turning into a pupa probably consumes some hundreds of mites.

This species also feeds on young Thrips, and doubtless also on the young of scale insects.

Scymnus vagans is known to occur in New South Wales, Victoria and Tasmania, sometimes in abundance. Mr. Albert Koebele of the U. S. Department of Agriculture, sent from Australia several consignments of this ladybird to California.

W. HARPER DEAN. **The Sorghum Midge.** — *U. S. Dept. of Agric. Bur. of Entomology.* Bull. N. 85. Washington, 18 April, 1911.

1565

The *Contarinia (Diplosis) sorghicola* Coq., the larvae of which injure the sorghum by nibbling the grains, is very extensively found in the Eastern States of the United States. Among the natural enemies of this insect, an ant must be mentioned, *Iridomyrmex humilis* Mayr, which destroys a large number of the larvae, killing them or dragging them into the ant hills.

United States

A Diptera, *Psilopodinus flaviceps* Aldrich, attacks and devours the adult.

Trochilus Alexandri, a humming-bird, also does good service to agriculture, being a great destroyer of insects.

G. MARTELLI. **Information on *Aphis Brassicae* L. and some of its Parasites and Hyperparasites.** (Notizie sull'*Aphis Brassicae* L. e su alcuni suoi parassiti e iperparassiti). — *Boll. del Labor. di Zool. gen. e agraria di Portici*, vol. V, pp. 40-54, 1910. — *Rivista di Patologia vegetale*, anno IV, n. 19-21, pp. 308-309. Pavia, 15 marzo 1911.

1566

The writer first describes the habits of *Aphis Brassicae* L., which lives in large colonies on leaves of cabbage and other Crucifers; from September to June it has about ten generations, each with four moults.

Italy

Its parasites include: *Aphidius Brassicae* Marsk., (Hymenoptera); *Lasiophthicus (Syrphus) Pyrastri* (Diptera), hyperparasite *Bassus albosignatus* Grav; *Syrphus balteatus* Deg., (Diptera), hyperparasite *Pachyneuron* sp.; *S. Ribesii* L.; *Allotria vittrix* Wes., var. *infuscata* Kieff., (Diptera).

1567   Natural Enemies of the Caterpillars of the Vine Hawk Moth
        (Deilephila Elpenor) see below no. 1590.

France

1568   E. L. PATTERSON: **Technical Results from the Gipsy Moth Parasite
        Laboratory. III. Investigations into the Habits of Certain Sar-
        cophagidae.** — *U. S. Department of Agriculture. Bureau of
        Entomology. Technical Series.* N. 19, Part. III, pp. 25-32. Wash-
        ington, March 22, 1911.

        A number of Experiments carried out at the Gipsy Moth Parasite
        Laboratory indicate very conclusively that the sarcophagids in New
United England do not destroy living gipsy-moth larvae or pupae in the
States field. From a collection of 2 666 specimens not a single sarcophagid
        was reared.
            In cages the flies would not oviposit on healthy or recently
        killed caterpillars or· pupae, but did so· freely after they became
        slightly decomposed. First-stage maggots, when placed artificially
        within living pupae, failed to develop in every instance, showing
        that the conditions were not favorable for their growth. When
        living and decomposing larvae or pupae were placed side by side
        in a cage, the flies selected the latter on which to oviposit, and
        normal larvae developed. In conclusion it must be understood
        that the writer has not attempted to work with any one species
        of the Sarcophagidae, nor to separate them into species; but, on the
        other hand, he has ·worked with them only as a family, taking for
        granted that if any of these flies are ever parasitic on the gipsy
        moth, they would naturally be found in the infested localities.
            Although all the experiments have given negative results, yet
        they are nevertheless of economic importance: because in Europe
        and Japan, where sarcophagids are more commonly associated with
        the gipsy moth than in the United States, it is possible that there
        may be several species that have the parasitic habit. If so, foreign
        investigations should ·be hastened ;· for if introduced into America
        these parasitic sarcophagids would be an important addition to the
        natural ·enemies of the " gipsy moth " *Porthetria dispar* L.

1569   **Natural Enemies of Citrus Pests in Florida.** (See Ns. 1556 and 1562
United of this *Bulletin*).
States:
Florida

A. A. Girault. The Chalcidoid Parasites of the Coccid *Kermes* 1570
pubescens Bogue, with Descriptions of two new Genera and
three new Species of *Encyrtidae* from Illinois. — *The Canadian Entomologist*, Vol. XLIII, N. 5, pp. 168-178. London,
May 1911.

The writer describes two new genera and three new species of
Encyrtidae found in Illinois as parasites of the common oak coccid   United
(*Kermes pubescens* Bogue).   States:
They are: Illinois
Cristatithorax gen. nov., *C. pulcher* sp. nov., *Aenasioidea* gen.
nov., *A. latiscapus* sp. nov., and *Microterys speciosissimus* sp. nov.
Associated with them he has found certain insects of the families
Pterolamidae (gen. *Pachyneuron* Walker) and *Eulophidae* (gen. *Gi-
rolasia* Foerster).

Insectivorous Birds of New of South Wales. — *The Agricultural Ga-* 1571
zette of New South Wales, Vol. XXII, Part I, pp. 36-38. Sydney,
January 1911.

The " Willie Wagtail " (*Rhipidura tricolor*) and the " Scissors
Grinder " (*Sisura inquieta*) are described in this number. Both   Australia:
destroy a great many insects harmful to crops and to domestic   N. S. Wales
animals in South Australia.

Birds destroying Locusts in South Africa. (See Abstr. 1521 of this 1572
Bulletin).   S. Africa

David E. Fullaway. The Use of Insecticides in Hawaii. — *Hawaii* 1573
Agricultural Experiment Station. Press Bulletin N. 27, pp. 1-8.
Honolulu, 1910.

At the Hawaii Agricultural Experiment Station, a number of
experiments were carried out on the use of insecticides and on   United
practical remedies for common pests.   States:
Attention is called to the subject of spraying for killing noxious   Hawaii
weeds. Two compounds were used with some success: ferrous sulphate and arsenite of soda.
Arsenite of soda for weed-killing is prepared as follows: 2 lbs.
of white arsenic and 6 lbs. of soda are dissolved in one gallon of

1567

Natural Enemies of the Caterpillars of the Vine Hawk Moth *(Deilephila Elpenor)* see below no. 1590.

France

1568

E. L. PATTERSON: **Technical Results from the Gipsy Moth Parasite Laboratory. III. Investigations into the Habits of Certain Sarcophagidae.** — *U. S. Department of Agriculture. Bureau of Entomology. Technical Series.* N. 19, Part. III, pp. 25-32. Washington, March 22, 1911.

United States

A number of Experiments carried out at the Gipsy Moth Parasite Laboratory indicate very conclusively that the sarcophagids in New England do not destroy living gipsy-moth larvae or pupae in the field. From a collection of 2 666 specimens not a single sarcophagid was reared.

In cages the flies would not oviposit on healthy or recently killed caterpillars or pupae, but did so freely after they became slightly decomposed. First-stage maggots, when placed artificially within living pupae, failed to develop in every instance, showing that the conditions were not favorable for their growth. When living and decomposing larvae or pupae were placed side by side in a cage, the flies selected the latter on which to oviposit, and normal larvae developed. In conclusion it must be understood that the writer has not attempted to work with any one species of the Sarcophagidae, nor to separate them into species; but, on the other hand, he has worked with them only as a family, taking for granted that if any of these flies are ever parasitic on the gipsy moth, they would naturally be found in the infested localities.

Although all the experiments have given negative results, yet they are nevertheless of economic importance: because in Europe and Japan, where sarcophagids are more commonly associated with the gipsy moth than in the United States, it is possible that there may be several species that have the parasitic habit. If so, foreign investigations should be hastened; for if introduced into America these parasitic sarcophagids would be an important addition to the natural enemies of the "gipsy moth" *Porthetria dispar* L.

1569
United States:
Florida

Natural Enemies of Citrus Pests in Florida. (See Ns. 1556 and 1562 of this *Bulletin*).

A. A. Girault. **The Chalcidoid Parasites of the Coccid** *Kermes* **pubescens Bogue, with Descriptions of two new Genera and three new Species of** *Encyrtidae* **from Illinois.** — *The Canadian Entomologist*, Vol. XLIII, N. 5, pp. 168-178. London, May 1911.

1570

The writer describes two new genera and three new species of *Encyrtidae* found in Illinois as parasites of the common oak coccid (*Kermes pubescens* Bogue).
They are:
Cristatithorax gen. nov., *C. pulcher* sp. nov., *Aenasioidea* gen. nov., *A. latiscapus* sp. nov., and *Microterys speciosissimus* sp. nov.
Associated with them he has found certain insects of the families *Pterolamidae* (gen. *Pachyneuron* Walker) and *Eulophidae* (gen. *Girolasia* Foerster).

United States: Illinois

Insectivorous Birds of New of South Wales. — *The Agricultural Gazette of New South Wales*, Vol. XXII, Part I, pp. 36-38. Sydney, January 1911.

1571

The " Willie Wagtail " (*Rhipidura tricolor*) and the " Scissors Grinder " (*Sisura inquieta*) are described in this number. Both destroy a great many insects harmful to crops and to domestic animals in South Australia.

Australia: N. S. Wales

Birds destroying Locusts in South Africa. (See Abstr. 1521 of this *Bulletin*).

1572
S. Africa

David E. Fullaway. **The Use of Insecticides in Hawaii.** — *Hawaii Agricultural Experiment Station.* Press Bulletin N. 27, pp. 1-8. Honolulu, 1910.

1573

At the Hawaii Agricultural Experiment Station, a number of experiments were carried out on the use of insecticides and on practical remedies for common pests.
Attention is called to the subject of spraying for killing noxious weeds. Two compounds were used with some success: ferrous sulphate and arsenite of soda.
Arsenite of soda for weed-killing is prepared as follows: 2 lbs. of white arsenic and 6 lbs. of soda are dissolved in one gallon of

United States: Hawaii

water and boiled for fifteen minutes. Dilute one pint of this mixture with ten gallons of water, when it is ready for use.

Ferrous sulphate dissolves in water and is used at the rate of 3 lbs. of sulphate to 1 gallon of water.

1574

M. VASILIEV, A. A. POMASKIIE, P. C. GRINAKOWSKII. **Treatment of Maize Grains with Kerosene.** (Vliianie Kerosèna na Vskhojesti Kukurusi), — *Khosiaistvo (Husba ndry)*, VI G., No. 5, pp. 140-144. Kiev, 3 Fevral 1911.

Russia

If maize grains' are treated with kerosene solution for 24 hours the germinative power is not lessened in the least, provided that the temperature never drops below 25° C. during the 5 or 6 days following the sowing.

The odour of kerosene remains in the soil for about a week, and keeps away from the seedlings harmful larvae of *Pedinus femoralis, Gonocephalum intermedium, Coprophilus striatulus*, and adult ants and millipedes.

1575

J. PERRAUD. **Treatments against Codlin Moth Maggots** (Les traitments contre les Vers des fruits). — *Revue Agricole, Viticole et Horticole*, 9ᵐᵉ année, No. 100, pp. 81-85. Villefranche (Rhône), 25 Avril, 1911.

France

The larvae of the Codlin Moth (*Carpocapsa pomonella*) and of *C. funebrana* spoil two-thirds or three-quarters of the crop of apples and pears in France.

American growers are now able to put sound fruit on the French and other European markets, by treatments with arsenical salts, which have given excellent results in the United States in the control of the " fruit maggot " (1).

---

(1) For the life-history and control of the Codlin Moth, and for the treatment with Paris green as recommended long ago by Prof. F. M. Webster, of Purdue University, Indiana, see: ELEANOR A. ORMEROD, *A Manual of Injurious Insects.* 2d Ed. London, 1890, p. 289.

« For the Codlin Moth, trees should be sprayed for the first time just after the bloom has fallen. The second application should follow in about ten days or two weeks ; and the third about ten days after the second. This late application may safely be dispensed with, however, if the season be dry. »

See also: *Arsenite of Lead Spray for Codlin Moth.* The Journ. of the Dpt. of Agric. of South Australia, Jan. 1907, p. 349. « In spraying with arsenite of lead, the spray should be misted finely on to the trees ; the liquid should not run down the limbs and trunk ».   (*Ed.*).

The writer has been able, during the past three years, to destroy an average of from 85 to 95 % of these maggots by the use of arsenical mixtures with a lead and iron base, in plantations where the trees were of all ages and shapes.

The most effective treatment is that made immediately after the flowers have set. But as the hatching of the codlin moths sometimes spreads over a very long period, it is advisable to give a second treatment ten or twelve days after the first, when the fruit is about ⅓ or ½ in. long. The flowers and fruit only should be sprayed, and a bent jet should be used.

The writer has found the following mixtures effective against the fruit maggot and also against the Flea beetle:

1) Arsenate of lead mixture:

> Anhydrous arsenate of soda . . . 200 gr.
> Neutral acetate of lead . . . . . . 600 »
> Water . . . . 100 litres
> (Equivalent to 2 lbs.: 6 lbs.: 100 English galls.).

Dissolve the arsenate of soda and the acetate of lead separately in 10 litres of water each. Pour the solution of acetate of lead slowly into the solution of arsenate of soda (and not inversely), stirring the mixture. The mixture should not be made until just before it is to be used, and should then be added to the remainder of the 100 litres of water.

2) Arsenate of iron mixture:

> Anhydrous arsenate of soda . . . . 200 gr.
> Crystallised sulphate of iron . . . 400 »
> Water . . . . 100 litres
> (Equivalent to 2 lbs.: 4 lbs.: 100 English galls.).

Dissolve the arsenate of soda and the sulphate of iron separately in 10 litres of water each. Pour the iron sulphate solution slowly into the arsenate of soda solution (and not *inversely*), stirring the mixture. As before, the mixture must be made up to 100 litres with water, and should not be made until needed.

ED. ZACHAREWICZ. **The Vine Flea Beetle and its Treatment.** (L'Altise et son traitement). — *Le Progrès agricole et viticole*, 29ᵉ année, n. 19, pp. 600-601. Montpellier, 7 mai, 1911.

1576

In a vineyard of the Hérault where there was a strong invasion of vine flea beetles the writer made a treatment, at the period when

France: Hérault

in combination with the following mixture:

Copper sulphate	1.5 kg.
Soap powder	1.5 »
Water	50 litre

He dissolved 200 gr. of ortho-arsenate of soda in a vessel containing 15 litres of water; and 600 gr. of crystallised neutral acetate of lead in another recipient, containing 35 litres of water, pouring the latter into the first solution. (Equivalent to 15 lbs. sulphate of copper and 15 lbs. soap in 50 galls.; 2 lbs. arsenate of soda in 15 galls., and 6 lbs. acetate of lead in 35 galls.). When ready, this combination was added to the mixture, and the vines treated at once with a spray. At least 2 hectolitres of the mixture should be used per hectare (of 4000 plants) if the treatment is to be efficacious.

In another vineyard, Bordeaux mixture with 200 gr. of arsenate of soda added was used.

In both these vineyards the Flea Beetles had disappeared at the end of two days.

1577   **Spraying for Plum Curculio (Conotrachelus nenuphar, Herbst) on Peach.** (See Abstr.1535 of this *Bulletin*).

1578   S. ACCARDI. **Controlling Locusts.** (Esame critico dei mezzi di lotta consigliabili per la distruzione delle cavallette). — *Estr. dal Boll. della Cattedra amb. d'Agricoltura per la Prov. di Girgenti. L'Agricoltore Agrigentino*, p. 576. Girgenti, 1910.

The conclusions of this study are the following:

a) The eggs must be collected and destroyed when a workman can collect and destroy more than 1500 in a day.

Italy:
Sicily

b) The best method of controlling the young locusts (larvae and small nymphs) is that of the benzene lamp, which the writer has used on a large scale; it is very economical, and by its use all the locusts in a zone which has been invaded can be destroyed.

c) The method of using large tents for collecting the full grown nymphs has already been profitably employed; it is very efficacious, especially when it is adopted in conjunction with the lamps. The tents are prepared beforehand by the workmen who carry the lamps, and while the lamps destroy all the larvae and small nymphs the full grown nymphs, escaping from the flame, are collected in the tents and then put into sacks, where they are crushed.

d) The use of insecticides is not advisable, either from the economic or the technical point of view.

e) The use of arsenates and arsenites would be very costly, and is in any case prohibited in Italy by the Ministry of Agriculture and the Superior Board of Health.

f) The full grown locusts may be controlled by being collected early in the morning when they are torpid and easily captured, and afterwards crushed. This system may be used up to September 10th or 15th (1).

S. ACCARDI. **Controlling the Locust in Sicily.** (Prepariamoci alla lotta contro le cavallette in Sicilia). — *Cattedra ambulante di Agricoltura per la provincia di Girgenti*. Girgenti, marzo 1911.

1576

The writer asks the Government to take measures for organising the control of the locust in Sicily, and as a consequence of numerous experiments, strongly advises the use of the Swedish lamp:

1) The strong flame constitutes a very powerful remedy against the locusts during the whole of the month of April and a good part of May.

Italy:
Sicily

2) The vegetation, still very backward, is not interfered with by this flame.

3) Even the most powerful of these lamps do not consume more than a $1/4$ litre of benzene per hour, instead of 1 litre, as asserted by some.

The Anti-Locust Campaign in South Africa. (See Abstr. 1521 of this *Bulletin*).

1580

S. Africa

---

(1) Compare with J. S. HUNTER, *Studies in Grasshopper Control.* California Exp. Stat. Bull. n. 170, Sacramento, 1905. « During the first few weeks of the work against the grasshoppers the method of destruction employed was that of fire... Burning is to be recommended only where the pasture burned over is of no great value and where the grasshoppers are seriously threatening orchards or other cultivated fields. Care will always have to be taken that the fire is kept under perfect control. » *(Ed.)*.

Insects Injurious to Special Crops.

1581   F. H. CHITTENDEN. **Papers on Insects affecting Stored Products. The Lesser Grain-Borer.** — *U. S. Dpt. of Agriculture. Bureau of Entomology.* Bull. N. 96. P. III, pp. 29-46. Washington, March 31, 1911.

United
States

The results of the series of experiments performed with carbon disulphide and hydrocyanic-acid gas against the Lesser Grain Borer (*Rhizopertha dominica* Fab.) and incidentally against other insects, are of considerable value and show in brief the following facts :

That the lesser grain-borer possesses less resistant power to both gases than do most other stored-product insects.

That fumigations at low temperatures, and especially below 50° F. (10° C) are practically ineffective, unless an excessively large amount of bisulphide of carbon or of a cyanide be used; and that it is still more desirable that from 48 hours to 3 days be the length of exposure, in order to kill all insects in even tight enclosures.

Experiments show that even with 10 pounds of bisulphide of carbon to 1000 cubic feet of space in a tight receptacle only a very small percentage of grain insects were killed in an exposure of 24 hours and with a temperature of about 48° F. (about 9° C); and that even with 20 lbs. of carbon bisulphide to 1000 cubic feet, or 10 times what may be now accepted as a standard, only 75 per cent of the insects present were destroyed in a 24 hour exposure.

It may be safely assumed that under ordinary conditions in moderately high temperatures, between 65° and 75° F. (16° to 24° C) 1 ½ lbs of bisulphide of carbon to 1000 cubic feet of air space is insufficient even for 48 hours exposure; and that we may adopt as a general standard 2 lbs. to 1000 cubic feet for 48 hours, or more or until the odour of the gas becomes entirely dissipated.

The Larger Grain-Borer (*Dinaderus truncatus*, Horn) is now very common in Mexico and in Guatemala, and may easily get introduced into Texas and into the other Gulf-States. Measures must therefore be taken to prevent the introduction of this noxious Borer, so harmful both to wheat and maize. The larvae feed on the young grain, before it attains maturity.

Snout Beetle Destructive to Maize. — *The Rhodesia Agricultural Journal*, vol. VIII, N. 3, pp, 436-438. Salisbury, 1911.

1582

In 1909-1910 the "Snout Beetle", a Curculionid, did serious damage to maize in the early stages of growth about Salisbury, Rhodesia. Sometimes the crops were completely destroyed before they were 6 ins. high ; and in some cases even a second seeding was badly damaged.

Africa:
Rhodesia

The beetle which does the damage measures about 0.35 in. in length and is of a reddish-brown colour. It is the adult which does the damage, by eating the leaves.

Nothing is known of the life-history, as far as the writer is aware, but he believes the larva lives in the soil, feeding on roots. This insect seems to be peculiar to Rhodesia, where it has long been known; but it was not till last year that it appeared in amy numbers.

It is generally believed that Storks (*Ciconia alba*) eat quantities of snout beetles, so possibly their great abundance may be due to the small numbers of the migrant storks last season.

Cotton-Boll Weevil *Anthonomus grandis* (1) **in the United States.** — (See Abstr. 1403 in this *Bulletin*).

1583
United
States

LEWIS H. GOUGH. **The Froghopper during the Wet-Season of 1910 in Trinidad.** — *Department of Agriculture, Trinidad. Bulletin*, vol. X, N. 67, pp. 4-59. Trinidad, January-March, 1911.

1584

An account of the history of the froghopper-blight of the sugar-cane in Trinidad (2) compiled from published records, together with the description, results and symptoms of the disease, the life history of the insect, and preventive and remedial measures.

Trinidad

The leaves of blighted canes first become lighter in colour and then take on a yellowish tinge. Frequently they show longitudinal yellow spots or patches, $^1/_8$ to $^1/_4$ inch broad, several inches long. The tips of the leaves droop, and their edges roll inwards.

The lower leaves wither and if the disease is very severe the top of the cane also. Usually, however, the disease does not progress so far, and the plant recovers.

---

(1) See Abstr. 1035 of the *Bulletin* for March, 1911.   (*Ed.*).

(2) See p. 379 of *Bulletin* for Dec. 1910 ; Abstr. 352 of *Bulletin* for Jan. 1911; Abstr. 649 of *Bulletin* for Feb. 1911 and Abstr. 1558 of this *Bull.*

The most important natural enemy of the *Tomaspis* is a mould, the Green Muscardine (*Metarrhizum anisopliae* (1) Sorokin). Other foes are birds, toads, treefrogs, scorpions and spiders. The larvae of a dipterous fly attack its nymphal stages.

1585
Tonking

The " Borer " *(Xylotrechus quadrupes)* attacking Coffee in Tonking. — (See Abstr. 1338 of this *Bulletin*).

1586

F. Z. **Agriotes lineatus a Tomato Pest.** (Un insetto dannoso al pomodoro). — *Giornale di agricoltura della domenica*, anno XXI, No. 21, p. 199, 1 fig. Piacenza, 21 maggio 1911.

Italy

Serious damage has been caused in a large Tomato plantation by the larvae of *Agriotes lineatus*, which devours the stems of the young plants close to the crown and kills them; good rotations and careful tilling of the soil would be important factors in the control of this insect.

1587

F. H. CHITTENDEN. **The Asparagus Miner, Agromyza Simplex.** — *U. S. Dept. of Agric., Bureau of Entomology*. Circular N. 135, pp. 1-5. Washington, March 25, 1911.

United States: New England

The Asparagus Miner (*Agromyza simplex*) is widely spread in New England and causes a good deal of damage to asparagus. The larva eats the tissue of the stalk below the skin and pupates in the cavity produced; if a plant is attacked by several larvae at once it may die.

The remedy recommended is to let some asparagus plants near the beds grow freely to act as traps; at a fixed time, varying from place to place, they are destroyed with the pupae inside them.

1588

P. NOEL. **The Enemies of the Raspberry.** (Les ennemis du Framboisier). — *Bulletin du Laboratoire régional d'Entomologie agricole*, Deuxième trimestre du 1911 (Avril-Mai-Juin 1911) pp. 4-9. Rouen, 1911.

France

The Raspberry, originally growing in the colder countries, is now to be found almost everywhere, in Normandy, Brittany, in the

---

(1) See Abstr. 650 of *Bulletin* for Feb. 1911.

environs of Paris (where 5 thousand tons of raspberries are consumed yearly), in Burgundy, Lorraine, England, Germany, and especially the United States.

The writer gives a list of the enemies of this plant. Amongst them are 8 Coleoptera, 9 Hemiptera, 7 Hymenoptera, 80 Lepidoptera, 7 Diptera, 4 Acari and 1 cryptogamic disease.

G. MARTELLI. **The Caper-bush Fly,** *Ceratitis Savastani* (Descrizione e prime notizie di un nuovo Zoocecidide : *Ceratitis Savastani,* mosca del cappero. *Mem. Classe Sc., Accad. d. Zelanti,* vol. VII, 8 pp. e 4 figg., 1910). — *Rivista di patologia vegetale,* anno V, num. 1, p. 7. Pavia, 1 Aprile, 1911.

1589

Under the name of *Ceratitis Savastani,* the writer describes as new a Dipteron which attacks caper bushes in Sicily.

The female of this insect lays her eggs in the new buds, deforming them and preventing them from opening regularly.

Italy:
Sicily

J. FEYTAUD. **Vine-Pests: The Vine Hawk Moth, Deilephila Elpenor.** (Les ampélophages. Le Sphinx de la Vigne). — *Le Cultivateur français,* 5ᵉ année, N. 14, pp. 5-6. Lyon, 8 Avril 1911.

1590

The caterpillar of the Vine Hawk Moth (*Deilephila Elpenor*) (1) feeds on the leaves of the vine. It is polyphagous, and also devours various other plants: willow-herb, bedstraw, purple loose strife fuchsia, etc.

The Sphinx has some natural enemies, parasites which live in the larval state in the body of the caterpillar; the chief of these are Ichneumons, such as various *Anomalon, Cryptus, Ichneumon,* etc. It is also hunted by other enemies, for instance, *Doria concinnata, Micropalpus comptus, Haemithacea erythrostoma.*

France

A very good method of control is to gather and destroy the caterpillars, and the chrysalids should also be sought for in the soil during the winter.

Two other Hawk-Moths have been found on the vine: the Striped Sphinx (*Deilephila lineata*) and the Small Elephant Hawk-Moth (*D. Porcellus*), but they are much rarer than the preceding species.

---

(1) Known in England as the Large Elephant Hawk Moth (*Cheirocampa Elpenor*).   (*Ed.*).

1591   FRED JOHNSON. **Typhlocyba comes, var. coloradensis, the Grape Leaf-hopper, in the Lake Erie Valley: Papers on Deciduous Fruit Insects and Insecticides.** — *U. S. Dept. of Agr., Bur.` of Ent., Bull.* N. 97, Part I, pp. 1-12. Washington, March 31, 1911.

United
States

For several years past, injury by the grape leafhopper (*Typhlocyba comes* var. *coloradensis*) in the vineyards of the Lake Erie Valley has been confined to limited areas.

Its increase and dissemination during the season of 1910, however, should be a warning to the vineyardist to be prepared to combat it during the coming season, if the adults are at all numerous when the vines " leaf out " in the spring.

On account of the inability of the nymphs to escape from the underside of the grape leaves and because of the soft and unprotected condition of their bodies, the nymphal period is the most vulnerable stage of the insect.

Unfortunately, this is the stage at which the insects are the least conspicuous to the casual observer. For this reason, in vineyards where the adults are common in early spring, an examination of the underside of the foliage should be made during the early part of July. If the nymphs are at all numerous, a single thorough spray application of black leaf tobacco extract, applied to the underside of the leaves, before the pests develop wings, will reduce their number to such an extent that those remaining will neither seriously curtail the growth of the vine nor impair the quality of the fruit.

1592   G. LÜSTNER. **Hawthorn Aphis (*Aphis Crataegi*) injuring Appletrees.** (Die Weissdornblattlaus (*Aphis Crataegi* Kalt.) als Schädling des Apfelbaumes). — *Geisenheimer Mitteilungen über Obstsund Gartenbau,* XXVI Jahrg., N. 5, s. 71-72, Abb. 23. Geisenheim, Mai 1911.

Germany

The writer deals with the damage done to apple trees in various parts of Germany by *Aphis Crataegi* Kalt. a species which is much less common than the others which attack this tree.

This parasite causes the leaves of the shoots to turn a red brown colour, while the leaves that still remain green are covered with light greenish yellow spots. The leaves also become more or less curled resembling peach leaves attacked by *Exoascus deformans*.

This Aphis may be controlled by spraying with quassia and soft soap.

H. Kurdiumoff. **An Acarus Pest of Young Fruit Plantations in** **1593**
the South of Russia. (Opreski vanié Dereviev Sierno-Isviestkovoi
smiesiu protiv Tcerviezow Chicitovok) — *Khosiaistvo (Husban-*
dry), VI. G., N. 8, pp. 248-250. Kiev, 24 Jevralia 1911.

An Acarus, *Lepidosaphes Ulmi* L., is doing serious damage to
the young plantations in the South of Russia.

The young apple trees, when attacked by a very large number **Russia**
of these insects, wither and die when the winter is cold and wet.

Practically nothing has been done so far to control this scourge;
but the writer advises the use of the lime-sulphur mixture which
has already been tried in North America and has given very satisfactory results.

G. del Guercio. **A New Deformity of the Branches of the Olive** **1594**
Tree. (Un'altra nuova alterazione dei rami dell'olivo). — *Cronache*
agrarie, anno I, N. 2, pp. 39-45, 2 figg. Firenze, 31 marzo 1911.

The writer has found some special deformities, either separate
or grouped without order, and extending from the top to the base
of the branch, in the young branches of the olive trees of the year **Italy**
and those of new formation.

These deformities at first take the form of projections from
the round contour, and are very small and almost pointed; afterwards the centre rises and takes the form of a nipple, sometimes
hemispherical and sometimes oval, while the bark of the branch cracks
and the excrescences turn a reddish yellow.

According to M. del Guercio these deformities are caused by
the puncture and suction of the Scolytus of the Olive (*Phloeothrips*
Oleae Costa).

H. von Jhering. **The Insect Pests of the Fig Tree in Brazil and** **1595**
their Control. (Os insectos nocivos da Figueira e os meios de com-
batel-os). — *Chacaras e Quintaes*, vol. III, N. 2, pp. 9-11, 4 figg.
S. Paulo, Brasil, Fevereiro de 1911.

The writer enumerates the following insect pests of the Fig
tree in Brazil: **Brazil**

Azochis gripusalis Wlk., *Trachyderes thoracicus* Oliv., *Stenoma*
albella Zell., and a beetle of the family of Cerambicidae which has
not yet been specifically determined. These insects damage the
wood of the plant, and even the young branches and leaves.

The following method of control is recommended against *Azochis gripusalis:* insert a piece of copper wire into the gallery hollowed out by the insect, in order to kill it, and then close the opening with wax. If this does not give satisfactory results, a mixture of kerosene and water, creoline and water, or lysol at 5 % should be injected into the canal, and the opening afterwards closed with wax and a piece of wood.

But it is not sufficient to kill the larvae wich are found. New individuals must be prevented from developing, and for this purpose sprayings should be made with Paris Green (50 gr. in 6 litres of water), or with the well known mixture of copper sulphate and lime (1.5 parts of each of these two substances in 100 parts of water).

1596   **A New Disease of the Mulberry Tree.** (Una nuova malattia del Gelso). — *Il Villaggio,* anno 36, N. 1822, p. 254. Milano, 27 maggio 1911.

A new disease of the mulberry has recently appeared in the Trento district (Mori, Calliano, Besenello), causing considerable alarm amongst farmers.

Austria: The new buds appear scorched, and have dry spots which
Trentine gradually spread over the whole leaf and end by stopping the growth and causing the young branches to dry up.

As soon as the disease appeared, Prof. Orsi was sent to the infected district by the Trento Section of the Provincial Council of the Tyrol, and he found an Acarus, *Tetranychus pilosus,* on the diseased mulberry trees; it lives as a parasite on the leaves. The parasitism of this insect, however, does not appear to be manifested except on feeble plants, which are dying off and are much affected by changes of temperature. The young mulberries, sheltered from the weather, were only attacked to a very small extent by this disease ; and the same thing was observed amongst the wild mulberries, so that there is no reason for undue alarm.

1597   P. NOEL. **The Enemies of the Hazel Tree.** (Les ennemis du Noisetier). — *Bulletin du Laboratoire régional d'Entomologie agricole,* Deuxième trimestre du 1911 (Avril-Mai-Juin 1911), pp. 10-15. Rouen, 1911.

France There are numerous enemies of the hazel tree, besides the squirrel and nuthatch. The writer gives a list of them, which includes 25 Coleoptera, 11 Hemiptera, 1 Hymenoptera, 59 Lepidoptera, 6 Diptera, 6 Acari and a cryptogamic disease.

P. LESNE. **Destruction of Wood-Leopard Caterpillars in Cork-Oak**   1598
Forests. (La lutte contre les chenilles xylophages de la Zeuzère
(*Zeuzera pyrina* L.) dans les forêts de Chênes-lièges). — *C. R. de
l'Acad. des Sciences*, t. 152, N. 19, pp. 1269-1271. Paris,'
8 Mai 1911.

The Wood-Leopard Moth (*Zeuzera pyrina* L.) has for some years
been known to damage cork-oak trees in the forests of the mountains
of the Edough, department of Constantine ; it has lately appeared   Algeria
also in the department of Algiers. It causes withering of the head
of the tree, and sometimes kills young trees.

The writer has succeeded in destroying the larvae by means of
carbon disulphide ; at first he injected this into the main gallery
with a syringe, using 6 to 8 cc.; but he found it more convenient
to introduce the disulphide within long narrow gelatinous capsules ;
after the capsule is in position, the hole is blocked with clay ; in
twenty-four hours the moisture in the tunnel has dissolved the gelatine and set free the carbon disulphide. This method can be
used with success in the trunk and large branches, and does not
injure the tree. If small branches are attacked it is better to cut
them off : the wounds should be painted over with Stockholm tar,
to prevent the entrance of other wood-borers, particularly the
longicorn beetle *Cerambyx Mirbecki* Luc.

BARRY BAND. **Some Insect and Fungoid Diseases of the Funtumia**   1599
Rubber Tree in Tropical Africa. — *Tropical Life*, Vol. VII,
No. 5, pp. 92-94, May 1911.

Insect Pests.

The larvae of *Glyphodes ocellata* cause much damage to *Funtumia* in Ceylon, but only occasionally attack these trees in cultivation in Tropical Africa. The moth lays its small inconspicuous   Gold Coast
eggs on the leaves, and the caterpillars sometimes cause total de-   Uganda
foliation.   Ashanti

Bordeaux mixture has been found on the Gold Coast to be a
successful remedy. London purple and Paris green are useful and
inexpensive.

Girdling beetles (superfamily *Cerambycides*, subfamily *Lamiidae*
Jemmet) have done harm to *Funtumia* trees in Uganda, in Ashanti,
and the Gold Coast. These pests should be destroyed by hand,
and the larvae can be killed by injecting into their tunnels kerosene

or sanitary fluid, and then closing up the hole with a mixture of clay and tar.

Termites (*Termes gestroi*) get underneath the laticiferous system of the stem and make channels throughout the wood. Their nests should be dug up, or destroyed by kerosene or hot water.

Fungoid diseases are neither numerous nor very destructive. They consist of a stem disease due to *Nectria funtumiae*, a root disease (*Hymenochaete* probably *noxia* Petch and Massee) and a leaf fungus (*Meliola* sp.). In many plantations, the young *Funtumia* trees are invaded by mistletoe (*Loranthus* sp.). This should be cut away and burnt and the wounds tarred over.

1600

T. E. Snyder. **Damage to Telephone and Telegraph Poles by Wood-Boring Insects.** — *U. S. Department of Agriculture. Bureau of Entomology.* Circular N. 134, 8vo, pp. 6. Washington, March 7, 1911.

It has recently been ascertained that serious and extensive damage is being done in certain localities to standing poles by wood-boring insects.

United States

The principal injurious species is the Pole-borer (*Parandra brunnea* Fab.). The Pole-borer has seriously damaged as high as 10 to 15 per cent of the chestnut poles which have been set in the ground for from 10 to 12 years in lines in North Carolina, Virginia, West Virginia, Maryland and the District of Columbia. It has only recently been determined that it has also seriously damaged a considerable proportion of the arborvitae (*Thuya occidentalis*) telephone poles in part of a line in Illinois.

A very common injury is by white ants (*Termes flavipes*). In lines from 10 to 12 years old serious damage by these insects occurred in 15 per cent of the poles, and their work is often present, at least superficially, in 75 per cent of the poles under all conditions of site.

Injury by a giant roundheaded borer is sometimes found in chestnut poles. Longitudinal weathering cracks in chestnut poles are often widened, and other defects enlarged, by large black carpenter ants and other small black ants, which thus hasten decay.

Methods of treating poles superficially by brushing with various preservatives have proved to be temporarily efficient in keeping out wood-boring insects.

An effectual remedy is to impregnate the poles with creosote by either the open-tank or cylinder-pressure process.

to be levied upon each of the registered horticultural establishments, and the rest of the sum is to be reimbursed by a charge made for the phytopathological certificate and proportional to the market value of the produce for which it is granted.

Should it prove impossible, (owing to the carelessness of the horticultuists, or for any other reason) to meet the principal expenses in the manner set forth in the above paragraph, the Minister of Agriculture reserves to himself the right of fixing, as seems most equitable to him, the amount to be contributed by those who have neglected to furnish the necessary information, while the balance will be contributed by the certificate-holders.

The sum adjudged to each horticulturist will be collected as a legal tax and remitted by the Ministry of Agriculture even in the case of the partial or total refusal of a phytopathological certificate. These contributions are to be entered in the Budget as « revenue from various sources ».

The officials of the proposed Department are to be appointed by the Ministry of Agriculture. They are as follows: 1) Inspectors, heads of sections, whose duties are:

a) The direction and scientific control of all sections of the Department.

b) The supervision of the work entrusted to deputy-inspectors and superintendents, whom they must provide with detailed instructions and with any information they may require.

c) To make every enquiry necessary for the carrying out of culture-inspections and to grant, when due, certificates of inspection.

2) Temporary agents, or deputy-inspectors, whose province it will be to visit and examine such establishments as are indicated to them with the view of ascertaining whether the plantations are in good condition, in order that all trees etc. may be sent out free of injurious insects, and of any cryptogamic disease likely to spread in orchards, or fields.

Further, the work of the Department requires: temporary agents or over-seers, whose duty it is to assist the deputy inspectors in such duties as have been especially entrusted to them, regarding the horticultural establishments in their neighbourhood.

The officials of the Phytopathological Inspection Department undertake, within the limits fixed by the Order instituting the Department, and the the instructions of the Ministry of Agriculture, the inspection of all horticultural establishments and their branches which are assigned to them. When inspecting the above, the officials are to be provided with their letter of nomination, or the identification card, given them by the Ministry of Agriculture.

Deputy-inspectors and agents are to be proposed by the inspectors and reelected annually. Their number is variable, depending on the requirements of the service.

The conditions of the enrolment of deputy inspectors and of over-seers are determined by a ministerial decree.

The offices of Chief Inspector of the Entomological and of the Cryptogamic Sections are bestowed upon Directors of State Scientific Establishments (Stations of Agricultural Entomology or of Vegetable Pathology), named by the Minister of Agriculture, who will decide upon the necessary qualifications.

Every horticulturist who wishes his plantations inspected, must send in a notice before April 1st each year. He must write upon stamped paper, according to a prescribed form and undertake:

1) To obey implicitly the instructions given him by the Minister of Agriculture (or his representative) in all matters relating to phytopathological inspection.

2) To send with his request a precise description of the situation of the plantations to be inspected, and to give the approximate area of each.

3) Not to send out any plants which have not come from the plantations under supervision, without first informing the inspectors of the Department.

4) To enclose with each request for a Certificate of Phytopathological Inspection a certified copy agreeing with his books, of the consular invoice which accompanies the plants sent out.

5) To furnish the officials, whose work it is to inspect the Horticultural Establishments, with every possible facility for discharging this duty.

6) To pay, within the prescribed time, the amount which is incumbent upon him in regard to the expenses incurred by the Department, in accordance with the provisions of art. 9 of the Statute of Dec. 16, 1910 and with those of the present Order.

The State accepts no responsibility, either as regards itself or its agents, with regard to the horticulturists outside of the organisation or of the work of the above-mentioned Department (which is sanctioned by this Order) or as regards the validity in foreign countries of the certificates of inspection.

Should the officers of the Department consider that the horticulturists have not discharged their obligations, they shall, after due notice, acquaint the Minister of Agriculture with the fact, who will decide as to the right course to be pursued.

Other Animal Pests.

S. B. DOTEN and PETER FRANDSEN. **The Potato Eelworm.** — *Agricultural Experiment Station, University of Nevada.* Bulletin N. 75; pp. 7. Reno, Nevada, March, 1911.

Several carloads of potatoes from Nevada have been recently rejected by the California Inspection Service on account of the presence of the potato eelworm (*Heterodera radicicola*). As the majority of the loads were passed as sound, it may be concluded that the disease is not as yet widely spread in the State.

L. ZUNINI (Italian Consul). **The Campaign against Rabbits in Australia.** (L'Australia attuale. Usi, costumi, agricoltura, industria e commercio). — Pp. XII + 343. Torino, S. T. E. N., 1910.

It is well known that rabbits are the worst pest of both crops and stock in Australia; they are harmful to stock because of the enormous amount of pasture they eat. Among the methods for destroying rabbits the spreading of cultures of infectious diseases should be mentioned. This has given a death-rate of 95 % in some places; but there is danger of the same diseases infecting stock, particularly sheep.

The invasion of rabbits began in the east about Melbourne and Sydney and spread gradually westwards. Western Australia has till lately been free owing to the desert belt which separates it from the other States; but some have now succeded in crossing this.

In 1907 in Western Australia fences with wire netting began to be raised to protect the arable region and part of the grazing land. In 1910 these fences were nearly finished, having cost about £ 328 000. There are three principal lines: No. 1 runs right across the country from south to north, and is the nearest to the eastern frontier: it is 1135 miles long. No. 2 is 75 miles away from No. 1: it runs from the southern ocean for 724 miles, finally joining No. 1; this is to protect the arable district, as some rabbits have been found between Nos. 1 and 2. No. 3, 160 miles long, runs east rom the west coast and joins No. 2.

About two-thirds of the State are undefended, namely the Kimberley, Eastern, and Eucla Divisions.

The fences are composed of uprights about 6 ft. high and 12 to 18 ft. apart, sunk about 2 ft. in the ground; they support four rows of wire, at equal distances apart, the top one being barbed. Wirenetting of 1 ¼ inch mesh and tarred below is also fastened to the uprights, reaching 3 ft. high and 6 inches below the soil: it is doubtful whether this is deep enough.

Every five miles special traps are constructed to catch the rabbits which, on meeting the fence, run along it to try and find a way through.

Gates 13 ft. wide are placed at road-crossings, at least one to every 10 miles.

1603   CLEVE. **Destruction of Tse-tse Flies with Euphorbia Glue.** (Die Vernichtung der Tsetse-Fliegen mit Leim). — *Deutsche Kolonial Zeitung*, N. 9, p. 144. Berlin, 4 März, 1911.

German W. Africa

A species of Euphorbia producing a glue containing a very powerful poison grows along the Usambara railway-line. This glue gives marvellous results against tsetse fly. Donkeys of little value are smeared with the Euphorbia glue and driven to the drinking places along the country roads; the tsetse flies settle on them and get caught in the glue and die. In a week a donkey can destroy 1 500 to 2 000 flies per day at first but only 15 to 20 later on.

Legislation for the Protection of Plants.

1604   **A French Department for the Phytopathological Inspection of Horticultural Produce.** — *Journal Officiel de la République Française*, N. 130 Paris, 13 Mai, 1911.

France

The President of the French Republic has issued a Decree insituting a Department for the phytopathological inspection of horticultural produce. It shall consist of an Entomological and of a Cryptogamic section.

The expenses incurred by the above department shall form part of the budget of the Ministry of Agriculture, being defrayed as follows: the chief outlay is to be met by an annual tax of £ 1 (25 fr.)

INTERNATIONAL INSTITUTE OF AGRICULTURE

BULLETIN OF THE BUREAU OF

AGRICULTURAL INTELLIGENCE AND

OF PLANT-DISEASES ✍ ✍ ✍ ✍ ✍

2nd YEAR - NUMBER 6

JUNE 1911

ROME, 1911 — PRINTED AT THE INSTITUTE'S PRINTING OFFICE

CONTENTS

FIELD CROPS. — INDUSTRIAL CROPS. HORTICULTURE. — ARBORICULTURE.

LIVE-STOCK BREEDING. — AVICULTURE.
BEE-KEEPING. — SILK PRODUCTION. — FISHERIES AND GAME.
ANIMAL INDUSTRIES.

PLANT DISEASES,
NOXIOUS INSECTS AND OTHER PESTS.

THE INTERNATIONAL INSTITUTE OF AGRICULTURE

The International Institute of Agriculture was established under the International Treaty of June 7th, 1905, which was ratified by 40 Governments. Eight other Governments have since adhered to the Institute.

It is a Government Institution in which each Country is represented by delegates. The Institute is composed of a General Assembly and a Permanent Committee.

The Institute, confining its operations within an international sphere, shall:

a) Collect, study, and publish as promptly as possible statistical, technical, or economic information concerning farming, vegetable and animal products, the commerce in agricultural products, and the prices prevailing in the various markets;

b) Communicate to parties interested, also as promptly as possible, the above information;

c) Indicate the wages paid for farm work;

d) Make known the new diseases of vegetables which may appear in any part of the world, showing the territories infected, the progress of the diseases, and, if possible, the remedies which are effective;

e) Study questions concerning agricultural co-operation, insurance, and credit in all their aspects; collect and publish information which might be useful in the various countries for the organisation of works connected wrth agricultural co-operation, insurance and credit;

f) Submit to the approval of the Governments, if there is occasion for it, measures for the protection of the common interests of farmers and for the improvement of their conditions, after having utilized all the necessary sources of information, such as the wishes expressed by international or other agricultural congresses or by congresses of sciences applied to agriculture, or agricultural societies, academies, learned bodies, etc.

The Institute publishes: *a*) a Bulletin of Agricultural Statistics; *b*) a Bulletin of Agricultural Intelligence and Diseases of

Plants; c) a Bulletin of Economic and Social Intelligence; d) a Bulletin Bibliographique hebdomadaire (published every Saturday).

It has also published a volume on " The Organization of Agricultural S atistical Services in the Several Countries ", and a volume on " Statistics of Cultivated Areas and of Vegetable and Animal Production in the Adhering Countries " (an Inventory drawn up from documents published by Governments), and " Studies upon the present condition of Agricultural Association in certain countries ".

Officers of the Institute
and List of the Delegates to the Permanent Committee.

President: Marquess RAFFAELE CAPPELLI, *Delegate of Italy*

Vice-President : M. LOUIS-DOP, *Delegate of France.*

General Secretary: Prof. PASQUALE JANNACCONE.

Delegates of the adhering States to the Permanent Committee..

	States adhering to the Institute	Groups in which adhering States are classified	Names and Rank of the Delegates
1	Germany . . .	I	Dr. T. MUELLER, Privy Councillor.
2	Argentine Republic	I	His Excell. E. PORTELA, Minister plenipotentiary of the Argentine Republic to H. M. the King of Italy.
3	Austria	I	Chev. V. DE POZZI, Government Councillor.
4	Hungary	I	E. DE MIKLÓS DE MIKLÓSVÁR, Secretary of State for Agriculture. Member of the House of Magnates.
5	Belgium	IV	O. BOLLE.
6	Brazil	I	A. FIALHO, Ex-Deputy; Ex-President of the National Agricultural Society.
7	Bulgaria	III	D. RIZOFF, Minister plenipotentiary of Bulgaria to H. M. the King of Italy.
8	Chile	I	S. ALDUNATE BASCUÑAN, Minister plenipotentiary of Chile to H. M. the King of Italy.
9	China	I	OU-TSONG-LIEN, Minister plenipotentiary of China to H. M. the King of Italy.
10	Costa-Rica . . .	V	R. MONTEALEGRE, Minister plenipotentiary of Costa-Rica to H. M. the King of Italy.
11	Cuba	V	C. M. DE CESPEDES Y QUESADA, Minister plenipotentiary of Cuba to H. M. the King of Italy.

	States adhering to the Institute	Groups in which the adhering States are classified	Names and Rank of the Delegates
12	Denmark	IV	H. H. KONOW, Secretary to the Danish Legation to the Italian Government.
13	Ottoman Empire	I	Dr. MEHMED DJÉMIL BEY.
14	Egypt	II	B. CHIMIRRI, Delegate of Eritrea and Italian Somaliland.
15	Ecuador	V	LOUIS-DOP, Delegate of France.
16	Spain	I	ENRIQUE RODRIQUEZ DE CELIS, Agronomic Engineer.
17	United States . .	I	DAVID LUBIN.
18	Ethiopia	V	Prof. G. CUBONI, Director of the Station of Vegetal Pathology of Rome.
19	France	I	LOUIS-DOP, Vice-President of the Institute.
20	Algeria	V	LOUIS-DOP, Delegate of France.
21	Tunis	V	LOUIS-DOP, Delegate of France.
22	Great Britain and Ireland	I	H. G. DERING, Counsellor to the British Embassy to the Italian Government.
23	Australia	IV	H. G. DERING, Delegate of Great Britain and Ireland.
24	Canada	II	H. G. DERING, Delegate of Great Britain and Ireland.
25	British India . .	II	H. G. DERING, Delegate of Great Britain and Ireland.
26	New Zealand . .	IV	H. G. DERING, Delegate of Great Britain and Ireland.
27	Mauritius . . .	V	H. G. DERING, Delegate of Great Britain and Ireland.
28	Greece	IV	A. CARAPANOS, Chargé d'affaires of Greece to the Italian Government.
29	Italy	I	Marquess R. CAPPELLI, Vice-President of the Chamber of Deputies, President of the Institute.
30	Eritrea and Italian Somaliland	IV	B. CHIMIRRI, Member of Parliament.

States adhering to the Institute	Groups in which the adhering States are classified	Names and Rank of the Delegates
31 Japan	I	NAOTOSHI MARUMO, First Secretary to the Imperial Japanese Embassy to the Italian Government.
32 Luxemburg . . .	V	O. BOLLE, Delegate of Belgium.
33 Mexico	II	G. A. ESTEVA, Minister plenipotentiary of Mexico to H. M. the King of Italy.
34 Montenegro . . .	V	G. VOLPI, Director General of the Monopolies of the Kingdom.
35 Nicaragua. . . .	V	V. E. BIANCHI, Consul General of Nicaragua at Rome.
36 Norway.	IV	Dr. G. FJELSTAD, Agricultural proprietor.
37 Holland	IV	H. DE WEEDE, Minister plenipotentiary of Holland to H. M. the King of Italy.
38 Peru	V	Dr. M. M. MESONES.
39 Persia	IV	A. DEL GALLO, Marquess of ROCCAGIOVINE.
40 Portugal	IV	LUIZ FILIPPE DE CASTRO, Professor of the Agronomic Institute at Lisbon.
41 Roumania. . . .	I	G. C. NANO, Minister plenipotentiary of Roumania to H. M. the King of Italy.
42 Russia	I	His Excell. G. ZABIELLO, Counsellor of State, Consul General of Russia at Rome.
43 Salvador	V	A. BALLO, Acting Consul General of Salvador at Genoa.
44 San Marino . . .	V	His Excell. L. LUZZATTI, Minister of State of the Kingdom of Italy.
45 Servia	III	B. I. SOUBOTITCH, Secretary to the Servian Legation to the Italian Government.
46 Sweden	IV	G. V. T. DE STRÅLE, Counsellor to the Swedish Legation to the Italian Government.
47 Switzerland . . .	IV	J. B. PIODA, Minister plenipotentiary of Switzerland to H. M. the King of Italy.
48 Uruguay	V	REQUEÑA BERMUDEZ, Chargé d'affaires of Uruguay to the Italian Government.

AGRICULTURAL INTELLIGENCE

NB. The Intelligence contained in the present Bulletin has been taken exclusively from the books, periodicals, bulletins, and other publications which have reached the Library of the International Institute of Agriculture in Rome during the month of June 1911.

The Bureau assumes no responsibility with regard to the opinions and the results of experiments outlined in the Bulletin.

The Editor's notes are marked (Ed.).

Development of Agriculture in Different Countries — Scientific Institutions — Education in Agriculture and Forestry — Experimentation — Biography — History of Agriculture.

S. FUNEK AND L. SCHMITZ. **The Conditions of Agriculture in Germany.** 1605
(Betriebsverhältnisse der Deutschen Landwirtschaft). — *Bearbeitet unter Leistung der Betriebsabteilung der Deutschen Landwirtschafts-Gesellschaft.* Stuck VIII der Sammlung, in 8º, pp. 128 +X+ 178. + 16 Uebersichte, Berlin, Pare^y, 1910.

This volume contains two parts.

I. — *The present condition of agriculture and dairying in Havelland.*

The cultivation of the soil, stock-raising and the industries de- Germany pendant on it, manual labour, capital invested,, and distribution of wealth in this district are discussed.

The first chapter deals with: soil (geographical, geological, agricultural, analytical); climate; crops; cultivation and manuring; rotations; yields and prices.

The second describes draught animals and other farm live-stock, particularly milch-cows, and the breeding and produce of pigs and sheep.

The numerous statistics are illustrated on seven large plates.

The following are the average yields of the principal crops :

	Cwt per acre	qls per hectare
Wheat	20.4	25.7
Rye	17.—	21.3
Barley	20 —	25.—
Oats	21.3	26.6
Potatoes . . .	132.—	165.—
Mangolds . . .	477.6	592.—

II — *The agricultural conditions of the Eifel, particularly the districts of Schleiden, Daun, Prüm, and Bitburg.*

For this region the natural and social conditions of farming, methods used, conditions of labour (including animal labour), capital invested, and distribution of profits are examined.

The average yield of the principal crops are:

	Cwt. per acre	qls per hectare
Wheat	15.7	19.6
Rye	13.7	17.2
Wheat and Rye	14.5	18.2
Barley	15.7	19.6
Oats	14.8	18.6
Peas	10.6	13.3
Lentils	15.1	18.9
Haricot Beans	20.—	25.—
Vetches	16.3	20.4
Clover hay	47.9	59.9
Potatoes	99.3	124.2
Mangolds	298.7	373.4
Swedes	305.—	381.5
Kohl-rabi	174.—	217.5

The work includes a bibliography and nine plates of statistics.

1606   WEIN (Austrian Consul). **Agriculture in Crete.** — *Berichte der k. u. k. Oesterr - Ung. - Konsularämter: — Kreta-Kanea,* p.. 1-29. Wien, Mai 1911.

The general agricultural situation in Crete has remained unchanged for some years. The lack of communications, capital, agricultural credit, and irrigation form serious obstacles to improvement.

In general there is too much rain in winter, and too little in summer and autumn. Very little dung is used, and practically no artificials. The forests and fruit-trees are ruined by goats.

The Cretan government is now making great efforts to improve these unhappy conditions. The agricultural section has sent experts all over the island to instruct the peasants, to teach them to graft fruit-trees, and to distribute seeds, artificial manures, eggs of selected silkworms, etc.

Olive oil, wine, raisins, fruits, locust beans, gall-nuts, and almonds are exported from the island. The oil, which reaches 25 to 30 million *oke* (oka = 2.82 lbs). goes even to Sweden and Norway; but

Crete

it is not well prepared and soon turns rancid.   It is also used in several industries, such as soap-making.

The yield of tangerines, oranges, and citrons is good; the exports
of the last-named reach 500 000 fr. (£ 20 000) per annum.   The almonds go to Hamburg.   About 1000 tons of gall-nuts are produced;
they are mostly sent to Austria.   The locust-beans exported are worth
abont 1 500 000 fr. (£ 60 000).   Silk-worm cocoons are sent mostly
to Italy, some also to France.   Over 300 000 *oke* of sultanas are
exported annually to Italy, Austria Switzerland and Germany (1).

ZUCULIN (Italian Consul). **Agriculture in the Vilayet of Kossovo,**   **1607**
European Turkey. — *Bollettino del Ministero di Agric. Ind. e
Comm.*, Serie, B, Fasc. 7, pp. 253-256. Roma, 10 Aprile, 1911.

The very fertile soil of the whole vilayet of Kossovo is still cultivated by primitive methods, and does not produce enough for local
consumption, whereas there might be a considerable exportation.   Ottoman
Under proper cultivation, lands (*ci/lik*) near the railways would give   Empire :
heavy crops.   Kossovo

Some improvement has taken place lately owing to the facilities
accorded by the Government to farmers purchasing machines.   Permanent exhibitions are held ln the chief centres.   Every purchaser
is allowed five years for payment; the machines pay no duty on
entry, and are carted free on the railway.

An agricultural school will shortly be opened at Trabarova near
Uskub.

The principal crop is wheat; but its acreage is yearly decreasing
in favour of tabacco and poppies, which pay better.   The approx-

---

(1) The chief product of Crete is olive oil, used partly in the manufacture of soap (annual produce 3 155 000 kilos), for which there are 18 factories.
Other products are carob-beans (1 560 00 frs.). valonea, dry and fresh fruits,
wine (1 110 000 frs. exported to Malta) chestnuts, hides and leather, cheese,
silk. There are about 400 000 sheep and 120 000 goats, besides 10 000 horses,
40 000 asses, 70 000 oxen, and 20 000 pigs. The chiefs exports were olive oil
valued £ 238 972 ; carob-beans £ 54 739; soap £ 47 324; raisins £ 42 291; wine
£ 24 162; valonea £ 4 608; sheep and goat skins £ 9 905.

The Statesman's Yearbook for 1911. p. 1288.   (*Ed.*)

imate yields of the crops in the vilayet are given below ; it should be
noted that the statistics are not very exact.

Wheat	100 000	tons
Rye	80 000	»
Barley	50 000	»
Grapes	50 000	»
Maize	40 600	»
Oats	30 000	»
Beans	25 000	»
Tobacco	5 000	»
Rice	4 000	»
Poppies	3 000	»
Hemp	2 000	»
Opium	20	»

Stock-breeding might be greatly extended, considering the excellence of the pastures and the large foreign demand. But at present
the export does not exceed about 70 000 head.

1608   JESZENSKY (Austrian Consul). **Agriculture in the Vilayet of Adria-
nople, European Turkey.** — *Berichte der k. k. Oesterr. - Ung.
Konsularämter,* J. 1911. - *Türkei - Adrianopel,* pp. 1-5. Wien,
April, 1911.

Agriculture in the vilayet of Adrianople suffers from the very irregular rainfall: some years it is very heavy; in others there are severe
droughts; in either case the cereal crops are ruined.

Ottoman
Empire :
Adrianople

Tobacco-growing has for some time been increasing; the yield is
about 4 000 000 k. (4 000 tons) of excellent tobacco; about half is
exported.

Wine-production used to be very profitable, but it is continually
decreasing owing to importation of foreign alcohol.

On the other hand, silk-worm rearing has attained great importance, owing to the initiative of the Ottoman National Debt. In 1910
the yield was 1⅓ million kilogs of cocoons; the silk is exported raw
or wound.

Cattle, buffaloes, horses, asses, goats and sheep are bred; only mutton is exported; the other stock are not enough for local requirements,
so that some come in from Bulgaria.

In 1910 measures were begun for the protection of the forests,
which had been partly destroyed.

Besides tobacco, silk and sheep, 80 wagons of eggs are sent to
Germany, sheep and goat skins to Trieste, fox and hare skins to Hamburg, and 300 000 kg. (300 tons) of wool to Servia and Bulgaria

The Trade and Agricultural Conditions of Arabistan, Persia — *The*   **1609**
G·og·aphical Journal - London - March 1911.

Potentially Arabistan is one of the richest provinces of Persia.
Apart from the transit trade, however, commerce makes little
progress, for the population is too scanty and apathetic to develop   **Persia:**
the great agricultural resources of the country, although thousands   **Arabistan**
of acres might be irrigated on the Hindijan and Jarraki rivers and in
the neighbourhood of Mohammerah.

The Arabs of the desert pursue a nomadic life, subsisting on the
produce of their flocks and on the wheat crops when the season is
favourable—an event which occurs about thrice in ten years. But
wherever irrigation is possible, and dates and rice can be grown,
a large permanently settled population is usually to be found.

A. Mc. KERRAL. — **Agricultural Survey of the Sagaing District.** —   **1610**
Dept. of Agric., Burma. Agricultural Surveys, N. 2, Sagaing
District, 4to, Pp. 39 (1-32), Rangoon, Burma, 1911.

The Sagaing District consists of a somewhat irregular area of
about 1860 square miles (4800 square kilometres), along the Irrawaddy river.

The annual rainfall is from 26 to 33 in. (660 to 838 mm.), with   **British India:**
maxima in May and September.   **Burma**

Water for irrigation is obtained from 1) rain-water tanks; 2)
dammed streams 3) reservoirs for catching the flood-waters of the
large rivers, and 4) direct from some of the rivers.

Cultivation of the land is usually begun before the rains set in,
any dung used being applied previously; the land is then left till it
begins to dry after the rains. On heavy land it is then ploughed,
but on light land only harrowed: two harrowings are generally given,
the first with a seven-toothed instrument, the second with a heavier
three-toothed one which works deeper; where a very fine tilth is
required, as for tobacco, a log of wood is used.

The principal *Field-Crops* are:

Paddy (*Oryza sativa*): numerous varieties; 60 000 acres (24 000
hectares.

Wheat (*Triticum sativum*): grown for a century at Ava, and has
now spread to other parts. Average crop 6 or 7 baskets per acre.

« Jowar » or Great-Millet (*Sorghum vulgare*): 115 000 acres
(46 000 ha).

Maize (*Zea-Mays*): grown on the islands of the Irrawaddy, sometimes mixed with « Pe-gya »: yield on good land 5 000 cobs per acre (12 000 per hectare).

« Pe-gyi » and « pe-pa-zun » (*Dolichos Lablab*), and « pe-bizat » (*D. biflorus*): 8 200 acres (3300 hectares).

« Pe-myit » (*Psophocarpus tetragonolobus*): grown near Mandalay·

« Pe-gya » (*Phaseolus lunatus*): 29,000 acres (11,600 hectares); yield up to 20 baskets per acre.

« Pe-yin » (*Ph. Calcaratus*): 1200 acres (480 ha.); yield about 10 baskets.

Gram (*Ph. Mungo* and vars.): 20 000 ac. (8 000 ha.): 5 to 6 baskets per acre per ha.

« Pe-lun » Cow-pea (*Vigna Catjang*): 2,300 ac. (920 ha.).

« Kalape » (*Cicer Arietinum*): 12 000 ac. (4 800 ha.): 6 to 15 baskets.

Earthnut (*Arachis hypogœa*): 8 000 ac. (3 200 ha.): 35 baskets per acre.

Cotton (*Gossypium neglectum verum*): grown pretty generally; there are two varieties — « wa-pyn » or « wa-gale » with white fibre, and « wa-ni » with brown fibre, 52 000 ac. (21 000 ha.); 120 « viss » of unginned seed per acre.

Deccan Hemp (*Hibiscus Cannabinus*), and other species of the genus, are grown to some extent for their fibre.

Tobacco (*Nicotiana Tabacum*); chiefly grown on islands in the river near Kyaukyit: 2 400 ac. (1000 ha.).

« Brinjals » or « kayan » the Egg-plant (*Solanum Melongena*) and Tomato (*Lycopersicum esculentnm*): the latter gives two crops in the year.

Chillies (*Capsicum annuum*): 2500 ac. (1000 ha.): yield, 120 «viss » per acre (440 kg. per ha.).

Cucurbitaceous plants: — Gourds, Melons, Pumpkins, and Cucumbers.

Sesame (*Sesamum indicum*): one of the most important crops: yield, 4 to 10 baskets per acre,

Sweet Potato (*Ipomœa Batatas*): yield, about 2000 « viss » per acre (7000 kg. per ha.).

Garden Cultivation is only practised near the large towns; except with Plantains and Betel-Vines it is never systematic. The fruits include seven species or varieties of Citrus, Betel-Nut, Plantain, Guava, Custard-Apples, Mango, Pomegranate, Grapes, Pine-Apple,

The Toddy Palm (*Borassus flabellifer*) is found all over the district, particularly on waste land; the preparation of jaggery (a kind of sugar) and various other products gives rise to a considerable industry in some places.

Livestock. — In the year ended June 30th 1909 the numbers of stock were as follows:

Bulls and Bullocks	69 235
Cows	79 609
Male Buffaloes	1 718
Female Buffaloes	1 952
Calves	81 859
Buffalo Calves	2 135
Sheep	9 087
Goats	3 177
Horses and Ponies	1 820

LOTZ (Austrian Consul). **Agricultural Progress in Siam.** — *Berichte der k. k. Oesterr. Ung. u. Konsularämter* - Asien-Siam-Bangkok, pp, 1-10 Wien. Mai 1910.

1611

The Government of Siam has begun to repair the irrigation and drainage works which had been allowed to fall to ruins. Numerous attempts at jute cultivation have been made, but so far without much result. In 1910 an agricultural exhibition was held, and another is planned for 1911. The exports are given in *ticals* under the following headings (a *tical* is about 1s. 7d.).

Siam

Rice	93 948 200	ticals
Teak	7 903 225	»
Various	8 497 396	»

There is a general crisis in the rice-milling industry. The export of teak has diminished, owing to increased internal consumption. The effects of the disastrous deforestations of previous years are beginning to be felt,; the Government has made stringent regulations against deforestation.

LEOPOLDO ZUNINI (Italian Consul). **The Australia of To-day. Customs and Usages. Agriculture, Industry and Commerce.** — (L'Australia Attuale: Usi e Costumi; Agricoltura, Industria e Commercio.) in 8º, pp. XII + 343, con 83 incisioni, Torino: S. T. E. N. 1910.

1612

Mr. Zunini was instructed by the Italian Emigration Office to study the question of making Italian agricultural settlements in Western Australia, and for this purpose to come to an understanding

Australia

with the local government. The volume before us gives the report of his work, in which three delegates were associated with him.

By the Land Act of 1898 Western Australia was formed into six great divisions: the Kimberley, the North-West, the Western, the Eastern, the South Western, and the Eucla.

Kimberley Division — Area: 144 000 sq. miles (372 672 sq. km. Mean temperature 83° Fahr. (28.3° C.) Annual average of rain: 24 inches (609 mm.) Though very hot the climate is not unhealthy. The soil, to a large extent alluvial, is excellent, and if irrigated bears all kinds of tropical vegetation. Cattle raising is very successful.

North-West Division. — 81 000 sq. miles (209 628 sq. km.) Mean temperature 76° Fahr.. (24.4° C.) Rainfall 13 inches (330 mm). There is great heat in summer, but the climate is very healthy. The country consists of a succession of grassy plains intersected by rocky hills and covered in many parts by *Triodia irritans* - the bush which is almost the sole vegetation of the central Australian desert. It is said to be well adapted for sheep raising - 2 per acre (5 per hectare) in the most fertile districts.

Western Division. — Area: 133 000 sq. miles (344 204 sq. km.) consisting almost entirely of boundless plains. Mean temperature: 72° Fahr. (22.2° C.). Rainfall: 8 inches (203 mm.) Climate hot, but healthy. There is not much water, except near the chief rivers, (the Murchison and Gascoyne), where it is easily found not far from the surface.

Eastern Division. — Area: 491 920 sq. miles (1 273 088 sq. km.) including all the interior of Western Australia. Although in some parts the soil is fertile, the want of water makes all regular cultivation impossible. There is however some good pasture land.

South Western Division. — Area : 77 850 sq. miles (201 475 sq. km.). The mean temperature varies from 66° Fahr. (18.8° C.) in the North to 59° Fahr. (15° C.) in the South. The rainfall is very regular, varying from 10 inches (254 mm.) at certain points of the North East to 53 inches (1346 mm.) in the South West : general average 22 inches (558 mm.).

This division includes the greater part of the zone of temperate climate, which stretches along the shore of the Indian Ocean to the South of the river Murchison, and to a certain extent, along that of the South Pacific.

The south west extremity is covered with vast and very dense forests. All European produce flourishes on the soil, which is very fertile, the light friable kind being considered the best. Here and there large stretches of sand are found, but even these, if properly irrigated, give a satisfactory return.

Eucla Division. — Area : 48 150 sq. miles (124 612 sq. km.). Mean temperature : 61 Fahr. (16.1° C.) Rainfall : 14 inches (355 mm.) Except a few sheep raising stations, this division is uninhabited. To the east of Cape Culver there is practically no water ; to the west of it, there is sufficient, but the soil is not very fertile. To the north there is a table land affording excellent grazing ground, though here too water is scarce.

These were the divisions of Western Australia up to last year. But certain changes have been made by an Act of Parliament just passed. The Western and North West Divisions are now united. The limits of the South Western Division (agricultural zone) have been pushed further to the East as far as the «rabbit-proof fence» (1). About a third of the Eastern Division has been made into a new district called the Central Division ; it includes the central gold-fields and Kalgoorlie is the Capital.

The South Western Division is practically almost entirely reserved for the so-called « settlers »: that is, for agriculturists who acquire land and settle there. The other divisions which, because of the tropical climate or the want of water, are specially, or solely, adapted for grazing, are chiefly inhabited by « squatters »: that is, cattle raisers, who do not acquire land, but hold it on long leases.

Land for cultivation can only be in those zones and districts which are expressly declared from time to time *open to agriculture.*

The conditions of rent are fixed by the « Land Act » and vary greatly in the different divisions. Thus, in the North West and Western Divisions the price is 10 shillings per 1000 acres (12.50 frcs per 404 hectares), the minimum amount being 20 000 acres (8080 hectares) : in the Eucla Division it is 5 shillings per 1000 acres (6.25 frcs. per 404 hectares); minimum amount 20 000 acres (8080 hectares). In the Eastern Division not less than 20 000 acres (8080 hectares) must be taken at half a crown for every 1000 acres, (3.125 frcs for 404 hectares) during the first seven years ; after that the price is doubled.

In Kimberley the minimum lot varies from 50 000 to 20 000 acres (20 200 to 8080 hectares) according to circumstances, the price being 10 shillings (12.50 frcs.) per lot. In the South Western Division the minimum lot is 3000 acres (1212 hectares), costing one pound or 10 shillings (25 or 12.50 frcs.) according to the situation.

The settlers' first work is to clear the ground of forest. Owing to the great distances, the difficulty of transport etc., the wood cannot

---

(1) See this *Bulletin*, Abstr. 1602, May, 1911. (*Ed.*).

be utilised ; it is therefore burnt on the spot.   For this purpose the
smaller trees are felled, and their stumps and roots pulled up, while
the larger ones are « ringbarked » ; that is a ring of bark is removed
from the trunk, and in a short time the tree withers, and is then easily
burnt.   The latter process is often adopted for all the trees when
the land is to be used for grazing.   The large quantity of water
absorbed by the trees, and especially by the Eucalyptus, is liberated
when they are dead, and the grass which was at first scanty and dry
then grows luxuriantly.   In the south only the smallest trees are
felled; the large ones, which grow to an immense size, are left
standing, after being « ringbarked ».   The land is then cultivated,
and the strange sight is seen of abundant crops growing in the
midst of gigantic white skeletons of trees.   The burnt wood serves
at least one purpose: its ashes are an excellent fertiliser.

   Among other differences in agricultural methods it may be noted
that in Western Australia it is considered indispensable to let the land
lie fallow every two years.

   The following table gives the yield in wheat of Western Australia
as compared with that of the other parts of the Commonwealth.

| | Average 1903-04 | | Ten year average. Average 1893-94, 1904 05 | |
	bush. per acre	hectol. per ha.	bush. per acre	hectol. per ha.
W. Australia . . .	13.60	12.23	11.03	9.92
Queensland	17.75	15.96	16.39	14.74
S. Australia	7.72	6.94	4.52	4.06
Victoria	14.49	13.03	7.23	6.50
N. S. Wales	17.51	15.75	9.85	8.86
Australasia	—	—	8.25	7.42

   The average yield of wheat in the neighbourhood of Northam
is 11 bushels per acre (9.89 hectol. per hectare).   In certain parts
of the district 20.25 and even 30 bushels (the latter very rarely)
are obtained par acre. (1)

   In the « gullies » near Perth, the soil, which is alluvial, is very
fertile and suitable for fruit-cultivation.   Harvey River is one of
the chief centres for the orange industry: the « Washington Navel »,
a very choice fruit which was brought from California, is the variety
cultivated.   It is sometimes very prolific.

_____

(1) 1 bush. = 36.347 litres = 0. 36347 hectolitres.

SPEMANN. **Agricultural Conditions in Samoa.** (Die Landwirtsch.   **1613**
Verhältnisse auf Samoa.) *Mitteilungen der Deutschen Landwirt-*
schafts. Gesellsch. XXVI J. N. 13 *pp.* 156-162 Berlin 25 März
1911 (1).

The climate of Samoa is tropical, the average temperature being
25°.7 C. The average annual rainfall is from 3419 mm. to 6000 mm.
in 196 wet days. The climate is, on the whole, healthy. The soil is
volcanic, ferruginous and poor in potash.   **Samoa**

As far as the soil and climate are concerned, all tropical cultivations are possible, but those which succeed best and are most saleable, are cacao, coco nuts and india rubber from *Hevea brasiliensis* and
Ficus elastica. After these come bananas and pine-apples.

The island produces some excellent species of wood for building
called *mamala* and *malili.* It is also suitable for raising cattle, most
of which are descended from Herefordshire stock from New Zealand.

Horse-breeding can be carried out successfully on a small scale,
good stud animals (mostly of English blood) are imported from New
Zealand and Australia. Pigs also stand the climate well.

The Agricultural Situation in New Caledonia. (Situation Agricole   **1614**
de la Nouvelle Calédonie). *Bulletin de l'Office Colonial,* N. 41
pp. 166-172. Melun. Mai 1911.

The future of New Caledonia depends largely upon the success of
its agricultural and industrial undertakings. The increased value of
the exports of 1910 is due to the higher market price of local products
such as *trocas,* coprah, india-rubber and even coffee.   **N. Caledonia**

There are two factories for preserving meat, one at Ouaco and the
other at Noumea. Breeders are obliged to supply cattle regularly
and of good quality.

The factories for making sugar, pea-nut-oil, coprah, and tapioca
have already a considerable output, and others could be started for
the extraction of castor-oil and cotton oil.

The neighbourhood of Noumea could support sufficient milch-
cows to make a butter factory profitable.

302,000 kilos (664 400 lbs) of hides were exported; these could
well have been tanned on the spot, as tanning substances are plentiful in the country. At Noumea there is a factory for steam-dry-
ing and silos for drying and preserving all kinds of seeds and of preparing coffee and cotton.

_____

(1) See this Bulletin for Dec. 1910 p. 191.

1615   SMITH. **The Conditions of Agriculture in Papua.** Papua. *Deutsche ·*
     Colonialzeitung, N. 20, S. 336-337. Berlin, 20 Mai 1911.

**Territory
of Papua**
:

Papua (formerly known as British New Guinea) generally enjoys
two good rainy seasons. The British part of the island is rich in minerals. The colony exports about £ 7 500 worth of coprah and £ 6 300
of sandalwood, besides gold and pearls.

Several experimental stations have been founded by the British
government. So far 7700 acres have been brought under cultivation;
of these 5200 are under cocoanuts, 4200 under rubber, and the
rest under sisal hemp, coffee, etc. The natural cocoanut groves occupy at least 350 000 acres. At present nothing has been done to utilize the resources of guttapercha. (1)

1616   **Budget of the United States Department of Agriculture for** 1911-12.
     — *The Journal of the Board of Agriculture*, N. 2, pp. 166-167.
London, May 1911.

**United
States**

The Budget of the United States Department of Agriculture
for the year ending June 30th, 1912, which was approved on March
4th, 1911, amounts to £. 3 520 800 (Francs 87 890 200). The expenditure is two and a half times that sanctioned for the year 1905-06,
and more than five times the amount for 1895-6.

The principal increase has taken place in the forest service,
including experiments in connection with forest fires, lumbering,
timber testing and preserving, the afforestation of treeless regions,
the maintenance of nurseries, collection of seed, planting etc.

Other work in connection with the national forests includes
construction and maintenance of roads, bridges, telephone lines,
and other permanent improvements.

---

(1) In Papua, 300 000 acres of land have been leased, principally by
planters, and plantation work has commenced with energy, the principal cultures being cocoanuts, rubber, sisal hemp, coffee, and Murva fibre. Cotton,
vanilla, kapok, cocoa, tapioca, cinnamon, tea, and tobacco are also being cultivated. On hundreds of square miles indigenous sago is growing and there
are at least 250 000 acres covered with native-owned cocoanut trees.

The forests contain valuable timbers, in most cases easily accessible by
river. Sandal-wood, ebony, gums, rattans, and other forest products are found·
The Stateman's Yearbook for 1911, p. 328.   (*Ed.*).

The amount allotted to the Bureau of Plant Industry includes about £. 100,000 (2,500,000 francs) for the investigation and control of plant diseases. Provision is also made for the improvement of grazing lands and the encouragement of improved methods of farm management, for dry farming experiments and the utilisation of reclaimed land, for the investigations and improvement of various crops, including breeding, seed testing, methods of production and sale and for the purchase and distribution of valuable plants and seeds.

The chief items in the expenditure sanctioned for the Office of Experiment Stations are for the establishment of stations and contributions towards the maintenance of experiment stations, including some administrative expenses for nutrition investigations, and for irrigation and drainage investigations.

The chief expenses of the Bureau of Animal Industry are for the inspection and quarantine of animals, eradication of southern cattle tick, dairying experiments, animal husbandry experiments, and cooperative experiments in breeding and feeding.

BENNETT. **Crops and Farm Products in 1910 in the United States. —**   1617
The Board of Trade Journal, N. 750, p. 100, London, April 13, 1911.

The value of the crops and farm products (including livestock sold, meat, etc.) of the United States in 1910 has been officially estimated at about £ 1 800 000 000 (£ = 25 francs 25 cent.). As compared with £ 1 752 000 000 in the previous year. The principal contributor to this huge total is Indian corn, which is put down at 3 125 713 000 bushels, (bushel = 35.102 litres) valued at not less than £ 304 000 000 as against 2 772 376 000 bushels and £ 330 546 400 in 1909. Cotton comes next with an estimated value of £ 140 000 000 as compared with £ 158 400 000 in 1909; hay is valued at £ 125 000 000 as against £ 137 869 000 in the previous year; and wheat is fourth at £ 124 000 000 as against £ 146 009 200 The yield of oats was over 1 000 000 000 bushels.

In consequence of the fall in prices, however, the total value of the cereal crops was less than in 1909, although the volume of the harvest has never been equalled.

The exportation of wheat was on a comparatively small scale, partly on account of abundant harvests elsewhere, but very greatly owing to the increased home demand for the feeding of a much larger population and of stock.

United
States

1618   HEARN (Brit. Cons. Gen.). **The Development of Agriculture in California. Sheep raising under Electrical Influence.** — *Diplomatic
and Consular Repor's*, N. 4650, pp. 1-46. London, May, 1911.

The investigations of the last few years have resulted in the
discovery of several wheats new to California. « Chul » is the leading
new variety, and it is believed that it will enable the wheat growers
of the State to increase their output. The irrigation investigation
branch of the Department of Agriculture, in co-operation with the
office of the State Engineer and the University of California, is beginning experiments in the production of wheat on irrigated land.

Much of the barley produced in California is highly esteemed for
brewing purposes on account of its light colour. The production of
beet sugar is steadily increasing, although it is understood that the
Sugar Trust have interests which enable them to control most, if not
all, the sugar beet factories in California. The Lima bean industry
is so profitable that it is extending from Santa Barbara and Ventura
Counties north and south along the coast. Beans of all commercial
varieties are raised in large quantities along the lower Sacramento and
San Joaquin Rivers.

The State Forester shows that the largest yield of Eucalyptus
discovered by his department was 57 820 board feet to the acre on
a plantation planted 32 years ago.

The canned fruit business of 1910 proved a disappointing one
for packers and dealers. The following table shows the quantity
and variety of fresh deciduous fruits forwarded from California by
rail in 1908 and 1910 (1).

		1908	1910
Apricots	Car-loads	232	290
Cherries.	»	208	250
Grapes	»	3816	4948
Peaches.	»	1980	2518
Pears	»	2702	2361
Plums	»	1763	1552
Various	»	2216	2153

(margin) United
States:
California

---

(1) The export of fresh fruits from California by rail amounted in 1909
to 15 265 car-loads (each about 10 tons), including 2599 car-loads of peaches,
2638 of pears, 1 527 of plums and prunes, and 5875 of grapes. In the year
ending Oct. 31st. 1909, 40 000 car-loads of oranges and lemons were sent from
Southern California. The dry-wine production in 1909 was about 25 million
gallons; sweet wine about 16 million.

The Staterman's Yearbook for 1911, p. 410.   (*Ed.*).

The quantity and variety of California dried fruits produced in the last three years is given below :

		1908	1910
Apples	Tons	3 350	3 000
Apricots	»	19 000	15 250
Figs	»	2 900	3 775
Peaches	»	23 000	25 000
Prunes	»	28 500	37 000
Raisins	»	65 000	62 000
Various	»	3 000	1 750

The average crop of almonds is 2200 tons, the walnut crop produced in 1910 was about 8500 tons, which is a good average for the last few years. Within the last few years it is known that the production of olives has largely increased in Fresno County, the number of trees having increased from 35 000 in 1899 to 100 000 at the present time.

The bearing acreage of oranges and lemons in Central California is each year being augmented, Owing to the more favourable commercial conditions the production in 1910 is not considered as being too great and appearances indicate that the long expected adjustment of the wine market is near at hand.

Fruit packing in the San Joaquin valley has been greatly facilitated by the introduction of a new type of packing-table: this is circular and rotary with a space in the centre ; outside it stand three or four sorters, who place the fruit on it; the packer is in the centre, and by turning the table round, he can rapidly reach any fruit he requires. Experiments in cotton growing are being conducted on the Pacific Coast from the Imperial Valley in southern California to Klamath Falls in the State of Oregon.

Encouraging reports as to the growth of cotton are being received from districts in the north where it was thought impossible to grow the crop.

Californian grape growers have apparently solved the question of successfully raising Persian grapes having the advantage over the American and European grapes.

That the soil and climate in the vicinity of Biggs, in Butte County, California, is peculiarly adapted to the growing of rice, has been fully proved by the experiments carried on there during the past three years with about 50 varieties.

Experiments have proved that electricity will more than double the lamb crop and greatly increases the yield of wool. A flock of 2 000 sheep was divided, one half being placed in a field under the power wires of the Great Western Power Company while the, other was removed from electric influences. In the field under the electric power line the production of lambs averaged a fraction over two lambs to each ewe. In the adjoining field where electrical influence was lacking the lamb average was less than one to each ewe. Similar differences were noted in the yield of wool from the sheep in the different fields ; the fleeces from the sheep in the electrically-influenced field proved 20 per cent. heavier.

1619   **The Agricultural Resources of Santo Domingo.** Hayti and Santo Domingo - *Diplomatic and Consular Reports - Annual Series* N°. 4638, pp. 36 (12-36) London, May 1911.

For many years one of the principal sources of wealth in Santo Domingo has been the timber industry. The mountain sides are covered

Santo   with great forests containing mahogany, *lignum vitae* (1), logwood (2)
Domingo   and other valuable hard woods and dye woods.
 The greater part of the soil lies fallow or is devoted to grazing.
 There are very few ploughs in Santo Domingo, except of the most rudimentary description, nor has the want of them been felt. Almost everywhere the earth responds generously to the slightest scratch of the hoe. The native agriculturist, on the little patch of tilled ground or « conuco » surrounding his cabin, raises with little or no labour the plantains, maize, yams, etc. required for his own sustenance, but not for the market. Consequently vegetables are very scarce; even onions, potatoes, beans, cabbages, etc. are imported, and all other kinds are practically unknown save when imported in tins.
 The position formerly held by the grazing industry explains the peculiar tenure by which much of the land of the Republic is still held. Each tract of land originally belonged to one proprietor and descended undivided among his heirs for generations, until it was owned in common by many individuals. Custom authorised any one of the co-own-

---

(1) Lignum vitae = *Guaiacum officinale.* A small tropical American tree. The greenish-brown, hard, heavy wood is used for pulleys, bearings in machinery, tenpin-balls, etc. From the stem (spontaneously or by incision) exudes the Guajacum resin.   (*Ed.*).

(2) Logwood = *Haematoxylon Campechianum.* The wood of this tree, containing the crystalline principle haematoxylin ($C_{16}H_{14}O_6$) is much used as a dyestuff to produce dark-red colors, violets and blues, and for giving a special lustre to blacks and greys. Logwood is so heavy as to sink in water.
                                                                    (*Ed.*).

●rs to enter upon as much of the land unoccupied as he pleased and to establish « conucos », the other tenants retaining a reversionary interest in the soil so taken up. Of late years there has been a marked tendency. to divide such «communero» lands among the rural co-owners.

It is only in comparatively recent years that a beginning has been made in the wider exploitation of the country's agricultural possi-bilities. The crops raised for export now comprise sugar, cocoa, tobacco, coffee and bananas (1).

The chief crops (apart from timber) shipped in 1910 from the two ports of Puerto-Plata and S. Pedro de Macoris were:

Tobacco, nearly 19 million lbs. (8 ½ million kgs.).

Cocoa, over 12 million lbs. (5 ½ million kgs.).

Coffee, nearly 1 ½ million lbs. (680 000 kgs).

Cotton, over 38 000 lbs. (17000 Kgs.)

Bananas, 591 000 bunches.

The port of Sanchez also ships cocoa, the above amount being only two-thirds of the total for this product.

The larger and more important sugar estates are situated on the southern coast, principally near San Pedro de Macoris (where there are seven) and Azua. There are no sugar refineries in the Republic.

The growing of cacao has become the chief native industry of the Republic. Especially is this the case in the rich Cibao region. Most of the cacao is raised on small plantations, the product of which is from

---

(1) Of the total area (18 045 square miles), about 15 500 square miles is cultivable. *Sugar*-growing is a flourishing industry; shipments in 1909, 155 642 109 lbs. to the value of 3 304 931 dollars, being an increase of 16 235 593 lbs. and 212 502 dollars over those of 1908. *Cocoa* was exported to the extent of 32 672 661 lbs. valued at 2 759 191 dollars a great decrease on the shipments during 1908. The exports of *tobacco leaf* in 1909 amounted to 24 822 461 lbs. value 1 239 486 dollars, being an increase of 6 156 867 lbs. and 229 878 dollars over 1908. *Cotton* showed a decrease of 2 539 085 lbs. and 196 951 dollars the figures for 1909 being 1 542 284 lbs. valued at 128 202 dollars, as against 4 081 369 lbs. and 325 153 dollars during 1908. *Coffee* exports are increas-ing; the quantity shipped in 1908 exceeded 4 000 000 lbs. Experiments are being made in cotton-growing; the cultivation of rice is being undertaken by a concessionaire, who has obtained an exclusive right for the purpose; some attention has recently been given to cattle-raising and dairy produce. Large sugar plantations and factories are at work in the south and west of the Republic. The country is rich in timber, including mahogany, satin-wood, logwood, cedar, iron-wood, sabina, and other woods; transport facilities, ho-wever, are wanting. (*Statesman's Yearbook for 1911*, pp. 1200-1201. London, Mac millan, 1911). (*Ed.*).

50 to 100 barrels, a barrel (96.90 litres) being worth about 8 dol (41.44 francs.)

The cultivation of coffee, which some years ago gave promise of rapid growth, has remained almost stationary. The principal coffee lands lie near Moca (to which circumstance that town owes its name), Santiago and Bani.

Tobacco is grown chiefly in the vicinity of Santiago and is generally of an inferior quality and no attempts are made to introduce the finer grades.

At Sosua, about 10 miles from Puerto Plata, is a large banana plantation owned by an American Corporation. Copra and cocoanuts from the groves which fringe Samanà Bay are exported from the port of Samanà. Elsewhere the bananas, oranges, limes, cocoanuts, pineapples and other tropical fruits which might grow plentifully throughout the country are entirely disregarded as articles of commerce.

Experiments lately made in growing cotton and hemp have given very satisfactory results. These commodities are produced with greatest success in the districts of Monte Cristi and Azua, where the lack of rain discourages the cultivation of other Dominican staples. Rice culture is also promising, though the quantity raised is not nearly sufficient for local consumption.

All of the articles above referred to are being produced either in the Cibao valley or in the vicinity of the coast. The interior districts where not entirely depopulated, are still given over to grazing. There is little traffic in cattle, however, but some hides are exported from most of the ports.

In the Azua and Monte Cristi districts much attention is given to goat breeding, and a considerable number of goat- skins are exported. The dairy industry does not exist in the Republic, all the butter and cheese consumed in the country being imported.

Apiculture is one of the best paying industries in the country as it yields as much as 1 per cent. every day throughout the year, there being no winter to check the activity of the bees, which are of Italian stock. Honey and beeswax are now produced in considerable quantities.

The waters surrounding the island teem with fish, yet these are almost completely disregarded even for home consumption.

1620   **The Conditions of Agriculture in Guadeloupe.** — *Bulletin de l'Office Colonial*, n. 41, pp. 163-164, Melun, Mai 1911.

Guadeloupe   In January 1910 the cultivated land in Guadeloupe amounted to 133 000 acres belonging to 12 660 plantations. The area under cocoa and coffee continues to rise. Sugar-cane extended somewhat in 1910 owing to the high price of sugar; whilst its export had been between 12 and 17 million francs (£. 480 000 to £. 680 000) for over fifteen years, it reached 21 839 764 fr. (approx. £. 835 000) in 1910.

Rum, tafia, cotton, annatto (1), vanilla, and pineapples are also exported.

Besides these crops for export other foods are produced for local use, such as manioc and other edible roots, bananas.

The sugar factories are modernising their plant, and the tafia industry is becoming increasingly important.

E. AXEIRO (Italian Consul at Campinas). **Agriculture in the State of Goyaz, Brazil.** (Lo Stato di Goyaz). — *Bollettino del Ministero degli Affari Esteri*, n. 405, p. 1-18. Roma, 1911.

1621

The State of Goyaz is abundantly watered, as its territory forms parts of the Amazon and la Plata basins.

It has a population of only 350 000 on 800 000 km² (310 000 sq. miles); consequently tillage is little developed.

Brazil : Goyaz

Cattle-breeding is prosperous; Goyaz furnishes most of the cattle for Rio de Janeiro and S. Paolo. The drivers (bojaderos) take the cattle in herds of thousands ; they are driven the whole way, over 620 miles, through forests and across streams, which are forded. The beasts are so tired by this journey that they are rested for some months before being slaughtered. Sometimes whole herds are lost on the way.

After cattle-breeding, sugar-cane growing has the next place in importance ; it is chiefly carried on in the districts of Corumba, Bomfim and Sa. Luzia. The product is not well prepared and is of poor quality, so that none is exported. Spade culture is still used. A tobacco, which is supposed to be good, is grown ; the dried leaf is rolled into rope form. Cigarettes wrapped in maize straw are made from it.

Preserved fruits, gum, and tanned hides are also exported in some quantity.

Tha land is largely occupied by squatters ; the occupiers are perpetually quarrelling about boundaries. The Government is at present endeavouring to put an end to this state of affairs.

Most of the immigrants are Syrians.

---

(1) Annatto, or annotto, or roucou: a shrub, *Bixa Orellana* (*Bixaceae*); provides a dye extracted from the pellicles of the seeds. This dye, of a high-orange or yellowish-red colour, dissolves readily in alcohol, and is used in varnishes. Annatto is used for colouring cheeses, as in the case of Dutch cheeses.   (*Ed.*).

1622   Sir W. Mather. **Resources and Development of Egypt and the Anglo-Egygtian Sudan** (An Address by the Rt. Hon. Sir Wm. Mather, delivered in Manchester). 1 vol., pp. 47. Southampton 1911.

Egypt.
Anglo-
Egyptian
Sudan

While the cultivated land forms a mere fraction of the total area of Egypt, its prolific quality is unequalled in the world, and it produces annually the richest crops of every product cultivated there.

Apart from the grain and vegetable crops, which are chiefly consumed by the population, the great staple product of Egypt is cotton. This product has risen in quantity since the great dam at Assouan was completed, the increase being chiefly in Lower Egypt, where the irrigation water is supplied by summer canals fed from barrages.

The raising of the height of the dam by 23 feet, now nearly completed, will produce no further increase in Lower Egypt; but in Upper Egypt the enormously increased storage of water will make the irrigation more constant and effective, so increasing the yield of cotton. The land is so fertile that with sufficient irrigation it will produce up to three green-crops a year.

When this work is finished, Lower and Upper Egypt will be irrigated as completely as can be accomplished by the waters of the Nile, so that no appreciable further increase in the area under cotton is to be anticipated.

At the same time, the completion of this reservoir will remove the restrictions hitherto imposed on the utilization of Nile water in the Sudan.

The boundary between Egypt and the Anglo-Egyptian Sudan is the parallel of 22°N.; Wadi-Halfa is the frontier town on the Nile.

The inhabitants of the Sudan are chiefly Arabs in the north, who form the trading class and occupy the desert, and negroes in in the south, who cultivate the soil and raise cattle where the rainfall is more abundant.

In the north of the Sudan, as in Egypt, the rainfall consists of a few passing storms, so that cultivation is entirely dependent on the Nile water. North of Khartoum the agricultural belt by the river is very narrow, and is watered only by the native water-wheels, except in seasons of exceptional flood; in places the hills come almost to the banks of the river.

In the provinces of Dongola and Berber the valley is wider, and there are some tracts below the level of the banks, so that water can easily be carried to a distance of several miles by canals. It is here that Government concessions have been granted, and attempts have been made to establish improved systems of agriculture. Cotton is being increasingly planted in North Sudan and with very promising results.

South of Wad Medani, the capital of the Blue Nile province, the rainfall becomes more abundant and regular, and the natives raise plentiful rain-crops of sesame, ground-nuts, and native cotton, and several varieties of sorghum, maize, and millet.

The provinces of Berber and Khartoum are the most productive at present, and the most suitable tract for cotton-growing in them is along the Nile north of Khartoum. The Concession at Zeidab will shortly be extended to 40 000 acres ; at present there are 3 000 acres under cotton, 3 000 under wheat, and 2500 under leguminous crops.

Between the Blue and White Niles, which meet at Khartoum, and reaching 150 miles south from there, is the great plain known as El Gezira; this will form the great field for cotton-cultivation in the Sudan ; it is estimated that it ought to yield 700 000 Egyptian bales per annum of the best cotton.

Plans for the irrigation of this plain from a dam to be constructed at Sennar have already been prepared by the Government of the Anglo--Egyptian Sudan ; it is suggested that the capital required might be raised on the security of the British Government.

PERROT. **Economic Value of Eastern Morocco**. (La valeur éco-   **1623**
nomique du Maroc Oriental). *La Quinzaine Coloniale*. N° 8,
P. 278, Paris 25 Avril, 1911.

The plain of Trifas, a fertile and alluvial stretch of land on the coast of Eastern Morocco, and which extends as far as the mountains of Beni-Suassen, is especially adapted for agricultural development. The neighboring region of Beni-Suassen would afford, with-   **Morocco**
out a doubt, many agreable surprises to prospective miners. As for the adjacent plateau of Udjida and Angad, they are distinctly arid and improductive, but water could be found at several points. Beyond this, to the south, the rough plateaux of Berguent follow, and it is only here and there that special cultivations could be undertaken.

Excepting the region of Beni-Suassen which con only be mined, these lands can only become valuable through agricultural development. Soon there will not be a single acre uncultivated in the Trifas plain, though in former years it was entirely deserted.

Eastern Morocco promises a very important economic development, but above all the water problem must be studied very carefully.

1624   MICKEL. **The Conditions of Agriculture in the District of Moschi, German East Africa.** (Die landwirtschaftlichen Verhältnisse des Bezirks Moschi). *Deutsches Kolonialblatt*, N. 10, s. 386-391. Berlin, 15 Mai, 1911.

Rubber and cotton are the two chief crops of the more mountainous part of the territory of Moschi ; cotton is grown between the rubber-trees while they are young. There is no doubt that the general yield of agricultural produce will increase greatly when communications and means of transport are improved.

German East Africa: Moschi

At present experiments are being tried to see whether the *hirsutum* species of cotton, which does so well in the humous soils of Uganda, can replace the Egyptian varieties in Moschi. It has been shown that cotton can be grown without irrigation.

For rubber, experiments have been made with *Manihot, Kickxia, Castilloa,* and *Hevea.*

Trials of lucerne, of *Desmodium,* and *Vicia* gave fairly good results.

To produce tanning substances, *Rumex hymenosepalus* and acacias have been planted.

Several species of *sisal* are cultivated, and *Cajanus indicus* is planted as shade for the young coffee trees.

In the marsh of Doloti, rice is grown.

The natives also cultivate an excellent local wheat, as well as maize and beans; the last two might give rise to a considerable export.

As the agricultural zone is left behind, the pastoral zone appears ; it has the characters of steppe. Attempts to introduce sheep for wool have not given good results so far, but there is no reason why sheep-breeding should not be successful in the future.

1625   **Third Congress of Cooperative Dairies at Udine, Italy. A Resolution regarding an International Agreement for the Inspection of Dairy Products.** (Risultati del III Congresso delle Latterie Sociali). *La Industria lattiera e zootecnica.* Anno IX, N. 9, pp. 137-139. Reggio Emilia, 3 Maggio 1911.

Italy

Among the subjects discussed by this Congress were three important problems of the dairy industry in Italy.

First, the question of dairy instruction. Deputy Bignami's report states that there is much room for improvement in the dairy experimental stations and schools already existing.

A discussion of the question of ferments necessary in the manufacture of cheese, ended in the following resolution:

« That systematic and comparative studies of cheese ferments be carried on either in the national scientific institutions or in private dairies under the direction of competent persons.

« It is hoped that these studies may demonstrate the necessity of new laboratories provided with the economic and scientific equipment necessary to solve problems that are of interest to the cheese industry in Italy ».

Finally a resolution of international importance sums up the opinion of the Congress on the question of an international agreement on certain hygienic and chemical regulations concerning the importation of products in general, and especially of dairy products. The following is the resolution as adopted by the Congress:

« In order to avoid the differences that often arise, and the difficulties that are met with in the international commerce of dairy products and in general of agricultural food commodities, it is necessary to establish exact methods of analysis and principles of valuation, by an international agreement.

« As this agreement must be arrived at, not by discussions and resolutions of international congresses, but by a special international conference of competent people chosen by the various governments ;

« The Congress expresses a wish that the initiative shall be taken either by the International Institute of Agriculture or by the Minister of Agriculture and Commerce of the Kingdom of Italy ».

The Rubber Commission of the German Colonial Economic Committee. (Verhandlungen der Kaoutschuk-Kommission des Kolonial-Wirtschaftlichen Komitees vom 30. März 1911). *Beihefte zum Tropenpflanzer*, Bd. XII, N. 3, s. 201-281 + figs. 5 + ch. 1. Berlin, Mai 1911.

1626

The formation of this Commission was primarily due to the manihot rubber cultivation in German East Africa ; but the Commission proposes to develop and consolidate the production of rubber and gutta-percha in all the German colonies.

Germany: German Colonies

The attention of the Commission will be devoted principally to the following questions.

1. Study of the rubber question. Regular reports on the state of the world's rubber market, the conditions and profits of rubber-growing, and the preparation of rubber and gutta-percha in the German colonies. Tabulation of the statistics relating to the above. Planning of expeditions through the rubber-producing districts. Foundation of rubber and gutta-percha stations. Guarantee of minimum prices to the natives of New Guinea.

2. Measures tending to encourage a good and uniform preparation of rubber and gutta-percha in all the German colonies.

3. Control and appraisement of the quality of the products, so as to obtain a valuation as favourable as possible from the commercial and industrial points of view. Arranging of exhibitions.

The Colonial Economic Committee considers that the collaboration of German rubber-planters and rubber-importers, and all those connected with the German rubber and gutta-percha industry, will be a sure means of encouraging and improving the production and preparation of rubber in the German colonies.

In the first meeting of the Committee, on the 30th of March 1911, the following points were discussed :

1. Generalities and organization. 2. State of the world's rubber market. 3. Spread of the use of rubber. 4. The economic value of manihot rubber. 5. Propositions for the fixing of « standards ». 6. Help to be given to the Central Rubber Bureau. 7. Rubber and gutta-percha stations in New Guinea. 8. Gold medal of the Colonial Economic Committee at the International Rubber Exhibition. 9. Synthetic rubber. 10. Examination of rubber, gutta-percha, and resins.

1627   **Florida's New Law providing for a State Horticultural Commission.**
California Cultivator, Los Angeles, Cal., April 6, 1911.

The State of Florida is considering the establishment of a State Horticultural Commission. The next session of the State legislature will have under consideration a bill, already formulated, whereby it is United provided that prior to the first of July, 1911, a State Commissioner States: of horticulture shall be appointed to serve a four-year term, with Florida salary of doll. 2 500 (12 875 fr.) per year, to maintain an office at the University of Florida, al Gainesville. He shall have one deputy, and may appoint a District Horticultural Inspector, who shall employ as many assistants as the County Commissioner may judge necessary. The district inspectors are to receive a salary of doll. 1500 (7725 fr.) per annum.

The duties of the State Commissioner shall be to exercise general supervision and permanent control over the horticultural interests of the State, especially to enforce laws relating to horticulture ; to disseminate information upon subjects pertaining to horticultural interests ; to hold meetings for instruction of horticulturists ; to publish and distribute bulletins ; and to grant licenses to nurserymen and tree dealers.

A French National Oleicultural Society.   (Une Société nationale   **1628**
d'Oléiculture de France).   *La Petite Revue agr. et hort.* 17e ann.,
n. 397, p. 138. Antibes, 2⁵ Juin 1911.

An Association for the study of all technical questions concerning
olive growing and the preparation of olive oil has just been formed
in France.

This Society will complete the work of the « Syndicat national   France
de défense de l'Oléiculture française » founded in 1906 ; its work will
extend to France, Algeria, and Tunis.   The administrative council is
composed of authorized representatives from all the olive-growing
regions of France.

The first work has been to bring the question of olive parasites
before the Society ; this subject will be discussed at a congress to be
held at Avignon on the 5th of next December.

Work of the Experimental Oil Station at Spoleto (Italy). —   **1629**
*R. Oleificio Sperimentale dalla Calabria all'Umbria. Attività.
Esperienze. Ricerche. Studi.* pp. XVI + 179. 5 Allegati. Spoleto :
1910.

The first Italian Experimental Oil Factory was instituted by the
Minister of Agriculture in 1889 at Palmi in Calabria. In 1898 it was
removed to Cosenza (Calabria) and thence in 1903 to Spoleto (Umbria)   Italy:
where it now remains.   Umbria

The director and his assistants carry out researches in the laboratory and also give courses of instruction. The latter are of two kinds:

(a) *occasional;* these are exclusively practical and intended for the
mill workmen and the olive pruners and grafters; and

(b) *theoretical and practical* courses, lasting about three months,
and including all branches of the work.

The work done at the oil factory is well evidenced by the different papers published by the staff in various journals and bulletins,
and collected in the present volume.

F. BRACCI. — 1) Contribution to the Chemico-agricultural Status
of Olive Cultivation.

2) Retrocession of Oil in the Olive to the Branches. — 3) New
Contribution to the Study of the Oil Formation in Olives. — 4) New
Researches on the Oil Formation in Olives. — 5) Fertilisers for the
Olive Tree. — 6) Effect of different Fertilisers on the Olive and on the
Oil — 7) On the Pickling of some Varieties of Olives from the Cosenza
District. — 8) Short practical Notes on the Carriage and Storage of
Olives and on the Presses with modern Crushers, as compared with
the old ones used in Umbria. — 9) On the Hot water Treatment

and on the Washing of Oil. — 10) The Immediate and Automatic Separation of the Oil from Pulp water. — 11) Separation of the Pulp from the Olive Stones. — 12) Researches on the Separation of the Pulp and on Almond Oil. — 13) The Quality of the Vessels used for keeping Oil. — 14) The Effect of Iron Implements and Utensils on Oil. — 15) The Removal of the Olive Stones and the Manufacture of Oil cakes. — 16) Determination of the acidity of Oils. — 17) The Experimental Olive Grove (Cultivation and Experiments). — 18) On the new Processes of the Extraction of Oil. — 19) Contribution to the chemical Analysis of Italian Olive Pomace. — 20) New Observations on the Reaction recommended by Villavecchia and Fabris.

F. BRACCI and G. FREZZOTTI — 1) On the Refractive Index of Olive Oil. — 2) On Cartelli's Thermoleometer.

G. FREZZOTTI — 1) Analysis of some Olive Pomace from the Marche. — 2) New Experiments on the Oil Content of Olives in connection with the Method of their Storage.

G. FREZZOTTI and DI MORI. — Researches on the Thermic Degree of vegetable Oils by means of Tortelli's Thermoleometer.

G. FREZZOTTI, DI MORI and S. PALMIERI. — Investigations on Olive Pomace.

P. SPERANZA. — Practical Observations on the Reproduction of the Olive by Seed.

1630   H. NEUBAUER. **Agricultural Experimentation and Control in Germany**. (Das Landw. Versuchs-und Kontrollwesen in Deutschland). — *Archiv des Deutschen landwirtschafstrats*, pp. 174-297. Berlin, 1911.

There are at present in Germany 75 Agricultural Experimental
Germany   Stations and kindred institutions which were founded at the following dates:

11 from	. . . .	1851 to 1860
11 »	. . . .	1861 » 1870
22 »	. . . .	1871 » 1880
8 »	. . . .	1881 » 1890
12 »	. . . .	1891 » 1900
11 after	. . . .	1900

There are also four Experiment Stations in the colonies.

The total number of the staff (excluding the officials of the colonial Stations) is 1378. The staff consists of:

Scientific Directors.	77
Scientifically-trained officials, chiefs of sections, assistants, chemists, botanists, etc.	456
Laboratory helps	142
Special technical foremen, as Farm bailiffs, gardeners, dairymen, brewers, etc.	78
Clerks. Cashiers etc.	180
Servants and attendants	211
Persons occasionally employed	234

One Institute is especially the property of the German Empire, of the others.

28 are dependent on the Federal States
6 »　　　»　　　» Provinces and Districts
29 »　　　»　　　«· Chambers of Agriculture
4 »　　　»　　　» Agricultural Associations
7 ,　　　»　　　» ˙ Other Associations
1 is private.

Total 75

The grants, calculated in pounds sterling, to the German Experimental Stations in 1909 were;

	State Grants	Province or District Grants	Agric. Chambers Grants	Fees and other direct income	Miscell. Income	Total Income
Prussia . . . . . £.	34 387	3 748	18 546	137 278	5 519	199 119
Bavaria . . . . . «	12 312	1 474	552	12 513	1 044	27 894
Saxony . . . . . »	4 401	318	44	2 514	819	8 097
Würtemburg. . . »	2 299	—	—	2 985	—	5 243
Baden. . . . . . »	2 258	—	—	676	54	3 244
Hesse. . . . . . »	2 514	—	—	2 399	98	3 770
Mecklenburg- Schwerin . . . »	1 273	—	511	2 446	1 575	5 834
Saxe-Weimar . . »	296	—	—	1 256	164	1 716
Oldenburg . . . »	206	—	122	1 978	206	2 512
Anhalt . . . . . «	1 086	—	1 327	319	245	2 976
Brunswick . . . »	—	—	—	—	—	—
Hamburg . . . »	387	—	—	4 176	—	4 563
Alsace-Lorraine . »	2 270	—	135	1 838	190	4 432
Imperial Institute »	14 307	—	—	—	—	14 307
Total £.	77 029	5 540	21 237	170 347	9 649	283 707

The total number of control and paying analyses in 1909 was:

Fertilizers.	152 587
Fodders.	55 380
Seed	62 906
Dairy Produce	660 122
Soils	2 807
Water	4 511
Human Foods	25 927
Sugar Beets	1 496
Plant Diseases, etc.	9 357
Live-stock Diseases	3 091
Various	27 493
Total	1 005 677

In 1888 the Union of the Experiment Stations of the German . Empire was established, with the object (art. 2 of the Statutes) of promoting the common interests of these stations in all scientific and practical matters, especially the control of fertilisers, fodders, seeds and other important subjects connected with agriculture.

Further, the Union (Art. 5 of the Statutes) appoints a Permanent Committee every three years, for the purpose of considering analytical questions relating to:

(1) Chemical fertilizers.
(2) Fodders.
(3) Seeds.
(4) Soil.

At present, 65 Stations belong to the Union, the organ of which is the important review entitled *Die Landwirtschaftlichen. Versuchssta-tionen* which was published for the first time in 1858.

The experimental work of the stations includes researches on the following subjects:

A.   ATMOSPHERE.

Besides the Central Office of the well equipped Physical Laboratory of the Royal College of Agriculture at Berlin, (*Königl. landwirtsch. Hochschule*) many other Institutes are engaged in meteorological observations, especially in such as concern vegetation and cultivation experiments.

B.   SOIL.

Thanks to the Soil-Improvement Stations, much uncultivated and peat land has been transformed into fertile fields and meadows.

Studies have been made at the Institute of Agricultural Chemistry at Breslau upon the power possessed by the soil of absorbing fertilizing substances.

The Geological Institute in Berlin has been engaged for some years upon a systematic geological- agricultural survey of Prussia and has already brought out maps of the greater part of the kingdom, the scale being 1: 25 000. A certain number of the Stations have also turned their attention to soil-improvement and to the study of the factors which determine its productivity.

The researches of Rodewald and Mitscherlich at Kiel deal with the physical properties of soils; while König at Münster has found that the electrical conductivity especially the osmotic pressure of the soil, afford the means of determining the solubility of its component parts.

Colloidal chemistry has proved to be of great assistance in determining the chemical changes which take place in the soil.

C. PLANT NUTRITION AND CULTIVATION — Cultural experiments with Knop's solution and those with sand (Hellriegel's system) have determined the first principles of plant-nutrition. These have been followed by researches on fertilizers, the study of agricultural bacteriology, the employment of the inoculation methods of the Tharandt school, the methods for the preservation of the nitrogen content of stable manure devised by Soxhlet of Munich, and the experiments with green manuring made at the Experiment Stations of Köslin and Halle.

Many Institutions applied themselves with success to the breeding of new varieties of cultivated plants.

Phytopathology is also an important branch. The study of the life conditions of animal and vegetable parasites is the chief work of the new Imperial Institute of Biology at Dahlem near Berlin. The Agricultural-botanical Institute at Münich and the Phyto-pathological Experiment Station al Geisenheim are engaged in similar researches.

Since 1906, uniform plant-protection throughout the Empire has been organised by the Imperial Institution of Biology at Dahlem, on the basis fixed in 1890 by the German Agricultural Society.

Investigations have been made at the Experiment Stations of Münster and Marburg (now Harleshausen) as to the harm caused to plants and animals by the waste water and gases from factories etc.

D. CATTLE FEEDING. — In addition to the epoch-making work of O. Kellner (Möckern), there are the labours of Zuntz (Berlin), which deal with the metabolism resulting from muscular exertion, the work on animal physiology carried on under the direction of Pfeiffer at the Agricultural Institute at Breslau, and of Morgan at the Hohenheim Experiment Station, and the attempts of Franz Lehmann a t Göttingen to increase, by means of a chemical process, the utility of different straw-varieties.

At Stations with experimental fields attached, many practical feeding experiments have been made according to a common plan and with the pecuniary assistance of the State.

E. AGRICULTURAL INDUSTRIES. — Promoting Agricultural Industries by means of research and scientific experiment has of late become the aim of a number of Institutes many of which have been recently established. The spheres of their activities are as follows.

1. Dairying.
2. Sugar.
3. The Milling Industry.
4. Fermentation industries (Brewing, Spirits, Yeast, Vinegar).
5. Manufacture of starch.
6. Vine cultivation and wine-making.
7. Fruit-culture, Horticulture.

AGRICULTURAL CONTROL. — With regard to agricultural control, the greatest success has attended the exertions of the Agricultural Council of Saxony (*Landes-kulturrat für das Königreich Sachsen*) to which all questions of control are referred. This Council has established an agreement between the agricultural authorities and

115 firms for the control of fertilizers, ·
106   »   »   »   of fodder,
35   »   »   »   of seeds.

The clearness and practical utility of the forms adopted for the purchase and guarantee of the products are remarkable.

In 1905, there was appointed, under the direction of the German Agricultural Council, a Committee for regulating trade in fertilisers, feeds and seeds. Its duty was to draw up general rules regarding the delivery of fertilizers, cattlefoods, and seeds. The Committee was appointed with the consent of the German Agricultural Council, the Imperial Federation of the German Agricultural Associations the German Agricultural Society, the Farmers' League, the Union of the German Peasants' Christian Association. The Union of the Agricultural Experiment Stations of the German Empire was constituted for the purpose of trade control into a Permanent Council.

The subjects of regulations were as follows:

a) The declaration and nature of the goods.

b) Analysis (exact determination of weight, of apparent defects of the goods, rules for sampling, determining minimum values; methods of analysis.

c) Indemnity for minimum values.

d) Expenses of analysis.

e) Arbitration.

By these means a sound honest basis is given to the trade in fertilizers, food-stuffs and seeds.

This Report on the German Agricultural Experimental Stations and on the system of controlling trade in the interest of agriculture ends with a comprehensive bibliography.

GIULLON. **The Winter Schools of Agriculture in France.** (Les Écoles   **1631**
d'Agriculture d'hiver en France). — *Bulletin Mensuel de l'Office de Renseignements Agricoles*, N. 4, pp. 419-432. Paris, Avril 1911.

The Winter Agricultural Schools in France are intended for young people who are at least 16 or 17 years of age. This should not be confused with the special Agricultural courses which may be established in all rural schools. Their number increases considerably.   **France**
The course of study and the subjects taught vary in different districts; they will be still more varied when the schools have extended into the South of France.

The organization of the winter schools in connection with universities appears very favourable. It is advisable to annex several winter schools to the Practical Schools of Agriculture already existing.

The principal Winter Schools are as follows:

Practical School of the College of Langres;

Winter School of Agriculture at the Lyceum of Troyes;

Practical Winter School of Agriculture at the Lyceum of Lons-le-Saunier.

Winter school of Agriculture at the Lyceum of Chartres.

Advanced course in practical Agriculture at the Lyceum of Chaumont.

Winter School of Vine-Cultivation of the College of Epernay.

Winter course in Agriculture at the Professional School of Montbrison.

Higher Agricultural Education and Technical Schools in Portugal.   **1632**
(Ensimo superior de Agricoltura). — *A Vinha Portuguesa*, n. 4, pp. 122-126 Lisbona, Abril 1911.

A government decree has laid the foundations of the organisation of higher agricultural education in Portugal.   **Portugal**

There will be two courses, one for agricultural engineers, the other for forest engineers. After the ordinary course of study, the agricultural engineers can take either agricultural chemistry or colonial agriculture. The forest engineers have to attend special courses on forest economics, hydraulics, regulation of torrents, roadmaking and transport, fisheries, game, and pasturage.

A second decree institutes a Practical School of Horticulture.

1633

V. Rümker. **Experimentation and Agricultural Instruction in the United States.** — *Das landwirtschaftliche Versuchs- und Unterrichtswesen in den Vereinigten Staaten von Nord-Amerika und in Preussen*, pp. 34. Berlin 1911.

After his journey to America to study and to complete a publication which he had prepared in collaboration with E.v. Tschermak (1), the author thus summarises the characteristics of experimentation and of agricultural instruction in the United States.

United States

1. The penetration of scientific knowledge and progress into the remotest corners and smallest enterprises, by the most appropriate methods.

2. In all grades of agricultural instruction, the best means for the preparation of all necessary apparatus for research can be found both for instruction in all branches of agricultural science and for encouraging intuitive and objective instruction. In the course of their studies young folks are not required to memorize all formulae, nor to recite their lessons from memory; but they must learn to see and observe accurately; and the teaching is done experimentally and by exhibiting objects.

3. The State is not alone in granting subsidies; but the larger the expenses are, the more must those classes contribute whom the outlay benefits most particularly, such as agricultural Corporations, Unions, Societies etc.

4. The conviction that the agriculturist, no matter what his condition and his instruction may be, needs and profits by a theoretical as well as a practical education. Their motto is: not to study too soon nor too briefly. It is only when the student possesses a good practical preparation, and can study thoughtfully and critically, that his studies bear a lasting and beneficial influence on his entire life.

5. An effort is made in the public schools to interest young folks in Nature. Love of Nature, which is the logical result of observation

(1) See Abstr. 726 of this *Bulletin* for March, 1911.   (*Ed.*).

and knowledge of natural phenomena, is perhaps one of the most efficient and permanent means of fighting against rural depopulation.

6. To encourage advanced experimentation and agricultural instruction, a Commission was formed in America in which the three following factors are represented :

a) The Society of Experiment Stations and Agricultural Colleges.

b) The Experiment Station Office of the National Department of Agriculture.

c) The Instruction Division of the Department of the Interior.

The work of this Commission, sanctioned by and in conjunction with the public authorities, is not limited to bringing about uniform and systematic work, but it also sees to the general efficiency of the public organizations.

Hr. Rümker has also ascertained that the field of operation of the American Agricultural Experiment Stations is greater that that of the German and European ones in general ; the Kaiser-Wilhelm Institute at Bromberg best compares with the American institutions.

American Stations, characterized by their excellent equipment, modern perfection, compactness, and the convenience and simplicity of their apparatus, usually consist of various departments : administrative, agricultural, zootechnical, special cultures, botany, chemistry, phythopathology, horticulture and fruit culture, forestry, study of the soil, practical agricultural experiments, etc.

Hr. Rümker, in conclusion, expresses the wish that the Prussian government should send a Commission to the United States to study the organization and endowment of agricultural experimentation and instruction.

LEROY ANDERSON. **The Teaching of Agriculture in the Secondary Schools of California.** *The University of California Chronicle*: N. 2, P. 164-176, Berkeley, April 1911.

1634

Fully one-third of the population in California is engaged in agriculture. The entire population, whether urban or rural, is interested in it and dependent upon it. To conserve and enrich the soil resources is the problem of modern farming ; to raise larger crops of better products and still maintain the soil fertility ; and the solution of this problem is largely a matter of education.

Agriculture ought to be taught in order that no young man or woman may leave the farm for another vocation, thinking that there

United
States:
California

is nothing worth-while in farming.   Interest in teaching agriculture is world wide; and all evidence points in the direction of its usefulness and of its success as a subject for secondary schools.   The main agricultural topics have been so well reduced to pedagogical form in the colleges that their presentation in secondary schools is a matter of adaptation, which in the hands of wise teachers is easily accomplished.

One marked advantage of the secondary agricultural school is the possibility of its securing the attention of the boy and girl at an age when the majority of boys and girls are finding the high school inadequate to their future as they see it, and when something vocational strongly appeals to them.

1635

Technical Education in Brazil. — *Journal of the Royal Society of Arts*. N. 3053, P. 744, London, May 26, 1911.

Brazil

The Brazilian Government have recently authorised a system of schools and stations to teach agriculture in the several States, in harmony with the plan for Apprenticeship Trade-schools. At the head is to be a High School of Agriculture and Veterinary Surgery, at Rio de Janeiro.   The school will give education fitting students for places as experts in the general extension of agricultural training. With the co-operation of the State Government, agricultural schools, experimental stations, model farms and stock ranches will be established as soon as the general working out of the plans justifies further extension.   Elementary instruction in rural industries will be encouraged in the existing schools for elementary education.

By demonstrations at Experimental Stations and elsewhere it is intended to instruct farmers in the use of modern implements and cultural methods.

1636

A. CHEVALIER. **Botanical Map of French West Africa** (Essai d'une Carte botanique, forestière et pastorale de l'Afrique occidentale française). — *C.R. de l'Acad. des Sciences*, T. 152, N. 23, pp. 1614-1617. Paris, 6 Juin 1911.

French W. Africa

The writer describes the great divisions of this map from the point of view of botanical geography.

I. *Saheli Zone*.

Between 17° and 20° N. lat. is the indefinite boundary between the Sahara and the Saheli zone.   The latter is characterized by a short rainy season, with 20 to 35 cm. (8 to 14 ins.) of rain in the year; large spaces are still desert, but thorny scrub appears, in places very dense, and consisting of *Acacia tortilis* Hayne, *A. Vereck* G. and P., *A. arabica* Willd., *A. albida* Delile, *Balanites aegyptiaca* Delile, and *Zizyphus Jujuba* Lam.

II. *Sudan Zone.*

a) Flood districts, largely covered in the rainy season by the waters of the Niger ,Bani, Volta, etc. Aquatic grasses are abundan t *Andropogon zizanioides*, var *nigritanus* Stapf, *Panicum stagninum* Retz, var. *Burga* A. Chev, *P.pyramidale* Lam., and a wild rice (*Oryza Barthii* A.Rhev.); these districts are considered suitable for cotton.

b) Districts of plains with thin scrub, and near the villages extensive fallows, which in the rainy season become pastures, chiefly composed of annual grasses.

c) Plateau districts covered with scrub and trees; the flora is somewhat varied — grasses, various species of *Andropogon* with perennial stocks, scrub trees often covered with *Loranthaceae*.

III. *Guinea Zone.*

a) Plateaux and valley systems from 300 to 800 m. (1000 to 2600 ft.), with permanent rivers, more or less embanked and bordered by tall forests: in these Ferns and Monocotyledons are abundant, some arborescent — Palms, *Pandanus*, *Dracoena*, Bamboos ,others as underwood — *Zingiberaceae*, or as epiphytes — Orchids. Between these fringing forests savannah formations occur; in places there are pure colonies of *Berlinia Heudelotiana* Baill., and of *Oxyanthera abyssinica* Munro.

b) Mountain chains stretching for 1000 km. (620 miles), from Conakry to the Central Sassandra, at 800 to 1500 m. (2600 to 5000 ft.); here grow a great quantity of ferns, some of them arborescent — *Cyathea*, numerous epiphytes — Orchids, *Begonia*, *Peperomia*, and plants belonging to the African sub-alpine zone — *Rubus, Hypericum, Hydrocotyle, Olea, Cardamine*; also *Eriospora pilosa* Benth. (*Cyperaceae*) which forms deposits of peat.

IV. *Lowland Plain zone.*

This extends over Baoulé, lower and middle Dahomey, and Lagos. It is the zone of the rich development of Oil Palms (*Elaeis guineensis*, Jacq.) in Dahomey, and the *Borassus* savanna h in Baoulé; everywhere are found yams, which are the staple food of the natives.

V. *Virgin Forest Zone.*

This comprises the south of French Guinea, Liberia, and parts of the Ivory and Gold Coasts; isolated patches in Dahomey connect it with the great equatorial forest. It is composed of over four hundred species of trees with numerous lianes and abundant underwood, in which occur *Zingiberaceae*, Ferns, and Dwarf Bamboos.

1637   **Crops in the State of Sâo Paulo.** (La polyculture dans l'Etat de Sâo-Paulo, Brésil). (1). — *Revue des Questions Scientifiques*, tome LXIX, p. 690. Louvain, 20 Avril 1911.

Brazil:
Sao Paulo

The cultivation of coffee, for which the soil and climate of Sâo Paulo are particularly adapted, met with such instant success that almost the entire territory was given up for the planting of coffee trees.

The severity of the coffee crisis was beneficial; the farmers of Sâo Paulo realized the danger of limiting themselves to the cultivation of only one crop.

A thorough change is in progress; and planters, aided by the government, are giving their attention to other crops, especially rice and certain starch plants. However, they reserve the most important land for coffee trees.

The cultivation of rice has already reached large proportions, two methods being employed—one without, and one with irrigation. The latter has given the better results.

---

(1) See Abstrs. 9 and 10 of this *Bulletin* for Jan. 1911.   (*Ed.*).

Agriculture. — Agricultural Physics, Chemistry, and Botany.

A. D. HALL. **The Progress of Chemistry of the Growing Plant during the Year 1910.** — *Annual Reports on the Progress of Chemistry for* 1910. *Issued by the Chemical Society*, vol. III, pp. IX + 303 (214-219). London, 1911.

1688

H. E. and E. F. Armstrong have published a paper on the action of chloroform and similar substances in stimulating enzyme action in living structures (1).

"Their results fall into line with the work of A. J. Brown on the semipermeability of the membrane surrounding the barley grain, and indicate that only those substances are active which succeed in penetrating into the leaf. The authors propose to extend Starling's term of "hormones" to these excitants, and they point out that they are all substances with but slight attraction for water; materials which react with water generally fail to penetrate the leaf (2).

Great Britain. Germany

"It is generally considered that in plant tissues the enzymes and glucosides are either contained in different cells or in different vacuoles in the same cell. Guignard states that in the cherry laurel the enzyme is stored in the endodermis, whilst the glucoside is in the parenchyma, and as the enzyme is not diffusible it is most probable that the glucoside is induced to travel to the enzyme".

The action is evidently bound up with changes in the concentration of the fluids within the leaf; in his paper, Guignard, compares the action to that of frost, which induces a concentration of the cell sap and at once sets up change. In the leaves exposed to vapours there is sufficient water to allow of the passage of the glucoside towards the hormone entering very close to the enzyme which lies near the exterior surface.

---

(1) See below Abstr. 1644, for an abstract of this article.

(2) Cp. with G. C. Bourne, *Animal Chemism: Enzymes and Hormones.* Address to Brit. Assoc. Sheffield, 1910. *Nature*, Sept. 22, 1910, p. 382.

See also, *The Science and Practice of Farming during 1910 in Great Britain.* Int. Inst. of Agric. Rome, p. 416. (*Ed.*).

"From solutions a considerable amount of water enters the leaf with the hormone, a leaf, for example, increases in weight by 20 per cent. after 18 hours' immersion in chloroform water, whereas it only gains 5 per cent. after 24 hours in pure water, and 2 per cent. after 45 hours in a 2 per cent. solution of sodium chloride.

"The authors discuss these results in the light of H. E. Armstrong's theory of the constitution of water, and then proceed to show their application to a number of phenomena in the life of animals and plants. As regards plants, one of the most significant facts is that carbon-dioxide itself acts as a hormone; it is easy to suppose that variations in the presentation of this substance to the cell may excite enzymic action in the direction of hydrolysis, or the reverse, the most significant of the processes in the metabolism of the cell. Moreover, a slight initial excitation may be sufficient to set in motion considerable change, because many of the products of hydrolysis, for example hydrocyanic acid and benzaldehyde, are themselves hormones and would extend the action. In the living plant, the hormone-excited changes can never be so large as in the experiments on the detached leaves, for A. D. Waller shows that the leaf is killed within a minute of the action of the chloroform, as may be ascertained from the abolition of electrical response.

"Doubtless from these experiments light will eventually be thrown on the physiological function of many of the ethereal oils, terpenes and scents secreted by plants so normally that they cannot be without significance.

"They also throw some light on the horticultural practice by which plants like lilacs intended for forcing are exposed to the vapour of ether for 24 hours or so. After the etherising process it is found that the plants can be forced into bloom a week or 10 days earlier than would otherwise have been possible. As cold acts in the same way by altering the concentration of the cell sap, we may also correlate the similar acceleration of flowering that is induced by a preliminary cold storage before forcing, and, again, the well-known fact that potatoes which have been frozen become sweet through an accumulation of enzyme-produced sugar.

"In a paper on the ripening of premature fruit, A. E. Vinson shows that dates which have reached a certain stage of development can be made to ripen by exposure to certain vapours or solutions, practically, the same substances which the Armstrongs have found to be active. Vinson similarly concludes that the ripening is brought about by the release of intercellular enzymes through substances penetrating the cuticle and stimulating the protoplasm.

" Various papers dealing with assimilation have been published during 1910. S, B. Schryver has taken up afresh the work of Priestley and Usher on the photochemical formation of formaldehyde by chlorophyll (1).

" Thoday has examined in detail Sachs' method of measuring assimilation by the difference in dry weight of comparable areas in the two halves of a leaf before and after exposure to light (2).

" R. Willstätter and his colleagues have continued their investigations on the constitution of chlorophyll. They had before established the existence of two chlorophylls, one amorphous — a phytol ester containing one phytol residue and one metoxyl group for each magnesium atom — and the other crystalline, yielding, on hydrolysis, phaeophorbin, which is a dimethyl ester. The authors have now examined the distribution of these chlorophylls in a number of plants from the various orders. From experiments with grass, plantain and nettles, they find that the nature of the chlorophyll is not influenced by the soil or the time of the year. The amorphous phytol ester, chlorophyll, is widely distributed and preponderates in some cases. Crystalline chlorophyll is not always found. Colorimetric determinations show that the leaves of various plants contain $\frac{1}{2}$ to 1 per cent. of chlorophyll in their dry material.

" The question of the action of small traces of metallic salts and other possible catalytic agents on the growth of plants has again received a good deal of attention during the year.

" W. E. Brenchley has examined the effect of the sulphates of copper and manganese on the growth of barley in water cultures (3).

" In the same line of work comes a paper by P. Ehrenberg on the effect of zinc salts on vegetation. (*Landw. Versuchs-Stat.*, 1910, 73, 15; *A.*, II, 236). Zinc he finds to be always toxic when the action is simply between the plant and the reacting substance. In his experiments on soil, however, cases were met with of apparent stimulus due to zinc, but the author considers that these can always

---

(1) Proc. Roy. Soc. 1910, B. 82, 226. Journ. Chem. Soc. April 1910, Abstr. 334. This paper wass ummarized in: *The Science and Practice of Farming during 1910 in Great Britain*. Int. Inst. of Agriculture. P. 127. Rome. 1910. (*Ed.*).

(2) See *Nature*, vol. 83, June 23, 1910, p. 511. This paper was summarized in: *The Science and Practice of Farming during 1910 in Great Britain*. Int. Inst. of Agric. P. 126, Rome, 1910. (*Ed.*).

(3) *Annals of Botany*, vol. XXIV, N° XCV, p. 571. London, July 1910. This paper was summarized in: *The Science and Practice of Farming during 1190 in Great Britain*. Int. Inst. of Agriculture. P. 129. Rome, 1910. (*Ed.*).

be explained by some indirect chemical or biological action of the zinc on the constituents in the soil, rather than to any stimulating action of the toxin on the plant. Ehrenberg concludes that zinc vessels ought never to be used in vegetation experiments.

"P. Hoenig (*Landw. Jahrb.*, 1910, 39, 775) also reports a long series of experiments on the action of chromium salts on vegetation, in which he claims to demostrate that both the chromium salts and the chromates, although normally toxic, may act as stimuli. However, Mr. A. D. Hall observes that the conclusion as to stimulus is vitiated by the fact that the additions of chromium were always made to soil in which the test plants were growing, and very involved actions are taking place in the soil.

"Otto and Kooper (*Zeitseh. Nahr. Genussm.*, 1910, 9, 10; A., II, 233) published a paper on the changes of the composition of fruit as it ripens after gathering. The experiments were made with sloes and the authors found that in the ripening process the laevulose increased while the dextrose decreased, and during the same time both the acids and the amount of tannin was larger than the net increase of sugar, the difference no doubt representing losses by respiration, and the authors considered that the other figures indicated a change from dextrose to laevulose, a change, however, which is very difficult to credit (1).

"Another paper, although a contribution to the study of genetics, is yet of general interest to plant-physiologists, because of its possible bearing on enzyme actions in living plants, is one by M. Wheldale(2) on the inheritance of colour in certain sweet peas and stocks".

1639 M. BRIDEL. **Meliatine: a New Glucoside from Bogbean, *Menyanthes trifoliata*.** (La méliatine. nouveau glucoside, hydrolysable par l'émulsine, rétiré du Trèfle d'eau) *C. R. de l'Acad. des Sciences,* t. 152, n. 24, pp. 1694-1696. Paris, 12 Juin 1911.

France In studying Bogbean (*Menyanthes trifoliata* L.) the writer applied M. Bourquelot's biochemical method to the fresh plant; he detected the presence of a glucoside capable of hydrolysis by synaptase.

---

(1) Cp. with LINDET's researches, *C. R. Acad. d. Sc.* 20 Mars 1911, and this *Bulletin*, Abstr. 1108, April 1911.

(2) Summarized in: *The Science and Practice of Farming during* 1910 *in Great Britain*. Int. Inst. of Agricltlture. P. 134. Rome, 1910.

This glucoside, which he calls *meliatine*, is a white crystalline body without smell, and with a distinct bitter taste which develops after a few seconds ; it is laevo-rotatory. Under the action of synaptase it yields δ-glucose. Meliatine contains no nitrogen. Organic analysis and cryoscopic tests suggest the formula $C_{15} H_{22} O_9$. On total hydrolysis Meliatine should yield 52.02 % of glucose.

F. T. Shutt.   **Flax Seed.** — *Experimental Farms, Report of the Chemist*, pp. 204-205. Ottawa, 1910. (App. to the Rep. of the Min. of Agr.).

1640

Considerable differences in composition are known to exist among consignements of linseed upon the market. Recognizing that the value of flax seed or linseed must depend to a large extent on its composition, the writer analysed twenty samples representing as many distinct strains grown by the Government Cerealist on the Experimental Farm, Ottawa, in 1909.

Canada

The percentage of oil varied from 34.50 to 42.20 averaging 37.10. The percentage of protein varied from 19.06 to 27.56, the average being 24.77. A study of the data shows that while there is a relationship between the oil and protein content no constant ratio exists. In a general way, however, the tendency is for the protein to vary inversely as the oil. The weight of 1 000 seeds varies greatly, the extremes being 3.9044 gr. and 8.8538 gr., the average being 4.9151 gr.

Attention may be directed to the results of varieties. La Plata A and B, which are very high in weight ; they are associated with a particularly large and plump seed.

An attempt at correlation of these data of seed weght with those for the oil and protein content did not reveal any relationship. It was, however very evident that the weight varied with the size.

F. T. Shutt.   **Wheat Straw at Different Stages of Growth. Early cut Straw to be preferred as Fodder.** — *Experimental Farms, Report of the Chemist, Wheat*, pp. 194-196. Ottawa, 1910. (App. to the Rep. of the Min. of Agr.).

1641

In relation to the investigation on the influence of environment on the composition of wheat, the writer thought it desirable to make a study of the composition, as regards nitrogen compounds, of the straw of the wheat plant at different stages, from the flowering period to that of dead ripeness.

Canada

A portion of a large plot of « Bishop », spring wheat, was investigated. In the collection of the samples the plants were cut 10 cm, from the ground and the ears were immediately removed in order to prevent migration of the nutrients from the straw. In all, seven cuttings were made, the first being on July 9, 1909, when the plants were in flower and the last on August 24, when the grain was dead ripe.

In the tabulated statement of data the following information is given : date of collection, stage of growth when sample was taken, the proportional weights of ears and straw, the percentage of dry matter; lastly, the percentage of total and albuminoid nitrogen present in the dry matter, from which the proportion of total nitrogen in the form of albuminoid has been calculated.

Considering first the proportional weights of ears and straw, it is observed that the weight of the ears increased from the beginning to the close of the collection period. The largest increase in this weight occurred between the « earlymilk » and the « dough » stages, and the next largest between the latter and the « late dough » stage, when the kernel was quite plump. The increases in proportional weight of the ears during the latter portion of the collection period are to be attributed more especially to the rapid drying out of the straw.

Coming to the changes in the composition of the straw during growth and ripening, the dry matter increased from the earliest stage of the collection, when the plant was in flower, until the grain was dead ripe. The total nitrogen in the fresh straw remained practically constant, until the kernel had reached the dough stage; it then declined somewhat rapidly, until the grain was ready for harvesting. From this on, there was a marked increase until the grain was dead ripe. Considering the total nitrogen content of the dry matter, a steady decrease was noticed until the grain was ready for harvesting, after which it remained practically constant.

The study of the character of the nitrogen compounds in the straw, as the plant proceeds from the flowering stage to that of complete maturity, is one of the most interesting features of the investigation. Until the late dough stage, the proportion of albuminoid to non albuminoid nitrogen remains fairly constant. When this period has been reached and the grain begins to mature, there is a sudden, though not very large, increase found as albuminoids. In these facts the writer finds a strong proof of the constancy of composition of the nitrogenous material of the dry matter during the earlier period of the grain development, when the straw is in full functional activity. Subsequently as the straw loses vitality, which is indicated by its turning yellow, there is appa rently a more or less rapid conversion into the albuminoid form.

From the stand point of the farmer who wishes to know what may be the feeding value of wheat straw cut at one or other of the final stages of the grains' development, this investigation shows that while the dry matter of the straw becomes poorer in nitrogenous compounds as the grain develops, the total amount of such nitrogen in the straw does not materially alter by reason of the ever-increasing storage in the straw of dry ma tter. The practical conclusions from this is that straw cut before the grain is fully ripe differs in feeding value from that cut later. Chiefly by reason of its greater digestibility, rather than from the presence of any larger proportion of the more valuable nutrients. The earlier cut straw is then the more nutritious fodder: not as some suppose by the possession of a large percentage of albuminoids, but from the greater availability of its constituents for the nourishment of the animal.

W. F. SUTHERST. **Sugar Content of Oranges.** — *California Cultivator.* **1642** Vol. XXVI, N. 20, p. 612, Los Angeles, May 18, 1911.

The writer carried out a number of analyses of Valencia oranges of varying degrees of ripeness, and dividing each into three parts estimated the amount of acid (as citric acid), grape sugar and cane **United** sugar. The work was carried out in the chemical laboratory of **States:** the Bonita High School, Arizona, on Valencia oranges taken from **Arizona** the neighboring orchards. The following results were obtained per cent.

I. Green.

	Stalk end	Middle	Top
Acid	2.49	3.32	2.27
Grape sugar	4.16	3.87	4.00
Cane sugar	3.24	4.60	5.32

II. Middle Ripe.

Acid , ...	2.41	2.66	2.13
Grape sugar	2.62	3.08	3.30
Cane sugar	2.54	4.82	5.34

III. Ripe.

Acid	2.57	2.61	2.06
Grape sugar	3.25	3.92	4.30
Cane sugar	4.73	5.45	6.02

From the results it is seen that 1) the acid decreases with age to a slight extent, with the larger percentage in the middle portion ; consequently to produce a fruit with the minimum amount of acid, a long, narrow shape is required ; 2) the grape sugar (glucose or dextrose) varies slightly in amount in different parts of the orange ; but as this substance does not add much to the sweetness of the orange, consideration of it may be neglected ; 3) the cane sugar generally increases throughout the fruit with age, but is more highly developed in the top (navel end) ; as a very little of this sugar serves to increase the sweetness, a development of this end would ensure a sweeter fruit.

1648   ERNST SCHULZE. **Protein Formation in Ripening Seeds**. (Zeltsch. physiol. Chem. 1911, 71, 31-48). *The Journal of the Chemical Society*, Abs. 322. London, April, 1911.

Unripe pods of the vetch (*Vicia sativa*) were gathered late in August and divided into hulls and unripe seeds ; these were analysed

Germany   separately. The hulls contained very much more asparagine than the unripe seeds, but less arginine, although the difference in this respect was not so great as with peas and with *Phaseolus vulgaris*, owing probably to the *Vicia* seeds being nearly ripe.

Asparagine in quantities varying from 1 to 2 % of the dried plant was found in young plants harvested during May and June of *Vicia sativa*, *Trifolium pratense*, and *Medicago sativa*. The two former also contained guanosine, whilst leucine was obtained from the *Vicia* and perhaps also from the *Medicago*. The amount of asparagine in young leguminous plants increases when they are stored for a few days in the dark.

A detailed investigation has shown that young leguminous plants only contain mere traces of arginine ; in peas a little was obtained from the roots, but none from the above-ground portions. It is considered that the influx of arginine to the seeds must at the best be very small ; and that therefore arginine is formed in the seeds. In the ripening seed as in young leaves, asparagine is used for the synthesis of protein ; in general, the synthesis of protein takes the same course in both parts of the plant.

A comparison of the non-protein nitrogen compounds in the unripe seeds and in the rest of the plants, shows that tryptophan is rapidly used by the seeds, glutanine only slowly. Further investigation in this direction is expected to indicate more completely those of the non-protein nitrogenous constituents which pass into the seed and are used for protein synthesis.

H. E. ARMSTRONG and E. F. ARMSTRONG. **The Function of Hormones in Regulating Metabolism**. *Annals of Botany*, Vol. XXV, N. XCVIII, pp. 507-519, London, April 1911,

1644

The invaluable series of observations made by Adrian J. Brown with blue barley, *Hordeum vulgare* var. *caerulescens* have shown that the grain is surrounded with a membrane of extreme tenuity which is penetrable by but few mineral substances and also not by sugars etc., and the writers' observations showed that the leaf is protected in a precisely similar manner. The protection is obviously afforded by what is perhaps best termed a *differential septum*, the term semipermeable membrane being far too narrow and misleading as an indication of the functional significance of the membrane. As it appeared to be desirable to give a special name to the class of substances that pass through differential septa such as are met with in the barley grain and laurel leaf, exciting activity within the cells when they have thus gained an entry, the writers have proposed that the term *Hormone* given by Starling to certain excitants of functional activity in the animal organism (including carbon dioxide) should be applied to all such substances. The hormones as a class are substances which have but slight attraction for water and may therefore be spoken of as *anhydrophilic*; hydrophillic substances generally fail to penetrate septa which are selective to the degree manifest in cereal grains and the laurel leaf. The writers believe this criterion to be one of special importance. In all their experiments freshly-picked leaves were either exposed to the vapour of the substance to be tried in corked tubes, or nearly immersed in solutions. The tests were made both at room temperatures and at 37° C., with leaves picked at different periods throughout last year (1910). Young leaves picked in the spring responded far more rapidly to stimulation than older leaves collected in the late summer and autumn.

Great Britain:

As in the case of the laurel leaf, the substances found to be inactive were: weak solutions of mineral acids, caustic soda and most metallic salts. The active salts were mercuric chloride (not nitrate nor sulphate) cadmium iodide (not chloride) sodium and potassium fluoride. Iodine, carbon dioxide and hydrogen sulphide act slowly; ammonia very rapidly.

Acids of the acetic series were found to be effective in the order observed by Loeb and others, activity being most marked in the case of the least soluble acids of highest molecular weight. The same may be said of the alcohols of the methylic series. Lactic, benzoic, picric and salicylic acids act slowly, oxalic, tartaric/ and citric acids are inert.

Volatile hydrocarbons, especially benzene and toluene, carbon bisulphide, chloroform, ethers and ethereal salts, aldehydes, acetone, camphor, piperidine and phenols, are all very active excitants; paraldehyde in aqueous solution is also very active.

The picture that the authors have formed of the mode in which hormones gain an entry involves the conception that the surfaces of the intermolecular spaces in the differential septa are coated with a protective sheath of molecules of " hydrone, " OH_2, the fundamental molecule of water.

The main effect produced by hormones when they gain entry into the living cell is the stimulation of enzymic artivity, and it is supposed that they exercice a determining influence in regulating metabolism in plants as well as in animals.

During the daytime, while regenerative changes prevail, the proportion of diffusible hormones in circulation must be relatively small and water will have little tendency to pass in through the leaf surfaces.

As the light diminishes, degenerative changes set in and gradually increase in intensity: these undoubtedly give rise to carbon dioxide and other hormones which serve to induce the entry of water at the leaf surface.

The development of perfume by flowering plants in the evening is clearly an external manifestation of the beginning of the degradation process; flowering in fact, marks the onset of the period when degenerative processes begin to prevail and the accumulated stores of material are set in circulation to develop the reproductive organs and seed. The perfume itself must exercise a stimulative influence on the plant in which it is produced.

The increased fertility in partially sterilised soils is with reason attributed by Russell to the destruction of Protozoa and the increased activity of Bacteria which perform the gradual break-down of organic matter. The writers are inclined to believe that the carbon dioxide and the ammonia which are present in partially sterilised soils, in larger quantity in comparison with the unsterilized, are of prime importance in facilitating plant growth by affording the stimuli required to determine the degenerative changes involved in the translocation of nutritive materials. They are also inclined to believe that in more or less effectually sterilized soils by heating the germination of seeds takes place much less rapidly than in unsterilized soils, because carbon dioxide and ammonia, the latter especially perhaps, are produced only in abnormally small amounts, if at all; and therefore the necessary stimulus to the inhibition of water and germination is lacking. Mr. Pickering attributes the slow germination of seeds in such soils to the production of substances which have a directly toxic effect.

The experiments made at the Woburn Fruit Farm by the Duke of Bedford and Mr. Pickering have brought into prominence the highly deleterious effect of grass on the growth of trees and the earlier annual maturity of trees the roots of which are covered with grass. Mr. Pickering, after testing various possibilities, has been led to assume that toxic substances are formed by the growth of the grass and that these affect the underlying roots of trees.

Here again, taking into account the pronounced aminophilic habits of the Gramineae, the writers are inclined to think that the roots of trees under grass suffer because they are more or less completely deprived of the stimulus afforded by the greater proportion of ammonia and carbon dioxide in bare soils. To the stimulative influence of ammonia may also be due the advantages which under certain conditions sulphate of ammonia shows over nitrate of soda as a nitrogenous manure. The writers also propose to make an experimental inquiry on the assumption that some part at least of the influence exercised by the nodules of leguminous plants may be due to their aminogenetic power.

Most leaves become more or less brown when exposed to the action of either chloroform or toluene. The most striking exemplification of this change is offered by *Aucuba Japonica*, the common spotted Japanese laurel and also by *Azara microphylla*. The leaves of *Drosera* become intensely black when placed in toluene vapour.

The brown-black colour of ripe banana is easily produced by exposing the fruit to an anaesthetic. The autumn coloration of leaves and their fall may well, at least in part, be conditioned by processes of a similar order, by a sudden outburst of hormones, which either determine the occurrence of special enzymic changes or hasten such changes. Similar considerations may apply to the ripening of seeds.

Discussing the physiological significance of glucosides especially of cyanophoric glucosides, the writers are inclined to take the view that in not a few instances at all events, the compound associated with glucose functions simply as a hormone. In some cases the cyanophoric glucoside disappears as the seed ripens, in *Linum* for example ; maybe hydrogen cyanide is of special service in hastening ripening; or when present in the seed, as in mustard, the glucoside may undergo hydrolysis during germination and furnish a hormone which serves to stimulate the growth of the seedling. The extent to which hormones are producible may have something to

do with the various degrees of readiness with which seeds germinate. From the writers' point of view, it is improbable that hydrogen cyanide is ever present as such except in minimal amount,
unless perhaps at certain special times; it would necessarily escape
at a rapid rate if it were thrown into circulation.

In their communication to the Royal Society, the writers have
contended that one effect of the entry of a hormone in a living
cell is to condition the introduction of water and that the consequent
dilution of the cell contents would determine the occurrence of
down- grade changes. It appears also probable that a primary effect
of the hormones is to condition the separation from each other of
the successive layers which may be supposed to constitute the pro-
toplasmatic complex; although deposited in close contact, these are
perhaps sheathed with thin layers of hydrone molecules, and disin-
tegration sets in when the aqueous layers are penetrated by the
hormone. A similar effect would be produced by freezing.

Assuming such changes to happen, enzymes previously stored
in the cells would be set at liberty, and by their action the proportion of molecules in solution would be rapidly and largely increased. In other words, the osmotic tension would be raised and a
flow of water determined to the region in which the hormone is
active.

1645   MAZÉ. **Influence on Plant Development of the Mineral Matter which
accumulates in the Organs as the Residue of Assimilation.
Absorption of Colloidal Organic Matter by the Roots.** — *C. R.
Acad. Sciences*, Tome 152, N. 12, pp. 783, 785. Paris, 20 Mars
1911.

France

Exosmose, by the roots, of unused mineral matter, and the
secretion by the leaves, of water saturated with salts, seem to be
the means of defence possessed by plants against the accumulation
of unassimilable matter.

The excessive absorption of soda and of sulphuric acid in the form
of nitrate or of ammoniacal salt is injurious to the evolution of the
plant, whereas hydrochloric acid behaves in a quite different manner
for reasons not yet discovered.

The writer has ascertained these facts by cultivating maize plants
in a nutritive solution, in which he varied the kind of nitrogen food
whilst keeping the proportion of nitrogen constant. He was thus
able to observe the effect of sodium nitrate, of the sulphuric acid,
and of the hydrochloric acid of ammonia salts.

In the case of crops raised on a large scale the result of such treatments pass, as a rule, unperceived: as the constituent elements of the soil neutralise the acids and bases thus excreted.

Other experiments were made to study the absorption of colloidal organic matter by the roots. Maize plants grown in the same nutritive solution, in which the nitrogenous food was a sulphate or a chloride of ammonium, and then placed in bottles containing either starch jelly peptone, and peptone with nitrate of ammonium, dissolved in distilled water, or humus dissolved in ammonia, absorbed organic colloidal matter. This assimilation is seen by examining the figures given in the table which summarises the results of these enquiries.

The writer draws attention to the fact that the starch shows no trace of liquefaction nor of saccharification; the starch jelly contains no amylase. Solutions of saccharose given to well developed plants contained no sucrase. Contrary to what the writer affirmed some years ago, the roots excreted no amylase nor sucrase; and the inversion of the saccharose, and the saccharification of the starch, take place slowly under the influence of the progressive acidification of the nutritive solutions.

J. STOKLASA. **The Chemical Nature of Root Secretions.** — *Seventh International Congress of Applied Chemistry*, London, May 27th to June 2nd, 1909, Section VII, Agricultural Chemistry, p. 83 London, 1910.

1646

The secretions from roots grown in moist air were investigated in parallel experiments, under conditions of abundant aeration, with ordinary air, and with deficient aeration with air containing nitrogen 94 % and oxygen 6 %. Under the latter conditions lactic, formic, acetic or oxalic acid (with *Beta vulgaris*) were found, either singly or together, in the culture liquids, or in the water with which the roots were washed. Under conditions of sufficient aeration none of these acids could be detected; and the conclusion is drawn that the acids must not be considered as normal secretions of the roots, but merely products of respiration with an insufficient supply of oxygen. The only acid which could be detected with aerobic respiration was carbon dioxide. The experimental plants, *Zea mays*, *Pisum sativum*, *Triticum vulgare*, *Phaseolus vulgaris*, and *Lupinus luteus* were kept under conditions of sterilisation from the beginning and were grown

Austria: Bohemia

in sterilised water. All experiments were made with careful exclusion of bacteria, so that no bacterial secretions could compromise the results.

1647   T. A. KIESSELBACH. **Transpiration Experiment with the Maize Plant. Preliminary Report.** — *Twenty third Annual Report of the Agricultural Experiment Station of Nebraska.* Appendix, pp. 125-139, Ch. II, pl. IV, fgs, 2, Lincoln, Nebraska, U. S. A. 1910.

United
States:
Nebraska

Experiments were made with 40 plants of the " Yellow Dent " variety of maize. Twenty of these were cultivated for 64 days on a rich clay alfalfa soil, watered with spring water ; and twenty others for 76 days on sand watered with a complete nutritive solution. The plants grown in the clay soil were divided into 5 groups of 4 plants each, and each group was kept at a different degree of saturation. The plants grown in sand were kept at an almost constant saturation of 100 %, and were divided into 4 groups of 5 plants each, each group being watered with a nutritive solution of different strength.

The amount of water consumed by these plants in obtaining a certain yield had no relation to the moisture of the soil, other factors remaining constant. Maize plants of the same variety when grown, some in a damp soil and others in a much drier soil, transpired a like amount of moisture, as long as the drought was not so severe as to endanger their life.

The amount of water required to produce the same weight of dry matter on dry soil is, indeed, a trifle less than on moist soil, but the effective yield is also reduced.

It would seem that the stomata have hardly any function of their own in reestablishing the equilibrium between external conditions and the proportion of moisture transpired.

This proportion is determined by climatic factors, the most important of which is the relative moisture of the atmosphere. The curve of transpiration corresponds pretty nearly to the curve of evaporation.

If the ratio of evaporation from a sheet of water in a given locality is known, an approximate idea of the conditions requisite for transpiration can be formed.

An experiment was made in growing maize plants from 2 to 5 months in pure river sand, watered with a complete nutritive solution ; but the results obtained showed no marked relation between the concentration of the solution and the amount of water required for the production of a unit of dry matter.

The root-development is relatively much more considerable in dry soil than in moist. Plants which have passed the first phase of their growth in a dry soil, are more likely to resist a subsequent period of drought, owing to the large absorbant surface they offer to the soil molecules.

J. W. LEATHER. **Transpiration of Water by Plants in Bengal.** — *Seventh International Congress of Applied Chemistry*, London, May 24th to June 2nd, 1909, Section VII, Agricultural Chemistry, pp. 100-105, London, 1900.

1648

Transpiration experiments by pot-culture methods were carried out at Pusa in Bengal, the following points being considered : the nature of the plant, the fertility of the soil, the proportion of water in the soil, the character of the season.

British India: Bengal

As a general conclusion the Author assumes that each plant has its own special transpiration ratio, which is the amount of water transpired per unit of dry matter produced during the whole growing period. The magnitude of this ratio is the outcome in part of the atmospheric conditions which have surrounded the plant during its life history through many generations, and this ratio is temporarily effected by such causes as fertility of the soil, manure, etc. Consequently it is impossible to form correct judgment as to whether the vegetation of a certain region transpires more or less, than in another, without accurate knowledge of the transpiration ratios of at least the chief plants included. Moreover, from the agricultural point of view, it is of equal importance to know the weight of crops grown, since this is the second chief factor which regulates the total water transpired in any region.

Turning to the special question as to whether transpiration is greater or less in the tropics than in Europe, it will be evident that there is so great a variation in transpiration ratio, among different plants, that it becomes necessary to exercise care as to how a comparison is made. The European ratios are taken from Lawes' and Hellriegel's data.

A comparison made on this basis shows that the four millets *Eleusine coracana*, *Paspalum scrobiculatum*, *Cyamopsis psoralioides*,

Cajanus Indicus have a rather higher transpiration ratio than the similar European crops, the difference being however only small. Finally, a comparison of the ratios of wheat, barley and peas grown in India during the cold period, with those grown in Europe, shows that the ratios found for the latter are much the lower; the climate, however, at this period is not hot, nor very moist, and cannot be called " tropical ".

1649   G. RIVIÈRE et G. BAILHACHE. **On the Increase in Weight of Long Turnips, of the « de Croissy » Variety, and of the progressive Increase of their Constituent Parts**. (De l'accroissement en poids des Navets longs dits « de Croissy » et de l'augmentation progressive de leurs principaux éléments constitutifs). — *Journal de la Société Nationale d'Horticulture de France*, 4ᵉ série, tome XII, pp. 186-191, Paris, Avril 1911.

France   By continuing during 1910 his experiments begun the previous year, the writer has been able to draw up the two following tables.

TABLE I.

Increase in weight of the Turnips of the « de Croissy » variety, from the 25th day after the seeds were sown till the date of gathering.

Dates	Weight of 10 whole turnips (Roots and leaves)	Weight of roots (10 roots)	Weight of leaves (10 leafy crowns)	Variation between two weighings		Remarks
				Roots only	Leaves only	
10 June	—	—	—	—	—	Sowing
5 July	160 grams	20 gr.	140 gr.	—	—	25ᵗʰ day
10 —	495 grams	110 gr	385 gr,	+ 90 gr.	+ 245 gr.	30ᵗʰ —
15 —	1010 grams	365 gr.	645 gr.	+ 255 gr.	+ 340 gr.	35ᵗʰ —
20 —	1880 grams	920 gr.	960 gr.	+ 555 gr.	+ 315 gr.	40ᵗʰ —
25 —	2140 grams	1220 gr.	920 gr.	+ 300 gr,	— 40 gr.	45ᵗʰ —

TABLE II

Increase, per 1000 parts of normal matter, of the several constituent parts of turnips of the « de Croissy » variety, from the 25th day after sowing until the 45th day, when they were gathered.

	25th day from sowing		30th day		35th day		40th day		45th day	
	leaves	roots	leaves	roots	leaves	roots	leaves	roots	leaves	roots
Water % . .	91.70	93.20	93.20	94.10	94.14	93.46	93.35	94.15	92.50	94.80
Dry Matter	8.30	6.80	6.80	5.90	5.86	6.54	6.65	5.85	7.50	5.20
Sugar % . .	0.73	1.70	0.55	2.20	0.40	2.47	0.45	2.77	0.75	3.60
Nitrogen . .	0.45	0.30	0.34	0.20	0.28	0.20	0.33	0.19	0.30	0.12
Corresp. Albuminoids	2.8125	1.875	2.125	1.250	1.750	1.250	2.0625	1.1875	1.875	0.75
Ash	1.75	0.95	1.50	0.75	1.24	0.83	1.46	0.75	1.45	0.55

This table clearly shows the increase of useful constituents, more especially of sugar, in the roots, and the decrease of ash, or useless matter. The proportion of nitrogen also decreases notably. The proportion of water is always considerable.

The writer has also drawn up a table giving the total weight of the principal constituents of ten « de Croissy » turnips, from the 25th day of vegetation, which show that on the 45th day:

1. The weight of the leaves is 6 ½ times greater than on the 25th day. 2. The root-weight is 61 times greater than on the 25th day. 3. The weight of sugar, in comparison with that on the 25th day, is 6 ½ times greater in the leaves, and 129 times greater in roots.

R. COMBES. **Current Opinions on the Physiological Phenomena which accompany the Fall of Leaves.** (Les opinions actuelles sur les phenomènes physiologiques qui accompagnent la chute des feuilles). — *Révue générale de Botanique.* t. XXIII n. 268, pp. 129-k 64. Paris, 15 Avril 1911.

1650

This review of current opinion on the changes which precede and accompany the fall of leaves, shows that if studies hitherto made are far from having settled all the points involved they have

France

at least shown beyond doubt that the leaves which fall in autumn still contain a considerable proportion of substances—as, for instance, starch and sngar compounds—which could have been utilised by the plants.

They have also shown that the substances which do not disappear or which even accumulate in the leaves in autumn in the period preceding their fall, should not be considered *a priori* as substances useless to the plants which contain them. Therefore, in interpreting the results obtained from the study of the immediate constituents of plants, either by microchemical methods or by quantitative analysis, the persistence or accumulation of such constituent parts in falling leaves must not be considered as evidence of the uselessness or poisonous nature of these substances.

1651   J. A. Le Clerc. and G. F. Breazeale. **Plant Food Removed from growing Plants by Rain or Dew**. — *Seventh International Congress of Applied Chemistry*, London, May 27th to June 2nd 1909., Section VII., Agricultural Chemistry, pp. 55-78. London 1910.

From previous researches of other investigators and from the authors' experiments it is shown that:

1. On ripening, the salts held in the sap of the plants have a

United States   tendency to migrate from the dying to the living tissue.

2. That this migration is upward and not downward: there being, in fact, little evidence to show excretion through the roots into the soil.

3. The plants exude their salts upon their surface; and rain or dew then washes these salts back to the soil.

4. The analysis of plants for ash ingredients may give erroneous results, especially if it is desired to arrive at the amount of plant food absorbed by, or essential to, plant growth, unless the amount of these ingredients removed from the plants by rain, dew, etc. be taken into consideration.

1652   E. East. **The Transmission of Variations in the Potato in the Asexual Reproduction**. — (*Connecticut Agr. Expt. St. Dep.* 1910, p. 119-160); *Zeitschrift induktive Abstammungs-und Vererbungslehre.* Band IV, Heft 5, pp. 374-395. Berlin, März 1911.

United States: Connecticut   This note shows the analogy between the inheritance of fluctuations in asexual reprodution of multicellular organisms and in the reproduction of *pure strains* (of Johannsen and Jennings). It has been found that the proportions of starch and of nitrogenous substances in the dry matter can neither of them be changed by the selection of fluctuations and their subsequent asexual reproduction.

It is the same with fluctuations in yield, except for certain cases which may be due to mutations.

The writer believes that all cases of bud-sports are due to the loss of an epistatic factor. In pink-tubered varieties, white tubers appeared and remained constant. In four other varieties the shape changed from oval to round, and in two of these the change was permanent.

In four others the eyes changed from shallow to deep, and the change proved permanent. A peculiar variation in the formation of the tuber was also partly retained. With the exception of the last, all these characters are recessive.

The writer concludes that Mendelian segregations are not confined to the divisions following on maturity of the germ cells.

F. MERKEL. **Spring Selection of Cereals, Beetroots, and Potatoes, in Germany.** (Zur Sortenauswahl in Fruhjahr.). — *Mitteilungen der Deutschen Landw. Ges.*, XXVI Jahrgang, Stuck 13, pp. 162 166. Berlin 25 März 1911.   1658

This is an account of the results of experiments made in 1910 by the Plant Selection Bureau of the German Agricultural Society. These experiments, made in several parts of Germany, deal with the most important and varied kinds of crops: cereals, root and tuber crops, pulse.   **Germany**

March wheat - the commercial varieties of March wheat can be subdivided into two groups: slow growing and quick growing wheat. The latter variety is in request for localities exposed for long periods to floods, and generally excessively damp, and also where it is desirable to have the wheat ripen at different dates so as to facilitate harvesting operations.

The characters of these two groups of varieties will be yet more evident if they are compared as follows:

a) slow growing: requires carefully selected soil and cultivation, and gives a high yield. The varieties of this group are suited to districts where intensive agriculture is practiced. The best results of this kind were obtained with the « Strubes roter Schlanstedter », selected from March wheat of Bordeaux (France), almost entirely immune to « smut »; and with « Heines Japhet », also selected from French types, but little inferior to « Rimpaus roter Schlans-tedter ».

b) quick growing: few requirements, but yield rather low. These varieties are specially suited to districts where extensive farming is practiced; they have few needs and ripen early: « Strubes begrannter »; « Galizischer Kolben »; and « Heines Kolben »

Barleys — These barleys can be classified, like the March wheats, into two groups: the slow growing and the quick growing. The varieties of the first group, with grains with a low proteid content, are used in brewing. Such are the « Imperial », « Pfauen », « Heines Goldthorpe », « Heydenreichs Goldthorpe », etc.

The varieties of the second group, with a high proteid content, are used as forage and for distilling alcohol. Amongst these are « Hannagerste » « Svalöfs Hannchen » and « Rethges Gerston I, II and III ».

Oats. — Of late years the varieties of oats have been constantly increasing in number. Experiments made by the « Society of German Agriculturists », from 1908 to 1910, aimed at obtaining types suited to heavy soils and types suited to light soils.

Amongst the first, « Svalöfs Goldregen » and « Strubes Schlunstedter » gave the best results. Of the second the « Leutewiter Gelb hafer » is the one which best resists drought.

« Svalöfs Siegeshafer » gains in favor and is a serious rival to « Svalöf-Goldregen ».

« Fichtelgebirgshafer », which is well suited to the cold high plateaus of Central and Southern Germany, yields well and its straw is stiff and strong.

Sugar Beets and Mangels Swedes, Carrots - These plants also need selecting for two types: those for use in districts where intensive farming is the rule (they have a high yield but require much care), and those intended for extensive farming (they yield less, but require no special care).

As a forage beet, or mangel, the « Eckendorfer gelb » is recommended.

Potatoes — The best varieties are:

1) for yield of tubers: « Hesse », « Eimbals Alma », and « Richters Fürstenkrone ».

2) For high starch-content: « Paulsens Agraria », «Graf Arnims » « Erste von Nassenheide » and « Eimbals Wohltmann ».

3) For yield of starch: « Eimbals Professor Wohltmann », « Böhms Erfolg », and « Dolkowski's Switez » and « Bohun ».

Pulse — Leguminous plants, particularly those for forage, were the subject of lengthy researches and interesting experiments.

JOSEPH BURTT-DAVY, **Inheritance of Row-numbers in Maize Ears.**
Nature, Vol. 86, N. 2167, pp, 347-348. London, May, 11, 1911.

1654

It is well known among maize-growers that the number of rows of grain on an ear of maize varies from 8 to 25, or even more, according to the breed; also that in the same breed the number may vary within certain limits, *e. g.* 8, 10, or 12 in some breeds, 12, 14, 16, or 18 in others, and 18, 20, 22 or 24 in yet others. In some breeds the range of variation is even greater, while in others it seems to be more closely limited. In some breeds an ear carrying more than 8 rows is considered untrue to type, but the writer is not aware that any South African grower has yet succeeded in fixing the number of rows in any breed to such a degree that *no variation* occurs in that respect.

S. African
Union

In the course of a series of breeding experiments which are not yet completed, Mr Burtt Davy has met with the following interesting case.

Thirty-three plants of «Arcadia» sugar-maize, each of which bore two well-developed ears, were studied as regards number of rows. On 21 plants the number on the upper ear was different from that on the lower, while on 12 plants the number was the same on each ear. Of the 21 plants on which the number of rows was different on the two ears, 13 had a larger number on the lower than on the upper, while 8 had a smaller number on the lower than on the upper.

The total number of ears producing any given number of rows was as follows:

Rows	. . .	8	10	12	14	
Ears	. . .	11	23	30	2	Total 66.

The «Arcadia» is a white sugar-maize, obtained from a cross between a normally 8-rowed «Black Mexican» and a white flour-corn normally bearing a large number of rows, but the writer does not know that either was pure bred for row numbers, and no subsequent selection in this line had been made.

It is generally supposed by maize-growers that the number of rows is a definite, heritable character. Results obtained by crossing two other breeds, an 8-row and 18-row (each believed to be pure as regards this character), have this year produced irregular results in the F_1 generation. However, the case described above seems to indicate that the development of rows is, within certain limits, a vegetative character, depending in part on seasonal conditions and on food supply. This view is strengthened by the fact that this is the first year in which 14-row ears have been noticed in this breed, all the parent ears for two or three generations having been 8-, 10-, or 12-rowed (so far as the author is aware). At the same time, there is ample indication that, within certain limits, row-numbers are inherited in the maize plant; but it is doubtful whether any South African strains are yet sufficiently pure-bred for this character to demonstrate the point with absolute certainty.

1655   D. Larionov. **Selection of a Sunflower resistant to certain Pests.** — See Abstr. 1951 in this Bulletin.

1656   F. Lafar. **Technical Mycology: The Utilisation of Micro-Organisms in the Arts and Manufactures etc.** Translated by Charles T. C. Salter. Vol. II. *Eumycetic Fermentation.* Part. II. pp. 10 + 191 + 748: London, 1910. Abst. Reviewed in *Nature*, N. 2161, Vol. 86, p. 140. London, March 3, 1911.

This is the English translation of the second part of the second volume of Prof. Lafar's well- known book. It succeeds the previous
.Austria   part after an interval of seven years, and completes the work.
In an introductory section Prof. Lafar takes up the general question of yeast nutrition and yeast culture, and brings his subject well up to date.
The Author points out the importance of the presence of certain mineral foodstuffs, and indicates the possible sources of organic foodstuffs, laying special stress on the sources of nitrogen and on the oxygen requirements of the yeast cell. Here, in connection with Hansen's experiments, he indicates the most favourable conditions for cell reproduction, and the oxygen requirements for both cell-reproduction and respiration.
Then follows a description of the effect of copper and its salts, inorganic acids and salts, organic stimulants and poisons, and of alcohol itself upon the yeast cells.
Some part of this is repeated by Albert Klöchar, of Copenhagen, who, treating the matter from a somewhat different point of view, gives an account of the life-history and variability of the Saccharomycetes and describes fundamental researches into the life-history of these organisms, temporary variations, and the production of sporing and non-sporing forms, and the development and mainte-

nance of these varieties under various definite conditions. Klöcher also contributes a full classification of the families Saccharomycetaceae and Schizosaccaromycetaceae.

In a chapter on the morphology and subdivision of the family Aspergillaceae, Prof. Carl Wehmer gives an account of the saccharification of starch, acid fermentation, formation of alcohol, and the degradation of proteids and their derivatives by the members of this family.

Special articles are also contributed by Prof. G. Lindau on *Cladosporium herbarum* and *Dematium pullulans ;* by Dr. H. Will on " The Torulaceae, Pink Yeasts and Black Yeasts "; by Prof. Richard Meissner on Mycoderma or " Mother of Vinegar "; by Prof. H. Müller-Thurgau on " The History, Morphology and Fermentation phenomena of *Saccharomyces apiculatus* "; by Dr. H. Wichmann on the Moniliae and Oidia ; and, in the section devoted to enzymes and enzyme action of yeast, by Dr. Rudolf Rapp on '· Alcoholase ", by Dr. Arminius Bau on " The Chemistry of Alcoholic Fermentation and on the Enzymes Decomposing the various Sugars "; Whilst Dr. Lafar and Dr. M. Hahn close the work with a chapter on " Endotryptase and Philotion ".

The bibliography given at the end of the book covers more than 130 pages, each page containing from 20 to 30 titles of papers. In this volume is contained the index of the whole work (vol. I and vol. II, part. I and II).

W. L. OMELIANSKY and O. P. SEWEROWA. **Pigment Formation in** some *Azotobacter chroococcum* **Cultures**. (Die Pigment bildung in Kulturen des *Azotobacter chroococcum*). — *Centrablatt für Bakteriologie* etc⎰ Jena, 8 april 1911. **1657**

The formation of pigments when growing in certain culture-media is characteristic of some forms of *Azotobacter chroococcum*.

Between the coloured and colourless forms there are intermediate ones in which pigmentation has been in some measure hindered. The age of the culture used for inoculation has an effect upon the pigmentation, which is produced sooner when old brown inoculation cultures are employed. The optimum temperature is about 30° C. The process only takes place in the presence of plenty of air. A culture medium of agar, dextrine, and chalk, with the addition of 2 or 3 % of dextrine is the best for the production of this pigmentation. The colouring-matter is insoluble in ordinary solvents. It dissolves in alkalis, but undergoes a chemical change.

Russia

No doubt the dark colour of vegetable soil is due, in some measure, to the action of this microorganism.

1658   F. H. SHUTT. **Inoculation Experiments with Nitragin for Legumes** (1) **Experimental Farm, Report of the Chemist.** — PP. 205-208. Ottawa, 1910. (App. to the Rep. of the Min. of Agr.)

Experiments with specially prepared cultures for the growth of legumes were commenced in the spring of 1902, and continued almost uninterruptedly since that date. In the spring of 1909, trials were begun with Hiltner's Nitragin as prepared by the Dr. Reiche Nitragin Company of Milwaukee, Wis. U. S. A., cultures being used for Red Clover, Alfalfa and Pease. The methods of both seed and soil inoculation were followed, the series comprising trials in pots and plots.

Canada

The soil used in the pot series was an extremely light, sandy loam. Its nitrogen content was 0.101 per cent.

The writer concludes that failure to obtain an increased crop of clover or other legumes does not necessarily imply the absence of the nitrogen-assimilating bacteria; it more often is due to deficiency of moisture, an unsuitable seed bed, an acid condition of the soil, or to a lack of proper drainage. Seed of a low germinating value has also been found answerable for an imperfect catch. Before concluding that inoculation is necessary it would, therefore, be well to enquire if the lack of success may not be due to one or more of these unfavourable conditions, or to poor seed.

1659   S. DEZANI. **Action of Gypsum on Nitrification.** (L'azione del gesso sulla nitrificazione). — *Le Stazioni Sperimentali Agrarie italiane.* Vol. XLIV, F. 2, pp. 119-137. Modena, 1911.

These experiments with *Nitrosomonas* and *Nitromonas*, showed that gypsum has no specific action upon the activity of the microorganisms of nitrification. The different proportions in which lime and magnesia were used in the experiments have likewise had no influence. Experiments with artificial soil (sand, clay, carbonate of lime, water) and with natural soil of the clay type have confirmed the hypothesis according to which the beneficial action that gypsum has on the nitrification of clay soils is due to a physico-chemical modification of these soils.

Italy:
Piedmont

---

(1) See Abstract 1125 in this *Bulletin*, April 1911.   (*Ed.*)

A. DISTASO. **A Microbe which breaks up Cellulose.** (*Bacillus cel-*   **1660**
lulosae desagregans n. sp.). Sur un microbe qui desagrège la
cellulose. — *C. R. de la Soc. de Biologie.* Tome LXX, N. 22,
pp. 995-996. Paris, 23 juin 1911.

A microbe has been isolated which occurs in the intestines of
the fowl and has been found to possess the property of breaking
up cellulose.   This microorganism is very minute, it is straight and   **France**
terminates at either extremity in a right angle.   It is a facultative
anaerobic form, and has oval sub-terminal spores.   In a saccharine-
gelatine medium its colonies much resemble those of *Streptococcus.*
Saccharine media are not favourable to this bacillus, which has
a feeble action upon glucose, and none upon lactose, maltose and
saccharose.

It also breaks up potatoes, lettuce, green peas and haricots
with the formation of sugars.

W. L. MOORE. **Meteorological Forecasts and Warnings in the United**   **1661**
States. — *Report of the Chief of the Weather Bureau for* 1909,
pp. 8-9.

The Mount Weather Observatory transmits each day to Washington the results of its observations on which the official forecast
is based.   **United**
By sounding the higher atmospheric strata (up to 4 000 metres),   **States**
the gradients are determined, and the normal and abnormal atmospheric currents studied.   These factors react in a constant ratio
on the progress of the weather in the Central States of the Atlantic
coast.

The average direction of the wind above 3 000 meters is to the
north-west.   Deviation to the South or South-west always precede,
by about 2 days, the beginning of the rainy reason on the Atlantic
coast (Central Coast Zone). Undoubtedly a long uninterrupted series
of observations in the higher atmospheric strata will lead to the
discovery of laws and rules of practical utility in forecasting the
weather.

By examining the isobaric maps, prepared each day from the
telegraphic reports for the northern hemisphere, it is possible to
forecast the weather, sometimes for as much as a week ahead.

Here is an example of the Bulletins drawn up by the Observatory :

Thursday, July 9, 1908: a heat wave will prevail on Friday in the Plain States, and will reach the Atlantic coast States on Sunday. The heat wave will last two to three days in the aforementioned regions, and will end in rains, which will begin on Sunday in the Plain States, on Monday in the Mississippi Valley and in the Western Lake districts, and on Tuesday in the Atlantic Coast States.

These rains will perhaps be heavy enough to determine the end of the drought in the Ohio valley and in the Central States of the Atlantic coast.

1662   V. J. GOMILEVSKII. **Late Spring Frosts and how to control them.** (Posdniie Vesennie Samaroski (ili Utenniki) i Vosmoxnaia Borba I nimi) *Khosiaistvo* (*The Home*). VI oi G. Isdaniia, N. 10, pp. 3000 - 303 Kiew, 10 ago Marta, 1911.

Late frosts in May, and sometimes even in June, do serious injury in Russia to the flowering fruit trees, to the young shoots, and to rye about to ear. These losses are principally felt in narrow

Russia   and low-lying valleys

In Germany and France, farmers have founded Societies organized to fight frost by means of an effective and inexpensive system of smudging. The approach of the danger is easily foretold by means of a special thermometer which the Germans call « *Frostwehrthermometer* », which gives sufficiently accurate readings on the frost-preceding evening. An observer provided with one of these thermometers, situated on a fairly high spot, announces about 7 or 7.30 in the evening the probability of a frost, by firing a gun.

At this signal, the neighbouring farmers hasten to take the necessary steps to combat the frost. They arrange in the right manner great heaps of hay, damp straw, rotten wood, and other fuel which produces much smoke, and set fire to it at dawn. A thick layer of smoke rises over the plantations covering the tops of the tallest trees, until the sun, risen high above the horizon, heats the air, and dissipates the danger of frost.

The mode of taking the observation is simple: a psychrometer with a wet-bulb thermometer is used; it is placed in the open, but in the shade. If at 1 p. m. the temperature is shown to be below a certain limit the probability of a frost increases proportionately.

The temperature limit varies with the season and the locality under consideration. Thus:

	St. Petersburg	Warsaw	Elisabetgrad	Astrakhan
In April . . .	4.0⁰ C.	4.0⁰ C.	5.5⁰ C.	4.0⁰ C.
In May. . . .	2.5⁰ »	4.0⁰ »	5⁰ »	2.5⁰ »
In June . . .	2.0⁰ »	3.5⁰ »	4.0⁰ »	0.5⁰ »

It is often desirable to take a second control reading at 9 p. m. At that hour the following are the « temperature limits ».

	St. Petersburg	Warsaw	Elisabetgrad	Astrakhan
In April . . .	2.0⁰ C.	2.0⁰ C.	3.0⁰ C.	2.0⁰ C.
In May. . . .	1.0⁰ »	2.0⁰ »	2.5⁰ »	1.0⁰ »
In June . . .	1.0⁰ »	2.0⁰ »	2.0⁰ »	0.0⁰ »

Unfortunately, everyone is not able to take these readings; and, on the other hand, it is not possible to adopt general rules, as the value of the temperature limit varies not only with the time of year and the locality, but also with the nature of the soil and the crops raised. The determination of this « temperature limit » requires a long series of observations, carried out over a series of years.

Mr. Brounof suggests for these observations the use of an aspirating psychrometer of the Ashmann type, and he points out a new sphere of activity for the agricultural meteorogical stations. The data collected by these stations should be forwarded to the Central Bureau of Meteorology, where they could be properly worked out, so as to determine the « temperature limits ».

D. B. Tedorov. **The Effect of Damp and Frost upon Winter Cereals.** (Vllianie suroveh Morosov na osimbie Posievi). — *Khosiaistro (Le Ménage), VI G. Isdaniia.* N. 12, pp. 365-367. Kiev, 24 Marta, 1911.

1668

It is well known that when the snow is not sufficiently deep, young cereals are often killed by frost on the arrival of spring.

Observations in many districts of Podolia, show that, as a rule, the harm is not caused by winter frosts but by late white frosts. Last winter was cold, damp, and stormy over almost all South Russia. Nevertheless, not much difference in development was observed between young plants of rye and wheat growing in places covered with snow and in others free from it. On the contrary

Russia

many strong plants succumbed to the cold March winds, against which the old maize stalks of the previous autumn would have afforded an excellent shelter; it is therefore recommended that these stalks should be left standing in the fields till April.

1664 R.STEPPES. **Damage done by Frost to Rye at Swalöf in Sweden** (Frostschaden an Schossenden Roggen). — *Landw.-Mitteilungen*, 60 Jahrgang, N. 6, pp. 82-83. Danzig, 16 März, 1911.

Severe frosts occurred in the experiment field at Svalöf on May 28th, 29th, and 30th, 1908, the effects of which were felt at the beginning of June.

Sweden

The tips of the rye shoots, and even the whole inflorescence, was to some extent whitened, the tissues attacked grew stunted, withered, and the yield diminished to a more or less noticeable extent.

All the varieties were not equally affected. Those varieties of which the ear had not yet come out of the sheath and those in which it had already come well out, suffered little ; whereas those which eared at the time of the frost suffered serious injury, for at that period the ear is rich in water and very sensitive to meteorological influences; such as frost. The inconstancy and variability of this factor makes it impossible to obtain frost resisting varieties.

In this case, as in that of storms, weather forecasts may be of great service; since they make it possible to take steps to restrict the injury done, as by placing in the fields vessels full of resin and oil, which are set fire to during the night.

1665 M. BUISSMANN. **The Power of Acclimatization possessed by some Imported Plants in Java.** (Bijdrage tot de Kennis van het Klimat van Oost-Java). — *Weersower-sichte van Februari, Cultura a 23ste Jaargang. N.* 272 pp. 222 - 223. S. Gravenhagen. April 1911.

This article gives general information concerning the climatic conditions prevailing in Feb. 1911 in the Eastern part of the island of Java, and data referring to plants which have been imported from other countries at some distance.

Dutch E. Indies: Java

Average temperature 18. 29⁰ C. with a maximum of 24⁰ C. on the 13th and a minimum of 13⁰ C on the 28th; 21 wet days. Very cloudy generally.

Solanum laciniatum imported from Australia and New Zealand, produced flowers and fruit during the month.

Oryza momtana from S. Africa ripened its seeds.

Sarothamnus scoparius from S. Europe has not yet flowered, although its stalks are 2 m. (6 ft.) high.

Canna Warsczewiczi has a large number of very beeatiful dark red blossoms.

A. D. HALL. **The Progress of Soil Chemistry and Soil Bacteriology during the Year 1910** (1). — *Annual Reports on the Progress of Chemistry for* 1910. *Issued by the Chemical Society.* Vol. VII, pp. IX + 303 (208-214). London, Gurney & Jackson, 1911.

1666

« *Soils.* — During the year F. K. Cameron, who has been associated with Whitney in the study of soil productiveness and action of fertilisers, has published a general survey of the whole field. The author's main object is to controvert the general idea that the principal function of the soil is to supply nutrients to the plant, and that fertilisers are added to the soil to supply the nutrients which are lacking or in deficient quantity. He begins by discussing the rôle played by the water in the soil in its relation to the solids, and after dealing with the physical actions in which it shares, he takes as a starting point the conclusion that the plant draws its nutriment solely from the solution formed by the action of the soil water on the soil particles. Now Cameron concludes, on physico-chemical grounds, that this solution must be always of approximately the same strength, whatever the soil or whatever the treatment it has received in the way of fertilisers, because the addition of a few pounds of phosphoric acid to a hundred thousand times its weight of soil already containing two or three thousand pounds of phosphoric acid, and with an enormous absorbing power for that material, cannot influence to any sensible degree the concentration of the soil water in the phosphoric acid. Similarly with potash and the o.her mineral constituents of the plant. The amount of nitrogen in the soil solution is governed by other considerations, and in the main the argument refers to the mineral and not the nitrogenous nutrient of the plant.

« The evidence points to the extracts from all soils being of approximately uniform composition. Moreover, plants flourish in

United States. Germany. Great Britain. India

(1) See also: A. STUTZER: *Progress in the Study of Soils during the Last Two Years.* This *Bulletin*, Abstr. 50. January, 1911. (*Ed.*).

water cultures of extremely low concentration, far below that prevailing in any of the natural soil solutions, nor is growth accelerated
by any increase in their strength.

« Putting aside the nitrogenous components, it would follow that
all soils must behave alike as regards their power of supplying
plants with their mineral constituents and that mineral fertilisers
can have no direct action in supplying the plant with its food.
As this conclusion does not agree with experience, some other factor
must be sought, which determines the differences undoubtedly existing between the response of crops on particular soils to mineral
fertilisers. The next step in the argument was the examination of
aqueous extracts from various soils by the method of water cultures. It was found that plants would grow in these extracts, where
they substantially behaved in the same relative fashion as when
growing in the soils themselves, either in the field or in pots. The
extracts from good soils yielded good plants, while the poor soils
transmitted their indifferent crop-producing powers to their aqueous
extracts. Nothing in the analyses of these extracts as regards
their concentration in plant nutrients would account for the differences in growth exhibited; in fact, dilution of some of the poor
extracts resulted in no falling off in growth, but at a certain stage
even an increase. Hence the author concludes that the poor extracts and in their turn the poor soils contain certain toxic substances which inhibit the growth of plants. This was confirmed by
finding that shaking up the poor extracts with such absorbent materials as animal charcoal, precipitated alumina, or ferric oxide
made them capable of carrying good growth, although these substances could not possibly have added to the nutrients in the solution.
Certain commercial fertilisers had the same beneficial effect on the
solution, as had treatment with minute quantities of pyrogallol and
lime. From this it was concluded that the toxic substances must
be complex organic compounds, which are destroyed or precipitated
by the treatment employed. A search was then made in some bad
soils for organic materials of a toxic nature, and several such
substances were successfully isolated, some of which proved to be
toxic to plants in water culture. The author finally correlates the
deterioration of soils under the continued growth of one crop with
an accumulation of such toxic substances characteristic of a particular plant, and concludes that the value of rotation, or a bare
fallow, or of the ploughing in of a green crop, is due to the op-
portunities afforded for the oxidation or precipitation of the toxins.
Furthermore, the usual fertilisers are considered to act indirectly

in fitting the soil for the growth of crops rather than in the direct supply of plant food (1).

" Although no absolute distinction can be drawn between available and total plant food in the soil, the opinion continues to grow that information that is of value towards forming an opinion of the fertiliser needs of the soil can be best obtained by a determination of the amount of phosphoric acid and potash soluble in an aqueous solution of carbon-dioxide, which is, after all, the chief solvent naturally at work in soils. In this connection, E. A. Mitscherlich has published a critical study on the solubility in water containing carbon-dioxide of the materials present in fertilisers and soils. He ascertained the influence on the resulting concentration of such factors as time, temperature, proportion of carbon dioxide and the ratio of the amount of solvent to that of material.

" In another paper E. A. Mitscherlich investigates the question of whether crop production is influenced at all by the strength of the soil solution in carbon-dioxide, which in the laboratory determines its solvent power over minerals. He arranged a series of pot experiments of given soils and manures, watering some with tap-water and others with water containing various amounts of carbon-dioxide, but obtained no increased yield for the carbon-dioxide. He concludes that a small amount of carbon-dioxide is sufficiently effective, and that under natural conditions there is always a sufficient production from the roots and from the oxidation of organic matter, hence the application of fertilisers designed especially to increase the amount of carbon-dioxide in the soil gases is needless. The use of carbon-dioxide saturated water as an analytical agent to deal with soils is also recommended by Biéler-Chatelan (2).

« Arising out of his work with Hutchinson on Protozoa (3), E. J. Russell has investigated the amount of ammonium compounds present as such in soils. Considerable uncertainty attaches to the determinations of ammonia in soils, because in the methods usually adopted the alkali attacks some of the organic nitrogen compounds, and there is a continuous evolution of ammonia as long as the

---

(1) For other papers on this subject, see: B. SCHREINER and J. J. SKIMMER. *Effects of a harmful Organic Soil Constituent.* This *Bulletin,* n. 2. December 1910, p. 217 ; and OSCAR LOEW. *Soil-Sickness.* Ibid. p. 218.   (*Ed.*).

(2) For other studies connected with this subject see: G. J. JONKOW, this *Bulletin,* Abstr. 754. March, 1911; and A. SUPRUNENKO: ibid. Abstr. 755. (*Ed.*).

(3) See: *The Science and Practice of Farming during 1910 in Great Britain,* p. 187. International Institute of Agriculture, Rome, 1910.   (*Ed.*).

distillation is continued. Russell finds that distillation with alcoholic potash (0,5 to 1.0 per cent.) at reduced pressures (32-35 mm.) shows a sharp end-point at which the evolution of ammonia ceases, and for soils not too rich in organic matter the same end-point is reached by a single distillation with magnesia and water at the same low temperature and pressure. This point Russell considers to represent the conclusion of the evolution of the nitrogen in the soil that was combined as ammonia. Only one or two parts of ammonia per million of soil are found in ordinary soils, rising in very rich garden soils to five or six. This is because the ammonia is kept down to a low limit by its conversion into nitrate by the nitrifying organisms. Thus under field conditions the factor limiting the formation of nitrates is really the preliminary ammonia producing process, and instead of the rate of nitrification it is really the rate of ammonia production that determines the amount of nitrogen available for the crop (1).

« As bearing on the soil materials available for growth, S. U. Pickering has continued his examination of the chemical changes brought about by heating the soil for a short time to various temperatures above and below 100°. He confirms his previous results, that at all temperatures, but especially at 100° and above, there is a considerable formation of soluble organic matter which will serve as plant food, but is toxic in its nature, as shown in injurious action on the rate of germination of seeds. This injurious material, however, gradually decomposes, probably by oxidation, because the injurious effect disappears when the soil in a moist condition is exposed to the air even under aseptic conditions.

« E. J. Russell has also been working at the often debated question of the value of earthworms in cultivated soils (2).

« H. Mieth tried a series of vegetation experiments in which he employed calcium silicates as sources of calcium. He found that plants easily decompose such precipitated silicates and can take up the calcium from them, so that these compounds may serve as sources of calcium to the plant instead of the carbonate; this fact the author correlates with the maintenance of neutrality in many soils which show on analysis only a trace of calcium carbonate

---

(1) See also: E. J. RUSSELL, *Factors which determine Fertility in Soils:* l. c., pp. 162-164.   (*Ed.*).

(2) This paper is summarized in: l. c., p. 160, and in this *Bulletin* No. 2, p. 215, Rome, December, 1910.   (*Ed.*).

" H. E. Annett (1) reports an interesting fact regarding the colour of certain black cotton soils which occupy an area of over 200 000 square miles 517960 km² in India. These soils are not rich in organic matter, and remain black after oxidation with sulphuric acid. The colour proves to be due to a large extent to a black magnetic compound containing 73 per cent. of ferric oxide and 18 per cent. of titanium dioxide (2).

" *Soil Bacteriology*. A. Koch has continued his work on the power of *Azotobacter* to accumulate nitrogen in soils to which sugar and other carbohydrates have been added, and has obtained further results in confirmation of former experiments. He has extended his experiments to small plots of soil, half a metre square, in the open air, and after treatment with sugar he has found that he obtained an increase of crop, which, although slight in the first year, was considerable in the second and third after application.

From other sources we have evidence that the fixation of nitrogen by *Azotobacter* in the open ground is much affected by the prevailing temperature; if this be too low, other organisms than the *Azotobacter* predominate as a result of the carbohydrate application. Koch has added one further link to the completeness of the demonstration by showing that the addition of sugar to soils destitute of the *Azotobacter* organisms results in no increase in their content of nitrogen.

"Koch has also studied a fresh the denitrification process in soils and finds that there is but little loss of nitrogen, although both nitrate and dextrose had been added, provided the amount of water in the soil is kept down. For example, when the water in a particular soil was below 18 per cent., there was no reduction of nitrate, but when it rose to 25 or 30 per cent., denitrification set in. In other words, anaerobic conditions must be established before the reducing organism comes into play.

E. J. RUSSELL. **Recent Investigations on Soil Fertility.** — *Nature*, N. 2167, Vol. 86, pp. 363-364. London, May 11, 1911.   1667

S. S. Peck, of the Hawaiian Sugar Planters' Experiment Station (Bulletin 34), has studied nitrogen fixation and denitrification, and confirms the general results obtained by C. Hoffman and B. W. Ham-

Hawaii.
S. Australia.
Victoria.
United
States:
Colorado.

(1) For other papers on this subject see: This *Bulletin*, *Abstr.* 61, January, 1911.   (*Ed.*).
(2) See: M. H. Krzemieniewska. *Influence of the Mineral Constituents of Nutritive Solutions on the Development of Azotobacter*: this *Bulletin*, N. 2, p. 211. Dec., 1910 and *ibid*. *Abstr.* 54 and 55, *ibid*. March 1911 *Abstr.* 745.   (*Ed.*).

mer (1), Gerlach and Vogel, Koch (2), and others. Molasses applied before planting stimulates nitrogen fixation, but applied to the growing plant it does harm by causing loss of nitrate or diminished nitrification.

He also confirms some recent work of Russell and Hutchinson (3), and finds that numbers of Protozoa harmful to bacteria occur in soil — he found amoebae, paramoecium, and others — all of which can be destroyed by moderate heat or antiseptics like carbon disulphide. Partial sterilisation of the soil is being studied in several directions. The *Journal of Agriculture of South Australia* states that farmers there have long recognised the advantage of burning the stubbles, and thus heating the soil ; investigations are in hand at the Roseworthy College to study the problem from this new point of wiew.

An apparatus for soil sterilisation suitable for gardeners is described in *The Journal of the Department of Agriculture of Victoria*, which is similar in principle to some that are working in England. The *Scientific American* recently gave an account of methods proposed in the United States.

Although nitrates are invaluable in the soil, an excess is injurious, because it causes plasmolysis.

Dr. Headden of the Colorado Agricultural College Experiment Station (Bulletins 155 and 160), reports analyses of soils in Colorado containing such excessive amounts of nitrates that they were sterile. He thinks their formation can only be explained as due to bacteria ; he supposes that nitrogen fixation has gone on to an excessive degree, and has thus led to disastrous consequences.

The phenomena of flocculation and deflocculation in soils have been much investigated, but are far from being worked out. E. E. Free has recently summarised (*Journal of the Franklin Institute*) the present position of our knowledge, and has shown that a marked influence is exercised by impurities present in the water in which suspensions are made for experimental purposes. He considers it probable that in absolutely pure water only a medium degree of permanence would be attained. In his view, any material can be suspended in water, flocculated, and deflocculated, if it can be got in a sufficiently fine state.

(1) See this *Bulletin*, Abstr. 54, January, 1911.   (*Ed.*).

(2) See this *Bulletin*, Abstr. 55, January, 1911.   (*Ed.*).

(3) See: *The Science and Practice of Farming during* 1910 *in Great Britain* (International Institute of Agriculture), pp. 187-189. Rome, 1910.   (*Ed.*).

A. G. Dojarenko. **The Formation of Assimilable Nitrogen during**   **1668**
the Oxyation of Humus, and its Solution in Alkalis (1). (Die
Bildung des von den Pflanzen assimilierbaren Stickstoffes beim
oxydieren der Huminstoffe und ihre Lösung in Alkalien). —
Seventh International Congress of Applied Chemistry, London,
May 27th to June 2nd, 1909 Section VII. Agricultural Chemistry,
pp. 11-16. London, 1911.

The writer has experimented on the formation of assimilable
nitrogen by plants during the oxydation of humic substances, and
their solution in alkalis, and has been led to the following conclusions:

1. During the oxydation of humic acids with peroxide of   **Russia**
hydrogen (30 %), part of the nitrogen separates from the humic
substances under the form of ammonia, of soluble amides, and of
amido-acids.

2. The nitrogen of the amides and amido-acids of hnmic acid
is transformed completely in oxidised forms of humic compounds.

3. What remains of the nitrogen of the humic acids (humic
nitrogen), is used in the formation of ammonia and simple amides,
which takes place as the result of oxidation.

4. The greater or lesser aptitude of humic acids to separate
assimilable nitrogen during the process of oxidation can be determined by their content of nitrogen in its different forms and
especially of " humic nitrogen ".

5. The solution of humic acids in alkalis forms, on the one
hand, crenates and apocrenates; and on the other, the nitrogen
separates under the form of simpler compounds (ammonia).

6. Apocrenates and crenates are formed at the expense of the
nitrogen of the amides and amido-acids; the " humic nitrogen ' is
used in the formation of soluble and simple nitrogenous compounds.

7. By separating the humic acids of the soil, humic acids are
obtained on the one hand which, on dissolving in alkalis, are transformed; and on the other hand, apocrenates and crenates and
soluble and more simple forms of nitrogen, are obtained as products
of the primitive humic acids.

8. As complete and accurate an analysis as possible of the
alkaline extract of the soil allows the composition of the primitive
humic acid to be determined; and to characterise the mobility of
the humic substance, so far as it affects the aptitude of assimilable
nitrogenous compounds to separate.

---

(1) See Abstr. 56 and 57 of this *Bulletin.* Jan. 1911.   (*Ed.*).

1669   W. O. Robinson & W. J. Mc Caughey. **The Colour of Soil.** —
             U. S. Department of Agriculture, Bur of soils, Bull no. 79,
             pp. 29, table IX, fgs. 2. Washington, 1911.

             The writers consider critically the importance of the colour of
             soils.
             The chief conclusions are:
             1. The colour of a soil has important agricultural signifi-
United   cance. Dark-coloured and red soils are generally warmer and better
States   drained than light coloured soils. Certain extreme cases are however,
             exceptions to the general rule: as is the case of bogs and peats, on
             the one hand, and stiff red clays on the other hand.
             2. Generally speaking, the colour of a soil is dependent upon
             the content of organic matter and ferric oxide, the latter being more
             or less hydrated.
             3. The thicker the film of organic matter and ferric oxide
             coating the soil grains, the darker the soil.
             4. Organic matter tends to blacken a soil. Intermediate shades
             of gray are fairly common. Ferric oxide tends to redden a soil.
             Intermediate yellowish shades are known, but not common. Organic
             matter and ferric oxide together produce shades of brown, which are
             very common.
             5. The degree of hydratation of the ferric oxide in red soils may
             be less than in yellow soils. That such is the case, however, has never
             been shown; and it is probable that the thickness of film sur-
             rounding the soil particles is the predominant factor determining
             colour.
             6. Ferric oxide is the soil component least soluble in pure water
             and most salt solutions. It is easily reduced to the ferrous condition
             by the soluble organic soil components, and is then soluble to a marked
             degree in the presence of carbon-dioxide. Its transportation in the
             soil is explained by these facts.
             7. Ferric oxide tends to segregate in surface soil and on or among
             the finest or « clay » particles.
             8. Generally, although not always, red soils are older than yellow
             soils, and the drainage is better (1).

             _____

             (1) Compare with Omelianski and Sewerowa's observations on the pig-
             ments produced by *Azotobacter Chroococcum* in mould. This *Bulletin*, Abstr.
             1657, June 1911.

G. Liuboslavskii. **The Influence of a Covering of Vegetable Growth**   **1670**
and of Snow on the Temperature of the Soil. (Vliianie Poverkh-
nostnago Pokrove na Temperaturu i obmien Tepla o Verkh-
nikh Sloiakh Potcvi). Isviestiia Imperatorskago Liesnago Instituta, Vep. XIX, str. 1-86. — *Journal opetnoi Agronomii* Gd. XI,
kniga 6, pp. 953-955. St. Petersburg, 1910.

The writer studies the influence of a covering of vegetable
growth and of snow on the temperature of sandy soils.

He has made use, in his studies, of the observations made during
15 years by the Forestry Institute of St. Petersburg on bare soils   **Russia**
and on those covered in winter with snow and in summer with
grass; the temperatures were taken at a depth of 4, 8, 16, 32 and
64 inches (10, 20, 40, 80 and 160 cm.).

1) In winter the heat increases the deeper one penetrates into
the soil. At a depth of 64 inches (160 cm.) the temperature rises
to 4°62 C. in snow covered soil, (about 22 inches or 55 cm. of snow),
and to 10°16 C. in bare soil, above the surface temperature.

2) In summer the reverse is the case; that is to say, the temperature falls, and the extent of the fall is 8°42 on soil covered with vegetation, and 12°14 C. in bare soil.

3) In April intermediate conditions prevail. The temperature
at the surface and at the maximum depth is a little higher than
that of the intermediate layers.

4) When the strata nearer the surface are very cold and the
temperature subsequently rises, heating takes place at the expense
of the layers of air nearest to the soil.

F. T. Shutt. **The Moisture Content of Packed and Unpacked Soils.** —   **1671**
Experimental Farms, Report of the Chemist, pp. 214-15, Ottawa,
1910. (App. to the Rep. of the Min. of Agr.)

The importance of sub-surface packing for the conservation
of moisture has been greatly emphasised in connection with soil culture in semi-arid districts, being the distinguishing feature of «dry-   **Canada**
farming».

To ascertain what additional amounts of water might be brought
up by packing and stored in the surface soil, determinations have
been made during 1909 of the moisture in the soil to a depth of
14 inches in areas packed and not packed.

The data from the packed and unpacked areas are as follows;

| | Percentage of moisture | |
| | Packed | Unpacked |
Date	Summer-fallow at Lethbridge	Alta, Exp. Farm.
July 16, 1909.	13.55	13.35
August 21, 1909.	13.68	12.36
October 1, 1909.	11.21	11.22
November 2, 1909	11.13	10.21
	Barley-soil of Lacombe	Alta, Exp. Farm.
May 14, 1909	11.93	11.55
August 23, 1909	7.59	7.48

It is not claimed that this preliminary examination furnishes data of conclusive character — it will be necessary to repeat the work under different seasonal conditions, probably determining the soil moisture more frequently — but it is pointed out that the results show no very great advantage from the use of the sub-surface packer.

1672   G. S. FRAPS. **Effect of Ignition on Solubility of Soil Phosphates.** — *The Journal of Industrial and Engineering Chemistry*, V. 3, N. 5, p. 335 Easton, Pa, May, 1911.

It is known that ignition of the soil increases the quantity of phosphoric acid dissolved out by acids.

The object of the work here reported was to study the effect of ignition upon mineral phosphates, such as may occur in the soil.

United States: Texas

The results of the experiment made at the Texas Agricultural Experiment Station, are summarised as follows:

1. Ignition increases about ten times the solubility of the phosphoric acid of some mineral phosphates, as wavellite, dufrenite and variscite, in fifth-normal nitric acid.

2. Ignition renders variscite, dufrenite and wavellite almost completely soluble in 12 per cent, hydrochloric acid,.

3. Ignition of the soil will probably render inorganic phosphates soluble in acid, and therefore it is not a method for estimating organic phosphoric acid.

4. Ignition of the soil renders considerable quantities of iron and aluminium oxides soluble in acid.

A. A. J. DE SIGMOND. **The Value of Soil Analysis in the Study of   1673
the Alkaline Soils.** — *Seventh International Congress of Applied
Chemistry*, London, May 27, to June 2nd, 1909. Section VII,
Agricultural Chemistry, p. 50. London, 1910.

The writer has studied the Hungarian alkali soils, called " *Szik-
land* ", and based on his own experiences as regards the value of
soil analysis, has drawn the following conclusions :   **Hungary**
    1) Chemical analysis is the only way of ascertaining the na-
ture and quantity of injurious salts in the soil.
    2) It is the only trustworthy scientific method in controlling
the reclamation of alkali land.
    3) It cannot be neglected in the surveying of such land.
    4) It also gives useful indications as regards the need of fer-
tilisers on alkali land.
    5) The complete chemical analysis of the soil, combined with
mechanical soil analysis, form the only scientific basis in classifying
and characterising the different soil types of this order.

W. E. BRENCHLEY. **Weeds in Relation to Soils.** — *The Journal of   1674
the Board of Agriculture*, Vol. XVIII, No. 1. pp. 18-24, London,
April, 1911.

Plants which spring up and flourish in a particular locality are
very definitely influenced by the character and composition of the
soil. But most of the facts already collected deal with grass land   **Great
vegetation. We have but little information concerning weeds on   Britain:
arable land, and this is scattered in many separate publications.   England**
So that it has never been systematically accumulated and classified.
    During the spring and summer of 1910, a systematic exploration
of the region between Harpenden and Bedford, where the Chalk,
Gault, Lower Greensand, and Oxford Clay appear in well marked
succession, gave interesting results.
    107 species, representing 74 genera, were collected from about
150 fields. A few were found everywhere; some grew exclusively
in certain fields; while others grew more or less abundantly according to the nature of the soil.
    A summary of the results is as follows:
    1. *Clay and Heavy Loam.* — In soils of this character, the number
of species is limited, especially in comparison with the varied and numerous flora on light and sandy soils. *Bartsia odontites* and *Mentha
arvensis* are found here exclusively; other species, such as *Brassica*

Sinapis, Chenopodium album, Matricaria inodora, Polygonum aviculare,
P. Convolvulus, Ranunculus arvensis, and *Veronica hederaefolia,* which
are all adapted for clayey soils, are found also in other places.

2. *Chalk.* — Plants widely distributed in other soils are entirely
lacking here. Plants almost confined to chalk soils are: *Bromus
mollis, Geranium pusillum, Scabiosa arvensis,* and *Sherardia arvensis;*
Brassica alba, Fumaria officinalis, and *Geranium molle* are also characteristic, but are found on other types of land as well.

3. *Light Lands.* — These are characterized by *Chrysanthemum segetum, Rumex Acetosella, Spergula arvensis.* Other plants that are often
found here are *Matricaria Chamomilla, Triticum repens, Viola tricolor, Polygonum aviculare, Chenopodium album, Rumex obtusifolius,
Lamium purpureum* and *Papaver* sp.

4. Common weeds of general distribution are: — *Capsella Bursa-
pastoris, Cerastium vulgatum, Convolvulus arvensis, Equisetum arvense,
Galium Aparine, Ranunculus, Rumex sp., Senecio vulgaris, Taraxacum
officinale, Tussilago Farfara, Cnicus arvensis.*

1675   THOMAS H. KEARNEY. **The Choice of Crops for Alkali Land.** —
U. S. Department of Agriculture, Farmer's Bulletin, 446, p. 32.
Washington, May 3, 1911.

Practically none of the important field crops can be profitably
grown where the quantity of white alkali salts (sulphates, bicarbo-
United   nates and chlorides) in the depth occupied by the roots exceeds
States   1 per cent of the dry weight of the soil.

Forage plants are usually to be preferred for growing in alkali
land. Many of the standard meadow and pasture grasses can be
successfully grown where the quantity of alkali within reach of the
plant roots form from 0.5 to 1 per cent of the dry weight of the soil.
Foxtail, millet, rape, kale and sorghum, as well as barley and rye
when grown for hay, will often give fair yields; and rye, when grown
for hay, will often give fair yields if the quantity of alkali does
not exceed 0. 8 per cent.

Certain leguminous forage plants, notably alfalfa, Canada field
peas, sweet clover (1) and vetches, should give a fair yield where the
alkali is not above about 0. 5 per cent. Success with these crops

---

(1) "Sweet clover" *Melilotus alba.* (BAILEY, *Cyclop. of Americ. Horticulture,* II, 101).   (*Ed.*)

depends largely upon planting at a time when the surface soil is relatively free from salt (after flooding or after heavy rains).

Alkali soils which have a tendency to puddle and form a hard crust on the surface can be improved by ploughing under green crops. Good crops for this purpose are sorghum, millet, barley, rye, rape and kale where the alkali content forms from 0.4 to 0 8 per cent; and vetches, Canada field peas, horse beans and sweet clover, where the alkali content is 0. 1 to 0. 4 per cent.

For alkali land that is being reclaimed by flooding, sorghum is probably the most satisfactory catch crop that can be grown during the progress of the work. In regions where the climate is suitable for its culture, rice is a good crop for this purpose, and the same is true of berseem (*Trifolium alexandrinum*) in localities having a mild winter.

In the presence of about 0. 5 per cent of alkali salt a profitable crop of sugar beets may usually be expected; and if other conditions are exceptionally favorable, as much as 1 per cent of salts can be tolerated. However, the quality of the roots for sugar manufacture is impaired by a quantity of alkali that does not hinder the growth of the plants.

Of the cereals, barley, rye, oats, wheat, and emmer are fairly tolerant of alkali, so far as the plants are concerned; but the presence of more than 0. 1 to 0. 2 per cent of alkali salts usually prevents the production of well filled and plump grain. Barley and rye are somewhat more resistant than other cereals.

Maize is much more sensitive. If grown in alkali land the stubble should be disked or ploughed in immediately after harvest, in order to prevent the baking of the ground and the accumulation of salts at the surface.

Cotton is decidedly resistant, so far as the growth of the plants is concerned, but good yields of fibre can not be expected where the alkali exceds 0. 6. per cent. Egyptian and other long-staple types should not be grown in the presence of more than 0.1 to 0.2 per cent alkali salts.

None of the truck crops and garden vegetables can be recommended for extensive planting on alkali land. Asparagus and onions may however be grown in a small way on land containing 0.4 to 0. 6 of alkali salts.

Of fruit trees only the date palm and pomegranate do well on strong alkali land. If the alkali salts present do not exceed 0. 4 per cent, pears, figs and grapes of the European type (*Vitis vinifera*) are likely to thrive and bear fruit of fair quality.

The following ornamental trees are reported to be successful in moderately alkaline land (about 0. 5 per cent): Cottonwood (1). blacklocust (2), honey locust, (3) and Russian mulberry. Of trees adapted only to regions having a mild winter the date palm and *Washingtonia* palm can tolerate a good deal of alkali, and the Umbrella tree (*Melia azedarach*), European plane tree (*Platanus orientalis*) Japanese varnish tree (*Koelreuteria*), and some species of Eucalyptus (*E. rostrata, E. tereticornis*) are also said to be fairly resistant.

Of shrubs suitable for hedges and windbreaks in alkali land, Russian olive and possibly golden willow, in districts having a severe winter, and tamarisk (*Tamarix gallica*), pomegranate, and the large-growing salt-bushes (*Atriplex Breweri, A. lentiformis*) in milder regions are the most likely to give satisfactory results.

1676   M. L. FULLER. **Underground Waters for Farm Use.** — U. S. Geol Survey, Water-Supply Paper. No 255, pp. 58; E. S. R. Washington, April 5, 1911.

United States   This paper states that of the needs of the farmers of the United States « few are greater than that of purer water supplies ». The paper discusses sources of water supply: underground waters, springs, and wells and their protection, cisterns, and the combination of wells and cisterns. Discussing the relative safety of water from different water-bearing materials, the author states that in general waters from sands and gravels if taken from a considerable distance below the surface are safe to use. Waters from clay are likely to be mineralized, but are as a rule free from contamination. Waters from limestone, particularly in the vicinity of buildings or settlements, are frequently contaminated and unfit for use. This is not because of the amount of lime dissolved, but because of the fact that the water, falling on the surface as rain, often plunges directly through basins, or sinks into the under ground channels, instead of slowly filtering downward through the soil and into the rock, as in most other materials. This water carries with it the

---

(1) Species of *Populus*, BAILEY, *Cyclopedia of American Horticulture*, New York, Macmillan, 1909.

(2) *Robinia pseudacacia*, F. H. KNOWLTON etc. in I. K. FUNK, *Standard Dictionary of the English Language*, p. 1044, London, 1910.   (*Ed.*).

(3) *Gleditschia triacanthos*. Contessa di SAN GIORGIO, *Catalogo Poliglotto delle Piante*, Firenze, 1870, p. 221.   (*Ed.*).

impurities washed or otherwise brought to the sink and bears them along through underground passages to distant points.

On account of the points and fissures which occur in granite, gneiss and schist, waters from these rocks are frequently contaminated, particularly in cities and other thickly populated regions.

Of the various sources of water supply the ground water is the most satisfactory for farm use, because it is least liable to pollution; and streams and ponds are the most unsatisfactory, because of the ease and frequency with which they are contaminated. Fortunately, however, the latter are very seldom used for drinking and domestic purposes, being utilised mainly for stock, on which the effect of moderate pollution is not apparent. The underground supplies, whether from wells or springs, although safe in many localities, are far from being universally so, the safety depending mainly on their location and on the nature of their protection.

When carefully made, cisterns are generally safe to use; and cistern water being very soft is highly prized for domestic purposes.

The Automatic Water-Finder. See Abstract 1879 in this *Bulletin*.   1677

J. R. Currie. **Experiments in the Storage of River Waters** (1). *Journal of the Royal Institute of Public Health.* Vol. XIX, No. 4, pp., 214-222. — London, April, 1911.   1678

The results of these experiments may be briefly stated :

Storage reduced the number of excretal bacteria in all cases.

Sunlight hastened reduction : diffused daylight did not appear to have this action.   **Great Britain**

Storage at 37° (2) was more effective than. at room temperatures in eliminating or modifying excretal germs.

Alike with slight and gross contamination excretal germs decreased in number under storage.

Storage eliminated excretal germs from 1 c. c. of the waters in 4 weeks' time or less, except in the presence of extreme pollution.

The work on these raw waters was done with bottled samples. It does not follow that the same waters, when treated on a large scale in the open, would react to storage precisely as they

---

(1) See this *Bulletin* Abstr. 408, February, 1911.   (*Ed.*).
(2) Presumably centigrade degrees.   (*Ed.*).

did under laboratory conditions; but it is reasonable to expect that they would follow the same general laws.

The possible effect of currents in reservoirs in raising germ laden ooze from the bottom was allowed for in the experiments. The samples were shaken before being examined, so that the test included the sediment together with the germs, if any, contained in it. Apart from the raising of ooze, it is unlikely that the slow movements of water stored in bulk, whether in circulation or quiescent, would have any appreciable effect on bacterial growth. The researches of Giuseppe Cao appear to show that the disappearance of germs from water kept in active movement takes place at the same rate as in comparatively still water.

It is probable that the principle of storage is capable of broad application; therefore how river waters in general would behave under storage treatment can only be determined accurately by experiment in each instance.

1679   F. DE CONDÉ. **Automatic Watering.** (Arrosage automatique). — *Revue horticole.* 83ᵉ année, N. 12, pp. 290-291. Paris, 16 juin 1911.

**France:
Lot-
et-Garonne**

An ingenious system is in force in Lot-et-Garonne. It consists of a raised reservoir with a principal pipe from which branch off, at right angles, secondary pipes, each of the latter being regulated by a tap, and having nozzles at certain intervals.

The space between the secondary pipes is the distance between the beds to be watered. The watering is effected by the automatic action of the taps. That of the first pipe is opened, setting in action all the nozzles of that line, which working as a hydraulic tourniquet, water the ground with a very regular fine spray. To the pipe is affixed a tube which discharges water into a bucket suspended by cables above the soil; the weight of the water overcomes the resistance caused by the friction of the supporting cables, the bucket descends, closes the tap automatically, and rises again, when a lever opens the regulating tap of the next pipe. This process is repeated every time.

The speed of watering is regulated by the speed of filling the buckets which depends upon a tap.

This apparatus, which only needs setting in motion, allows of irrigation at night.

With a charge of water of 6-7 m. (19 ft. 8 ins. to 23 ft.) each nozzle irrigates a circle with a radius of about 6 m. (19 ft. 8 ins.) therefore 140 to 150 nozzles are required per hectare (56 to 61 per acre) the entire cost of installation is about 4000 fr. per hectare (about £64 10s. per acre).

F. Duvieusart. **The Irrigation of Grazed Meadows**. (Irrigation des   **1680**
prairies pâturées). — *Annales de Gembloux*, 21e a., 5e b., pp. 248-
251, fgs. 2., Bruxelles, 1er mai, 1911.

Hitherto irrigated meadow lands in Belgium have not been used to any practical extent for grazing, in spite of the advantages of such a mode of exploitation in certain cases. Sloping lands are now irrigated by means of level ditches cut in straight lines between points   **Belgium**
determined some distance apart on the contours. The edges of these channels are left quite sharp, so that they can easily be broken down by animals; consequently it is impossible to graze live-stock on these lands.

The writer suggests the following alterations:

1) The channel excavated between two intermediate points, by means of a surveyor's level with telescope, instead of being recti-linear, should follow horizontal surface curves, rectified at a series of points, at a short distance one from the other.

2) The section of the channel should be so shaped that the ridge over which the water flows is at least as wide as an animal's hoof.

The author thinks that if this were done, animals could be allowed to graze freely without injuring the channels to such an extent as to interrupt the regularity of irrigation.

A description is given of a simple apparatus by means of which the level can be traced exactly between definite points.

Drainage Works in Rumania. (Rumänische Entwässerungsarbeiten),   **1681**
— *Oesterreichische Monatsschrift für den Orient*, n. 4, s. 56-57.
Wien, April 1911.

The Rumanian parliament has in view a scheme for the improvement and drainage of vast stretches of land liable to be flooded by the Danube. The State owns 450 000 ha. (over a million acres) of *balten* (submerged land) and 300 000 ha. (750 000 acres) perio-   **Rumania**
dically flooded ; besides this, private individuals own 100 000 ha. (250 000 ac.) of submerged land and 80 000 ha. (200 000 ac.) of periodically flooded land.

The Government intends to appropriate 150 milllon *lei* (6 million £) for draining and improving a total of 350 000 ha. (870 000 ac.),

6

of which half is State land and half private. On the lowest estimate the land should bring in 50 leï per ha. (16s. per acre) per
annum after the improvements. The work will be so arranged that
the profits of the first years can be used for further work in the
following years.

1682   **Irrigation in Burma.** — *The Indian Agriculturist*, N. 3, p. 91. Cal-
             cutta, March, 1, 1911.

On most of the land watered by the Mandalay Canal only one
rice crop is grown. The area irrigated in 1910 amounted to 58 097
acres as against 55 953 in 1909.

British   The area irrigated from the Shwebo Canal during the year was
India: approximately 147 556 acres as compared with 148 123 in 1909.
Burma   The Mon and Ye-u Canals are still under construction and no irri-
             gation was done from them.

The area recorded as having been irrigated and cultivated in the
Kyaukse District from the canals fed by the Zawgyi and Paulaung
rivers is 128 854 acres. The total area irrigated in the Meiktila
and Yamethin Districts amounted during the year 1910 to 94 098
acres against 53 471 in 1909.

The area protected by embankments during the year amounted
to 645 761 acres.

1683   **Irrigation Project in Cuba.** — *Bulletin of the Pan American Union,*
             p. 787. Washington, April 1911.

The Secretary of Agriculture, Commerce and Labor, of Cuba,
is actively engaged in carrying out the preliminary arrangements for
irrigation on the island. To this end he has asked the Foreign Of-
Cuba   fice to request the United States and British Governments each to
             recommend an engineer whose services could be secured by the
             Cuban Government. These two irrigation experts, together with a
             Cuban engineer, will constitute a Commission which will study the
             subject in general, and make a detailed investigation of the possi-
             bilities of irrigating the Province of Pinar del Rio.

1684   **Irrigation Project in Chile.** — *Bulletin of the Pan American Union,*
             pp. 779-780. Washington, April 1911.

Chile   An extensive irrigation project for watering the rich agricul-
             tural zone between Peña Blanca and El Salto is now under way.

The plan includes the formation of an artificial lake at Quebrado de Escobar, near Peña Blanca, with a storage capacity of 10 000 000 cubic meters of water. This reservoir, from which the entire district can be advantageously irrigated, will be 80 meters wide and 25 meters deep.

This will give a fall of 100 meters, which can be utilized in developing electric energy for motive power, electric lighting, and for conveying water to the villages and farms in the district.

The districts that will be especially benefited by this irrigation plant are Peña Blanca, Villa Alemana, Zuilpue and the new settlements that are forming at Las Palmas.

Rothamsted Experimental Station in 1910. 67th year of Wheat culture. Liming in Permanent Pasture. Effects of Green-Manuring.
— *Mark Lane Express.* London, April 17 1911.

1685

The annual report for 1910 of the Rothamsted Experimental Station (Lawes' Agricultural Trust) has now been issued. Dealing first with the weather and crops it states that the season of 1910 was a very unfavorable one for most crops; the yield of wheat on thrashing proved exceptionally low; on the unmanured plots it fell to 7.5 bushels per acre, and only on three occasions during the sixty seven years of the experiment has it been lower. The highest yield was on the dunged plot, but that only gave 28 bushels per acre. In the barley experiments, an exceptional increase was produced by superphosphate. This is in accordance with previous experience: phosphoric acid has its maximum effect in wet and cold seasons.

Great Britain: Rothamsted

The permanent grass plots also yielded much smaller crops than usual, and the proportion of the leguminous herbage was considerably below the average. The effect of lime was not so marked as usual, though its value was very apparent to the eye on the plots on which the soil has become sour through continual applications of ammonium salts. On the limed portions, the peat that had accumulated previously has almost entirely disappeared, and a close sward is beginning to form again.

The yield from the mangold field was above the average, though not so high as in the preceding year, and the usual attack of ·*Uromyces betae* on the high nitrogen plots was very marked.

The trials of the new nitrogenous fertilizers were repeated, but the yields in this field were all so low that much weight cannot be attached to the results. Both the nitrate of lime and cyanamide gave poor results, nitrate of soda being the most effective source of nitrogen applied.

As in the previous trial, the value of the leguminous crops as a preparation for wheat was very marked, the yield of grain being 60 per cent. better after either vetches or crimson clover, than after rape or mustard (1). The yield of straw was even more in favour of the leguminous crops, and it was noticeable that on all these plots following green manuring there was none of the blight which characterized the wheat elsewhere.

The investigations on the effect of heating and of antiseptics upon the fertility of soils, which were described in the last report, have been continued. None of the trials made in the open field yielded positive results, while other attempts toward the practical application of the previous investigations have not yet reached the stage for report. Dr. Hutchinson and Mr. T. Goodey have now accumulated a good deal of material regarding the life history and members of the protozoa associated with the soil.

1686   VIZIRANU. **Cultivation Experiments at the Agricultural Station of Nucet-Dâmbovita in Rumania. Wheat varieties, Maize, etc.** (Resultate obtinute en plantele cultivate în câmpule de îucercari al scoalei de agriculturâ Nucet-Dâmbovita în vara onului 1910). — *Câmpul*, N. 6, pp. 176-180. Bucarest, June, 1911.

Experiments were carried out at the school of Nucet-Dâmbovita on the cultivation of several varieties of wheat, rye, spring

Rumania   barley, maize, French beans, beets, etc.

The yields of the most productive of the 25 varieties of wheat were as follows:

	Bush. of 60 lbs. per acre	Kilograms per hectare
Shireff	42.4	2824
Chiddam	36.0	2400
Milanese	32.9	2196
Clovers.	26.0	1733
Ortowa.	22.1	1476
Rogen	21.8	1456
Prolifique	21.75	1450

Of the five varieties of rye grown, «Vasu» yielded 54 bushels (of 54 lbs.) per acre (3240 kg. per hectare) of grain, and 8 tons of

_____

(1) See this *Bulletin* for May 1911. Abstr. 1389   (*Ed.*).

straw (20 360 kg. per ha,) ; « Hama » 17 bush. (1035 kg.), and « Zélande » 8 ½ bush. (514 kg.).

Experiments with oats and barley gave no results, as the sowing
was done under very adverse conditions.

The best yield of maize was obtained from « Dent de cheval »,
with 38.3 bushels (of 60 lbs.) per acre (2552 kg. per hectare) of·
grain, 3 ¼ cwt. of leaves (414 kgs.), and 20 tons (50 000 kg.) of
stalks and cobs.

Seven varieties of beets were tried, the best yields being
« Mamouth rose » 28 tons per acre (70 000 kg. per ha.), « Eckendorf »
tankard 24 tons (60 000 kg.), and « Corne de bœuf » 22 tons
(55 000 kg.).

Of the French beans, « Capacioasa » gave the best results —
1203 lbs. per acre (1348 kg. per ha.), while « Suisse blanche » gave
only 268 lbs. (300 kg.).

A. D. HALL. **Work on Fertilisers during the Year 1910.** — *An-   **1687**
nual Reports on the Progress of Chemistry for 1910. Issued by the
Chemical Society.* Vol. VII, Pp. IX + 303 (219-221). London, 1911.

The changes taking place when cyanamide is applied to the
soil continue to attract a good deal of attention, and C. Ulpiani
gives an account of a long series of experiments on this question.   Italy.
He dismisses the idea originally suggested by Löhnis that bacterial   France.
action plays any considerable part in breaking down the cyanamide   Great
to the stage of ammonia. He regards the action as chiefly brought   Britain
about by the colloidal surface of soil particles, which acts as a ca-
talyst. The change ceases when this is destroyed either by heating
the soil or by treating with acids or alkalis, but can be restored
by the addition of precipitated silica. The cyanamide changes first
into carbamide and then into ammonium carbonate ; but Ulpiani
can find no evidence for Löhnis' idea that a formation of ammonium cyanate precedes the carbamide. The change takes place in
the presence of antiseptics and with sterilised materials ; it also goes
on with increased velocity at 100° ; and it is most rapid at first,
then falls off. It also increases with the concentrations of the solution taken. None of these facts agrees with the theory that the
change is brought about by bacteria. The soil absorbs the ammonia as it is formed, and this removal of the products accelerates
the rate of change, and also prevents polymerisation into dicyanodiamide.

Because of the susceptibility of cyanamide to change in moist air and the formation of the toxic dicyanodiamide, C. Brioux (1) has worked out a method for the analysis of the altered product. This method depends on the fact that the precipitate which cyanamide gives with silver nitrate is insoluble in ammonia, whereas the precipitate similarly formed by dicyanodiamide is soluble (2).

Methods for the estimation of nitrates continue to attract a good deal of attention, because the determinations with the nitrometer or as nitric oxide by Schloesing's process are not particularly convenient. It is obviously preferable to reduce the nitrate to ammonia, which can be rapidly and accurately measured by the routine methods of the laboratory. M. E. Pozzi-Escot employed for this purpose aluminium together with a little mercuric chloride, so as to form an aluminium-mercury couple which reduces the nitrate to ammonia in a few minutes.

This method has, however, been severely criticised; Cahen dismisses it as untrustworthy, and would replace it by Devarda's method, in which the reduction is effected by 2 or 3 grams of alloy containing 45 per cent. of aluminium, 5 of zinc, and 50 of copper. This is digested with the nitrate-containing material for half an hour in the presence of concentrated sodium hydroxide, the digestion flask being connected from the outset to the distilling apparatus. The distillation is then completed and the ammonia collected in the standard acid as usual.

J. M. Wilkie has discussed a method of determining ammonia, which may on occasion become useful to the agricultural analyst. The solution is rendered exactly neutral and neutral formaldehyde is added. The acid which results from the abstraction of the ammonia by the formaldehyde is titrated with baryta water, using phenolphthalein as indicator.

1688   **Guano Deposits of Assumption Island, Seychelles.** — *Bulletin of the Imperial Institute*, vol. IX, N. 1, pp. 39-44. London, 1911.

Seychelles:
Assumption L.

Summary of a report prepared by Mr. R. Dupont, Curator of the Botanic Station in the Seychelles, on the guano deposits of the Island of Assumption.

---

(1) This paper was summarised in this *Bulletin*, Abstr. 414, February, 1911.
(2) For other researches on Calcium Cyanamide see this *Bulletin*, 1. Year, p. 35 (Fr. REIS, *Physiological Action of Calcium Cyanamide and Derivatives*) November, 1910; *ibid.*, I. Year, N. 2, p. 232. (P. HANNSCH, *Calcium Cyanamide as a Fertiliser*), December 1910; *ibid.* Abstr. 72, January, 1911; *ibid*, Abstr. 412, February, 1911.   (*Ed.*).

In estimating the extent of the deposits, two chief modes of occurrence have been recognised: 1) in pits; 2) a shallower formation on the general surface, still in course of formation by birds.

Seven analyses of the guano found at one locality in seven different pits gave the following average result; the large amount of water present is attributed to the fact that the samples were collected and analysed after a shower of rain:

	Per cent.
Calcium phosphate	61.04
Moisture	19.57
Iron oxide and alumina	3.67

The following analyses of two samples, one taken from an old deposit and the other from one of recent formation, show the variability in the amount of calcium carbonate to which these surface-guanos are liable:

	Older bed Per cent.	Newer bed Per cent.
Calcium phosphate	72.83	8.94
Iron oxide and alumina . . .	0.60	0.50
Calcium carbonate	1.20	60.00
Moisture	8.70	10.00

The total amount of pit-guano available is estimated at about 106 000 tons, and of surface-guano at 270 000 tons. Further, it is estimated that 46 000 tons of high-grade guano, suitable for export to Europe, could be obtained: and about 50 000 tons of low-grade guano, which could not be exported to Europe at a profit under present conditions. The deposits at the north end of the island are already being worked. The right to collect guano in Assumption Island and in the other islands of the Aldabra group is held under a lease which expires in 1931.

Concession for Working Guano Deposits in Mexico. — *The Board of Trade Journal*, N. 749, p. 47. London, April 6, 1911.

1689

The British Minister at Mexico City reports the publication of a concession for working guano deposits and phosphate and sulphate of lime in the Islands of the Gulf of California and the Pacific Ocean, between 22° N. latitude and the parallel of the United States frontier. The working of the deposits must be begun within a year dating from 20th February 1911.

Mexico

1690 H. Holland. **Phosphates in India.** — *Journal of the Royal Society of Arts*, N. 3051, p. 651. London, May 12, 1911.

One of the most extraordinary features in connection with the trade of India is the large export of phosphatic manures in the form of bones.

British India The exports during the past five years have grown to nearly 90 000 tons per annum. The loss of fish manures and oil-cake can be made good by reproduction, but the phosphate of lime sent out in the form of bones has been derived from the soil; and, as India is singularly deficient in deposits of mineral phosphates, such a loss is serious for a country dependent almost solely on agriculture. When sulphuric acid is manufactured on a larger scale in India, and the chemical industries generally become thereby developed, it is probable that this loss of phosphate will be curtailed and the material turned to account in the country.

1691 Sencial. **Coffee Pulp as Fertilizer.** (Aprovechamiento de la pulpa del Café come abono). *El Hacendado Mexicano*, vol. IX, p. 191. Mexico, Mayo 1º de 1911.

Coffee pulp, as other industrial residues, is a good fertilizer, provided it is prepared properly. In putting away a large quantity

Mexico to decompose, sawdust, urine and a little lime should be added. It should then be left covered for a year.

Prepared in this way, coffee pulp is a relatively cheap fertilizer and its use cannot be highly enough recommended especially where coffee is grown.

1692 J. P. Street. **The Solubility of Organic Forms of Nitrogen Fertilizers.** — *Connecticut State Sta. Rpt.* 1910. E. S. R. Washington n. 5, p. 322. April 1911.

As preliminary to a study of the availability to crops of water-

United
States:
Connecticut soluble and permanganate-soluble forms of nitrogen and to devise if possible a laboratory method for determining the agricultural value of organic forms of nitrogen, the ammonia evolved on distillation with magnesia, the water-soluble and the permanganate soluble nitrogen were determined in 117 samples of organic nitrogenous materials used in fertilizer mixtures.

The average results obtained with the principal materials are given in the following table.

SOLUBILITY OF NITROGEN OF FERTILIZING MATERIAL.

Material	Number of samples	Nitrogen					Solubility of organic nitrogen	
		Total	As Ammonia	As water-soluble organic	As permanganate - soluble organic	As insoluble organic	Total	Water insoluble organic
		%	%	%	%	%	%	%
Dried blood.	6	11.67	0.11	0.32	10.77	0.47	96	96
Hoof meal.	2	15.00	0.35	1.19	12.78	0.68	95	95
Cotton-seed meals . .	5	7.03	0.08	0.68	5.85	0.42	94	93
Bone	3	3.84	0.00	1.12	2.56	0.16	96	93
Dried fish	22	7.94	0.67	1.69	5.07	0.51	93	91
Tankage (1)	29	5.80	0.27	1.52	3.61	0.40	93	90
Tankage (alleged) . .	2	5.57	2.33	0.65	1.63	0.96	70	63
Castor pomace. . . .	9	5.24	0.08	0.68	3.95	0.53	90	88
Peruvian guano . . .	2	5.40	1.77	1.11	2.02	0.28	92	88
Garbage tankage. . .	5	2.54	0.07	0.40	1.06	1.01	59	50
Sheep manure	5	2.42	0.39	0.38	0.79	0.86	58	48
Peat	4	2.89	0.09	0.08	1.13	1.59	43	42
Tobacco stems. . . .	4	2.51	0.27	0.52	0.44	0.68	59	39

(1) Under the name of *tankage*, a kind of flesh-meal is prepared in the United States from the refuse-meat, entrails and other offal that accumulate in slaughter-houses. These materials are steamed in tanks to remove grease, and the residue is dried down and reduced to a fine mechanical condition. When well prepared, this product should contain no more than 10 or 12 % of moisture, though sometimes it has been found to contain as much as 30 %. Usually it contains more water and more phosphoric acid, some 5 to 7 % namely, but less nitrogen, some 7 to 7 ½ %, than pure dried blood. Since much of the tankage nitrogen is easily decomposable, tankage is to be regarded as a valuable manure. H. STORER, *Agriculture in some of its relations with Chemistry.* New York, 1906, vol, II, p, 21,   (*Ed.*).

These results indicate that digestion with a 2 per cent neutral solution of potassium permanganate may offer a means of determining the approximate relative value of the organic nitrogen found in commercial fertilizers. The method was applied to 252 samples of mixed fertilizers and the solubility of the nitrogen of the mixed fertilizers agreed closely with that of the nitrogen of the material used in the fertilizer, and showed that with few individual exceptions the high grade fertilizers (those containing the most nitrogen) had a higher nitrogen solubility than the low grade goods. Pot tests of several of the nitrogenous materials on rye showed that all of the materials classed as inferior by determination of solubility in permanganate showed a decided inferiority to dried blood, which was used as a standard for comparison. Peat appeared to be almost worthless as a source of nitrogen; and the nitrogen of the other materials was found to be from about one-fifth to two-fifths as available as that of dried blood.

1698   E. B. VOORHEES & I. G. LIPMAN. **Investigations Relative to the Use of Nitrogenous Fertilizer Materials,** 1898-1907. — *Seventh International Congress of Applied Chemistry, London,* May 27th to June 2nd, 1909; Section VII., *Agricultural Chemistry,* pp. 91-95. London, 1910.

United States: New Jersey

Data collected in the course of ten years experiments carried on in 20 series of three large galvanized iron cylinders open at both ends and sunk in the ground. The experiments were planned to determine whether losses of nitrogen really occur in field practice.

The results secured are summarised as follows :

1. There was a marked falling off in the yields between the first and second rotation, especially in the soils which have received no applications of animal manure.

2. The nitrogen compounds in liquid manure were much superior to those in solid manure as a source of nitrogen to crops.

3. Larger applications of nitrogen were invariably followed by larger yields of this constituent in the crops.

4. Nitrate, ammonium sulphate and dried blood, when applied in equivalent amounts, were found to possess an unequal value, Nitrate was superior to ammonium sulphate, and the latter was superior to dried blood as a source of nitrogen to crops.

5. In the presence of nitrate, the nitrogen in the manure and in the humus were utilised more thoroughly than in its absence.

6. Under certain conditions · nitrates or other readily available nitrogen compounds, may hasten the depletion of the soil nitrogen.

7. Ammonium sulphate and dried blood intensified the development of acidity in the cylinder soils.

8. The proportion of nitrogen in the crops was readily affected by the nitrogen treatment. It was also affected by the character of the crop itself.

9. In the first rotation, the fresh manures produced dry matter relatively richer in nitrogen than that produced by the leached manures ; in the second rotation this relation was reversed.

10. The solid and liquid manure, fresh, produced dry matter relatively somewhat richer in nitrogen than that produced by the solid, fresh.

11. The smaller application of nitrate, when used together with manure, produced dry matter relatively poorer in nitrogen than that produced by the larger application of nitrate under the same conditions.

12. The wide range in the proportionate content of nitrogen in the crops, shows clearly that greater care should be exercised in measuring out the nitrogen to our cultivated crops.

13. Out of every 100 pounds of nitrogen in the form of nitrate, there were recovered in the first rotation 62.76 pounds, and in the second rotation 61.42 pounds. The corresponding returns for ammonium sulphate were 49.51 pounds and 37.01 pounds respectively. This indicated that the acidity in the soil increased sufficiently to interfere with the normal growth of plants.

14. Out of every 100 pounds of nitrogen applied in the form of animal manures, there were recovered in the first rotation less than 25 pounds, and in the second rotation less than 39 pounds.

15. A comparison of the crop yields in the first and second rotation, shows that the animal manures have a marked cumulative effect.

16. The maize crops seem to have utilised a smaller proportion of the nitrogen applied than was utilised by the oats and wheat.

17. The fresh manures were utilised better than the leached manures.

18. The solid and liquid, fresh, was utilised better than the solid, fresh.

19. The solid and liquid, leached, was utilised better than the solid, leached.

20. The smaller applications of nitrate were utilised to about the same extent as the larger applications.

21. The equivalent quantities of nitrate, ammonium sulphate, and dried blood were utilised in the order named.

22. The animal manures when used together with the larger applications of nitrate, were used to better advantage than when used together with the smaller application.

23. The proportion of nitrogen recovered in the crops ranged from 62.09 to 22.31 per cent.

24. With the returns from the nitrate nitrogen taken as 100, the relative availability of the other nitrogenous materials was as follows

	First Rotation	Second Rotation	Both Rotations
Sodium nitrate.	100.0	100.0	100.0
Ammonium sulphate	78.9	60.3	69 7
Dried blood	76.3	52.2	64.4
Solid manure, fresh.	32.9	39.2	35.9
Solid and liquid, fresh	50.4	55.6	53.0
Solid manure, leached	33.8	44.0	38.9
Solid and liquid, leached . . .	33.6	49.7	43.1

25. Nitrate and ammonium sulphate showed practically no residual effect. Dried blood showed a slight residual effect.

26. The animal manures showed a very pronounced residual effect.

27. Notwithstanding the annually repeated applications of manure, together with relatively large amounts of nitrate, there is no marked evidence of denitrification.

28. All of the cylinder soils lost considerable quantities of nitrogen.

1694   G. AMPOLA. **Experiments with Various Nitrogenous Fertilizers.** (Sui vari concimi azotati). — *Annali della R. Stazione Chimico-Agraria Sperimentale di Roma*, S. II, Vol. IV, 1910, pp. 73-115. Roma, 1911.

Italy: Latium   The following are the results of experiments on various nitrogenous fertilizers made in the laboratory and in plots at the Royal Experimental Station of Agricultural Chemistry in Rome, in 1909-10.

1. Amongst nitric fertilizers, nitrate of calcium has been found more useful than sodium nitrate.

2. With calcium nitrate the yield of straw and grain has been often greater than with sodium nitrate. This is accounted for by the fact that calcium nitrate is the natural product of nitrification.

3. The repeated use of sodium nitrate makes the soil alkaline. In clay soils, carbonate and bi-carbonate of sodium are formed.

4. Good results have also been obtained with calcium-cyanamide, although the yield was somewhat less than with ammonium sulphate.

5. Calcium cyanamide proved more efficacious as a top-dressing than if applied before sowing.

6. The more absorbable phosphatic fertilizers have most effect. Superphosphates are therefore more satisfactory than phosphorites and basic slag.

7. Lime combined with nitric acid is more efficacious than when combined with sulphuric acid or with the cyanamide group.

J. A. VOELCKER. **Top-dressing with Nitrogen Fertilisers.** (Experiments with Nitrogenous Top-dressing 1910). The Woburn Experimental Station of the Royal Agricultural Society of England. Field Experiments, 1910. *The Journal of the Royal Agricultural Society of England*, V. LXXI, pp. 335-338. London, 1910.

1695

A series of experiments on the effect of different top-dressings on oats. The previous crop was barley, and the manures applied were : calcium cyanamide, calcium nitrate, nitrate of soda, and sulphate of ammonia.

Great Britain : Woburn

The results confirmed those obtained in previous years with corn crops, as wheat and barley ; *i. e.* that when the same money value — or, as it is better stated, the same amount of nitrogen — is applied, it does not, in the case of corn crops, matter much in which form of these nitrogenous top-dressings it is given.

In the case of mangolds both the experiments of 1909 and 1910 proved that calcium cyanamide and calcium nitrate answer perfectly well for the mangold crop, and are quite as good, or, possibly, slightly better for them than nitrate of soda supplying the same amount of nitrogen. Sulphate of ammonia, on the other hand, would appear to be less beneficial than the other nitrogenous top dressings for a mangold crop.

In comparing the different nitrogenous top dressings the writer considers not only the effect produced upon the particular crop to which they were applied, but also whether they, or any of them, left any residue over for the use of subsequent crops. All the plots had been manured for mangolds, in 1909, with dung, mineral superphosphate, sulphate of potash and common salt, the nitrogenous top-dressing being given additionally. In 1910 after the mangold experiment a wheat crop was grown.

From the results it appears that the residue left over for a second crop was in no instance of material value. Nitrate of soda and sulphate of ammonia showed no residue, but rather gave a lowering of the produce. Calcium cyanamide was responsible for a surplus of 2 bushels per acre (1.8 hl per ha.) of corn, and calcium nitrate for 3 bushels (2.7 hl); and, possibly, this was connected with the fact of their both supplying some lime to the land. At best, however, the influence was not very marked. There is nothing at present to lead to think that, in regard to the new nitrogenous materials, their lasting effect requires to be taken into serious considerations.

1696   C. A. MOOERS. **The Utilization of Various Phosphates**. (Fertility Experiments in a Rotation of Cowpeas and Wheat Part. I.). — *Bulletin N. 90 pp. 1-90 of the Agr. Exp. Sta. of the University of Tennessee. Knoxville, Tenn.* December 1910.

United
States :
Tennessee

In connection with a green-manure and liming experiment in which cowpeas as a summer crop were followed by winter wheat, the writer planned a series of trials with various phosphates, which has now been carried out at the Experiment Station Farm of the University of Tennessee for five years with the production of ten crops. The phosphates used were the following :

Kind of phosphates	Total Phos. Acid (P₂O₅)	Available phosphoric acid (P₂O₅)		
		By Official Method %	By Wagner Method %	By Dyer Method %
Acid phosphate	17.25	16.90	—	—
Steamed bone meal.	23.85	—	—	—
Thomas slag meal	17.75	—	10.52	—
Phosphate rock.	33.90	—	—	10.5

The chemical analyses of the soils used for these experiments indicate that all four soils are similar with respect to content of lime and magnesia, which were low in each. None of the soils contained more than a « trace » of carbonate of lime. All four series were conducted therefore on soils distinctly poor in lime, so that a similarity of results, especially with regard to the effect of liming on the relative availability of the different phosphates, might be expected.

In order to make a satisfactory field test of this nature, a prime essential is a soil in great need of phosphoric acid. Because of the good supply of this element, the soil of the first series of experiments was poorly suited to this purpose; but even here it was found that there is a distinct tendency of liming to lower the availability of the phosphate rock, but not to affect the acid phosphate, whose relative standing is appreciably advanced.

Series II was on a soil which gave fair response to phosphating and, as in Series I, the rock acted well where no lime was applied and the financial results of the experiment were in its favor. But under liming the standing of the two materials was reversed to such an extent that the rock was next to unprofitable, while the acid phosphate was highly profitable, in particular where the removal of the cowpea crop exhausted the soil supply of phosphoric acid to the greatest extent.

In Series III, where the soil was poorest in phosphoric acid, although there is the same marked tendency of the phosphate rock to give inferior returns under liming, there is a difference from the results of the first two series in that on the unlimed plots the rock was decidedly inferior to acid phosphate. The explanation which the writer thinks most plausible for this result is that in Series I and II the solvents, such as acid humus and carbonic acid in the unlimed soil, were present in greater quantity than in either Series III or IV. This is indicated by the amounts of both humus and acidity, as determined by chemical analysis:

Series	I	II	III	IV
Humus	1.36	0.96	0.78	0.73
Acidity by the Veitch method	0.07	0.083	Neutral	0.04

In each series the liming was ample to correct acidity and at least in Series III and IV. would be expected to render the soil slightly alkaline, a condition which is recognized as unfavorable to the solution of the so-called insoluble phosphates. With acid phosphate however, a moderate excess of lime in the soil is not considered detrimental; for the precipitated phosphate of lime which would then be produced is known to be highly available to plants, and much superior to the phosphates of iron, aluminium etc. which would otherwise be formed.

The steamed bone meal, although included among the relatively insoluble phosphates, appeared in these experiments to occupy an

intermediate place, with returns little inferior to those from acid phosphate. But the influence of the nitrogen contained in the meal must
not be overlooked, and probably gives it a higher standing than can
be attributed to the phosphoric acid alone.

The experiments with Thomas slag were not sufficiently extended
to afford all the evidence desired; but results are very much in
its favor, especially if a large enough application be made to take
the place of liming, in which case it promises to be the most profitable
of all the phosphates. Of course, the initial cost of such an application is large, but otherwise there does not appear to be any objection
to it.

A comparison of the last crops harvested throughout the series
gives little ground for the opinion that phosphate rock increases
appreciably in effectiveness with the lapse of time after incorporation
with the soil. There seems therefore to be little promise in phosphate
rock on soils like those under consideration, unless liming, which
should be considered necessary be omitted; and even then the results
of Series III and IV show that acid phosphate may be much more
profitable than the untreated rock.

Analyses of the soils and full details of the results obtained are
given in tabular form.

1697   A. Gregoire and G. Hendrick. **The Fertilizing Value of some
Phosphatic Substances.** (La valeur fertilisante de quelques
matières phosphatées. *Annales de Gembloux* 21ᵉ année 4ᵉ 1.
pp. 166-183. Bruxelles 1 Avril 1911.

Belgium   A series of cultural experiments with some commercial phosphatic
substances. Of these, the first was a compound put foward by the
agricultural Syndicate of Selzaete under the name of « precipitated
mineral phosphate » and guaranteed to contain 28 to 30 % of phosphoric acid, soluble in alkaline ammonium citrate.

Two other fertilisers were made at the Haren factory, and also
called « precipitated mineral phosphates », one of them being said
to contain ammonia.

The firm of Bernard of Mesvin offered two samples of phosphates
which they put on the market as « Bernard phosphate » and which
are sold according to their content of phosphoric acid soluble in mineral acids.

The culture experiments were carried out in stone-ware pots containing 16 kg. (45.264 lbs) of soil.

There were two series of experiments: in the one, sodium nitrate wes used, in the other ammonium sulphate. The chief fertilizer contained 1.5 gr. of nitrogen and 1.5 gr. of potassium (1 gr. = 15.43 grains Troy).

Chemically pure dicalcium phosphate was taken as a control. The plant used was barley, except in one case when mustard was tried.

A general statement is made to the effect that when nitrogen is given in the form of nitrate of sodium the phosphoric acid of the fertilizer has more effect than when nitrogen is given as ammonium sulphate. The difference amounted to 15 %.

With regard to the phosphates, it was found that :

1). The phosphoric acid of the precipitated mineral phosphates, whether containing ammonia or not, and even though soluble in alkaline ammonium citrate, have a relatively weak fertilizing power. The latter only amounts to about 4/10 of that possessed by phosphoric acid from pure dicalcium phosphate.

2). The precipitated mineral phosphates cannot be used in the feeding of animals, as they are distinctly poisonous.

3). « Bernard phosphates » have no fertilizing action upon normal soils.

V. I. Sazanov. **Experiments on the Assimilation of Phosphorites.** **1698** (Opœtœ po Isutcheniiu, Usvoiaemosti raslitchnœkh Fosforitov). — *Annales de l'Institut agronomique de Moscou,* G. XVIII, Kniga 1⁰, pp. 100-112. Moskva, 1911.

Report of the results obtained from the experiments which were made, to ascertain the degree of assimilation of certain raw phosphorites of the government of Kostroma: Vershnik phosphorites with 24.50 % of $P_2 O_5$; Nijniak with 29 %; and Gliantsev, 28 %. For the sake of control and comparison, they also experimented with Kasan phosphorites, 27 %, and Ryasan 20 %, as well as with basic Slag, 13 %. **Russia**

These experiments were made with oats and buckwheat, planted in pots containing sandy soil and rich humus soil.

Results of experiments with sandy soil :

Oats. — The action of all the phosphorites are almost the same ; there was hardly any degree of assimilation. If normal manuring gives a surplus of 34 % of yield, scarcely 3 % of it is with phosphorites. The following table indicates this:

YIELD	Without P2 O5		K Cl + Ca (NO3)2 + Mg SO4 + Fe2 Cl6 Phosphorites of										Basic Slag		Usual manuring	
			Riasan		Kasan		Nijniak		Vershnik		Glian-tsev					
	1	2	1	2	1	2	1	2	1	2	1	2	1	2	1	2
Grains in grams.	0.15	0.10	0.35	0.17	0.10	1.17	0.22	0.27	0.10	0.22	0.27	0.29	13.10	10.50	13.89	14.75
Straw in grams..	0.75	0.85	1.20	1.00	1.29	1.08	1.13	0.95	0.91	1.04	1.13	0.96	19.10	17.65	19.50	20.12
Total ..	0.90	0.95	1.45	1.17	1.39	1.25	1.35	1.22	1.01	1.26	1.40	1.25	32.20	28.45	33.39	34.87
Average	0.93		1.31		1.32		1.28		1.14		1.32		30.17		34.13	

Buckwheat. — Results obtained with buckwheat are quite different. There is an increase of 35 % in the yield.

Experiments with oats in rich organic soil:

Soils. — Black soil, sandy soil rich in humus, clay soil.

Fertilizers. — Nitrogen, 0.5 gr. in the form of nitrate of soda; phosphorus 0.25 in acid phosphate of potassium, or in phosphorites; potassium, 0.75 in potassium chloride.

A good deal of phosphorus was necessary in the black soil; without phosphorus the yield (portion above ground of seven plants in each pot) is 18.82 gr.; while with acid phosphate of potassium and with basic slag, 35.43 and 32.75 grs. are obtained respectively.

But, in spite of these conditions, the Ryasan phosphorites and also Nijniak phosphorites are not assimilated; the yield is even lower than from those pots which do not contain any phosphates.

Again, while ammonium sulphate increases the degree of assimilation of phosphates in sandy soils, it is valueless — from this point of view — in b lack soils, due probably to the large amount of lime that they contain.

Phosphorites increase the yield in sandy soils containing decomposing organic matter; for instance, a yield of 17 gr. without phosphates is raised to 27 grs. by using phosphorites.

Phosphorites produce no effect in clay soils. Indeed, in these experiments, the yield is less than from plants where phosphates were not used.

In sandy soils of forest-lands, phosphorites increase the yield from 34 to 39 grams.

The following table gives a summary of the results, and shows the yield obtained by using phosphorites and phosphates, as percentages of those without fertilising with phosphates.

OATS	Yields in grams of straw, leaves and ears of plants in each pot		
	Without P$_2$O$_5$	Phosphorites	Acid phosphate of potassium
Black soil with nitrogen fertilizer, Na NO3	100	85	188
» « » » » (NH4)2 SO4	»	113	214
Clay — 0-13 centimetres deep (0 to 5 inches)	»	93	99
» 14-27 » » (5.5 to 11 inc.)	»	106	119
Sandy soil, containing decomposing organic matter - Depth 0-9 centim. (0 to 3.5 inc.)	»	145	181
» 9-27 » (3.5 to 11 inc.)	»	427	1300
Sandy soil of forest-land - Depth 14 cm. (5.5 inc.)	»	113	118

HENDRICK. **Lime in Basic Slag** (1). *Jour. of the Society of Chemical Industry*, pp. 520-522. London, May 15, 1911.

1699

Great Britain

In a paper communicated to the Society of Chemical Industry in 1909 by the writer, it was shown that there is a much smaller percentage of free lime in ordinary commercial samples of basic slag than is commonly represented, and that calcium carbonate is practically absent. At the same time it was shown that there is in such

---

(1) See also Abstr. 75 in this *Bulletin* for Jan. 1911. (*Ed.*).

slag a considerable amount of lime available as a base, that is lime which is capable of neutralising acidity in the soil and of acting as a base during nitrification.

It was pointed out that what is desired in the soil is not free alkali, but lime in a form such as carbonate, in which it is not free and does not render the soil strongly alkaline, yet is available to neutralise acidity when required.

An endeavour was made to measure the available base in basic slag and different methods were tried for this purpose. In one of these the amount of citric acid neutralised when shaken with basic slag in the cold was measured and calculated into its equivalent of lime. Another method used was to distil solutions of ammonium sulphate and ammonium chloride with the slag and estimate the basicity from the amount of ammonia given off.

The investigations reported in this paper were undertaken by the writer to find out how far the previous experiments were vitiated by a source of error possibly due to the fact that the ammonia obtained in those experiments might have been given off, in large part at any rate, not because of the basic action of the slag, but on account of hydrolysis of the ammonium salts used.

These further experiments provide further evidence in favour of the writer's conclusions, that basic slag contains a considerable proportion of lime capable of acting as base in the soil, part of it being readily liberated, while other portions are liberated with greater difficulty and slowly. A further conclusion reached was, that as the conditions are complex, it is impossible to draw any line, and state an exact percentage of basic lime in slag, except in terms of a strictly defined method of determining it.

It may also be concluded that distillation with a solution of ammonium chloride provides a better method of determining the available base in slag than distillation with a solution of ammonium sulphate.

1700   J. A. VOELCKER. **The influence of Magnesia on Clover and Beans.** (The Woburn Experimental Station of the Royal Agricultural Society of England). Pot-Culture Experiments, 1909, 4. — *The Journal of the Royal Agricultural Society of England,* Vol. LXXI, pp. 348-349. London, 1910.

Great
Britain :
England:
Woburn

Pot-culture experiments were made to try the effect of magnesia on clover and beans, magnesia being added to the soil in quantity to make the soil percentages of magnesia respectively 0.05,

0.10, and 0.20. In each case addition of magnesia retarded the germination though not ultimately affecting the final stage. Along with this were noticed changes in the root growth, similar to those observed with wheat, the roots becoming more fibrous as the magnesia was increased. It was also noted that nodule formation in the case of the beans was reduced. The general result obtained is that as the quantity of magnesia in the soil is increased so is the produce lowered. This was more marked in the first cutting of clover than in the second, and not so clear in the straw of the beans as in the corn.

G. Masoni **Action of Manganese Sulphate on Plants.** (Saggio sul-   **1701**
l'azione del solfato di manganese in rapporto alla vegetazione. Se esiste qualche relazione fra l'azione del ferro e quella del manganese nel terreno). — *Le stazioni sperimentali agrarie italiane,* XLIV, f. 2, v. pp. 85-112. Modena, 1911.

The experiments were made with maize and lupins in sand cul-   **Italy:**
ture, watered with different solutions of manganese sulphate. The   **Tuscany**
article contains a critical consideration of the question, and a bibliography.
The chief conclusions are:
    1) Any beneficial action exerted by manganese sulphate is due directly or indirectly to the sulphuric acid radicle, and in general to the salts added, rather than to the manganese; this appears, indeed, to retard plant growth.
    2) Where iron and manganese are used together, the action of the sulphuric acid, soluble salts, and iron neutralizes the harmful action of the manganese,

E. Takenchi & S. Ito. **Note on the Injurious Effects of Chlorides**   **1702**
on Vegetation. The Botanical Magazine, Vol. XXV. N. 392, pp. 132-33. Tokyo, May, 1911.

Chloride of magnesium, as well as chloride of sodium, exerts a beneficial action on the yield of crops when used in small quantities in heavy soils, rich in calcium carbonate. In poor soils, on the contrary, the injurious action of the chloride is added to that of magnesia   **Japan**
which in this way is added to soil already suffering from an excess of this element.
    In order to ascertain the injurious effects of chlorides without taking into consideration the relative proportion of lime and magne-

sia, the author made experiments applying jointly calcium and magnesium chlorides. The results of one of the first experiments are as follows:

Plants of rice (plants in a pot) were planted in 10 pots holding 10 kilos clay soil, rich in humus, with 6% Ca O and 5% Mg O. Each pot received the following general manure:

> Ammonium nitrate . . . . 6 grams
> Bi-calcium phosphate . . . . 10 »
> Potassium sulphate . . . . 6 »

Some of these pots received 0.05% of both chlorides; others 0.1% The harvest, gathered in October, gave the following weights in average of two pots:

	Straw	Grains
0.05 % Ca Cl₂ + 0.05 % Mg Cl₂ . .	67.5 grams	61.4 grams
0.1 % Ca Cl₂ + 0.1 % Mg Cl₂ . .	23.9 »	28.6 °
Without chlorides	85.2 »	61.0 ›

Thus a great depression is noticed on the increase of the chlorides.

A second experiment was made with pots containing 4 kilos sand manured as follows:

> Potassium sulphate . . . . 0.5 grams
> Ammonium nitrate . . . . 0.8 »
> Bi-calcium phosphate . . . . . . 3.0 »
> Ferric hydroxide . . . . 1.0 »

The results of the first experiment were here confirmed.

It seems probable then that chlorine in any form interferes with certain vital functions of plants as soon as its quantity increases beyond a certain limit.

1708   J. A. VOELCKER.   **The Influence of Salts of Lithium and Caesium on Wheat.**   (The Woburn Experimental Station of the Royal Agricultural Society of England).   Pot-Culture Experiments, 1909. 1. Hills' Experiments. — *The Journal of the Royal Agricultural Society of England*, Vol. LXXI, pp. 344-345. London, 1910.

A series of experiments was made with lithium and caesium, used in the form of different salts. The experiments were carried on in pot-culture of wheat with Woburn soil.

The author concludes that salts of lithium supplying it in not greater quantity than 0.002 % of the soil, will do no harm; but that when given above that quantity, they will have an injurious effect

Great
Britain:
England:
Bedfordshire

on the wheat plant. Caesium salts, on the other hand, would, so far, appear to have no injurious effect, even when in amounts corresponding to 0.0036 parts of the metal to 100 parts of soil.

P. KOENIG. **Stimulating and Toxic Action of Chromium Compounds.** 1704 (Studien über die stimulierenden und toxischen Wirkungen der verschiedenen Chromverbindungen auf die Pflanzen, insbesondere, landwirtschaftiche Nutzpflanzen). — *Landw. Jahrbücher* XXXIX B., H. 6. pp. 775-916. Berlin 1911.

The following are the results obtained from experiments made, in 1907 to 1910, with ten cultivated plants and many weeds, grown in Germany various nutritive solutions and in the soil.

1. All chromium compounds are absorbed by plants.

2. Chromium salts in small doses are not injurious. Indeed, they often have a favorable stimulating action.

3. Chromium sulphate by itself is less injurious than chrome alum, which produces poisonous compounds: that is, chromates, bichromates, and chromic acid.

4. In the soil and in nutritive solutions, chromic acid is less injurious than chromates.

5. Among the chromates, potassium bichromate is the most toxic; potassium chromates, calcium chromate and manganese chromate are less so.

6. Calcium chromate is as toxic as potassium chromate, although less soluble.

If carbonate of lime be added to potassium chromate this becomes less poisonous to lime-seeking plants, but more so to plants that do not prosper in calcareous soils.

7. Plants which grow in good organic soil best resist the toxic action of chromium.

8. Bichromates are excellent destroyers of weeds.

9. Plants rich in silica and in oxalates are less affected by toxic chronium compounds.

L. J. BRIGGS. **Dry Farming in Relation to Rainfall and Evapora-** 1705 **tion** (1). — *U. S. Dept. Agr., Burreau of Plant. Industry, Bull.* 188, pp. 71. E. S. R. Washington March 1911.

This Bulletin was prepared to aid prospective settlers in regions of United limited rainfall. It contains a discussion of the relation of the quantity States: Great Plains Western U.S.

---

(1) Cf. this *Bulletin*, p. 234, Dec. 1910; Abstr. 82-87. January 1911; Abstr. 423, February 1911; Abstr. 782-786, March 1911. (*Ed.*).

and distribution of the rainfall and of evaporation to crop production under dry-farming methods, in various sections of the Western United States, including the Great Plains, Intermountain and Pacific coast regions and Southern Texas.

.   In the discussion, account is taken of seasonal distribution of the rain, the rate at which the rain falls, the amount lost through run-off from the surface and the proportion lost by evaporation. Tables are given which show the normal rainfall at every station in those regions where precipitation records are available.

It is shown that while the method of alternate cropping and summer fallowing is the most highly developed dry-farming method, it is not the best method for all dry farming regions. In dry-farming sections where the rainfall is not so limited as in Utah, and especially in regions having a summer rainfall, other methods give as good or better returns.

1706   **Water required for Crops on Rich and Poor Soils.** *U. S. Department of Agriculture, Farmers' Bulletin* 435. — *Experiment Station Work*, LXII. pp. 24 (5-6). Washington, March 17, 1911.

Prof. J. A. Widtsoe of the Utah Experimental Station has stated (in the Utah St. Exp. Bul. 105) that the amount of water actually required for the production of a pound of dry matter becomes smaller as the available fertility of the soil increases. This law is not new, but it does not seem to have been applied to the cultural methods in a conntry where the limiting factor is the water supply.

United
States
Utah

Prof. Widtsoe found that thorough hoeing or cultivation throughout the season increased materially the yield of dry matter and decreased the amount of water required per pound of dry matter produced; that resting the soil for several years had the same effect; and that on infertile soils the water requirements of crops could be materially lowered by the addition of manure or commercial fertilizers. He believes that in every case the result is to be attributed largely to the plant food set free by the hoeing or fallowing, or that added in the fertilizers.

In the Utah experiments it was found that maize required a third less water, to mature a pound of dry matter, on soil which had been manured or fertilized with nitrate of soda than on the same soil without such treatment.

The important lesson from this work, briefly stated, is that if the farmer wishes to conserve a scanty water supply and use it to best advantage in the growth of crops he must keep his land rich.

K. Fruwirth. **Experiments on the New Methods of Cereal Cultiva-**   1707
tion. (Weitere Erfahrungen über die neuen Getreide-kulturverfah-
ren). *Wiener Landw. Zeitung*, 61 J., N. 33, pp. 385-387. Wien,
26 April 1911.

The writer reconsiders the usefulness of the different methods
used in the cultivation of cereals, and compares covering with soil
(*Zuschüttverfahren*), (Zickmantel, Zehetmayr, Jäger, Schönner) with   **Austria**
banking up (*Behäuflungsverfahren*) (Demtschinsky, Jäger, Kessler).
He gives, in particular, the results of several experiments with
authentic Petkuser winter rye, made at Chlumetz-a-Cidlina.

Plots	Treatment	Seed in Kg. per ha.	Yield in Kg. per ha. corn	straw	Difference caused by filling in method corn	straw
	Unmanured					
1.a	covered on Dec. 10th. . . cm. 18	125	2660	6040	+ 260	+ 1040
2.a	» » March 9th. . » 18	125	2540	5860	+ 140	+ 860
3.a	ordinary drilling . . . . » 10	167	2720	5880	—	—
4.a	» » » » 18	125	2400	5000	—	—
	With superphosphate					
1.b	covered on Dec. 10th. . . cm. 18	125	2780	6320	+ 530	+ 1670
2.b	» » March 9th . . » 18	125	2520	5980	+ 270	+ 1330
3.b	ordinary drilling . . . . » 10	167	2630	5370	—	—
4.b	» » » . » 18	125	2250	4650	—	—

Plots	Treatment	First quality. Percent passing through sieve of 2 mm.	2.25 mm.	2.5 mm.	2.75 mm.	Weight in gms 1000 grains	Weight of 1 hectol.	Second quality. Percent
1.a	covered on Dec. 10th . cm. 18	21	35	32	12	24	66	19.2
2.a	» » March 9th . » 18	19	36	33	12	23	64.2	12.7
3.a	ordinary drilling . . . » 10	14	34	37	15	25	67	18.8
4.a	» » » » 18	10	29	37	24	29	69.6	18.2

After giving the results of other experiments with wheat, oats
and barley at Chlumetz, the author also sets forth his results at Wald-
hof with winter barley.

Plots	Treatment	Yield in kg. per are corn	straw	Ears per plant	Date of first ear showing	Date of Ripening
1	ordinary drilling, 1 kg. p. a. cm. 18	29.72	21.10	3.79	11.V	12.VII
3	covering up, 0.6 kg. per are » 18	38.16	22.73	3.19	14.V	14.VII
8	earthing up, 0.6 kg. per are cm. 27 × 20 × 20 × 27	9.53	9.02	4.39	19.V	20.VII

	Weight of 100 ears in gms.	Percent through sieve						Weight of 1 000 grains in gms
		$2\,^5/_8$	$2\,^1/_2$	$2\,^3/_8$	$2\,^1/_4$	$2\,^1/_8$		
Ordinary drilling	150	46	17	9	21	6	1	37.7
Covering np	171	48	13	3	18	10	8	39.8
Earthing up	169	16	9	27	21	19	8	35.9

Another experiment made with winter wheat, Strube's Squarehead, in plots of 2.5 sq. m. gave the following results:

	Number of plants sown	at harvest
Ordinary drilling	370	234
Covering up.	370	237
Earthing up	370	180

The writer only confirms the conclusions given in a previous article, and taking into consideration the results obtained by Schneidewind, Depke, Krüger, Augstin, Bohutinsky, Windisch, and von Kerpely, he states that the recent very severe criticisms of these methods are not more justified than the former excessive enthusiasm. However, covering presents, in every instance, a greater chance of success than earthing up. At the same time, a marked diminution in the seed sown is not recommended; and good condition in nourishment and cultivation are necessary.

Finally, unsuccessful crops are found more frequently in inland than in maritime climates. Furthermore, unfavorable soils are particularly injurious to the earthing up method.

In these experiments, the most difficult things to determine are the distance between the rows and the amount of seed to be used.

1708   DEMTSCHINSKY. **Demtschinsky's Method of Earthing Wheat by Machine** (Behäufelung des Getreides nach Demtschinskyscher Methode). — *Deutsche Landw. Presse*, no. 25, p. 293. Berlin, 29 März, 1911.

Germany

Concerning his method and the agricultural machines used for it, M. Demtschinsky gives the following information. The aim in earthing-up wheat, and cereals in general, is to preserve the moisture. The Chinese earth-up wheat three or four times before the ears develop; they earth-up again before the flowering and call this process " earthing up for milk ", which means preserving the moisture to facilitate the formation of the milk-like sap in the grain.

The second aim is to promote the development of adventitious roots. In general, his method has been misunderstood. The cereals must not be completely covered with earth, but only partially.

For this purpose potato moulding implements cannot be used.

A very good implement for this purpose, is mark D (Demtschinsky Model) manufactured by Laas and Co. at Magdeburg, Germany. With one horse, a man can earth up from six to seven hectares (about 15 acres) per day with it.

HÖSTERMANN. **Experiments in Electro-Culture at Dahlem, in Germany** (1). (Elektrokulturversuche). — *Bericht der Kgt. Gärtnerlehrnstalt zu Dahlem bei Steglitz für die Jahre* 1908-09, pp. 137-144. Berlin, 1911.

1709

In the summer of 1909 the Imperial Biological Station at Dahlem undertook experiments to determine the exact effect of electrical discharges on the growth of plants.

The experiments were divided into the following groups:

1) Controls, exposed to atmospheric electricity only.

2) Intensification of atmospheric electricity by currents on overhead wire.

3) Application of high-tension electricity of different strengths.

4) Cultures covered by a wire cage, arranged to exclude natural atmospheric electricity.

Group I: Control.

Culture plants: spinach, radish, « rapünzchen » (2), cabbage lettuce.

Taken as normal and valued at 100.

Group II: Intensified atmospheric electricity.

Culture plants: carrot, « rapünzchen » (2), radish, spinach. Increase of yield by 15 to 40 %.

Group III: Artificially-produced high-tension electricity (direct current). Culture plants: as in *Group* I.

a) Strong current.

Yield 90 to 105 - slight average decrease.

b) Weak current.

Yield 100 to 125 - increase up to 25 %.

Germany
Germany

---

(1) See Abstr. 81 of this *Bulletin* for Jan. 1911. (*Ed.*).

(2) « Rapünzchen » is apparently used for *Valerianella olitoria* (Corn Salad, Lamb's Lettuce) and *Campanula Rapunculus*; the former is grown as a salad, the latter for its roots. (*Ed.*).

Group IV: Wire cage.
Culture plants: Dwarf French beans.
Yield 86.5 - reduction 13.5%.
The following conclusions may be drawn from these and other experiments:

1) The electricity normally present in the air exerts a considerable influence on plants; if it is excluded, growth is retarded. (The author remarks that expt. IV will be repeated, to observe whether the shading of the wire-cage has any effect in decreasing the yield).

2) A powerful high-tension current has a very slight favourable, or an unfavourable, action on growth.
A weak low tension current gives better results, but the optimum is not yet known.

3) Applications should not be made during hot sunshine; in summer early morning and evening are best; in spring and autumn 7.30 to 9.30 a. m. and for two hours before dusk; in winter only in the morning from 9.30 to 11.30. These times coincide with those of the potential optimum of atmospheric electricity and the greatest humidity. Applications during rain are useless, but foggy weather is most favourable.

With strawberries unquestionable results have been obtained in hastening ripening by several days; these would come in for the higher prices at the beginning of the season.

The author considers that the researches must be continued before definite conclusions can be drawn. He warns growers against too readily taking up schemes for electroculture, which would be sure to lead to disappointment; for it has not yet nearly reached the practical stage, and it will be a long time yet before sufficient is known about it to obtain dependable results.

1710
Congo

A. LONAY. **The Problem of Motocûlture. The Question of Tillage in the Congo.** (Le Problème de la Motoculture). See Abstract 1875 in this *Bulletin*.

1711

G. LAKON. **Retarded Germination of the Seeds in Conifers.** (Beiträge zur forstlichen Samenkunde. 1. Der Keimverzug bei den Konifern und hartschaligen Leguminosensamen. — *Mitteil. aus dem Bot. Inst. der Kgl. Forstakad. zu Tharandt.). Naturwissensch. Zeitschr. für Forst-und Landw.*, 9 J. H. 5, pp. 226-237, figs. 3, tab. 14. Stuttgart, Mai 1911.

Germany:
Saxony

Results of experiments made for the purpose of comparing the softening, and the absorption of water and of sulphuric acid, in seeds of *Pinus sylvestris, P. Strobus, P. Peuce, P. Cembra*, with that of seeds of the leguminous plant, *Gleditschia triacanthos*.

The Author has come to the conclusion that in the case of conifer seeds it cannot be a question of hardness of the tegument, and that all treatment with that in mind is entirely useless. Also that the retarded germination of Conifer seeds is due to natural conditions. This fact should be remembered when making experiments for the purpose of finding remedies.

As in the case of other seeds, it is necessary to study the action and effect of temperature, chemical agents, anaesthetics, etc.

The writer has already studied the effects produced under very many conditions, such as drying, heating, ether, chloroform, saline solutions, diluted acids; but he is still unable to give a definite result.

So much interest has been aroused during the process of ascertaining the causes of the retarded germination of the seeds of conifers and certain broad-leaved species, that the writer is preparing to undertake a series of researches on the chemical processes that take place in the kernels of these seeds.

Field Crops. Industrial Crops. Horticulture. Arboriculture.

H. HITIER. **Varieties of Barley for the Brewery** (1). — *Bull. de la Soc. d'Encourag. pour l'Industrie Nationale*, 110ᵉ an., N. 5, pp. 702-703. Paris, Mai 1911.

1712

The barleys grown for malting belong to three species or well-marked varieties.

1. FOUR-ROWED BARLEY. — *Hordeum tetrastichum pallidum*. — This is characterized by a covered grain, by ordinary husks or glumes, long awns, and ears of a fine pale yellow color. There is only one variety; the French common name is " escourgeon " or square barley. It is found in a wide range of territory: from Norway to Servia, to Catalonia and as far as Japan.

France

In order to give a good yield, it needs a deep and well prepared soil, so that the effects of different climates and soils may be lessened by manuring and by careful treatment; that explains why no

---

(1) See p. 49 *Bull*. Nov. 1910.

large number of varieties exists. There is a winter and a spring
" escourgeon ".

The square winter barley produces straw in abundance; sown at
the end of August, it is often cut, as forage, in May, and then
gives a second crop of poor ears.

The ears of the *common, long, winter barley* are much longer
(9-11 cm.) and more slender ; its rank straw has a tendency to
lodge ; its very long grains (10-12 mm. or .4 to .5 in.) have thick
husks.

The four-rowed summer barley has loose ears (7-10 cm. = 3-4
in.); but it does not lodge because of the shortness of the straw
(80-90 cm. = 32-36 in.). This is grown extensively in northern
countries and also on mountains because of the rapidity of its growth,
which takes about 100 days.

1. TWO-ROWED BARLEY. — The e is grown most generally,
as it is more accomodating, thriving best on calcareous or
sandy plains, very dry in June and July, where wheat can ripen
only with difficulty, and also because barleys with adherent husks
and plump grains are in demand for brewing.

a) H. distichum erectum (erect ears). — The ears are compact, very stiff, usually supported by solid and flexible stalks. They
do not lodge and give a large yield when grown in clay soils. The
grains are very plump but not compact.

The Italian or *Alpine barley* has a stem about 43 inches (110 cm.)
long, very thick at the base ; it is moderately early. The ears are
long (about 4 in.), compact and covered with a large number of very
close, full, round, large and heavy grains.

Jerusalem Barley has whiter, shorter (3 to 4 in.) but more compact ears. *Goldthorpe*, an English variety, also gives good results.

b) H. distichum nutans (drooping ears). — This is without doubt
the best barley for the brewery. The ear bends down because the
grains, which are long and have thin pellicles, are further apart on
the rachis.

The *Hanna* barleys have a bluish base ; they ripen somewhat
late (110 days after sowing on the 15th of March). The ears are
long (4 to 5 inches) and fairly compact ; grains large and somewhat
long ; pale thin, glume rather coarse.

Chevalier Barley, of French origin (1), is considered the best for
brewery purposes ; the grain is heavy, and round, richer in flour,

---

(1) " The *Chevalier* variety [was] raised by the Rev. Dr Chevalier of
Debenham, Suffolk, [England] in 1819 ".

J. PERCIVAL, *Agricultural Botany*, p. 506. London, 1910.   (*Ed.*).

and more easily ground than Hanna barley; it germinates very quickly and very regularly, but it is a late barley. In fact, it has been known, for a long while, that of the English and French barleys of the latter part of the 19th century, the former mature more quickly and need richer soil than the latter.

C. W. WARBURTON. **Winter Oats for the South of the United States** (1). — *U. S. Department of Agriculture, Farmers' Bulletin*, 436, pp. 32. Washington, April 15, 1911.

17.8

Only a small part of the sections known as " South Atlantic " and " South Central States " in the United States, is devoted to the production of oats. During the last ten years, the average production in 16 States has been about 870 000 000 bushels, or about 8.5 per cent of the entire crop of cereals in the United States. The average yield to the acre was 21.8 bushels and the average acre value $ 10.09.

United States

In the South, winter oats are in great favor, and their value there is greater than that of spring oats. Two varieties are commonly grown : the " Red Rustproof " and the " Winter Turf. " The former is a little less resistant than the latter, but it is more productive and matures earlier.

The " Winter Turf ' is recommended for the northern regions of the winter-oat belt, for the purpose of pasture and hay production. Winter Oats can be grown in all the Southern States, as far north as the following States : Delaware, Maryland, Kentucky and the Southern part of Missouri. It is not certain, however, whether this crop will be able to survive the winter over a large portion of this area.

---

(1) Other pamphlets on oats published by the U. S. Department of Agriculture: Farmers' Bulletin no. 424, " Oats ; Growing the Crop "; no. 420, " Oats; Distribution and Uses "; no. 395, " Sixty Day and Kerson Oats " and concerning two varieties of spring Oats adapted to the maize belt of the United States. Circular no. 30, *Bureau of Plant Industry*. " Improvement of the Oat Crop " and containing a detailed plan for testing individual selections.

See also: M. A. Carleton. " Ten years Experience with Swedish Select Oat ". *Bureau of Plant Industry, Bull. 182*. Washington, 1910. Mr. Carleton made his experiments in the northern States and also in Alaska. This *Bulletin*, Nov. 1910, p. 51. — E. G. Montgomery, *Oats Variety Tests, Bull.* 113 of the Agric. Exp. Station of Nebraska, Febr. 15, 1910. See Abstr. 1400, of this *Bulletin*, May, 1911.

An excellent three-year rotation, in cotton growing States, is as follows: Maize aud cow-peas (*Vigna Catjang*), winter oats followed by cow-peas, then cotton. Outside the cotton growing section, wheat and some forage crop could take the place of cotton.

On good soil, it is not rare to have a yield of 30 to 60 bushels per acre ; occasionally it has even reached 100 bushels.

1714   LAIGUE. **Maize Cultivation in Bessarabia**. (La Culture du maïs en Bessarabie). — *Bulletin mensuel de l'Office des Renseignements Agricoles*, N. 4, p. 480-485. Paris, Avril, 1911.

In Bessarabia, the following species of maize were chosen for the purpose of selection : *Funk, Leaming, Boone County White, Longfellow, Funk 90 days* and *Cinquantino.*

Russia:
Bessarabia

In general, a high grade of maize is rarely seen in Bessarabia. In order to better these conditions, provisions are being made throughout the province for organized work in the selection of maize seed.

This work of selection is especially being carried on at four country schools, where each pupil is obliged to choose ten maize plants.

Russia supplies the European market with only 11.5 % of the maize needed for consumption, while the United States exports 56 % of it. Trials with several species of American maize which have been received from 40 different parts of the United States, will be made in Bessarabia in 1911. A study of the soil in which each variety has been grown in the United States will be made, and according to that, each one will be planted in soil best adapted to it.

There are three good varieties of maize in Bessarabia, namely : *Bessarabian, Orangée* and *Cinquantino.* However, it is difficult to say whether they can be grown with as much success as can the American varieties.

Next winter, a laboratory will be establishesh at Kishinev by means of which it will be possible to begin a careful study of the soils of Bessarabia, in order to ascertain which variety can be grown with the greatest success.

For this purpose enquiries will be made from the Zemstvos for farmers who will be prepared to study the American varieties, and at the same time, by their knowledge of the various soils, will be able to facilitate the introduction of new varieties.

DEVEY (British Consul). **Chickpea Production in Damascus District.**
— *The Board of Trade Journal*, N. 755, p. 360. London,
May 18, 1911.

1715

The chick peas which are produced in the district of Damascus
are classed in two qualities: viz., «nature», a variety used sometimes to feed cattle, horses and goats; and «qualité puissante»
largely consumed as a human food. The total value of the average
quantity of chick-peas exported exceeds 30 000 £ (about 750 000 fr.).
The exports go mostly to France, Italy and Egypt.

Ottoman
Empire:
Syria

P. G. HOLMS (British Consul at Guadalajara). **Chickpea or Garbanzo
Production in Mexico.** — *The Board of Trade Journal*, N. 755,
p. 361. London, May 18, 1911.

1716

The chief chickpea (*garbanzo*) producing States are Sonora, Ja-
lisco, Guanajuato, Michoacan and Queretaro. Practically the whole
crop in the first named State is grown in the Jaqui valley, with
natural irrigation from the overflowing of the Jaqui river. Garbanzo
cultivation is new to Sonora, having reached importance only within
the last three or four years.

Mexico

The annual value of the Sonora crop is probably about
500 000 pesos (about 51 000 £ = 1 275 000 francs). A considerable
quantity of the Sonora garbanzo is exported to the United States.
The crop is mostly purchased, however, by travellers, specially sent
from Spain, who travel from hacienda to hacienda.

H. P. HUTCHINSON. **The Soy Bean as an English Crop.** —
The Journal of the S. E. Agric. College, Wye, Kent. N. 19, 1910,
pp. 318-321. London and Ashford, Kent.

1717

In 1910, the author made trials of Soy Beans (obtained from
America) in the open, on a chalky loam at Wye. The plants grew
well till flowering-time, but then turned yellow; however, a certain
amount of seed was produced. Examination showed that the roots
were free from nodules.

Great
Britain:
England:
Kent

In some pot-cultures in the open, soil in which Soy Beans
had grown in America was added to half the pots: the plants in
these pots continued growing well and produced a good crop of
seeds; examination showed that nodules had formed plentifully on
their roots. The plants in untreated soil behaved like those in the
field-trial.

From these experiments the writer concludes that it is possible to obtain a crop of Soy Beans in England. " Early Tennessee " was the better of two varieties tried. Inoculation with the special nodule bacteria is, however, necessary.

The distance apart of the plants should be 4 or 5 ins., with 12 to 15 ins. between the rows.

1718   **Cultivation of Soy Beans in the Caucasus.** (Culture du Soja au Caucasus. — *L'Engrais*, 26ᵉ année, No. 20, p. 550. Lille, 19 Mai, 1911.

The first crop of Soy Beans grown in the Caucasus was sold to Hamburg; 500 tons were forwarded, the price at Batum being **Russia:** 2s. 2d. (2.80 fr.) for about 40 lbs. (18.078 kg.) The freight to Ham-**Caucasus** burg is 13s. (16.25 fr.).

At this price, the cultivation of Soy is very remunerative to the farmer and it is estimated that 16 000 tons of this year's crop will be exported, judging by the number of seeds reserved for planting purposes.

If this demand continues, it is certain that in a few years the production of the Soy bean in Caucasus will rise to very large proportions.

1719   G. RITTER. **Nitrogenous Manuring for Lupins.** (Beiträge zur N-Er-nährung der Leguminosen. Versuche mit Lupinen auf Schwerem Boden). — *Centralblatt für Bakteriologie*, 29. Bd. N. 23-25, pp. 650-968, 2 Taf. Jena, 8 April, 1911.

Mr. Ritter has drawn the following conclusions (which have a very practical import) from his experiments with lupins: When **Germany** lupins are grown for the first time in virgin soil recently brought under cultivation, especially on heavy land without inoculation, the soil must be well supplied with nitrogen in the form of nitrates, or of ammonia salts.

Where inoculation is used, a small addition of a nitrogenous fertilizer will further the growth of lupins considerably. The best results will be obtained by spreading over the soil, before planting, a very small amount of soil from fields under lupins or serradella.

Lupins can also be cultivated in heavy soils rich in lime.

**Experiments with Taro (*Colocasia antiquorum* Schott and escu-   1720
lenta).** (Essai de culture rationelle du Chou caraïbe, *Arum esculentum*, Linn.). *La Côte d'Azur agricole et horticole* 3ᵉ a., n. 5,
p. 5. Hyères (France), Mai, 1911.

Very specialized study was made with Taro, or Colocasia, or
Carib cabbage at the State Experiment Station of South Carolina.
The Taro plant flourishes abundantly in Central and Southern Ame-   United
rica, in the equatorial regions of Africa, in the Indies, in China, in   States:
Japan etc. It is not confined to tropical regions, being found as far   S. Carolina
as the Himalayas; but it is most abundant in the tropics and
millions of people there use it as food. Its cultivation for profit in
the Hawaii Islands has only been attempted since they have become
possessions of the United States.

The tests made by the Experiment Station of South Carolina
prove already the Taro crop should yield about 10 to 14 tons
(English) per acre (25 000 to 35 000 kg, per hectare).

The process of cultivation costs less than that of potatoes; and
with an equal outlay, the yield is greater in quantity and value.

It is probable that this crop will scarcely be found beyond the
warm regions of North America; for the plant loves heat and
humidity and is somewhat similar to rice in this respect. It could
be easily acclimatized in Italy and in Algeria and Tunis.

The tubers, large as the thumb, have an entirely peculiar and
very agreeable taste and are very rich in starch.

**B. Schmidt. The Production of Forage for the increasing Live Stock   1721
of Germany.** — *Die Futterbeschaffung für Deutschlands anwach-
senden Viehstand*, pp. 143. Berlin 1911.

In this study on the production of forage in Germany, and the
German colonies, in its relation to the development of the live-stock
breeding industry in that country since 1870, the writer comes to   Germany
some conclusions of general importance.

At present the forage required for German livestock is still largely imported from abroad. Nevertheless it would be quite possible
to develop the production of forage in Germany to such an extent as
to obviate this necessity.

The yield of permanent meadows and grazing lands could be intensified by better cultivation, by regulating irrigation, and by
manuring. The yield of meadows per unit of area, could be much
heavier than it now is. In the case of grazing lands not only could

the yield be intensified, but the area could be extended, especially i n.
moorland districts where there is a good rainfall, and also by utilising the vast peat-bogs, which naturally produce forage.

The yield of cultivated grass-land can be increased by selecting
the best kinds of forage-plants, and by precautions against drought
and frost, loss from which can be obviated by cultivating mixed forage. The area under forage-crops can also be increased by gradually
and persistently substituting them for fallow.

Besides this, the progressive cultivation of suitable plants on the
vast areas still unused in the German colonies will make it possible
to increase still further the national output of concentrated forage.
There are, therefore, grounds for believing that the demand for forage
in Germany will soon by supplied by its home production.

From 1907 to 1908, the imports of forage had already fallen 18.5%
(from 943 000 000 frs to 770 000 000 frcs); and during this same period German colonial production increased in relation to the home
demand in the ratio of from 0.72% to 1.07%.

1722   Aug. Chevalier. **Forage Plants of West Africa.** — *J. d'Agriculture*
Tropicale, XI année, N. 118, pp. 97-99. Paris, 30 Avril 1911.

More than 150 kinds of graminaceous plants grow in the Western
Sudan, but only some thirty of these have real value as forage.
Amongst the forage-plants preferred by cattle should be noted:

West-Africa   1. *Pennisetum setosum* Rich., an annual graminaceous plant, from
30 to 50 cms. high, very common in the Sahelian zone. This forage
is much liked by cattle and is sometimes cut and dried for horses.

2. *Rottboellia exaltata L. f.* - This annual graminaceous plant
with an easily digestible straw grows to a height of 2 or 3 metres.
It is cultivated by the natives as a forage for cattle and horses.
It is sown in beds at the beginning of the rainy season. When it
has grown to 10 or 15 cms. it is transplanted into the maize fields.
It is reaped after flowering, from August 15th to September 15th.

3. *Dactyloctenium aegyptiacum* (L.) Wild. — An annual graminaceous plant that grows in tnfts. Excellent forage for cattle and horses.

4) *Digitaria sanguinalis,* (L), Scop. - Annual or biennial grass,
fonnd nearly all over the world. In the Sudan this plant multiplies
on tilled and fallow land. It makes a good feed for cattle and horses,
which when fed on this hay can do without sorghum seed.

5. *Zornia diphylla* Pers. - An annual leguminous plant, of the
group *Hedysareae.* Its small leaves are formed by only one
pair of lanceolate leaflets. It is very common in Senegal and the

Sudan, where it grows at the beginning of the rainy season and lasts sometimes the whole year on damp soil. When dried and stored as hay this plant is much liked by horses, and some natives say that it is a better forage than pea-nut straw.

6. *Alysicarpus vaginalis* D.C. - Another of the *Hedysareae*, hardier than the one above mentioned; it grows all over West Africa. It also grows in India and has been introduced into America.

Besides these wild plants there are two cultivated leguminous plants which are grown on a large scale throughout the savannah zone of West Africa, and are dried and stacked after the cereal harvest is over; one is the common pea-nut, the other is a variety of the Chinese dolichos, *Vigna nilotica* Benth., which is extensively cultivated in the Sudan.

E. LINDHARD. **Cultural Experiments with Red Clover**, (Dyrknings- **1728** försög med Rödklöver 1898-1910, 54. Beretning fra Statens Forsögsvirksomhed i Plantekultur.) *Tidsskrift for Landbrugets Planteavl*, 18 b., I. H.; pp. 1-95 + tab. 45. Köbenhavn, 1911.

Experiments were made, from 1898 to 1900, in clay and sandy soil by the Experiment Stations of Askov, Tystofte, and Lyngby, at **Denmark** Vester Hassing, Tystrup, and Aakirkeby, with the following varieties of red clover:

Late varieties: Swedish, Norwegian, Courlandish, Bohemian, Polish.

Early varieties: Russian, Polish, Danish, Bohemian, Moravian, Rhenish, North American, Hungarian, Transylvanian, Dutch, and French.

The writer notes that red clover is very widely spread throughout Europe, North America, South America and Australia. The late and the early varieties, are those mostly grown and they are almost always cultivated simultaneously. The late variety only grows once in a year, so that it can only yield one crop, whereas the early variety grows up several times in the same season, and yields several crops: it flowers from 15 to 20 days earlier than the late variety.

In Italy and France only early clover is grown as a rule; in the Austrian and German mountains the late and semi-late varieties are also grown; but the further North we go we find that the late clover is preferred to the early, and in countries where the winter is very severe and the summer short, only late clover, in its more characteristic varieties, is raised. This is the case in Norway, in most parts of Sweden, in Finland, North Russia, and Siberia. Denmark is a border land where both varieties can be raised and where, in normal years,

the clover of different countries can be advantageously cultivated. Now
Denmark consumes 2 000 000 kgs of clover seed per year, most of
which is imported. The main purpose of the experiments above referred to was to determine which countries and regions supply the
best seed. Since 1870, the Danish Government has experimented
at Orslev with 2000 samples of clover seeds from all parts of the world.

As the result of these experiments the author classifies the varieties of clover from the different countries as follows:

Early Red Clovers. - In Little Russia and its neighbouring provinces, a clover is grown which resembles the late varieties of early
clover grown in Danish meadows. The development of this clover
in the meadows is feeble, but is is vigorous and relatively speaking
hardy. Further West, in Galicia, Silesia, Poland, Posen, Holstein,
and Denmark, a rather earlier kind of clover grows but it flowers somewhat later than the Russian clover. Not only does it develop
sooner, but it grows up again more abundantly, and yields more hay,
than the Russian clover and is no less hardy. From the highlands
of Bohemia comes a similar kind of clover, which is rather more constant than that above mentioned, and develops more vigorously the
first year, but rarely yields as much as the Russian clover in the second year.

It would seem that the Carpathian mountains mark a limit, and
that the clover growing to the South and West of these mountains is
progressively less and less hardy. Thus, Hungarian clover is much
earlier than the above, but it is less profitable and does not stand the
Danish climate. Moravian clover yields better and is nearly as early.
Austria and Styria produce a similar clover which flowers as early,
but is unsatisfactory from the point of view of hardiness. From this
same region comes the red clover of Styria, a rather later and even
semi-late variety, which yields excellent crops but is not hardy enough
for Denmark.

The clover grown on the plains of Germany is raised from imported seed; but in the mountain districts of the Rhine, Eifel, Hünsruck,
Pfalz, and Würtemberg, an earlier clover than the Russian and Bohemian is grown, but it is not so hardy. The Dutch clover is still earlier, with plenty of green stuff and more tufted, but less hardy. French
clover is still earlier, but its hardiness decreases towards the West
and South. The earliest but least hardy clover of European meadows
is the Italian; next to it comes the clover of Southern France and England: but in England semi-late clover is grown, the early variety
being seldom raised.

The red clover of North America has hairy stalks and leaves.
The kind most generally grown is about as early as the Russian clo-

ver; there is another kind which is a little earlier, and in the more northerly districts, a larger semi-late, or late, clover is grown. Clover for seed is mostly grown in the States and in Southern Canada, where the climate is similar to that of Kiew and Orel in Russia. American clover is hardier than early Russian clover, but the results obtained in experiments made with it are less uniform, and in some cases it has been more subject to disease. The clover placed on the market includes early and semi-early seed.

A hairless meadow clover is raised in Chile, similar to Dutch clover in its early development and hardiness. Some samples, however, contained seed of the hairy variety.

A yet earlier variety comes from New Zealand, but it cannot stand the Danish climate.

The best early clover was found to be the one from Russia, then those from Galicia, Silesia, Poland, Holstein, and Denmark. The highest yield was obtained from Holstein clover, then Danish and Russian, followed by North American, Austrian and Moravian, which is especially suited to two year leys.

Late Red Clover. — This variety is cultivated in the Eastern highlands of Central Europe, on the shores of the Baltic, in Scandinavia, Finland., and the Northern sections of the United States and Canada. As a rule, European clover develops later and is hardier and of smaller growth as one goes North and West. The seeds are more expensive, as the market supply is less, and they are often mixed with early clover.

Early clover grows quickly in spring; it is in full flower from the 2nd to the 24th June, grows again rapidly after the first cut, and under normal conditions of rainfall yields a second and relatively speaking early and abundant crop; besides which it is suited to mixing with other forage plants. Late clover, on the contrary, grows later; it is in full flower from the 5th to the 10th July, yields a late and abundant crop, grows again slowly, and only occasionally yields a second good crop. These qualities make it less suited for grazing, but it is in better condition the second year than early clover. Late clover is specially suited to sowing with timothy-grass and other late-flowering forage plants, but not with early-flowering ones. Under the conditions above stated, it yields a better crop than early clover, it has fewer requirements, and succeeds better in cold, damp soils.

The best late clover comes from Denmark. Danish clover has yielded in two years 400 kgs of hay per Td. L. (1) more than Swedish

---

(1) Tønde Land = 0.5516 ha. = 1.365 acre .   (*Ed.*).

clover, 550 kgs more than Norwegian clover, and 500 more than Silesian and Bohemian clover. These latter kinds were more bulky
but less hardy, whilst the Norwegian was later and hardier, but less
developed. Experiments show that the seed produced in Denmark
is of very different kinds, varying as much as 20% in yield. The
writer believes that the production of Danish seed would acquire
more importance if the best varieties only were cultivated.

For two successive years, at Orslev and Tystofte, red clover seed
was grown with the following results per Td. L. *Late*, first cut 59.5 to
272 kgs; average 180.5 Kgs. *Early*: first cut 51.5 kgs to 126 kgs; average 82.5 kgs.; second cut 36.5 to 109 kgs; average 62 kgs.

Finally, experiments were made with samples taken from the biggest lots of seed sold in 1904, 1905, and 1906, by the most important
Danish firms. The lots thus inspected represented for the last two
years, 1/5 of the total consumption of early clover seed in Denmark.
The results obtained showed that the several firms have offered, on
the same terms, clover seed of a uniform average quality.

The name of the place of production may justifiably serve in
practice, as an indication of the quality of the clover, specially in the
case of mixed lots grown on the same territory, so large that the difference of local varieties disappears. When the purity of the variety
cannot be guaranteed in the strictest sense, there should at least be
the guarantee afforded by a knowledge of the place whence the seed
comes, in default of other data to designate the variety.

1724   A. D. McNair and W. B. Mercier. **Lespedeza Striata, or Japan
Clover.** — *U. S. Department of Agriculture, Farmers' Bulletin* 441,
pp. 19. Washington, May, 1911.

United
States

Lespedeza striata, or Japanese clover, introduced into the United
States from Asia, about sixty years ago, now occurs from New Jersey
westward to Kansas and southward to the Gulf of Mexico.

Lespedeza is an annual, and is esteemed as a constituent of pastures, being especially valuable for this purpose on poor or thin soils,
where other plants do not thrive. It withstands drought well, and matures seed under very severe grazing; hence, it is rarely necessary to
resow it on pasture lands.

Artificial inoculation with nitrogen-fixing bacteria is necessary
only when the seed is first sown on new land.

At the present time Lespedeza can be recommended in the United States as a hay crop only on the fertile lands of the lower Mississippi Valley, and on certain silt soils, where it frequently attains a height of from 12 to 30 inches and yields from two to four tons of hay per acre. Only one cutting of hay can be obtained in a season.

With Bermuda grass (*Cynodon dactylon*) Lespedeza produces excellent pastures in the South of the United States, materially improving the quality of the hay without perhaps increasing its quantity.

Under conditions where it thrives, Lespedeza has increased the carrying capacity of permanent pasture lands of the South of the United States by at least 25 per cent. Under favourable conditions, the yields are from 5 to 12 bushels of seed per acre, which command a price of $ 3 to $ 3.50 a bushel.

Alfalfa is more productive than Lespedeza; but is scarcely suitable for short rotations and is not so generally adapted to Southern soils.

P. Passalacqua. **Experiments on sowing Sainfoin** (La Lupinella). — *Giornale di Agricoltura della Domenica*, An. XXI, N. 18, p. 170. Piacenza, 30 Aprile 1911.   .   **1725**

These experiments were made on the 31 st. of March 1910. Milled and unmilled sainfoin was sown in marly soil, in parallel plots, at depths of 1, 2, 4, 6, 8, 10, and 12 cm. (·4, ·8, 1·6, 2·3, 3·1, 3·9, and 4·7 ins). The seedlings on each plot were counted after 10, 20, and 25 days.   **Italy**

From the result the writer concludes:

1. Milled seed gives a larger germination than unmilled seed.

2. The seed should be covered; the best depth for germination is 4 cm. (1.6 in); at 6 cm. (2.3 ins) and more the seed may be considered as lost.

3. Below 4 cm. (1.6 in), the deeper the seed is sown the slower is the germination; a depth of 2 to 4 cm. (·8 to 1.6 in) gives the quickest germination.

G. Paris. **Atriplex Halimus L**. (Sull'*Atriplex Halimus* L.). — *Le stazioni sperimentali agrarie italiane*, vol. XLIV, f. 2, pp. 140-156. Modena, 1911.   **1726**

Atriplex Halimus L., commonly known in South Italy as Salzolla, is quite an important plant in Apulia, where it is not only used for making thick, close hedges, but also as a forage plant, its leaves and flowers being used as food for domestic animals.   **Italy: Apulia**

This chenopodiaceous plant, which is generally considered a, seashore plant, flourishes also in the central regions of the southern Apennines, at 70 kilometers from the sea and at an altitude of 800 m.,

It preserves its halophytic characteristics even whilst growing in soils which contain only a small quantity of chlorides.

The accumulation of salt in the tissues is essential to the life of halophytes, for it enables them to overcome the high osmotic pressure of the saline solutions in the soil, and thus to utilise their water.

It is not unlikely that the accumulation of salt in *A. Halimus*, and other halophytes which grow in normal soils, is the result of the persistence of the special anatomical structure of their leaves, and accounts for the fact that these plants, whilst continuing to be halophytic, preserve the characteristics of xerophytes.

This has probably determined the localisation of the individual in an environment which was not originally its own, and has made it possible for this plant to withstand against other species.

1727

Ch. K. FRANCIS. **A Study in Oklahoma of Bermuda Grass *(Capriola (Cynodon) Dactylon Per.)*** — *Oklahoma Agricultural Experiment Station*, Bull. N. 90, Stillwater, Okla.

The chemical analyses relating to a series of experiments with Bermuda grass, covering a period of three years, are given in this paper, together with the results of experiments on the nutritive value of this forage. The conclusions are the following:

United States: Oklahoma

Bermuda grass grows rapidly, is the best pasture grass grown in the Southern States of America and is particularly suited to the climatic conditions of Oklahoma. It makes a good lawn, prevents land from being washed away, and grows on almost any soil.

The most practical method of planting Bermuda grass is to set out small pieces of the sod. This grass makes a hay which is remarkably high in protein, being excelled by but few hays.

The nutritive ratio of Bermuda hay varies from 1:3.06 to 1:6.4. It is easily digested and has no equal as a cheap food for cattle. (1)

1728

J. A. VOELCKER. **The Woburn Experimental Station of the Royal Agricultural Society of England. Field Experiments 1910. Manuring of Old Pasture Land (Broad Mead) 1910.** — *The Journal of the Royal Agricultural Society of England*, V. LXXI, pp. 341-342. London, 1910.

Great Britain: England

Experiments in manuring pasture land with farm-yard manure, basic slag, superphosphate, lime, sulphate and nitrate of potash.

_____

(1) See Abstr. 786, *Bulletin*, March 1911.

The plots on which these experiments were made were all chain-harrowed and rolled ; and then mowed.

The highest production of hay was given by farmyard manure; but the quality was coarse, and there was but little clover in it. The next highest yield was from the use of basic slag with sulphate of potash, mineral superphosphate with sulphate of potash, yielding nearly 9 cwt per acre less. All the manured plots, with the exception of the limed one, gave an increase over the unmanured plot ; on the limed plot the finer herbage and fresher appearance were very marked, though the hay was less in amount.

Prof. Biffen's botanical examination shows that the plots to which sulphate of potash had been applied contained more Leguminosae than any of the others, the plot treated with superphosphate and sulphate of potash giving the most. The lowest proportion of Leguminosae was found on the unmanured plot and on that manured with nitrate of potash and basic slag.

The most marked changes from previous years were:

1. The increase in the leguminous herbage on the farmyard manure plot.

2. The general increase all round of Leguminosae and of " miscellaneous " plants.

J. HENDRICK. **Improvement in Scotland of Hill Pasture as determined by the Effect on Stock. Experiments from 1901 to 1911.** — *Transactions of the Highland and Agricultural Society of Scotland*, V. Ser., vol. XXIII, pp. 190 2,67 + tabl. VII. Edinburgh, 1911.

1729

Experiments on the improvement of poor hill pasture by the application of manures and by cake-feeding were begun in 1901, and have therefore been continued for ten years. The experiments were started at the suggestion of the Board of Agriculture, which gave each year a grant towards the cost.

Great Britain: Scotland

The Highland and Agricultural Society and the West of Scotland Agricultural College co-operated in laying down experiments on a uniform plan at seven different centres. Four experiments were discontinued, only three experiments in the East of Scotland have been continued.

In the East of Scotland experiments, plots of 4 acres each were laid off and fenced. These were grazed every summer with sheep, or with cattle as well as sheep. At each centre there were 5 plots, one of which was untreated, and the others were treated as decribed below.

At each centre a preliminary season's grazing was undertaken before any of the plots were treated, so as to test the equality of the plots.

The treatment of the plots was as follows:

Plot A. — Sheep were fed on the plot with a mixture of equal parts of decorticated and undecorticated cotton-cakes during 4 years. Then, during 2 years, the cake feeding was discontinued in order to measure how much improvement had been produced by the residual manurial matter. Then, 10 cwt of slag was applied. The effect of this addition of slag was measured during the following three seasons.

Plot. B. — Basic slag, 10 cwt per acre, applied in the second year.

Plot C. — Basic slag, 10 cwt per acre, and sulphate of potash. 210 lb. per acre, both applied in the second year.

Plot D. — Superphosphate, 9 cwt per acre and ground lime, 10 cwt per acre, both applied in the second year.

The slag applied to Plot A amounted to about 158 lb of phosphoric acid per acre, whereas the slag applied to Plots B and C amounted to about 200 lb. phosphoric acid per acre.

In the first seven years the sheep in each plot were weighed regularly at intervals of about a month: in the eighth year they were weighed only at the beginning, middle, and end of the season. But in the following two years the regular weighing was resumed.

The chief results of these experiments are as follows:

1. The lime-phosphatic manures — a) basic slag and b) superphosphate, applied along with lime — have in every case effected a marked and long-continned improvement on the poor pastures to which they were applied.

2. Basic slag applied alone has on the whole given the best return of all the manures.

3. Potash used along with basic slag has not generally paid its way.

4. Even in the case of basic slag, on an average, three or four years elapsed before sufficient result was obtained to pay for the slag. On the other hand, the effect of the slag was not exhausted even after nine years.

5. Though a dressing of superphosphate and lime effected a considerable improvement, it did not pay so well as basic slag. The original cost of the dressing was greater, and on the average the return obtained was no greater than that from slag alone. The effect of the dressing was not exhausted in nine years.

6. The feeding of cake gave the worst return of all for the expenditure. In no case did it pay, either in the direct increase made by the sheep or in the improvement effected in the pasture. Generally

·speaking, very little result is recoverable on these soils from the manurial residue of the cake used.

7. When the soil is covered with a very thick coarse sod of grass of poor quality, clover plants and the fine grasses have no room to develop, and the effect of the manure is shown only very slowly.

On such pasture, sheep alone are unable to eat down the grass properly, and better results are obtained when sheep and cattle are grazed on the same land. On such land cattle make far greater live-weight increase per acre than sheep.

The main result of all these experiments is to support the view that the chemical constituent most needed by the poor pastures experimented on is phosphate, and phosphate in a basic form combined with excess of lime; as slag, or perhaps ground mineral phosphates, containing a slow-acting phosphate combined with a considerable excess of lime (1).

The Production of Cotton in Cyprus (La production du Coton à Chypre). — *Bulletin de l'Office du Gouvernement Général de l'Algérie* N. 11, p. 166. Paris, 1 Juin 1911.

1780

The cotton output of Cyprus is estimated at:

315 553	kgs in 1908	(310.6 tons)	
405 720	» 1909	(400.3 tons)	
455 560	» 1910	(448.4 tons)	

Cyprus

This cotton is exported solely from Larnaca. The chief producing centres are Dali, Kytraea, Morphon, Prastion, Kiti, Perivolia, Asha, Tricomo, Lefkonico, and Carpas.

Since new ginning machinery has been imported into Cyprus the cotton is cleaner than it was formerly.

It is thought that if the tendency, which has been registered for some time past, for a heavier rainfall continues in Cyprus, the local cotton industry will be able to develop profitably. (2).

---

(1) Compare: E. PARKE and B. DYER, *Mauuring of Grass-land.* The Journ of the Board of Agriculture, Oct. 1909, p. 591. See also *The Science and Practice of Farming during* 1910 *in Great Britain.* Intern. Inst. of Agricul_ture. Rome, 1910, p. 260.   (*Ed.*).

(2) Only one third of the arable soil of Cyprus is cultivated. The prin-·cipal products in 1909 were: wheat, 684 000 hl. (1 900 000 bushels) barley, 864,000 hl., (2 400 000 bushels) vetches 43 200 hl (120 000 bushels) oats, 136 000 hl· (380 000 bushels). Carobs, olives, cotton and grapes are produced in large ·quantities. Irrigation works, for storing and distributing rain water, were

1731   E. LEVASSEUR. **The World's Production and Consumption of Cotton** (1). (Production et consommation du Coton dans le Monde). — *Revue Economique Internationale*, Vol. II, n. 13, p. 30-50. Bruxelles, Avril 1911.

United
States.
India.
Egypt.
Asiatic
Russia

In the last 40 years the production of cotton has nearly quadrupled. From 1250 million kgs (1 234 000 tons) in 1870, it has risen to 4783 million kgs, (4 706 000 tons) in 1909.

The following are the estimates of the United States cotton crop during the last five years;

	Millions of kil'ograms	Thousands of tons (English)
1905	2 252	2216
1906	2 882	2836
1907	2 410	2381
1908	2 874	2828
1909	2 189	2154

Texas is in the first rank, Georgia, the Carolinas, and Mississippi in the second. The plantations are made preferably in new regions, where the soil is not exhausted by long years of production.

The extension of the area under cotton in India has not been as rapid as might have been hoped for, and the yield per acre in the United States is double that obtained in India. The average production, from 1899 to 1908, was 756 million kgs. (744 000 tons).

In Egypt the heaviest crop was that of 1907 which amounted to 1011 million kgs. (995 000 tons).

The Asiatic possessions of Russia have become important cotton producing countries. The production of Turkestan, with that of Khiva and Bokhara and of the Caucasian Provinces was estimated. in 1908, at 355 million kgs (349000 tons) circa. Fergana alone supplies more than half this quantity. The railways have greatly contributed to this increase.

---

completed in 1901. During the 1906-07 season, 1945 acres (778 hectares) were irrigated for winter crops, and 86 acres (34.40 hectares) for summer crops. The Forestry Department is attending to replanting denuded districts. There were 301 669 sheep and 277 357 goats in Cyprus, in 1909. In 1898, there were 47 242 head of cattle and 62 174 horses, asses and mules. *The Statesman's Year-Book, for 1911,* p. 112.

— See also p. 251 of the *Bulletin* for December, 1910.   (*Ed.*).

(1) See also Abstr. 1403 of this *Bulletin* for May, 1911,   (*Ed.*).

The world's production of cotton in 1909-10, in bales of 225 kgs. (495 lbs) each, amounted to:

United States	10 155 000
East Indies	4 186 000
Russia in Asia	768 000
China	1 200 000
Mexico	125 000
Brasil, Péru, Persia, Turkey,	
Antilles, Africa	645 000
Egypt	940 millions of kgs.

The producing countries export and consume at the same time in various ratios.

Exporting countries (in millions of kilogr).

	1880	1908
United States	742	1840
British India	212	450
Egypt	132	260
China	?	35 ?
Brasil	r	5 ?

The countries in which the proportional rate of increase in the cotton imports has been highest are Germany (133%) Italy, (351%), Austria-Hungary (180%) and Russia (132%). Galveston is the largest world centre for cotton exports.

The cotton crop of 1909 was estimated at 4783 million kilogrammes (4 707 000 tons). As the average price per kilog. is reckoned at 1.50 frs, as the spinning more than doubles the value of the raw material, and as the weaving of the thread into materials from the plainest to the handsomest, is supposed to double the value of the thread, it would not appear to be an exaggeration to estimate that each kilogram of raw cotton, acquires a value of about 5 frcs. by the time it reaches the ultimate consumer. This, would give to the world cotton crop a total value of about 24 000 millions of francs. No other textile comes anywhere near this value.

1732   **The Cultivation of Cotton in Russia.** (Obsor Diicatelnosti. Depar-
tamenta Semledielia v 1909. G.-Khlopkovostvo: Report of the
work of the Department of Agriculture in 1909). — *Exegodnick
Glavuago Upravlenia Semlenstroistva i Semledielia po Departamentu Semledielia.* (Year-Book of the General Direction of
Rural Organization and Agriculture at the Ministry of Agriculture). G. Tretti, p. LXXI-LXXIII, St. Peterburg, 1910.

Russian
Empire

The production of cotton in the agricultural districts of Turkestan and Transcaucasia supplies a good half of the Russian demand for this raw material, whereas, ten years ago, the Russian
Empire, like almost all European countries, was dependent on the
American market. The gradual rise in the customs' duties, and
the reduction of taxation on land planted to cotton, have constantly
favoured the prosperity and profit of this crop in Russia. The importation of the raw material from the cotton·producing to the cotton-
spinning centres of the Empire is shown in the following table :

	Asiatic cotton	Caucasian cotton (in tons)
1890	29 036	3 149
1895	49 904	5 413
1899	73 035	9 646
1903	109 749	12 894
1906	152 203	14 469

The most important centre of production in Asia is the territory of Fergansk, specially adapted to this crop by the nature of
the soil and by meteorological conditions.

About one third of the area in irrigated districts is planted in
cotton, as is shown by the following table, in acres :

	Total area of irrigated land cropped	Area under cotton
1904	1 589 773	504 388
1905	1 801 467	448 633
1906	1 780 185	495 936
1907	1 801 270	538 336

Yet. in spite of these favourable conditions, one half of the
cotton required by Russia is imported, as has been seen. As the demand is constantly growing, the need of extending the cotton
crop, wherever it can be profitably raised, is keenly felt.

Such extension can be obtained by two means:

1) By improving the culture-methods, by agricultural experiments, by advancing capital to the rural population, and by organizing the control of cryptogamic diseases and injurious insects.

2) By irrigating the regions of Turkestan and Transcaucasus best suited to cotton.

The Committee appointed for studying this question held two meetings in 1910, in which it examined :

1) The proposal of Colonel Volikov for irrigating the " hungry, steppes ".

2) The problem of irrigating by means of Artesian wells. Experiments made in Turkestan have already given most satisfactory results.

But all these undertakings imply heavy expenditure, which places the Russian producer on a footing of inferiority to his American rival, who can raise his cotton without recourse to irrigation works.

For this reason the Government promotes and favours experiments for the creation and selection of varieties of cotton which can flourish under the natural conditions prevailing in Turkestan and the Caucasus.

Encouraging and exact results, are due to the Experimental Station at Odessa, directed by Mr. V. G. Roturistrov. The importance of these experiments is all the more evident when we remember that the meteorological and soil conditions of the Experiment Field at Odessa are similar to those prevailing over an immense zone which stretches along the coast of the Black Sea, in the Northern regions of the Caucasus and on the Western shore of the Caspian. This zone comprises 6 ½ million dessiatines (18 millions of acres) of arable land. With a four-year or five-year rotation, 1 ½ million dessiatines (4 millions of acres) could be planted each year to cotton.

If we estimate the yield at only 10 puds (361 lbs) per dessiatine, the total yield would still amount to 15 million puds (241 153 tons), which would entirely cover the demand of the Russian home market: for in 1908, 14.5 million puds, (223 436 tons), for a value of 119.1 million roubles, or £ 12 593 075, were imported.

The Development of Cotton Cultivation in Turkestan (Zur Hebung der Baumwollkultur in Turkestan). — *Deutsches Kolonialblatt*, No. 11, p. 436. Berlin, 1. June, 1911.

1733

Since last spring the Russian Government has sent agricultural experts to the three principal districts of Turkestan, with instructions

Russian Empire: Turkestan

to develop the cultivation of cotton. At the same time the number of teachers has been increased so that each agricultu ral district may have its own.

The agricultural districts are Margelan, Ándishan, Namangan, Kokand, Katta-Kurgan, Khodshant, Samarkand, and Taschkend.

The first four are in Ferghana, the three next in Samarkand, and the last in Syr-Darya.

The experts are to assist the planters, watch over the teachers, inspect the crops, and prepare plans for the further development of cotton production in Turkestan.

1784   FULFORD.   **Exports of Raw Cotton and Wool from Tient-sin.**   *The Board of Trade Journal*, No. 750, p. 100. London, April 13, 1911.

The total exports of raw *Cotton* from Tient-sin during 1910 amounted to 145 627 piculs (19 416 633 lbs) as against 25 126 piculs **China**   (3 350 132 lbs) in 1909. Unfortunately the trade is being spoiled by the methods of the native dealers, who not only mix seed and leaf with the staple, but have adopted the plan of soaking the stuff in water, to increase the weight, to such an extent that when bales have been opened solid lumps of ice have been found in the middle. The remedy, of course, lies in the foreign buyers agreeing to refuse all such cargo, but it sems that the present demand is too great to allow of any such agreement being made.

The total export of *Wool* (of camel and goat) from Tient-sin during 1910 was 174 935 piculs (23 324 000 lbs.) as against 264 166 piculs (35 222 133 lbs.) in 1909.

Both camel hair and goats' hair have met with a good demand, but it is worthy of note that the former is now going very largely to continental manufacturers.

1785   SANSOM. (British Consul). **Cotton Growing in Korea.** — *The Board of Trade Journal*, No. 757, p. 480. London, June 1, 1911.

The cotton growing of Korea is one on which great hopes are set, and considerable efforts are being made to foster it. A Cotton Culti-
Japanese Empire: Korea   vation Association, formed under official auspices in 1905, devotes itself to encouraging the cultivation of the Upland species of Ame-rican cotton. It produced, in 1909, about 400,000 lbs from 1000 acres, and this year the plantations will cover 7 500 acres. The ground available for cotton in Korea is estimated at 1 300 000

acres, of which it is said that 600 000 acres will be planted with Upland cotton by 1917.

Reports are now to hand of the proposed formation of a company for raising cotton in Korea, promoted by business men in Japan, and approved by the Government General. The capital will be £ 500 000 and operations will commence with the purchase of 12 500 acres of cotton lands to be cultivated by tenants. Should anticipations be realised, Korea will, before long, be able to supply a good proportion of raw material to the Japanese mills. The cotton district will be served by the Honam Railway.

COLDWELL. (British Consul). **Encouragement of Cotton Growing in San Salvador.** — *The Board of Trade Journal*, No. 757. p. 479, London, June 1, 1911.

1786

An Act has recently been passed in San Salvador for the encouragement of cotton growing and manufacture in the Republic. The Government is empowered to appoint an agricultural expert who shall make a study of the lands in San Salvador suitable for cotton cultivation.

San Salvador

Agriculturists and manufacturers, undertaking respectively the cultivation of cotton and the manufacture of textiles, are to be allowed to import, free of duty, the necessary seed and machinery. An exhibition of fabrics and other products of cotton is to be held every five years.

Cotton Growing in the Leeward Islands W. I. — *Journal of the Royal Society of Arts*, No. 3044, p. 495. London, 1911.

1787

From various causes the cotton industry in the Leeward Islands received a check last year. In his report on the Blue Book of the Leeward Islands just issued, Mr. H. E. W. Grant, the Colonial Secretary, directs attention to this check, which he attributes partly to low prices and partly to bad weather and heat. Blister mite (1) was very prevalent and adversely affected the crop, whilst the unwise habit of leaving old cotton bushes on the land aggravates the evil. Fortunately the islands have hitherto escaped serious visitation from the cotton worm (2). In the Virgin Islands there remain large num-

Leeward Islands

---

(1) *Eriophyes Gossypii.*   (*Ed.*).
(2) *Alabama argillacea.*   (*Ed.*).

bers of cotton plants of an inferior type, and the Government is doing what it can to persuade the planters not to use the local seed for planting, but to import. In Antigua the acreage under cotton has been decreased, owing to losses sustained from the attacks of the « Flowerbud maggot » (1), and in St. Kitts only 1 100 acres were planted, owing probably to the fall in prices in the previous year. From Nevis and Montserrat the returns are more satisfactory, but the exports of cotton from the Leeward Islands are never likely to be large.

1738   **Cotton Cultivation in South America.** — *The Board of Trade Journal.* No. 751, p. 154. London, April 20, 1911.

S. America There are extensive tracts of territory in the neighbourhood of the River Magdalena in Colombia, which are very suitable for cotton cultivation, and in Venezuela and Guiana there are large unexploited areas in the interior on which cotton could be profitably ´grown, especially in the vicinity´ of the Orinoco. The climate and soil of Argentina are exceptionally suitable for cotton cultivation, but owing to a lucrative business in grain and cattle breeding, the production of cotton has not yet been undertaken on an extensive scale. This may also be attributed partly to scarcity of labour. Peru is one of the oldest cotton producing countries of South America, and a great deal more could be done in this direction by suitable irrigation.

1739   LAVALLE Y GARCIA. **The Cotton Production of Peru** (2). — *Peru- To-Day*, No. 2, p. 23-28. Lima, April, 1911.

Peru Few situations offer better conditions for the production of cotton than the coast of Peru. In the valleys irrigated by rivers ., of intermittent flow, the cultivation of cotton is made possible by the great absorbent capacity of the fine sandy deep soils. In these valleys is generally cultivated the native cotton *Gossypium Peruvianum*, the great root development of which makes it resistant to drought.
Peruvian coast lands are alluvial and are very suitable for cotton. In Peru are obtained the greatest cotton harvests per unit of area.

(1) *Contarinia Gassypii.*
(2) See p. 252 of this *Bulletin* for Dec. 1910.   (*Ed.*).

In the Valley of Lambayegue the average production of Upland cotton (*Gossypium hirsutum*) varies from 484 to 553 lbs. per acre. In new lands, recently opened to cultivation, as high as 1384 lbs. per acre have been obtained.

Sea-Island cotton in the valley of Pativilea gives a production varying between 386 and 442 lbs. per acre. Mit-affifi cotton has yielded in the valley of La Chira 498 lbs. per acre.

The production of the native cotton, *Gossypium Peruvianum*, is noticeably less than that obtained from the Upland cotton, Mit-affifi and Sea-Island.

Practically, one may take as an average of Peruvian production per acre, 484 lbs., against the highest average in the United States of 390 lbs. and in India of 70 lbs. per acre.

The excellent conditions which the coast of Peru offers for the cultivation of cotton, have caused a notable continuous increase in production, which in the short period of six years has almost tripled. The exportation which in 1903 was 7 651 358 kgs of fibre, had reached proportions three times as great in 1909, being then 21 370 256 kgs.

The Cultivation of Cotton in the State of Sergipe, Brazil. (Baum-wollanbau im Staate Sergipe). — *Deutsches Kolonialblatt*, No. 11, pp. 435-436. Berlin, June 1st, 1911.

1740

After sugar-cane, cotton is the most important crop of the State of Sergipe. In this State the cotton grows on the high table-lands of the interior, in the regions of Itabajana, Siamo, Djasetassan, and Seuhora. The quality, as a rule, is not excellent. The annual output fluctuates between 20 000 and 50 000 bales. The cotton is carried to Aracaju, first on mules and then by water. At Aracaju there are five factories which spin about 25 000 bales. In good years cotton is exported to Bahia and Rio de Janeiro; but in bad years it has to be imported from other States to keep the local factories going.

Brazil:
Sergipe

The surplus seed is used partly as fuel for the ginning machinery, partly as a feed for cattle, and partly as manure. It is exported when the price it fetches covers the cost of carriage to the sea coast.

O. F. Cook. «**Hindi**» **Cotton in Egypt.** — *U. S. Dept. of Agr., Bur. of Plant Industry.* Bull. No. 210, pp. 7-52. Washington, May 1911.

1741

The standards of uniformity are higher with the Egyptian cotton than with American short staples, because the Egyptian cotton is used for superior fabrics, and for other industrial purposes where

Egypt.
United
States:
Arizona

strength is required. The prospects of establishing a successful Egyptian cotton industry in America depend on the possibility of producing a uniform crop and avoiding the need of subsequent sorting of the fibre. In the Egyptian industry the requirement of uniformity is met, in part, by a system of careful grading and sorting, made possible by cheap labor, not available in the United States. Inspection of the fields in Egypt during the early growing season shows a large and very general contamination with the inferior type of cotton known as the « Hindi », that produces only a short, sparse, white lint, quite unlike the Egyptian cotton. The Egyptian system of roguing the plants only at the time of thinning would not effect a complete elimination of the « Hindi » cotton, even if it were generally applied, as many plants, not readily distinguished as « Hindi » hybrids at earlier stages of growth, give later indications of hybrid nature.

An increase of the « Hindi » contamination is supposed to have taken place in Egypt in spite of the selection that has been directed against it, and this, along with the diminished fertility of the soil, rise of the water level in the soil, plant diseases, and insect pests, would account for the lessened production of the Egyptian fields.

The supposed increase in the proportion of « Hindi » cotton may prove to be due to the naked seeds that permit a more rapid absorption of water and a more prompt germination than fuzzy seeds. Prompt germination would allow the « Hindi » seedling plants to make more rapid growth in the earlier stages and thus gain an advantage over Egyptian seedlings in the same hill. It is also possible that the « Hindi » characters are prepotent over the Egyptian, like the Upland characters in the later generations of Egyptian-Upland hybrids.

Breeding experiments have shown that it is possible to secure a much higher degree of uniformity in Arizona than now exists in most of the cotton fields in Egypt. Attention to the external characters enables the « Hindi » cotton and other undesirable variations to be removed from the fields before the flowers open, and hence before cross fertilisation becomes possible.

The greater popularity of the brown-linted varieties of Egyptian cotton may be explained by the advantage that the color gives in sorting out the inferior «Hindi» white fibre. The exclusion of the « Hindi » cotton by a more efficient system of selection will enable white varieties to be grown in Arizona and thus produce longer and stronger fibre than brown varieties are likely to produce. A study of many variations and hybrids of the Egyptian cotton shows a distinct tendency for the brown colour to be associated with short fibres.

It is possible that the reversions to the « Hindi » characters may continue to appear in small numbers, even in carefully selected stocks, as in analogous naked-seeded variations occasionally found in uniform selected varieties of Upland cotton. Nevertheless, experiments indicate that such reversions to the «Hindi» characters are not likely to interfere with the development and preservation of uniform strains of Egyptian cotton in the United States if the proper methods of selection are applied.

World Flax Production. — *Journal of the Royal Society of Arts.* No. 3046, p. 536. London, April 7, 1911.

1742

The need for encouraging the cultivation of flax in all coun tries, where conditions are favourable, is being made evident; and the « Union of European Flax-Spinners» has, during the past year, obtained samples of flax from Japan, Canada, Mexico and several of the South American States, the retting operations being carried out under proper supervision in Belgium, France and Holland. The results are said to be very satisfactory, and to indicate clearly that much may be done if cultivators in those countries receive expert assistance in the best methods of retting and general treatment of the fibre for export. At present, three-fourths of the world's supply comes from Russia, but the quality of the fibre is inferior.

Russia.
Ireland

The extent of flax cultivation in Ireland (1) is still considerable; but the acreage has been gradually diminishing during recent years.

Flax from the East Africa Protectorate — *Bulletin of the Imperial Institute*, Vol. IX, No. 1, pp. 11-14. London, 1911.

1743

Various supplies of flax, grown in the Highlands of East Africa, have been examined from 1908 to 1910 at the Imperial Institute.

The results indicate that flax can be grown there successfully. In order to obtain a product of good quality, however, it is advised that considerable attention should be devoted to the processes involved in the preparation of the fibre, and particularly to the methods of retting (2).

British
East Africa

---

(1) See Abstr. 1161 of this *Bulletin* for April 1911. (*Ed.*).

(2) The British East Africa Protectorate has an area (roughly estimated) of about 200 000 square miles; population estimated at 4 038 000. The agricultural products of the lowlands are essentially tropical, and include rice, maize, various native grains, cassava, cocoanuts, etc. The cultivation of sisal

1744   Wm. Trealase. **The Species of Agave Cultivated during Recent Years in Mexico.** — (*Transactions of the Academy of Sciences of St. Louis.* Vol. XVIII, No. 3. Abs.) Nature, No. 2170, Vol. 36. London, June 1, 1911.

Mexico

Many species of *Agave* have been cultivated during recent years in Mexico under the name of " zapupe ". Of the various forms for which numerous local popular names exist, five different species, all new to science, are delimited according to spine characters, and these fall into three groups. They may be distinguished as " azul ", " tepezintla ", " ixtle ", " cimarrón ", and "green zapupe; " and are probably all referable to the section *Euagave*. As cultivated plants they rarely set capsules, and appear to be freely bulbiferous after flowering.

1745   **Production of Esparto Grass in Tripoli.** (Produzione dello sparto in Tripolitania). — *Bollettino del Ministero di Agric. Ind. e Comm.* Serie B. Fasc. 6. pp. 237-238. Roma. 15 Marzo 1911.

Tripoli

22456 tons of esparto grass (1) were brought, in 1910, from the interior of Tripoli to the market of the vilayet. The supply was much below that of previous years.

Esparto grass has to be sought for more and more in the interior, as the bad habit the natives have of gathering it carelessly and pulling up the roots, prevents the reproduction of the young plants. All the export trade is with England.

Whilst the production of esparto grass is gradually declining in Tripoli, it is increasing in Algeria and Tunis, as a result of the improved facilities for communication and of the measures taken by the Government. Besides, the esparto grass of Tripoli only yields from 42 to 43% of pulp, whereas that of Tunis yields from 43 to 45%, that of Algeria from 45 to 48% and that of Spain 55%.

---

hemp and Ceara rubber is now being undertaken on an extended scale. Cotton growing is receiving attention on the banks of the Yuba River. Other plants of economic value are being experimented with. In the highlands almost all crops of the temperate zone are grown, viz: oats, barley, wheat, potatoes, all European vegetables, beans, peas, linseed. There is now a large acreage under wheat. Maize culture is rapidly extending. Many coffee plantations are established. The growing of black wattle is also receiving attention. Ostrich farming has practically become an established industry. *The Statesman's Yearbook for 1911*, p. 175.   (*Ed.*).

(1) A mixture of *Stipa tenacissima* and of *Lygeum Spartum*, locally known as « Alfa ».   (*Ed.*).

The Palm-Fibre Industry in Venezuela. Palma de Cogollo. — *Journal of the Royal Society of Arts*, No. 3053, p. 744, London, May, 26 1911.

1746

The palm-fibre, or, as it is locally known, the *cogollo* industry, has for many years been of great economic importance in Venezuela, particularly in the Maracaibo district.

Venezuela

The fibre is obtained from a small palm called *palma de cogollo*. Only the young shoot or centre leaves are gathered. The first cutting can be made when the plant is one year old, and thereafter from two to three times a year.

The leaves are soft and pliable and are split into narrow ribbons, which, when moistened, may be rolled into a string-like form, and then woven into hats.

The hats made from the Venezuelan *cogollo* are practically the same as the so-called *Panama* hats, but are seldom so fine-grained or well made as the Ecuadorian or Colombian hats.

Utilising Fibrous Plants in Argentina. Caraguata and Ibera. — *Bulletin of the PanAmerican Union.* p. 549. Washington, March, 1911.

1747

The Government of the State of Corrientes has authorised a private person to utilize the fibrous plants found in great quantities on the islands of the Parana River and along the boundaries of the Province of Corrientes. The fibrous plant which will be exploited most extensively is called " caraguata " and is a species of wild thistle, very abundant, which sometimes grows seven feet high. *Ibera* a strong and fine fibre, much used in the manufacture of gunny or jute sacks, will also be utilized.

Argentina

KRüGER. **Experiments in the Manuring of Sugar Beets.** (Untersuchungen über die Ernährungsbedingungen der Zuckerrübe). — *Zeitschrift des Vereins der Deutschen Zucker-Industrie*, 664, 1fg, *Berichte der Zweigvereine, Halberstädter Zweigverein*, Feb. 27 th, 1911. pp. 460-467, Berlin, May, 1911.

1748

The results of experiments, begun in 1905 at the Experimental Station of Bernburg, on the nutritive requirements of sugar beets, are here examined. The experiments were made respectively with insufficient, sufficient, and excessive quantities of manure.

Germany: Anhalt

In the case of nitrogenous manures:

With insufficient nitrogenous fertilizers, a product is obtained with a high sugar content, easily preserved, which can be stored without fear of decomposition, and which is also easily worked. Sufficient nitrogenous manure increases the crop, but not the sugar content.

In the case of phosphates: a good crop, both for quantity and quality can be obtained with manures relatively deficient in phosphates.

With regard to potassic fertilizers: a heavy crop can be obtained without potassic fertilisers, but the sugar content is unsatisfactory: the beets are difficult to preserve and also to work. On the other hand, by applying potassic fertilizers sparingly a good crop from all points of view is ensured.

As to the important question of an excess of nutritive substances: phosphoric acid can be used in great quantities without any bad effects, as long as the conditions of the soil are not impaired. When the soil will tolerate it, an excess of potash has no injurious effect on the quality or quantity of the beets. On the other hand, nitrogen must not be used to excess, as by so doing it is impossible to obtain ripe beets, the leaves remain green till the autumn, and if the weather is favourable they may so continue till October.

Nitrogen should be so administered that at the end of the season it is reduced to a minimum leaving none to be assimilated.

1749   W. R. Beattie. **The Peanut.** (**Arachis hypogoea**). — *U. S. Department of Agriculture. Farmers' Bulletin* 431, pp. 39. Washington, March, 11, 1911.

The peanut is worthy of more general cultivation throughout the Southern part of the United States, especially in the boll-weevil (1) districts, where it will in many cases be found more profitable than cotton.

United States

The demand for peanuts to be used in the preparation of human foods is constantly increasing. The United States is a heavy buyer of peanut oil produced abroad, while there are thousands of acres of waste lands in the Southern States that would produce enough peanuts to keep the cotton-seed oil mills running and furnish more than enough oil for home consumption.

While the average yield of peanuts is only about 34 bushels an acre (31.6 hectolitres per hectare) with proper methods a yield

(1) *Anthonomus grandis*. Both. See Abs. 1583 of this *Bulletin*, May, 1911.
(*Ed.*).

of 60 bushels (54 hl. p. hectare) ofpeasand 1 to ½ tons (25.1 to 37.6 metric quintals per hectare) of forage may reasonably be expected.

The dry matter of peanut hay averages 11.75 % protein, 40.95 % carbohydrates and 1.84 % fats. The dry matter of the entire plant of peanut contains 13.48 % protein, 36.28 % carbohydrates and 15.06 % fats.

The peanut vines, after the removal of all the first-class peas, have a feeding value practically equal to the cost of the field culture of the crop.

An acre of first-class peanuts, calculating the yield at a ton of vines (25.1 metric quintals per hectare) worth from 8 to 10 dollars, and 60 bushels (54 hl. per ha) of peas, worth 40 to 60 dollars, will give an income of 48 to 70 dollars (621 to 906 francs per hectare). The cost of growing an acre of peanuts is variously estimated at 12 to 25 dollars (155 to 325 francs per hectare), including seed and fertilizers.

The net return of 36 to 45 dollars (466 to 581 francs per ha) is above the average for the crop as now grown in the United States, but decidedly lower than may be expected under favorable conditions and proper cultural methods.

Insects Injurious to the Peanut. Recently a species of *Aphis* has been reported as working upon the roots of the peanut plants. Its presence is indicated by patches of what appears to be a white mould upon the roots and pods of the peanut and is generally not observed until digging time. Thus far no great injury from this insect is apparent (1).

Fungus Diseases. The peanut crop has thus far been remarkably free from disease. About the only disease that has been prominent is a form of leaf spot (*Cercospora personata* (B. & C.) E. & E.) which appears in the form of small brown spots on the leaves. This disease is especially noticeable on the young plants during a wet spring.

Notes on Ground Nuts, Arachis hypogoea, in the West Indies. — 1750
West Indian Bulletin Vol. XI, No. 3. *Imp. Agr. Dep. Barbados,* 1911.

A summary is given of the results that have been obtained up to the present in the experiments on the cultivation of imported varieties of ground nuts. These have been conducted at various

West Indies:
Dominica
Montserrat
Nevis

(1) See Abstr. 1542 of this *Bulletin* May, 1911.   (*Ed.*).

Botanic and Experiment Stations in the West Indian Islands during the last few years. An account of them is given in the Annual Reports of the Botanic Stations.

The general conclusions reached by these experiments are the following :

The disinfection of ground nuts by immersion for five minutes in a solution of corrosive sublimate of 1 per 1 000 of water before planting is highly to be recommended.

The varieties most suitable to the different islands vary somewhat with the locality; but the Spanish and Carolina Running varieties are likely to prove most generally useful.

An application of 1 200 to 2 400 lbs. of lime per acre to the soil in which this crop is to be grown is likely to prove advantageous, at any rate in the islands of Dominica, Montserrat and Nevis.

The effect of gradual acclimatization may do much to reduce the harm inflicted by fungi, and, in conjunction with seed selection, to increase the yield given by the different varieties ; so that a really useful addition to the agriculture of the islands will accrue by the extended cultivation of ground nuts.

1751   **The Cultivation of the Castor-Plant; Production, Preparation and Utilisation of Castor Seed.** — *Bull. of the Imperial Institute,* V. IX, No. 1, pp. 17-35. London, 1911.

From the information reported it appears that, whilst there is a very large demand for castor seed and castor oil, this demand is met from comparatively few sources, and that many of the importing countries are in a position, as regards climate, to produce **British** all the castor seed they require. This aspect of the question has **Colonies** been seriously considered in recent years, in Australia and certain of the South African States, but, so far as is known at present, but little has been done to establish an industry in either of these countries. The manufacture of castor oil in the United Kingdom has been established comparatively recently, and this has given a further incentive to the production of castor seed in various British tropical and sub-tropical countries besides India, the principal producing country, and cohence the bulk of the castor seed that enters international trade is drawn.

For these reasons a large number of inquiries has been received at the Imperial Institute in recent years, on the one hand from manufacturers desiring new sources of supply of castor seed, and on the other from planters in the colonies desirous of undertaking the production of this seed. In connection with these various inquiries, a considerable number of samples of castor seed grown in Uganda, Anglo-Egyptian Sudan, East Africa Protectorate, Rhodesia, Ceylon and Fiji. have been received and examined in the Scientific and Technical Department of the Imperial Institute. The results of these investigations show that in many parts of the Empire the production of castor seed of good quality could be undertaken. Notices are therefore given respecting the climate and soil, the cultivation, the harvesting and the fungoid and insect pests of the castor plant, at present largely grown only in India, Java, Brazil, the United States and Italy.

KOCHS. **Spindle tree (*Evonymus europaeus*) Seed Oil.** (Oel der Samen von *Evonymus europaeus*). — *Bericht der Königl. Gärtnerlehranstalt zu Dahlem bei Steglitz. Berlin, für die Jahre* 1908-1909, pp. 192. Berlin, 1911.

1752

Germany : Prussia

The seed of the *Evonymus europaeus*, including the aril, contains 35.2% of a fluid oil, of the following composition:

	In the aril	In the seed
Water	2.71 %	3.10 %
Fatty substances	56.41 %	43.63 %
Nitrogenous matter	20.56 %	26.85 %

The specific gravity of the oil extracted from the seed is 0.9738, that extracted from the aril, 0.9272.

Utilisation of Para Rubber Seed. — *Bulletin of the Imperial Institute,* V. IX, No. 1, pp. 35-38. London, 1911.

1753

British Colonies

Reference is made to the fact that the kernels of these seeds contain about 42 per cent. of a liquid drying oil very similar in properties to linseed oil and capable like that oil of being used in the manufacture of important industrial products.

Since these kernels were first investigated at the Imperial Institute in 1902-3, small consignments have been received from time to time in London and sold as oil seeds; but there has been no large development of this trade, mainly because the demand for seed for planting has been so large as to preclude the collection of seed for industrial use, and, further, the profits from sales of rubber on developed estates have been so large in recent years that little or no attention has been given to the utilisation of by-products. Now, however, when the area of productive Para rubber plantations is increasing rapidly every year, it seems likely that this indifference to the possibility of using these kernels will disappear, and already the expression of oil from the kernels has been undertaken at one or more mills in the East Indies.

It is believed, therefore, opportune to call attention to several practical difficulties which may occur in dealing with these kernels, and to the methods of overcoming them.

Considerable difference of opinion exists as to the cost of collecting Para rubber seeds.

For shelling the seeds, the installation of machinery is desirable.

Kernels for exports should be thoroughly dried in the sun before being packed in bags for shipment.

In expressing Para rubber seed oil trouble may arise from the presence of a fat-splitting enzyme in the kernels; as this is taken out with the water expressed along with the oil, and if this aqueous layer is left in contact with the oil, the latter will be rapidly hydrolysed. As with castor seed, it may be assumed, however, that with due care no trouble will arise with Para rubber seed kernels from this cause.

In determining the value of an oil seed the amount of oil present is the factor of prime importance, but much also depends on the nature of the cake left after expression of the oil.

Unfortunately Para rubber seed contain a cyano-genetic glucoside and an enzyme which decomposes this in presence of water, yielding prussic acid. As with linseed cake, however, the mere production of small quantities of prussic acid affords no ground for suggesting that cake from Para rubber seed kernels will be unsuitable for feeding cattle. Nevertheless, it is considered of the greatest importance, to determine as soon as possible the average maximum yield of prussic acid from cake made from these kernels under industrial conditions; and to make extensive preliminary feeding trials.

1754

P. J. S. CRAMER. *Coffea Robusta* in Para Rubber Cultivation in Java (1). — *The Agricultural News.* Vol. X, No. 235, pp. 132-133. Barbados, April 29, 1911.

Dutch
East Indies:
Java

Coffea robusta is considered by Dr. Cramer to be identical with *Coffea Laurentii*. It was first obtained from Brussels, in 1900, for

---

(1) See also this *Bulletin*, November 1910, p. 72. (*Congo Coffee and Investigations on Rubber-culture*) and *ibid.* Abs. 462, February 1911. (*Ed.*).

planting in the east and centre of Java, where this species of coffee plant was considered as a curiosity until two years later, when its large power of production came under observation.

Since 1907 there has been a great extension of the area of *Coffea robusta* in Java; the estimated area in 1907-1908 was 5000 acres and 1908-1909 from 20 000 to 30 000 acres, and it is probable that this estimate is below the actual extension. No other kind of coffee is being planted at present, to any extent, in Java.

Experiments in Java show that this coffee will flourish from sea-level to an altitude of 3 000 feet. The best plantations are found in the humid districts of East Java, where there is a large rainfall, distributed equally during the year. These estates are situated from 1000 to 1500 feet above sea-level and the soil is deep and rich in vegetable mould. In Java, *Robusta* coffee is always planted under shade. The plants suffer severely if exposed to the wind, and where such exposure is likely to occur, it is useless to attempt to grow it unless measures are taken for its protection, The plant grows very quickly on volcanic soils and on those which are rich in vegetable mould. The growth is much slower in compact and clay soils.

Coffea robusta planted with Para rubber trees grows as well as that which is being raised alone, and does not interfere with the development of the rubber. *Robusta* coffee, planted between rubber, gives a small yield two years after planting; and, usually, a complete crop in the third year, averaging 15 cwt. per acre (1884 kgs. per hectare). Nurseries for *Coffea robusta*, planting out, topping, pruning and care of a young plantation, time of flowering, yield, and preparation for market and quality of the product are here described.

Insects and Diseases. The only insect dangerous to *Coffea robusta* that has been noticed so far is *Xyleborus coffeae* Wurth (1), which bores holes in the branches; the damage from this is lessened by topping the tree and encouraging the formation of secondary branches.

The most serious disease is caused by *Corticium javanicum*. In the tratment for this it is advised that the trees be cut down, and the sucker which arises be topped and allowed to take the place of the old plant. Lastly, *Coffea robusta* is only slightly attacked by *Hemileia vastatrix* (2); and the root disease which is so serious

---

(1) See this *Bulletin*, Abs. 1585, May 1911.   (*Ed.*).
(2) See this *Bulletin*, December 1910, p. 362 and Abs. 615, February, 1911.
                                                        (*Ed.*).

in regard to Para rubber is never found on the living roots of the coffee, so that there appears to be no fear of an increase in the amount of this disease in Para rubber through the intercalary cultivation of *Coffea robusta.*

1755   **Coffee Plantations in Bukoba, near Victoria Nyanza Lake.** (Kaffeekultur in Bukoba). — *Deutsche Kolonialzeitung* No. 19, p. 319. Berlin, May 13, 1911.

After many attempts, the German Colonial Government has at last succeded in introducing coffee as a staple crop in the district of Bukoba.

German East Africa

The berry of the Bukoba coffee tree is small, and is very similar to that of the Arabian tree. Most of it is exported to Marseilles and Aden.

European firms have introduced machinery into this zone for the commercial treatment of this coffee, thus improving its trade value.

The value of the exports rose from £2550 (63.750 frs.) in 1905, to £5450 (136.250 frs.) in 1909.

1756   **Chinese Tea Exports.** — *Journal of the Royal Society of Arts,* No. 3052, p. 710. London, May 19, 1911.

The total quantity of tea exported from China in 1909 was 199 792 400 pounds, a decrease of over ten million pounds as compared with 1908. This reduction was due principally to a decreased demand for common black teas, due to the abundant supply from India and Ceylon.

China

The Viceroy and Governor of Kiangsi has been asked to supply the growers of these teas with fertilizers, as their decline is largely due to farmers having neglected to clean the ground, turn it over and fertilize it. In the Keeman district, where strict attention has been paid to these matters, the teas produced have attained great popularity, and the production, which amounted to 20 000 half-chests a few years ago, reached 95 000 half-chests in 1909.

Owing to the absence of suitable storage facilities for the crop, especially that of the Hankow variety, which is stored in junks and subjected to all kinds of weather, etc., the Ministry has been petitioned to build a go-down capable of holding at least 200 000 half-chests of tea.

Tea Growing in Sumatra. — *The Tropical Agriculturist.* p. 182, Colombo, February, 1911,

1757

Land suitable for tea-growing is reported to be plentiful on the west coast of Sumatra, in the province bearing that name, and large areas have been applied for. Short crops in Java have led tea planters there to secure land in this section of Sumatra, where the climate is in every way favourable for the tea-growing industry.

Dutch
E. Indies:
Sumatra

Regulations for Control of Tea Industry in Japan. — *The Board of Trade Journal*, No. 758, p. 531, London, June 8, 1911...

1758

Regulations came into force on 5th May forbidding, under penalty of a fine of not more than 100 yen (about £10) the manufacture of and trade in: 1) tea manufactured by using adhesive substances, or tea so manufactured mixed with other tea ; 2) tea coloured with any ' kind of colouring matter, or tea so coloured mixed with other tea; 3) putrefied tea, or putrefied tea mixed with other tea ; 4) tea mixed with sand or other impurities.

Japan

The Cultivation of Tobacco in Russia. (Tabakovodstvo). — *Exegolnik Glavnago Upravlenia Semlieustroistva i Semliedielia po Dapartamentu Semledielia.* (Year Book of the General Direction of Rural Organization and Agriculture in the Department of Agriculture). G. III, pp. LXX-LXXI. St. Petersburg, 1910.

1759

The Department of Agriculture has of late made efforts to improve the tobacco crop in Russia and introduce scientific modes of handling the product. The Government entrusted the realization of its scheme to the agricultural teachers of the Governments of Cernigov, Taurida, Kutai, Poltava, and Kuban. Experiments in methods of cultivation were made in two plantations, at Lokvitz (Poltava) with common tobaccos, and at Osurgeti (Caucasus) where the quality of the soil and the climate lend themselves to the raising of high-class tobaccos.

Russia

Of the several varieties of tabacco experimented with, the best results have been obtained with the « Herzegovina » variety in Crimea; with the « Kentucky » variety in Cernigov, and with the « Sumatra » variety in the Caucasus (Osurgeti).

The Ministry of Agriculture has appointed an expert as general inspector for the tobacco plantations, begun in 1909, in the Governments of Taurida, Cernigov, Volhynia, Poltava and Kuban.

1760   W. M. HINSON and E. H. JENKINS. **The Management of Tobacco Seed Beds.** — *Connecticut State Sta., Bul.* 166. *E. S. R.* Vol. XXIV Abstr. No. 4. Washington, April 5, 1911.

United States: Connecticut

This Bulletin reports the results of work in cooperation with the Bureau of Plant Industry of the Department of Agriculture on tobacco cultivation. It discusses the advantage of sterilizing tobacco seed beds, the use of fertilizers, and the apparatus for and the operation of steam sterilizing.

A pressure of 70 lbs. (4.9 atmospheres) maintained for 30 minutes sufficed to kill all seeds of weeds. The cost of labour of sterilizing 180 sq. yds. of seed beds was $ 6, while that of weeding 90 sq. yds. of unsterilized beds until the seedlings were taken up was $ 12. Steam sterilization is more convenient, and more effective in killing weed seed, if a boiler can be used. On a small scale the formalin treatment may be more feasible and is best applied to a dry soil in the fall.

The rate of seeding, use of sprouted and dry seed and the watering and ventilation of seed beds are also discussed.

1761   E. S. SALMON. **Notes on Hops.** — *The Journal of the South Eastern Agricultural College, Wye, Kent,* No. 19, 1910, pp. 362-375, 382-384). London and Ashford, Kent.

Great Britain : England, Kent

On the raising of New Varieties of Hops from Seed. — The writer has continued his experiments on crossing different varieties of hops with pollen obtained from various selected male hops, 12 066 seeds being obtained from twenty - nine crosses in 1909. The female parents used were the Canterbury Whitebine, the Tolhurst, the German variety « Stirn », and five different varieties of seedling origin. The male hops used were selected for different special characters.

The most vigorous varieties of male hops obtained up to the present have been some sent to the writer from Oregon, U. S. A.

Brambling and Fuggle Hops not " growing out ". — A case was investigated where some Brambling hops in a garden near Canterbury had not " grown out ".

It was found that the sole cause was the insufficient pollination of the hops when " in burr ".

Such cases show the necessity of emphasizing the point that the supply of male hops in a garden must be looked upon as of primary importance ; and further that the male hops planted must be in flower during all the time the female hops are producing " burr ".

R. H. CARTER. **The Estimation of Soft Resins in Hops** (1). — *The*   1762
Journal of the South-Eastern Agricultural College. Wye, Kent.
No. 19, 1910. pp. 375-382. London and Ashford, Kent.

Messrs. Briant and Meacham (2) differentiated hop resins into
two classes: " soft " and " hard " resins, and showed that the former,
which are extracted with petroleum ether, contained preservative   Great
resins, whilst " hard " resins, which are extracted by subsequent   Britain:
treatment with sulphuric ether, had no antiseptic properties. In   England,
view of these facts Messrs. Briant and Meacham suggested a method   Kent
of valuing hops on the basis of their " soft " resin content.

In connection with Salmon's experiments on the breeding of
hops, it seemed desirable that some information should be obtained
as to the amount of soft resins present in the various parent
plants used and the seedlings obtained from them.

The writer's analyses showed that the German hops from Hol-
ledan — which were practically seedless — show the highest percentage of soft resins, while certain samples of Oregons — which
were well seeded — come second. Among the hops grown at Wye
in the College plantation, two German varieties " Late Bavarian "
and " Elsass " show a higher percentage, viz., over thirteen per
cent., than any English variety, except one sample of " Canterbury
Whitebines " grown at the College. Of the seedlings, two show over
thirteen per cent. of soft resins.

The Rose as a Staple Crop. (Die Rose als landwirtschaftliche Kul-   1763
turpflanze). — *Deutsche Landw. Presse*, No. 44. pp. 516-517. Berlin,
3 Juni, 1911.

Proposals have been made in France to check the crisis in the
wine trade by substituting the rose for the vine in districts suited
to its cultivation. Experiments have shown that 4,000 rose-trees   France.
can be planted per acre, which will yield, at the end of two or three Bulgaria.
years, 150 blossoms per tree. Each rose tree will produce about 600   Turkey.
grammes of rose petals per year; 1 acre will produce about 530 lbs. Germany.
of blossom from which 4 kgs of essence of roses can be distilled,   Russia.
worth from £18 to £54 per lb. This represents an average gross   Luxemburg

---

(1) Cf. this *Bulletin*: Abstr. 566 Frb. 1911, and Abstr. 843, March 1911.
(2) *Journal Fed. Institute of Brewing* 1897, p. 233.   (*Ed.*).

income of £128 per acre. It must be noted that the annual production of essence of roses is inadequaté to meet the demand (1).

Bulgaria now produces about 11 000 lbs. of essence of roses and is doing all it can to increase its output. (2). Turkey also produces a small quantity, and now has rivals on a small scale in Russia and Germany.

The best roses for this purpose are the « Damask rose » of Bulgaria and the « cabbage rose » of Provence.

Roses are also extensively cultivated in Luxémburg, but not for their essence.

In Luxemburg there are from 30 to 40 farms, covering an area of about 425 to 500 acres, where only roses are raised. The exports are valued at about 1 million frs. per year, for 2 500 000 rose-trees exported. The rose-trees of Luxemburg have been obtained exclusively from the wild rose (*Rosa canina*), which is indigenous to that country and to the Belgian Ardennes.

1764   Eug. Collin. **Marjoram and its Adulterations**. (La Marjolaine et ses Falsifications). — *Annales des Falsifications*, IVᵉ année, No. 29, pp. 127-131. Paris-Généve, Mars, 1911.

Southern France   Marjoram, (*Origanum Majorana* L.), the flowering tips of which are inscribed in the Pharmacopaeia and are used in medicine as stimulants, is gathered in the South of France, in the Department of Vaucluse, at Grasse, and Nice, and can yield as much as 520 gr. of essence per 100 kgs. of fresh flowers. The plants which grow in the neighbourhood of Paris do not yield more than 370 grammes.

In several departments in the South of France, marjoram is grown on a fairly large scale. The flowering tips which are gathered there are almost all exported to Germany, where they are used as seasoning. This export is adulterated by the addition of fragments of the leaves of *Cistus albidus* and *Cornus sanguinea*.

--- --

(1) In metrical quantities: One rose-plant gives in one year 600 grammes of petals. One hectare should therefore give a yearly yield of 600 kgs. of rose-flowers; which by distillation ought to produce 4 kgs. of attar, valued from 1000 to 3000 frcs. per kilogr.   (*Ed.*).

(2) The exports of essence of roses from Bulgaria amounted to 4394 kgs. in 1904, 5316 kgs. in 1905, 7098 kgs. in 1906, 5295 kgs. in 1907, 4565 kgs. in 1908, and 6050 kgs. in 1909, but these figures are for the amount after adulteration. *The Statesman's Year-book: 1911.* p. 675.   (*Ed.*)

The writer points out the use that can be made, in detecting such adulteration, and generally in examining mixtures of bruised leaves, of carefully observing: 1st, the way the leaves behave when boiled in an alkaline solution at 5 %; 2nd, the distribution and arrangement of the stomata; 3rd, the presence or absence and form of the protective and glandular hairs; and the appearance and shape of the epidermic cells (1).

" Karambusi " Oil. — *The Chemist and Druggist,* N9. 1634, vol. LXXVIII, p. 84, London, May 20, 1911.

1765

The bark of the karambusi-tree (*Warburgia Stuhlmanni*) (2) is offered in the markets in Zanzibar along with the wood of the African sandal-tree. It yields an essential oil, which is very similar to ordinary sandal-wood oil, to the extent of 0.5 to 1.0 per cent. It is a viscous, yellowish-red oil, with an odour typical of sandal-wood oil and having the following characters:

Zanzibar

Sp. Gr. at 20° 0.9864
Optical rotation . . . . minus 41°.8
Refractive index at 20° 1.5127
Saponification value 11.2
Acetyl-ester value 100.2
Soluble in its own volume of 90 per cent alcohol.

Vegetables as Field Crops in Prussia. (Der feldmässige Gemüsebau in Preussen), — *Mitteil. der Zentralstelle der Preuss. Landw. Kammern* n. 22. p. 139. Berlin, 29 Mai, 1911.

1766

Growing vegetables as field crops is gaining in importance in Prussia. Out of a cultivated area of 16 787 225 hectares (41 464 445 acres) 175 746 (434 092 acres) are under vegetables. The best results are obtained on holdings of from 5 to 20 hectares (12 to 50 acres). Besides this, market gardening is also steadily increasing in Prussia, where in 1906 there were already 4073 such undertakings employing 12757 market gardeners.

Germany
Prussia

---

(1) The preparation of essence of marjoram is of interest to several Mediterranean countries. Recently a marjoram oil from Greece was studied by Schimmel. See *Ber. von Schimmel u. Cie*, Miltitz. bei Leipzig, April, 1911, p. 88.

(2) *Warburgia*. ENGLER. *Pflanzenw.* Ost-Afr, C. (1895) 276; and in ENGLER & *Prantl., Natürl. Pflanzenfam.* III, 6 (1895) 318. Cinnamoneae. *W. Stuhlmanni*. ENGLER II, cc. Afr. trop. or. (*Index Kewensis. Supplementum primum*, p. 459. Bruxelles, Castaigne, 1901-1906).   (*Ed.*).

1767   **Tomato Culture in Indiana (U. S.).** (Growing Tomatoes for the Canning Factory). — *U. S. Department of Agriculture. Farmers' Bulletin* 435. *Experiment Station Work LXII.* pp. 24 (8-12). Washington, March 17, 1911.

United
States:
Indiana

The annual pack of tomatoes in the United States is probably not less than 10 000 000 cases. The growing of tomatoes for canning is therefore an important agricultural industry. A large part of the crop for this purpose is grown by the general farmer rather than by a specialist, and as a rule not as much care is taken with it as is necessary to yield the greatest profit.

A Bulletin (No. 144) of the Indiana Experiment Station, by J. Troop, C. G. Woodbury and J. G. Boyle, summarizes the results of a study of tomato growing for canning in Indiana.

It is stated that with proper care and a good season, without exceptional losses from insects and diseases, yields may be expected of from 6 to 12 tons per acre (15 060 to 30 120 kg. per hectare) in Indiana.

The opinion is expressed that the yield could easily be raised to 12 or 15 tons per acre (30 120 to 37 650 kg. per ha.) by following improved methods of culture. Roughly speaking, it requires a yield of at least 5 tons per acre (7550 kg. per ha.) to pay expenses at the usual contract prices. The cost of growing depends largely upon the methods followed and may be estimated at from 25 to 50 dollars per acre (323 to 646 francs per hectare) ; probably 35 dollars (453 francs to the hectare) may be considered a fair estimate.

The price received for the crop varies from 7 to 8.5 dollars per ton (3.55 to 4.35 francs per metric quintal).

It thus appears that under the best conditions a profit of from 50 to 75 dollars per acre (about 650 to 975 francs per hectare) may be realized.

1768   W. R. Beattie. **The Production in the United States of Onion Seed and Sets.** — *U. S. Department of Agriculture. Farmers' Bulletin* 434, p. 24. Washington, 27 March 1911.

United
States

Production of Onion Seed. Many of the leading onion growers of the Northern States are now raising their own supplies of seed, for by so doing they can procure a better grade than is obtainable in the general market. Complete directions for growing and harvesting onion seed are given in this Bulletin.

The yield is generally from 3 to 4 pounds of seed for every bushel of bulbs (standard bulbs) planted (about 3.5 to 5 kgs. of seed for every hectolitre of bulbs) and as a rule will be about 400 pounds to the acre (448 kgs. per hectare), although as much as 800 or even 1000 pounds (896 or 1120 kgs.) have been secured.

Production of Onion Sets. The term " set " as applied to the onion, indicates a small, undersized bulb which, when replanted in the ground, will produce a large onion. The common method of producing sets is to sow a large quantity of seed on a small area of rather rich land, and thus produce bulbs that are undersized owing to crowding ; the ideal set is almost globular and about half an inch (12 mm.) in diameter.

In the United States the onion set industry is confined to a few areas. The crop is extensively grown near Louisville, Ky., Chillicote, Ohio, and Chicago, Ill., in the Platte River Valley of Nebraska, in Southwestern New Jersey, and in Southern California. The entire area devoted to this enterprise in these localities is estimated at from 2 500 to 3 000 acres (1 000 to 1 200 hectares). The yield per acre varies with the locality, but will average about 300 bushels (270 hl. per hectare).

Climate and soils adapted to onion set-growing and cultural methods are described.

In his conclusions the writer states that no large profit can be obtained from the production of either onion seed or sets, and the greater profits are obtainable from comparatively small plantings.

Enemies of the Onion. — Onion smut (*Urocystis cepulae* Frost) propagates itself almost indefinitely in the soil when this once becomes infested. In such infested soils, the smut attacks the young seedling onions, but cannot attack sets or transplanted healthy bulbs. The explanation seems to be that the smut hyphae are only able to penetrate the leaves of the young tender seedlings. The best method of control has proved to be that of formalin (1 pound of 40 per cent. formalin to 25 to 33 gallons of water); this is applied by a drip-attachment to the drill.

The onion maggot (*Anthomyia ceparum*, Bouché) is often very destructive in fields that are just sown. This insect works at the roots of the young seedlings and is difficult to control. A carbolized form of kerosene emulsion is effective in controlling this pest. Mineral fertilizers (kainit, nitrate of soda, potassium sulphate or chloride) are useful as deterrents.

The onion thrips (one of the *Thysanoptera*) has proved very destructive, especially throughout the Southern States, and is now becoming quite a serious pest in Texas. Kerosene emulsion, whale-oil soap and some of the nicotine preparations have been found useful in controlling this pest.

1769   S. T. PARKINSON. **A New Method of Forcing Plants.** — *The Journal of the South-Eastern Agricultural College, Wye, Kent.* No. 19, 1910, pp. 245-247, London and Ashford, Kent.

Great Britain

From actual practice in plant forcing the inference may be drawn that there is a stage in the resting period of most plants when the ordinary forcing methods are useless and that this period, due to inherent character of the plant, varies in the case of each kind of plant. Further great importance must be attached to influences at work on the plant previously to the actual forcing. For example, rhubarb is best forced after the crown has been exposed to frost, and bulbs after they have been placed in a cold frame to harden and form roots.

These experiments were carried out as a test, under conditions at the disposal of any florist ; and Molisch's « Dipping » or « Warm Bath » method, was used. which consists in placing plants, or certain portions of them, in lukewarm water of a definite temperature, leaving them there for some hours and then removing and forcing them in the usual manner.

The duration of the dipping was usually 12 hours (a shorter time if the plants were tender or near the end of their resting period) and the temperature was about 95° F. (35° C.) for most plants, and not more than 85° F (about 29° 5 C.) for soft plants such as Seakale. Rhubarb withstood a temperature of about 100° F, (about 37 ½° C.) without apparent ill-effect.

The best time for applying the treatment is just as the plant is emerging from the period of deepest resting. Speaking generally, the last half of November or the beginning of December is a good time.

Lilac (*Syringa vulgaris*), *Spirea, Iris Germanica*, and Rhubarb responded in a remarkable manner to the treatment.

With Seakale the results were not so good, whilst with Lily-of-the-Valley, Tulip, Narcissus, and Snowdrop the treatment was quite unsuccessful.

Strawberry Cultivation in Great Britain (Strawberry cultivation) — **1770**
Board of Agriculture and Fisheries Leaflet No. 207, p. 6, London,
Feb. 1910: revised March, 1911.

The cultivation of strawberries has of late years greatly extended
in Great Britain. The area under strawberries, in 1909, was 30 065
acres (12164 hectares). Of this total 25 937 acres (10494 hectares) were **Great**
in England, the leading counties being Kent, Cambridge, Hampshire, **Britain:**
Norfolk and Worcester. Although considerable initial capital is re- **England**
qnired, the industry is a very suitable one for small proprietors as a
family may be provided for on a holding of 4 acres (1,6 hectares).
Gross returns may be said to be between £40 and £60 per
acre (2500 to 3750 francs per hectare) but may fall as low as £20
(1250 frs. per ha.), while in a favourable season they may rise to as
much as £100 (6250 frs,. per ha). Strawberry growing, however, is
attended by considerable risks due to late frosts, or to insect or other
pests.

J. VERCIER. **Chief Causes determining an Increase in the Straw-** **1771**
berry Crop and a Modification in the Chemical Composition
of the Fruit. (Principales causes déterminant dans les cultures
de fraises une augmentation de récolte et une modification de
la composition chimique des fruits). — *Le Progrès agricole et*
viticole, 28ᵉ année, No. 24, pp. 742-747, Montpellier, 11 Juin, 1911. **France**

CAUSES WHICH MAY DETERMINE AN INCREASE IN THE CROP.
The Variety selected. — The greatest variations are determined by
this factor. The writer has obtained the following yields :

	per 100 sq. m.	per acre
Noble Laxton	Kg. 103	82.4 cwt
Sharpless	» 125	100 »
Quatre Saisons remontantes.	» 88	70 »
Red Pearl	» 76	60 »

Mr. de Vilmorin reckons an average of 150 kgs. Mr. Henry of
275 kgs. (large berry varieties), and 330 kgs. (small berry varieties),

whereas **Mr.** Bussan estimates from 100 to 150 kgs. for the large and 150 to 250 kgs. for the small fruit.

The usual average is 100 kgs. (80 cwt. per acre).

2. *Nature of the soil.* — The « Sir Joseph Paxton » suffers from chlorosis in calcareous soil, and only yields 35 kgs. per 100 sq. metres, instead of from 100 to 110 kgs. in vegetable mould. The « Pearl » which yields 100 kgs. when grown in the garden, only produces from 60 to 70 kgs. when grown in the field. The *Hericart de Thury* yields from 50 to 60 kgs. on sandy soil, and 90 on vegetable mould.

3. *Watering and irrigation.* — The following results have been obtained with the « Royal Sovereign » :

1.721 kgs. per 3 sq. metres 3.79 lbs per 3.588 sq. yards without watering

1.950 » » 3 » 4.30 » » » » with 1 watering

2.340 » » 3 » 5.16 » » » » with 2 »

2.400 » » 3 » 5.29 » » » » with 3 »

4. *Mode of cultivating.* — Under similar conditions in other respects, forcing on the bed is less profitable than early growing under frames, except in the case of a few varieties specialised for forcing.

5. *Fertilizers.* — The following results were obtained with the « Sharpless » variety :

No. of lots	Fertilizers used par 100 sq. metres	Cost	Yield per 100 sq. metres		Difference as compared to test lot. kg.
			kg.	frs.	
I	Test lot —	—	93.400	60.70	—
II	Slag : 5 kg. Sulphate of potash: 3 kg.	1.21 fr.	97.600	63.40	+ 4.2
III	Slag: 5 kg. Sulphate of potash: 3 kg. Nitrate: 2 kg.	1.80 fr.	109,300	71.00	+ 15.9

6. *Climate.* — Damp weather is preferable. Hoar forests are very injurious when they occur at the time of the first flowers, as these are the blossoms which produce the large berries.

CAUSES WHICH MAY LEAD TO A MODIFICATION IN THE CHEMICAL COMPOSITION OF THE FRUIT.

1. *Variety.* (Extract from the tables of 35 analyses made at the Oenological Station at Beaune).

Name of variety	Weight per 100 gr.		Chemical Composition of juice per litre		Colour grade of the juice
	in juice	in dry matter	Reducing Substances calculated as glucose	Acidity, calc. as sulphuric acid	
Gloire de Mans . . .	67.40	32.60	66	7.6	50
Eléonor	55.00	45.00	77	8.4	100
Mary	71.60	28.40	64	9.1	100
St-Antoine	69.80	30.20	74	4.7	83
Quatre-Saisons . . .	54.70	45.30	84	6.4	—
Small wild strawberry.	53.60	46.40	90	8.6	—

2. *Soil.* — With the « Sharpless » variety the writer obtained :

Nature of Soil	Yield % of juice gr.	Sugar per litre gr.	Total acidity per litre as sulphuric acid gr.
Semi-Sandy	57	65	5.2
Sandy (hilly) , ...	54	63	6.0
Very Sandy	77	56	4.7
Garden organic soil	86	86	6.4

3. *Fertilizers.*

No. of lots & manure used	Fertilizers	Weight per 100 gr.		Chemical composition of juice, per litre	
		of juice gr.	of matter dried by pressing gr.	Reducing substances calculated as glucose gr.	acidity calc. as sulphuric acid gr.
I. Test lot	—	86.00	14.00	86	6.4
II. Without nitrogen	Slag and sulphate of potash	85.50	14.50	81	6.4
III. Complete	Slag, Sulphate of potash, nitrate.	79.70	20.30	83	6.3
IV. Without potash	Slag and nitrate	75.10	24.70	80	6.3
V. Without phosphoric acid	Sulphate of potash and nitrate .	81.30	18.70	80	6.3
VI. Organic fertilizer	Mould; blood and oil cake . . .	60.20	39.80	78	6.2

4. *Degree of ripeness in the Strawberries:*

(*Quatre Saisons* Strawberry).

	Weight per litre of juice	
	Reducing subst. calc. as glucose	Total acidity calc. as sulphuric acid.
Partially ripe	78	12.3
Ripe	83	7.5
Over ripe	84	7.2

1772   L. GRANATO. **The Cultivation of the Pine-apple in Brazil.** (Cultura do Ananaz). — *Boletim de Agricultura*, N. 11, p. 969, Sâo Paolo, 1910.

Brazil

Whilst no fewer than 25 million pine-apple plants are cultivated in Florida, and over 6 million of these fruits are exported, Brazil has still much to do to develop this crop.

The following varieties of the *Ananassa sativa* are known in Brazil: *abacaxi amarello, branco; roxo, vermelho,* and *abacaxi de Tinger*. There are some special varieties from Guatemala, Havana, Martinique, Jamaica, etc.

All these kinds can be traced back to two varieties:
1. the common pine-apple with spiky-edged leaves ;
2. the smooth leaved pine-apple.

Loamy soils, rich in humus, and sufficiently moist, are best suited to this plant. It can be grown between the rows of wheat, potatoes, or other plants. A hectare can produce from 1000 to 1500 fruits. Its worst enemies are kinds of scale insects, *Diaspis Bromeliae* and *Pseudococcus Bromeliae*.

CECIL H. HOOPER. **Observations on the Blossoming of our Hardy Cultivated Fruits.** — *Journal of the Royal Horticultural Society.* Vol. XXXVI, Part. III, pp. 548-564. London, May 1911.   **1773**

The earliest fruits to flower are cob and filbert nuts; gooseberry is the next, and red currant usually follows it, but is not so regular in its flowering-time. Black currant starts flowering next and is about a month in bloom.

Among plums the Japanese variety is the earliest to flower, coming into bloom a week before the earliest of the European varieties.. The average length of time in flower for plums is 19 days, and they are in full bloom on the 7th and 8th days after commencing. An individual flower is about five days between the opening and the falling of the petals. Mr. W. O. Backhouse concludes from his observations this year that varieties of plums are on the whole self-fertile ; he finds hybrids, however, tend to be completely sterile. The average order of blossoming of plums in Great Britain is as follows : *Early blossoming plums:* 1. Japanese plum; 2. Grand Duke; 3. Damascene; 4. Black Diamond; 5. Prince of Wales ; 6. Monarch : 7. Rivers' Early Prolific ; 8. Greengage ; 9. Victoria ; 10. Drooper ; 11. Pershore Egg Plum. *Late blossoming plums:* 12. Bradley's King of Damsons ; 13. Sultan; 14. Oullin's Golden Gage ; 15. Jefferson ; 16. Farleigh Damson ; 17. Cox's Emperor ; 18. Coe's Golden Drop; 19. Prune Damson; 20. White Bullace; 21. Pond's Seedling; 22, Late Orleans ; 23. Belle de Louvain.

In 1909, cherries were in flower at Wye, Kent, from April 21 to May 19. The different varieties were in flower an average of 22. days each, and in full flower about the 7th or 8th day. Cherries of different varieties come into flower at nearly the same time.

At Wye the average length of time in flower for pears is about 18 days with full bloom on the 8th day. M. B. Waite of the U. S. Department of Agriculture found that of 36 varieties tested by him 22 were self-sterile, and although a few varieties of pear were

Great Britain: England

productive with their own pollen, yet even with these varieties self-pollination seemed to be less certain than cross-pollination.

Mr. Chittenden's experiments, made in Essex, proved that among pears the proportion of self-sterile varieties is quite as large in England as in America.

The quince, which flowers later than the pear, seems to fruit nearly as well with its own pollen as with that of another variety; whereas apples were found to be more likely to be sterile to their own pollen than pears.

The average length of time in flower of the different varieties of apples at Wye is 17 to 18 days, with full blossom on the 7th day. Individual flowers take about seven days from opening to fall of petals.

The time of blossoming does not appear to be influenced by the stock on which the variety is grafted. Observations made in Victoria, Australia, in New York State and in Great Britain show that in general the order of flowering of different apple varieties is similar in different continents, but the average duration of flowering is different.

For strawberries the length of time in flower observed at Wye was about 52 days and for raspberries 44 days.

The raspberry frequently fertilizes itself; bunches of flowers placed by the writer in paper bags fruited almost as well as those in the open.

With this and other few exceptions cross fertilization greatly increases the production of the orchard, and intermixed plantation of 2 or more varieties flowering at the same time is to be recommended in a general way.

As bees are of great value in pollination, especially in unseasonable and changeable weather, it seems advantageous to place hives of bees in different parts of a plantation; the writer suggests one hive to 2 acres of fruit plantation (1).

---

(1) " It would be useful to observe the action of bees on almonds, which are of so much importance in Italy, particularly in Puglia and Sicily, and in the Mediterranean countries generally. Also in the case of olives, where the crop is often reduced by lack of fertilization, it would be well to study the action of bees to see if they can increase the production. Bees are useful to the Locust, or Carob tree ". I. GIGLIOLI, *Malessere agrario ed alimentare in Italia*, p. 700. Portici, 1903.   (*Ed.*).

T. IKEDA. **The Pruning and Training of Fruit Trees in Japan.** — *Journal of the Royal Horticultural Society*, vol. XXXVI, part III, pp. 581-586. London, May 1911.

1774

The systems of training and pruning fruit trees followed by the Japanese differ widely from those adopted by Western nations. The prevalent mode of training fruit trees is that called « tana-zukuri » (literally, « table cordons »). It is a mode of training on overhead supports, and is mainly used for pears and vines, sometimes also for apples and plums.

Japan

Peaches are also regularly trained nowadays ; they require no support and form dwarf bushes. They receive some pruning every year, and are trained onthe « open-centre » system. Citrus fruit trees, loquats, date plums, cherries, apricots, hazelnut trees, plums, quinces, chestnuts, walnuts, pears and apples in some localities are left quite unpruned.

In « tana » training the trellis is made of bamboos or wire fitted on wooden posts at a height of 5 ¹⁄₂ feet and 1 or 2 feet apart; the pruning is very light, and is generally done in winter.

« Tana »-training offers advantages in the convenience of management, harvesting and control of pests, in early fruit production and for protection from wind and rain storms.

A more vigorous system of pruning is adopted in the case of Kaki trees, *Diospyros Kaki*, that appears to have arisen out of the practice of pulling the fruit with a portion of branch suitable for hanging it up to dry.

The fruiting shoots are broken at the base, while the sterile shoots are left intact to produce spurs the next year.

FRANK MOORE. **Profitable Grape Growing in Kent County, Delaware.** — *American Agriculturist*, p. 261. New York, February 18th, 1911.

1775

Grapes are being grown on a number of farms in Kent County, Delaware at a profit seldom exceeded by vineyards in any other state. From a vineyard of nine acres planted in the spring of 1907 the writer harvested 4 ¹⁄₂ tons of grapes an acre in 1910. He sold the grapes through the Delaware produce exchange and received $ 1900, or $ 211 an acre. Grapes in Delaware are ready to harvest from August 15 to September 20. The flavour of the

United States : Delaware

grapes grown in Kent County is equal if not superior to that of grapes grown in any of the eastern States both for eating and for the manufacturing of grape juice.

1776   A. Tournier. **Vine Culture in the Parras District, Mexico.** (La Viticulture au Mexique). — *Revue de Viticulture,* 18ᵉ an., no. 913, pp. 705-711. Paris, 15 Juin, 1911.

The district of Parras is the only part of Mexico where vines are grown to any extent (1112 acres or 450 ha.) and nearly all these vineyards belong to the San Lorenzo Hacienda, an estate on which 9500 native Mexicans live.

The climate is temperate, very dry and very healthy, the average temperature of the year not exceding 20º C. (68º F.). A great drawback is the rain, which, falling in summer, favours the development of diseases and yet does not supply enough water for the soil, so that irrigation is necessary.

Mexico : Parras

Anthracnose is the most destructive of these diseases : to combat it the vines are sprayed in winter with iron sulphate and sulphuric acid.

The soil of the vineyards is calcareous, clayey, deep and compact ; the proportion of lime reaches 65 %, although on an average it does not exceed 20 %.

The principal grafted varieties grown on the estate are:

Muscat (from which muscat wine is made, containing generally 10 % of sugar and 16 % of alcohol), Grenache and Rose du Pérou (from which Port with 18 % alcohol is made), Pedro Ximenès and Golden Clairette (from which Sherry is made), Mission (from which « Evaporado de Uva » is made), Carignan and Mourvèdre (for ordinary wines), Malvoisie, Folle (from which « Sauternes » are made), Cornichon and Flamm Tokay for the table and for early shipments.

At present the land is irrigated four times (November, March, April, June) ; this could be reduced to two, before the buds break and a fortnight after flowering. Conditions for wine-making are poor, and the products do not keep well. Only the manufacture of « Evaporado de Uva » is of interest.

A certain quantity of must pressed immediately after picking is concentrated to 56º Baumé, in coppers of large surface and little depth. This concentrated juice is then added to fresh must till a mixture of 20º Baumé is obtained.

This is then allowed to ferment; it begins slowly and usually stops when there is 18 % of sugar and 10 % of alcohol. The liquor is finally put in barrels placed in warm chambers (45° C, 113° F) for six months; here fermentation continues slowly, then ceases when there is 14 % of sugar and 12 % of alcohol. The wine is then filtered and bottled. A priest appointed by the State Bishop inspects the process of the manufacture of this wine, which according to the religious law, must contain only grape-juice; in fact, most of this wine is used as mass wine («para consagrar»). Its flavour is similar to that of Banyuls; it is sold at 0.75 fr. (7d a bottle).

Progress in Olive Growing in the State of California. — *The Agricultural South-West*, n. 51 p. 8. — Wichita, Kansas, March 10th, 1911.

1777

Not more than a quarter of a century ago, there were no olives grown in any part of North America, except in botanical gardens. Experiments proved that olive trees would thrive well in parts of California. Numerous orchards were planted, and at the present time, there are approximately 25 000 acres devoted to olive growing within the State of California. Olive orchards are scattered along the California coast from Mount Shasta to S. Diego. The olive which thrives best in California is known as the Mission Olive and differs from the fruit grown in Europe. During the past year more than a million quarts of ripe olives were marketed from Californian orchards, and about one and a half million quarts of pickled green olives. Even with its present magnitude, the olive growing industry of California is but in its infancy; and olive growing offers a wide field for the exercise of enterprise and the investment of capital.

United States: California

Experiments on the Manuring of Olives in Spain. (Essais d'engrais dans les Oliveraies en Espagne). — *Feuilles d'Informations du Ministère de l'Agriculture*, N. 13. Paris, 28 Mars, 1911.

1778

There are already many olive growers in Spain, who are interesting themselves in chemical fertilizers and are making practical tests to convince themselves of their value and efficiency. Gradually Spanish agriculturists are being persuaded that it is necessary to use fertilizers in order to obtain good yields of olives and to ensure a crop each year.

Spain

Among the many experiments carried out in Spain mention is made of one at Valdepeñas de Jaen, a noted olive region, in an olive grove a hundred years old, on clay soil.

Plot	Manure per hectare (1)	Yield per hectare
I.	1 Unmanured 1	2500 kg.
II.	Superphosphate — 350 kg. . . . . Sulphate of Ammonia — 100 kg. . . . . Nitrate of Soda — 100 kg.	3750 »
III.	Superphospate — 350 kg. . . . . Sulphate of Ammonia — 100 kg. . . . . Nitrate of Soda — 100 kg. . . . . . . Sulphate of Potash — 100 kg.	4620 »

The complete manure with potash thus gives nearly double the crop of the unmanured plot.

1779   **Importation of Chestnuts and Hazelnuts into the United States.** (Importazione di castagne e nocciuole negli Stati Uniti). Italian Consular Report. — *Bollettino del Ministero di Agricoltura, Industria e Comm.*, Serie B, fasc. 7, p. 242. Roma, 1° aprile, 1911.

The consumption of chestnuts and hazel nuts in the United States is sustained, to a large extent, by importation. Piedmont sends large French chestnuts (" marrons ") for the confectionery in-

United States   dustry. In the exportation of " marrons", chestnuts and hazel nuts to the United States, Italy ranks first.

The value of the annual importation from Italy amounts to about 3 500 000 frs. (£140 000) ; from Spain and France about 650 000 frs. (£26 000) and 150 000 frs. (£6000) respectively.

Shipments are made in barrels or in cases. The cases are so constructed as to allow ventilation.

The « marrons » of Piedmont are shipped in barrels and the chestnuts of Naples in cases.

1780   **Cocoa-nuts in the Federated Malay States.** — *The Tropical Agriculturist*, vol. XXXVI, No. 2, p. 172. Colombo, February, 1911.

In Selangor a Company is now being formed to enter on

Federated Malay States   cocoa-nut cultivation on an extensive scale. This Company will

---

(1) 100 kg. per hectare = 89 lbs. per acre   (*Ed.*).

have a nominal capital of $ 500 000 (1). It has obtained the right to select land in the Kuala Langat district. It is proposed to open up 1000 acres in the first year and another 1000 in the second year and possibly more later. The original applicants for the land are willing to hand over their rights without taking any profit of any kind, either directly or indirectly.

Fruit Trade in Germany. (Der Obsthandel Deutschlands). — *Das Handelsmuseum*, N. 19, pp. 291-292. Wien, 11 Mai 1911.

1781

The following information is taken from a report of the Austrian Consul in Hamburg on the fruit trade in that city.

The fruit from overseas is unloaded into large sheds whose temperature can be regulated ; it is then mostly sold by auction.

Germany

In 1909 temperate fruits ('' Obst '') were landed at Hamburg to the value of 25.4 million marks (£ 1 240 000), warm-temperate and tropical fruits (''·Südfrüchte '') 54.5 million marks (£ 2 670 000).

The total imports into Germany showed a considerable decrease in 1910 — 75.1 and 65.6 million marks (£ 3 675 000 and £ 3 210 000) for the two classes, as against 99.1 and 74.9 million marks (£ 4 870 000 and £ 3 665 000) in 1909.

The fresh fruit from America and Australia arriving in Hamburg is examined for San José scale : from 1.25 to 13.37 per cent. of the American fruit is found to be attacked.

Prunes are imported from France, Austria-Hungary, Bosnia, Servia and California, dried apricots and peaches from California, and dried apple slices ('' Ringäpfel '') from North America. Their value in 1909 was 14 million marks (£6 850 000). Dried figs, raisins, currants, dates, almonds and nuts also form a large part of the Hamburg import.

Austrian fruit ripens a good deal later than French and Italian, and consequently does not catch the best market in Hamburg ; only apples, pears and quinces (particularly from Bohemia and Steiermark) are of much importance in the trade.

Apples in 1910 showed a great diminution, particularly from Italy, Belgium, France, and Holland; from Austria, Switzerland, and the United States there was little falling-off.

Pears and quinces came to little over half the amount of the previous year, all countries but France showing a decrease.

---

(1) The dollar in use in the Malay States is that of the Straits Settlements, value 2s. 4d. The *Statesman's Yearbook*. (*Ed.*).

Strawberries showed a considerable increase, due to imports from Holland, for France sent rather less.

Other small fruits showed a decrease; this was primarily due to the shortage of cow-berries from Sweden. Holland also sent fewer small fruits, whilst Austria-Hungary and Italy sent more.

Dessert-Grapes showed a diminution, particularly due to smaller imports from France and Austria-Hungary; Spain, on the other hand, sent more.

Nuts also shared in the decrease; this was almost entirely due to the fact that France sent only a quarter of the previous year's amount ; Brazil also showed a decrease, while other countries had an increase.

Dried plums showed a decided increase from the United States, but this was more than balanced by decreases elsewhere.

The fact that the German imports of fresh fruit in 1910 did not come up to those of the three previous years should be attributed to the good crop in Germany in conjunction with the smaller crops in the exporting countries.

1782   **Belgian Exportation of Forced Fruits.** (Exportation belge des Fruits Forcés). — *L'Agriculture Commerciale*, N. 10, pp. 245-246. Paris, 28 Mai, 1911.

The geographical and economical superiority of Belgium is shown by the increase in the sale of its agricultural products in England. The present Belgian exportation proves that Belgium is likely to become the garden of Europe for early fruits and vegetables.

Belgium

The Hoyalaert region is steadily developing. One of the directors of the syndicate for the production of forced fruits places the number of glass-houses constructed annually at 1 000. The demand for early forced fruit is ten times as great as the production.

The following gives, in detail, the distribution of the Belgian forced fruit exportation in 1909 :

Germany . . .	410 131	lbs. or	186 423	kg.
United States .	76 534	» »	34 788	»
France. . . .	13 581	» »	6 173	»
England . . .	755 580	» »	343 445	»
Netherlands. .	57 548	» »	26 158	»
Sweden . . .	14 909	» »	6 772	»
Other countries	20 775	» »	9 443	»

Forestry.

The Russian Timber Industry. — *Journal of the Royal Society of Arts*, No. 3052, p. 706-707. London, May 19, 1911.

1788

The Russian Empire occupies the first place among the nations of the world in the extent of its timber resources, the value and quality of two-thirds of which are practically unknown. The total area of the Russian Empire is 8 647 657 square miles, and 39 per cent. of the surface of the Empire is under forests. Those in European Russia (1) cover an area of 474 000 000 acres ; Finland, 50 500 000 ; Poland, 6 700 000 ; Caucasus, 18 600 000 ; total 549 800 000. In the Ural provinces, forests cover 70 per cent. of the area ; in the northern provinces 60 per cent., and in the four lake provinces 57 per cent. The Government owns 65 per cent. of these forests, possessing in European Russia, 285 598 941 acres ; Caucasus, 12 826 387 ; Asiatic Russia, 560 519 435 ; Amur region, 288 742 000 ; total 947 686 763. Of the forests 23 per cent. belong to the landed proprietors and 9 per cent. to the peasantry. It is estimated that in Western Siberia alone there are 465 000 000 acres in virgin forest, and Eastern Siberia, although not quite so rich in timber, has sufficient forests for the world's supply of timber for years to come.

Russian Empire

The largest timber districts in European Russia are in the north. The four Governments of Olonetz, Archangel, Vologda and Viatka, comprising a total area of 650 000 square miles, are almost entirely covered with timber, but the greater part has never been explored by civilised man, though expeditions are now being formed for the purpose of investigating the immense resources of the country. The State forests, during a recent year, yielded 1 286 560 000 cubic feet of lumber, the Department of Forestry realising in round numbers for the sale of timber, rent of lands, etc., £ 6 500 000. The expenditure, including £ 160 000 for cutting trees and sawing logs, amounted to £ 1 400 000, thus leaving a profit to the State of £ 5 100 000. It is stated officially that

---

(1) See this *Bulletin*, May, 1911. Abstr. 1439.   (*Ed.*).

the reafforestation of State lands provides for more than the amount cut from the forests each year. The above figures do not include the timber lands owned by private persons in European Russia. They are divided as follows: Imperial appanages, 14 274 500 acres; private landowners, 151 072 000; peasants, 29 210 000; joint-stock companies, factories, works, churches, etc. 6 853 500 acres. The Russian timber industry comprises 1428 factories, saw-mills, planing establishments, wooden-box factories, piano factories, etc. This industry is one of the greatest in the Empire.

1784　　　R. LELORRAIN. **Utilization of Timber in Indo-China** (1). (Utilisation des bois en Indo-Chine). — *Bulletin de l'Office Colonial*, N. 41, pp. 156-161, Melun, Mai 1911.

Forests extend over about 57 775 000 acres (25 000 000 ha.) of the area of Indo-China, or a proportion of 33 % of wooded land. The action of the forest service is necessarily slight and it limits itself **Indo-China** especially to prohibiting the felling of trees under a certain diameter.

Teak is floated down the rivers. Besides the many important companies for forest exploitation, there are the European and native timber merchants who saw up the timber intended for local use. The value of the timber dealt with represents a turnover in the colony of more than 15 000 000 francs (£600 000); it is likely to increase in proportion to the development of exportation.

The principal species are as follows:

TONKING AND NORTH ANNAM: *Lim* is the best species and the most resistant. 25 000 to 30 000 cubic metres of it are used each year, especially as a building timber and for railway sleepers. Is is already used in France to a considerable extent.

Gu is excellent for cabinet-making.

Xoan-dao resembles mahogany, and is often veined like walnut.

Caoi is very similar to oak, and has all its qualities.

Gie, an excellent kind of oak; it is used in local industries.

Sang-le is hard but light. It is much sought after by natives who make long and flexible oars out of it.

CENTRAL ANNAM: *Kien-kien* and *Cho* are the best forest species in Central Annam and are in great demand for local industries. *Cho* would make good railway sleepers.

---

(1) See also Abstr. 1338 of this *Bulletin* for May 1911.   (*Ed.*).

Boi-Loi is excellent for furniture as it takes a good polish.

Huynh is the Mahogany of Indo-China. For some years it has been sold in London and Liverpool as mahogany.

SOUTH-ANNAM, COCHIN CHINA, AND CAMBODIA: *Sao* is similar to *Lim* and can be used for the same purposes.

Dau has several varieties; the best is *dau-mit*, which is useful for joinery.

Dang-Huong and *Son* are mahogany-like woods.

Cam-Xe and *Cam-Lai* are rare : they are used for high-class work, such as pianos.

Huynh-duong is a scented, straw-yellow wood, also used for high-class work.

Assam Forests. — *The Indian Agriculturist*, No. 3, pp. 87-88. Calcutta, March 1, 1911.

1785

At the close of the year 1909-10 the total area of reserved forests under the direct control of the Forest Department was 6477 square miles. The reservation of the Narpuh and Nongkhyllen forest in the Khasi and Jaintia Hills Division resulted in an increase of 62 square miles in the Western Circle; in the Eastern Circle there was an increase of 104 square miles, due not to the formation of new reserves but to a more accurate computation of areas in the Cachar and Sylhet Divisions by the Survey Department.

British India: Assam

Two areas in Lakhimpur were selected during the year for the growth of *Simul* (*Bombax Malabricum*) to supply the tea-box industry, but it has been considered advisable to vest the control of these areas in a political officer.

Further progress was made in bringing the reserved forests under systematic management.

In the Charduar rubber plantations 5542 trees were tapped, the yield being the highest yet obtained. The experiment with *Ficus elastica* seedlings in the Lushai Hills was successfully continued and the young plants are reported to have done well. Nine new forest villages were established during the year. These villages have proved extremely useful, but, as pointed out by the Conservator of the Eastern Circle, the greatest care must be exercised in the choice of settlers, as many tribes are useless.

1786   E. A. SMYTHIES. **Some Aspects of Fire Protection in Chir Forests,**
              Pinus longifolia, in India. *The Indian Forester,* vol. XXXVII,
              No. 182, pp. 54-62, Allahabad, Jan. and Feb. 1911.

Mr. Smythies considers three classes of Chir (*Pinus longifolia*)
forest, according as they are protected against fire for 35 years or
15 years, or are burnt annually. A comparison between the three
British India classes brings out several points of extreme interest :
              1) After the year of burning, fire protection gives an extraor-
dinary and universal stimulus to regeneration ;
              2) Successful regeneration is possible under the most favour-
able conditions without fire protection ;
              3) Long continued fire protection has always an adverse
effect on regeneration ; so much for the consequences of fire protection on regeneration. Further :
              1) Annual burning does not cause any damage to anything
above the seedling and young plant stage. Accidental fires, on the
other hand, sometimes kill the tallest trees ;
              2) In the typical forests of *Pinus longifolia,* fire protection is
useful as far as regeneration is concerned, but only when the conditions are favourable, and it is not always necessary ;
              3) When fire protection commences, regeneration takes place
practically everywhere ;
              4) With the contrary method, regeneration is not required
everywhere at once, but should be restricted to the regeneration
areas and to blanks ;
              5) There is only one way to do this : namely to protect the
regeneration areas, and to burn the remainder. Blanks whether protected or not, would fill up, provided the conditions are not unfavourable ;
              6) When an area has been successfully regenerated, it should
be carefully burnt early in the year, when fires are not intense, and
thereafter fire protection abandoned ;
              7) It is possible that long continued fire protection causes
the power of the forest to deteriorate.
              However, fire protection would certainly be advantageous under
the following conditions ;
              1) In all regeneration areas ;
              2) In all areas where the protection of the soil is of para-
mount importance. Undoubtedly, the thick layer of grass and needles
obtained in fire protected forests gives more efficient protection to
the surface soil than the more scanty covering of burnt areas ;
              3) In all plantations ;

4) In certain special cases where the crop has become so thin and scattered that it is advisable to have a complete regeneration even in the areas which are not in regular regeneration coupe.

5) In precipitous areas under the selection system.

Mr. Smythies dwells on the differences between European and Indian forests.

H. R. MACMILLAN and G. A. GUTCHES. **Forest Fires in Canada.** —   **1787**
Bulletin No. 9, Forestry Branch, Department of the Interior. Ottawa, Canada.

This is an illustrated pamphlet of 40 pages prepared for the purpose of arousing interest in the question of preserving forests from destruction by fire.   **Canada**

The subject is dealt with under the following heads: Classification of Lands; Destruction of the Forests; Effects of Forest Fires; Causes of Forest Fires; Forest Fires in 1909, and Conclusions.

The writer points out that the original forest areas covered nearly two million square miles divided as follows: From the maritime provinces westward to South Eastern Manitoba was an unrivalled stand of pine. In Southern Quebec and Southern Ontario were large bodies of valuable hardwoods, the only hardwood forest Canada possessed. From Nova Scotia to the Yukon stretched the great spruce belt of America, hundreds of thousands of square miles of pulpwood and saw timber, broken in its continuity only by reservoirs, driveable streams and water-powers. From the east slope of the Rocky Mountains to the Pacific coast and Vancouver Island stretched in a solid body a pure coniferous forest containing the largest trees and the greatest amount of timber per acre of any timber lands in Canada.

By a series of calculations the Bulletin shows that timber equal to 2 185 billion feet of sawn lumber has been destroyed by forest fires, an amount 437 times as large as is yearly cut in the whole of Canada. The loss thus sustained is estimated to approach a sum equal to about one billion of dollars.

The following conclusions are reached by the writer:

1. The area of merchantable timber has been, until within a very few years, grossly overestimated. The quantity of merchantable timber, never as large as is popularly believed, has been reduced more by forest fires than by any other cause.

2. These fires, though largely preventable, are still occurring. This is due not so much to lack of laws as to lack of enforcement

of existing laws. The laws cannot be enforced unless they are supported by public spirit, backed by generous legislative appropriations and administered by permanent skilled officials free from political interference.

3. The destruction of the existing timber by fire is not only reducing the present timber supply, but is destroying the value or possibility of a future crop, laying waste large areas of forest land, exercising a deleterious effect on navigable streams, water-powers and irrigation reservoirs, and is in every way directly opposed to the national welfare represented by a progressive conservation policy.

1788

The Electric Current and Trees.—*The Gardeners' Chronicle*, vol. XLIX, No. 3694, p. 324. London, May 27, 1911.

In England damage by electric current is at present almost confined to street trees. Direct current is more dangerous to trees than alternating, but it is hardly used except for trams. A direct current of low intensity may kill a tree without showing any signs of burning, apparently by disorganizing the protoplasm. Alternating current exerts only a local effect; it is only in wet weather that there is much danger of current grounding through the trees; when it does so, people touching the trunk may get severe shocks.

Great
Britain

The practice of fixing wires to trees should not be allowed, as the best insulators are liable to fail when the air is saturated with moisture. The grounding of a slight alternating current may cause the death of a line of cambium the whole length of the trunk; this soon heals over, but it can be detected by a ridge of bark that forms over it.

1789

C. G. ROGERS. **The Agri-Silvicultural Method: Report on the Raising of Forests with Field Crops in Berar.** — *The Indian Forester*, vol. XXXVII, No. 1 and 2. Allahabad, Jan. and Feb. 1911.

From 1902-03 to 1909-10 attempts were made to restock blank areas in the Chirodi Reserve, Amraoti Division. On land sufficiently good for cultivation, field crops were sown (chiefly sesamum, cotton, and arhar(1)) with forest seeds in every fourth or sixth drill; sometimes a crossdrilling of forest seeds was carried out in the second season; cultivation was continued for three seasons.

British India
Berar

---

(1) Arhar: *Cajanus indicus* Spreng. Sir G. WATT. *The Commercial Products of India*, 1908, p. 196.   (*Ed.*).

It was found that in only a few cases had the seedlings been able to withstand cultivation, and after three years they were generally not strong enough to compete with the growth of grass and weeds.

The trees sown were Babúl (*Acacia arabica*), Bhosi (*Bacchinia racemosa*), Ber (*Zizyphus Jujuba*), Goti (Z. *Xylopyra*), Khair (*Acacia Catechu*), Tiwas (*Ongeinia dalbergioides*), Tendu (*Diospyros Melanoxylon*), Ain (*Terminalia tomentosa*), Kahn (*F. Arjuna*), Palás (*Butea frondosa*), Sálai (*Boswellia thuriferia*), Achár (*Buchanania latifolia*), Hewar (*Acacia leucophlœa*), Nin (*Azadirachta indica*), and Bharati (*Gymnosporia montana*) Of these, Khair always grew best.

In those cases, on the poorer soils, where the saplings were not strong enough to compete with the grass after three years of cultivation, it was found that a very light grazing (one cow to the acre or less) could be employed to advantage.

In general, however, the writer recommends that the lines of seedlings should be left, and only the intermediate spaces should be cultivated. With some weeding along the rows, this method gives a good stand of young trees after three or four years on fairly moist soil; on very poor soil the cultivation must be continued longer.

LENT. **Forest Manuring in the District of Sigmaringen, Hohenzollern.** 1790
(Forstdüngungsversuche im Regierungsbezirk Sigmaringen). — *Mitteilungen der Deutschen Landwirtschafts-Gesellschaft*, XXVI J., St. 17, pp. 204-206. Berlin, 22. April 1911.

This article describes experiments in manuring spruce (« Fichten ») on a plateau of Black Jura (Lias) at 600 metres (1970 ft.).

In one experiment, four plots were treated as follows: Germany :
Hohenzollern

h) Unmanured.

i) Alsike Clover, 30 kg. per ha. (27 lbs. per acre), sown in May 1906, inoculated with « nitragin ».

k) Clover as on *i*); ground quick-lime 2000 kg. (16 cwt. per acre), applied in March 1906.

l) Clover as on *i*); kainit 400 kg. (3 ¼ cwt.), basic slag 800 kg. (6 ½ cwt.), applied in March 1906.

All planted with 4 year spruces (pit-planting), 1.2 m. (4 ft.) each way.

In another experiment the plots were:

a) Ground quicklime 1000 kg. (8 cwt.).

b) Ground quicklime 2000 kg. (16 cwt.).

c) Basic slag 800 kg. (6 ½ cwt,) ; kainit 400 kg. (3 ¼ cwt.).

e) Sulphate of ammonia (20 % N.) 200 kg. (1 ½ cwt.) in year of planting.

f) As *e*), in year after planting.

g) Unmanured.

The lime and mineral manures were applied part in the pits in March, and part as a top-dressing in July; the ammonia in the pits at planting time and as a top-dressing in July.

The trees and planting (in the middle of April 1907) were as in the other experiment.

Measurements in the autumn showed the following average growth per annum on plot *c*):

$$
\begin{aligned}
1907 &. . . . . \quad 34.6 \; (1)\\
1908 &. . . . . \quad 50.6\\
1909 &. . . . . \quad 73.0\\
1910 &. . . . . \quad 107.3
\end{aligned}
$$

The results on all the plots in both series, regarding the growth of each year on plot *c*) as 100, are as follows:

Season	*a*	*b*	*c*	*d*	*e*	*f*	*g*	*h*	*i*	*k*	*l*
2nd	84	91	100	97	90	95	88	89	93	89	125
3rd.	67	74	100	108	70	75	71	76	81	76	134
4th.	53	59	100	109	58	61	64	67	73	67	131
5th.	46	50	100	104	51	55	58	—	—	—	—

These figures show that phosphate alone produces a decided increase, which becomes still greater when potash is added; further, the long-continued action of basic slag is well seen; the effect of quicklime, on the other hand, rapidly falls off.

1791 LOJACONO. **Cork-Oak Plantations and Cork Industry in Italy** (I sugghereti e l'industria del sughero in Italia). — *La Rivista Agraria*, N. 9, p. 117-118. Napoli, 5 marzo, 1911.

Italy: Sardinia, Sicily

In spite of repeated attempts to introduce cork-oak cultivation into California, Australia and Cape Colony, the monopoly of cork still rests with Portugal, Spain, France and Italy.

Of the 4 165 000 acres (1 683 000 ha.) under cork-oaks all over the world, Italy has 250 000 acres (100 000 ha.), i. e. 5.95 %, while

---

(1) No measure is stated: presumably centimetres. (*Ed.*).

it produces only 4 920 tons (50 000 quintals) of the 110 000 tons (1 120 000 quintals) produced by the entire world, i. e. 4.55 %; this yields about £100 000 (2 500 000 fr.) a year.

Cork of excellent quality is furnished by the principal centres of production : Caltagirone in Sicily and Tempio Pausania in Sardinia. The low yield is due to the fact that Italy does not produce cork of the thickness required for the manufacture of champagne corks, because of the seven-year contracts in the cork districts which make it necessary, to use the bark before its complete formation To prevent this injury and loss, the contracts should be made for at least eight to twelve years, as in Spain and France.

PURAN SINGH. **Tanning Extracts in India.** — *The Indian Forester*, vol. XXXVII, No. 344, pp. 160-171 (Indian Trade Journal), Allahabad, March and April, 1911.

1792

The Report of the Fifth Indian Industrial Conference, which met at Lahore on Dec. 30th., 1909, contains a useful paper on Indian materials suitable for the manufacture of tanning extracts.

British India

I. *Tamaricaceae*.

The galls of three species of *Tamarix*, namely, *T. gallica* Linn., *T. articulata* Vahl, *T. dioica* Roxb., contain about 50 per cent. of tannic acid. A sample of the bark gave about 8 per cent. of tannin.

II. *Dipterocarpaceae*:

In 1898, an extract was prepared from the bark of *Dipterocarpus tuberculatus* Roxb. in Burma, and gave 24 per cent. of, soluble tannin. It may be noted that this bark is capable of yielding a much richer extract if prepared on scientific lines.

The bark of *Shorea robusta* Gaertn. or *sal* is a valuable tanning material. Large quantities can be had as waste product from the forests of the United Provinces and Bengal. The tannin calculated on the dry bark of the old trees is 5 per cent. and of the young trees 9-12 per cent.

The fruits of *Vateria indica* Linn. gave 25 per cent. of tannin with only 12 per cent. of soluble non-tannin.

III. *Sterculiaceae*:

The bark from *Heritiera littoralis* Dryand is reported to be remarkably free from any objectionable colouring matter and has 14 per cent. of tannin.

IV. *Anacardiaceae*:

The bark of *Odina Wodier* Roxb. has 9 per cent. of tannin. *Mangifera indica* Linn. has 16 per cent. of tannin.

The galls of *Pistacia integerrima* Stew. contain 75 per cent of tannin, and are very useful in preparing mixed tannin extracts.

The bark of *Rhus paniculata* Wall., gives about 22 per cent of tannin and an extract with 82 per cent. of tannin, the average being 60-70.

V. *Coriaceae:*

All parts of *Coriaria nepalensis* Wall. are said to be rich in tannin; the leaves contain 20 per cent.

VI. *Leguminosae:*

The bark of *Acacia arabica* Willd. is one of the most popular tanning agents in India. The bark contains about 17 per cent. of tannin and 6 per cent. of soluble non-tannin. The pods are said to contain quantities of tannin varying from 5 to 20 per cent.

Both the bark and the wood of *Acacia Catechu* Willd., the famous "Katha" yielding tree, can be utilised for manufacturing tannin extracts. Simultaneously with the manufacture of Katha from the wood, the writer is of opinion that a good light-coloured tannin extract can be prepared as a by-product from the wood. The bark is also capable of yielding a good tannin extract.

The bark of *Acacia leucophloea* Willd. contains 21 per cent. of tannin and is reported to be as good as the bark of *Acacia arabica*.

Caesalpinia coriaria Willd. is the American sumac or dividivi. It was introduced in India in 1834 and has been cultivated in many districts with considerable success. The pods from the Indian-grown dividivi give 30-50 per cent. of tannin.

Caesalpinia digyna Rottl, is an indigenous species of dividivi growing freely in Burma, Assam and Bengal. It can be cultivated with great ease. The pods from which the seeds have been removed show over 50 per cent. of tannin, and in certain samples the percentage rises as high as 60; it is considered one of the richest tanning agents, possessing properties of special value which render it of more importance than the South American dividivi.

The bark of *Cassia auriculata* Linn. is a valuable tanning material which in mature trees contains 11 per cent.

Xylia dolabriformis Benth., is the famous pynkado of Burma, Bombay and other places. A large quantity of pynkado timber refuse or dust is available. The specimens of saw dust and chips of pynkado gave 6 and 5 per cent. of tannin respectively. With regard to its tanning properties Prof. Procter reports: « In its low percentage of soluble non-tannin as well as in colour it resembles quebracho ».

VII. *Rhizophoraceae* (Mangrove Family):

The species of this family are reported by far the most abundant and richest tannin-yielding trees. The efforts of the Government of Burma are also concentrated on the production of extracts from mangrove. So far the extracts yielded by *Rhizophora mucronata* Lam. have proved to be the richest in the market; the only objection is that their colour is too red, but the objectionable colouring matter may be found susceptible of elimination. The bark of *R. mucronata* contains 26-30 per cent. of tannin, and the extract prepared from the same has 72 per cent. of tannin with a water content of about 6 per cent.

VIII. *Combretaceae:*

Next to the mangrove family, the various species of *Terminalia* deserve a short description. *T. Chebula* Retz is distributed in many parts of India and Burma. The fruits are mostly exported and very good pale-coloured extracts can be made from them. They contain from 31.00 to 43.74 per cent of tannin. The bark of *T. Oliveri* Brandis contains 31 per cent. of tannin while its leaves show about 15 per cent. The bark of *T. tomentosa* Bedd may be considered quite as good as the *Shorea robusta* bark.

IX. *Myricaceae*:

The bark of *Myrica Nagi* Thunb. has 27 per cent. tannin.

X. *Cupuliferae:*

The dry bark of *Quercus glauca* Thunb. contains 12.20 % of tannin, that of *Q. dilatata* Lindel 7.94 %, *Q. incana* Roxb. 23.36 % anb *Q. semecarpifolia* Sm. 8.60 %.

XI. *Coniferae:*

The bark of *Pinus longifolia* Roxb. contains about 13 per cent. of tannin.

From the description of these various tanning materials, the writer presumes that a fairly correct idea can be formed as to the tannin resources of India, and that there is no reason why a well-organised and flourishing tannin industry should not be developed.

H. R. MACMILLAN. **Tan Bark and Tanning Extracts used in Canada.**   **1798**
— *Bulletin No. 20, Forestry Branch, Department of the Interior.*
Ottawa; Canada.

From reports received from 67 tanneries which represent 90 per cent of the vegetable tanning consumption in Canada, Mc. Macmillan   **Canada**
calculates that in 1909 there were $ 1 126 000 worth of vegetable

tanning materials used, consisting of 76 792 cords (1) of bark valued at $ 646 679 ; 17 313 500 lbs. of liquid extract valued at $ 51 042.

It is claimed that until a few years ago bark was practically the only tannin used in Canada. Hemlock and oak were the chief barks used. Measured by value, bark, now represents very little more than half the vegetable tannins used in the country ; no bark is used except hemlock and there are very few tanneries depending altogether upon bark.

In 1909 the forests of Canada produced tanning materials to the value of $ 889 894 ; 73.3 per cent of this was used at home, the remainder was exported. Taken together, bark and extract used in Canada or exported in 1909, represent a production of 110 000 cords of hemlock bark. There was cut in Canada that year 278 985 000 board feet of hemlock. This amount should have given 168 000 cords of bark. Since only about two-thirds of this quantity was used, it is argued that there must have been a waste of bark amounting to a value of about $ 2 072 000. The purpose of the bulletin is to call attention to this source of wealth that is allowed to waste year by year.

1794   Wattle Bark Industry in South Africa. — *The Board of Trade Journal*, No. 758. p. 530. London, June 8, 1911.

The production and exportation of wattle (2) bark continue to expand. The total exports from Durban last year, as compared with the previous year, were as follows :

S. Africa
Union

1909 .	. . . . . .	tons.	35 771
1910 .	. . . . . .	»	41 344

The demand from the United Kingdom is slowly increasing, but the chief ports of destination of the bark are Hamburg and Antwerp.

During 1910, several companies were established in Natal for the purpose of planting large areas with wattle, and individual farmers also have been actively extending their plantations. The annual production is likely to increase considerably within the next few years, as the new plantations arrive at maturity.

---

(1) The Cord of wood varies greatly in size in different counties in England, from 96 to 216 cub ft; the most used are 125 and 128 cub ft.
I. NISBET in WRIGHT's *Standard Cyclopedia of Modern Agric.* London 1909.

(2) See Abstr. 499 *Bulletin* for February 1911.   (*Ed.*).

BOOTH-TUCKER. **Eucalyptus in India.** — *The Indian Agriculturist,*   **1795**
No. 5, p. 149. Calcutta, May 1, 1911.

With a view to encouraging and popularising the cultivation
of the Eucalyptus in India, it is suggested:

1) That nurseries should be established in as many places
as possible for the cultivation and distribution of young plants of
suitable varieties.

2) That the Forest, Canal and Railway Departments be en-   **British India**
couraged to establish plantations.

3) That an Annual Arbour Day Celebration shall be fixed on
a date suitable for each Province or locality, when this and other
valuable varieties of trees may be planted by school children.

4) That an Eucalyptus Association be formed for the purpose
of pushing the cultivation of the Eucalyptus.

5) That special concessions and grants of land be made to
persons, companies, societies, villages or associations willing to
establish at their own expense nurseries, groves, avenues, or plantations of Eucalyptus (1).

I. RODWAY. **Trees of the Tasmanian Forests of the Order** *Myrtaceae,*   **1796**
the Genus *Eucalyptus.* — *Agricultural and Stock Department,*
Bull., No. 17, pp. 15. Tasmania, 1910.

The writer states that Eucalyptus wood varies considerably according to the conditions of its production. He asserts that it would
be advantageous to classify it according to the species, the age,   **Tasmania**
and the conditions of development. He divides the Eucalyptus trees
of Tasmania into two groups:

(a) Those with kidney-shaped anthers:

E. obliqua L'Her. (Stringy-bark); *E. obliqua* var. (Gum-topped
Stringy); *E. regnans* F. v. M. (Swamp Gum); *E. amygdalina* Lab.
(Black Peppermint); *E. linearis* Dernh. (White Peppermint); *E. Ris-
doni* Hook. (Blue Peppermint); *E. Risdoni* var *Hypericifolia* (Bastard
Blue Gum, Cabbage Gum); *E. coccifera* Hook. (Mountain Peppermint);
E. Sieberiana F. v. M. (Ironbark, White-topped Stringy); *E. pauci-
flora* Sieber (Weeping Gum).

---

(1) See Abstr. 500 in the *Bulletin* for Feb. 1911.   (*Ed.*).

12

(b) Those with parallel anther-cells : E. *globulus* Lab. (Blue Gum); *E. viminalis* Lab. (Maima Gum or White Gum) ; *E. acervula* Hook. (Red Gum); *E. Stuartiana*, F. v. M. (Apple-scented Gum); *E. Gunnii* Hook. (Cider Gum); *E. Muelleri* Moore (Brown Gum); *E. cordata* Lab. (Heart-leaved Gum); *E. urnigera*, Hooker (Urn Gum); *E. vernicosa* Hook. (Dwarf Gum).

Eucalypts are very accomodating with regard to soil and moisture, while the size is influenced largely by protection from excessive influence of drying winds. Given this protection, a gum-tree will grow well, even with a 12 inch (300 mm) rainfall. Eucalypts are bad soil protectors and poor soil producers, because of the vertical position of the leaves and the fact that leaf shedding is not copious and the leaves do not rapidly decompose.

In Tasmania , they are distributed over three zones according to altitude:

1st. Below 1200 ft. altitude : *E Globulus, E. viminalis, E. obliqua, E. Amygdalina, E. linearis* and *E. Risdoni.*

2nd. About 2000 to 3000 ft.: *E. urnigera, E. Muelleri.*

3rd. Above 3000 ft: *E. coccifera.*

E. regnans and *E. obliqua* connect the first and second zones. Eucalypts of the upper zones will not thrive at a lower altitude.

A Eucalypt forest will readily regenerate itself provided that the seedlings are not subjected to drought.

The evergreen character of the Eucalypt leaves makes it difficult to determime when the tree should be cut and the wood seasoned.

To dry a tree before cutting is not approved of. The durability of these woods depends on the tannin that they contain; some of these gum-woods are naturally impregnated with tannin. In a diseassed condition the trees produce « kino », a tannic secretion which results from the combination of the lignin of wood fibres, after it has been reduced to sugar by bacterial decomposition, and tannic acid (which is always present in the wood).

In all cases, the timber produced on alluvial flats is of less dense fibre than that of rocky hills, and is in consequence more difficult to season.

Some Eucalypts consist of straight fibres: *E. regnans, E. obliqua, E. amygdalina, E. Muelleri*; these can be cut easily. Others on the contrary have a considerable curvature of the fibre, and to such an extent in some kinds that the wood is rendered nearly worthless as timber; this is also true of wood with fibres that run in various directions.

Rubber Plantations in Java (Anpflanzung Kautschukliefernder Bäume auf Java). German Consular Report. — *Deutsches Kolonialblatt*, No. 9, p 356. Berlin, 1 Mai 1911.

1797

The total area given up to rubber cultivation in Java is about 49 050 *bouws*, that is about 84 902 acres, as a *bouw* is equal to about 1 3/4 acres. Of this area 6400 *bouws* are planted with *Ficus elastica* and 25 500 *bouws* with *Hevea brasiliensis*, while the remaining 17 100 *bouws* contain these two plants and also *Manihot Glaziovii* and *Castilloa elastica*.

Dutch East Indies: Java

The Government also possesses the following plantations:

	Bouws	Acres
Ficus elastica	10 929	18 903
Hevea brasiliensis.	1 816	2 151
Castilloa	78	140
	12 823	21 194

Plantations owned by natives are not included in this list. The Government has also planted 1500 *bouws*, about 2595 acres with Guttapercha trees (*Palaquium*) (1).

Exotic Rubber Cultivation in the Congo State. — *The Board of Trade Journal*, No. 755, pp. 358-359. London, May 18, 1911.

1798

A certain number of plantations of rubber vines have been abandoned in the Congo State as not worth keeping up. Some of these vines, however, are so far advanced as to be capable of growing without further care.

The experimental cultivation of *Hevea brasiliensis* is to be greatly extended in the equatorial regions, and particularly in the districts of the Equator and Dangala, where the rainfall is most abundant and most regular. At the beginning of 1911, twelve centres had been fixed upon, of which five were in the Dangala and two in the Equator districts. The choice of suitable lands is very important, as the rainfall is only moderate, even in the equatorial region. Considerable quantities of *Hevea* seed have been imported from Ceylon.

Belgian: Congo State

---

(1) *Palaquium Gutta*, = *Dichopsis Gutta*, called at Perak « Taban Merah » Cf. H. SEMLER, *Die tropische Agrikultur*, II. Bd. p. 725. Wismar, 1900.

(*Ed.*).

The cultivation of *Manihot Glaziovii* is to be extended at the station of Dokala (Middle Congo). The growth of this species is rapid there, and rubber extraction from trees of ten years' growth has given satisfactory results. Certain stations in the Uele district are also suitable for the extensive cultivation of this rubber tree, the climate being characterised by a pronounced dry season.

Funtumia elastica, while developing satisfactorily in some regions of the Congo, does not appear to be capable of bearing repeated tappings over a long period so well as *Hevea*. The yield of latex at the first tapping is greater than from *Hevea*, but at the end of a few days the secretion ceases. Regular experiments have been made at Libenge with encouraging results, though the quantity of rubber obtained is much less than from *Hevea*.

1799   THURSTAN (Brit. Cons.). **Rubber Plantations in the Kasai District, Congo State.** — *The Board of Trade Journal*, No. 758, p. 513. London, June 8, 1911.

Belgian : Congo State

Rubber plantations have been in existence for some years in the Kasai District, which at present produces a large proportion of the wild rubber exported from the Congo. These plantations are, however, few in number and apparently unprofitable.

The period of experiments is now ended, and it is considered established that *Hevea* is the most suitable tree for plantation in the Kasai. The soil and climate of this district seem to be admirably adapted for rubber plantations.

The price of land has been fixed by the Belgian Government at 10 francs per hectare if purchased, or at 5 per cent. of the sale price if rented. To obtain full rights of ownership or to rent land at these prices, an applicant must occupy it provisionally for five years, meanwhile paying a rent equivalent to 5 per cent. per annum of the purchase price. At the end of five years land thus occupied provisionally and developed will be sold or let to the occupant at the above-mentioned prices if it is planted with trees to the extent of fifteen trees per hectare or covered to the extent of one tenth by buildings. In cases where land is rented from the Government the lease is for a maximum period of fifteen years, renewable at will at prevailing prices. The above regulations do not, of course, apply to plantations already in existence and belonging to private companies or individuals.

The greatest difficulty in the way of making rubber plantations in the Kasai District profitable is that of transport. The confluence of the Kasai and Lulua rivers is some 800 or 900 miles above Stanley Pool, whence all goods are conveyed by rail to Matadi lower down on the Congo River, at the head of navigation for ocean-going steamers.

H. S. SMITH. **The Castilloa Industry in Mexico and Central America.** — *Department of Agriculture, Trinidad: Bulletin*, Vol. X, No. 67, pp. 81-93. Trinidad, January, March, 1911.

1800

The variety of *Castilloa* which is cultivated in Mexico is the same as that cultivated in the West Indies. General conditions, climatic and economic, are equally favourable in Mexico to *Castilloa* culture and it has been proved that its culture can be made a commercial success.

C. America : Mexico

From actual experiments and from information given by planters in Mexico, there is nothing to justify the statements made that 10 to 12 years old *Castilloa* trees yield an average of about 2 pounds (906 gr.) per year, but everything shows that the average at this age is nearer ½ lb. (226.5 gr.) per tree.

In tapping, a knife with a V shaped blade is used. The trees are tapped with long V cuts, connected by a shallow vertical channel to carry the latex to a single cup at the base of the tree. After making the cut with the V tool it is opened down to the wood with the point of a sharp knife. Tapping is done up to a height of 30 feet (10 metres).

In the writer's opinion, by tapping higher up the tree, as is done in Mexico, the yield in Trinidad can be considerably increased, and by adopting some modification of the Mexican methods of tapping and collecting, the cost of production can be reduced materially.

The percentage of resin in rubber from trees of similar age is probably the same in Trinidad as in Mexico, but the resin contents of the average rubber shipped from Mexico is lower, on account of the number of large wild Castilloas scattered through the plantations, which are tapped at the same time as the young cultivated trees and the latex mixed.

On the whole, the *Castilloa* tree in Mexico is singularly free from disease. " Collar rot " which attacks it in the West Indies, is not to be found in Mexico. " Die-back " is fairly common in some places, but where it is not due to actual poverty of soil or to the effect of strong dry winds, it has been found to be amenable to treatment. Canker gives some trouble and sometimes kills fine trees on the Atlantic side (with humid climate), but the long dry spell of the Pacific slope seems to keep it in check.

1801

H. H. COUSINS. **Castilloa Cultivation in Jamaica.** — (*Journal of the Jamaica Agricultural Society*, Sept., 1910), *Nature*, London, April 6, 1911.

Suggestions are given as to the cultivation of *Castilloa* rubber in Jamaica. It is first pointed out that plants were brought to Jamaica from Kew in 1881 and that a tree from these, growing in the Royal Gardens, was used for purposes of propagation. This makes it fairly certain that all trees of Castilloa in Jamaica, more than fifteen years old, were planted from material obtained from this tree.

Plants have been subsequently raised from seed obtained from British Honduras. All these have been shown to be plants of *Castilloa guatemaltica*. An account is given of Costa Rica Castilloa (*Castilloa costaricana*) and it is mentioned that on the Pacific side of Costa Rica, there exists a drought-resistant Castilloa possessing olive-green flowers ; this seems to be suitable to conditions in Jamaica and will be tried there shortly.

Attention is given to climatic and geographical conditions which make it appear likely that the first-mentioned species of Castilloa would be much more suited for growing in Jamaica than the latter, and planters are advised to give due regard to these considerations before they employ, in any quantity, Costa Rican seed in their Castilloa plantations. Experience is showing that to grow Castilloa as a shade for cacao is not sound practice, and that this rubber tree should be planted by itself if the best results are desired.

Jamaica

1802

The Utilisation of Hevea Seed. See Abstract 1753 in this *Bulletin*.

1803

BADERMANN. **Production of Guttapercha in Siam.** (Gummigewinnung in Siam). — *Gummizeitung*, N. 29, p. 1082. Berlin, April 21, 1911.

The " Gettania " (Guttapercha) gum of Siam is an excellent insulator for sub-marine cables. But little care is taken in Siam of the " Taban " (1) trees which grow wild, especially near the seashore.

Siam

---

(1) " Taban " in Malay. The trees which produce guttapercha are *Palaquium Gutta*, *P. oblongifolium* and *Payena Leerii*. See note to Abstract 1797. in this *Bulletin*.

For *Palaquium optimum*, the best Gutta-percha producing tree in Sarawak, Borneo, see: ODOARDO BECCARI, *Nelle Foreste di Borneo, Viaggi e Ricerche di un Naturalista*, Firenze, 1902, p. 152.   (*Ed.*).

Live Stock Breeding. -- Aviculture. — Beekeeping.

Silk Production. — Animal Industries.

G. Moussu. **Drainage and Liming of Grass-land for the Prevention of Liver-Rot in Sheep and Cattle.** (Sur le traitement de la cachexie aqueuse par distomatose). — *Journal d'Agric. pratique*, 75ᵉ an., N. 22, pp. 684-686. Paris, 1ᵉʳ Juin 1911.

1804

The measures against liver fluke should be of two kinds, 1) preventive, 2) curative.

In prevention the chief requirement is to avoid the conditions which allow the hatching and development of the embryos. If this is impossible, the life-cycle must be broken at some point, either by killing the embryos on the pastures or by destroying the molluscs (*Limnaea*) which are their hosts.

France

The pastures must therefore be made healthy by draining, deep drainage if possible, or at any rate surface drains and ditches to carry off stagnant water. This will prevent the eggs hatching.

If the water cannot be run off, the pasture may be disinfected. To effect this, quicklime should be spread in all hollows and stagnant pools, and along surface-drains, ditches, streams, and rivers to a distance of 10 or 15 yards each side. 1 lb. of quicklime or 4 ½ lbs. of carbonate of lime (chalk dust) per 100 gallons of water is enough to kill the fluke-embryos and the molluscs; but five monthly applications are necessary (May to September); this should only be done on grazing land. No stock should be let on the land for a few days after the dressings.

There is no certain remedy; the best medicine is ether extract of male fern (1).

---

(1) See this *Bulletin*, May 1911, Abstr. 1454.   (*Ed.*).

1805   GUILLERMO GANDARA. **The Control of Acaridian Parasites and the Prevention of Pyroplasmosis.** (La plaga de las garrapatas). — *Boletin de la Camara Agricola nacional de Tamaulipas, Mexico.* Tomo III, V. 4, pp. 51-54. Taumalipas, 1 Abril 1911.

In South America several kinds of Rhipicephalous acari-parasites on horses and cattle, are designated under the name of " *garrapatas* ". The most injurious of these pests in Mexico, and more especially on **Mexico**   the Atlantic sea-coast, is *Aracboophilus*, I. Ac. R. de Say, a blood-sucking insect, producing bad anaemia in the animals it fastens on, and sometimes causing their death. It is also the propagating agent of the heamatozoan protozoan *Pyroplasma bigeminum*, which is the cause of a very serious kind of pyroplasmosis, locally known as " *Ranilla* ".

Several preventive measures have been proposed. One of the remedies suggested is to smear the hide of the animals with 1 kg of fat, 250 grammes of petroleum, 100 gr. of oil of Cade, and 100 gr. of creoline. Special care should be taken to smear the inside of the flap of the ear with this ointment, as the insects are in the habit of settling there.

Another remedy is to spray the animals with an emulsion consisting of 15 litres of petroleum and 500 grammes of ordinary soap, dissolved in 5 litres of boiling water.

These remedies are, however, rather costly. The Department of Agriculture of the United States suggests two others.

One consists in dipping the animals in a tank with vertical trapezium-shaped sections, of a cubic capacity of 72 metres, filled with an insecticide consisting of a mixture of 187.5 litres of petroleum, 12.5 kgs. of soap, and 125 litres of water. The beasts should be dipped twice a year in March or April and again in August or September, so as to correspond with the two periods of development of the parasites. 5 litres of insecticide are reckoned necessary for each head of cattle.

The other remedy consists in removing the cattle from one grazing land to another during the months in which the parasites infest them (from November to January) and lay their eggs in the soil; care is afterwards taken to burn the fields where the insects have fallen. If the grazing lands available for the cattle are divided into three sections, subjected each year in succession to fire, the parasite will be got rid of at the end of three years, provided that all the drovers over a large zone adopt the same method for their destruction.

CH. DOUGLAS. **Influence of Temperature on Milk Yield. Ventilation**   1806
of Cow Byres. — *Transactions of the Highland and Agricultural
Society of Scotland*, V. Ser., Vol. XXIII, pp. 170-189. Edinburgh, 1911.

In this article a second series of experiments on the ventilation of byres and its influence on milk yield is described.

The experiments were carried on at five centres. The cows were
of the Ayrshire breed, mixed Ayrshires and cross breeds. The ge-   Britain:
neral period of the experiment was from November 21 to March 27.   Scotland

The general result of this second series of experiments corresponds closely with that obtained in the first series. Both series
have dealt exclusively with the practical question of the influence
of greater or less ventilation in combination with the natural body-
heat of the cows. Within these limits, the experiments are held
to have established with the utmost certainty the fact that the
production of milk can be carried on at least as profitably in byres
ventilated down to 50° F (10° C.) as in those whose temperature is
kept 10 degrees F. (5°.5 C.) higher by undue restriction of ventilation.

Further, it is brought out:

1. That any restriction of ventilation sufficient to bring the
temperature of a byre up to 60° F (15.°05 C.) leads to a degree of
atmospheric impurity inconsistent with the conditions of perfect
health.

2. That in byres in which the temperatures have been kept
down by thorough ventilation in autumn, cows do not suffer either
in health or milk yield, even from very low temperatures in winter.

3. That whatever waste of food may be entailed in the maintenance of the body-heat of cows in colder byres, this is more than
counteracted by the influence of fresher air; while it is evident
that the health of animals is much more likely to be promoted by
active digestion than by the mere prevention of loss of body-heat.
It is also observed that the colder temperature in autumn causes
the cows to grow and to retain thick coats of winter hair: so that
it is not even certain that the body-heat is better conserved in the
less ventilated byres than in those which permit the animals to retain their natural coverings.

From these results the following conclusions are given:

a) A careful attempt should be made to give such a degree
and kind of ventilation as will, without creating draughts, keep the
temperature of the byre always down to 50° F. (10° C.).

b) Special care should be exercised to keep the temperature of the byre well below this point in autumn and early winter.

1807 A. D. HALL. **The Progress of the Chemistry of Animal Nutrition during the Year 1910.** (1). — *Annual Reports on the Progress of Chemistry for* 1910. Issued by the Chemical Society. Vol. VII, pp. IX + 303 (221-224). London, 1911 (1).

Great Britain. Germany. United States

" In some earlier papers, T. B. Wood has shown that certain constant differences exist in the composition of the various kinds of mangolds usually grown. Their average content of dry matter varies from 10.7 per cent in the " Yellow Globe " to 13.1 per cent. in the " Long Red " and yellow-fleshed varieties. Since the " Long Red " yields on the average as large a crop as the " Yellow Globe " and a much larger one than the yellow-fleshed varieties, it produces the most dry matter per acre, and should be the most profitable mangold to grow. To make this conclusion valid, however, it was necessary to show that the dry matter of the " Long Red " variety possesses equal feeding value to that of the others; accordingly Mr. Wood carried out a series of experiments on fattening cattle, using 37 animals in all, comparing in each case the effect of equal weights of " Long Red " and " Yellow Globe " mangolds. The final result shows a superiority of the " Long Red " as compared to the " Yellow Globe " of 116 to 100, in their power of producing live-weight increase, the proportion of dry matter being approximately the same in the two varieties. The limits of experimental error obtaining in the trials are discussed, and the final result may be taken as conclusive, that the feeding value of the mangold is determined as closely as it can be measured in practice by the percentage of dry matter in the roots ".

" In the field of animal nutrition interest is now chiefly fixed on the proteins and their cleavage products, as it is felt that the main lines of the energy question are settled ".

" Abderhalden and his co-workers continue to improve upon their attempts to feed animals with the cleavage products instead of the proteins themselves and have now attained a much greater measure of success. They found that dogs could maintain their nitrogen equilibrium on the deficient cleavage products of meat, whether hydrolysed by trypsin, pepsin and erepsin, or by acid, provided that care was taken to remove the trace of barium which acted preju-

(1) Cp. this *Bulletin*, No. 200, January, 1911. (*Ed.*).

dicially in their former experiments. When the products of acid hydrolysis are administered, it is desirable to add tryptophan, because this substance is to a large extent destroyed by the acid. '

" Osborne has continued his work on the cleavage products of proteins, and in an important paper, in which he sets out as fully as possible the cleavage products of zein, he shows a recovery of something like 80 per cent. He discusses at length the sources of loss which still exist in all methods of protein hydrolysis ".

« Kellner has continued his work on the value of non-protein nitrogen compounds in the nutrition of ruminant animals. Lambs were fed as to their nitrogenous requirements exclusively on asparagin and ammonium acetate ».

« The result showed that these substances can be so converted by the bacteria of the intestines into protein that they can replace some of the protein required for maintenance. There was however, no evidence of production of flesh from these non-proteins, but when fed together with protein they can increase the formation of flesh by saving the protein required for maintenance. The same question has also been investigated at the Hohenheim Station, where ammonium acetate and asparagin were fed to milch cows. The authors conclude that these substances do not lead to any increase in the undigested protein in the faeces, although they are converted by bacterial action into proteins, which may be utilised by the animal, not merely for maintenance, but also for milk production » (1).

« Among other papers interesting to the agricultural chemist is one by Siegfeld on the constitution of butter fat ».

« He finds that trybutyrin is soluble in alcohol, by which it can be extracted from a mixture of beef butter. Butter, however, yields very little fat to alcohol and that of much the same composition as the original fat : from which he concludes that Bell's original conception of butter fat as mixed glycerides is most likely to be correct ».

« T. Weyl has examined the precipitation of proteins by acetone as a basis for analytical processes. He finds that acetone precipitates the protein from milk completely, the milk is diluted with an equal volume of water, 4 volumes of acetone are added, and the collected precipitate, after washing. is extracted with ether, dried, and weighed. It is possible that this method of precipitating proteins with but little change may become useful in plant analysis.

---

(1) Cp. this *Bulletin*, Abstr. 200, Jan. 1911. (*Ed.*).

« As regard the nutrition of farm stock, the most notable event of late years has been. the soy bean from Manchuria and the considerable trade in soy bean cake that has thus developed » (1).

« F, Honcamp (*Landw. Versuchs.-Stat.*, 1910, 73, 241) now reports certain determinations of the digestibility by sheep of soy bean meal, made both from the pressed cake and from the residue after the oil had been chemically extracted. The following table will show that the meal is the most concentrated of all feeding stuffs in common use, with the exception of linseed, from which the oil has not been extracted :

	Soy Press cake		Residue	
	Total	Digestible	Total	Digestible
Crude protein	47.9	43.3	52.2	48.0
Nitrogen-free extract .	32.8	31.1	34.6	34.6
Crude fat	7.9	6.9	1.8	1.2
Crude fibre	5,6	4.4	5.3	5.2
Starch equivalent . .	92		86	

« It has long been recognised that a certain amount of care must be exercised in feeding stock with cottonseed cake ; from time to time injurious results have been reported, as though the feeding stuffs contained some toxic substance, but the experiences were not consistent, and attempts to isolate a poisonous constituent have not been succesful, although cholin and betain have been found and credited with the harmful action. In practice, farmers have found it wise not to feed cotton cake to milch cows near calving, nor to young stock ».

« A. C. Crawford, after a series of chemical and physiological experiments, now attributes the toxic results to salts of pyrophosphoric acid, the compounds being in some meals inorganic, in others probably organic. Seed of Upland cotton is more generally poisonous than that of Sea Island cotton, although the latter becomes toxic if it is heated in the process of extracting the oil, due to the conversion of ortho- into pyro-phosphates ».

----

(1) Cp. with: Feeding Experiments with Soy Bean Cake, *Journ. of the Board of Agriculture*, Dec. 1909, vol. XVI, No. 9, abstracted in *The Science and Practice of Farming during* 1910 *in Great Britain.* Int. Institute of Agriculture, Rome, 1910, p. 426.   (*Ed.*).

J. MACKINTOSH. **First Report on the Cost of Food in the Pro-**   1808
duction of Milk in the Counties of Kent and Surrey. — *The Jour-*
nal of the South Eastern Agricultural College, Wye, Kent, No. 19,
1910, pp. 35-54, London and Ashford, Kent.

During the winters 1908-9-10 the Wye College conducted an
inquiry into the feeding of dairy cows in the counties of Kent and
Surrey. The main object of the inquiry was to obtain information
regarding the cost of food in the commercial production of milk.

The following prices per ton were used in all the calculations.   Great
Mangels and Swedes 10 s.; Turnips 8 s.; Hay 60 s.; Oat Straw 40 s.   **Britain:**
Barley Straw 25 s.   **England:**
        Kent

Home-produced meals were taken at the estimates given by the
farmers, and purchased meals and cakes at market price.

The lowest cost of food per gallon of milk was 3.83 d. the
highest 10.54 d.; the average cost (from 59 farms) 6.58 d.

The lowest cost per cow per day during the first week of May
was 7.8 d.; the highest 24.1 d.; the average (from 66 farms and
2097 cows) 14.88 d..

The lowest daily yield per cow was 1.37 gallons; the highest
3.41 gallons; the next highest 2.88 gallons; the average daily yield
from 60 farms and 1957 cows) was 2.24 gallons.

As to the relation of daily yield of milk per cow to cost of
production, it was seen that the cost of food per cow per day is
lowest where the cost of food per gallon is highest, and both of
these are associated with the lowest daily yield per cow. On the
other hand, where the daily yield per cow is highest it is found
that the cost of food per cow per day is also highest, and the
cost per gallon of milk lowest.

The cost of food per gallon of milk decreases steadily as the
daily yield increases, but apparently the milk from the farms where
the daily yield per cow averages over 2.5 gals. is not produced at
an appreciably cheaper rate than the milk on the farms where the
daily yield per cow averaged from 2.35 to 2.50 gals.

The cost of the ration fed to the cow is a factor of relatively
greater importance in influencing the cost of production than is the
daily yield of the cow.

As to the relation of quantity of food to cost of production
the following general conclusions were arrived at: The chief factors
contributing to a high cost of food per gallon of milk are:

a) The use of an excessive amount of long hay. Where more
than 15 lbs. is fed per day it would materially reduce the cost to
replace half of it by oat straw; and the change would have little

or no effect on the daily yield of milk. The more extensive use of chopped or chaffed hay would also tend towards economy.

b) The use of an excessive amount of roots ; 40 to 70 lbs. of mangels per day to milking cows is a sufficient and satisfactory quantity.

1809 St. Wojciechowski. **On the Relative Valuation of Forages according to Prof. Kellner's Table**. (Ueber relative Wertbestimmung des Futters nach Prof. O. Kellners Tabelle I.) (1). *Fühling's Landw. Ztg.* 66, 48, H. pp. 265-282. Stuttgart, 15 April, 1911.

Russia : If the production value of 100 kgs. of a unit of forage be V;
Poland the production value of 1 kg. of digestible albuminoid (A D) be x; the production value of 1 kg. of starch value (VA) be y, (x and y being expressed in the same units as V) ; if a be a coefficient indicating how many kgs. of AD are contained in 100 kgs. of forage; b another coefficient indicating the same thing for VA, both a and b being taken from Prof. Kellner's Table I, the writer calculates the following general algebraic formula for the production value of 100 kgs. of given forage :

$$V = ax + by \dots$$

The writer draws the following deductions from the analytical development of this equation :

1. The maximum value of production of 100 kgs. of a given forage is equivalent to double its effective production value.

2. In the case of forages in which the ratio AD : VA differs; no real scale of values exists; or rather there is a scale of special values for each value V', V'', $V''' \dots V^n$.

3. Equivalent amounts of forages having the same ratio AD : VA are in inverse proportion to their content in AD and VA respectively.

4. On the other hand, the production values of 100 kgs of forages having the same ratio AD : VA are directly proportional to the content in AD and VA respectively.

The writer applies the above formula to two practical examples.

---

(1) O. Kellner, *Die Ernährung der landw. Nutztiere. Tab. I. Zusammensetzung. Verdaulichkeit, u. Stärkewert der Futtermittel.* Fünfte Auflage. Berlin, 1909.   (*Ed.*).

N. W. **Dairying and the Silo.** — *California Cultivator.* Los Angeles, March 2, 1911.

1810

In the Eastern States where dairying is more prevalent than it is in the Central West one very seldom finds a farm on which there is not a silo. This is due to the fact that the experience of practical dairy farmers, as well as experiments carried on by the experiment stations, prove conclusively that milk and butter fat can be produced more profitably where a portion of the ration consists of properly made maize silage than on any other ration that can be produced. The increasing value of farm lands in the maize belt indicates that dairy farming will be much more prevalent in the future than it has been in the past. As this condition gradually comes about, silos and alfalfa will spring up on every farm. No combination of factors is more conducive to prosperity, wealth, fertile farms, and good homes than that of well-bred dairy cattle, capacious silos and productive alfalfa fields.

United States

N. HANSSON. **Comparative Feeding-Value of the Dry Matter of Different Roots.** (Hat die Trockensubstanz verschiedener Futterrüben denselben Futterwert?) — *Fühling's Landw. Zeitung,* J. 66, H 9, pp. 297-313. Stuttgart, 1 Mai, 1911.

1811

It is generally reckoned that 10 kgs. (22 lbs.) of mangolds, carrots, and turnips, and 12 kgs. (26 ½ lbs.) of swedes form one nutritive unit. At the same time the great variability in water content (1) has made some other basis desirable ; the use of the content in dry matter as the basis rests on thorough experiments carried out at the Royal Veterinary and Agricultural School at Copenhagen. As, however these experiments were made on pigs, it was desirable to try them also on cows.

Denmark Sweden

The writer analysed six varieties of mangolds, two of turnips, two of swedes, and two of carrots; he carried out the trials simultaneously at two farms and on twenty groups of animals.

In general, the figures adopted in Sweden were confirmed, viz. 1 feeding-value unit (*Futtereinheit*), *i. e.* 1.1 kg. of the dry matter of roots, = 3 kg. of milk.

Further :

---

(1) Cf. *The Science and Practice of Farming in 1910* in *Great Britain,* p. 248. Int. Inst. of Agric., 1910.   (*Ed.*).

1) The dry matter of different roots has essentially the same composition, except in sugar content.

2) In mangolds, turnips, and swedes the content of digestible nitrogenous matter is 0.4 to 0.5 %.

3) The difference in the roots fed showed no influence on the fatty content of the milk.

4) The differences of live-weight due to the differences in the dry matter of the different roots are so small as to be negligible.

5) As the different roots also cause no difference in the yield of milk, the same nutritive value may be attributed to the dry matter of all the ordinary roots.

The experiments were controlled by one in which sugar-beet slices were used.

1812

A. STUTZER. **The Loss of Nutritive Matter in the Ensilage of Potatoes.** (Beobachtung über den Verlust an Nährstoffen beim Einsäuren von Kartoffeln), — *Fühling's Landw. Ztg.*, 60 J., 7 H., pp. 239-241, Stuttgart, 1. April, 1911.

Germany:
Prussia

The writer notes that there are few data available on the loss of nutritive matter due to the ensilage of potatoes. In 1910 he made some enquiries and analyses on a large estate in East Prussia equipped with a distillery.

Whilst no appreciable loss was observed in steamed potatoes, except a smaller proportion of starch, the ensilaged potatoes lost 11.8 % in all and 25 % of their non-nitrogenous extractive matter. The following calories were obtained in relation to the dry matter:

Untreated potatoes	4361 calories.
Steamed 〃	4031 〃
Steamed and ensilaged potatoes .	4154 〃

In view of these results, which require further confirmation, the author questions whether it would not be advisable to dry part of the potatoes intended as fattening foods.

1818

Alfalfa Meal as a Feeding Stuff. — *Hay Trade Journal*, No. 46. Canajoharie, N. Y. May 12, 1911,

United
States

Within the past few years considerable alfalfa hay has been ground into a meal and offered as a substitute for grain for horses, cattle, sheep, swine and poultry. Though sometimes sold on the market just as it is ground, it is more commonly mixed with molasses, corn chop, wheat screenings, chaff, weed seeds, or other waste products.

The advantage of alfalfa meal lies in the fact that it is fed with less waste than hay and has a higher percentage of protein than ordinary hay. It is in a convenient form for special purposes, snch as city trade, and there is a considerable reduction of freight charges when shipped to a distance; but a pound of alfalfa hay does not contain any more nutrient when ground into rreal than it did before, and for home consumption it is doubtful if the advantages are enough to pay for the grinding.

The value of alfalfa meal has been widely advertised, and many expensive plants have been installed for the purpose of grinding alfalfa hay to meal. This is an expensive operation and it is doubtful whether the benefit derived from it justifies the purchaser in paying the increased price of the ground material.

F. T. SHUTT. **Wheat Straw at Different Periods of Growth.** — See Abstract 1641 in this *Bulletin.*

1814

A. GOUIN. **Pea-Nut Oil Cake as a Food for Cattle.** (Le Tourteau d'Arachides dans l'alimentation des bovidés). *Journal d'Agric. Pratique,* 75 année. No. 25, p. 779-790, Paris. 22 Juin, 1911.

1815

The writer discusses the figures given by Mr. E. Poher (1) in his table of the quantities of oil-cake to be given to cattle, and thinks the amounts excessive. In his opinion pea-nut oil-cake should be reserved for breeding animals and milch cows, and even then not more than from 1 to 2 kgs. a day should be given. He also emphasises the fact that pea-nuts contain very little lime, and that the phosphoric acid in this seed is contained in combinations of much less importance for nourishing bone-making tissues than phosphate of lime (2).

France

(1) See Abstr. 1459, this *Bulletin,* May, 1911.

(2) The mineral content of the pea-nut (*Arachis hypogaea*) barely equals on an average half that of other Leguminosae. TH. DIETRICH & J. KÖNIG, *Zusammensetzung, u. Verdaulichkeit der Futtermittel,* p. 977. Berlin, 1891. (*Ed.*).

13

1816   CH. BRIOUX. **Essence of Mustard in the Oil-cakes of Cruciferous Plants.** (Essence de moutarde des tourteaux de Crucifères). — *Annales de la Science Agronomique*, 28 An. No. 3, pp. 323-337, Paris. Avril et Mai, 1911.

The factory by-products supplied to agriculture by cruciferous plants are utilised in two ways. The oil-cakes of native colza and rape seed are used as a food for cattle, those of foreign or Indian

France   colza, camelina, cole-seed (*ravison*), white mustard and black mustard are used as manures, as their strong odour and bitter taste and the fact that, when steeped with water, they produce in fairly high proportions a poisonous essence, essence of mustard, makes them unfit for fodder.

This essence of mustard is produced by the action, in the presence of water, of a soluble ferment, myrosine, on a saline glucoside, myronate of potash. This myronate is specially plentiful in black mustard seed (*Brassica nigra*) and Sarepta mustard (*B. juncea*). The separation of this body is determined by the temperature at which it is steeped; the best is about 37° C. and the essence ceases to be produced at about 70° C, owing to the myrosine coagulating without affecting the myronate.

As a result, oil-cakes manufactured by a hot process are much less likely to cause accidents than those made by cold processes, for the essence forms very rapidly in those prepared by the cold method, as is shown by the following table:

	Duration of Steeping and Percentage of Essence							
	1 hour	2 h.	3 h.	5 h.	7 h.	15 h.	20 h.	24 h.
	grams	gr.	gr.	gr.	gr.	gr.	gr.	gr.
Oil-cakes prepared by cold process . .	0.376	0.311	—	—	—	—	—	—
Oil-cakes prepared by hot process . .	0.081	0.118	0.171	0.217	0.316	0.373	0.420	0.411

Mr. Moussu's experiments show the very poisonous nature of this essence, 2 gr. of which, per 100 kgs of live weight, are enough to produce rapid poisoning.

Oil-cakes of native colza and rape seed, free from black mustard or foreign colza seed, are not generally poisonous in the quantities in which they are usually consumed.

Cases of poisoning, which always occur when a new supply of oil-cake is first taken into use, can be avoided by observing the following precaution :

1. Each time that a new supply of colza oil-cake is purchased only give it in a dry condition, after crushing and mixing with other food.

2. Begin to give it *in small quantities,* starting with from 300 to 400 grams per day for adult cattle, then increase the quantity gradually till an ordinary ration is reached. In case of intestinal irritation stop giving the oil-cake.

A more radical method is to treat the oil-cake with boiling water, as it causes decomposition of the myrosine and this prevents the formation of the essence.

The ordinary quantity of colza and rape seed oil-cake fed to milch cows is 1 kg. or at most 1.5 kg.; in the case of animals which are fattening the ration can be raised to 2.5 or 3 kgs., but gradually, and the health of the animal should be watched.

It is advisable not to give, colza oil-cake uninterruptedly.

The writer proposes to replace the old method of analysis, based on the oxydation by bromine of the products of the distillation of oil-cake infusion by that of determination by means of the silver reaction, which he has found accurate, rapid and simple

L. PALMAS. **General Remarks on the Microscopic Analysis of Oil-cakes**. (Considérations générales sur l'analyse microscopique des tourteaux). — *Annales de Gembloux,* 21 à 41, pp. 184-200, Fgs. 12, Bruxelles, 1st Avril, 1911,   1817

The purpose of this work is, 1) to describe the internal morphology of seeds employed in making the oil-cakes commonly used in Belgium ; 2) to propose a method of investigation preferable to that now in use in the recognized laboratories and the analytical laboratories of the State,   Belgidm

Morphological study implies :

1) Examination of a transverse section of the spermoderm ;

2) Examination of a transverse section of the albumen and the cotyledons.

3) Examination of a horizontal projection of the constituent parts of the spermoderm, the albumen and the cotyledons.

This last enquiry shows the general graphic construction of the oil-cake.

The seeds studied were: *Cocos nucifera, Papaver somniferum, Sinapis nigra. Sinapis alba, Sinapis arvensis, Brassica napus oleifera, Camelina sativa, Arachis hypogaea, Linum usitatissimum, Ricinus communis, Gossypium* spec., *Sesamum indicum.*

The method of investigation proposed comprises the following processes:

1. Making an average sample of the oil-cake and then taking from it a weight of 2 grammes;

2. Passing this test sample through a silk sieve;

3. Examining the sample thus sifted for the presence of starch and mineral matter;

4. Treating the unsifted portion with 100 cc. of a cold solution of caustic potash at 1 %, in a glass beaker;

5. Bringing to boiling point after stirring well with a glass rod;

6. As soon as the mixture boils, pour it all into a conical shaped vessel containing a certain quantity of cold water. Stir with a glass rod. Let the mixture settle, decant. Wash it several times with cold water, In these conditions the fragments of the spermoderms. which generally are alone characteristic, and the fragments of albumen or dense cotyledons. settle at the bottom of the vessel;

7. Take from this sediment the test sample for analysis. Mount it in glycerlne. Crush with the rounded back of a pair of microscopic tweezers so as to break up and cleave the parts under observation; place it on a slide;

8. Examine this final preparation magnified to 97 and 390 diameters.

If a general examination at 97 diameters shows spermodermic fragments not properly clarified by the potassic treatment above described, a new preparation should be made, with 2 grammes of the oil-cake added to 100 cc. of a solution of caustic potash at 10 % to be boiled slowly for 5 or 10 minutes.

1818   HENNET. **British Exports of Horses and Breeding Stock**. (Grossbritanniens Ausfuhr an Pferden und Zuchtvieh), — *Mitteilungen der Fachberichterstätter des k. k. Ackerbauministeriums*, N. 13, pp. 103-104, Vienna, 1911.

Great Britain   The importance of British exports of horses and breeding stock is due not so much to the quantity, as to the high price fetched by the animals exported for cross-breeding abroad. At the Liverpool exhibition 50 000 frcs. (£ 2 000) was paid for a bull.

The exportation of horses is the most important. In 1910, 59 150 were exported for a value of £ 1 294 238. Of this total, 30 206 (1) went to Belgium, 19 957 to Holland. 2354 to France, and 6633 to other countries. This exportation alarmed the Government which proposes to give awards so as to keep the best specimens from leaving the country.

In 1910, 3482 bulls were exported, valued at £ 170 893; 1701 of these went to the United States, 684 to Argentina, 212 to Canada, 179 to Uruguay, 97 to Australia, and 599 to other countries.

The number of pedigree sheep exported rose to 7839 head, valued at £ 62 558. Of this total, 3811 went to Canada. The United States imported twice as many as the preceding year, and Argentina only half. Germany came next with 675 head.

Besides these, 851 pigs were exported.

NYLANDER, **Native Cattle in Finland**. (Das einheimische Rindvieh Finlands). — *Deutsche landw. Presse*. N. 31, pp. 370-371, Berlin, 19, April 1911.

1819

The white, hornless cattle of Finland are of the same stock as the Swedish *Fjäll* breed, and those of North Russia and Norway.

The spotted hornless breed of Finland, the *Zoros* breed of Norway also belong to a common stock, as do the Swedish breed of Gotland, and the brown breed of the South.

Russian Empire: Finland

These three breeds are affected by the general, local influence of climate and diet. The cattle are small, ungainly, but hardy and inexpensive to keep, and very susceptible of improvement.

The cows yield a good supply of milk for 20 years.

---

(1) The high figures for horses exported to Belgium and Holland are due to old and diseased draught horses which are sold off in England. This accounts for their low price per head. Negotiations are going on between the three Governments concerned to put a stop to this exportation., as a result of the active agitation carried on by the British Society for the Protection of Animals

On the traffic of decrepit horses to the Continent, See *The Science and Practice of Farming during 1910 in Great Britain*. Intern. Inst. of Agric. Rome, 1910, p. 452. (*Ed.*).

By putting the cattle out to graze for three or four weeks in the spring they recover from the deplorable condition to which they are reduced during the winter months, and fatten well.

The Finnish cattle are already crossed, expecially in the south, with Holstein, Friesland, and Ayrshire cattle.

The Government is now trying to improve the cattle by selecting the native breed and crossing them with the Ayrshire. Over 300 000 frcs. have been distributed in awards for this purpose during the past 5 years.

The West Finland cattle are chiefly met with in West and North Tavastland, North Satakunta, in Finland proper and in the North of Nyland. Their colour is dun, sometimes fawn. When fattened, the animals weigh as much as 320 to 400 kgs. (700 to 880 lb.). The horns are short and curved forwards. A cow yields, on an average, 2000 litres (440 gals) of milk per year.

The East Finland breed is common in the greater part of East Finland, in Karelen, Savolax, Central Finland and Kajana. These animals are duncoloured but their backs are white. A cow weighs from 300 to 350 kgs. (660 to 770 lbs.), and yields an average of 2000 litres (440 gals) of milk per year.

The North Finland breed. It is mostly white with black or brown ears and sometimes its sides are spotted, it is found in the more northerly parts. The cows are not more than 112 cms. (44 inches) in height. But they yield on an average 2500 litres (550 gals) of milk a year.

1820   **Cattle and Dairying in the Punjab.** (*Civil and Military Gazette*). — *The Indian Agriculturist*, No. 4, pp. 115-116. Calcutta, April 1, 1911.

British
India:
Punjab

During the past twenty years in the Punjab the great canal colonies have come into existence, irrigation from the older canals has expanded, and the pressure of population has brought under the plough large areas of formerly uncultivated land. The cultivated area in the Punjab has grown from 35 000 to 44 000 square miles, the percentage of this area receiving irrigation has increased from 30 to 41, the number of wells has risen from 240 000 to 280 000, and the population has increased by several millions. To a great extent therefore large parts of the Punjab have been transformed from pasture to arable land. These changes necessarily introduced profound modifications in the conditions of cattle supply. While on the one hand there was a great increase in the number of bullocks required to work the ploughs and the wells, and in the number of cows to provide milk for the growing population, expanding cultivation meant diminishing grazing grounds, while in addition, at the worst of the transition period, the country for a series of years suffered severely from drought, so that even the grazing grounds normally available were largely curtailed.

The experiment recently undertaken by the Deputy Commissioner of Montgomery of leasing land for breeding depôts for cows of the Sahiwal type is one that should be watched with interest, and the grant of lands on special terms for a similar purpose might well be kept in view when distributing the area to be irrigated by the new canals.

There can be no doubt that the milk supply to the Indian population of towns and cities is unsatisfactory.

To encourage stock-breeding the extension of the Civil Veterinary department is urged. It is also recommended that attention should be paid to sheep-breeding both for wool and *ghi*; and that goats, though less important, should not be neglected.

Cattle Raising in Chiriqui, Panama. — *Bulletin of the Pan-American Union.* pp. 643-651. Washington, April 1911.

1821

The province of Chiriqui, lying on the Pacific side of the Continental Divide, is admirably adapted for cattle raising. The land is covered by light forest which may be cleared with the *machete*. At intervals this growth gives place to level expanses of grass-covered *llano*. The prevailing herbage of the *llanos* is *jenjebrillo*, which bears a close resemblance to the famous " blue grass " of Kentucky (1).

Panama:
Chiriqui

The region is abundantly watered. Stock raising is the principal industry of Chiriqui and there are in the province more cattle than in all the rest of the Republic's territory. There can not be more than 50 000 head, all told, in Panama, although there is land in the Republic that would sustain 5 000 000 head of cattle.

There is no better country for economical cattle raising. One acre of its *potrerò* will fatten a steer, whereas 3 acres of the western grazing land in the United States are required to support one.

---

(1) Cf. A. N. M. ALPINE: *Poa compressa* L.; much like *P. pratensis*, and is suited to poor sandy soil. R. P. WRIGHT, *Standard Cyclopedia of Modern Agriculture*, vol. 2, p. 164, 1909.   (*Ed.*).

A *potrero* is a fattening ground, made by clearing away the natural growth, save for a few shade trees, and, after burning over, planting in the several kinds of fodder plants suitable to the soils.

Cattle can be raised in Chiriqui, and *potreros* maintained, at any elevation between sea level and 4 500 feet above it.

The price of fatted steers is steadily rising, stimulated by a protective tax imposed by the Government. Cattle are raised in Chiriqui at a cost of slightly more than 1 dollar per head per annum, and it is quite evident that this figure could be reduced by 20 per cent. On a fenced ranch the stock need hardly any attention. One man, with intermittent help, will look after 1 000 head.

1822   BIEBER. **Stock-Breeding in Kafa, Abyssinia** (Jagd. Fischerei und Viehzucht bei den Kaffitscho). — *Deutsche Rundschau für Geographie.* 7 Heft. Vienna, 1911,

Stock-breeding and agriculture are the chief sources of wealth in Kafa, where the natives raise cattle, sheep, goats, horses, donkeys and poultry.

Abyssinia   The cattle belong to the zebu variety, which is bred for its m lk, butter, meat and hides. The sheep are of the breed known as Fat-rumped breed (*Ovis. Aries*, var. *steatopyga*); they are very large and fat. The same is true of the goats. The horses, of average size, resemble Arab horses.

The fowls are small and lay but few eggs, which the natives never eat. Each native keeps on an average from 30 to 100 head of cattle but owners of 1000 head of cattle are not rare. The cattle are kept and fed in the meadows all the year round.

The only mode of fattening resorted to is that of not working the best cattle. The pasture lands are neither cared for nor improved. Oxen are only used for ploughing, horses for riding and asses and mules as pack-beasts. Milk is used solely for making butter. An ox hide can be purchased for about 3 shilliugs, a goat skin for 9*d.* Leather bottles are made with the sheep-skins.

Live-stock is abundant and cheap:

an ox costs from 14*s.* to 25*s.* 6*d.*
a sheep   »   10*d.* to 4*s.*
a mule   »   67*s.* to 147*s.*
a fowl only costs 1 ½*d.*

Civets (*wonge, Viverra civetta*) are bred on a large scale, but only the males are kept; as the females do not yield the product utilised in perfumery and tobacco factories.

E. H. RILEY. **A Note on Zebra Hybrid Breeding.** — *U. S. Dept.*   1823
of Agric., XXVI Annual Report of the Bureau of Animal In-
dustry, pp. 229-232. Washington, 1911.

Attempts to obtain Zebra hybrids have been made for several
years at the Experiment Station of the U. S. Bureau of Animal   United
Industry.   States
  A male Grévy's Zebra (*Equus Grevyi*) from the National Zoological Park was used. He was placed with five mares, four of
them pedigree Percherons, the other of a rather heavy carriage type.
But the zebra took no notice of them.
  A large Kentucky jennet and four burro jennets were then
substituted for the mares ; after eight months the zebra mated with
one of the burros, and since then there has been no difficulty in
getting a service.
  Attempts to impregnate the mares artificially were also made;
in only one case was success obtained, and then the mare aborted
after four months. Further attempts will be made, and for this
purpose several more zebras have been obtained from Abyssinia.
  The zebra-ass hybrids have been more successful: six colts and
five fillies have been obtained. The period of gestation averaged
378 days.
  These hybrids show an improvement over both parents in
action, conformation and disposition. The sire weighed 800 lbs. and
was 13 ½ hands high ; the dams averaged 550 lbs. and 12 hands.
The hybrids averaged 48 lbs. at birth; at one year two of them
averaged 500 lbs. and 12 hands. They have good action and a
neat and clean-cut appearance ; they are as easily handled as horse
foals of the same age.
  Their fertility will be tested *inter se* and with horse, zebra,
and ass.

E. MASCHERONI. **Friuli Cattle** (I bovini Friulani). — *Il Corriere dei*   1824
Macelli. Anno II, N. 2. pp. 15-20. Palermo, 1911.

  The Province of Friuli holds the first place in Italy for the
improvement of the breed of cattle. In the north of Friuli the
cattle belong to a breed of the Carnian Alp and of Slavia. The Italian   Italy:
Slavia variety is not distinguished by a single and constant   Friuli
type. In the west, and even on the south-western slopes of
the province the gray breed (similar to that of Belluno) predominates, but is constantly decreasing ; nevertheless, nearly 3/4 of the

cattle of the central, southern, and south-western parts of Friuli
are of the red piebald variety (Jurassic variety).

In 1870 the oxen of the plains of Friuli belonged to the
specialised type of draft cattle, tallish, strongly built, with powerful
muscles. Here are some measurements :

	Cow	Ox	Bull
Average height at withers	4.49 ft.	5.08 ft.	4.92 ft.
Girth, behind shoulder	6.16 »	7.21 »	6.56 »
Length of back	3.44 »	3.77 »	3.61 »
Average live weight (butchers' beasts)	8.55 cwt.	11.4 cwt.	13.3 cwt.

The dead weight is about 50 % of the live weight.

In 1878 Simmenthal cattle began to be crossed with the local
breed ; good results were obtained and they continued to be imported
regularly. The present breed was thus obtained; it is characterised
by an improvement in shape, by a change in the colour of the
coat from yellowish (*froment*) to red piebald, and by the higher yield
of the animals. They unite, better than any other Italian breed, the
three qualities of aptitude for work, high production of meat, and
of milk.

There are about 250 co-operative dairies in the Province of
Udine, of which more than 100 use the milk of the Simmenthal-
Friuli cows, representing about one half of the milk produced in
the province, which is valued at about 7 000 000 frs. (£. 280 000)
a year.

These cattle are generally fattened in from 2 to 3 months, beginning with an extra ration of maize waste, sorghum, or bran, or less
frequently with oil-cake, of which from 2 to 3 kgs. (4 ½ to 6 ½ lbs.)
are given per day, to begin with, increasing to as much as from 8
to 9 kgs. (17 ½ to 20 ½ lbs.) by the end of the period of fattening.

Oxen are fattened when about 5 years old, cows when from 9
to 10 years old. As a rule, fattening is not continued until the
animal is thoroughly fat, as in practice it is found more profitable
in these districts to stop fattening somewhat sooner.

About 70 000 calves are exported each year from the province'
valued at nearly 12 million frcs. (£. 480 000). They are sent more
especially into Tuscany and Emilia, where they are fattened. They
then weigh from 13 to 16 cwt. at 2 to 3 years of age, and about
19 cwt. at 4 years of age, and their net yield in meat is from 60
to 63 %.

This article is illustrated.

NICOLAU ATHANASOF. **Brazilian Caracù Cattle**. (Estudo sobre o gado   1825
Caracù). — *Secretaria des Negocios da Agricultura, Commercio e
Obras Publicas do Estado de Sao Paulo. Relatorio apresentado ao
Exmo. Snr. Dr. Antonio de Padua Salles*. In 8°, pp. LV 153. 1910.

The cattle of the State of S. Paul are classified by breeders
into two breeds: one is called the " Legitimate Caracù ", " *Caracù
Legitimo,* " the other simply " Caracù " The writer considers that
the first named descend from the Aquitanian breed, through the
Portuguese Minhota and Alemtejana ; it is characterised by remark-   Brazil:
St. Paul
able size, by strong, pointed horns, by the light colour of the
nostrils, muzzle and mouth, by the light coloured hair of the head,
and by a yellowish coat. The second kind are connected with
the Iberian breed, and are characterised by the black or black
spotted colour of the muzzle, and by a black tail, head, orbits,
nostrils and lips. Both breeds of Caracù cattle grow slowly, but
their meat is excellent. They are well suited for fattening. The
writer obtained an average daily increase of 787 grammes per head,
feeding them on poor forage and a little good hay. The average
live weight is as follows:

                    2 year heifers . . . . . 2.85 to 7.6 cwt.
                    2 year oxen . . . . . . 7.6 » 8.55 »
                    2 year cows and over . 8.55 » 9.5 »
                    2 year bulls and over . 11.4 » 14.25 »

The net yield of meat is from 50 to 55 %.
The yield of milk is low, generally from 5 to 6 litres per day
during the period of abundant lactation, and about 2 litres towards
the end of this period. The milk is, however, very rich, containing from 5.5 to 6 % of fat. Oxen are used in field work from 4 to
12 or 15 years old ; but it would be better to slaughter them some
years earlier.
The most noticeable feature of these cattle is their capacity for
work, for which they are admirably suited by their heavy build,
vigorous muscles, and great hardiness.
Careful selection and more especially better feeding would greatly
increase their strength ; for instance, instead of breeding these animals
entirely in the open they might be raised in stables or at least
some shelter might be provided for them.
Though they are very hardy, the Caracù cattle are not exempt
from disease: anthrax, (*manquiera*) foot and mouth disease, introduced into Brazil in 1895, scouring in calves, rickets, are the most

common diseases. Much harm is also done by the *Ripicephalus an-nulatus* (garrapatas) (1), an insect of the *Ixodiae* family, which is the principal agent in transmitting *Pyroplasmosis* (*tristeza*).

1826   **Sheep-Dipping Order of 31st March, 1911, in Ireland.** Dublin, 1911.

United Kingdom: Ireland

· This Order of the Department of Agriculture and Technical Instruction for Ireland, dated the 31st. of March 1911, applies to the whole of Ireland, hereinafter referred to as the Dipping Area in which annual dippings of sheep are prescribed. Two dipping periods are prescribed, the " Summer dipping period ", commencing on the 15th. of June and terminating on the 31st. of August, and the " Autumn dipping period " commencing on the 1st. of September and terminating on the 15th. of November. The mode of dipping prescribed is by thorough immersion in a sheep-dip approved by the Department of Agriculture of Ireland for sheep-scab, by the Sheep-scab Order of 1905.

Exceptions to dipping requirements for sheep intended for exhibition, slaughter and other special circumstances are only granted provided a Veterinary Inspector of the Local Authority shall previously have certified after examination and enquiry in to the case, that the sheep are free from disease and that the grounds on which the exemption is sought are satisfactory. Prescriptions are given for the clipping of sheep before dipping, for the isolation of sheep after dipping, for the modalities regulating Declarations and Certificates etc,

1827   S. R. SHERWOOD. **Suffolk Sheep.** *The Journal of the Royal Agricultural Society of England*, vol, LXXI, pp. 64-78 + plate 1. London, 1910.

Great Britain: England

The progenitors of the present Suffolk sheep are stated to be the Norfolk ewe and the Southdown ram. In 1886 the Royal Agricultural Society gave the breed its recognition by establishing separate classes for it at their show. East Anglia is the home of the Suffolk breed.

The hair on the face and legs below the knees and hocks of the Suffolk sheep should be glossy, jet black, fine, and free from

---

(1) See Abstr. No. 1805, in this *Bulletin*, June, 1911.   (*Ed.*).

any coarseness of hair. Breeders are very particular as to this texture and colouring, for it denotes quality and gives a smart thoroughbred appearance. Further, it almost follows that this, one of the most distinctive features of the breed, proves to be associated with sheep having the character of good mothers and milkers, as well as showing them to be animals which, when slaughtered, cut full of lean, juicy flesh.

The " Scale of Points" published by the *Suffolk Sheep Society* is as follows :

Head. — Hornless; Face black and long, and muzzle moderately fine, especially in ewes. (A small quantity of clean white wool on the forehead not objected to). Ears, a medium length, black and fine texture. Eyes, bright and full. . . , ... , ...   25

Neck. — Moderate length and well set. In rams stronger, with a good crest)   5

Shoulder. — Broad and oblique   5

Chest. — Deep and wide . . . . , ...   5

Back and Loin. — Long, level, and well covered with meat and muscle. Tail broad and well set up. The ribs long and well sprung, with a full flank   20

Legs and Feet, — Straight and black, with fine and flat bone. Woolled to knees and hocks, clean below. Fore legs set well apart. Hind legs well filled with mutton   20

Belly (also scrotum of rams). — Well covered with wool   5

Fleece. — Moderately short; close, fine fibre, without tendency to mat or felt together, and well defined, *i. e.* not shading off into dark wool or hair . , ...   10

Skin, soft, and pink colour   5

Total . . .   100

The average percentage of dressed carcass to live weight of wether lambs under 12 months old recorded for the Suffolk entries is 62.91, the average live weight being 141.2 lb. (kg. 59.96) ; the average percentage for wether sheep under 22 months old is 65.35, and the live weight 179 lb. (kg. 80). Further, the Suffolks are mutton producers of the highest quality.

Many Suffolks have been sent to France, Germany, Spain, Italy, Russia, Switzerland, North and South America, Canada, Australia, and South Africa.

The average prices obtained in 1910 were for ram lambs from
£7 12s. 11d. (fcs. 191.15) to £11 7s. 4d. (fcs. 284.15). Much higher
prices have been made previously.

The Suffolk Sheep Society has flock competitions annually, and
every flock is subject to inspection once in four years. This practice has a great tendency to obtain uniformity and also to keep
up a high standard of excellence.

Suffolks cross well with many other pure bred sheep, particu-
arly with Lincolns and Cottswolds, improving the mutton quality of
these long-woolled sheep. They also mate well with South-down
and Cheviot. The Cheviot cross is an excellent one.

The writer concludes that careful in-breeding, with judicious
selection for constitution and stamina, is the fundamental practice
of the successful breeder; and that harm is often done through not
paying enough attention to line-breeding (1).

1828   P. A. PAKHOMOVIM. **Present Status of Sheep-breeding in Russia.**
(Sovrem ennoe Sostoianie Orzevodstva v. Rossii). — *Exegodnik
glavnago Upravleniia semlenstroistva i semledielia po Departamentu semledielia.* (Year-Book of the General Direction of Rural
Organization and Agriculture of the Department of Agriculture),
1909, pp. 472-484. S. Peterburg, 1910.

Sheep breeding in Russia is susceptible of improvement, both
as regards quantity and quality.

There are about 40 million sheep in European Russia, or 40
head of sheep per 100 inhabitants; whereas there are 66 in Eng-

Russia   land, 35 in Denmark, and 1830 in Australia. With the exception
of some million merinos and other selected and improved breeds,
the great mass consists of several stiff-woolled varieties, which may
be classified as follows:

I. *Wool-growing varieties: Ziganskiia and Voloskiia.* — Their
wool is known as " Don wool " and is chiefly used in making army
cloth, characterised by its strength and lustre.

The *Ziganskiia* breed comes from Asia Minor, whence it spread
through Bessarabia and other countries bordering on the Black Sea;

---

(1) See also ROBERT WALLACE, *British Breeds of Sheep* (Board of Ag.
and Fisheries) in *British Breeder of Live Stock*. London, 1910, summarised in
The Science & Practice of Farming in Great Britain, pp. 479-499. Internat. Inst.
of Agric. Rome, 1910.   *(Ed.).*

the average length of the wool is from 3 to 4 cm. and a fleece may weigh as much as 3.20 kg.

The *Voloskiia* breed is found in the Caucasus and along the shores of the Caspian Sea ; the length of the wool varies from 10 to 17 cm. and a fleece weighs about 2.5 kg.

2. *Fur-growing breeds.* — The *Romanovskaia* is only found in the Government of Jaroslav, to which it is restricted by the special nature of the soil. When exported elsewhere it rapidly degenerates, even if the same meteorological conditions prevail. This breed has specialised from that commonly found in the North of Russia, *Ovis brachyura borealisi*; from this thoroughbred breed come the North Russian varieties such as the "*Polinskaia*" (Viatka), and "*Eselskaia*" (Liflandia).

3. *Breeds for Lamb-skin Production.* — *Riescetilovskaia and Socolskaia;* the wool of the first is black, fine and lustrous, the second has brown wool. The fur industry flourishes mostly in the Government of Poltawa, where the *Riescetilovskaia* breed was greatly improved by crossing it with the " Karakul " sheep of Bokhara.

In some of the Caucasian centres of the *Taurida* and the Don, wool-growing breeds are still raised; the " *Electoral-Negretti* " and " *Negretti Rambouillet* " in South-western Russia, and the " *Infantado* ' in the Government of Yekaterinoslav.

But the finest of these wool-growing breeds is undoubtedly the Russian merino sheep of the Black Sea (*Electoral Înfantado*), which besides its high yield of wool (as much as 20 lbs. per clip) supplies excellent meat and good skins. At present over 100 000 sheep of this breed are raised in Siberia, which is destined to become an important sheep-breeding centre.

It should not be supposed that sheep-breeding is possible only with a system of extensive farming. It is equally profitable and possible in countries cultivated intensively; as fallow lands and such bye-products as straw, husks, etc., can thus be put to good use.

If sheep-breeding in Russia is to improve and progress the following points must be attended to :

1) the varieties best suited to given localities and to certain kinds of production must be selected. The *Romanovskaia* variety can be used as the basis for skin producing breeds ; the *Bokhara Karakul* for milk and lamb-skins.

2) Some Russian varieties should be crossed with English meat-producing breeds.

3) Shows should be organized, grazing lands improved, etc.

1829   SCHWARZ. **Breeds of Pigs Suited for Breeding on a Small Scale.**
(Welche Schweinarten eignen sich besonders für den Kleinbesitz?)
— *Arbeiten der Landw.-kammer für die Provinz Pommern.*
XXII Heft, pp. 22. Stettin, 1911.

There were 22 080 008 pigs in Germany in 1907, valued at over
£175 226 893 (3 532 800 280 marks). 10 % of this total was supplied
by wholesale breeders, 45 % by average breeders, and 45 % by
Germany   small breeders.

The German Agricultural Society (*Deutsche Landwirtschafts Gesellschaft*) has classified German pigs into three groups, pure breds,
improved native breeds, and unimproved native breeds. The German White Pure-Bred and Berkshire breeds belong to the first group.

German Whites are descended from crosses between white native pigs and Yorkshires, Lincolnshires and Suffolks. They have lost
the ugly pug-nose of the Yorkshire, and the face is only slightly
dished. This breed requires concentrated food, to realise its remarkable precocity so that it can only be profitably reared where
it can be carefully attended to.

German White pigs require a generous diet during the first
period of growth, after which the breeding stock can be put to
graze. Contrary to the usual practice, this breed should only be
half fattened, as the return decreases as fattening progresses. These
pigs should therefore be kept till 9 or 12 months old, until they
weigh from 120 to 150 kgs. (260 to 330 lbs.). This breed is suited
to places where the market demands meat for immediate consumption, that is to say tender, well-flavoured pork that is not
too fat.

Though the Berkshire breed is rather less prolific than the
German White, it equals it in all other qualities. It occasionally
yields from 85 to 90 % of its live weight in meat. But it is not
much esteemed in Germany, perhaps on account of its black bristles.
A cross with the Meissner breed ought to give good fatting pigs.

The improved native breeds are the product of crossing with
pure-breds. Large sized pigs have thus been obtained, which mature rather slowly, but are very hardy and prolific, and need less
attention than the pure-breds. They are the best grazing breeds,
and are specially suited to localities where the pasture lands are
plentiful and where the market calls for cheap rather than high-
quality pork. The best improved native breeds are the following:
Westphalian improved, Marschschwein, Hannoverian improved, Old-
enburg, Alsener, Holstein, Meissner. This latter is noted for its
fertility.

The unimproved native breeds are constantly making way for the improved ones, and they are rarely found except in their native localities. They can, however, be profitably reared for sausage meat, and are surpassed by none for excellency and ready preservation. It would therefore be desirable to select and cross these native breeds so as to make them more precocious and profitable, rather than to let them disappear. They should not however be over improved, as it is desirable to preserve their local characteristics.

It is therefore not possible to lay down general rules as to the pigs best suited for breeding on a small scale, as in making a selection one must be guided by the locality, the industries carried on there, the kind of farming, and the requirements of the market.

The Growth of Dairy-industries in New Zealand. (Le développement laitier de la Nouvelle Zélande). — *Laiterie et Elevage*, 6e an., p. 95. Louvain, 15 juin, 1911.

1880

New Zealand now possesses 1 773 326 head of cattle, of which 536 629 are milch cows. Mechanical milking apparatus is more and more used.

New Zealand

Butter and cheese are manufactured on a large scale in co-operative dairies which secure an output of a constant and superior quality.

There are 189 butter factories, producing about 475 000 cwt., of which 323 000 are exported ; 191 factories are engaged in cheese-making, producing 437 000 cwt., of which 408 500 are exported.

H. RABILD. **Cow-Testing Associations.** — *U. S. Dep. of Agric. XXVI Annual Report of the Bureau of Animal Industry*, pp. 99-118

1881

The cow-testing movement in connection with dairying originated in Denmark in 1892 and the first co-operative cow-testing association was organized in 1895 on the farm of Soren Peter Knudsen at Lille Skovgaard, Vejen. Another association was organized later during the same year and since then the movement has expanded wonderfully. From Denmark it has spread to other European countries. In 1909 in Denmark 530 such associations existed; in Germany 207 ; in Sweden 662; in Norway 146 ; in Finland 99; in Russia 52; in Scotland 13; figures for the other countries not being available. The primary purpose of the cow-testing movement was

Denmark.
United
States

14

to obtain records of the yearly production of milk and butter from each individual cow in the herds of the members, and with these data as a basis, by the selection of the best producing cows for breeding purposes, to develop a strain of cows which would produce a large quantity of milk rich in butter-fat. Later it was found that to judge the quality of the individuals it was necessary in addition to keep account of the amount of food consumed by each cow, in order to learn which of them utilized the food to the best advantage. Many of these associations do not take into consideration the cost of the feed nor the price of products, but use the feed-unit system for this determination and that cow is considered best which combines the greatest yield of milk per 100 feed units with the largest production of butter-fat. The cow-testing movement in the United States was inaugurated by the writer, and the first association was organized at Fremont, Mich. in 1905 and consisted of 31 members owning 239 cows. In 1910 there were 52 such associations in the Union; 12 of them in Wisconsin, 9 in Vermont, 6 each in Michigan and Maine, 3 each in California, Iowa and Ohio, 2 in Pennsylvania, and one each in Washington, Colorado, Connecticut, Nebraska, New Hampshire, Oregon, New-York, Maryland; while in 1908 only 12 existed.

The United States Department of Agriculture through the Dairy Division of the Bureau of Animal Industry has been largely instrumental in encouraging the inauguration of cow-testing associations in the various dairy States in co-operation with the State authorities. In many States no funds have been available for conducting the work and the Department has furnished the services of an organizer and has supplied blanks and record books free of charge, in the hope that when the value of the work has been demonstrated the States would appropriate sufficient funds to carry it on.

1882   I. M. KRASSER. **Trial Milkings twice a day** (Das Ergebniss täglich zweimäliger Probemelkungen bei sechs Kühen. Ein Beitrag zur Beurteilung Milchfälschungen. *Mitteilung der Landw.-chem. Versuches u. Lebensmitteluntersuchungsanstalt des Landes Vorarlberg in Bregenz).—Zeitschr. für das Landw. Versuchswesen in Oesterreich,* XIV J., H. 4, pp. 711-721, tab. II. Wien, April, 1911.

Austria: Experiments and investigations to determine the contingent
Vorarlberg   variations in trial milking, taken twice a day, at 6 a. m. and 6 p. m., with six cows in different periods of lactation, gave the following results :

1) No appreciable difference was found between morning and evening milk, either as to quantity or quality. In localities such as the Vorarlberg, where the cows are milked twice a day at regular intervals, trials to determine the yield can be made with mixtures of equal parts of morning and evening milk.

2) The daily variations noticed in the quality of the different milkings, as the result of circumstances which are little known, may be such, that, as a rule, it is practically impossible to determine adulteration by means of trial milkings (1).

R. T. HEWLETT, S. VILLAR and C. REVIS. **On the Nature of the Cellular Elements present in Milk**. Part. II. Quantitative and Qualitative Results. Part. III. The Milk of Animals other than the Cow. — *Journal of the British Dairy Farmers' Association* Vol. XXV., pp. 34-75. London, 1911.

1833

A preliminary report (1) of an " Investigation into the Cellular Elements present in Milk " was issued by the writers last year (2).

They have continued and extended their researches and from the results obtained, have come to the following conclusions : " It is difficult to formulate any general conclusion from this survey of the kinds of cells present in different conditions. All that can be said is that in the milk of healthy cows in full milk and which do not give a high cell connt, the majority of cells tend to be of the type termed '· large uni-nuclears " with a small admixture of other cells. At the beginning and end of lactation, or when the cell count is high, the multi-nuclears tend to be the predominant cell, and this is the case whether the high cell count is without discernible cause, or whether a definite mastitis is present. That is to say, a high cell count seems to be due to an increase of the multi-nuclears, and may or may not be associated with mastitis ".

Great Britain

Substituting the word " polymorpho-nuclear leucocyte " for " multi-nuclear cell ", these results are in general in accord with Savage (3) but the writers differ entirely as to the nature and

---

(1) This variation has long been known, See H. RIEVAL : *Handbuch der Milchkunde*, p. 66. Hannover, 1910 ; and A. MOUVOISIN : *Le Lait, son Analyse, son Utilisation*, p. 114, Paris, 1911. (*Ed.*).

(2) Cfr. *The Science and Practice of Farming during 1910 in Great Britain*, pp. 548-549 International Institute of Agriculture, Rome, 1910. (*Ed.*).

(3) *Journal of Hygiene*. 1906, p. 123; *Reports to the Medical Officer, Local Government Board*, 1907 *et seq.*

origin of the actual cellular elements. Even in the deposits from the serous fluid in catarrhal mastitis they do not find the presence of polymorpho-nuclear leucocytes and must conclude that the cells of the deposit are not " pus cells " in the ordinary acceptation. In the writers' opinion *it is not possible to recognise diseased conditions by means of a microscopical examination of the cells present.*

The general consideration of the results obtained investigating the milk of animals other than the cow (ass, goat, human milk) only tends to confirm the conclusions already arrived at. A uniform type of life evidently tends to a fairly uniform excretion of tissue cells from the udder. The effect of outside causes in increasing temporarily this excretion was emphasised also in the case of goats, while some of the samples of human milk showed plainly that very high cell counts are not by any means necessarily connected with any diseased or disordered condition of the mammary gland.

The writers again emphasise the view that in the cow the udder must be looked upon as an organ which has by breeding and selection been brought to an artificial condition of milk secretion and that this has been accompanied by a stimulation of the tissues to cell proliferation, and that this proliferation may quite easily become abnormally great, leading to the appearance of an increased number of cells in the secretion. In support of this view the writers lay great stress on the fact constantly noticed by them, viz, that when the cell count is high for *any* reason the cells themselves are always well-defined, showing little sign of degeneration, and also stain in a much more characteristic and definite manner, a fact which is difficult to explain if they are considered to be blood elements.

1834   **The Composition of Evaporated Milk.** *Food Inspection Decision* N. 131. — *U. S. Dept. of Agr.* Washington, February 27, 1911.

This decision gives the requirements of the U. S. Agric. Department with respect to the manufacture and composition of unsweetened condensed milk.

United States

1) It should be prepared by evaporating the fresh, pure, whole milk of healthy cows, obtained by complete milking and excluding all milkings within 15 days before calving and 7 days after calving, provided that at the end of the 7 day period the animals are in a perfectly normal condition.

2) It should contain such percentages of total solids that the sum of two shall not be less than 34.3, and the percentage of fat shall not be less than 7.8 per cent. This allows a small reduction in total solids with increasing richness of the milk in fat.

3) It should contain no added butter or butter oil incorporated either with whole milk or with the evaporated milk at any stage of manufacture.

A. J. J. VANDEVELDE, **Adulteration of Milk with *Cocoline*.** (La Falsification du lait par la Cocoline). — *Bull. de la Soc. Chim. de Belgique*, 25ᵉ an., N. 3, pp. 135-136. Gand, Mars 1911.

1885

The writer quotes the two following analyses:

1) Milk presenting the appearance of homogenized and pasteurised milk. By coagulation with acetic acid it was possible to separate, with some difficulty, a curd which, after extraction with ether from the mass to which sand was added, and when slowly dried, yielded 28 gr. of fat per litre. On analysis this fat gave the following constants:

Belgium

Index of soluble volatile acids (Leffmann-Beam) 20.7

   »   »   insoluble »   »   (Polenske) . . .   5.7

   »   »   refraction at 40⁰ C. (Abbé-Zeiss) . . .   40.2

   »   »   critical dissolution (Crismer) 45.7

Optical examination (Cesaro) showed crystals of cocoline.

2) Milk presenting the appearance of homogenized and pasteurised milk.

The curd, which formed slowly and with difficulty, yielded after treatment with ether, and heating (*étuve*) 18 gr. of fat with the following constants:

Index of soluble volatile acids (Leffmann-Beam) 22.9

   »   »   refraction at 40⁰ C. (Abbé-Zeiss) . . .   40.8

   »   ▸   critical dissolution (Crismer). 43.7

Optical examination (Cesaro) showed crystals of cocoline.

1886   LARSEN and WHITE, **Milk Powder Starters in Creameries.** — *Agricultural Experiment Station.* Bul. N. 123, p. 1-14. Brookings, South Dakota, Dec. 1910.

Experiments made in South Dakota show the practicability of using milk powder solutions in place of natural milk as a medium for growing starters for buttermaking. In making butter from sour, hand separated cream and in making butter from sweet, fresh cream the milk powder starter has produced the same good flavor as natural milk starter, so that the one may replace the other in practical creamery work.

United
States:
S. Dakota

The cost of the milk powder is greater than that of natural milk under normal creamery conditions, but the location of many big central plants in large cities makes conditions such that an ample supply of good milk cannot be obtained at the usual price. It is under these or similar conditions that milk powder has its value for starter-making (1).

1887   J. R. MOHLER, H. J. WASHBURN and L. A. ROGERS. **The Viability of Tubercle Bacilli in Butter and Cheese.** — *U. S. Dep. of Agr. XXVI Annual Report of the Bureau of Animal Industry,* pp. 179-191. Washington, 1911.

As a result of the various experiments made by the Dairy and Pathological divisions of the U. S. Bureau of Animal Industry, evidence has been obtained that constant storage in an icy temperature does not destroy the dangerous tubercle bacilli which may be contained in butter. The application of the tuberculin test to all cows that supply milk for butter-making purposes, with the subsequent removal of all tuberculous animals from the dairy herds is desirable, but where this can not be done recourse may be had to pasteurization, as it has been found that subjecting cream to a temperature of 140° F. (60° C.) for a period of twenty minutes or of 176° F. (80° C.) momentarily will effectually destroy all of the

United
States

(1) In South Dakota dairy industries are of great importance. There were in the State, in 1910, 656 000 milch cows, besides 1 341 000 other cattle. The chief manufacturing industries of South Dakota are the making of butter, cheese and condensed milk, and flour and grist milling. The dairy-work output is calculated at $ 2 182 653. *The Statesman's Year-book for* 1911, p. 521.

(*Ed.*).

tubercle bacilli present. Moreover the manufacture of butter out of pasteurized cream has the· advantages of increasing the keeping capacity of the butter and of improving the quality. No dependence should be placed upon the action of the salt that is added to butter as an agent in the destruction of tubercle bacilli. Evidence was obtained that the bacillus of tuberculosis retains its virulence also in cheese for a considerable period of time.

The removal from dairy herds of all tuberculous animals cannot therefore be too strongly urged.

HENNET. **Swiss Cheese Exports in 1910** (1). (Der Käseexport der Schweiz im Jahre 1910). — *Mitteilungen der Fachberichterstatter des k. k. Ackerbauministeriums*, N. 7, p. 53. Wien, 1911.

1838

In 1910, 597 282 cwt. of cheese were exported from Switzerland, for a value of £ 2 496 900 showing an increase of 1 546 cwt. over 1909 (2).

Switzerland

The countries which import most cheese from Switzerland are France, the United States, and Germany. Exports to Italy, on the other hand, have notably declined, as Italy is more and more supplying her own demand for dairy products. The exports of condensed milk continue increasing.

Prices have risen, which somewhat compensates the Swiss cheese industry for the competition of Italian cheeses in the South of France and Austria.

Neufchâtel Cheese. French and American Methods of Manufacture. — *U. S. Department of Agriculture, Farmers' Bulletin*, 435 - *Experiment Station Work*, LXII, pp. 24 (21-24). Washington, March 17, 1911.

1839

The soft-curd rennet cheese known as Neufchâtel, made extensively in the Department of Seine Inférieure, France, from cow's milk, either whole or skimmed, has become very popular in the United States, where the process of manufacture has been considerably

France.
United
States

---

(1) See also this *Bulletin* January 1911, Abstr. 226.

(2) The total value of Swiss animal food exports in 1909 was 93 764 667 frs; in 1910 it amounted to 100 051 562. *The Statesman's Year-Book for 1911* p. 1261· (*Ed.*).

changed, so that as now made it represents a different type and is ready for use as soon as made, whereas the French variety is allowed to ripen for several weeks.

The French method of manufacture is as follows: Fresh milk is set at 85° F. (29.4° C.) with sufficient rennet to cause a thorough coagulation in 24 to 36 hours. The curd is then placed in cheese cloth bags and allowed to drain for some 12 to 24 hours. The draining is assisted by the application of light pressure. When the curd is dry enough, it is pressed into cylindrical shapes 1 ³/₄ by 3 inches (4 ½ by 7 ½ cm.) and salted from the outside. It is then allowed to drain for several hours and is placed in a ripening room where in a few weeks it becomes covered with white and blue mould. The cheese is then placed in a cellar for further ripening and when spots appear on the outside it is wrapped in paper and tinfoil and marketed.

The American method of manufacture is as follows: Fresh sweet milk is heated to 165° F. (77° C.) for 10 minutes and then cooled immediately to 72° F. (22.2° C.) Until very recently, the milk used was not pasteurized, but the great difficulty in securing reliable milk together with the advantages of pasteurization and the use of a commercial starter, have made the heating method very popular.

In large factories the cheese is made in large vats, but on the farm it can be made in smaller quantities in shot-gun cans holding about 30 pounds (13.6 kg.) of milk ; after the milk is cooled to 72° F. (22.2° C.), a small amount of commercial starter is added and enough rennet to ensure a thorough coagulation in 18 hours.

Usually about 1 cubic centimeter of commercial starter and ½ cubic centimeter of rennet extract is sufficient to 30 pounds (13.6 kg.) of milk if the temperature is mantained at 72° F. (22.2° C.). As soon as the milk is firmly coagulated it is placed on a cotton covered strainer rack or in cotton bags to drain. The acidity of the exuding whey at this time should be not over 0.3 per cent or the flavour of the cheese will be too acid.

The draining process requires several hours and should be kept up until all free whey has escaped. Light pressure, such as can be obtained in a small cheese press, aids materially in expelling the whey. During the draining process the curd on the outer surface of the strainer should be stirred occasionally to ensure even drying. As soon as the curd is sufficiently dry, salt is added at the rate of 2½ ounces to 10 pounds (14 gr. to 1 kg.) of curd. At this time the acidity of the whey should be not over 0.5 per cent. The cheese should then be

(1) North Carolina Station. *Bulletin* 210,

pressed for a short time to expel excess of whey. It is then kneaded by hand and finally pressed into small cylindrical shapes 1 $^1/_4$ by 2 $^3/_4$ inches (3.1 by 6.9 cm.), weighing $\frac{1}{4}$ pound (113 gr.) each. These are wrapped in parchment paper and tinfoil, and are then ready for market.

J. Michels (1) states that American methods of making Neufchâtel cheese are unsatisfactory because they are too slow, the souring process is not properly controlled, with a consequent lack of uniformity of product, and the product is not properly packed. He suggests a method of procedure which he found was not subject to these objections: 1000 pounds (4 $\frac{1}{2}$ quintals) of milk containing 4 per cent of fat will yield 34 eight-ounce (226 $\frac{1}{2}$ grams) tumblers of cheese.

When such milk is re-enforced with cream as suggested by Prof. Michels, 1000 pounds (4 $\frac{1}{2}$ quintals) of it will yield 38 eight-ounce tumblers of cheese. A price of 10 cents (52 centimes) per tumbler net, will yield a good return to the producer and furnish the consumer a wholesome food at a very reasonable cost.

G. SQUADRINI. **Returns at the Modena Slaughter-house.** (Il rendimento di macellazione dei bovini abbattuti nel macello di Modena). — *Il Corriere dei Macelli*, Anno II, N. 3, p. 32. Palermo, Aprile 1911.

1840

In order to compare the net returns from the slaughter of the breed of cattle from the Modena lowlands and that of cattle of other breeds, the writer, who is the manager of the Modena Slaughterhouse, registered the live weight and the net weight of all the cattle killed there during the year 1910.

Italy: Modena

These figures show again that the Modena lowland breed is superior, in net returns, to the Modena mountain breed : they also show the former is surpassed, in net returns, only by the Bologna, Romagnole and Friuli breeds.

The Modena breed has smaller bones, as is shown by the following table:

Reggio . . . . . . ox 20 % bone
Mantua and Bologna . » 19 % »
Modena . . . . . . » 16.5 % »
Servia . . . . . . » 15.5 % ›

The results in the tables prepared by Dr. Ferrarini in 1902 show that the Modena breed gave for that year:

For fat	oxen a return of			57.3 %
For half-fat	»	»	»	51.4 %
For lean	»	»	»	49.6 %
For fat	cows	»	»	51.2 %
For half-fat	»	»	»	48.7 %
For lean	»	»	»	40.4 %

In 1910 these figures were surpassed: the net returns from fat oxen reached 66 % ; the average returns for cows, 54.6 % ; and the maximum return for fat cows, 65.3 %.

These figures show the progress made in the province of Modena in stock breeding and the prospects of a diligent and continuous selection of the local breed.

1841   **Prevention of Damage to Hides, Skins and Wool.** — *Board of Agriculture and Fisheries, Leaflet,* No. 246. London, March, 1911.

Warble-Fly (1). — One of the most destructive insect pests in Great Britain is the Warble Fly, which is injurious to the living animal, to the hide and to the meat. Various estimates have been made of the loss caused by this pest, but there are no reliable data on which an opinion can be formed. The Board of Agriculture was recently informed that in the case of a tannery, 30 per cent. of the hides dealt with in one year were damaged by Warble Fly ; but in another case only 7.5 per cent. were damaged.

Great Britain

The best method of destroying the maggots is to extract them when „ ripe " by squeezing the warbles with both thumbs and squashing them under foot.

If the practice of destroying the maggots be systematically followed, it must result in an appreciable reduction in the number of adult flies. The method has been tested in the course of some experiments carried out, for the Irish Department of Agriculture and Technical Instruction, by Messrs. Carpenter and Steen, and

(1) Warble Flies, *Hypoderma lineata* and *H. bovis*. (*Board of Agriculture and Fisheries, Leaflet* No. 21, Sept. 1894; Revised, July 1905. London).

(*Ed.*).

seemed to result in a substantial local reduction in the prevalence of the fly.

The use of strong-smelling dressings was recommended, with the idea of deterring the flies from laying their eggs. But Ostertag has stated that such dressings are not efficacious.

Damage to Hides owing to Dirty Condition of Animal. — This spoils the hair and makes the grain of the hide tender, with the result that the quality of the leather is depreciated.

Tar Branding of sheep must be done when the sheep are in the early stages of growth of the fleece, as only in this case the marking material becomes nearly worn off by the time the fleece comes to maturity. When tar and paint marks have to be clipped off by the wool-sorter, the loss in this way is about 1 oz. (28 gr.) per fleece.

Various Parasites and Dips. — The injury due to the parasite causing sheep-scab (1) is well-known. Keds (2), ticks (3) and lice as well as the maggot of the sheep maggot-fly, also cause serious injury.

Broadly speaking, sheep dips are more or less effective against the first three of these parasites. For the destruction of keds, two dippings at intervals of 3 weeks are necessary; for ticks, arsenical dips appear to give the most satisfactory results; while any dip which is suitable for sheep-scab is effective also against lice.

Dipping is also useful against the larvae of the sheep maggot-fly (4), but is not permanently effective in preventing the flies from egg-laying or " striking ".

Dips must be used at the proper strength, as at a greater strength they cause injury to the wool and skin.

Flaying. Hides and skins are often removed in a defective manner, the result being a lowering of their value. In Ireland a number of demonstrations of the most approved methods of flaying hides were given in 1908-9 by an expert flayer at the principal centres of the fresh meat trade and of the tanning industry in Ireland.

---

(1) *Dermatodectes ovis*, or *Psoroptes communis* (Acarina) (Board of Agric. and Fish.-Leaflet No. 61, November 1899; Revised, August, 1906, London.

(2) *Melophagus ovinus* (Diptera).

(3) *Ixodes ricinus* and *Haemaphysalis punctata* (Acarina). (Ibid. Leaflet No. 145, July, 1905. Revised July, 1908. London).

(4) *Lucilia sericata* (Ibid. Leaflet No. 126, February, 1905. London).

(*Ed.*).

1842   FULFORD. **Camel and Goat's Wool of Tien-Tsin**. See Abstract No. 1734 in this *Bulletin*.

1843   **Keeping Poultry Free of Lice.** — *Poultry Success*, vol. XXII, No. 3, pp. 26-27. Springfield, Ohio, March, 1911.

United
States:
Ohio,
Maine

Experience has shown that the best way to rid poultry of lice is by the use of a dusting powder to be worked into the feathers, following up a first application of powder with a second at an interval of 4 days to a week. If the birds are badly infested at the beginning it may be necessary to make still a third application. The lice powder experimented with very good results at the Maine Agricultural Experiment Station, Orono, Maine is made by incorporating the liquid mixture of 5 parts of gasoline (1), 1 part of crude carbolic acid 90-95 per cent strength, or if the 90-95 per cent strength crude carbolic acid cannot be obtained, the mixture of

3 parts of gasoline
- 1 part of creosol

in sufficient plaster of Paris to take up all the liquid.

To free the cracks and crevices of wood-work from lice and vermin a liquid spray or paint is the most desirable form of application.

1844   L. E. RICE and C. NIXON. **Seven Methods of Feeding Young Chickens.** — *New York Cornell Station Bulletin*, 282, pp. 415-452, figs. 25. *E. S. R.*, Washington, March 1911.

United
States:
New York

The purpose of this experiment was to test the efficiency of chick rearing by 7 different kinds of ration and methods of feeding. The eggs used were from vigorous mature single comb white Leghorn stock on free range. The methods of incubating and brooding are described.

---

(1) Gazoline is a colourless, volatile, inflammable product of the distillation of crude petroleum.

(*Ed.*).

The cost of rearing the different flocks of chicks for the first six weeks is given in the following table :

Average gain and cost of feeding chicks the first
6 weeks by different methods.

RATION	Number of chicks in experiment	Number of chicks at end of 6 weeks	Average weight of chicks at 6 weeks. —— Pounds
Cracked grain and bran	110	90	0.370
Cracked grain	110	85	0.375
Cracked grain dry mash	110	97	0.343
Dry mash	110	94	0.345
Wet mash powdered milk	110	106	0.542
Wet mash skim milk	110	102	0.511
Variety ration	110	110	0.503

Total amount of food consumed —— Pounds	Cost per pound gain.	Cost of food per 100 chicks	Cost of labour per 100 chicks.
129.73	$ 0.160	$ 2.940	$ 1.423
125.88	» 0.173	» 3.228	» 1.507
166.13	» 0.193	» 3.589	» 1.320
167.56	» 0.196	» 3.608	» 1.362
193.91	» 0.115	» 3.805	» 1.505
232.93	» 0.123	» 3.725	» 1.565
196.57	» 0.117	» 3.571	» 1.464

Considering the number of chicks reared, the vigour of the chicks and the continued palatableness of the ration the variety ration gave best results for the first 6 weeks. In total weight of flock, average weight of chicks, rapid growth and development, cost per pound gain and per pound weight, the wet mash powdered milk ration gave best results.

In feeding the wet mash rations and the variety ration, great care must be taken that the chicks are not over-fed and that they do not get spoiled or mouldy food. After the first 3 weeks there is less danger of overfeeding on the variety ration. At the end of 6 weeks all flocks were gradually accustomed to a fattening ration and the results are shown in the following table:

Summary per flock for 6 weeks of fattening.

RATION	Number in fattening experiments	Number died in 6 weeks	Average weight chicks marketed	Total amount of food consumed	Total cost of food consumed	Total cost of labour	Total cost per pound gain
			lbs.	lbs.	$	$	$
Cracked grain and bran	90	2	1.093	250.8	5.58	1.21	0.108
Cracked grain	85	2	1.204	243.1	3.38	1.21	0.097
Cracked grain dry mash	97	4	1.153	261.4	5.83	1.21	0.094
Dry mash	94	7	1.114	260.8	5.86	1.21	0.109
Wet mash powdered milk.	107	2	1.204	280.6	6.21	1.22	0.107
Wet mash skim milk.	102	4	1.137	271.4	5.82	1.22	0.118
Variety ration	110	3	1.139	286.5	6.32	1.21	0.113

The cost of rearing a chick to 6 weeks averaged $ 0.098 for all flocks or $ 9.80 per 100 chicks. The average total cost per pound of gain in the fattening experiment was $ 0.106.

1845   **Poultry Industry in Great Britain and Ireland.** — *Nature*, London, March 23, 1911.

Great Britain and Ireland

The Journal of the National Poultry Organization Society, N. 1, vol. V, mentions that considerable progress has been made, during the last 12 months, in the organization of this industry. Mr. Brown estimates, in fact, that Great Britain produces now a value of £ 5 000 000 per year more eggs and poultry than 15 years ago.

Great progress has been made, especially in Ireland, where it is estimated at present that the production is proportionally greater than in any other country.

Nevertheless, Wales and Scotland are only now becoming aware of the share they can have in this industry. The supply of cheap foreign eggs, apparently can not be relied upon to continue indefinitely and an increase in the production of Great Britain will certainly prevent a scarcity.

F. B. NASMYTH-MILLER. **The Irish Poultry Industry.** — *The Illustrated Poultry Record.* Vol. III, N. 8, pp. 341-345. London, May, 1911.

1846

Poultry-keeping has made a steady advance in Ireland during recent years.

Ireland now occupies the premier position as supplier of eggs and poultry to Great Britain, the total value of the export being estimated at £3 720 497 for 1909. Adding to this the value of feathers exported, amounting to £32 968, a total value of £3 753 465 is reached. During the past 20 years the trade in poultry products has more than doubled itself. The following figures show the quantity and value of eggs, poultry and feathers exported for the years 1904 and 1909:

United Kingdom: Ireland

	Eggs Great Hundred (1)	Value	Poultry Cwt.	Value	Feathers Cwt.	Value
		£		£		£
1904 . .	5 738 129	2 044 208	278 553	779 948	12 153	36 459
1909 . .	6 362 714	2 863 221	306 170	857 276	15 457	32 968

It is probable that in 1910 the value of the imports into Great Britain of poultry from Ireland exceeded that of the imports from all other countries combined.

In 1900 the Department of Agriculture put into operation a scheme for encouraging improvement in the poultry-keeping industry. Provisions were made under this scheme for the establishment of egg-distribution stations (of which there are now 619), of turkey stations (532 in 1910) and of egg-distribution stations for geese (140 in 1910).

___

(1) Great Hundred = 120 eggs.

In 1905 a supplemental scheme entitled " Tutorial and Practical Classes in Poultry-Keeping " was introduced. The programme
of work in connection with these classes may be briefly stated as
follows : The instructor remains at a given centre for 2, 3 or 4
weeks as the case may be and holds one class daily of not less
than 2 hours' duration. The instruction is essentially o a practical nature and is followed by practical work in which the pupils
take part.

White Wyandotte, White Leghorns and Barred Plymouth Rock
are the chief breeds of poultry kept; the Indian Runner is the
chief breed of ducks.

At the Department's Poultry Fattening Station at Avondale,
Rathdrum, County Wicklow, training is afforded to young men who
wish to qualify in this work. The breeding of poultry also receives
special consideration at most of the Department's instititutions,
notably at the Albert Agricultural College, Glasnevin ; the Munster
Institute, Cork; at the Ulster Dairy School, Cookstown. The two
last-named establishments are the chief training centres for women
desirous of qualifying as instructors in poultry-keeping and dairying.
A model Poultry Farm was established in 1902 at Cullybackey,
under the Antrim County Council, with the following objects : (1)
Providing poultry-keepers in County Antrim with a practical means
of studying improved methods of poultry-keeping ; (2) supplying
hatching eggs and stock birds of pure breeds of poultry ; and (3)
producing first-class laying strains of fowls. Its efforts havebe en
rewarded with considerable success.

1847   **Poultry-Keeping in the French and Belgian Colonies.** (Geflügelzucht in
den französischen und belgischen Kolonien). — *Landw. Umschau,*
3 J., N. 26, pp. 639-640. Magdeburg, 30 Juni, 1911.

Without a doubt, England ranks first among the nations that
have striven to encourage poultry-keeping these last few years, but
France and Belgium come soon after.

**French
Colonies.
Belgian
Congo**

In the French colonies of Tonking, Annam, Cochin-China, Dahomey and Guinea, poultry-breeding has become a good source of
income in many districts. Types, very productive of eggs and
furnishing also a good quality of meat, have been obtained by crossing the native races with the French Houdan, Mantes and Bresse
breeds. Lately, many incubators have been introduced and the
methods of breeding have been perfected more and more.

In Indo-China, the breeding of ducks has reached a high standard and the dried meat is sent in enormous quantities to China.

The crossing of native breeds with those of Rouen and Peking has given very satisfactory results.

The French Agricultural Ministry furthers the progress of this agricultural industry in every possible way, by instituting experimental Stations and by furnishing breeders with specimens of pure breeds, etc.

In Belgian Congo, till recently, there was only one native type of fowl: brown, small and producing but a small quantity of eggs (50-60 per year). At present this type has been very much improved by crossing and selection. The following breeds were imported from Belgium and have become well acclimatized :

Campines, known for its production of eggs, and Coucou de Malines which can be fattened easily.

Importation of Eggs in Great Britain. (L'importation des Œufs en Grande-Bretagne). — *L'Agriculture commerciale*, N. 6, p. 128. Paris, 26 Mars, 1911.

1848

Importation of eggs into Great Britain has increased very considerably : the figures for 1910 are : 18 344 137 cases of 120 eggs, value £7 296 145 (183 000 000 fr.) which shows an increase of 633 696 cases (76 043 540 eggs) over 1909.

Great Britain

It is distributed among the different countries as follows :

Imported from	Importation of cases of 120 eggs	Value £	Per cent of each country
Russia	9 217 586	3 282 194	50.25 %
Denmark	3 647 139	1 732 107	19.90 »
Germany	507 307	200 860	2.77 »
France	907 599	417 545	4.96 »
Italy	746 841	350 238	4.07 »
Austria Hungary. .	1 370 121	555 998	7.47 »
Canada	1 860	1 097	0.01 »

These figures show a marked increase for Russia. Denmark and Austria Hungary show a slight increase. Importations from other countries have diminished.

The price of eggs has been going up constantly since 1898, in which year a case of eggs sold for about 5s.10d. (7.36 fr.) whereas it cost 8s. (10.10 fr.) in 1910.

1849

Exportation of Eggs from Bulgaria. (Bulgariens Eier Export). — *Das Handels Museum*, N. 21, p. 327. Wien, 25. Mai, 1911.

Bulgaria

The value of eggs exported from Bulgaria amounted to 8 846 028 frs. in 1910, as against 9 211 646 frs in 1909. The following were the export figures for preceeding years: 1908, 7 297 461 frs, about half of which represented the value of exports to Germany ; in 1906, 10 648 810 frs, of which about 6 millions worth were exported to Germany. It was only in 1905 that about 6 million frs. worth of Bulgarian eggs were imported into Austria, out of a total exportation valued at 9 112 678 frcs. As a rule Germany is Bulgaria's best client for eggs.

1850

Trade in Plover's Eggs. (1) — *The Agricultural Record*, N. 896, vol. 39, p. 145. London, June 1911.

Great Britain

Mr. C. Bathurst has called the attention of the Home Secretary to a trade which is rapidy developing in the eggs of the peewit, or lapwing (*Vanellus cristatus*). It is stated that American agriculturists are buying them in large quantities because of the usefulness of the birds in destroying wireworms, and various insects destructive of roots, cereal crops and pasture. The Gloucestershire County Council have obtained an order to protect the birds and their eggs for 5 years.

1851

Uruguayan Ostrich Feathers. — *Journal of the Royal Society of Arts*, N. 3052, p. 711. London, May 19, 1911.

Uruguay

The feather industry is of considerable importance in Uruguay. The native ostrich or *nandu* of Uruguay (2) is smaller than that of Africa.

A still smaller species is found in Patagonia (3), and seems to range much further north; each male has five cr six females with him, and they generally keep together in flocks of fifteen to thirty. These are found roaming throughout the open country of Uruguay. The average height is five feet, and the weight 80 to 100 lbs. each.

---

(1) See also : *The Science and Practice of Farming during 1910 in Great Britain*, p. 594. Rome, International Institute of Agriculture, 1910. (*Ed.*).

(2) *Rhea americana*. (3) *R. Darwini*. KNOWLTON: *Birds of the World*, edited by RIDGWAY, pp. 67-69. (*Ed.*).

To secure the feathers, which have become an important article of export, the birds, at the time the plumage is full, are driven into previously arranged nets and their feathers pulled out. The majority of the feathers are very fine, sometimes equalling, and even excelling, the African in quality, but smaller. To increase the size three feathers are joined together.

Some years ago there were nearly 100 000 native ostriches in Uruguay, but this number has recently fallen off, owing to the migration of the ostriches to Argentina.

CASTELLOTTI. **The Improvement of Silk-growing in Italy.** (Pel miglioramento della Sericoltura Italiana). — *Bollettino di Sericoltura*, N. 19, p. 184. Milano, 13 Maggio 1911.

1852

A greater spread of improved methods in all the silk-growing provinces of Italy would so much increase the yield and reduce the expenses, that competition with foreign silk could be entertained and the crisis in silk-growing would thereby be prevented.

Italy: Lombardy

Experiments were made at Piacenza and Cremona, in several places, and under favourable conditions, with eggs of hybrid Chinese silkworms ; the results were compared with those from ordinary eggs grown on the Italian peasants' system. The lots were dried in the same apparatus.

The averages of ten trials were as follows :

	Improved culture	Ordinary culture
Double cocoons	4.3 %	8.2 %
Weight of cocoons per oz. (1) of eggs . . .	72 kg.	45 kg.
Dry crude silk in cocoons	34 %	30 %
Finished silk per kg. of dry crude silk . . .	332 grams	287 grams
Yield of finished silk per oz. of eggs . . .	8.127 kg.	3.874 kg.
Floss-silk (" bourre ") in cocoons	14.12 %	27.75 %

It appears that improved cultivation would give more than double the present yield of silk in Italy ; so that the cultivator could sell his cocoons at a lower price and yet realize a good profit, whilst the spinners would be able to compete with Asiatic products.

---

(1) The " oncia " used for silkworm eggs is 30 gms.; the English ounce is 28.3 gms.　　　　　　　　　　　　　　　　　　　(*Ed.*).

1853   **Silk-worm Breeding in Croatia-Slavonia.** (La Sericoltura nella Croa-
zia-Slavonia). Italian Consular Report. — *Bollettino del Ministero di Agricoltura, Industria e Commercio.* Serie B., Fasc. 9.
pp. 285-286. Roma, 1º maggio, 1911.

In 1910 there were in Croatia about 10 000 cultivators of the
silk-worm; from about 7 000 ounces of eggs (ounce = 30 gr.) they
obtained a product of 546 000 lbs. (248 000 kg.) of cocoons.

Hungary:
Croatia-
Slavonia

The eggs come from the province of Ascoli and from Brianza in
Italy. There is a tendency for silk-worm nurseries to develop
more in the districts of Sirmio, Posségha and Virovilica, especially
since the abolition of the monopoly of silk-worm breeding which
in the preceding years was held by a Hungarian Company and two
Croatian banks.

For the past two years, the Croatian cocoons have appeared on
the Milan market, where they are distinguished for the elasticity
of their thread.

A spinning mill will soon be put into operation at Posszéga.

1854   **The World's Output of Artificial Silk.** (Die Weltproduktion von
Kunstseide). — *Das Handelsmuseum,* N. 14, p. 124. Wien,
6 April, 1911.

Austria

The output of artificial silk for the whole world now amounts
annually to about 5 ½ million kgs. Of this, Germany produces
about one third, valued at 24 000 000 marks. More artificial silk
is, however, imported into Germany than exported.

1855   **Apiculture at the Trappist Convent at Maristella, S. Paulo, Brazil.**
(A apicultura na Trappa de Maristella). (Taubaté. S. Paulo). —
Characas e Quintaes, Vol. III, N. 3, pp. 35-36. S. Paulo, Brasil,
Marzo, 1911.

Brazil:
S. Paulo

The Trappist convent of Our Lady of Maristella, the most ancient in South America, is noted for the excellency of the crops it
raises and for the spirit of initiative which animates its members in
agricultural matters.

For some years past the most scientific systems of apiculture
have been adopted. In spite of many drawbacks, the number of hives
has increased from 4 in 1906 to 300 in 1910. These hives are of
a special kind, based on the method of Layens; they are horizontal

and divided into two sections, one measuring 16 inches for the brood, the other measuring 8 in. for storing the honey ; these two sections are divided by a perforated cloth, and some openings are arranged so as to ensure good ventilation. The size is such as to be adequate even in the busiest period.

Excellent results are thus obtained, due not only to the flora of the vicinity, and to the kind of hive used, but also to the good organization of the apiary.

Act for the Protection of certain Insectivorous and other Wild Birds in Natal. — *The Natal Agricultural Journal*, Vol. XV., N. 7, pp. 72-73. Pietermaritzburg, January, 1911.

1856

Act N. 33, 1896. For the Protection of certain Insectivorous and other Wild Birds in Natal.

British
S. Africa:
Natal

1. No person shall kill, catch, shoot at, or attempt to kill, catch, or aid in killing, catching or shooting at any of the birds specified in the schedule to this Act, and no person shall at any time take, injure, or destroy the eggs of any of the said birds except by express permission of the Governor for the purpose of scientific research.

2. It shall be lawful for the Governor in Council to add to the list of birds specified in the schedule to this Act the names of any others which it may be deemed desirable to protect. The official sanction of such addition to be published in the Natal Government Gazette.

3. Any person contravening any of the provisions of this Act shall, upon conviction, forfeit a sum not less than half-a-crown and not exceeding £ 1 sterling, and in default of payment thereof shall be imprisoned with or without hard labour for a period not exceeding one month.

Schedule

Locust-bird (large) (1)
Locust-bird (small) (2)
Tick-bird (red-beak) (3)
Swallows (all varieties)
Wagtail (4)
White Stork (5)

(1) Locust bird = *Glareola melanoptera* (F. H. KNOWLTON-R. RIDGWAY, *Birds of the World*. Westminster, 1909).

(2) Small Locust Bird, a Grackle = *Creatophora carunculata* (L. N. GILL, etc. in I. K. FUNK, *A Standard Dictionary of the English Language*, p. 1045, London, 1910).

(3) Tickbird = *Buphaga erythrorhyncha* (KNOWLTON-RIDGWAY, *l. c.* p. 790;

(4) Wagtails = *Motacilla* spp. (KNOWLTON-RIDGWAY, *l. c.* p. 651).

(5) White stork = *Ciconia ciconia* (*l. c.* p. 154).   (*Ed.*).

1857

Development of Pisciculture in Hungary (Hebung der Fischzucht in Ungarn). — *Oesterreichische Fisherei Zeitung*, No. 8, p. 134. Wien, 15. April 1911.

Hungary

The Hungarian Government spares no efforts to develop ˙pisciculture and thus mitigate the rise in the price of food and of meat in particular. ˙A decree of the Department of Agriculture grants substantial financial subsidies to all the communes, and to private persons interested˙ in pisciculture. Many Societies have already been formed and many fish ponds which had been abandoned have been restocked from fishery reservations.

Excursions have been organized to visit the important modern establishments for pisciculture abroad.

1858

A New Government Institution for Salmon Breeding in Sweden. (Eine neue staatliche Anstalt für Salmonidenzucht in Schweden). *Deutsche Landwirtschaftliche Presse*, No. 27, pp: 323-324. Berlin, 5. April 1911.

Sweden

A Government station for salmon-breeding will shortly be opened in Sweden on the Wättern Lake, where the water is very good and clear and attains a depth of 126 metres.

Particular attention will be given to the breeding of a variety known as the " Wättern Salmon ", which is a very fine .variety of lake trout. The Government will stock this lake each year with several million eggs of the salmon and of the " Coregon " salmon.

As Sweden already has ponds for breeding carp at Anedoba and another for trout at Engelsberg, the station on the Wättern Lake will be used exclusively for breeding the fish of the country.

1859

Expansion in Alaska Salmon Packing Industry. — *The Canner and Dried Fruit Packer*, N. 14, pp. 44-46. Chicago, April 13, 1911.

United States: Alaska

The salmon canning industry of Alaska will undergo a high expansion during the coming season as the result of the marked increase in the number of canneries and the extension of the facilities of many of the older ones. A survey of the field at the present time indicates that eleven new canneries will be installed this spring with a possible total of fourteen or fifteen different lines of machinery which, with a great supply of fish, may increase the pack by 400 000 cases.

Most of the new canneries are being erected in South Eastern Alaska. In Central and Western Alaska and Bristol Bay, the best locations have long ago been well taken up, as the streams and protected harbours are few and far between and the good fishing grounds fewer.

Agricultural Industries.

The Wine Trade in Mexico and South America. (Le Commerce des vins dans les différents états de l'Amérique Latine). — *Bulletin de l'Office du Gouvernement Général de l'Algérie*, N. 10, pp. 150-153. Paris, 15 Mai, 1911.

1860

Mexico. — Mexico is a large consumer of wines and liqueurs, most of which are imported from Europe. The total imports of foreign wines entered at the port of Acapulco, in 1909, were valued at about 42 000 frs., namely:

Mexico
Guatemala
Costa Rica
Panama
Honduras
Columbia
Venezuela
Ecuador
Chile
Argentina
Paraguay
Uruguay
Brazil
S. Domingo
Hayti
Cuba

14 400	from	Spain
14 000	»	France
4 135	»	Germany
2 822	»	United States
1 277	»	England
643	»	Holland

Guatemala. — The following quantities of wine were imported nto Guatemala :

175 645	frs. worth from			France
88 873	»	»	»	Spain
54 075	»	»	»	United States
46 195	»	»	»	Germany
25 724	»	»	»	Italy
31 698	»	»	»	other countries.

Costa Rica. — The total wine imported into Costa Rica was valued at about 444 000 frs., contr.buted as follows:

France	150 915 frs.
Germany	54 100 »
Italy	50 454 »
United States	7 627 »

Panama. — In 1909 the port of Colon entered :

150 828 frs.	worth of wine from					France
85 716 »	»	»	»	»	»	Spain
44 753 »	»	»	»	»	»	Germany
10 433 »	»	»	»	»	»	Italy
6 380 »	»	»	»	»	»	England.

Honduras. — The future of the wine-trade in Honduras is in the hands of the Californian producers.

Columbia. — About 700 000 gallons (gallon = 3.78 litres) of foreign wines were imported into Columbia. The Columbians prefer European wines.

Venezuela. — The total value of wines imported through the port of Guaira amounted to about 914 418 frs. of which Spain sent 445 433 and Germany 196 333.

Ecuador. — In 1909 Ecuador imported 2 717 119 frs worth of wine ; the United States share was insignificant.

Chile. — Chile itself produces a considerable quantity of wine. The value of the wines imported into Chile, in 1909, amounted to 696 037 frs. None came from the United States.

Argentina. — The preference is given in Argentina to a wine produced by blending the native Mendoza wines with 25 % of French, Spanish or Italian wine.

Paraguay. — The wines imported into Paraguay come mostly from Italy, Spain, Germany and France. In 1909 only 1 138 010 frs. worth of wine was imported.

Uruguay. — Although Uruguay produces wine to some considerable extent, large quantities of Spanish, Portuguese, Italian and French wines are imported into this country.

Brazil. — Though the State of Rio Grande produces a large quantity of wine, most of that drunk in Brazil comes from abroad.

The wine trade with Brazil fluctuates between 36 and 40 million francs. Portugal is the largest exporter, followed by Italy and then by France.

St. Domingo. — Of 66 000 frs. worth of wine imported at Puerto Plata, only 1 600 frcs. came from the United States, and the remainder came, in order of importance, from France, Spain and Italy.

Haiti. — As the result of a commercial treaty with France, little except French wine is drunk in Haiti.

Cuba. — Notwithstanding a preferential tariff in favour of Californian wines, most of the wine drunk in Cuba comes from France, Italy, Germany and Spain.

The opening of the Panama canal is likely to reduce by 50 % the cost of carriage of Californian wines.

Japanese Wines (Les vins du Japon). — *L'Agriculture Commerciale,* N. 11, pp. 279-280. Paris, 11 Juin, 1911.

1861

The alcoholic drinks of Japan are *saké*, made from fermented rice, (10° to 14° of alcohol). *shoku*, also prepared from rice, at 20° alcohol, and a liqueur called *mirin.*

Japan

The vine is cultivated in Japan and has succeeded to some extent; but as the native grapes are very inferior to foreign ones, the best varieties of American and European vines have been planted. There are already in Japan some vine growers who produce red, white, and sparkling wines, but their flavour is disagreable to the palate. The only wines which have any importance on the Japanese market are European, of which 220 000 gals. were imported in 1909, half of which came from France, and most of the remainder from Spain.

Phosphoric Acid and the Quality of Wine. (L'Acide phosphorique et la qualité des Vins). — *Journal d'Agriculture pratique,,* 75ᵉ année, Tome I, n. 14, p. 443. Paris, 6 Avril, 1911.

1862

Mr. A Müntz was the first to express the opinion that the superior quality of wine is proportionate to its content of nitrogenous matter and phosphates, and that this is not perhaps without effect on some of those organoleptic qualities which make such a difference in the prices of wines.

France

Mr. G. Paturel, who has tried, since 1901, to verify the accuracy of this relationship, has observed that the average richness of the

wines of the Beaujolais-Mâçonnais in phosphoric acid declines from
the 1st to the 4th quality, following the order of the quality and commercial value of the wines, whatever may have been the prevailing
quality of the year's vintage.

The average content of wines in phosphoric acid differs very
much from one year to another, (for instance 0.308 gr. per litre in
1906, a good year, and 0.150 gr. in 1905, a poor year), which still
further confirms the views of Mr. Müntz.

Mr. Pasturel concludes that the best test of the quality of a
wine is supplied by determining its phosphoric content, which affords analytical data of a much more reliable kind than those supplied by its alcoholic strength (1).

_____

(1) This opinion agrees with that expressed by Weirich and Ortlieb in
their study of the Greek wines of Thyre in the Cyclades, which contained in
all as much as 900 milligrammes per litre of phosphoric pentoxide, of which
about 350 milligrammes were in organic combination.

Since 1895 many studies have been made in Italy on the phosphoric
compounds in wine, and on the total amount of $P_2 O_5$ they contain. A. FU-
NARO and G. BARBONI found, in 1904, that Tuscan wines contained a maximum of 434 milligrammes of $P_2 O_5$ per litre; of which only 55 mgr. were in
organic combination. As a rule, red wines are richer than white wines in
organic phosphorus.

Until recently it was thought that the main organic compound in wines
was lecithine, similar to that existing in eggs and milk.

But the investigations made by A. FUNARO and A. RASTELLI show that
wines do not contain lecithine but glycero-phosphoric acid derived from lecithine, which is really present in the grape must.

MARCO SOAVE, when studying the Piedmontese wines, in 1906, demonstrated the presence of an organic phosphorated compound (already discovered by Posternak in many vegetable substances), which on decomposing is
thought to produce inosite, a special saccharine compound found in muscular
flesh, but which is also present in very small quantities in wine.

See: A. FUNARO and G. BARBONI, _Sulla lecitina nei vini_. Le Staz. sper.
agr. ital. vol. 37, 1904, p. 881.

A. FUNARO and A. RASTELLI, _Sullo stato di combinazione organica del
Fosforo nei vini_, Id. id. vol. 39, 1906, p. 35.

MARCO SOAVE. _Sul Fosforo organico nei vini_. Id. id. vol. 39, 1906, p. 438.
(_Ed._).

L. Roos. **Utilisation of currants in Greece. " Blutwein ''.** (Utilisa-   1863
tion des Raisins secs en Grèce. Le Blutwein). — *Annales des*
Falsifications, 4ᵉ Année, N. 29, pp. 113-126. Paris-Genève,
Mars, 1911.

This is a description of the organization resulting from the
Agreement of July 8, 1905, between the Greek Government, the
Vine-Growers's Bank of Greece, and the Bank of Athens to promote
the production and trade in currants. This agreement led to the
formation of the Privileged Company for the Protection of Currant   Greece
Production and Trade, which utilises the currants supplied either
from the tax in kind which amount to 35 % of the currants crop,
or from its purchases. These currants are so utilised as to prevent
them from competing with the trade in currants.

The Greek Company for Wines and Spirits, founded on the
initiative of the Privileged Company, prepares from these currants:
 1) fine flavoured alcohol for exportation ;
 2) denatured alcohol ;
 3) jellies, sweets, syrups, grape-sugar;
 4) wine.

33 000 tons of currants are consumed in the distillation of alcohol, of which 2 320 000 gals. are produced.

The Greek Company has succeeded, by able propaganda, in
considerably increasing the industrial uses to which alcohol is applied,
especially for illumination, for which purpose it has been adopted
by several municipalities for street lighting. Currants denatured
with salt are imported into Italy for the distillation of alcohol.
From 950 to 1410 tons of currants are used in the manufacture of
grape sugar, for the preparation of a popular sweetmeat made of a
mixture of this sugar with crushed sesame seeds. Lastly, these two
Companies purchase a certain quantity of fresh currants from which
they make wine, thus deflecting from their normal use a certain
quantity of currants.

These wines are more profitable to the Greek Wine and Spirit
C.º than the dried currants would be, as they are much preferred by
the foreign market. At present wine made from dried currants is
only prepared:
 1) in small quantities, as a cheap wine exported to Malta,
Turkey, and Egypt;
 2) for raisin syrup, exported to England where it is duty
free. A branch of the Company in London ferments this syrup
and prepares from it a kind of Port wine which is becoming more
and more popular ;

3) for preparing musts which are fermented up to 6-8° of alcohol, remaining sweet at 5 or 6° Baumé, these are then blended with strong red wines, mixed with alcohol to bring them up to 16 %. This product, which is known as " Blutwein ", is exported in large quantities to Hamburg. The consumption is considerable, and in 1910-11 the Greek C° will export 550 000 gals.

1864   R. L. ADAMS. **The Sugar Beet Industry in California.** — *California Cultivator.* Vol. XXVI, N. 20, p. 611. Los Angeles, May 18, 1911.

United States: California

To-day California vies with Michigan for first place in greatest sugar production in the United States. In total production of sugar beets California takes second place, the higher sugar content of California's sugar beets, however, offsets Michigan's greater tonnage.

Eight factories handle the California beet crop. These are situated at Alvarado, Los Alamitos, Spreckels, Betteravia, Chino, Oxward, Hamilton city and Santa Ana. In addition two new mills will probably be completed in time for the coming season, one at Anaheim and the other at Huntington Beach. The first is capable of grinding 600 tons of beets per day and the other 750 tons.

The following averages are for the four years 1907-1909 and are computed from the figures in the United States Department of Agriculture Year-Books:

STATE (1)	Sugar Lbs per acre	Yield Tons per acre	% Sugar in Beet	% Purity of Juice
Utah	4164	13.89	14.99	84.03
California	3809	10.60	17.97	83.65
Colorado	3264	11.24	14.52	81.03
Other States of the Union	3165	10.12	15.64	94.45

In 1910 California planted approximatively 87 000 acres with sugar beets, which brought to the growers the sum of 5 millions of dollars.

---

(1) See also Abstr. 833 of this *Bulletin*, March 1911 and Abstr. 1411, *ibid.*, May 1911.   (*Ed.*).

PRINSEN GEERLIGS. **The Sugar Industry in Brazil.** (La Industria
Azucarera en el Brasil). — *El Hacendado Mexicano*, Vol. IX,
p. 170-173. Mexico, Mayo 1 de 1911.

1865

There are two kinds of sugar mills in Brazil, the *usinas*
(modern mills) and the *ingenios* (those with antiquated plant).
From the point of view of output, Brazil can be divided into three
zones : north, central, and south. In the first two, modern systems
of cultivation are in use. In the northern zone, the Cayenne, Cristalina, Salangore, Bambo, and other varieties requiring a dry climate are preferred, whereas in St. Paul the Louziers variety is
mostly raised. The yield of the cane varies greatly ; it depends on
the soil and climate, and fluctuates between 400 and 560 cwt. per
acre. The sugar content of the cane is very high ; it can be estimated at 15 %. Four kinds of sugar are recognized in Brazil, White
Crystalline, Orange Crystalline, *Mascavinhos* (inferior product of a
light colour), and *Macavos* (inferior product of a dark colour).

Brazil

The Government does all it can to encourage the sugar industry.
Recently the *Coligacao Assucareira* (Sugar Company) was formed
which aims at improving the product and regulating the market.

G. CIAPETTI. **The Utilisation of Grape Pips.** (L'utilizzazione dei
vinaccioli. — *L'Italia vinicola ed agraria* - 1 an. N. 5, pp. 65-68.
Casalmonferrato, 4 Giugno, 1911.

1866

The fiscal laws now in force in Italy make it necessary to utilise as
fully as possible all the bye-products of wine-making. So far it has
been very difficult to make use of the pips and to extract oil from
them, and all the processes advocated were more or less defective.

Italy

This problem is now solved by the use of a small apparatus
with direct heating for the extraction of the fatty substances by
means of dissolvents. Direct heating is made possible by using
tetrachloride of carbon, easily obtained in Italy in the preparation
of electrolytic soda. This dissolvent is a colourless liquid, insoluble
in water, uninflammable, and its strength as a dissolvent is equal
to that of benzine or carbon sulphide. It also has the advantage
of being less easily decomposed, and of boiling at a temperature
of 76° C.

Fatty bodies treated with tetrachloride take from it no flavour or special, disagreeable smell. Their quality remains good.
The vapours given off by this substance are not poisonous, nor explosive when mixed with the air. There is less waste than with

benzine ; and the oil-cakes obtained can be used without danger as a food for cattle.

˗ The apparatus used is so made as not to be attacked by the tetrachloride ; it is very simple, and so constructed that all the solvent can be recovered. It can also be used for treating olive stones and several other oil seeds, such as linseed, sun-flower seeds, etc.

1867   **British Government Report on Flour Bleaching.** — *Modern Miller St. Louis Mo.* April, 22. 1911 (1).

The Report of the British Government in regard to the bleaching of flour is given in the conclusions of Dr. J. M. Hamill, which have recently been issued by the Local Government Board as follows :

Great Britain   It may be concluded that the alterations in and the additions to flour which result from a high degree of bleaching by nitrogen peroxide cannot be regarded as free from risk to the consumer, especially when regard is had to the inhibitory effect of the bleaching agent on digestive processes and enzymes.

Even in the case of flour which is bleached to the small extent which is at present ordinarily practiced, it would in present knowledge be unwise to conclude that the process is attended by absolute freedom from risk.

The fact that bleached flour has been shown to be something more than natural flour, the color of which has been modified, is also of importance in considering whether bleached flour may properly be represented as genuine flour.

1868   F. T. SHUTT. **Bleached Flour. Bread from Bleached and Unbleached Flours.** — *Experimental Farms, Report of the Chemist,* pp. 196-203. Ottawa, 1910. (App. to the Rep. of the Min. of Agr.).

The wide spread interest at the present time in bleached flour as a wholesome article of food, pointed to the desirability of **Canada**   obtaining data respecting the influence of the bleaching agent commercially used—nitrogen peroxide—on the flour and resultant bread. Consequently the writer, in conjunction with the Canada Cerealist,

----

(1) Cp. this Bulletin, Abstr. 569, Febr. 1911.   (*Ed.*).

has made a preliminary study comprising the chemical and physical examinations of bleached flours and their breads.

Firstly a series of six flours were bleached by the Alsop process. An outline of the operation is as follows : a current of air is made to pass between rotatory electrodes emitting flaming discharges, this so-called electrified air is conducted into a drum or agitator through which the flour is passed in such a manner as to bring it into intimate contact with the bleaching agent, chiefly nitrogen peroxide; the flour in passing through the agitator occupies from 8 to 15 seconds.

These, together with samples of the same flour unbleached were submitted to examination in the laboratory, the following determinations being made : moisture, total nitrogen, gliadin nitrogen, wet and dry gluten, the nitrogen in nitrite-reacting material and, in certain instances, the ash and the fat.

In every instance the bleached flour was the lighter in colour ; being also the drier, the difference in moisture-content being 0.66 per cent. The bleaching process did not affect the ash-content, and it did not appreciably affect the percentage of fat. The most careful testing of total and gliadin nitrogen did not disclose that there had been any influence on the nitrogen compounds by the bleaching agent. The amount of wet and dry gluten were appreciably the same for the unbleached and bleached samples of flour, and no differences could be discerned in their resiliency and elasticity ; the gluten from the bleached flour being however of paler colour. Finally ten of the eleven bleached flours contained less than 0.5 p. p. m. nitrite nitrogen; not a single sample of unbleached flour giving any reaction, but accidentally.

Since the consumption of flour is chiefly in the form of bread, it becomes a question of very considerable interest to learn whether bread from bleached flour contains an appreciable amount of nitrites. The process of bread making in its latter stages is such as would tend to a certain dissipation of the bleaching agent, provided the bread in baking were not exposed to the products of combustion. On the other hand, it would seem possible that in the operation of making bread from unbleached flour, free from nitrites, there might be produced or absorbed sufficient nitrites to give the reaction. Experiments in baking were therefore made. From the results it is concluded that flour free from nitrite-reacting material baked in an electric oven will yield bread free from nitrites; and that from flour containing considerable amounts of nitrite nitrogen the bread if similarly baked, may or may not be free, but in any case the amount will be very considerably reduced.

Considering that bleached flour was found slightly drier and its absorptive capacity somewhat greater than unbleached flour, the writer contends that a slightly larger amount of bread would be obtained from the former.

Certain experiments of a preliminary nature have been made by the writer with the view of learning the influence on flour of sunlight and air, separately and together, as bleaching agents. The results gave direct evidence of the bleaching action of sunlight, and of the air in the absence of direct sunlight. Both the samples experimented on were found to contain nitrite nitrogen to the extent of 0.05 p. p. m.

1869

F. J. G. Beltzer. **Vegetabie Milk and Cheese. Studies on the Vegetable Casein of the Soy Bean and its Uses.** (Etudes sur la caséine végétale du Soya et ses applications). — *Revue Scientifique*, 49 an., N, 23, pp. 716-720. Paris, 10 Juin, 1911.

The natives of Indo-China have prepared for years past a vegetable casein from " soy " milk, by the two following processes :

French Indo-China : Annam

Vegetable milk. — The soy seed is washed in cold water, steeped in cold water from 24 to 48 hours till soft, then crushed and ground under millstones, with enough cold water to mix it to a thick milky liquid. It is then filtered through a cloth, and the residue is again treated as above. The ultimate residue is used as a feed for live stock. the milk obtained from the first and second treatment is used as it stands for food or in the preparation of vegetable cheese.

Vegetable cheese. — This milk, when treated with a mineral salt or with an acid, coagulates into clots, and when strained and washed yields a kind of white cheese much eaten in the Far East.

In Indo-China the milk is coagulated, when it reaches boiling point, by adding a small quantity of powder called Tchoch-Kao, or plaster obtained from a selenite pulverised by subjection to heat.

There are 3 principal varieties of cheese in Annam :

1. The fermented kind, gray or yellow coloured, tasting something like Roquefort ;

2. The white or salted kind, like goat's cheese ;

3. The cooked or smoked kind, like Gruyère in appearance.

In its industrial utilisation soy beans should be subjected to the following processes :

1. Extraction of the oil by pressure ;

2. Extraction of the casein by precipitation of the milk prepared with crushed pulp ;

3. Mixture of the residuum oil-cake with fodders or molasses.

The extraction of casein for industrial purposes is obtained by the following process :

The pulp coming from the oil-press is ground under mill-stones with cold water, and the homogenous milky matter thus obtained, after kneading in vats, is passed, through a filter press. The residuum is subjected to the same process and a second lot of milk extracted.

The milky liquid is poured into cylindrical wooden vats, and heated to boiling point by tinned copper worms. To each 1000 litres of liquid, 1 kg. of plaster of Paris is added ; the caseinous coagulum clots; and is collected on cloth filters. It is dissolved in diluted soda lye, weak enough for the reaction to be neutral or very slightly alkaline, then, after filtering, it is precipitated with acetic acid, left to evaporate in the open air, and the precipitate dried at a low temperature.

The casein thus obtained is similar to that of milk.

100 grams of seed yield about 25 grammes of casein.

Uses of vegetable Casein. — Medium for painting, dressing for textiles, size for paper, Galalith, waterproofing for textiles, etc., and as a food it is used as Soy-casein, a flour like Nestlé's, with which sauces, bread, jam, milk, fermented milk, cheese and concentrated biscuits may be made.

International Cotton Statistics. (Internationale Baumwollstatistik). **1870**
— *Das Handelsmuseum*, N. 15, p. 231. Wien 13, April 1911.

The *Internationales Verband der Baumwollspinner und Weber-vereinigungen* publishes the following data on the cotton-spinning industry throughout the world.

The cotton industry of the whole world kept 135 596 724 spindles busy, distributed as follows :

Great Britain	53 859 247
United States	28 500 000
Germany.	10 299 597
Russia	8 600 000
France	7 200 000
India	6 195 671
Austria-Hungary	4 686 433
Italy	4 215 000

Of this total number, 18 781 960 spun Egyptian cotton, the others American, Indian, and other cottons,

One thousand spindles used in

England	63.50 bales
United States	166.04 »
Germany, ...	165.69 »
Russia	264.99 »
France	133.01 »
India	360.35 »
Austria-Hungary	176.54 »
Italy	192.44 »

On March 1st, 1911, manufacturers held in stock

2 565 000	bales of	American	cotton
707 767	»	Indian	»
203 247	»	Egyptian	»
582 226	»	cotton from various parts	

The number of spindles in the world increased in one year by 2 million.

1871   New Meat Chilling Process. — *Cold Storage.* London, May 18, 1911.

Great Britain

On the 4th inst the Tyser liner *Muratai* brought into dock in London among its refrigerated cargo 72 quarters of beef carried under a new patent chilling process. At the Central Meat Market the meat, which comprised 62 hind quarters and 10 fores attracted the attention of all the prominent dealers and was generally admired, the points most commented upon being its softness and dryness, the firmness of the fat and the absence of any objectionable odour. Part of a quarter that had purposely been sent a considerable distance and then cooked in the ordinary way for the table, was found to be tender, full of flavour and equal to any beef wherever grown. Further portions exposed to the atmosphere for six days have kept in very good condition. Representative men on market, including North and South American importers, have spoken in strong terms of praise of the condition of the shipment. As to the system under which this promising experiment has been made it has been patented under the names of Sir Montague Nelson,

Mr. Walter Tyser and Mr. John Dicks. One of the main principles involved in the system is the securing of the absolute dryness of the air in which the meat is stored.

Cold-storage for Mushrooms. (La conservation des champignons de couche par le froid). — *Revue générale du Froid.* 3. an., T. III, n. 6, pp. 298-299. Paris, Juin, 1911.

1872

Experiments showed that after a month's cold storage, mushrooms had neither deteriorated in appearance nor lost any of their nutritive qualities. At the end of this time they could be placed on the market, exactly like other mushrooms picked a day or two and left in the open air, and they could not be distinguished the one from the other. The only difference from freshly gathered mushrooms is that on leaving the cold-storage their skin is grayer and their water content rather less.

France

This is the only way of preserving mushrooms so as to retain their full flavour and aroma.

Agricultural Engineering and Farm Machinery and Implements.

Agricultural Machinery in Asia Minor. — *The Board of Trade Journal,* N. 756. P. 385. London. May, 25, 1911.

1873

There are exceptionally good openings for agricultural machinery in the interior of Asia Minor, particularly in the vilayet of Konia. A German agricultural machinery depôt, which was established a short time ago in Konia, has been a great success. The farmers of Anatolia were particularly impressed by the fact that, although there was an excellent harvest in 1910, a large portion of the crops was wasted owing to scarcity of labour and of labour-saving implements. Furthermore, irrigation schemes are being proceeded with the object of bringing more land under cultivation. so that there is every prospect of a good trade in Agricultural implements during the next few years.

Turkish
Empire
Asia Minor

Manufacturers would be well advised to combine for the purpose of sending an experienced traveller to the above-mentioned
districts, in order to become fully acquainted with the conditions
of the market.

1874   **Progress in the Agricultural Machinery and Implements in British India.** — *The Board of Trade Journal*, N. 751, p. 114-115.
London, April 20, 1911.

British India

Progress must take place rather along the lines of improvement
of the indigenous types of agricultural implements than by the introduction of those which have been found suitable in Europe. The
demand in India is for light and simply constructed implements, capable of being repaired locally, and suitable for bullock traction.
For these reasons, in addition to that of their cost, heavy European
implements have in most cases been found unsuitable for India.
The agricultural associations which have been formed in the various
provinces, have given much help in the introduction of useful implements and machines, while the agricultural shows and exhibitions
that are being held all over India have also been instrumental in
popularising their use. The problem of implements for wheat
threshing has been left in the hands of private engineering firms.
Experiments made by the Department at Lyallpur have led to the
hope that it may be possible to produce a moderate cheap bullock
power threshing machine that might become popular. In the United
Provinces the principal demand is for low chain-pumps and ploughs.
In the Southern Circle of the Central Provinces, for bullock-gears
and turnwrest ploughs; in Bombay, for ploughs and iron cane mills,
in Bengal, for iron mills for crushing sugar cane and in Burma, for
angle harrows and appliances for harvesting ground nuts.

1875   A. LONAY. **The Problem of Motor Culture.** (Le problème de la motoculture). — *Annales de Gembloux*, 21e a., 5e l., pp. 242-251.
Bruxelles, Ier Mai, 1911.

**Belgian
Congo**

The writer studies the methods of cultivating by motor-power
in their bearings on the exploitation of the Congo.

He thinks one should go further than merely applying motor-
power to the plough. The best methods and implements for preparing the soil in the best and most economical manner must be
studied, using a mechanical motor as the driving power.

The new implement, worked by the motor, if it is to answer the purposes of a practical plough must:

1) Plough the soil to the required depth, which one should be able to regulate according to the nature of the soil, crop, etc., the increased depth of the cultivation, which can be attained through the motor-power of the mechanism, will often secure a much heavier yield.

2) It should be able to reduce the ploughed soil to the required degree of division; it should be able to turn over the soil in clods as required for winter cereals, or reduced almost to fine dust as is required, for instance, in sowing flax. Proper preparation of the soil may largely increase the yield of the crops.

3) It should turn in straw and grass, as also manure, which it should mix as much as possible with the cultivated layer; this is an essential condition.

4) It should pulverize the soil evenly for the whole depth, so as to do away with the need of subsequent use of the cultivator and harrow.

5) It should work well, whether the soil be heavy or light, dry or moist, at least up to a certain degree of moisture, as beyond a certain degree of moisture, clay soil becomes plastic and cannot be cultivated.

6) it should be able to work, in spite of the stones and roots which are present in some soils. These should not be able to prevent the working of the plough or injure it too easily.

7) It should be so constructed as not to be easily injured by soil or dust getting into it. This will be the case with a cultivator fitted with the smallest possible number of attachments and cogs near the surface of the soil.

L. W. Ellis. **Traction Engine in Dry Farming**. — *Farm and Ranch.* Dallas, Texas, April 1, 1911.

1876

In the great southwest of the United States, in all the hottest and driest of the dry farming regions, the only ploughing that can be done economically during the greater part of the year is with the traction engine. It is at its best in the hottest weather. The steam engine produces its steam more economically, the internal-combustion engine its gas more perfectly in the highest temperatures.

United States: Texas

For the preparation of the seed-bed under every dry farming condition, the traction engine is profitable. It enables the farmer to do quick work when delay means loss of moisture and lower yields. It shortens his period of operation and increases his volume of work at the rare times when all natural conditions effect a combination for his advantage. Seeding may be done properly and speedily on days when from every acre sown on that day a bushel more will be reaped than from those sown the day following. Where seeding follows quickly after ploughing a disc ahead of the drill wipes out the wheel tracks of the engine and mellows the soil, the drill drops the seed at a given depth, the packer firms the earth around it to bring moisture quickly, and the smoothing harrow levels all and leaves the surface mulch.

At harvest time the engine in twenty hours may travel 30 to 35 working miles and cut nearly five acres to each mile travelled, with one driver and one or two men to watch the binders. The grain may be cut neither too early nor too late, the ground disked to check needless exhaustion of the soil moisture and the entire task completed before the toiling horses have bound the grain out of the way of sun and storm. A recent bulletin of the U. S. Department of Agriculture estimates the average cost of breaking prairie in the Northwest with a gasoline engine to be $ 1.70 per acre, including liberal allowances for interest, depreciations and repairs. W. M. Jardine, dry land cerealist of the Department of Agriculture, reported on an outfit seen in Montana breaking heavy sod land to a depth of four inches at a cost, including labor, of about 80 cents per acre. According to the same authority, the contract price for breaking varied from $ 4 to $ 5 per acre; and the cost with horses was not less than $ 4 per acre. To a greater or less degree, this difference in cost prevails over the entire semiarid region.

There is much to be said in favor of both steam and internal combustion tractors.

Steam engines were developed earlier and reached a high state of perfection before the internal combustion tractors became a commercial success. Now however, the latter have developed with greater relative rapidity than the former and are offering serious competition.

The internal combustion engines are usually lighter in total weight, hence can be used for work where steam engines would be less convenient. They represent less time lost in taking supplies than steam engines. The latter, however; are somewhat more reliable, and generally less expensive in first cost on the basis of equal brake horsepower.

The convenience and price of fuel is often the deciding factor. If a coal mine and plenty of water are convenient, it is possible for one man to supply the engine with both coal and water, and for three men to operate the entire outfit. The expense in this case would be limited to about $ 15 a day for an outfit capable of ploughing 25 acres, or about 60 cents per acre. In Montana, gasoline sells as high as 22 to 25 cents per gallon, and coal oil or kerosene as high as 18 to 20 cents per gallon.

From two and one-half to three gallons of fuel will be required per acre, hence the fuel cost alone may range from 45 to 75 cents per acre. Labor, board, lubricating oil and repairs would add 25 to 35 cents per acre. On this showing, the steam engine would be the more profitable.

However, instead of three men, it might easily take five, and instead of one team at least two, to operate a steam outfit.

The running expenses then would be close to $ 1 per acre and if a good quality of water were not obtainable for use in the boiler the depreciation would be at a much greater rate than for the internal combustion engine. The amount of water required for the latter is so small as to be almost negligible. Straw is often burned in steam engines during fall ploughing. The first cost of the coal is saved, the labor of supplying straw being equal to that of hauling coal.

At the present time, gasoline may be had delivered in the field in North Dakota for 16 cents a gallon. At this price, the cost per acre for ploughing would be about 80 cents, covering the labor and board of two men, fuel, lubricating oil and repairs. In the Southwest, where low-grade kerosene distillates may be had for less than four cents per gallon, the cost of fuel is as low as 12 cents per acre.

In these same sections, coal costs from $ 7 to $ 9 per ton and the cost of hauling coal and water, together with the greater labor cost, make the cost of operating steam traction engines greater than for the kerosene or gasoline tractors.

The tractor is a relatively new departure in crop production. Ten years for steam and five for internal combustion engines mark their serious use in general farm work.

The past development of traction engines has been merely an indication of greater things to be expected in the near future.

It is not idle prophecy to state that dry farming methods will soon have been standardized around the traction engine as the most effective factor under human control in the entire system of dry land agriculture.

1877   **A New Harrow for Marsh Lands.** — *The Implements and Machinery Review.* London, February 1, 1911.

The cultivation of the extensive marsh lands in the North of Germany, which are now being put under certain kinds of crops is requiring new implements and machines.

While the ploughing of much of this land presents no difficulty, it leaves a serious problem as to how the furrows should be broken up, since implements like the ordinary type of harrow would have the effect of merely scouring the surface without breaking the

Germany   soil to allow of the moisture draining to the bottom. The J. Kemna Steam Plough Company of Breslau has designed a special type of harrow for the Prussian Ministry of Agriculture. Being intended to be drawn by a tractor or by a steam ploughing engine, the harrow is suspended from a frame carried on four broad wheels in the form of drums, this shape having been given to them to allow of their travelling over the soft land without danger of sinking.

The machine is steered by hand wheels at either end. The harrow is fitted transversely under the centre of the machine in sections made up of a number of disks, each of which has six triangular sections cut away at the periphery. The efficiency of the machine for breaking up marsh land lies in the form of these discs. Instead of merely scratching the soil, the teeth of the disks apparently bite deep into the ridges and level them out in the form of light clods. The disks are flexibly connected and follow any irregularities of the land, and the tractive effort on them is exerted by chains attached to a loose frame which in its turn is fixed by chains to brackets on the main frame. An illustration of this special type of harrow is given.

1878   **The Comparative Cost of Travel by Horse and Wagon and Automobile.** — (Boston Evening Transcript 1910 Oct. 8) E. S. R. March 1911. Vol. XXIV, No. 3, p. 288.

This is a report of a six day test between a Maxwell automobile and a horse and wagon. The automobile covered 457.9 miles

United   (736.7 km.) at a cost of $ 6.20 (fr. 32) and the depreciation was $ 8.24
States   making a total cost per mile of 3.15 cts (fr. 0.162) and the cost per passenger mile 1.57 cents (fr. 0,081). The cost of oats and hay for the horse one week was $ 5.80 (fr. 29.87) the number of miles traveled 193.3 (km. 311) and the depreciation $ 1.47 (fr. 7,57), making the total cost per mile 3.68 cts (fr. 0.188) and the cost

per passenger mile 1.84 cts. (fr. 0.094). There were no repairs in either case. The depreciation in the case of the automobile was rated at 20 per cent a year on the basis of 10 000 miles a year which amounts to 1.8 cts a mile (fr. 0.092). The depreciation of the wagon, harness, and horse was based on the original cost of $ 275 (fr. 1416), the outfit being supposed to last 10 years and to be capable of 10 miles travel every day, making a depreciation of 0.75 cts per mile (fr. 0,038).

The Automatic Water-Finder. — *Agricultural Journal of Indai*, Vol. VI, Part I. Calcutta, January, 1911.

1879

This is a simple apparatus supplied by Messrs. Mansfield and C⁰ of Liverpool, by which any person may readily ascertain whether a subterranean spring of water exists under a spot where it is desired to sink a well. It indicates the presence of subterranean flowing springs at depths up to 1000 feet.

Great Britain. Brit. India

The instrument has been tried by the Bombay Department of Agriculture in the trap areas of the Deccan, where under ground streams traverse the country in various directions " The results so far obtained though not absolutely conclusive indicate an almost certain success ".

There are however, certain difficulties in the way such as expense and delicacy in the instrument.

The principle on which the instrument works is the measuring of the strength of the electrical currents which are constantly flowing between earth and atmosphere and which are always strongest in the vicinity of subterranean water-courses, the flowing waters of which are charged with electricity to a certain degree.

PLANT DISEASES

NOXIOUS INSECTS AND OTHER PESTS.

INTELLIGENCE

Non Parasitic Diseases of Plants and their Control.

H. Molisch. **Action of Tobacco-Smoke on Plants** (Ueber den Ein- 1880
fluss des Tabakrauchs auf die Pflanze). (*Sitzsber. d. k. k. Ak. d.
Wiss. in Wien. Math. naturw. Kl.* Abth. I Wien, 1911). — *Rivista
di Patologia vegetale*, an. V. n. 3, p. 42. Pavia, I Giugno, 1911.

The writer has investigated the action of fumigations with
tobacco, used to rid plants from insect parasites.

He has noticed that tobacco-smoke has a really injurious effect   **Austria**
on small germinating plants. Young vetches, peas, beans, pumpkins, etc., present an abnormal aspect, and their growth is arrested.

He has also noticed that plants grown in water are more sensitive than those grown in the earth to the harmful effects of
tobacco-smoke. He was unable to determine what element in the
smoke exercises this action.

Bacteria, amoebae, flagellata, and infusoria are still more sensitive
to the noxious effects of tobacco-smoke, and these microorganisms
soon die when subjected to it.

1881

G. Köck and K. Kornauth. **Contribution to the Study of " Leaf Curl '' in Potatoes.** (Beiträge zum Studium der Blattrollkrankheit. *Monatsch. Landw.*, III, p. 365. 1910). — *Botanisches Centralblatt*, Bd. 116, N. 15, pp. 388-389. Jena, 1911.

The writers submit to a severe criticism the work of Bokutinsky, entitled " *Beiträge zur Erforschung der Blattrollkrankheit* " (contribution to the study of " leaf roll " in the potato), and more especially Vañha's work " *Die Krauselkrankheit oder Blattrollkrankheit der Kartoffel, ihre Ursache und Bekämpfung* " (Leaf-Roll in potatoes, its causes and control). These books, of recent publication, come to conclusions which the writers do not accept.

Germany

In view of the inadequate and debatable description of the new fungus (*Solanella rosea*), which Vañha considers the pathological agent of the disease, the writers express doubts as to the existence of this fungus as a separate species, and as the cause of the disease.

The writers then set forth the results of their mycological investigations on this subject, laying special stress on the observations they have made in infected soils with some varieties of the " Dolkowski " potato. Varieties which had been selected as healthy the previous year, presented towards the middle of August acute symptoms of disease. Microscopic investigations revealed the presence of a mycelium in the whole vascular system, which confirms the hypothesis of the criptogamic nature of the disease. Artificial culture of the mycelium showed that it belongs to the genus Fusarium.

1882

R. S. Horne. **On Potato Leaf Blotch and Leaf Curl.** (1) — *Journal of the Royal Horticultural Society*, Vol. XXXVI, Part. III, pp. 618-623. London, May, 1911.

Great Britain: Scotland

Leaf Blotch, — This disease was imported into Scotland on three different occasions with the « President » variety of potatoes (in 1908, 1909, and 1910), and it shows a great tendency to spread in England. In 1904 Vañha described a potato disease « Potato Leaf Blotch » which he ascribed to a fnngus, *Sporidesmium Solani varians* Vañha. This fungus is said to produce in its life-cycle several kinds of spores, including *Macrosporium*.

---

(1) See the *Science and Practice of Farming during* 1910, *in Great Britain* Int. Inst, of Agric. Rome, 1910. p. 352, and Abstr. 286. Bull. Jan 1911.   ·(*Ed*).

Massee ascribes a form of Potato Leaf Curl to *Macrosporium Solani* Cooke. He says that a parasitic fungus exists in the tissues of the seed tubers ; as the plant develops the fungus gradually passes along the conducting tissue, from the tuber to the young stalk and finally attacks the leaves. Meanwhile the mycelium passes down the stalk to the roots and young tubers.

The writer, however, has been unable to observe a series of phenomena similar to those described by Massee. In the cases he has studied, the disease spread from the surface of the leaves to the deeper tissues; he noted several kinds of fungoid spores on the surface of leaves gathered late in the season, and amongst them those known as *Macrosporium*. He found in the diseased tissue the reproductive bodies of an animal organism. No conclusions as to the nature of the cause of the disease can be drawn from these merely preliminary investigations.

In 1906, L. R. Jones and C. S. Pomeroy described a Leaf Blotch disease of the Potato prevalent in some parts of the United States. This disease was due to a fungus, *Cercospora concors*. Published reports would seem to show that this disease is caused by more than one fungus and perhaps by different combinations of fungi.

Leaf Curl. — The potato leaves may be creased, curled, rolled, or shrivelled in different ways when they are not otherwise affected. This circumstance has been recently recorded by Massee (1910), C. Appel (1908) Schleh (1909) and Steglich (1909) in Germany ; by Ducloux and Héliard in France, and by several other men of science.

Rolling or shrivelling of the leaf associated with « Blackleg » was recorded by the writer in 1909 at Cleadon, in Durham. « Blackleg » is the English name for a disease described by Erwin Smith (1896) (1) as a bacterial disease of the tomato, egg-plant and Irish potato, and described by Grotenfeld (1901), O. Appel (1903) and others under the name of « Schwarzbeinigkeit ».

Steglich has recently studied the connection between Leaf Curl and a bacterial disease.

The rolling or shrivelling of the potato leaves may also occur unaccompanied by other visible symptoms of disease, or accompanied by distortions of the stalk, or by a brown discolouration of the stalk above ground or by blotches and scabs on the leaf.

---

(1) See the *Science and Practice of Farming in Great Britain during* 1910, Intern. Inst. of. Agric. Rome, 1910, p. 353.   (*Ed*).

P. de Caluwe (1908) in Holland, and Remy and Schneider (1909) in Germany, report that the Leaf Curl disease is widespread in their respective countries where it causes much loss of the crop.

1888   R. AVERNA-SACCÀ. **Contribution to the Study of the " Roncet " of the Vine.** (Contributo allo studio sul "Roncet"). — *Atti del R. Istituto d'Incoraggiamento di Napoli,* MCMX, serie 6ª - vol. LXII, degli Atti, pp. 115-143. Napoli, 1911.

The writer points out that " roncet " is a constitutional dis-

Italy   ease, characterised by partial degeneration of the parenchyma and by the production of a substance which becomes mucilaginous after passing through a pectic stage, a non infectious gum producing disease, caused by sudden changes of temperature in the young shoots forming in the spring. This disease is distinguished from " distorting and punctated anthracnosis " by the absence of the pustules caused by *Gloeosporium ampelophagum,* and from « black rot » (*mal nero*), by the fact that the gum is not infectious.

" Roncet " produces anomalies :

a) in the internodes, which are slender and sometimes affected with fasciation, the nodes being more or less pronounced than normally ;

b) in the leaves, which are misshapen and more deeply lobed than normally ; they are always chlorotic, withered at the edge or all over, sometimes marked with black spots, or perforated or split;

c) in the bunches of grapes, which are more or less distorted or abortive.

1884   RALPH E. SMITH. **The Relation of Climatic and Soil Conditions to Cases of So-called Mottled Leaf, Withertip, Dieback, Little Leaf, in Oranges, Peaches, Walnuts.** — *California Cultivator.* Vol. XXXVI. No. 21, p. 635-648. Los Angeles, May 25, 1911.

The most prominent and important troubles which have pre-

United States : California   vailed in California during the past winter and spring have been the " Mottled Leaf " and " Dieback " of the orange in certain portions of Southern California, the so-called " Little Leaf " of the peach in the San Joaquin Valley and the " Yellows " or " Dieback " of the walnut in the southern part of the State,

The calendar year 1910 was one of the dryest on record in Southern California and in the San Joaquin Valley, the rainfall for the year in these sections averaging only from 4 to 5 in. (102 to 127 mm.).

Mottled Leaf of Citrus Trees. Affected trees show near the end of the shoots a yellowing of the leaves between the veins, with the green colour only along the midrib and the lateral veins, giving the leaf a mottled appearance. There is no Chlorophyll, or but very little in the yellow areas. If the trees are badly affected there also occurs a decided shortage in the amount of fruit. Mottled leaf is to be regarded as simply a temporary setback in the development of the leaves and with warm weather the leaves soon put on their natural appearance.

The most prevalent and typical form of citrus mottled leaf is due to an irregular supply of moisture and plant food.

Withertip. In citrus groves, mostly on the lighter, gravelly and sandy soils there is now occurring a great deal of dieback, chlorosis, poor growth, lack of fruit and similar trouble.

Much of this trouble is now ascribed to the so called " withertip " fungus (1). The writer's experiments, however, have shown that it is absolutely impossible to infect a healthy citrus tree with this fungus. On the other hand, it is a most common inhabitant of trees injured or diseased from any cause whatever.

Little Leaf of the Peach. In the San Joaquin Valley much anxiety is felt on account of this comparatively new trouble. The disease is characterized by the development of spindly, yellow, sickly looking shoots on the new growth, with small, narrow, yellow leaves. The leaves along the shoots drop off during the summer, leaving tufts at the ends. Fruit fails to develop, shrivels and drops. It is worst on trees from 3 to 7 years old. This trouble also attacks other stone fruits, walnuts, pecans and other trees. Here again subsoil examination showed that the disease was practically confined to trees on light, sandy soil or subsoils, where the effects of the dry year of 1910 had been more pronounced.

Walnut Dieback and Yellows. Large numbers of young trees, from 2 to 10 years of age, have shown a sudden dieback on the tops, some or all of the limbs dying back to the forks of the tree, or, in some cases, whole trees dying to the ground.

---

(1) Withertip of Citrus trees has been attributed by Mr. E. O. Essig, to the parasitism of *Colletotrichum gloeosporioides*, Penzig. See this *Bulletin*, Abstr. 1547, May, 1911.   (*Ed.*).

Much of the wood thus affected is not entirely dead, but sends out belated, weak-growing, yellow shoots and leaves.

The lower part of the limbs or trunk sends out strong, thrifty suckers, showing that the root is still active.

All the troubles alluded to above are the direct result of subsoil drought during 1910, and are to be overcome only by maintaining and improving the moisture content and water-retaining capacity of the soil. Many other similar effects in various plants are being constantly met with which are attributed to parasites, lack of fertilizers and all sorts of obscure conditions, whilst they are really due to nothing more than a deficient or irregular supply of water.

Parasitic Diseases. — Generalities. — Parasitism. — Parasitic and Saprophytic Bacteria and Fungi. — Resistant Varieties. — Remedies.

1885　　E. S. SALMON. **Report on Economic Mycology.** — *The Journal of the South Eastern Agricultural College, Wye, Kent*, No. 19, pp. 325-361. London & Ashford, Kent, 1910.

The American Gooseberry-Mildew (*Sphaerotheca mors-uvae* (Schwein.) Berk).

Great Britain : Kent, Surrey　　This lately introduced disease has spread to a serious extent. In Kent not only has the acreage of infested plantations more than doubled itself in 1910, in comparison with 1909, but the general intensity of the disease has increased in 1910.

The area now attacked in Kent is 2 863 acres, or about ²/₃ of the total acreage under gooseberries.

The winter stage of the mildew has been found on leaf stalks and young leaves of gooseberry and on leaves of black currant.

Lime-Sulphur Washes for use on Foliage (1). Bordeaux mixture continues to be the best fungicide known for the control of apple

---

(1) See Abstr. 688 *Bulletin*, Feb. 1911, and Abstr. 1000 and 1001 *Bulletin*, March, 1911.　　　　　　　　　　　　　　　(*Ed.*).

" scab " or " black spot " (*Venturia inaequalis*) (1), and should be constantly used for this purpose except on those varieties of apples subject to " Bordeaux injury " (2). In these cases the use of a lime-sulphur wash may be recommended, as experiments made in the United States show that this wash is almost as efficacious as the Bordeaux mixture. The writer tried spraying apples, goose-berries, and hops with a lime-sulphur wash. The foliage of some varieties, such as the " Worcester Pearmain ", is not injured by spraying with a solution diluted to a specific gravity of 1.01. Other varieties such as " Cox's Orange Pippin ", " Charles Ross ", " King of the Pippins ", " Blenheim Orange ", and " Besspool " (Tower of Glamis) were badly scorched by a wash of this strength. For these varieties wash diluted to a specific gravity of 1.005 should be used when they are sprayed in June or later, though possibly the full strength wash is safe to use in May.

The writer had no occasion to test the efficacy of the lime-sulphur wash against apple " scab ". The experiments noted above give evidence that the lime-sulphur wash is efficacious against « powdery mildews ».

Although the wash has been used at « full strength » (sp. gr. 1.01) in May on the foliage of gooseberries without causing any injury, it is advisable at present to use the wash at « half strength » (sp. gr. 1.005) ; later in the season a weaker wash is necessary when used on certain varieties of gooseberries, — a point which requires further investigation.

" *Sooty Blotch* " : *a new fungus disease of Apples.* During the past four or five years the attention of the writer has been called to a disease which will frequently develop on apples after they are stored. The apples attacked show sooty looking blotches on the skin. Microscopical examination shows that these blotches are due to the presence of a species of *Leptothyrium* not previously recorded in Great Britain. These sooty blotches are composed of straggling threads (*hyphae*) of the blackish spawn (*mycelium*) of the fungus. This spawn is wholly superficial but grows so closely attached to the skin of the apple that the sooty patches cannot be easily wiped off. Near the sooty patches, compact circular masses of spawn (*mycelium*) of a shining black colour are formed. No spores are found

---

(1) See Abstr. 1021 and 1024, *Bulletin* March, 1911.
(2) See Abstr. 1002, *Bulletin*, March, 1911.

on these spots. The name "flyspeck" (1) disease has been given in America to this fungous growth. Where the disease appears, systematic spraying with Bordeaux mixture should be given, except on certain varieties like " Cox's Orange Pippin " and " Duchess 's Favourite ", on which a lime-sulphur spray should be used on account of their susceptibility to injury from Bordeaux mixture.

New York Canker. In 1899, Prof. W. Paddock established the fact that the fungus *Sphaerospis Malorum* (2) long known in the United States as the cause of the Black Rot of the fruit of the apple, pear, and quince, is capable of attacking also the trunk and branches of the same fruit trees, producing an injury of the nature of a canker, to which the name of " New York Canker ' is given.

Recently the writer observed the same disease on the branches of a pear-tree from Surrey.

1886　　V. DUCOMET. **Investigation of Some Diseases of Cultivated Plants in France.** (Recherches sur quelques maladies des plantes cultivées en France). — *Extr. des Annales de l'École nationale d'Agriculture de Rennes,* t. IV, 1910, pp. 1-29, 15 figg. Rennes, 1911.

A. — A new parasite of the almond-tree: *Fusicladium Amygdali,* sp. nov.

France:
Ille-et-
Vilaine,
Lot-et-
Garonne
The writer found on Almond-trees in the Experimental Garden of the National School of Agriculture at Rennes, and afterwards on trees growing in the open in Lot-et-Garonne, a fungus which he considers related to *Fusicladium Cerasi,* Rhb. and to *F. Pruni* Ducomet, but which he distinguishes from these by the name of *F. Amygdali,* sp. nov.

It is a parasite which attacks the leaves and small branches. It has not yet been noticed on the fruit.

It does very little harm on the leaves where it is hardly noticeable. On the small branches, the buds which are situated on the spots formed by this fungus frequently wither within the year of their formation. The same may be said of the extremities of the branches, when the fungus is wide-spread.

---

(1) The disease called «Sooty-blotch» in America is due to *Phyllachora pomigena* (Schw) Sacc. and " Flyspeck " to *Leptothyrium Pomi.* (Mont et Fr.) Sacc. STEVENS & HALL *Diseases of Economic Plants,* p. 93. New York, |1910.
(*Ed.*).

(2) See page 367 of *Bulletin* of Dec. 1910.

The writer advises disinfecting the branches during the winter, or, better still, at the beginning of the spring, immediately before the buds open. This, of course, will not prevent making use of anticryptogamic preparations during the period of vegetation.

B. — A *Peronospora*, parasite of buckwheat.

In 1910, an experimental crop of buckwheat, grown at the National School of Agriculture at Rennes, was suddenly damaged by a formidable invasion of a *Peronospora* of a kind not yet known; so far it has not been possible to determine whether this *Peronospora* belongs to a new species, or to a species already known as a parasite of other Polygonaceae.

Notch-seeded buckwheat suffered most severely, but common buckwheat and Tartarian buckwheat, cultivated in its immediate vicinity, were also attacked shortly after the first named.

The leaves attacked frequently withered from the edge inward. Brown points often appear on the withered patches. These are the conidial spores of a *Heterosporium*, which is undoubtedly related to the *Heterosporium variabile* of spinach. In this case it has only an accessory rôle; it is rather a saprophyte than a parasite.

C. — A little-known parasite of the potato : *Cercospora concors* (Casp.) Sacc.

In June 1910, the writer noted on the leaves of a potato of the " Early Rose " variety, a number of little round spots, of a dark brown colour, and therefore quite distinct from those of *Phytophthora infestans* both as regards colour, shape, and dimensions.

This is a parasite first noted in Germany in 1855, by Caspary, and described by him under the name of *Fusisporium concors*, and afterwards connected with the genus *Cercospora* (*C. concors* (Casp.) Sacc.).

The writer believes this parasite had never been noticed in France.

The fungus only attacks the lower leaves which are already fading, and therefore does not seem likely to do serious injury to the plant.

D. — On the simultaneousness of the action of some parasitic fungi of cultivated plants.

The writer calls attention to cases of the simultaneousness of the action of some parasitic fungi, due to a simple form of commensalism, from causes dependent on nutrition.

Such is the case in the association of *Cystopus candidus* and *Peronospora parasitica* on cabbage and sea-kale; of *Exoascus deformans* and *Clasterosporium carpophilum* on the peach-tree; and of *Puccinia Rubigo-vera* and *Tilletia Tritici* on wheat.

These three examples clearly indicate the influence of predisposition on the development of parasitic diseases. The essential factor in predisposition is, in this case, the internal chemical nature modified by the growth of the first parasite, or, to be more precise, as a result of the stimulus caused by the first parasite on the cells of the host-plant.

E. — Observations on *Clasterosporium carpophilum* (Lév.) Adh. in its bearing on " gummosis ".

It is known that *Clasterosporium carpophilum* (Lév.) Adh. (= *Cl. Amygdalearum* (Pass.) Sacc. = *Coryneum Beijerincki* Oud. = *Asterula Beijerincki* Wuill.?) causes on the several Amygdaleae, and more especially on the peach, such an abundant exudation of gum that the upper parts of the young branches die in full vegetation.

On the other hand, careful inspection, at the time of the great invasions in the early spring of all the young branches which have died from the ravages of this parasite shortly after the opening of the buds, frequently shows that these branches are situated under a gummy mass caused by the previous year's attack on the mother branch.

This leads at once to the supposition that the spores of the parasite, born in the lesion which gave rise to the gummy exudation, have been carried by the rain water into the small cavity in the angle formed by the bud from which the twig has grown with the branch which bears it. This is evidently the case, at least in many instances.

Microscopic examination of the gummy mass shows that the gum, as might have been supposed, acts as a culture in which the initial sowing of the conidia of the *Clasterosporium* is preserved as it is given off. The conidia develop there with the greatest facility when, as the result of moist weather, the gum is adequately softened.

It is thus seen to be necessary to subject the trees in winter to an anticryptogamic treatment, which shall poison the culture medium and prevent the development of the conidia of the fungus. The cupric-hydrate of Bordeaux mixture is doubtless one of the best.

1887   D. PINOLINI. **Diseases and Pests of Crops in the Province of Macerata in Italy.** (Provincia di Macerata. Cattedra ambulante di Agricoltura. L'attività della Cattedra nel suo primo decennio. Relazione del Direttore). 91 pp. (Malattie delle piante, pp. 36-38), 4 tav. Macerata, 1911.

Italy:
Macerata

In the Report on the work of the itinerant Agricultural teaching in the Province of Macerata, during its first ten years, the writer briefly enumerates the diseases of plants met with in this Province.

Besides the phylloxera of the vine and *Diaspis pentagona* of the mulberry, the writer mentions other causes which injuriously affect the crops. Fortunately the Elateridae have done little harm to the wheat and maize crops. The injury done by *Carpocapsa* and *Anthonomus* to pear-trees and by *Schizoneura lanigera* to apple-trees was much more severe.

The olive has suffered from a serious invasion of Cantharides. The following insect pests were studied with a view to their control: *Hyponomeuta padella, H. malinella, Pieris Brassicae, P. Rapae, P. Napi, Sesia apiformis, Cossus ligniperda, Zeuzera pyrina, Liparis dispar, Bombyx Quercus, Agrotis segetum, A. Tritici, A. fimbria.* Many experiments have been made to control the mole-cricket, which does serious damage to many crops in the province.

In 1905 an invasion of *Arvicola arvalis* was recorded.

In conclusion, attention is called to broomrape, *Orobanche speciosa*, which injures the bean crops seriously each year, and which is constantly spreading.

A. A. JACZEWSKI. **General Account of the Distribution of Crypto-** **gamic Diseases in Russia in 1909.** (Ocerk Rasprostraneniia Gribnik Boliesnei Rastenii V Rossii V 1909 Godu. Boliesni Sadovekh i Dekorativnekh Rastenii). — (*Year-Book of Rural Organization and Agriculture of the Department of Agriculture*), G. III, p. 589. S. Peterburg, 1910.

1888

Sphaerotheca pannosa is widely spread in rose-gardens, and attacks by preference *Rosa suaveolens*. As this plant, which is grown in nurseries, is much used for grafting, the disease is spread by this means. Infected plants should be treated with flowers of sulphur and grafts with copper sulphate.

Russia

Heterosporium gracile Sacc. and *Ascochyta orientalis* are notified in the Government of Kourk as injuring respectively *Iris* and *Silene*.

Mr. Bondarziev has discovered on yellow acacia a new fungus *Ascochyta Borjomi*, which produces round, whitish blotches, circled with a dark ring, on the leaves.

Fungoid attack of Crops in Sagaing District of Burma. See Abstr. 1942 in this *Bulletin*.

1889
British India:
Burma

1890   F. G. B. OSBORN. *Spongospora subterranea (Wallroth) Johnson.*
           — *Annals of Botany*, vol. XXV, No. XCVIII, pp. 327-341. Lon-
           don-Oxford, April 1911.

The organism producing the « Corky » or « Powdery Scab »
of potatoes (*Spongospora subterranea*) has recently been described by
Great   both Johnson (*Econ. Proc. Roy. Dublin Soc.* vol. I. pt. 12, April 1908;
Britain   *Sci. Proc. Roy. Dublin Soc.* vol. xii, N. S. No 16, July, 1909) and
Massee (*Journal of the Board of Agriculture*, vol. xv, 1908, p. 592), but
the results of their investigations are not in agreement (1).

Briefly stated, our present knowledge of *Spongospora* is as
follows:

Uninucleate myxamoebae are observed in young potato cells,
though this is disputed by Johnson. These subsequently form a plasmodium, while it is stated that fresh cells are invaded by a passage
being bored through their walls. At the approach of spore formation the plasmodium becomes very vacuolar, and then, according to
Massee, a hollow sphere is formed, in the walls of which lacunae
appear, while later polygonal cells (spores) are cut off, arranged in a
single layer.

Johnson has corrected this statement, pointing out that the

---

(1) See *The Gardener's Chronicle*, Febr. 19, 1910, p. 122:

« Corky Scab » or « scurf », is the well-known surface scurf which,
though quite superficial, takes away from the market value of the potato.
Organisms are found in the places affected by « Scab », but it is doubtful
whether these actually cause the disease. This is favoured by some alkaline
soils, and those which have been manured with night-soil and ashes. « Scab »
occurs more frequently in light than in compact soils. The disease is less
severe when sawdust is mixed with the soil at the time of planting, and if
quick-lime is applied to non-calcareous soils.

« Powdery Scab » is recognized by the fact that the spots it causes penetrate deeper into the tuber, and in the later stages dry rot cavities are found.
These cells contain the spores of a slime-fungus: *Spongospora*. As a preventive measure against « Scab » the seed tubers have been plunged before
planting in a solution of corrosive sublimate (1 oz. in 10 gals. or 28 gr to 45
litres of water), but this treatment is not always succesful. It is more
advisable to use « boxed » or « greened » seed tubers, wich have been carefully
selected and occasionally sorted during the winter. Tubers thus kept are
in a better hygienic condition than those stored in heaps, and the strong
short shoots are less subject to infection. G. W. SMITH, *Potato Tuber Diseases*,
in R. P. WRIGHT'S *Standard Cyclopedia of Modern Agriculture*, vol. X, p. 32.
London, 1910.   (*Ed.*).

spore mass is a « sponge-like » body. He further states that each spore contains a number of nuclei, comparing this with Jahn's (*Ber. d. deutsch. bot Gesell.* vol. xxvi-a. 1908) and Olive's (*Trans. Wiscon, Acad. Arts Sci. Litt.* vol. xv, pt. ii, 1907, p. 653) observations on *Ceratiomyxa*. Massee saw only a single amoeba which escaped on the germination of the spore.

As the investigations of Johnson and Massee are discordant it would seem desirable that other studies should be made on this subject. In this article the writer only gives an account of the biology and cytology of *Spongospora*, with some remarks on its affinities. The conclusions may be summarised as follows :

Spongospora subterranea is an intracellular parasite of the potato tuber, living in the cells in an amoeboid condition, and invading the daughter cells as they form in the process of cell-division.

The nuclei of the amoebae divide in an amitotic manner during the vegetative phase ; on its conclusion the amoebae fuse to form a plasmodium.

Plasmodium formation is followed by a degeneration and disappearance of the vegetative nuclei, chromidia appearing in the protoplasm. This is the akaryote stage.

On the conclusion of the akaryote stage the nuclei are formed on different sides to the previous ones, some of the chromidia being used in the process while the remainder degenerate.

Karyogamy occurs between pairs of the nuclei, and is succeeded by a temporary enlargement of the nuclei and a contraction of the chromatin, which is possibly a condition of synapsis.

Two karyokinetic divisions of the nuclei follow each other rapidly ; the first is marked by its length of spindle ; the spindle of the second is shorter, with more sharply defined fibres, and has eight chromosomes.

The spores are uninucleate, and are aggregated in rounded masses traversed by fissures, and marked by irregular depressions, but remaining attached in structures known as « spore balls ».

Spongospora is a member of the Plasmodiophoraceae, which group has many points of relationship to the Mycetozoa, differing chiefly in the parasitic habit, the method of division of the vegetative nuclei, and by the less constant presence of a flagellum on spore germination.

A bibliography of 21 papers is given and a plate containing 35 drawings.

1891

R. Ewert. **The Resistance to Cold of Conidia formed in Summer.**
(Die Bedeutung überwinterter Sommerkonidien für die Früh-
jahrsinfektion). — *Jahresbericht der Vereinigung für angewandte
Botanik*, Siebenter Jahrgang, 1909, pp. 91-92. Berlin, 1910.

Germany

As no perithecium has yet been found for *Oidium quercinum*
Thüm., which is rapidly developing in Germany, the writer has
made experiments with a view to determining the power of resistance of the conidia to cold.

The results show that the conidia of *Mycosphaerella sentina*
Kleb. preserve their germinating power throughout the winter until
the beginning of spring. And in summer, when subjected to a temperature of 5°-16° C, they do not lose their infectious qualities nor
their germinating faculty. The conidia of *Gloesporium Ribis* and
of *Fusicladium* behave in a like manner.

1892

V. Peglion. **On the Wintering of the Oak-Oidium.** (Intorno
allo svernamento dell'Oidio della quercia). — (*Rendiconti della
R. Accademia dei Lincei, Classe Scienze*, vol. XX, pp. 505-507.
Rome, 1911). *Rivista di Patologia vegetale*, an. V, n. 3, p. 37.
Pavia, 1 Giugno, 1911.

Italy

The investigations made by this writer show that the mycelium of the Oidium of the Oak can winter inside the buds of this
tree, thus living from one year to another as a parasite of the
organs in a state of latent vitality.

1893

V. Peglion. **On the Wintering of Certain Erisyphaceae.** (Intorno
allo svolgimento di alcune Erisifacee). — (*Rendiconti della Regia
Accademia dei Lincei, Classe Scienze*, vol. XX, pp. 687-690.
Roma, 1911). *Rivista di Patologia vegetale*, an. V. n. 3, p. 37.
Pavia, 1 Giugno 1911.

Italy

The writer notes that, like the Oidium of the Oak, the Oidium
of the Apple-tree (*Oidium farinosum*, conidial form of *Podosphaera
leucotricha*) and the Oidium of the Rose (*Oidium leucoconium*, conidial form of *Sphaerotheca pannosa*), winter as parasites in the
buds of their respective host-plants, thus confirming the observations already made by Mr. Laubert.

R. J. Kellermann. **The Relation of Crown-Gall to Legume Inoculation.** — *U. S. Dept. of Agric., Bureau of Plant Industry, Circular, No. 76*, pp. 3-6. Washington, March 30, 1911.

1894

The crown-gall organism has been found in tumors somewhat resembling the normal nitrogen-fixing nodules, upon the roots of alfalfa, crimson clover, and alsike clover.

It is usually possible to distinguish the tumors produced by the crown-gall bacteria from the nodules formed by the nitrogen-fixing bacteria by their external appearance. The nitrogen-fixing nodules do not modify the root-structure, whereas the crown-gall tumor causes much distortion of the root; frequently forcing it to branch into many small roots. Bacteriological examination makes it always easy to distinguish between the two.

It is not known what other leguminous crops are susceptible to crown-gall infection. It is believed, however, that there is reason to suspect all the clovers.

United States

H. S. Fawcett & O. P. Burger. **Diplodia causing Gumming of Peach and Orange.** — *Mycologia*, vol. III, No. 3, pp. 151-153. Lancaster, Pa. May, 1911.

1895

A species of *Diplodia* has been isolated in pure cultures from both peach trees and orange trees in Florida, and by inoculation tests has been shown to produce copious gumming on healthy individuals of these hosts.

As far as known to the writers this is the first time that any of the species of *Diplodia* have been shown to produce gumming in trees. This same fungus was also isolated a number of times from rotting fruits of orange and of grapefruit. It may cause softening and decay of various fruits.* Oranges, lemons, and apples, after being inoculated with a bit of the mycelium, softened in from one to two weeks.

United States : Florida

An examination of the description of this fungus by I. B. P. Evans (1) appears to show that the Florida *Diplodia* on peach and citrus may be the same as *Diplodia natalensis* Evans. Further study, and a comparison of cultures of the two fungi will, however, be necessary to determine this point.

---

(1) See Abstr. 323, *Bulletin* January, 1911.   (*Ed.*).

1896

ELLSWORTH BETHEL. **Notes on some Species of Gymnosporangium in Colorado.** — *Mycologia*, Vol. III, No. 3, pp. 156-160. Lancaster, Pa. May, 1911.

United States: Colorado

Colorado possesses 9 distinct species of cedar rusts (10, counting the new species described below), which is about one third the number of teleutospore forms known to occur in the United States. The new species causes the dense, globose "witches' brooms" (2 in. to 2 ft. in diameter) on the Utah cedar (*Juniperus utahensis*). The cause of these conspicuous "brooms" has been attributed to some of the numerous insects such as coccids, aphids, etc. which inhabit them. The studies made by the writer, however, show that a small *Gymnosporangium*, *G. Kernianum* sp. nov., was the cause of the fasciation, and that the presence of the insects is merely incidental. There are no clues as to its roestelial connection, though it probably belongs to *Amelanchier* and *Peraphyllum*, which form extensive chapparal around the infected trees.

The presence in the immediate vicinity of *Aecidium gracilens* Peck, on *Philadelphus occidentalis*, and of *Gymnosporangium speciosum* Peck on *Juniperus utahensis*, led the writer to think that *A. gracilens* may be considered as a true *Roestalia*. Thus the relationship of *A. gracilens* to *G. speciosum* is merely inferential, and is based on field observations, distribution, and the apparent roestelial characters of the *Aecidium*. Further, the fact that sowings of *G. speciosum* have been tried unsuccessfully on *Amelanchier*, *Crataegus*, and *Sorbus* supports the inference that it may have its roestelial stage outside of the Malaceae. This would be a very interesting connection if once established, since the only known case of a *Roestalia* outside of the ligneous Malaceae, is that of *G. exterum* Arth., which occurs on *Gillenia stipulacea*, a herbaceous annual of the Rosaceae, while *Philadelphus* belongs to the Hydrangiaceae. *G. speciosum* occurs in woody 'tissue of old branches, emerging through the bark in long longitudinal, sinuous masses of a reddish or orange colour, which ultimately fades to a white colour. It causes large hypertrophies, sometimes six to ten inches in diameter, superficially resembling those of *Peridermium Harkensii* Moore, on species of pine.

1897
Germany

A Smut-resistant Wheat. See above Abstr. 1653.

J. ERIKSSON. **The Red Colour of the Epidermis of Apples and Pears** **1898**
and Scab Disease. (Die rote Farbe der Fruchtschale und die
Schorfkrankheit der Obstsorten). — *Zeitschrift für Pflanzen-*
krankheiten. XXI Band. Heft. 3' pp. 129-131. Stuttgart, 1911.

In a study on the struggle against *Scab Fungi* (*Fusicladium*
dendriticum and *F. pirinum*) (1) E. Voges states that the red skin-
ned varieties of apples are immune against the attacks of fungi. **Sweden**
He supposes this immnnity is due to the presence of repellent
matter in the skin-cells.

The author of this article quotes a number of facts in disproof
of this hypothesis. The "*Rote Winterkalvill*" in the south of Sweden, suffers severely. In a fruit plantation near Matmô the following
were the worst attacked varieties of pears: "*Larsmässe Birne*"
early yellow, "*Jacobes Birne*", early, reddening on the side turned
to the sun, "*Fulleö Birne*", early, yellow and "Flemish Beauty",
late, reddening on the side turned to the sun.

This fungus winters on fallen leaves and on the latest grown
wood.

The following remedies are recommended:

1) Gather and burn all infected leaves;

2) Wash three times with a liquid fungicide: once before the
leaves appear, again immediately after their appearance, and a third
time towards the end of the flowering period.

Bordeaux mixture and a solution of from 2 to 3 % (early) and
from 1 to 2 %, (later) of chloride of sodium were successfully used
as fungicides.

3) Washing with milk of lime during the winter kills the
wintering portion of the stroma of the fungus.

LAURENT. **Conditions determining the Resistance of the Vine to Mil-** **1899**
dew. (Les conditions de résistance de la Vigne au "Mildew") —
Bulletin mensuel de l'Office de Renseignemenis Agricoles, N. 4,
pp. 464-471. Paris, April, 1911.

Numerous observations show that the sensitiveness of the vine
to mildew is very variable, and the multiplicity of the factors which **France**
may come into action is very disconcerting.

---

(1) On *Fusicladium* see Abstracts 1021-1024, *Bull.* March, 1911. They should
be called *Venturia inaequalis* (Cooke) Aderh., and *V. pirina* Aderh., now that
the ascigerous stages are known. Cf. P. SORAUER, *Handbuch der Pfanzenkrank-*
heiten, II Band, p. 248. Berlin, 1905. (*Ed.*).

Vineyards which have been directly manured with farm-yard manure are those most severely affected in that same year; phosphatic and potassic fertilisers have the opposite effect. The young leaves are most affected by the parasite. Resistance varies also according to the method of pruning, nipping, and the nature of the stock.

All these factors act indirectly by modifying the chemical and physical qualities of the vine-cells.

Resistance to mildew increases with the molecular concentration of the vine-sap. Dressings of farm-yard manure should always be corrected by a dressing of superphosphate.

We are far from having a reliable remedy against mildew such as vine-growers wish for, but by improving the usual conditions of culture, vines can be rendered relatively immune, which will greatly increase the effectiveness of preventive measures.

1900
West Indies

Fungus Parasites of Scale Insects.   See below, Abstr. 1952.

1901
Great
Britain

Species of *Cordiceps* parasitic on Larvae of Swift Moths (*Hepialus*).   See below, Abstr. 1948.

1902
N. America

***Empusa (Entomophthora) Sphaerosperma*, parasitic on Pupae of *Phytonomus nigrirostris*.**   See below, Abstr. 1974.

1903

G. H. GARRAD. **Nicotine Wash.   The Growing of Tobacco for Nicotine Extraction.** — *The Journal of the South Eastern Agricultural College, Wye, Kent*, No. 19, pp. 262-317. London and Ashford, Kent. 1910.

Great
Britain:
Kent

Nicotine wash, at a strength of about 1 oz. or 1 ⅓ oz. of 95 % pure nicotine per 10 gallons of water, with the addition of a small quantity of soft soap, is used with most deadly effect against many insect pests, including the Apple Sucker (*Psylla mali*) all kinds of Aphides, Thrips or Thunder Flies, the larvae of the Winter Moth (*Cheimatobia brumata*) and most young caterpillars. Among the Aphides are included such pests as Hop Damson Aphis or Hop Fly (*Phorodon humuli*), the Leaf Curling Aphis or " Green Fly " (*Aphis Pomi*), the Cherry Aphis or " Black Fly " (*Myzus cerasi*), the Woolly Aphis or " American Blight " (*Schizoneura lanigera*), and the two

Currant Aphides (*Rhopalosiphum ribis* and *Myzus ribesiae*). Against all these, nicotine is the best remedy that has yet been discovered.

And yet this wash is very seldom used as it is much too expensive. Experiments have, therefore, been made to see whether it would not be practicable and profitable for the fruit or hop-grower to grow his own tobacco and manufacture his own insecticide, in a simple way and at a low cost. With this object in view the crop is being grown at Wye on a fairly large scale ; and attempts are being made to find or to breed a very heavy-yielding type of tobacco, containing a high percentage of nicotine, which shall be particularly suited to this purpose of nicotine extraction.

The experiments have led the author to the following conclusions :

Tobacco can be grown to maturity in Great Britain, if care be taken to use suitable varieties such as *Erba-santa*, Clardy, Blue Pryor, *Rustica*, from Ireland, and Little Hill. On a good soil, a crop of from 1600 to 2000 lbs of dry leaves may be expected per acre.

The cost of growing an acre of tobacco may be estimated at £21 12s 6d, with a yield of 1800 lbs, of dry leaves, containing 4 % of nicotine = 72 lbs. of nicotine. Therefore the cost of producing 1 lb. of nicotine is 6s.

Spencer Pickering, working on the Apple Sucker (*Psylla mali*), found that a 0.075 % solution was the weakest strength of nicotine that could be effectively used.

If we allow 133 gallons as the amount of wash required to spray one acre, the cost of spray per acre of ground will be the cost of one pound of nicotine. We want therefore to be able to produce nicotine at a cost of something under 8s. per lb. and if nicotine wash is to be brought into general use its price must be reduced at most to 8s per acre of hops or fruit sprayed. This year's experiments worked out at a slightly higher price (including cost of extraction), so there is good cause for hope that this may be accomplished. Experiments will be continued next year on the same line.

The ideal soil for tobacco is a good rich loam and the land must be well worked. The best manure is dung combined with a heavy dressing of complete artificials, containing an excessive quantity of nitrogen.

The best distance apart to put the plants appears to be 3 ft by 1 ½ ft. This distance was found to give a larger crop without diminishing the nicotine content.

The plants must be topped low, leaving a stalk bearing only about a dozen leaves. This considerably increases the nicotine content without seriously diminishing the yield. It is very important to remove the side shoots (suckers) as fast as they appear, as this removal has a great influence on the nicotine content. The plants should not be cut until the leaves begin to assume a yellowish hue.

The best varieties tried were the *Erba-santa*, from Italy, *Rustica* and Blue Pryor from Ireland. One Sucker from the Transvaal, *Rustica* from India, and Clardy, Little Kill and North Carolina Bright from America.

1904   B. T. P. BARKER & C. T. GIMMINGHAM. **Fungicidal Action of Bordeaux Mixtures**. — *The Journal of Agricultural Science*. Vol. IV, Part I, pp. 76-94. Cambridge, May 1911.

A review of the many publications on this subject shows that the various theories on the fungicidal action of Bordeaux mixtures can be classified in three groups :

Great Britain

1) The copper is dissolved by atmospheric action, more especially by the action of atmospheric carbon dioxide ; purely chemical action.

2) The leaves sprayed with the mixture have a dissolvent effect on the copper compounds ; plant action.

3) The fungus itself dissolves the copper by which it is at last poisoned ; fungicidal action.

The writers discuss these three theories. There is nothing new in the conclusions arrived at, but they could not fail to have a practical influence on spraying, and their importance has already been confirmed by the results obtained.

In the first place they clearly point to the need of thorough spraying, so that the surfaces subject to attack may be well coated. In the second place they show the importance of using precipitate of copper in a state of very fine division so that it may adhere more completely to the foliage. In the third place they account for the fact that Bordeaux mixture may have an immediate effect; this is the opinion expressed by Clark and Crandall in their publication, and it is generally endorsed by experts. Nevertheless Pickering is of another opinion, but he adduces no facts in support of his views. No accurate conclusions have yet been arrived at as to the effect of an excess of lime in the mixture. It would seem that when other conditions are equal, the greater the excess of lime, the less closely the mixture adheres to the leaves, as the particles of copper are more widely separated; but a number of other factors evidently come into play in this matter.

In conclusion, the results of these investigations point to the importance of the adhesive quality of the mixture.

A. W. OLDERSHAW. **Experiments on the Spraying of Potatoes in Co. Louth, Ireland.** — *Dept. of Agric. and Techn. Instruction for Ireland: Journal*, vol. XI, No. 3, pp. 446-450. Dublin, April 1911.

1905

Experiments were carried out in 1908, 1909 and 1910 to test the efficacy of Woburn Bordeaux mixture (as described in the 8th and 11th Reports of the Woburn Experimental Fruit Farm (1) against potato blight (2), in comparison with soda-Bordeaux (Burgundy) mixture and milk-of-lime Bordeaux.

Ireland

In 1908 and 1909 the blight was very slight, so that the results could not be considered conclusive.

In 1910, however, the blight was very virulent, so that the conditions for testing spraying materials were almost ideal. The experiments were carried out on four farms. The plots were $1/20$ acre, except at two stations (B and D) where the sprayed plots were $1/3$ acre. The mixtures used were: Plot I, unsprayed; Plot II, Woburn Bordeaux Paste, 15 lbs. to 100 gallons; Plot III, Soda Bordeaux mixture, 8 : 10 : 40 ; Plot IV, Milk-of-lime Bordeaux mixture, 8 : 4 : 40.

At station C the plots were sprayed once (2nd week of July), at the others twice (1st week of July, and a fortnight later). In all cases 120 gallons per acre for each spraying were used.

The following are the results, expressed in cwts. per statute acre:

Station	I. Unsprayed		II. Woburn		III. Soda		IV. Lime	
	Saleable	Diseased	Saleable	Diseased	Saleable	Diseased	Saleable	Diseased
A	189	9	188	9	188	3	221	2
B	132	3	146	3	171	1	212	1
C	88	2	97	5	108	1	—	—
D	—	—	102	1	157	1	—	—

In all cases the Bordeaux mixture plots remained green longer than the Woburn paste plot, and the latter longer than the unsprayed plot.

---

(1) See: *The Science and Practice of Farming during* 1910 *in Great Britain*, p. 393. Rome, 1910. (*Ed.*).

(2) *Phytophthora infestans.* (*Ed.*).

18

1906
Germany

Carbolineum in the Control of *Sclerotinia fructigena, Botrytis ci-nerea, Penicillium glaucum,* **and the** *Peronospora* **of Vines.** See Abstract 1962 in this *Bulletin.*

Parasitic Diseases of Various Plants and Means
of Prevention and Control (1).

1907

E. C. JOHNSON. **Floret Sterility of Wheats due to Fungi, in the South West United States.** — (*Phytopathology*, Vol. I, pp. 17-18). *Annales Mycologici*, Vol. IX, No. 3, p. 307. Berlin, 1911.

United
States

The wheat crop in the States of the South-West of the United States is much reduced; ears of normal appearance are sterile.

The writer investigated the cause of this sterility with the help of artificial cultures, and concluded that it is due to the action of fungi, first of all *Stemphylium Tritici* and then *Puccinia graminis.* A third fungus, *Cladosporium graminum,* is only of secondary importance.

1908

Rye *Fusarium.* **Depressaria nervosa on Cumin.** *Hylemyia coarctata* **on Cereals.** — *Deutsche landwirtschaftliche Rundschau.* N. 9, pp. 97-99. Berlin, 15. Mai 1911.

Germany

I. FUSARIUM DISEASE OF WINTER RYE. — In bad years, especially when the moisture is excessive, cereals are backward in earing and are more severely attacked by a whole series of fungi known as " antagonistic symbionts. " On cereals these are chiefly " black fungi, " such as *Alternaria (Sporodesmium), Cladosporium* and *Fusarium.*

Other crops have other parasites, as *Ascochyta Pisi* on Peas; *Phoma Betae* on Beets and Mangels; the genera *Alternaria, Cladosporium,* etc., on various other plants.

---

(1) The plants are arranged in the same order as in the first part of this *Bulletin.*

The above mentioned " black fungi " appear each year on the grains of cereals, where they can be seen under the microscope in the form of slender threads. They are also found on beet seeds. In view of the fact that these fungi have adapted themselves to live on the host plant and to pass the period of repose on its seed, the writer proposes that they be known as injurious rivals (*schäd-liche Mitläufer*). In accordance with a general biological law, the weakening of the higher plant is particularly favourable to their development. This is why cold, damp, starvation, drought, and other enfeebling conditions contribute to spread parasitic diseases. This can be demonstrated experimentally with great exactness.

For instance, by selecting favourable conditions root-scab (*Wurzelbrand*) of beets caused by *Phoma Betae*, can be produced to any degree of intensity, using the same seed. If the environment is favourable to the higher plant the fungus scarcely develops, and vice versa.

The same laws hold good in the case of the species of *Fusarium* which attack cereals. According to the conditions under which they ripen, the cereal seeds will be more or less infested with the spores of *Fusarium* (in the ratio of 5 to 60 % and even more) according to Hiltner's observations. If the conditions following on sowing are favourable to the cereal, the fungus will develop but little and will cause no serious injury ; if they are not, the fungus will multiply to such an extent that it may even kill the young plants. Wheat-seeds, originally affected by *Fusarium* in the ratio of 60 %, sown on unmanured quartz sand, produced a maximum of diseased plants, about 60 %. When lime, potash and phosphates were added to the sand, only 30 % of the plants were slightly affected, although the manurial conditions were by no means perfect.

In the field, plants are at some time or other under unfavourable conditions, and it is then that the fungus may attack them severely.

When the seed is sown too late, the cereal develops but little, as it is at once subjected to winter conditions. Rye sown in October was so severely attacked that in some localities it was ploughed in. If it had been sown in September it would have been almost immune. Almost absolute immunity is secured for rye sown early and treated with a 1 ‰ solution of corrosive sublimate, according to Hiltner's advice (1).

(1) See Abstr. 993, *Bulletin*, March, 1911.

The disinfection of seed thus helps to defend the crops, even when conditions are unfavourable to them, against antagonistic symbions.

II. OBSERVATIONS ON THE CUMIN MOTH. — *Depressaria nervosa*, one of the Micro-lepidoptera, attacks the crops of cumin in Saxony so severely as to render its cultivation impossible. Kuhn advised that sheep be grazed in the infected fields in the spring. Dietrich has tried this remedy for several years with good results. This spring, moths came out from their hibernation about the end of March and laid their eggs on the upper leaves and stalks of the cumin from then on to the 10th of April; the larvae hatched in nine days. The sheep should be turned in at the end of March and in the first half of April.

The young larvae are very delicate, and can be destroyed by a thick dusting of slaked lime; and perhaps cyanamide or basic slag. Lime and basic slag do not injure the plants.

III. THE WHEAT-BULB FLY ON WINTER CORN. — The maggot of Wheat-bulb Fly (*Hylemyia coarctata*) lives in the hearts of wheat and rye plants, and generally destroys them. Cases have been found of 80 % loss in large fields of October-sown wheat.

The species has two broods, of which only the winter one attacks cereals.

The flies swarm and lay their eggs in late autumn, up to the end of October. The eggs laid on the tender plants hatch before winter, but the chief feeding time is in the first warm days of spring, and it is then that most of the damage is done. The maggot goes to the earth to pupate at the end of May; the adult emerges in a few weeks.

The new generation lays its eggs on meadow-grasses. For this reason, fields bordering on meadows are most subject to attack.

It is also well ascertained that wheat following peas is specially susceptible; but no explanation of this can be given, as the fly has apparently no connection with peas.

Again, some parts of fields may escape, for instance the ridges. This seems to be due to the more rapid development of the plants there, owing to the firmer soil. Firm soil is evidently advantageous to the crop.

Thin crops of winter-wheat may be cross sown in spring with Galician spring-wheat; this is better than dressing with nitrate, which only encourages rust and mildew in the healthy plants.

Mid-season sowings seem to be the best against this fly; wheat should be got in at the end of September if possible.

T. CARROLL. **An Inquiry into the Potato Disease** *(Phytophthora*   1909
infestans). — *Nature*, No. 2171, vol, 86, p. 506. London,
June, 1911.

Experiments were carried out by the writer at the Albert
Agricultural Institution, Glasnevin, Dublin, to ascertain whether the
disease, *Phytophthora infestans*, is carried to the tubers of the potato
plants from the leaves through the stems, and with the object of   United
proving the value of preventive spraying and suggesting its *raison d'être*.   Kingdom :
                                                                        Ireland :
    a) A case, protected by cotton-wool from the entrance of   Galway
disease spores, was placed in a field of potatoes. The potatoes
planted in the case belonged to a variety liable to the disease ; but
the haulms and tubers of these protected· potatoes were not attacked, whilst the surrounding unprotected crop was badly affected.

    b) A portion of ground in which potatoes were growing was
completely covered with cotton-wool immediately after the plants
had made their appearence, when it was found that the tubers of
the crop were completely free from disease, although the surrounding
crop was as much diseased as were the haulms of the protected
potatoes.

    c) Between the drills, holes were made 12 in, 6 in. and 3
in. deep, into which immature potato tubers were put, the haulms
of the potatoes being placed over them. The potatoes from the 12
in. hole were free from disease: those from the 6 in. and 3 in.
holes were one third and two thirds diseased respectively.

Experiments with diseased tubers were also undertaken:

    a) These were planted in a cool conservatory ; disease did
not appear in the plants nor in their tubers, although crops in the
neighbourhood were badly diseased.

    b) One of the tubers of a plant grown in the conservatory
showed no sign of disease up to September of the following year.
The haulms of this plant were removed, and, the soil having been
carefully removed from the tubers, diseased haulms from a plant
grown outside were shaken over the exposed tubers after they had
been sprayed with pure spring water. Almost all the tubers con-
tracted the disease on their exposed surfaces.

G. H. PETHYBRIDGE. **Investigations on Potato Diseases in Ireland.**   1910
Second Report: — *Department of Agriculture and Technical
Instruction for Ireland. Journal.* Vol. XI, No. 3, pp. 417-449.
Dublin, April, 1911.

    In 1909, the Department established a temporary station at   United
Clifden, County Galway, for investigating the various diseases to which   Kingdom :
                                                                        Ireland

the potato is subject in Ireland. The Department's Journal for January 1910 (Vol. X. Nº 2) published an article on the first season's work at this station. The following account deals with further work carried out there last season. (1910).

1. The ordinary " Blight " or " Black Blight " (*Phytophthora infestans* De Bary). — This disease is still the most serious one on potatoes in Ireland. However, great progress has been made in recent years in preventing it by spraying with Bordeaux or Burgundy mixtures, prepared from copper sulphate with the addition of lime and soda respectively. The investigations made last summer aimed principally at ascertaining the comparative values of different spraying mixtures, the number of times it is necessary to use them during the season, and the dates at which the spray should be applied.

It was abundantly clear that spraying, to be properly efficient must be carried out before *Phytophthora* has made its appearance on the foliage; and that the best times of application of the spray were those preceding a spell of wet weather ; and it was also clear that a single spraying is insufficient in Ireland, a second one is absolutely necessary, and in many cases a third one would be of advantage.

It has been suggested that some saving in cost might accrue if the mixtures contained a smaller proportion of copper sulphate with a correspondingly smaller proportion of soda or lime, than is used in the typical Bordeaux and Burgundy mixtures (2 lbs. of copper sulphate per 10 gallons of water with 2 ½ lbs of washing soda and 1 lb of lime respectively). Judging from experiments made by the writer it would, however, seem unwise to reduce the strength of the copper sulphate.

Prof Kelhofer suggested that by the addition of a small quantity of sugar to Bordeaux mixture its efficacy would be retained for a long tine on standing, and that the necessity for making fresh mixture each time it was required would be obviated. Experiments made by the writer however show the advantage of using freshly-prepared Bordeaux and Burgundy mixtures, and do not lead to the conclusion that the disadvantages of a stale mixture are adequately compensated by the addition of sugar at the time of preparation.

Spraying with a mixture made up with sea-water is better than not spraying at all; but the use of sea-water for preparing a spray results in a considerable loss of efficiency as compared with fresh water.

The " Shamrock " and " Clifden seedling " varieties possess a high degree of resistance to blight, but are not immune. But each of these varieties suffered considerably from the attacks of Black

Stalk Rot and Stalk Disease (*Bacillus melanogenes* and *Sclerotinia sclerotiorum*).

The spores produced by *Phytophthora* during the season are extremely sensitive to external influences and soon lose their power of germination, so that they cannot exist over the winter from one season to the next. When potato tubers are affected with blight the greater number of them are completely killed during the winter. If the remainder be planted, a very large proportion of them will also die or " miss ". Of those that do produce sprouts overground by far the greater number give rise to plants which remain perfectly healthy until they become infected in the usual way by means of air-borne spores. A few may produce feeble sprouts above ground which become diseased by means of mycelium derived from the planted tuber. On such affected sprouts spores may be developed if the conditions of moisture and warmth in the surrounding air be favourable, hence they may be regarded as dangerous centres of infection for the neighbouring plants, but they can scarcely be of frequent occurrence in the fields.

2. " Yellowing ", or " Yellow Blight ". — No fungus or other parasite has been found as the cause of this disease; soil conditions seem to play the most important part in producing it. " Yellowing " is common on wet, undrained bog land, and on light shallow soils where the underlying rock comes up close to the surface. Draining and good cultivation are the best preventive and curative measures.

3. " Stalk " or " *Sclerotium* " Disease. — The investigations made by the writer show that the attack of the potato plant by this disease takes place chiefly from air-borne spores, and not, as has hitherto been maintained, through the soil. The fungus enters the plant through the older yellowing leaves. The fungus is not infrequently found on them, and makes its way down the leaf-stalk, and thus its mycelium reaches the stem of the plant and enters it. The second point of entry is the series of wounds left on the stalks by the falling leaves. The chances of infection are much fewer when they are crowded together. Treatment of soil and of leaves and stalks of the plants with Burgundy mixture and with lime had little effect against this disease. Spraying with liver-of-sulphur solution is the only treatment which seems to have had any effect, and this but a slight one.

4. *Botrytis*. — *Sclerotinia* is often accompanied by another but less serious trouble, *Botrytis*, which, nevertheless, in some seasons may do considerable damage. The spores of this fungus infect the yellowing leaves and the mycelium passes thence to the stems.

No completely satisfactory remedial measures have yet been discovered with which to combat this disease, but burning the stalks at the end of the season would diminish somewhat the number of *sclerotia.*

5. Black Stalk Rot (*Bacillus melanogenes*). — This disease is not confined to Ireland, for similar diseases have been described for Germany, France, Holland, Canada, and the United States.. The writer isolated the particular organism which causes this disease in a pure culture, and found it allied to those described for .other countries but not identical with them. The spread of this disease is mainly due to the unsuspected planting of already infected " seed " potatoes. A healthy tuber may become infected by mere contact with material in which the organism is growing; experiment has proved that the bacillus can pass through the skin of a healthy tuber even in the absence of wounds, through the lenticels, or breathing. pores. Turnip Rot and Black Stalk Rot are different diseases caused by distinct organisms. A practical method of preventing the disease is to remove and burn all plants seen to be affected, so as to prevent the soil from becoming contaminated, and to see that no diseased tubers get into the pits.

6. "Corky ", " Powdery " .or *Spongospora* Scab. (*Spongospora subterranea* Johns) (1). Spongospora Scab presents two forms of attack, in the one case that of small spots on the surface of the tubers, and in the other the form of a " canker " or eating away of the tuber. The latter is the more serious, but there are all degrees of transition between it and the spot form. There are no immune varieties. Experiments seem to show that the spore-balls of this organism pass unharmed through the digestive tract of the pig and that the manure from pigs fed on diseased potatoes may be a source of infection to a potato crop treated with it.

Lime rather favours the disease than acts as a cure for it. Complete disinfection of " seed " tubers was obtained by soaking them in 1) formalin solution (1 : 600) for 3 hours, 2) copper sulphate solution (1 %) for 3 hours ; 3) d°, followed by rolling in slaked lime ; 4) soaking in and covering with precipitate of Burgundy Mixture for 5 hours ; 5) wetting the surface and rolling in flowers of sulphur. The best results were obtained with the formalin treatment, and the next best with sulphur.

---

(1) See above, Abstr. 1890
. Also *The Science and. Practice of Farming during* 1910, *in Great Britain.* Intern. Inst. of Agriculture. Rome, 1910, p. 352.   (*Ed.*).

The results obtained with soil disinfection were unsatisfactory. The amount of disease was increased by lime, chloride of lime and gas lime. Treatment with copper sulphate brought about a partial reduction of the scab but also some reduction of the total yield. Judging from the results obtained with sulphur and with superphosphate, it would seem probable that acidity may have something to do with the checking of the disease. Up to the present time the organism has not been found on any other plant than the potato.

7. " Black Speck " or " Rhizoctonia " Scab. (*Hypochnus Solani* Prill & Delacr.). — It is quite common to find on the surface of potato tubers little dark brown bodies of irregular shape, which become jet black when wetted and which resemble particles of soil. This fungus apparently does but little harm ; it is claimed by some observers that it causes a wet-rot of potato tubers, but this has not yet been found to occur in Ireland. It does not appear to be capable of penetrating the skin of the potato as is certainly the case in the nearly allied species *R. violacea*. Experiments made by the writer clearly show that the Collar fungus (*Hypochnus Solani*) is merely the fructifying stage of what has hitherto been known as *Rhizoctonia Solani*. These observations confirm the work of Rolfs in America, (*Potato Failures, Agric. Expt. Sta. Colorado, Agric. College Bull.* 91, 1904).

8. " Leaf Roll " and " Curl " (1). — It is possible to distinguish clearly in what is commonly called " Curl " two distinct diseases, for one of which the name " Curl " may be retained, the designation " Leaf Roll " being a suitable one for the other. Observations made by the writer show that " Curl " is not a parasitic disease but a condition of the plant in which the foliage is perfectly green and apparently healthy but owing to the absence of proper growth in the veins the leaflets remain crumpled and the plants as a rule remain dwarfed.

" Leaf Roll " is generally characterised by a lightness in the colour of the newer foliage accompanied by a rolling inwards of the leaflets from their edges, so that the under surface becomes exposed to view. The disease is probably parasitic as the vascular tissues of the plant were found to be invaded by the fungus *Verticillium alboatrum*. This disease is spread by tubers.

(1) See Abstr. 1882, in this *Bulletin*. (*Ed.*).

1911

Experiments in the Control of the Potato Pest *Synchytrium endo-biotlcum* **Percival, with Flowers of Sulphur.** — *Zeitschrilt für Pflanzenkrankheiten*, XXI Band, Heft 3, pp. 186-187. Stutt-gart, 1. April, 1911.

The Agricultural Section of the Sulphur Manufacturers (*Agri-kultur Abteilung der Schwelel-Produzenten*) of Hamburg, has expe-

Germany

rimented in the efficacy of flowers of sulphur as a remedy against Potato Black Scab or Wart-Disease (Schorf Krankheit) (1). The results have been most satisfactory (2).

Each of the Six experiments made, showed a reduction of 50 % in the total number of diseased tubers in the plots thus treated. But the good effects of the sulphur do not stop there; it improves the condition of the soil, kills weeds, and increases the yield of the tubers, especially when 40 % of potash is added to the mixture.

1912

W. BUSSE. **Investigations into the Diseases of Beets.** (Untersuchungen über die Krankheiten der Rüben). — *Arbeiten aus der kaiserli-chen biologischen Anstalt für Land-und Forswirtschaft*, VIII Band, Heft 2, pp. 221-302. Berlin, 1911.

The three kinds of fungi (*Pythium de Baryanum, Phoma Betae,* and *Aphanomyces laevis*) which are generally recognized as the cause

Germany

of root disease in beets (*Wurzelbrand*), are found all over Germany.

In most cases this disease is caused by *Phoma Betae* which is brought into the field with the seed.

The severity of the attack varies with the degree of develop-ment of the plant. *Pythium de Baryanum* is found on seedlings which have just taken root, whereas *Phoma Betae* and *Aphanomyces laevis* only attack the plants much later on.

The percentage of disease due to each of these fungi differs from year to year. The considerable variations sometimes noted seem

---

(1) A cryptogamic disease caused by *Chrysophlyctis endobiotica* Schilb. Cf. P. SORAUER, *Handbuch der Pflanzenkrankheiten*, II Bd. p. 116, Berlin, 1905. See also this *Buletin* Dec. 1910, p. 361; and Feb. 1911, Abstr. 610. (*Ed.*).

(2) Trials made under the direction of the Board of Agriculture of Great Britain have shown that sulphur has very little effect against this disease. See E. S. SALMON in *Journal of the S. E. Agric. College*, 1909, pp. 313 and 315. London, and Ashford, Kent, 1909.   (*Ed.*).

to be due largely to weather conditions in the spring. When the weather is damp *Pythium* and *Aphanomyces* prevail, when the weather is dry the, attacks of *Phoma* are more frequent.

The following soils are those on which root-disease of beets is most commonly found :

    1) very clayey soil;

    2) peat soil rich in humus, and as a rule all very moist soil.

    3) sandy and loamy soil.

Uromyces Betae on Mangolds in England. See Abstract 1685 in this *Bulletin*.

    1913

A New Disease of Cotton in Dahomey. — (Krankheiten Tropischer Nutzpflanzen). — *Zeitschrift für Pflanzenkrankheiten,* XXI Band, Heft 4, p. 218. Stuttgart, 3 Juni, 1911.

    1914

Of recent years a very injurious disease of cotton has appeared in West Africa and in Dahomey; according to Fron's observations the young shoots and lateral branches are those which are most affected.

Patches of decayed tissue form on the affected parts in which the mycelium of *Phoma Roumii* multiplies freely amongst the decayed cell tissue.

    Dahomey

The bark over the diseased patches splits and falls aways in strips, showing the pycnidia of the fungus. These are black pustules from which, on opening, fall spores easily carried by the wind, and which thus rapidly infest the plantations.

This parasite withers the leaves and seedvessels.

F. W. SOUTH. **Arrowroot Disease in St. Vincent, W. I.** — *The Agricultural News.* Vol. X, N. 237, pp. 174-175. Barbados, May 18, 1911.

    1915

The fungoid disease known as " burning " of arrowroot (1) has been recognized in St. Vincent for many years, and appears to be

    Windward Islands: St. Vincent

---

(1) Arrowroot is obtained from *Maranta arundinacea,* and other kinds of Maranta, as well as from *Zamia, Tacca, Curcuma, Manihot,* etc. See BAILEY. *Cyclopedia of American Horticulture.* Vol. II, p. 983.

Maranta arundinacea is cultivated on a large scale in the Bermudas; a value of £2 162 was exported in 1908; at St. Vincent, in the Windward Islands a value of £31 492 was exported in 1909. Maranta is also cultivated in British India, and in Natal. Bermuda Arrowroot is considered the best and fetches the highest prices. (*The Statesmans's Year Book,* 1911, pp. 238 and 272. London, 1911 ; H. A. NICHOLLS and E. RAOUL, *Petit traité d'Agriculture tropicale,* p. 354. Paris, 1911).   (*Ed.*).

of fairly wide distribution. In patches here and there in the field, the plants appear to have fewer leaves than the healthy ones growing in their vicinity, while these leaves are often rolled up and somewhat wilted. When such plants are dug up it is seen that the scale leaves of the rhizome are blackened almost throughout. The disease penetrates to the rhizome and there forms small black spots, which become wider in extent and eventually cover most of its surface. On cutting through such a diseased rhizome, it is seen that narrow, dark-brown streaks, 1/3 mm. wide. run inward from the surface in a radial direction for varying distances, which may be as great as the complete radius of the section. The dark lines originate from the black spots on the epidermis of the plant-stem. On examining carefully the outside of the scale leaves, it is found, in some instances, that a brown mycelium is present, running in narrow strands along their surfaces, while, under damp conditions, a white mycelium may often be found between the surface of the creeping stems and the inner surface of the scale leaves. The component hyphae often occur in a small tuft springing from the black spot on the surface of the rhizome, which marks the extremity of one of the black lines mentioned. These observations and the fact that a white mycelium starting from diseased plants was to be found in the soil itself, leave little doubt that the disease is of fungoid origin.

The infected spots in the fields appear to extend but slowly in the majority of cases — a fact which would seem to be due to the comparatively slow growth of the fungus. They vary in area from a few to several hundred sq. feet, and appear to be fairly constant in position from year to year. The symptoms of the disease do not make themselves apparent in affected spots until the rhizomes are nearly ripe for digging. The host-plants of this fungus appear to be extremely numerous; the following are attacked: cassava (2), tannia (3), yam (4), bananas, and cocoa seedlings; it is also said to

---

(2) Bitter Cassava = *Manihot utilissima ;* Sweet Cassava = *Manihot Apii* (Euphorbiaceae). See BAILEY, *l. c.* p. 981.   (*Ed.*).

(3) *Colocasia antiquorum* (Aroideae) is known as "inhame" in Brasil, "tania" (spelt also *tanier* or *tannier*) in the Antilles, "kachu" or "kuchu" in British India "alcoleaz" in Spain, "tallus" in Java (SEMLER, *Die tropische Agricultur,* 11 Band, p. 812, Wiesmar, 1900). Also Taro, see this *Bulletin,* Abstr. 1720, June 1911.   (*Ed.*).

(4) "Yam" is one of the many species of Dioscorea (*Dioscoreaceae*). The kinds generally grown are *D. sativa* and *D. aculeata,* natives of India and the neighbouring countries, and much cultivated there ; they have been introduced into the Antilles and other hot countries.   (*Ed.*).

infect Indian corn, pigeon-peas (1), plantains, the coffee bush and the Avocado pear-tree (2). It is worthy of record that this disease has certain symptoms in common with the well-known West Indian root-disease of cocoa, which also attacks avocado pear-trees. No definite statement, however, can be made as to the connection between the arrowroot fungus and the root disease of cocoa until much further investigation has been carried out.

A case is recorded in which it seems likely that the fungus causing this disease was continually present in the soil during 25 years. So far this fungus has not been found to produce any definite fructifications. Prof. Marshall Ward referred ˙ this fungus (*Kew Bulletin*, July 1893, N. 80) to the form genus *Spicaria*, but no other fructifications were obtained from which its systematic position could be definitely determined.

The writer suggests as remedial measures to dig up the affected arrowroot as thoroughly as possible and burn it. Infected fields might be isolated by a trench 3 ft. deep, and 2 ft. wide, the fields and trench to be covered with bush and the whole, including the diseased arrowroot, to be set on fire, so as to produce sufficient heat to sterilize the soil to the depth of a few inches. The field should then be thoroughly ploughed, stirred once a fortnight with a cultivator or hoes, and a crop of cotton planted. When the cotton has been harvested, the plants, mixed with a large amount of additional bush, should again be burnt. On sugar estates, sugar cane might be used as a rotation for the eradication of the arrowroot disease.

Leaf Spot (*Cercospora personata*) **injurious to Pea-nuts in the United States.** See above, Abstr. 1749.

1916

Corticium javanicum **and** *Hemileia vastatrix*, **injurious to** *Coffea robusta*, **in Java.** See above, Abstr. 1754.

1917

---

(1) " Pigeon-pea ", is a pea-like seed of an East Indian bush (*Cajanus indicus*), now cultivated in most tropical countries ; it is so called in the East Indies as it is often used to feed pigeons. There are two varieties, *C. i. bicolor* (The Congo pea or Angola Pea) and *C. i. flavus* (the No-eye pea). See G. WATT. *Dict. of the Econom c Products of India.* Vol. II.

(2) Avocado pear-tree = *Persea gratissima, Lauraceae* (BAILEY, *Cyclopedia of American Horticulture*, London & New York, 1902-1909).

1918   W. M. RAE. **The Jaindhara Disease, Soft Rot of Ginger, in the Rangpur District, Eastern Bengal.** — *The Agricultural Journal of India,* Vol. VI, Part II, pp. 139-146. Pusa, April 1911.

There is a disease of the ginger plant (*Gingiber officinale*) known in British India as Jaindhara disease. The tips of the leaves turn yellow, and this yellowing spreads towards the leaf-sheath; the leaf tissue dies, till finally the whole shoot becomes dry and withered. Meantime, the collar, that part of the erect stem between the place where it arises from the rhizome and where it emerges from the ground, becomes of a pale, translucent brown colour, and by the time the leaves are well yellowed it is very watery and so soft that the whole shoot can easily be lifted off, breaking away at this point, though not falling over spontaneously. Both the discolouration and softening extend to the whole rhizome, which gradually rots and disintegrates.

The disease appears with the advent of the rains in August and becomes epidemic only when the rains have set in and the ground is wet.

Although experiments in artificially inoculating the disease have not yet been carried out successfully, the careful investivations made by Dr. Butler, point to a parasitic fungus, *Pythium gracile* as the cause of the disease. The hyphae of this fungus ramify in the diseased tissues.

The remedies recommended for the control of this disease are:

1. — On harvesting the crop all the rhizomes should be removed from the ground, diseased ones should be burnt or buried deeply in a place where ginger will not be grown.

2. — Ginger should not be grown on the same land for at least three years.

3. — Great care should be taken to ensure that the seed is healthy, and it should be got from a place that is free from disease.

4. — The affected plants should be burnt. Care must be taken that no portion of the diseased rhizomes remains in the soil.

5. — Water should never be allowed to lie or stagnate in a ginger field.

British India: Eastern Bengal

1919   **Onion Smut (*Urocystis Cepulae*) in the United States.** See Abstr. 1768 in this *Bulletin.*

L. Peters. **A Common Disease of Pelargonium Slips** (Eine häufige Stecklingkrankheit der Pelargonien. *Gartenflora*, p. 213, 1 Taf. 1910). — *Botanisches Centralblatt*, Bd. 116, N. 14, p. 368. Iena, 4 April, 1911.

1920

Pythium de Baryanum, Hesse, is the cause of the blackening of those parts of Pelargonium slips which are buried in the soil. The writer advises as remedies for the control of this parasite, 1) the destruction of the infected plants, taking care not to use the soil in which they were growing, as the mycelium continues to live in it ; sand should be used ; 2) if the cuttings are still serviceable, the lower part should be cut away and the remainder placed in sand ; 3) only thoroughly decomposed and old mould should be used.

Germany

Sphaerella Fragariae and *Sphaerotheca Castagnei* **injurious to Strawberries.** See Abstr. 1991 in this *Bulletin*.

1921

Great Britain

The Sclerotinia (*Botrytis*) Disease of the Gooseberry or " Die Back '' (1). — *Board of Agriculture and Fisheries*, Leaflet, N. 248, pp. 8. London, April, 1911.

1922

The " Sclerotinia disease " of the gooseberry, or '' die-back '' as it is called in some districts in Kent, is widespread in England. The gooseberry bush may be attacked in four distinct places, viz. the main stem and base of the branches, the young wood of the current year, the leaf or the berry. As regards the main stem, the spawn (*mycelium*) of the fungus penetrates into the tissue (permeating the cortex and bast), and at the end of a season's growth causes the bark to crack and peel off, often in large pieces. The part of the stem first attacked is usually that portion situated at the ground level or a little above it; eventually the spawn of the fungus " rings " the stem at this place, and the whole bush is killed. Before this occurs the spawn of the fungus spreads upward in the stem to the base of the branches. Here it frequently attacks some of the branches so severely that they die. It is at this time that steps should be taken to stop the disease.

Great Britain

(1) See also Abstr. 319 *Bulletin* Jan. 1911.   (*Ed.*).
Cp. *The Science and Practice of Farming during 1910 in Great Britain.* Intern. Inst. of Agr. Rome 1910, p. 339.

Renewed growth of the spawn of the fungus in the stem takes place every spring, and it s at this time that the manner in which the fungus exists and spreads can be most easily seen. Small tufts of the fungus occur on the main branches nearly down to their base, and also on the younger wood. Little hard, blackish bodies, named *sclerotia*, are also produced, which are able, under certain conditions, to give rise to another form of fructification in which winter-spores, *ascospores*, are produced. In this stage the fungus has been known under the name of *Sclerotinia*, while the name *Botrytis* has been applied to the stage where summer spores only are produced. It is probable that the *Sclerotinia* stage with its winter spores only rarely occurs. It is certain that the disease can be perpetuated from season to season in its absence by means of the *Botrytis* stage, which by means of summer-spores, spreads the disease during the growing season, and then remains dormant in the form either of *mycelium* in the stem, or of *sclerotia* on its surface. Very commonly the spores affect the leaves, which then show a discolouration at their edges. If the attack spreads from the edge of the leaf inwards, until the greater part of the leaf is affected, the fall of the leaf soon takes place. The under-surface of the leaf is the part attacked. In the case of young bushes especially, a considerable proportion of the young shoots may be attacked and much weakened or killed. Infested dead shoots constitute a prolific source of infection. Lastly, the fungus occasionally attacks the berry and turns it rotten.

The best means of getting rid of the disease are the prompt removal and burning of all dead bushes or dead branches in the plantation. Where the disease has been allowed to become severe and widespread spraying must be resorted to, in addition to the prompt burning of all dead bushes. A heavy spraying with a solution of copper sulphate (4 lb. dissolved in 100 gallons of water) should be given just before the buds burst so as to destroy the tufts of *Botrytis*. The infection, or premature falling off, of the leaves, may be prevented by spraying, directly the fruit is set, with Bordeaux mixture composed of 8 lb. copper sulphate, 8 lb. quicklime, and 100 gallons of water. In this spraying it is essential that the under-surfaces of the leaves should be sprayed as much as possible. No injury follows the application of Bordeaux mixture of this strength, and if the spraying be done at the time indicated no spotting of the berries occurs. Any treatment which induces the bushes to make vigorous growth tends to stop the attacks of the fungus.

Anthracnose of the Vine in Mexico. See Abstract 1776 in this *Bulletin*.

1923
Mexico

C. W. EDGERTON. **Two new Fig Diseases.** (*Phytopathology*, Vol. I, pp. 12-17, 1 fig. Tab. IV, 1911). *Annales mycologici*, Vol. IX, N. 3, p. 306. Berlin, 1911.

1924

Two new cryptogamic diseases have been recorded on *Ficus Carica* in Louisiana. The first is produced by *Tubercularia Fici* sp. nov. which produces a sort of canker on the branches. Artificial cultures of this fungus are easily obtained.

The second disease is produced by *Corticium laetum* Karst. It appears first on the tips of the branches whence it extends to other parts of the tree; but it does little harm.

United
States:
Louisiana

J. B. RORER. **A Bacterial Disease of Bananas and Plantains.** — *Board of Agriculture, Trinidad*, pp. 1-5, pl VII-X. Trinidad, April, 1911.

1925

The writer describes a new bacterial disease of the banana and plantain which appeared for the first time in Trinidad on the " moko " variety, and which has since spread to other varieties of *Musa paradisiaca* and *M. chinensis*.

Trinidad

The leaves slowly turn yellow, and then the petiole of one of the leaves gives way just at the base of the leaf-blade, and all the other leaves quickly break down in a similar manner.

A transverse section of the pseudo-stem shows that practically all the vessels are discoloured, the color ranging from pale yellow to dark brown, and filled with bacteria. The discoloured bundles run back into the true stem and thence into the young suckers and buds. Sometimes in badly diseased plants the tissues of the leaf-stalks and stems are broken down completely so that fairly large bacterial cavities are formed.

If the disease is not severe the plant may live; the fruit, however does not ripen, but becomes black and rotten.

The writer succeeded in isolating the organism which is the cause of the disease and has given it the name of *Bacillus musac*. Experiments in inoculation carried out on a large scale have given positive results. The variety *Musa textilis* is resistant to this disease, inoculation only producing a few discoloured bundles in some of the leaves, but the plants still remained perfectly healthy in appearance.

1926   F. LAGERBERG. **A Disease of the Pine caused by " Hypodermella sulcigena "**. (Om gräbarrsjukan hos tallen, das orsak och verkningar. *Forstl. Versuchs. Schwedens*, Vol. VII, 6, p. 14, fig. Stockholm, 1910). — *Rivista di Patologia vegetale*, anno V, n. 3, p. 35, Pavia, 1º Giugno, 1911.

Sweden   This is a description of a disease of pine needles which are attacked and killed before they have fully come out of the sheath.
     This disease is caused by one of the *Hysteriaceae, Hypodermella sulcigena* (Link.) Tubeuf. The pycnidia of this fungus are the same as those of *Hendersonia acicola*, which in Germany attacks the Pine.
     In the writer's opinion *Lophodermium nervisequum* and *L. macrosporum* also belong to the genus *Hypodermella*.
     Pinus sylvestris, the needles of which last from 5 to 7 years, is more resistant to the disease than the Norwegian Pine, which loses its needles after 3 years.

1927   P. VUILLEMIN. **Observations on a Disease of the Weymouth Pine, Pinus Strobus, L.** (Remarques sur une maladie du Pin Weymouth). — *C. R. Acad. des Sciences*, t. 152, n. 22, pp. 1497-1498. Paris, 29 Mai, 1911.

France   The needles of the Weymouth Pine (*Pinus Strobus* L.) are
Calvados attacked by a fungus belonging to the *Hysteriinae* to which Mr Rostrup has given the name of *Lophodermium brachysporum*, and which Mr. von Tubeuf connects with the genus *Hypoderma* D. C. (1). This parasite, which is well known in Denmark and Germany, has been recorded by Mr. G. Fron in the nurseries of the West and of Calvados. This is the first time *Hypoderma brachysporum* has been recorded in France.
     The writer expresses the opinion that it is not a case of a new pest of French forests, for on October 6, 1888, in the same year in which Mr. von Tubeuf recorded the *Hypoderma brachysporum* in Bavaria, he noticed this fungus on the dry pine needles lying on the ground in the valley of Olima, near Épinal.

_____

(1) See Abstract 334, in this *Bull.* for January, 1911.   (*Ed.*).

The writer concludes that this parasite is as old in France as in Germany, and that it lives in the depths of the forests. He also considers it as a species which has long been indigenous, and which may occasionally invade nurseries when it finds the conditions especially favourable.

Blister Rust (*Cronartium ribicola*) of White Pine *Pinus Strobus*. — *Farm and Ranch*, vol. 30, N. 20, p. 10. Dallas, Texas, May 20, 1911.

1928

The dangerous European disease (*Cronartium ribicola*) of White Pine (1) recently introduced into America, was, by the prompt and active co-operation of all concerned, eradicated as far as found; but there is no evidence that all the cases have been found, nor is there any means of preventing the importation of more diseased white pine nursery stock. The reafforestation movement has created a market for a considerable amount of white pine stock. Many American nurseries regularly import their one-year-old coniferous seedlings; and it is safe to say that in the spring of 1909, ten million coniferous seedlings were imported from Europe, and of these several millions were white pine. The U. S. Department of Agriculture has issued a report on this disease (*Bureau of Plant Industry, Bull.* 206), in which a full and detailed account of the fungus producing it is given ; America is advised to raise its own white pine seedlings, and the opinion is expressed that importations from affected countries be prohibited.

United States

The preference of this parasite (*Cronartium ribicola*) for the five-leaved pines is of special importance to America, since the species are naturally present through the western, northern, and northeastern forests, and are planted more or less commonly throughout the country. The chances of great losses if this fungus should even approximate its past record in Europe are very great. The U. S. Department of Agriculture should be informed promptly and accurately of every importation of white pine and ribes.

G. H. PETHYBRIDGE. **The " Bladder Rust " of Scotch Pine *Pinus sylvestris* —** *Department of Agriculture and Technical Instruction for Ireland* : *Journal*, Vol. XI, N. 3, pp. 500-502. Dublin, April, 1911.

1929

A serious case of disease in Scotch Pine was observed during the past season in woods at Cappagh, County Waterford, where a large

United Kingdom: Ireland, Waterford

---

(1) Called Weymouth Pine in England. See SCHLICH's *Manual of Forestry*, Vol. II, p. 372. London, 1904.   (*Ed.*).

number of trees were attacked by one of the " bladder rust " fungi.
The position of attack by the disease is in most cases high up on
the main trunk, but the branches are also in many cases affected.
The attack takes the form of a blistering or swelling and cracking
of the bark, accompanied usually by a copious flow of resinous
matter. It apparently commences at one side of the trunk or branch,
but ultimately encircles it so that it becomes ringed. The ring of
dead bark was found extending to a width of a couple of feet or
more, and as time goes on, it gradually extends further. The
gradual progress of the disease down the bark generally leads to
the death of the whole tree.

The fungus which causes this disease is probably *Cronartium
Peridermium-Pini* (Willd.) Liro. The secondary stage of this blad-
der-rust was formerly known under the name of *Uredo Pedicularis*,
and was found on the leaves of certain species of Lousewort (*Pedicularis palustris* and *P. sceptrum carolinum*). *Pedicularis palustris*
and *P. sylvatica* are common in Ireland.

1980   A. A. ELENKIN. **Timber injured by** *Ceratostomella pilifera.* (Glav-
niieisciie Saprosci, Postupivsciie v Zentralnuiu Fitopatologhi-
ceskuiu Stanziu sa srok Iul Dekabr 1910). — *Xurnal Boliesni
Rastenii* (Journal of Plant Diseases), 5. G., N. 1-2, p. 15. St. Petersburg, 1911.

Timber stored in warehouses in the district of Podolsk. (Government of Moscow) has been found damaged by *Ceratostomella*
Russia   *pilifera* (Fr.) Wint., which causes bluish patches to form in the
woody tissue.

C. Pini, C. Piceae, C. cana, C. coerulea, and *Endoconidiophora*
coerulescens have also injured the timber.

The preventive measures suggested are the following :

1) That the timber be used as soon as felled, and the supplies stored in well-ventilated rooms ;

2) That the trunks be preserved, before use, by immersion
in tanks of water.

1981   *Zythia resinae* **(Fr.) Karst, a Fungus Injurious to Timber.** *(Zythia
resinae* (Fr.) Karst als unangenehmer Bauholzpilz). — *Jahresbericht der Vereinigung für angewandte Botanik.* VIII. J. 1910,
pp. 164-170, 8 Textabb. u. 2 Taf. Berlin, 1911.

In May, 1910 several spots of a sky blue or dark blue colour
Germany   were found in the pine timber used in building a house of recent

date at Hamburg-St. Paul. When examined under the microscope several tufts were seen consisting of from 4 to 7 pycnidia, measuring from 100 to 250 μ in diameter.

The pycnidia contained numerous spores from 3.5 to 5 μ in length and 2.5 to 3.5 μ in breadth.

This fungus is *Zythia resinae* (Fr.) Karst, belonging to the family of the *Sphaeroideae*. The blue discolouration of the wood penetrated 25 centimeters into the woody tissue. Numbers of ramified hyphae are found in the resin-canals and sometimes, though rarely, in the tracheids.

T. PETCH. **The Physiology and Diseases of** *Hevea brasiliensis*, **the premier Plantation Rubber Tree. Surinam Leaf Disease; Climatic Leaf Fall in Hevea** — Pp. 268, XVI pl. London, Dulau and C⁰., 1911.

1982

In this book, the author, mycologist to the Government of Ceylon, after describing the structure of *Hevea brasiliensis*, its cultivation, and the different modes of tapping the latex and obtaining the rubber, gives a detailed account of the diseases which attack this tree (1).

Ceylon

The author treats of this subject under the following headings: *a*) General Sanitation of the Plantations. *b*) Leaf Diseases. *c*) Root diseases. *d*) Stem diseases. *e*) Abnormalities in *Hevea*. *f*) Fungi on prepared rubber. *g*) Other Fungi on *Hevea*.

Amongst the root diseases are *Fomes semitostus* Berk.; Brown root disease (*Hymenochaete noxia* Berk) ; *Sphaerostilbe repens* B and Br.

Amongst the Stem diseases are Canker (*Phytophthora Faberi* Maubl.), Pink disease (*Corticium salmonicolor = C. javanicum* Zimm.); a stem canker, (*Coniothyrium* sp.) ; " Dieback " (*Botryodiplodia Theobromae*); *Fusicladium* sp. ; *Pestalozzia Palmarum* Cooke.

Amongst the Leaf diseases are : *Helminthosporium Heveae* Petch.; a cryptogamic disease known as " Surinam Leaf Disease ", which has not yet been identified ; *Glaeosporium heveae* Petch.; and a physiological disease causing the leaves to fall, known as " Climatic Leaf Fall in Hevea ".

Amongst the abnormalities in *Hevea* the writer mentions twisted seedlings, nodules, fasciation, and modifications caused by a certain slug (*Mariaella Dussumerii* Gray).

---

(1) On this subject see previous Bulleti ns. *(Ed.)*.

Phanerogamous Parasites and Weeds. — Their Control.

1933

E. V. WILCOX. **Killing Weeds with Sodium Arsenite.** — *Hawaii Agricultural Experimen' Station, Honolulu. Press Bulletin,* N. 30, pp. 15.

Hawaii

At the Agricultural Experiment Station of Honolulu (Hawaii), experiments have been carried on to test the effect of Sodium arsenite upon a number of weeds, including "oi", (*Stachytarpheta dichotoma*), *Lantana*, spurge (*Euphorbia peplus*), "pualele" or sow-thistle, pigweed, purslane (1), cockle-bur (*Xanthium strumarium*), "glue" (*Acacia Farnesiana*) dodder, Japanese nutgrass, "honohono" (*Commelina nudiflora*), *Crotalaria*, and other weeds. In these experiments the solution used was made by boiling 1 lb. of white arsenic and 2 lbs of sal soda per gallon of water for from 15 to 20 minutes, and dissolving this stock solution in from 15 to 20 parts of water. The effect of the spray was manifest in most instances within 2 or 3 hours, but on Japanese nut-grass the leaves did not turn brown until the second day. On all these weeds the leaves and stems ultimately died as a result of a single application.

In spraying alfalfa infested with dodder, the alfalfa was killed as well as the dodder.

For the complete destruction of *Lantana* a second, third, or even fourth treatment was found necessary. Sow-thistle and Japanese nut-grass although entirely destroyed above ground, promptly grew up again from the crown and the underground bulbs.

Experiments made by farmers show the good results obtained by spraying Hitchcock Berry or Thimble-berry (2), German Ivy

---

(1) Purslane - *Portulaca oleracea.*

(2) Thimbleberry - *Rubus occidentalis* & *R. odoratus.* L. H. BAILEY, *Cyclopedia of American Horticulture,* vol. III, p. 1466, New York, 1907, and Vol. IV, p. 1795, London, 1902. *(Ed.).*

(*Senecio mikanioides*), nettle (*Hesperocnide sandwicensis*), Passion vine, the air plant (*Bryophyllum calycinum*), and red sage (*Salvia coccinea*).

It should however be remembered in using this solution, that in addition to the danger of stock becoming poisoned from grazing on sprayed vegetation, too much arsenic in the soil may be injurious to all kinds of crops, and therefore Arsenite of Soda should not be used in very large quantities.

G. GOLA. **A new Weed which infests the Rice-fields of Piedmont, in Italy.** (Sopra una nuova pianta infesta alle risaie del Vercellese). — *Annali della R. Accademia di Agricoltura di Torino*, vol. LIII, (1910), pp. 541-547, 1 fig. Torino, 1911.

1984

For some years past the Experiment Station for Rice at Vercelli has recorded a new weed which has invaded the rice-fields in the neighbourhood of Vercelli; it is evidently an exotic plant and has been brought over with new varieties of rice.

Italy:
Piedmont

Examination of many specimens show that this plant belongs to the var. *uliginosa* Miq., of *Rotala indica* (Willd.) Koehne (1), (syn. with *Peplis indica* Willd., *Ammannia peploides* Spreng., *Ameletia indica* DC.).

R. indica is already known in Transcaucasian Russia where it was evidently imported with the rice, but this is the first time it has been recorded in Europe; this variety (*R. indica* var. *uliginosa*) was only known hitherto in Japan.

This weed injures the rice-crop as its roots spread over the surface of the rice-field, forming a thick matting which hinders the growth of the roots of the rice plants; and interferes with the flow of the water, and therefore with the ventilation of the soil, which, as recent experiments have shown, plays such an important part in the etiology of rice diseases.

This weed is an annual, but the enormous quantities of seed which each plant produces suffice to propagate it in the rice-fields. It develops late, so that it escapes weeding, which would, moreover, be very expensive if an attempt were made to extirpate this plant. On the other hand, winter work in the fields makes it impossible to destroy the seed.

---

(1) A plant belonging to the family of the *Lythraceae*. It is a native of tropical Asia. Cf. *Index Kewensis*. (*Ed.*).

It has been noted that *R. indica* grows most rapidly when the fields have been only slightly flooded, and so it may be that the depth of the water constitutes an unfavourable condition for the growth of *Rotala*.

In the writer's opinion, scientific rotation of crops is an effective remedy against this weed; when the soil is left dry for some years most of the harmful species disappear. The greater development of *R. indica* at Vercelli than elsewhere is probably due to the neglect of rotation of crops. In other zones, such as Novara and Lomellina, where rice is grown, this weed has not done the injury it has caused at Vercelli.

As *Rotala* is certainly due to the direct importation of Eastern Asiatic rices, great care should be taken in introducing new varieries of rice.

1985 N. NOVELLI. **The Control of Algae in Ricefields.** (Contro le alghe della risaia). — *Il Giornale di Risicoltura*, anno 1, n. 1, pp. 13-15. Vercelli, 1º Giugno 1911.

Italy : Piedmont

This year most of the rice-fields are infested by algae to an unusual extent. They form on the surface of the water a greenish layer of a filamentose or slimy description, called *nitta, litta, erba ragnèra* etc. in the rice-fields, consisting usually of a mixture of various algae.

These algae are injurious to the young rice plants, as they hinder their growth and tillering by intercepting the light and heat, thus retarding vegetation and keeping the temperature of the water lower.

These water weeds should be controlled by properly regulating irrigation at the time the rice is sown, and by wisely profiting by the need the rice has for low water or even dry land at the time of taking root and during the first period of growth: when the water is shallow its temperature is higher, and less propitious to the growth of algae, which can be quite destroyed by drawing off the water once or twice when the algae have not yet developed and only form a thin layer.

This nuisance can also be controlled by having recourse to the opposite extreme : by raising the depth of the water considerably and raking the layer of weeds to the edges of the rice-field.

Dry powdered sulphate of iron has also been used, but the results have been doubtful and unsatisfactory.

Dodder in Clover Seed from Chile. — *The Farmer's Review*, vol. XLIII. n. 12, p. 306. Chicago, March 25, 1911.

1936

Since July 1, 1910, twenty-three lots of clover seed, of probable Chilean origin, aggregating 370 000 pounds, have been imported into the United States. In all of these shipments two kinds of dodder seed characteristic of Chilean red clover seed are present. At a normal rate of seeding, these shipments are sufficient to seed approximately 46 000 acres, and at this rate of seeding an average of approximately 450 dodder seeds would be sown on each sq. rod. The sowing of this Chilean seed means that the clover crop on a considerable area will be destroyed by dodder, and farmers should be on their guard.

United States

Most of these importations have gone into the southern part of the clover-producing region. This Chilean clover seed is especially fine looking, being dark coloured and approximately 50 % larger in size than ordinary red clover seed produced in the United States (1).

W. FAWCETT. **A Parasitic Flowering Plant from Jamaica.** (Conversazione of the Royal Society, June 14) — *Nature*, N: 2137, Vol. 86, p. 570. London, June, 22, 1911.

1937

Scybalium jamaicense Schott and Endl. is one of the *Balanophoraceae*, a family of phanerogamous parasites growing on the roots of trees in tropical forests. "They do not develop chlorophyll and are therefore altogether dependent upon their host for sustenance. The seed contains an embryo of the simplest structure, having neither cotyledons nor radicle; it germinates in the soil, the embryo grows in length, thread-like, until it touches the root of a tree and then penetrates it. When established on the root it forms a tuberous rhizome, from which flowering stems are produced. The flowers are

Jamaica

---

  (1) This and other recent cases (compare this *Bulletin*, Abstr. 1553, May, 1911) show the growing importance of controlling the trade of leguminous forage seeds. As proposed by the Intelligence Office of the International Institute, the question should be taken in consideration from an international point of view. See: *Institut Intern. d'Agriculture. Service des Renseign. Agricoles et des Maladies des Plantes. Rapport de la II Division*. Novembre, 1909. Impr. Chambre des Deputés, Rome, 1909, p. 20. (Etudes preliminaires, etc. *Cuscute*). (*Ed.*).

very small, numerous in heads, on a stalk còvered with scales, male and female flowers on distinct heads.   This species is found in Jamaica, Cuba, and Hispaniola.

Other species occur in Brazil and Columbia.

1938   D. LARIONOW. **Broom-rape** (*Orobanche cumana*) **as a Parasite of the Sunflower in Russia** (Nieskolko Slov o Podsolnetknikie). — *Khosiastvo* (Husbandry), VI G., n. 20, pp. 642-644. Kiew, 29 Maia 1911.

Russia   Broom-rape (*Orobanche cumana*) is very injurious to sunflower plantations in South Russia, especially in the Governments of Poltava, Kursk, Voronezh and Saratov.   This plant lives as a parasite on *Xanthium* and *Artemisia*, whence it easily passes into the sunflower plantations.

The spread of this parasitic plant in Russia is hindered by the presence in the soil of the larvae of a Dipteron, *Phytomyza Orobanchia* Kalt., which destroys a large amount of its seed.

Many remedies have been proposed against this flowering parasite ; the best seems that obtained by Budbergen by selecting resistant varieties of sunflower, called « Selenciuk » the roots of which grow down very deep into the soil, thus preventing the development of the broom-rape seeds.

1939   **Bartsia latifolia, a Parasitic Weed in South Australia.** — *The Journal of the Department of Agriculture of South Australia*, vol. XV, n. 8, pp. 729-730. Adelaide, March, 1911.

The pasture-lands of South Australia suffer much from the inroads of a red-flowered weed, common Bartsia (*Bartsia latifolia*).

Australia: The roots of this weed are parasitic on grass roots to which
S. Australia   they attach themselves by means of little lateral suckers.   Many experiments have been made with a view to its destruction, but the results are unsatisfactory.

Prof. Ewart considers that the most effective way of eradicating Bartsia from an affected pasture is to bring it under cultivation.   The manure used and the working of the soil will leave the ground in far better condition to produce a strong, luxuriant pasture than it was before, and at the same time will reduce the parasitic Bartsia almost to vanishing point.

Insects and other Injurious Invertebrates.
Their Biology and Control.

G. GIANELLI. **The Microlepidoptera of Piedmont.** (I Microlepidotteri del Piemonte e specialmente della Valle d'Aosta, con i bruchi nocivi alle derrate e all'agricoltura ed il nome delle sostanze di cui si nutrono). — *Annali della R. Accademia d'Agricoltura di Torino*, Vol. III, (1910), pp. 3-143. Torino, 1911.

1940

The writer gives a list of the Microlepidoptera found up till now in Piedmont, and more especially in the Val d'Aosta.

Of the 925 species he mentions, a large number are new to Italy and Piedmont. The writer mentions in each case the time they live, the season they prefer, and the plants or other substances on which they feed.

This list includes a long series of insect pests which are injurious, in their larval stage, to agricultural produce.

Italy :
Piedmont

FRED. V. THEOBALD. **Report on Animals Injurious to Fruit Trees and Bushes in Great Britain.** (Report on Economic Zoology for the year ending September 30th, 1910). — *Journal of the South Eastern Agricultural College, Wye, Kent*, No. 19, pp. 88-183, and 210-211. London and Ashford, Kent, 1910.

1941

APPLE ENEMIES.

The Pale Brindled Beauty (*Phigalia pilosaria* Hb.) is as yet unrecorded as a fruit-tree insect. The normal food plants of this moth in its caterpillar stage are oak and white-thorn, but it has been found on a variety of other trees. It is wide-spread over Britain. Wherever met with no other treatment than grease-banding is necessary for this insect. The grease-bands should be kept in proper working order until after April.

Great
Britain :
England

The Light Emerald Moth (*Metrocampa margaritaria* Linn.) is quite a new apple enemy. Its larvae cause great havoc by chewing the bark and eating out the leading shoots. Its normal food plants are oak, beech, birch, and hornbeam. This insect is widely distributed throughout Great Britain. Treatment should consist of winter destruction, whilst pruning, and spraying with arsenate of lead.

The Small Egger Moth (*Eriogaster lanestris*, Linn.), is another injurious fruit insect. Its natural food plants are the whitethorn and blackthorn, and its distribution is very wide.

The Lackey Moth (*Clisiocampa neustris* Linn.) was not as common as usual in 1909 and 1910. The larvae die two days after spraying with arsenate of lead.

The larvae of the Lappet Moth (*Gasteropacha quercifolia* Linn.) attack both apple and plum. It is also common in hawthorn hedges.

Gold Tail Moth (*Porthesia similis* Fues.). A considerable amount of this insect was reported in 1909 on apple, pear, roses and hawthorn hedge from Kent, Surrey, Hampshire, Sussex, Yorkshire, and Worcestershire. Damage is caused by the larvae which eat holes in the young apples.

Lobster Moth (*Stauropus fagi* Linn.). In a plantation at Amberfield Chart Sutton, caterpillars of this moth were found feeding on apple foliage. Its normal food plants are the beech, birch and oak. It can easily be destroyed by arsenate of lead spraying.

Figure of Eight Moth (*Diloba caeruleocephala* Linn.). The larvae of this insect eat holes in apples, it is also very common on aloe and damson.

Winter Moth (*Cheimatobia brumata*, Linn.). A bad attack of this pest was reported in the Isle of Wight, and in 1909 the Winter Moth was very harmful to oaks, quite as bad as the Green Oak Tortrix (*Tortrix viridana*). It is also very injurious to cob-nut bushes, gooseberries and plums. The grease bands employed against these insects should not be placed too near to the ground (1).

The Bud Moth (*Hedya ocellana* Fab.) attacks all fruit trees in England, but mainly the apple and cherry. Treatment consists of spraying with arsenate of lead, but it is not nearly so effectual for this pest as nicotine wash. The writer thinks this pest can best be dealt with by autumnal spraying to kill the young larvae before they form their tents.

---

(1) See p. 173 of this *Bulletin* for Nov. 1910.   (*Ed.*).

Simaethis (*Choreutes*) *pariana* Clerk. This is a new apple pest which had never been recorded before as feeding in sufficient numbers to do harm. The larvae live in colonies and feed off the epidermis of the leaves which they spin together with quite a thick webbing, and gradually skeletonise the leaves and then move on to others. Treatment consists in handpicking the leaf nests in nurseries and spraying with arsenate of lead where they had taken up their abode in plantations.

The Pith Moth (*Blastodacna vinolentella* H. S.) seems to have been less harmful in 1909-10 than in previous years.

The Apple Blossom Weevil (*Anthonomus pomorum* Linn.). This pest baffles all treatment. It has been very harmful again in 1909 and 1910.

The Apple Twig Cutter (*Rhynchites coeruleus* De Geer), was reported as destroying the young shoots of plants at Wester Hill, Linton. The only way to prevent this damage is to jar the beetles off. All cut tips should be taken off and destroyed.

The Raspberry Weevil (*Otiorhynchus picipes*) sometimes eats the foliage, at other times the buds or blossoms or soft young shoots of raspberries, loganberries, hops, ferns, vines, roses, etc., and has recently been reported as devouring the bark of apple trees. These beetles are easily trapped by placing pieces of sacking on the ground. The beetles are found during the day sheltering beneath the sacking and can then be collected and destroyed.

Leaf Weevils (*Phyllobius oblongus*, Linn.) are particularly harmful to young grafts, and often do as much damage as *Otiorhyncus* Weevil. Experiments made with arsenate of lead as a remedy have given good results. Grease bands are also useful.

The Raspberry Beetle (*Byturus tomentosus* Fab.) is reported as injuring the blossom of apple trees.

The Apple Sawfly (*Hoplocampa testudinea* Klug.) continues to be a serious apple enemy.

The Apple Sucker (*Psylla mali* Sch.) is reported as doing serious damage in Canterbury. General reports show that the lime and salt wash has done a good deal in connection with this pest. This, and nicotine wash, can completely control it. A case is reported in which drenching with quassia and soft soap has given success.

The Rosy Apple Aphis (*Aphis sorbi* Kalt.) appeared in some localities in 1910. It has been noted that the larvae of the large Hover Fly (*Catabomba pyrastri*) were found eating this aphis.

The Leaf Curling Aphis (*Aphis pomi* Linn.) was very harmful all over Great Britain in 1909. When the leaves are once curled even nicotine wash has slight effect.

Woolly Aphis (1). Several apple trees which had been badly infested with Woolly Aphis were completely cured in two years by planting a nasturtium against each. The idea came from an old book. The experiment was renewed by the writer with like success.

A Green bug (*Lygus Sp.?*) attacks apple stocks and currants. Prof. Schoyen of Christiania sent the writer similar specimens of damage to currants and apples due, he said, entirely to Land Bugs (*Plesicoris rugicollis* and *Orthohytus marginalis*, etc.).

The Brown Scale (*Lecanium capreae* Linn.) attacks the leaves of the apple. The great variety of its food plants, which include poplars, willows, limes, hawthorn, alder, sycamore, roses, etc. makes it difficult to deal with in regard to prevention.

The Red Spider (2) has recently been frequently reported as injurious to apple trees.

CHERRY ENEMIES.

The Cherry-Stem Borer (*Semasia woeberiana* Schif).

The Cherry Fruit Moth (*Argyresthia nitidella* Fab.) first attacked cherry trees in Great Britain in 1910. No preventive treatment is known.

The Cherry Black Fly (*Myzus cerasi* Fab.) has been abundant in 1909. It causes the leaves at the tips to curl and die.

CURRANT ENEMIES.

The Currant Clearwing (*Asgeria tipuliformis* Linn.); the Currant Shoot-Borer (*Incurvaria capitella* Fab.); the Big Bud Mite (*Eriophyes ribis* Nalepa); the Brown Scale (*Lecanium persicae v. sarothamni* Douglas); the White Cushion Scale (*Pulvinaria vitis var. ribesiae* Signoret) the Gooseberry Aphis (*Aphis grossulariae* Kalt) should be mentioned.

Failure of Liver of Sulphur for Red Spider and Effects of Paraffin Jelly (3). So frequent are the reports of failure of liver of sul-

---

(1) Woolly Aphis, or Apple Root Louse, *Schizoneura lanigera*, (*Board of Agriculture and Fisheries*, Leaflet, No. 42).   (*Ed.*).

(2) Red Spiders, *Tetranychus, Bryobia* and *Tenuipalpus*, (*Board of Agriculture, Leaflet, No. 42*).   (*Ed.*)

(3) Paraffin jelly is prepared as follows: Paraffin 5 gallons, soft soap, 8 lbs. Boil the soap and paraffin together in a copper, and when boiling add a pint of cold water. Pour out in a barrel and this on cooling becomes a jelly. Add 10 lbs of this jelly to every 40 gallons of water. THEOBALD, *Insecticides*, in P. WRIGHT *Cyclop. of Modern Agric*. London. 1911, vol. VII.   (*Ed.*).

phur, the orthodox remedy for Red Spider, that it should never be recommended for that pest. It is now pretty well assured that liver of sulphur only acts under certain climatic conditions. On the other hand the generality of reports show that paraffin jelly has proved satisfactory in dealing with this pest. Good results were also obtained with nicotine wash, (nicotine, 96 %, 1 $^1/_5$ oz. soft soap 3 ozs, water 10 gallons); with liver of sulphur; with soft soap and quassia (soft soap 6 ozs, quassia 1 lb, water, 10 gallons). These washes were used against the red spider of ivy, (*Bryobia pretiosa*), the Red Spider of Gooseberry, (*Bryobia Ribis*) and the Red Spider of Apple (*Bryobia sp.*). Paraffin jelly alone gave satisfactory results in destroying these acari.

LOGANBERRY ENEMIES (1).

Leaf-Hoppers (*Typhlocybidae*). The species doing the damage were *Chlorita flavescens* Fab. There was no sign of parasitic attack amongst them such as the writer found in those attacking plums, the parasite being a species of *Aphelopus*, a genus of Prototrupids which form external galls on the Chloritae etc., called Thylacia.

The Bramble Shoot Moth (*Aspis udmanniana* Linn.), is one of the *Sericordiae*, and normally lives in its caterpillar stage on the bramble. In May 1910, however, it attacked the Loganberry. The larva tunnels into the shoots of the loganberries and feeds on the tips of the shoots, uniting the young leaves together with silk. It feeds in the same way on the bramble.

ANTS EATING RASPBERRY AND LOGANBERRY BLOSSOMS.

Numerous *Myrmicae ruginodes* smother the open raspberry blossoms to obtain the juice, and in so doing scrape with their mandibles the bottom skin. These wounds more or less heal and produce shiny scars.

NECTARINE AND PEACH ENEMIES.

A Red Spider, which proved to be *Tetranychus telarius*, was reported from Esher, for the first time in 1910, on the leaves of nectarines and peaches.

---

(1) The Loganberry is a hybrid resulting from the crossing of the raspberry with the blackberry, obtained in 1881. in California, by Judge Logan. See Page 83, *Bulletin*, November 1910.   (*Ed.*).

NUT ENEMIES.

The Nut Sawfly (*Croesus septentrionalis* Linn.) has appeared in parts of Kent.

PEAR ENEMIES.

The Slugworm (*Eriocampa limacina* De Geer) was reported for the first time as harmful in the Isle of Wight in 1910.

The Pear Midge (*Diplosis pyrivora* Riley) becomes more and more widespread every year especially in the south of England,

The Leaf-Curling Pear Midge (*Diplosis pyri*, Bouché) and the Pear Leaf Blister Mite (*Eriophyes pyri* Nalepa) seem still to be on the increase.

PLUM ENEMIES.

The March Moth (*Anisopteryx aescularia* Schiff), the Plum Fruit Sawfly (*Hoplocampa fulvicornis* Klug.), the Mealy Plum Aphis (*Hyalopterus pruni* Fab.), and the Plum Leaf Gall Mite (*Eriophyes phloecoptes* Nalepa) must be mentioned.

RASPBERRY ENEMIES.

The Raspberry Beetle (*Byturus tomentosus* Fab.) has again proved a serious menace. A series of trials have been made to find some treatment for it. Spraying with arsenate of lead or with soft soap and quassia produced certain results, but too unsatisfactory to be of any real value. There is no doubt that all that can be done at present is handwork, either by jarring several times or by sending women round to shake the beetles off into paraffin tins. The Large Sword Grass Moth (*Calocampa exoleta* Linn.), has attacked raspberries severely in the Isle of Wight. This is the first record the writer has of this insect attacking fruit. It normally feeds on various low plants. Its occurrence on raspberries is probably unusual, but this moth is wide spread in Great Britain.

STRAWBERRY ENEMIES.

The Strawberry Eelworm (*Aphelenchus fragariae* Ritz. Bos.) causes the so-called cauliflower disease in strawberries, characterised by the curious deformed growth of the strawberry. No treatment is known for this disease.

Vine Enemies.

The Vine Weevil (*Otiorhynchus sulcatus* Fab.) and the Mealy Bug (*Dactylopius citri* Risso) frequently get into vineries and glass houses.

Thrips or Black Fly (*Thysanoptera*) attack fruit trees. The damage caused to blossom and foliage of greenhouse and garden plants by Thrips has been known for the last 150 years, but it is only in the last two years that they have been so abundant in England. In 1909 and 1910 there were bad attacks of Thrips on plums, apples, cherries, and pears, also spreading to loganberries and raspberries in Worcestershire, Gloucestershire, and to some extent in Kent on cherries. In America *Euthrips pyri*, Daniel, does considerable damage. *Phlaeothrips mati* Fitch has been recorded as gouging into young apples, whilst *Thrips Tritici*, Fitch, has been observed attacking apple blossom and also has done much harm to strawberries.

Some years ago many naturalists looked upon Thrips as beneficial, believing that they were carnivorous. We now know most are herbivorous and can cause much loss. We may now definitely say that Trips do considerable harm to fruit and may even cause the entire loss of crops in Great Britain just as they do in California. Unfortunately they damage buds, blossom, foliage, strigs, and the fruit itself during their life-cycle, lacerating the tissue and sucking out the sap. The female lays her eggs in the plant tissue. The Thrips which does most damage to fruit trees in Great Britain is the *Euthrips Pyri* Daniel. This insect attacks all kinds of fruit trees.

The writer found one kind on apples, and another on gooseberries, but neither have yet been named.

The life-history of the *Euthrips pyri* is described by the writer as follows :

The winter is passed in the larval stage in the soil or under any refuse lying on the soil. By February they are all in the pupal stage, and by March the mature winged Thrips are seen on the ground.

The females crawl out in late winter and early spring and fly about, enter the buds and feed as soon as the buds show a tip of green, or even white in the case of plum blossom; they then lay their eggs in little slits cut in the young tissue. The eggs hatch in from six to eight days. From these ova come little pale larvae with no wings, and it is these that get into the blossoms and attack the fruit. By May these larvae fall to earth, and in the soil

20

they become pupae with long wing-buds and by the second week in June another brood of adults appears. These attack fruit and foliage, and lay their eggs in the fruitlets and in the leaves. The larvae may be found up to July, when they fall to the earth and enter crevices, and remain there all the winter turning to nymphs irregularly, and then to winged females for some weeks before they emerge above ground. In California this Thrips seems to be single-brooded, the larvae of the first brood remaining in the soil for a very great length of time and taking no food. In Great Britain there are evidently two broods and may even be three: Thrips migrate at a certain time in large numbers. This applies to the fruit species as well as to many others found in Britain.

The food plants of the Thrips seem very varied, not only fruit trees of all kinds, but practically all deciduous trees serve for its pabulum. It seems, however, that it only oviposits on apple, pear, plum, peach, cherry, apricot, nectarine, and other fruits.

The writer doubts whether spraying can be used successfully against these pests. More beneficial results are likely to accrue from attacking the wintering larvae and nymphs and so preventing an attack.

GENERAL.

The Red Haired Bee (*Andrena fulva*, Schrank), is very common in Britain. It helps to fertilise currant, gooseberry and apple blossom, but at the same time distributes a very serious fruit pest.

Destruction of Apple Blossom by Birds, was recorded in some localities, chiefly by sparrows and greenfinches.

The Usefulness of the Hedgehog. Observations show that the Hedgehog eats a large number of insects, including *Carabidae*, the *Otiorhynchus* Weevils, and many slugs. On the other hand it will consume eggs, and it takes young chickens, gamebirds, mice, even young rabbits and hares, etc. In conclusion, it may be said that this nightfeeder is useful if he can be confined where he does good.

Damage done to Pears by Birds and Squirrels. Blue Tit (*Parus coeruleus*) ; Ox-Eye or Great Tit (*Parus major*) and Blackbird (*Turdus merula* Linn.) damage and eat pears. A case is recorded of a tree almost stripped of fruit by Squirrels (*Sciurus europæus*).

ANIMALS INJURIOUS TO CORN CROPS.

Tulip Root (*Tylenchus devastatrix*) of oats. A great many data gathered by the author show that winter oats are not subject to Tulip Root nor to Frit Fly (*Oscinis frit*), whilst spring oats are badly attacked. This *Tylenchus* is controlled by applying sulphate of potash at the rate of 2 cwt to the acre. The effect of nitrate of soda and salt appears also to be very beneficial in this disease. The frit fly (*Oscinis frit* Curtis) was more or less prevalent all over England in 1909-1910. The only palliative for frit fly is sowing winter oats instead of spring.

ANIMALS INJURIOUS TO ROOT CROPS.

The Turnip Fleas (*Halticidae*), the Pigmy Mangold Beetle (*Atomaria linearis* Stephens), the Turnip Seed Weevil (*Ceutorhynchus assimilis*) destroy cabbages, turnips and Kohl Rabi. The Turnip Gall Weevil (*Ceutorhynchus sulcicollis* Gyll.) the Turnip, Mustard, and Cabbage Blossom Beetle (*Meligethes aeneus* Fab.), the Chafer Larvae (*Rhizotrogus solstitialis*) and the Mangold Fly (*Pegomyia betae* Curtis), attack mangolds and swedes. The many English *Melegithes* seem to attack the blossom of Fruit trees as well as cruciferous plants. The writer received from Dundalk, County Louth, specimens of swedes attacked by a new species of insect pest, of which no similar attack had been recorded before. It produces a regular galled growth on the plants causing very marked deformities.

ANIMALS INJURIOUS TO PULSE.

The Bean Beetles (*Bruchus rufimanus*) the Summer Chafer (*Rhizotrogus solstitialis* Fab.) and Eelworm (*Tylenchus devastatrix* Kuhn) have been noted on Peas. The Summer Chafer also attacks beans, apple, medlar, and rose.

ANIMALS INJURIOUS TO HOPS.

The damage done by the Eelworm (*Heterodera schachtii*) in hops is gradually getting worse, not only in Europe and America, but in Japan and Egypt. Even bananas are now suffering from the same disease. The Strig Maggot (*Diplosis humuli*) seem still to be increasing. The Fever Fly (*Dilophus febrilis* Linn.), which appeared for the first time among the hop cones in Rainham in 1882, again appeared at Whitstone, in Hereford, in 1910. The larvae feed on all kinds of roots, including those of hops.

ANIMALS INJURIOUS TO VEGETABLES.

Knot Root in cucumbers and tomatoes is due to an eel-worm (*Heterodera radicicola*) which in Jersey has attacked all the roots of figs.

This disease seems to be as general as ever in England, and occurs in America, South Africa and Japan. No remedy for it is known.

The Death's Head Moth (*Acherontia atropos* Linn.), the Brassicae Petiole Maggot (*Phytomyza flavicornis* Meig.), the Ground Aphis (*Pemphigus lactuarius*), *Forda formicaria* Heyden, an Aphis of Artichokes, Aptera (*Achorptes rufescens*, Nicolet), attacking mushrooms and a mite (*Rhizoglyphus spinitarsus*) which also attacks mushrooms, are referred to.

ANIMALS INJURIOUS TO FLOWERS.

Rose Enemies : The Raspberry beetle (*Byturus tomentosus*, Fabr.), seems to be extending its attention to other plants than its natural host plants of the genus *Rubus*, and it has been found eating the petals of roses.

Weevils (*Otiorhynchus picipes*) eat the buds out of newly budded rose plants and killed the plants.

The Garden Chafer (*Phyllopertha horticola*) and the Summer Chafer, (*Rhizotrogus solstitialis*) attack the blossoms.

The Swallow Tail Moth (*Uropteryx sambucaria*, Linn.) ; larvae of this moth were found feeding on rose-bushes at Romford, Essex. It has not before been recorded as a rose insect in England nor does Lucet mention it in his book *Les Insectes Nuisibles aux Rosiers sauvages et cultivés en France*, 1898. The caterpillar feeds normally on oak, ivy, bramble, elder, etc.

The Wood-boring Rose Sawfly (*Emphytus cinctus*, Linn.) the Leaf-rolling Sawfly (*Blennocampa pusilla* Klug.), the Rose Slug Worm (*Eriocampa rosae* Harr.) Soft Brown Scale (*Lecanium capreae* Linn.) and the Rose Leaf Hopper (*Typhlocyba rosse* Linn.) are also mentioned.

Other flower pests are the Chrysanthemum Leaf Miner (*Phytomyza geniculata* Macq.), and the Ivy Red Spider (*Bryobia pretiosa* Koch).

A beneficial beetle (*Clytus arietis* Linn.) : This beetle in its larva stage preys upon the wood-boring insects, especially Bark Beetles and Shot Borers, and has become an important enemy of such pests. Steps are being taken to introduce it into Ceylon to check the Tea Scolytus.

Hairworms (*Mermis Sp.*). *Mermis albicans* has been shown by Von Siebold to be found in the caterpillars of *Hyponomeuta evonymella*. The writer is led to believe that one species must be parasitic in grasshoppers, but unfortunately have no effect on their hosts.

A. McKerral. **Insect and Fungoid Attack on Cultivated Plants in Sagaing District, Burma.** — *Department of Agriculture, Burma, Agricultural Surveys.* No. 2, Sagaing District, pp. 39 (32-36). Rangoon, Burma, 1911.

1942

Insects. — The insect which does the most damage is the Poti-gaung, or cock-chafer grub, which is the most omnivorous feeder. The Ku (*Diacrisia obliqua* Wlk.) is wide-spread and attacks sesamum cotton, groundnut, and peas and beans. It usually feeds on leaves and, in Sagaing, attacks the capsules of sesamum and often does serious damage.

British India: Burma

The Nga-hmyaung-daung (*Spodoptera mauritia* Boisd.) is the larva of one of the Noctuid moths and attacks paddy, principally in the young stages of growth. Occasionally it damages pyaung (*Sorghum vulgare*) by eating the young central shoot, and is also known to eat sesamum and cotton.

The Poti or Po-di-gaung is one of the chafer grubs. The systematic name of the local variety is as yet uncertain. Both grub and beetle do damage, the former mostly to the roots of pyaung, and the latter to the leaves of various plants.

The Po-laung-mi, known in Pegu as Yve-phya, is the Rice Hispa (*Hispa aenescens*) (1).

The Po-daung-da attacks seedlings of paddy and jowar (Sorghum vulgare). It has not yet been identified. It is a green caterpillar which usually appears in November or December and attacks the plants, commencing from the top of the stalk and eating away all the tender parts.

The Set-po (probably *Nonagria uniformis*), is a stem-borer which attacks the paddy plant.

The Pya (*Aphis Gossipii*) clusters in large numbers on the shoots and leaves of the cotton plant, sucks the sap, and so interferes with the growth and development of its host. Another species attacks peas and beans.

The Wa-thi-win-sa-po are the cotton boll-worms and apparently comprise three different species, viz: *Earias fabia, Earias insulana,* and *Gelechia gossypiella.* These insects bore into the cottonboll and eat the seeds.

Fungoid diseases. — Wheat Rust (*Puccinia*) is known to Burmans in Sagaing as San-nwin-po. It has been sometimes recorded, but is nowhere widespread.

(1) See p. 175, *Bull.*, Nov. 1910. (*Ed.*).

Smut (*Ustilago*) is known to Burmans as Pya-kya-the; it does considerable damage to ears of wheat and jowar (sorghum).

Other Blights which are now being studied are Pothé, or sterility of the sesamum plant, and the Paw-win-the of sorghum.

1943   D. E. FULLAWAY. **Insects of Field Crops. Annual Report of the Hawaii Agricultural Experiment Station for 1910.** — *Hawaii Agricultural Experiment Station* 1910, pp. 21-22. Washington, 1911.

The greatest hindrance to the diversification of agriculture in the Hawaii islands has been the ravages of insects. They have been studied on the experiment field at Kunia, belonging to the

Hawaii   Kunia Development Co. which is typical of much of the land available for diversified farming.

The crops under observation were maize, wheat, barley, oats, jack beans and cotton.

The following insects were observed to attack maize: Cutworms (*Agrotis ypsilon* and *A. crinigera*), Army worm (*Cirphis unipuncta*), Grass army worm (*Spodoptera mauritia*), Looper (*Plusia chalcites*), Angoumois grain moth (*Sitotroga cerealella*), Corn leaf aphis (*Aphis maidis*), Corn leafhopper (*Peregrinus maidis*), Rice weevil (*Calandra oryzae*), Wireworm (*Simodactylus cinnamomeus*), Tenebrionid beetle (*Epitragus diremptus*), *Cryptoblabes aliena, Batrachedra rileyi, Amorbia emigratella, Opatrum serratum, Adoretus tenuimaculatus, Araecerus fasciculatus, Plodia interpunctella, Ephestia elutella, Setamorpha* sp., *Catorama mexicana*, Nitidulid.

On wheat: Cutworm (*Agrotis crinigera*), Army worm (*Cirphis unipuncta*), Grass army worm (*Spodoptera mauritia*), Looper (*Plusia chalcites*), Leaf roller (*Omiodes localis*), Corn leaf aphis (*Aphis maidis*), *Opatrum serratum, Epitragus diremptus*, Wireworm (*Simodactylus cinnamomeus*).

On Barley: Corn leaf aphis (*Aphis maidis*).

On Jack Bean: Grass army worm (*Spodoptera mauritia*), Leaf miner (*Agromyza* sp.).

On Cotton: Cutworm (*Agrotis crinigera*), Grass army worm (*Spodoptera mauritia*), Cotton aphis (*Aphis gossypii*).

1944   **Insect Pests in Uganda, the Gold Coast and West Africa.** (The Entomological Research Committee). — *The Agricultural News*, vol. X, No. 332, p. 90. Barbados, March 18th, 1911.

Uganda. Gold Coast, etc.   The agricultural papers so far printed in the *Bulletin of Entomological Research*, published by the Committee of Entomological

Research appointed by the British Colonial office, have been on fruit flies (two articles), Coccidae (five), and Hemiptera injurious to cacao (two).

The notes on Coccidae are based on collections from Uganda forwarded by Mr. C. C. Gowdey (1) and Mr. Newstead. These are of scientific interest as they contain several new species ; and small Hymenopterous insects which are stated to be fairly abundant, occur as parasites of the Uganda scale insects.

The notes on *Hemiptera* injurious to cacao include an account of a species of *Helopeltis* from the Gold Coast, which occurs as a pest in certain localities. The mosquito blight of tea in India is due to a species of this genus (*Helopeltis theivora*), which rendered large areas of tea plantations in India unproductive. The injury is caused by the punctures the insects make in feeding. These cause many young pods to die, and often injure the older pods to such an extent that, although they survive on the tree until they reach maturity, the seeds are worthless.

Another Hemipterous insect, injurious to cacao on the Gold Coast, is the cacao-bark sapper (*Sahlbergella theobroma*), with which is often associated a nearly allied species (*singularis*). These insects are reported as destroying cacao trees in certain localities. The injury to the trees results from the punctures of the bark made by the insects with their sucking mouth parts while feeding. Experiments indicate that spraying with kerosene emulsion, at a time when the immature insects are abundant, is an efficient and practical measure.

A paper by Dr. W. M. Graham on West African fruit flies (*Tryperidae*), states that these pests belong to two genera: *Ceratitis*, of which nine species have been recorded, and *Dacus*, of which eleven species are known. Very little seems to be described of the habits and food plants of most of these species, but they are all liable to prove serious pests to fruit cultivation.

The remedies suggested are the destruction of all fallen fruit and the use of the poisoned sweet mixture which has given such good results in Cape Colony. This is prepared by mixing sugar 2 ½ lbs, arsenate of lead (paste) 3 oz, and water 4 gallons, and is applied by being sprayed on the foliage of infested fruit trees. The adult flies feed upon this mixture and are killed.

In the second paper on fruit flies, Mr. E. E. Austen describes a new genus and two new species from Uganda. It is expected that

---

(1) See Abstr. 1935 *Bull.* March 1911. (*Ed.*)

these insects will prove to be pests of fruit, but nothing is known of their life history and habits.

1945   MAISONNEUVE. **On the Fecundity of Cochylis** (1). (Sur la fécondité des Cochylis). — *C. R. de l'Acad. des Sciences*, t. 152, n. 22, pp. 1511-1512. Paris, 29 Mai, 1911.

The writer's observations on the fecundity of the Cochylis lead him to believe that the total number of eggs laid by the female varies considerably according as the biological conditions are favour-

France   able, or the reverse.

Anyhow, the fact that females have been known to lay 120 well formed eggs explains the extraordinary way in which the larvae multiply, both in the first and second brood of Cochylis, even when the number of moths seems small.

Supposing a female to lay 120 eggs, half of which become females of the next brood, and lay 120 eggs each, the progeny of one female moth in a season will be 7200 larvae.

1946   MAISONNEUVE. **On the Ovaries of the Cochylis**. (Sur l'appareil ovarien des Cochylis). — *C. R. de l'Acad. des Sciences*, t. 152, n. 24, pp. 1702-1703. Paris, 12 juin, 1911.

The writer on making his first investigations of the ovaries of Cochylis which had hatched out on the previous day (May 13th), noted in each of the six ovarian ducts some twenty eggs, or 120

France   eggs in all (2).

But he also noted behind these fully formed eggs, between them and the blind end of each duct, a residual mass of undifferentiated protoplasm which he said could doubtless be used in elaborating new germs so that the number of 120 could very easily be exceeded.

In confirmation of this, a dissection of a female made on May 28th, 8 days after its hatching out showed that the living matter contained in the ovary ducts had been entirely transformed into eggs, growing smaller and smaller as they neared the extremity of each duct, the blind end of which contained a last egg, the most recently formed and the smallest of all.

---

(1) See Abstract 340, this *Bull.* Jan. 1911.   (*Ed.*).
(2) See preceding Abstract.   (*Ed.*).

This showed that each duct can contain not 20, but 25 or 30 eggs, which, multiplied by 6, gives a total of 150 to 180 eggs.

According to the age of the Cochylis moth dissected, the number of eggs borne by a single female is seen to vary. If all the eggs are laid and hatched out one can easily account for the formidable invasions of this moth which often occur quite unexpectedly.

F. PICARD and H. FABRE. **A Curious Change of Food Recorded for Cochylis and Eudemis.** (Sur un curieux changement de régime de la Cochylis et de l'Eudémis). — *Le Progrès agricole et viticole,* 28ᵉ année, n. 25, pp. 767-769, Fig. 1-2. Montpellier, 18 juin, 1911.

1947

It is generally admitted that Cochylis and Eudemis, unlike Pyralis, feed exclusively on the bunches of grapes. Specimens bred at the School of Agriculture at Montpellier show that there may be exceptions to this rule: In a cage containing Cochylis not only were the bunches of grapes eaten but the young shoots themselves contained the larvae; the caterpillars generally enter the axils of the leaves and their presence is revealed by a hole covered with a web and excrements. If the vine shoot be split it will be seen that the Cochylis bore holes in the pithy part of the stalk, or in the petioles of the leaves; tendrils are also often perforated. Almost all the vine shoots are attacked from the base to the extremity at each knot, not by one, but by twenty or thirty larvae, and sometimes more. In each knot can be seen the entrances to one or more tunnels.

France:
Montpellier

The writers think that the larvae may have been so numerous as to be starved and so spread over all the organs and bored into the stalks. They also noticed several caterpillars climbing up the shoots, whilst others were busy boring into them.

The writers also found some shoots perforated by Eudemis caterpillars. The tendrils were riddled by Eudemis as by Cochylis. In the case of Eudemis the phenomenon is more interesting than in that of Cochylis. The eggs were not so numerous, the bunches of grapes contained only a few grubs, and some were even free from them. This change of diet cannot therefore be explained solely by starvation.

1948

R. STEWART McDOUGALL. **Swift Moths (*Hepialidae*)** (1). — *The Journ. of the Board of Agriculture*, Vol. XVIII, No. 2, pp. 116-120, 1 pl. London, May, 1911.

Two very destructive British moths, the Small Garden Swift (*Hepialus lupulinus* L.) and the Ghost Swift (*Hepialus Humuli* L.), belong to the family of the Swift Moths (*Hepialidae*).

United Kingdom

The larvae of these two moths attack the underground portions of plants, causing great injury to them.

The larvae of the Small Garden Swift attack narcissus, paeony dahlia, chrysanthemum, oats, colchicum, gladiolus, lilies, pea, bean, strawberry, gooseberry, celery, parsnip, parsley, potato, mint, lettuce, etc.

The Small Garden Swift is widespread in England and Wales but less common in Scotland; it is also found in Ireland.

The larvae of the Ghost Swift are especially harmful to carrot, hop, potato, oats, asparagus, etc.

The writer gives the systematic description of these two species and the means for their control. Vaporite (2) has been tried with good results. Birds and moles also assist in the destruction of these moths; there are also two parasitic fungi, *Cordyceps militaris* and *C. entomorrhiza*.

1949

F. V. THEOBALD. **Springtails (*Collembola*). Their Importance, with Notes on Some Unrecorded Instances of Damage.** — *The Journal of the South Eastern Agricultural College, Wye, Kent*, No. 19, pp. 183-199. London and Ashford, Kent.

The importance of the Collembola or "Springtails", one of the two divisions of the order Aptera, as destructive insects, was

Great Britain

referred to by Sir John Lubbock and John Curtis, and since then in many parts of the world references have been made to them in connection with the damage they do to plants. Recently some fresh facts have come to light through the researches of Prof. Carpenter in Dublin, in connection with apteran injury".

Very many are harmless, but certain species, especially in the genera *Sminthurus* and *Lipara*, are undoubtedly injurious, attacking both leaves and stems : others damage roots (*Templetonia*),

---

(1) See Abstr. 1307, *Bulletin* for April 1911.   (*Ed.*).
(2) Insecticide composed chiefly of naphthalin   (*Ed.*).

and others seem to so disturb the soil (*Achorutes*) that seedlings suffer. They injure the plants in two ways: by so opening the plant tissue that it is easily invaded by bacteria and fungoid pests; and, as many are found feeding on diseased and fungus growths, it is quite possible that they may act as distributors of bacterial and vegetal disease germs.

The following is a list of the injurious species: *Lipura armata* Tullberg; *L. ambulans* Linn.; *L. Burmeisteri* Lubb.; *L. fimetaria* Linn.; *Achorutes armatus* Nicolet; *A. manubrialis* Tullberg; *A. longispinus* Tull.; *A. rufescens* Nicolet; *A. purpurescens* Lubbock; *Anurida granaria* Nicolet; *Isotoma palustris* Müll; *I. tenella* Reuter; *Orchesella cincta* Linn.; *Entomobrya nivalis* Tullberg; *E. multifasciata* Tullberg; *Lepidocyrtus sp.*; *Sminthurus fuscus* Linn.; *S. luteus* Lubbock; *S. niger* Lubbock; *S. pruinosus* Tullberg; *S. hortensis;* *Templetonia nitida* Templeton; *Degeeria annulata* Fabricius.

From recent observations made by the writer it seems quite likely that *Sminthurus luteus* may play some part in distributing potato disease (*Phytophthora infestans*).

It also attacks currants, apples and potatoes.

Sminthurus luteus and *S. niger* Lubbock attack the turnip crop (1); *S. pruinosus* Tullberg attacks beans and sweet peas; *S. hortensis* (2) attacks tobacco in America; another species of *Sminthurus*, probably an undescribed native species, appeared in great numbers in lucerne paddocks in South Australia in 1896 doing great damage (3).

Species of *Orchesalla* have been known to attack orchids (4); White Springtails (*Lipura ambulans* Linn,) attack peas, beans, and the roots of garden flowers and succulent vegetables (5); they also attack the roots of celery and cauliflower (6) and have been observ-

(1) E. A. ORMEROD, *Reports and Observations on Injurious Insects for 1894*, p. 110 (1905).

(2) RILEY and HOWARD, *Insect Life*, Vol. 3, p. 151, 1891.

(3) *Australian Insects*, p. 10.

(4) F. V. THEOBALD, *First Report on Economic Zoology* (British Museum), pp. 108-112 (1903) and F. V. THEOBALD, *Second Report on Economic Zoology* (Brit. Mus.), p. 76 (1904).

(5) CARPENTER, *Economic Proceedings of the Royal Botanical Society*, I, part 6, p. 293 (Plate XXVI-*A*) 1905.

Ibidem, I, part 8, p. 340, 1906.

Ibidem, I, part 8, p. 442, 1907.

(6) F. V. THEOBALD, *Second Report of Economic Zoology* (B. Mus). p. 158 (1904).

ed (1) on narcissus bulbs; *Lipura fimetaria* is found throughout
the year in damp earth, engaged in feeding upon carrots, potatoes,
and other roots.

Templetonia (Heteromurus) nitida Temp. attacks the roots of
the strawberry; *Digeeria aunulata* Fab. feeds on the leaves of
currant bushes; *Achorutes rufescens* N. attacks mushrooms; *A. armatus*
Nicolet, attacks seeds; *A. purpurescens* Lubb. attacks cabbage; *A. armatus*
Nicolet and *A. longispinus* Tullberg (2) are said
to damage roots and seeds of healthy plants, and other *Achorutes* (3)
are said to prevent the germination of seeds.

Entomobrya nivalis Linn. attacks hops; one of the *Poduridae*
was reported as very harmful to mushrooms; *Isotoma tenella* Reuter
destroys tobacco seedlings in Ireland. A species of *Isotoma* attacks
poultry (4); a *Lepidocyrtus* infests houses in the United States (5).
A *Sminthurus* was found feeding on Uredo spores of the common
wheat rust *Puccinia rubigo-vera*. It was proved also to distribute
spores, so any good done is neutralised.

The experiments made by the writer in the control of these
pests lead him to the following conclusions: *a*) the springtails may
be poisoned with arsenate of lead or nicotine at 1 1/5 oz. to 10 gallons
of water; *b*) the ground treatment is necessary also, and as
they do not feed on the soil the drying caustic effects of lime and
soot are better than the mere spraying of the ground by the several
insecticides; *c*) where they attack asparagus and sea-kale they may
be kept down by being trapped with half scooped-out orange rinds.

1950   A. J, Cook. **The Peach Aphis** *(Aphis persicae-niger)*. — *California
Cultivator*, Vol. XXVI, No. 20, p. 614, Los Angelos, May 18, 1911.

We have much to learn of this insect, as we know neither the
eggs, nor the sexual form nor its full life history.

It works on both the twigs and the roots. As it is on the
roots all the year, it does more harm to the roots fom than the
twigs, where it remains only for a short time in the spring. While on

United
States :
California

        (1) COLLINGE, *Report on the Injurious Insects and other Animals observed
in the Midland Counties during 1905*, p. 10, 1906.
        (2) CARPENTER, *Proceedings of the Association of Economic Biologists*, Vol. I,
Part I, p. 14, 1905.
        (3) GUTHRIE, *The Collembola of Minnesota*, p. 4, 1903.
        (4) F. V. THEOBALD, *Parasitic Diseases of Poultry*, p. 37, 1896.
        (5) *Canadian Entomologist*, XXVIII, 1896.   (*Ed.*).

the twigs, some of the lice grow wings and fly to other trees. By this means and by the planting of infected trees from the nursery the pest is spread. This aphis is widely spread all over the United States.

Several insects prey upon these aphids, so that often the lice are kept down by natural insect enemies. Sometimes the lice will disappear, both the root forms and those above ground, without control work being necessary.

D. LARINOW. **The Selection of a Variety of Sunflower Resistant to the Larvae of** *Homeosoma nebulella*. (Nieskolko Slov o Podsolnietcnikie). — *Khosiaistvo* (The Home) VI G., No. 21, pp. 667-675. Kiew, 2, Junia 1911.

1951

In 1896 and 1897 the sunflower plantations in district of Saratov were almost completely destroyed by a Lepidoptera, *Homeosoma nebu'ella* Hb. This insect is now widespread throughout Russia, except in the most northerly sections of the Empire.

Russia: Saratov

The females of the first brood (May-June), feed on the thistle (*Carduus*), aster, and *Cirsium*, of which they suck the honey; then they lay their eggs on the inflorescence of the sunflower. The larvae, which hatch out after a few days, attack the still unformed fruit, and destroy the seed. They then turn into chrysalides on the flowers or leaves. The second brood of moths lay their eggs on the wild flowers of the same family, more especially on *Carthamus*, (*C. lanatus, C. tinctorius*, and *C. glaucus*). The larvae of the second brood winter in the fields and complete their development the following spring.

J. M. Karsin noted that the double-flower variety of sunflower, cultivated as an ornamental plant, is unaffected. He crossed these varieties with those grown for their oil, and obtained a resistant variety known as the " armoured sunflower ". The larvae of the *Homeosoma nebulella* Hb. are unable to perforate the pericarp of this sunflower.

Investigations and analyses led Karsin to suppose that this species of invulnerability of the ornamental and " armoured " sunflower was due to the presence of a larger proportion of silica in their pericarps than in those of other varieties; but the writer's studies clearly show that varieties having gray achenes with white streaks, of which the pericarps contain a high percentage of silica are more subject to attack than those with metallic blue achenes which contain less silica.

The invulnerability of the " armoured " sunflower is not accounted for by the toughness of the pericarp nor by its high silica
content. All resistant varieties are characterised by a subcutaneous
layer of highly pigmented cells, which the larvae can uncover, but
which they can never perforate.

As the American and Californian sunflowers have this characteristic in a marked degree, the writer points to these two varieties
as affording excellent material for a process of selection, in view
of obtaining a type of *Helianthus* resistant not only to the attacks
of these insects, but also, may be, to those of rust and broom-rape.

1952   **Recent Work with Fungus Parasites of Scale Insects in the
West Indies**. — *The Agricultural News*, vol. X, No. 232, p. 94.
Barbados, March 18th, 1911.

In Grenada many trees, particularly mangos, have been subject to bad attacks of scale insects, accompanied by black blight
fungus. The scales are generally « soft shield scales », of the
genus *Coccus*.; these are attacked by the « shield scale fungus »
(*Cephalosporium Lecani*). As this fungus was confined to the
extreme leeward end of the island, it was sent out to various
places where black blight was present. As a result the fungus
has become definitely established at two places in the interior of
the island ; in the successful cases the trees were almost freed
from scales, and were consequently much less severely attacked
by black blight. The fungus was also observed to attack the
« mealy shield scale » (*Pulvinaria pyriformis*) on a cinnamon tree:
this had not been recorded before.

In Barbados the shield scale fungus was found attacking
black scale (*Saissetia nigra*) on Hibiscus. The use of this material
to infest green and mango shield scales (*Coccus viridis* and *C.
mangiferae*) on guava and mango plants at two places was very
successful, so that after three months it was difficult to find
unattacked scales in the trial trees.

As a result of the discovery of this fungus on the mealy
shield scale in Grenada, search was made on trees of Java plum
(*Eugenia Jambolana*) and rose apple (*E. Jambos*) in Barbados, and
individual scales were found to be attacked there also. Branches
of Barbados cherry (*Malpigia glabra*) on which the scales had
been killed by the fungus were then tied into the Java plum and rose
apple trees, with the result that the fungus gradually increased.

West Indies :
Grenada
Barbados

Much work will have to be done in ˙ distribution before the fungi give general results against the scales, and re-infection may be necessary after unfavourable seasons.

The Larvae of certain *Tachinidae* and the White Stork the Natural Enemies [of *Laphygma exempta*, injurious to Gramineae. See Abstract 1970 in this *Bulletin*.

1953
Rhodesia

Hypostema variabilis, and *Bracon* sp. **Natural Enemies of *Phytonomus nigrirostris*, Injurious to Forage Crops in North America.** See Abstract 1974 in this *Bulletin*.

1954
N. America

The Larvae of *Microphtalma disjuncta*, Parasites of the Larvae of *Rhizotrogus solstitialis*, Injurious to the Vine in Russia. See Abstract 1997 in this *Bulletin*.

1955
Russia

G. MARTELLI. **Native and Foreign Parasites of the Mulberry Pest,** *Diaspis pentagona* Targ., **so far known and introduced into Italy.** (Parassiti indigeni ed esotici della *Diaspis pentagona* Targ. finora noti ed introdotti in Italia). pp. 1-15, 9 fig. Acireale, 1910.

1956

Of recent years the director, Prof. F. Silvestri, and his assistants of the Laboratory of Agricultural Entomology of the Royal High School of Agriculture of Portici, near Naples have: made a special study of the natural control (artificial control is always more expensive) of *Diaspis pentagona* Targ. (1).

Italy :
Naples

The writer gives a list of the several native and foreign parasites of the *Diaspis* known or introduced up to now into Italy.

Parasites introduced from abroad are the following : *Prospaltella diaspidicola* Sil., *Aphelimus diaspidis* How., *Prospaltella Berlesei* How., *Archenomus orientalis* Silv., *Rhizobius lophantae* Blaisd., *Chilocorus Kuvanae* Silv., *C. distigma*, *Platgnaspis Silvestri* Sichard.

To these parasites must be added 4 species of *Cecidomyidae* (dipterous insects of prey), *viz. Tricontarinia ciliatipennis* Kieff. and *T. japanica* Kieff., obtained from specimens coming from Japan,

---

(1) See also, p. 375 *Bull.* Dec. 1910. (*Ed.*).

and *Arthrocnodax moricola* Kieff. and *A. silvestri* Kieff., obtained from specimens from South Africa.

The native parasites are *Chilocorus bipustulatus* L. *Exochomus 4 — pustulatus* L.. *Cybocephalus rufifrons* Reitt.

Besides this, the Portici Laboratory has recently received from California other specimens, such as *Rhizobius*, which will be bred in the hope that they also can be acclimatised in Italy for the control of *Diaspis* and of the *Diaspinae* in general as also of the *Lecanium*.

1957

J. W. JEFFREY. **Efficiency of *Vedalia cardinalis* against the '' Fluted Scale '' *Icerya Purchasii*.** *California Cultivator*. Vol, XXVI, No. 21, p. 613. — Los Angeles, May 18, 1911.

United 9tates: California

The report of the Californian State insectary (1) shows that less than 100 orders were received for *Vedalia cardinalis* during 1910. When one considers the billions of plants in California that are subject to attack by the fluted- scale (2) this scarcity of orders shows what a marvellous hold the Vedalia has secured in California, Perhaps the white scale (*Aspidiotus* spp.) has not been exterminated in a single locality throughout this range, and yet the work of its arch enemy is so effective that only 3336 Vedalia have been called for in 12 months.

1958
California

***Scutellista cyanea*, a Parasite of *Saissetia Oleae*, injurious to Citrus Fruits.** — See Abstract 1967 in this *Bulletin*.

1959

A. A. GIRAULT. **An Egg-parasite of the Codling-Moth.** *The Canadian Entomologist*, vol. XLIII, No 4, pp. 133-134. London, April, 1911.

United States: Georgia. Illinois

The writer gives a description of a Mymarid (*Anaphes gracilis* Howard), which, from an old record from Georgia, is shown to be a parasite of the eggs of the Codling Moth (*Carpocapsa pomonella*).

---

(1) See Abs. 1563 of this *Bulletin*, May 1911.   (*Ed.*).

(2) *Icerya Purchasii* is also called «Cottony-Cushion Scale» - See Abstr. 1967 this *Bulletin*.

(*Ed.*).

The species was originally described as a parasite of *Lepidosaphes ulmi*.

The writer took a specimen on August 25th, 1910 in a pig-shed at Centralia, Illinois.

"Hairworms" *(Mermis sp.),* Parasites of Grasshoppers. — See Abstract 1941 in this *Bulletin*.

1960
Great
Britain

The Hedgehog as a destroyer of Insect Pests and Slugs. — See Abstr. 1941 in this *Bulletin*.

1961
Great
Britain

E. Molz. **Carbolineum in the Control of Plant Diseases**. (Untersuchungen über die Wirkung des Karbolineums als Pflanzenschutzmittel). — *Centralblatt für Bakteriologie, Parasitenkunde und Infektionskrankheiten*, 30 Bd., No. 7-12, pp. 181-232. Jena, 30. Mai 1911.

1962

Carbolineum is a general designation for tar oils in commercial use as insecticides and fungicides.

This study describes the results of a series of experiments made to determine the value of these products in the control of plant diseases.

Germany

Diaspis Piri and *Aspidiotus ostreaeformis*. — Volatile oils are much more efficacious than heavy oils in the control of these insects. A 30 % aqueous solution is used for the complete destruction of *Diaspis* and *Aspidiotus*; though fairly satisfactory results are obtained with a 15 % solution.

Schizoneura lanigera Hausm. — Undiluted tar oils destroy the *Schizoneura* but also kill the surrounding tissues. Heavy oils are less injurious than light oils. A 10 % solution to be sprayed on after the fall of the leaves is therefore advised.

Eryophyes Vitis Nal. — A 20 % solution of unrefined tar oil injures the young vine shoots, which remain intact when oil freed from phenol is used.

For the larvae of *Pieris Brassicae* L. and *Euproctis chrysorrhea* L. : ,

1) 1 % solutions of tar oils, with the exception of unrefined phenols, do not completely destroy these larvae.

2) In the case of *Euproctis*, the best results are obtained with unrefined phenols and their bases.

3) A solution of unrefined phenols at 0.5 % suffices to destroy the developed larvae of *Pieris Brassicae*. The great efficacy of this insecticide makes it the most advisable for use in sylviculture.

Carbolineum as a means of keeping the larvae of certain insects off leaves they attack. This result can be obtained by using a 1 % solution.

Carbolineum in the control of insects and larvae concealed in the soil. — Carbolineum is much less effective than sulphide and tetrachloride of carbon in the control of insects which burrow deep into the soil ; but satisfactory results are obtained when it is used against Nematodes concealed in the surface soil.

Many experiments have been made in the control of fungoid diseases. Here are some of the more important results:

1) Tar oils can be used successfully against *Sclerotinia fructigena* and to some extent also against *Botrytis cinerea* and *Penicillium glaucum*;

2) Carbolineum acts against the *Peronospora* of the vine, but cannot take the place of sulphur or copper sulphate.

Tar oils spread on the soil some time before sowing, act as a soil disinfectant and stimulate seed germination.

It is said that carbolineum smeared on the bark of fruit trees assists their growth and increases their yield.

Copper solutions used for the control of fungoid diseases damage the green parts of peach-trees, whereas carbolineum destroys the fungus without attacking the tree.

Finally, heavy tar oils may be used with success in treating wounds in trees, to whatever cause they be due; the best results are obtained in the case of apple trees.

1968　　V. VERMOREL and E. DANTONY. **A Wetting Nicotine Solution.** (La Nicotine mouillante). — *Le Progrès agricole et viticole*, 38ème année n. 25, pp. 772-773. Montpellier, 18 Juin 1911.

France　The writers advise the use of a new nicotine spray for the control of Cochylis. The formula is the following, the mixture having the advantage of acting as a wetting solution:

Water	50 gals.	— (225 litres)
Carbonate of Soda Solvay . .	0.5 lb.	— (225 grams)
White oleine soap.	1 lb.	— (450 grams)
10 % Nicotine solution . . .	5 pints.	— (3.00 litres)

This spray has the advantage of being much less expensive than nicotinised copper solution and its high wetting capacity allows of a more thorough distribution of the insecticide over the grape-clusters which is a point of recognized importance.

By the use of a hose-nozzle fitted with a tap, it is possible to spray the grape clusters (the only parts which require protection) to the exclusion of all others and thus effect an important saving in nicotine, which cannot be done when nicotinised copper mixtures are used, as these have to be sprayed on to the leaves on which the nicotine is not required.

The carbonate of soda acts as a dissolvent of the nicotine salt, freeing the alkaloid. It has long been recognized that free nicotine is much more effective as an insecticide than salts of nicotine. For this reason nicotinised alkaline copper mixtures are more active than simple aqueous solutions of nicotine salts.

The solution here described wets the webs of the Cochylis and the Eudemis (which is not done by nicotinised copper mixtures), the insecticide thus coming into direct contact with the grub.

The quantity of soap mentioned is for use with rain water; and would have to be increased if ordinary water were used, in the ratio of about 0.1 lb. per degree of hardness and per 100 gals. of water. Anyhow, it is very easy to test whether the quantity of soap is sufficient, as soap should be added until the grape-clusters are visibly wetted by the solution.

Insecticidal Value of Ordinary Tobacco Juice. (Valeur, des jus de Tabac ordinaires). — *La Petite Revue agricole et horticole.* 17ᵉ année, N. 396, p. 127. Antibes, 11 Juin, 1911,

1964

It is a mistake to suppose that ordinary tobacco juices are injurious to plants and that only standard extracts are efficacious.

The opinion is doubtless due to the drawbacks of the old system of selling tobacco juice according to its specific gravity, which is not in direct relation to its nicotine content. This mistaken opinion was a source of failures, which are now obviated by the new system of guaranteeing the nicotine content of the juices sold.

France

Careful analyses show that the diluted juices (in which condition they should be used) contain no substances injurious to plants. Moreover they have always been used with success and in large quantities in the neighbourhood of Nice to control the insects which attack flowers.

Now, undoubtedly, the treatment of flowers is generally much more delicate than that of vines or of fruit-trees. Ordinary tobacco juice may therefore be considered an excellent remedy against Cochylis, Eudemis, and caterpillars. It costs less than standard extracts of nicotine and is equally good.

Viticulturists and órchardists in France will moreover find it all the more to their advantage to use tobacco juice for the protection of their plantations, as the French Tobacco Administration is quite unable to transform into extracts all the nicotine available for 1911.

If farmers refrain from using the ordinary tobacco-juices which are available, they will deprive themselves, to their great loss, of most of the alkaloid which has been prepared for the express purpose of protecting their crops.

1965   C. BACON. **Paraffin Emulsion as an Insecticide.** (L'émulsion d'essence de pétrole comme insecticide). *Revue de Viticulture*, 18e année, N. 914, p. 741, Paris. 22, Juin; 1911

France   The writer has remarked that as soon as this insecticide is sprayed on, all the Cochylis larvae come out of their silky cocoons, driven out by the odour; they remain motionless, and then, smothered in the soapy solution, turn brown and die. The young shoots and inflorescence of the vines are in no wise affected by this solution.

This insecticide is prepared as follows :

1 kg. of black or white soap is dissolved in 10 litres of hot water, then from 3 to 5 litres of essence of paraffin are poured in whilst the mixture is vigorously stirred. After emulsioning, 100 litres of water are added to the mixture. A neutral or basic copper solution may be added to this emulsion so as to make it more effective against other insects (*leaf-roller, flea beetles*, etc.), No flavor is imparted to the grapes by this emulsion.

As soon as this spray has been used the writer advises sulphuring with 50 % of powdered hydraulic lime, so as to take advantage of the remarkable wetting and penetrating qualities of this emulsion which make it of value for fixing the dusting.

1966   C. C. Mc DONNELL. **Chemistry of Fumigation with Hydrocyanic Acid Gas.** — *U. S. Department of Agriculture. Bureau of Entomology, Bulletin. No. 90.* Part. III, pp. 91-104, Washington, May 10, 1911.

The writer studies the proportion of potassium or sodium cyanide, sulphuric acid, and water required for the best yield of gas;

the action of mineral acids (sulphuric acid and hydrochloric) on cyanides and hydrocyanic acid; the effect of the presence of sodium chloride in cyanide on the yield of hydrocyanic-acid gas in fumigations; the formation of ammonia from the decomposition of the cyanide; the effect of presence of sodium nitrate in cyanides; on the effect of the presence of sodium nitrate in cyanides on the yield of hydrocyanic-acid gas. The results obtained on the evolution of hydrocyanic-acid gas under different conditions are given in a table.

These experiments show conclusively that the presence of chlorides and nitrates in cyanides which liberate hydrochloric and nitric acid respectively, together with hydrocyanic acid on treatment with sulphuric acid cause very marked decomposition of the hydrocyanic acid. The effect produced by hydrochloric acid is much more marked than that produced by nitric acid.

As practically all commercial potassium and sodium cyanides contain sodium chloride in greater or less amount, for fumigation work an analysis of a cyanide is of little value unless the chlorine content is also determined.

The amount of hydrocyanic-acid gas that can be used in fumigations falls within narrow limits. If the, application is too strong, serious injury will result to the trees, while, on the other hand, if too weak, many of the insects will escape the poisonous action of the gas, thus necessitating a second fumigation or giving inefficient results. It is therefore necessary that the strength and quality of the reagents be known and that the conditions under which the work is done be uniform.

R. S. Woglum. **Hydrocyanic-Acid Fumigations in California.** — *U. S. Department of Agriculture, Bureau of Entomology, Bulletin* No. 90, Part I & Part II, pp. 90. Washington, May 3, and May 10, 1911.

1967

I. *Fumigation of Citrus Trees.* — In 1886 Mr. D. W. Coquillet, experimenting on the cottony-cushion scale (*Icerya Purchasi* Mask.) in orange orchards in Calfornia discovered that hydrocyanic-acid gas was a most efficient insecticide for scale-insect pests of citrus trees. In 1890 it had commenced to be employed quite extensively. The use of this gas was restricted to California until 1892-93 when Prof. H. A. Morgan gave it a trial on orange trees in southern Louisiana. In 1893 it was on trial against the San José scale in Virginia and against citrus insect pests in Florida, Montserrat

United
States:
California

(British West Indies), and in Cape Colony (South Africa). To-day fumigation of citrus trees is carried on in California, Florida, Australia, Japan, and the Colonies of South Africa, and is now being introduced into Spain and Porto Rico.

This gas was first tried on deciduous trees by Mr. D. W. Coquillet in 1894 at Charlottesville, Va. The same year it was first used in the treatment of nursery stock. To-day the fumigation of deciduous stock before it is planted is required in many States by law.

The use of hydrocyanic-acid gas against insects affecting greenhouse plants has been successfully carried on for a number of years, and is also successfully used in the treatment of mills, various other buildings, and stored products infested with insects.

The introduction of the distillate spray (1) in 1901, simultaneously with the introduction from South Africa of the *Scutellista cyanea* Motschulsky, the parasite of the black-scale (*Saissetia oleae* Bern.) and its splendid showing, led many people to desist from the use of fumigations with hydrocyanic-acid gas. But Dr. G. Harold Powell's investigations, and past experience, showed that the distillate spray and the *Scutellista* parasite were inadequate to control the scale, and fruit growers took a renewed interest in fumigation.

The commercial fumigation of citrus trees in California is confined to six counties, Ventura, Los Angeles, Orange, Riverside, San Bernardino, and San Diego. Approximately 36 000 acres were treated during the year from July 1909 to July 1910.

Calculating the cost of fumigation on the basis of 30 cents a tree, the cost of fumigation of the citrus orchards of Southern California during the season 1909-1910 approximated $ 1 000 000.

Each of the citrus-fruit-producing counties of Southern California has a Board of Horticultural Commissioners, consisting of three members, whose duties are to supervise the destruction of insect pests, plant diseases, and noxious weeds within their respective counties. In the three greatest citrus fruit producing counties,

---

(1) Compound of Bordeaux mixture and tar oil. The following is another formula:

Ferrous sulphate 10 oz	284	gram.
Quick lime 5 oz.	142	»
Heavy tar oil. 24 oz.	681	»
Water 10 gal.	45,4	litres

F. V. THEOBALD in (P. WRIGHT, *Standard Cyclopedia of Modern Agriculture*, vol. VII, p. 133 London, 1910).   (*Ed.*).

Los Angeles, Riverside, and San Bernardino, numerous inspectors are also employed to assist in carrying out this important work, and advise when the trees shall be fumigated.

There are several different systems under which the work may be done: by contract, by association, by counties, and by private individuals.

The largest number of pests most injurious to citrus fruit in Southern California belongs to the *Coccidae*, or scale insects. Among those which are generally so destructive as to require extended efforts for their control are the purple scale (*Lepidosaphes Beckii* Newm.), the red scale (*Chrysomphalus Aurantii* Mask), and the black scale (*Saissetia Oleae* Bern). The yellow scale (*Chrysomphalus citrinus* Coq.), considered as a variety of the red scale, is much less destructive generally, though sufficiently destructive in some localities to be considered a pest of primary importance The Citrus mealy bug (*Pseudococcus citri* Risso), has recently been very injurious in certain quarters. Other insect pests attack citrus trees to a greater or less extent, but those just mentioned are generally the most injurious, and the principal method of their control is fumigation with hydrocyanic-acid gas.

When hydrocyanic-acid gas was first employed in treating orchards the apparatus used consisted of bell-shaped tents, manipulated by a high derrick mounted on a waggon. In 1892 Mr. C. W. Finch devised a much simpler and cheaper apparatus, consisting of flat sheet tents, octagonal in shape. The materials now generally used for sheet tents in southern California are 6 ½ or 7-ounce special drills and 8-ounce special army duck, though 10-oz, army duck is sometimes used in very large tents. These cloths are spoken of in ounces, meaning such a weight per yard, 30 in. wide. Drills are used as freely as ducks. In South Africa cloth even heavier than 10-oz is sometimes used. The writer would advise either a 7-ounce or an 8-ounce weight for commercial fumigation as superior to any cloth he has seen.

Mr. C. E. McFadden has devised an elaborate and ingenious machine for placing tents on trees. A description and drawing of this machine and of the supply cart, supply wagon and generating vessels is given. The process of fumigation consists in covering trees with cloth tents, and generating beneath them hydrocyanic-acid gas. After exposing a tree to the gas for an hour or thereabouts, the tent is removed to the next tree, and the process repeated. The work is carried on at night. Before fumigating, the orchard should be cultivated recently so that the ground shall be clean and smooth. The amount of chemicals to use, or the dosage varies not only with the size of the tree but also with the character of the insect to be destroyed.

The writer has worked out the following formulae giving the measurements around the bottom and over the top of tented trees:

$$\frac{C^2}{4\pi} \left[\frac{O}{2} - \frac{C(3\pi-4)}{12\pi} \right]$$

In this formula C equals the circumference of the tree, O equals the distance over the top of the tree, measured on the tent from the ground at one side to the ground at the other. If a person works out

and notes down in a table the values of $\frac{C^2}{4\pi}$ and $\frac{C(3\pi-4)}{12\pi}$ for different values of which he is apt to make common use, it is possible by its use in connection with the formula to determine the contents of the tree with fair rapidity. The distance around the bottom of a tent is easily secured by the use of a tape-line; the distance over the top was much more difficult to determine until Dr. A. W. Morrill invented a method of marking tents for this purpose.

For the generation of hydrocyanic-acid gas in fumigation, potassium cyanide, sulphuric acid, and water are necessary. The water is first measured and poured into the generating vessel. The required amount of acid is then added to the water. Whilst the mixture is hot it should be placed beneath the tree and the cyanide added. 1 fluid ounce of commercial sulphuric acid, and 1 ounce (avoirdupois) of 96 or 100 per cent potassium cyanide, in combination with 3 fluid ounces of water, give a complete reaction.

The preferable months for general fumigation are from August to December; the treatment can, however, be carried on with both safety and efficiency from December to April, provided the work be carefully done.

Common ladybird beetles (*Coccinella californica* Mann. and *Hippodamia convergens* Gué) are less easily killed by hydrocyanic-acid gas than the scale insects of the citrus, and large numbers of these insects on a tree at the time of fumigation survive the treatment. Fumigation destroys most of the *Scutellista cyanea* Morich. (*Hymenoptera*) in its adult and pupal stages. The majority of the larvae, however, which feed on the eggs of the black scale, are unaffected. One of the greatest benefits of the *Scutellista* is its work in trees which have been fumigated, as it devours the eggs of the black scale which have not been destroyed by the gas treatment. The average cost of fumigating a California citrus orchard is from 25 dollars to 40 dollars per acre. Large trees are much more expensive, while young trees cost considerably less.

II. *The value of sodium cyanide for fumigations.* — The writer points out that sodium cyanide at 124 to 130 % (1) purity can be used in fumigations instead of potassium cyanide, designated as 98 or 99 % pure. The following formula is given : 750 gr. of sulphuric acid, and 500 gr. of sodium cyanide per litre of water.

C. W. WOODWORTH. **The Control of the Argentine Ant.** (*Iridormyrmex humilis*) — *College of Agriculture, Agricultural Experiment Station, Berkeley, Cal. Bull.* No. 207, pp. 53-82. Berkeley, October, 1910.

1968

The Argentine Ant now occupies about 5 000 acres in California. There are more than forty separate colonies, varying from one acre to nearly 2 000 acres in extent.

United States : California

Except when carried by human agency they spread at about the rate of an eighth of a mile a year. Manure and nursery stock are particularly liable to be the method of transportation, though they may go with all sorts of merchandise.

Natural spread is not accomplished by flight. Migration normally occurs when the numbers exceed the food supply. Eradication is a possibility, and should be undertaken.

Control measures consist of barring ants out, and methods of killing. The best barrier consists of water treated with creosol, and makes possible a practical ant-proofing of rooms or houses.

In many cases their nests may be destroyed by the use of carbon bisulphide, potassium cyanide, or oil.

A syrup containing a very small quantity of arsenic is recommended as the most available poison, and the only really satisfactory method of killing the Argentine ant.

(1) Chemically pure sodium cyanide is commonly said to be 133 % pure; which means that an equal weight of pure sodium cyanide contains $\frac{1}{3}$ more cyanogen than potassium cyanide.   (*Author's note*).

Insects Injurious to Special Crops.

1969   I. A. PORCINSK. **Insect Pests of Cereals and Fruit Trees in Russia** (Vrediteli Rhelbnisk Slavok). — *Exegodnik Glavnago Upravlenia Semelustroistva i Semledielia po Departmentu Semledielia* (Year-Book of the Direction of Rural Organization and Agriculture of the Department of Agriculture). G. III, pp. 68-69. St. Peterburg, 1910.

An invasion of *Agrotis* (1) occurred in 1909 in many Governments, but only caused serious loss in the Governments of Tula and Ryasan.

Russia:
Tula.
Ryasan

Severe invasions of *Diplosis Tritici* in the wheat fields were recorded in the district of Beleev in the same year. As a remedial measure against this pest, farmers are advised to harvest early when possible and have the grain ground as soon as possible, also to burn the chaff immediately after threshing, if it contains larvae.

In Eastern Russia serious loss was incurred as the result of an invasion of *Hylemyia coarctata*, the larvae of which devoured the young spring-wheat seedlings.

In Southern Russia *Rhynchites pauxillus* which partially destroys the foliage of fruit-trees, is reported to be spreading.

1970   **Black Caterpillar Pest.** — *The Rhodesia Agricultural Journal*, Vol. VIII, No. 4, pp. 602-603. Salisbury, April, 1911.

During April 1910 about 150 sq. miles in the district of Umtali were invaded by a blackish caterpillar (*Laphygma exempta* Wilk.).

Rhodesia:
Umtali

This appears to attack only gramineous plants.

The White Stork is the most valuable of the natural enemies of this caterpillar, and certain parasitic Tachinid flies, the larvae of which might be advantageously scattered about the fields.

---

(1) Larvae of Noctuid moths — *A. exclamationis* and *A. segetum* — which occasionally do much damage to cereals.   (*Ed.*).

The most promising remedy for this pest appears to be the following locust poison :

> Arseniate of Soda. . . . 1 lb.
> Sugar . . . . 4 lbs.
> Water . . . . 8 gallons

The caterpillars devoured this most eagerly, sucking up the drops and dying in a short time.

The Wheat-Bulb Fly (*Hylemya coarctata*) **and Frit Fly** (*Oscinis frit*), **Attacking Winter Wheat.** See above, Abstr. 1908.

1971
Germany

O. OBERSTEIN. **Larvae of *Oscinis pusilla* Damaging Young Maize.** (Ueber Schädigungen von Fritfliegenlarven an jungen Maispflanzen. *Centralbl. Bakt.* 2. Abt. XXVIII, 4-5 pp. 159-160, 1910). — *Botanisches Centralblatt*, Bd. 116, No. 14, p. 367. Jena, 1911.

1972

The writer has had under observation young maize plants with deep longitudinal scars on their leaves ; the inner leaves were attacked at the base and were easily detached. Here and there on the shrivelled leaves small yellow Dipterous larvae were found, whence small, shiny black flies developed. These were recognized as *Oscinis pusilla*, which had only been recorded once before in Germany.

Germany

A. H. COKAYNE. **The Potato-Moth in New Zealand.** *The Journal of the New Zealand Department of Agriculture.* Vol. 2, No. 4, pp. 179-186. Wellington, N. Z. April 15, 1911.

1973

A severe outbreak of the potato-moth, *Gelechia operculella* (also known as *Lita solanella* (1), *Gelechia Solanella* and *Phthorimaea oper-*

New Zealand:
South Island

---

(1) Cf. this *Bulletin* No. 1047, March 1911.   (*Ed.*).

culella) has been experienced in the South Island, New Zealand. This insect is especially prevalent in North Otago and Canterbury, two of the most important potato-growing districts of New Zealand. Some 17 years ago the South Island crop was seriously affected, but between that date and this season the potato-moth has not been reported as causing any appreciable loss in the South Island, although it has long been recognised as a serious and annually recurring potato trouble in the North Island.

According to Meyrick the potato-moth was probably originally a native of Northern Africa, feeding on a variety of plants, until, on the introduction of the potato into the Old World, it transferred its attention almost entirely to that crop. At the present day it is in many countries the most serious insect enemy of the potato and it is especially serious in the Mediterranean regions, South Africa, California and Australasia. In Tasmania and in many parts of the Australian mainland it annually occasions great loss and seriously depreciates the crop, especially after it has been stored. In New Zealand it is now widespread throughout the North Island and in the South as far as Dunedin.

The tubers are the parts chiefly affected, becoming tunnelled with the galleries of the larvae of the moth and rendered unfit for consumption. Some may be affected before the tubers are lifted, but the majority of the damage is caused after the crop has been harvested.

The potato-moth can live on other plants besides the potato, such as many solanaceous plants, like the black night-shade (*Solanum aviculare*) and tobacco. In parts of Australia and the Southern United States, where it is a common tobacco-pest, it is designated as the « tobacco-leaf miner ». Allan Wight reported the larvae as feeding plentifully on the leaves of the native bulrush (*Typha angustifolia*).

The potato-moth, under the mame of *Lita solanella*, is included in the New Zealand Orchard and Garden Diseases Act, 1908, and foreign affected potatoes are liable to be prevented from landing and are either reshipped outside the Dominion or destroyed on arrival at one of the inspection ports.

The keynotes in control lie in the use of clean seed, thorough moulding up, destruction of all affected material, storing in moth-proof stores and carbon-bisulpide fumigation where necessary.

F. M. WEBSTER. **The Lesser Clover-Leaf Weevil.** — *U. S. Depart-*   **1974**
ment of Agriculture, Bureau of Entomology, Bull. No. 85, Part. I,
pp. 1-12. Washington, April 3, 1911.

The lesser clover-leaf weevil (*Phytonomus nigrirostris* Fab.), is
wide-spread throughout North America and is very destructive of   **United**
forage crops, devouring their leaves. It attacks red clover (*Tri-*   **States**
folium pratense), mammoth clover (*T. medium*), crimson clover (*T.*
incarnatum), white clover (*T. repens*), alsike clover (*T. hybridum*)
and alfalfa (*Medicago sativa*).

Amongst the natural enemies of this insect are one of the Tachinidae, *Hypostena variabilis* Coq., which is parasitic on the larva
of *P. nigrirostris;* and a hymenopterous parasite, *Bracon* sp. The
pupae are destroyed by a fungus (*Empusa Entomophtora sphaero-*
sperma).

Experiments with Cotton Stainers (Dysdercus spp.). — *The Agricul-*   **1975**
tural News, Vol. X, No. 235, p. 138. Barbados, April 29, 1911.

A series of experiments to determine the effect on the lint and
seed of cotton of the feeding of cotton stainers (*Dysdercus* spp.)
was outlined early in 1910 by the Entomologist of the Department   **Leeward**
of Agriculture to be carried out in several of the cotton-growing   **Islands**
islands of the West Indies.

The experiments made by Mr. W. Robson at Monserrat, show
that practically no effect on germination was produced by the feeding of stainers on seed which had been protected during growth,
and exposed to the feeding only after being harvested ; while the
seed produced in bolls attacked during growth showed a very small
relative germinating power. The lint was also affected to a very
serious extent where the stainers were abundant during the development of the cotton.

Average weight of 100 seeds attacked by stainers : 9.52 grams
on ten tests ; average weight of 100 seeds not attacked : 11.4 grams
on 5 tests.

The average germination on the tests of the seeds attacked by
stainers was 21 per cent; while of the seeds not attacked the average
germination on four tests was 94 per cent.

While the results seem to show that the stainer is capable of
doing serious damage to cotton, the writer is not of opinion that
it can be regarded as a serious pest in Montserrat at present. It

seems to become prevalent in certain localities in particular seasons, but does not assume the nature of a pest over large areas until after the bulk of the crop has been gathered, that is after December.

1976

Leeward Islands

The Blister Mite (*Eriophyes Gossypii*), the Cotton Worm (*Alabama argillacea*), and the Flower-bud maggot (*Contarinia Gossypii*) injurious to cotton in the West Indies. See above, Abstr. 1737.

1977

LEWIS H. GOUGH. **The Palm Weevil as Sugar-cane Pest.** — *Department of Agriculture, Trinidad, Bulletin*, Vol. X. No. 67, p. 59-64. Trinidad, January-March, 1911.

Trinidad. Barbados. British Guiana

The Palm weevil (*Rhinchophorus Palmarum* L.), the grubs of which are locally known as Grugru worms, is one of the oldest parasites of the sugar-cane, and has been repeatedly observed in various parts of the West Indies. It was observed at Barbados in 1847, in British Guiana in 1880, and in Trinidad in 1900.

The female beetle, having chosen a cane, bores a hole into the parenchymatous tissues with her ovipositor, and lays an egg at the bottom.

The beetle does not seem able to bore through the rind but always attacks from the exposed cut surface. The softer kinds of cane appear to be most frequently attacked. The eggs hatch in less than 48 hours.

The larvae grow to about 2 ½ or 3 in. in length ; they pass through at least 7 stages before pupating, the total period appears to be about 3 months (1). The grubs live singly in their tunnels ; should two tunnels meet, one of the larvae is invariably killed and eaten by the other. They tunnel very rapidly, a grub can completely hollow out a piece of cane a foot and a half long in a week.

When they have reached their full growth they leave the cane-plant and build a cocoon of fibres in the ground.

The pupal stage lasts from 2 to 4 weeks ; the adult stage for about 2 months. The adults burrow into cane or other vegetable matter (decaying palm-trees or banana stumps) in search of food.

---

(1) The last stage has been minutely described by W. F. H. BLANDFORD, *The Palm-Weevil in British Honduras*, Kew Bulletin, 1893).

Up to the present, Palm-weevil does not seem to have done much damage to cane cultivations in Trinidad, except on one estate, the beetles are, however, frequent on all estates, and the damage done by them may have been only on a very small scale or not been noticed.

As it is hopeless to expect to control the Palm weevil by poisoning its eggs or newly hatched grubs, the only method remaining is to prevent eggs being laid in the cane-plants. Various methods to effect this suggest themselves : extermination of the adults, coating the cut surface of the cane with a substance repellant to the beetle, or with a substance which would prevent the insertion of the eggs, and finally planting in such a manner that the beetle could not find the cut surface of the plant. Felling palm-trees to attract beetles which are then captured and destroyed, followed by the destruction of the log when the larvae have not yet reached maturity, has been recommended (see Hart, *Kew Bulletin Miscellaneous Information*, 1905, p. 159) and practised. In 1900 Hart recommended wounding grugru trees (2) to attract the beetles away from the sugar-canes. (*Kew Bulletin Miscellaneous Information*, 1900, p. 289).

T. BAINBRIDGE FLETCHER. **The Cane and Rice Grasshopper.** — 1978
The Agricultural Journal of India, Vol. VI, Part II, pp. 149-154.
Pusa, April, 1911.

The sugar plantations in many parts of India have been seriously damaged by grasshoppers (*Hieroglyphus furcifer.*). The winged females lay their eggs as the land dries up after the rains, at the **British India** beginning of the cold weather, and they remain dormant in the soil until the beginning of the next year's rains. As soon as the rains commence to moisten the soil, about the end of June, the eggs hatch out, and the young hoppers make their way up through the soft earth. At first they feed on any tender vegatio n which they find close at hand; especially small millets such as *Panicum frumentaceum, Eleusine coracuna, Paspalum scrobiculatum,* and *Setaria italica;* then they work their way to the sugar-plantations. Here they feed and grow till they reach their final winged stage, when they become a real pest, going from field to field, devouring all the

---

(2) Grugru-palm = probably au Astrocaryum palm tree. See BAILEY. *Cyclop. of American Horticulture.*

leaf of a field in a short time, every part of the leaf except the midrib being eaten up.

The following methods of fighting this grasshopper are recommended :

1) dragging bags over the young crops and killing the insects thus collected.

2) digging up the old *ukh* (1) roots and burning them so as to destroy the egg-masses ;

3) ploughing the soil up about March and so exposing the egg-masses to the light and heat of the sun.

1979
United
States

An *Aphis* injurious to Pea-nuts in the United States. See above, Abstr. 1749.

1980
Java

Xyleborus Coffeae, injurious to *Coffea robusta* in Java. See above, Abstr. 1754.

1981

E. E. GREEN. **Entomological Notes - Tea Tortrix**. *The Tropical Agriculturist*. Vol. XXXVI, No. 4, pp. 328-330. Colombo, April, 1911.

Ceylon

The Tortrix (*Capua coffearia*) is now very troublesome in the tea-plantations in the districts of *Ambagamuwa* and *Dikoya*.

The caterpillars of this insect feed on the leaves of the tea plant, which leads to their deterioration and sometimes kills them.

If unchecked by artificial means, the pest usually runs a course extending over two or three years. Its final disappearance is principally due to a disease which appears to be of a bacterial nature which kills the caterpillars; their bodies decompose, liberating a mass of spores which infect the surrounding foliage.

As direct remedial measures by insecticides cannot be used against this pest for fear of poisoning the tea leaves, it is advisable :

1) To collect and destroy the egg-masses of from 200 to 500 individuals concealed in the foliage. To facilitate this work the tea

---

(1) Vernacular for sugar cane: G. WATT. *Dictionary of the Economic Products of India*.

bushes should be pruned in December so that they are practically leafless during the egg-laying season.

2) To screen the plantations with barriers of trees, preferably with the *Acacia decurrens*.

3) To keep the plantations well-manured and as healthy as possible.

F. W. URICH. **The Cacao Thrips**. *Heliothrips rubrocinctus* Giard.   **1982**
— *Department of Agriculture; Trinidad, Bulletin*, Vol. X, N. 67, pp. 66-73. Trinidad, January-March. 1911.

This insect (*Heliothrips rubrocinctus* Giarp), formerly named *Physopus rubrocincta* one of the *Thysanoptera*, has always been present on cacao estates in the West Indies, but it was not until 1898 that attention was drawn to the " blight " it was causing to cacao pods. Up to now severe attacks have not been frequent, but in some districts it has a tendency to multiply rapidly and sometimes occasions loss. The cashew-tree (1) seems to be one of the favourite food plants of Thrips, which also feeds on cacao, guava, roses, almond, and mango.

West Indies.
Uganda

Its distribution seems to be a wide one also. It has been recorded from Granada, St. Vincent, St. Lucia, Dominica, Guadeloupe, Virgin Islands, Tobago, and Uganda. The insect recorded from Ceylon does not seem to belong to the same species.

This insect occasionally attacks the pods of these host-trees, but the most serious damage is done to the leaves, which are sometimes so seriously attacked that they drop off and a so-called " change of leaf " takes place, causing all young pods to wither.

This species is not found on the flowers of cacao or any other plant. The Thrips supposed to fertilize the cacao flower, and also found in immortelle flowers (2), belongs to quite a different genus. The writer

(1) Cashew-tree - *Anacardium occidentale* Linn. (*Anacardiaceae*), is extensively grown in tropical America. The kernels of the nuts are edible when roasted, and an oil is obtained from them. A gum is obtained from this tree which is used in preparing a varnish for the protection of books and furniture against white ants and other insects. The tree attains a height of from 20 to 25 ft. Cf. L. H. BAILEY, *Cyclopedia of American Horticulture*, Vol. 1, p. 61, New York. Macmillan, 1909.   (*Ed.*).

(2) Immortelle flowers, grown in American and English gardens, are *Helichrysum bracteatum*. Other immortelles are *H. aremarium* (French immortelle). *grandiflorum* (Fleur du Cap), etc. Cf. L. H. BAILEY, *l.c.* Vol. II, p. 567.   (*Ed.*).

has studied the life history of this *Heliothrips*. 3 days after the
eggs are laid young larvae were observed, 9 days after prepupae,
and pupae were present, and three days later adults appeared, making a total period of 12 days from hatching of egg to perfect insect. The prepupa stage lasts about 24 hours and that of pupa 48
hours. Generation seems to be continuous, but during a heavy rainy
season the numbers are smaller than in the dry season, which appears to be the time most favourable for their development.

No natural enemies of any importance have been observed. A
small staphylid beetle has been noted among colonies of larvae,
and mites have been noticed but none of these were actually seen
preying on the larvae or adults.

Rain appears to exercise some natural control on Thrips. Prevention is better than cure and a thoroughly well cultivated estate
is less liable to be attacked than one in a poor condition. Two
methods of artificial control are mentioned, fumigation by fire of
green wood, and spraying with an insecticide consisting of kerosene, 2 gallons, water, 1 gallon, hard soap, ½ lb. Whale oil soap,
used in the proportion of ½ lb. to the gallon of water is also
effective.

The spraying of pods for pod-rot appears to keep *Thrips* off;
especially if the Bordeaux mixture sticks well.

A bibliography of 13 works is in the appendix.

1983   G. N. KELLER. **Tobacco Growing in Ireland.** — *Department of Agriculture and Technical Instruction in Ireland, Journal.* Vol. XI,
N. 3, pp. 488-494. Dublin, April, 1911.

In warm climates insects which feed upon the leaves of the
tobacco plant cause great destruction. Ireland so far has been
United   favoured in this respect by the absence of any insect which injures
Kidgdom: tobacco after the plants have once become established and started
Ireland   vigorous growth.

A few caterpillars of the species *Hadena oleracea* and *Mamestra
brassicae*, which are very general feeders. have been noticed, and
occasionally large slugs may seriously injure single plants adjoining
headlands, but such attacks are of no practical importance.

1984   B. WAHL. **Two New Hop-Pests in Bohemia.** (Ueber zwei neue
Hopfenschädlinge). — *Wiener Landw. Zeitung,* 61 J., N. 36,
p. 416. Wien, 6 Mai, 1911.

Austria: Two very dangerous insect pests, *Hydroecia micacea* Esp., and
Bohemia   one of the *Cecidomyidae*, not yet determined, but probably to be

identified with *Diplosis Humuli* already found in England, have been recorded in the hop-gardens of Bohemia.

The larvae of *Hydroecia micacea* burrow into the soil and climb up inside the bine, eating the pith; they then bore holes out into the open air. Sometimes the tips of the plants are attacked and the leaves wither like the stalks.

The larvae of the second insect devour the inflorescence of the hops.

Careful cultivation is resorted to for the control of *Hydroecia;* in England when the injury caused by the Cecidomyid is not very serious the hops are picked early and dried.

If the injury done is more serious sheep are turned into the hop-gardens so that they may crush the larvae on the soil, or insecticides are used such as Vaporite (about 25 % of naphthaline and 75 % of gas lime).

O. W. BARRET. **The Control of** *Solenopsis geminata* **Fab. an Ant** **injurious to Cinchona** (Remedios contra la hormiga brava, *Solenopsis geminata* Fab., en las plantaciones de Chinas). — *Republica Dominicana. Revista de Agricultura*, Año VI, N. 10, pp. 255-257. Santo Domingo, Enero, 1911.

1985

Solenopsis geminata(1) is the most formidable enemy, after the Aphids, of the young cinchona plantations. These ants have seriously injuried the orange orchards at Porto Aico and elsewere. They live in colonies of from 5 000 to 15 000 individuals. They make their nests at the foot of the trees, excavating tunnels 15 centimeters below the level of the soil, from which they gain exit by one, two, or three holes at the foot of the tree. The working ants, escorted by soldier ants, come out of the nest and climb up the trunk of the tree where they gather the waxy substance emitted by the larvae of insects known as "*piojos*" and "*querezas*" they also puncture the bark of the branches and shoots from which they obtain a certain gum. The ants often damage the blossom of the young fruit, and the top branches; the young shoots are frequently cut right off. The wounds made at the base of the trunk are gradually enlarged until they form a complete circle denuded of bark; this completes the destruction of the tree.

Santo Domingo

(1) The « Brown Ant » of India. H.MAXWELL-LEFROY. *Indian Insect Life* Calcutta and Sinla, 1909.

To control this pest, planters are advised to circle the trees with grease bands 2 centimeters above the soil so as to form a ring 3 to 5 centimeters in breadth, using a mixture, prepared hot, of 3 parts of rosin, one of soda, and one of decoction of tobacco (just enough for the resultant mixture to be sticky). A second such grease-band should be placed 15 centimeters above the first.

For the destruction of the ant-nests a mixture is recommended consisting of 2 parts of rosin, one of soda, and one of tobacco decoction, to be injected with a syringe. In the case of young trees the quantity of soda should be reduced, as it might injure the young roots if it reached them.

1986   *Depressaria nervosa,* an Insect Pest of Cumin. See above, Abstr. 1908.

1987   **An Insect Pest of Pigeon-Peas, Cajanus indicus, in British Guiana** — *The Journal of the Board of Agriculture of British Guiana.* Vol. IV, N. 4, p. 239. Demerara, 1911.

In the Pomeroon district of British Guiana, pigeon-peas (*Cajanus indicus*) (1) are attacked by a skipper butterfly (*Eudamus* aff. *proteus*), the larvae of which are very destructive to young plants, devouring the leaves and sometimes causing the death of the plant.

British Guiana

The remedial measures suggested are hand-picking, and dusting the plants with Paris Green or spraying with arsenate of lead.

1988   **Turnip Sawfly (*Athalia spinarum* Fabr.) in Rhodesia.** — *The Rhodesian Agricultural Journal,* Vol. VIII, N. 4, pp. 600-602. Salisbury, April, 1908.

This insect has been abundant and destructive in the turnip-fields of Rhodesia this year. The larvae devour the leaves of turnips, kohl-rabi, and mangold wurzel, leaving only the midribs intact.

Rhodesia

Experiments made so far with different insecticides, especially with arsenical poisons, have not given satisfactory results.

---

(1) See Note to Abstr. 1915.   (*Ed.*).

Anthomyia Ceparum. Bouché (*Phorbia cepetorum* Meade) and the Thrips pest of onions. See above, Abstr. 1768.   1989

Diaspis Bromeliae and *Pseudococcus Bromeliae,* Enemies of the Pineapple in Brazil. See above, Abstr. 1772.   1990

Strawberry Pests in England. — *Board of Agriculture and Fisheries, Leaflet,* N. 207, pp. 6. London, February, 1910. Revised, March, 1911.   1991

The most prevalent and destructive of the insect pests which attack strawberries is the wireworm (1).

Where new ground is broken up and not over-deeply trenched, the grubs commence their ravages on newly formed plantations, and continue to work havoc among the roots so long as the plantations exist. When new plantations immediately succeed old ones the young plants are often completely destroyed.   Great Britain

Surface caterpillars (2) and the caterpillars of the Common Swift Moth (*Hepialus lupulinus*), are destructive to underground parts.

The Green Rose-Chafer (*Cetonia aurata*) is also injurious. As a grub it feeds on the roots, while in the adult stage as a beetle it destroys leaves and blossoms.

Tho Otiorhynchus Weevils (*O. sulcatus, O picipes* and *O. tenebricosus*) do considerable damage, the grubs feeding on the roots and the weevils on the shoots and runners.

Another weevil (*Anthonomus Rubi*), known locally as the Elephant or Snout Bettle, is harmful both as adult and as grub. By means of their proboscis or rostrum the adults puncture the stalk below the flower-buds, causing the latter to droop and become detached; they also puncture leaves and shoots. The grub lives inside the blossom buds, which as a result are destroyed.

---

(1) Name given to the larvae of insects belonging to the family *Elateridae.* The commonest is *Agriotes lineatus; A. sputator* and *A. obscurans* come next. (*Board of Agriculture and Fisheries, Leaflet* N. 10, Dec. 1894, Revised May, 1907, London)   (*Ed.*).

(2) The caterpillars of *Agrotis segetum* and *A.exclamationis,* etc. are named ' surface caterpillars ", because they hide just below the surface of the soil, and attack a large number of plants at soil level or just below it, almost always during the night. (*Board of Agriculture and Fisheries, Leaflet* N. 33, July, 1896. Revised September 1904. London).   (*Ed.*).

The ground beetles, *Pterostichus vulgaris, Steropus madidus, Harpalus ruficornis* and *Calathus cisteloides,* feed at night on the fruits. Occasional damage is done by other beetles and the caterpillars, of some moths..

Slugs and snails are also enemies of the strawberry, both fruit and leaves being attacked.

Eelworms (*Tylenchus devastatrix* Kuhn and *Aphelenchus fragariae* Ritz.-Bos.) also cause much loss among strawberries, the former damaging the roots and crown of the plant, while the latter species causes a somewhat cauliflower like growth and prevents the proper development of the buds.

Strawberry Leaf Spot (*Sphaerella fragariae* Tul.) causes dark brown spots to appear on the leaves. These spots gradually increase in size, becoming whitish at the centre and surroundend by a red margin. The leaf then turns yellow and soon dies, and as the disease spreads quickly much injury follows. As soon as the disease is observed the plants should be sprayed with Bordeaux mixture (10 lbs suphate of copper, and 8 to 10 lbs of lime in 100 English gallons of water). Later in the season, after the fruit has been picked the foliage should be thinly covered with straw and burnt over. Experience has shown this method to be highly successful and followed by a luxuriant growth of healthy and vigorous foliage.

Strawberry Mildew (*Sphaerotheca Castagnei,* Lev.) has caused serious loss to strawberry growers during recent years. Where the disease appears the plants should be sprayed with Bordeaux mixture. Where hops are grown great care should be taken to prevent this fungus from spreading to the hops as it causes hop-mildew.

1992   G. Lüstner. ***Nematus ventricosus* a Saw-Fly injurious to the Gooseberry.** (Habt acht auf die gelbe Stachelbeerblattwespe !) — *Möller's Deutsche Gärtner Zeitung.* 26 Jahrg, N. 25, p. 290, 2 Abb. Erfurt, 24. Juni 1911.

Germany   In the last few months almost all the gooseberry plantations of Germany have been attacked by the Sawfly — *Nematus ventricosus.*

The larvae of the first brood appear in May, those of the third in July.

They cause serious loss, as the larvae completely strip the branches of their leaves, only leaving the ribs or petioles.

The berries wither and fall, the branches do not develop fully, are more sensitive to frost, and will yield but little or no fruit for the ensuing year.

This insect can be controlled by spraying the bushes with an emulsion of soft soap and quassia wood infusion, which is applied to branches already attacked. The grubs should also be collected and destroyed along with the leaves on which the eggs or young larvae are found.

V. P. POSIEIELOV. **Experiments in Russia on the Control of Insect Pests of Fruit and Forest Trees.** Report of the Entomological Station of Kiev. (Otciet Kievskoi Entomologhiceskoi stanzii ob opetakh Borbi e vrediteliami sadovodstva i liesovodstva v. 1910 Godu). — *Khosiaistvo* (Husbandry). VI G., n. 9. pp. 277-284. Kiew, 3 Marta, 1911.

1998

Many experiments were made in 1910 at the Entomological Station at Kiev to determine the best remedies against some of the more destructive insect pests of fruit and forest trees.

Amongst the latter are :

1) *Anthonomus pomorum*, the larvae and adults of which injure pear and apple trees by attacking the tissues of the young shoots or the young leaves ;

Russia

2) *Rhynchites bacchus*, *R. pauxillus*, *Sciaphilus squalidus*, *Notoxus monoceros*, which devour the young shoots and snap off the infloresence of many fruit trees.

Notoxus monoceros is also found in beet and clover fields, and sometimes on forest trees.

Good results are obtained in the control of these insects by repeated sprayings with a mixture of Schweinfurth green and lime, in the following proportions: 17 gms. of Scheinwarth green, and 68 grammes of lime, in 12 litres of water ($=$ 1.4 lb. and 5.7 lbs. in 100 English gallons).

The best means of destroying *Hyponomeuta malinella* is a mixture of 17 grammes of *azurine* dissolved in ammonia, in 12 litres of water ($=$ 1.4 lbs in 100 gallons).

As remedial measures against *Carpocapsa pomonella* are suggested, besides washing, the use of grease - bands round the trunk, especially at the time the fruit ripens, as Schweinfurth green then has an injurious effect on them.

1994

J. A. Porcinskim. **Insect Pests of Fruit Trees in Russian Central Asia.** (Ocerk Rasprostranienia v Rossii Vaxnieiscikh Vrednekh Xivotnekh v 1909 Godu-Vrediteli Plodovekh Dereviev). -- *Exegodnik Glavnago Upravlenia Semlieustroistva i Semledielia po Departamentu Semledielia* (Year-book of the Direction of Rural Organization and Agriculture of the Department of Agriculture), G. III, pp. 602-604. S. Peterburg, 1911.

Russian Empire. Central Asia

There are many fruit-tree insect pests in Central Asia, as besides the native species almost all the European are found there, imported with consignments of fruit and plants since the opening of the railways.

This is the case with *Carpocapsa*, formerly unknown, and which has become very destructive in apple orchards throughout Turkestan, where it has no natural enemies to prevent its spread. *Tingis Pyri*, which attacks the pear-tree in Russia, only attacks the apple in Turkestan. Smearing the trees with soapy water is suggested as a remedial measure against this insect. One application kills from 90-95 %. Fallen leaves on which the insects conceal themselves to hibernate should also be collected and burnt.

Oxythyrea cinctella, which attacks the flowers of fruit-trees, passes the winter in dung heaps, where it can easily be found and destroyed.

Lastly, mention is made of *Coleophora alcyonipenella* and *Agelastica*, sp.; the latter is injurious to walnut and almond, of which it devours the foliage.

Grease-bands are recommended as remedial measures against these insects.

1995

Rhynchites pauxillus, **a Pest of Fruit Trees in Russia.** — See above Abstr. 1969.

Russia

1996

A. C. Romanovski-Romanko. **The Control of *Rhizotrogus solstitialis* L. in Russia.** (Boroa s Julskim Khrusticem). — *Exegodnik Glavnago Upravlenia Semlieustroistva i semledielia po Departementu semledielia*, God. III, pp. 128-131. S. Peterburg, 1911.

Russia

Rhizotrogus solstitialis L. is wide-spread in the sandy districts of the Dnieper, where it is very destructive to the vineyards.

The larvae of this insect live below the surface of the soil, devouring the roots of the plants they meet with on their way, more especially of vines.

Different systems of control have been studied at the experimental vineyard at Alesckov: getting children to collect the larvae; insecticides; cultivation of the soil, etc. The best results were obtained by the introduction of the larvae of *Microphtalma disjuncta*, which attack the larvae of *Rhizotrogus*, penetrate into their bodies, and soon cause their death.

Umbelliferous plants are sown here and there in the vineyards to attract the insects, who lay their eggs in them. As the larvae cannot burrow deep into the soil to reach the larvae of the *Rhizotrogus*, the following device is suggested: shallow trenches should be dug in the vineyards, in which wood, branches etc., are laid and covered over with very moist sand; by this means two purposes are attained: the larvae collect in these trenches and are thus drawn off from the vines; and in the trenches they are easily attacked by the larvae of *Microphtalma*.

A. A. JACZEWSKI. ***Coleophora alcyonipenella* an Apple Pest in Russian Central Asia.** (Isliedovania nad Gribnimi Parasitami). — *Exegodnik Glavnago Upravleniia Semlieustroistva i Semledielia po Departementu Semledielia.* (Year-Book of the Direction of Rural Organization and Agriculture of the Department of Agriculture), G. III, pp. 70-71, S. Peterburg, 1910.

1997

Serious injuries caused by *Coleophora alcyonipenella* are recorded on fruit-trees, more especially apple-trees, in Central Asia.

Good results have been obtained in the control of this insect by grease-bands on the trunks.

Russian Empire: Central Asia

H. P. STABLER. **The Control of Red Spider (1) on Almonds and Prune trees. Red Spider on Almonds.** — *California Cultivator* Vol. XXXVI, N. 18, p. 551. Los Angeles, May 4, 1911.

1998

The writer advises the application of sulphur to almond trees, when the leaves appear and again later.

United States !

(1) Red Spider is the name given to several species of the genera *Tetranychus*, *Bryobia* and *Tenuipalpus*. The injury they do is always due to the perforation of the plant tissues by their sharp mandibles. (*Board of Agriculture and Fisheries, Leaflet*, N. 41. London).

The first sulphuring should be done as soon as the leaves appear in March. Prune-trees should be treated as soon as the spider appears.

Full grown trees require about 1lb. of sulphur, which should be thoroughly distributed throughout the foliage. In normal seasons the spider is easily controlled by dry sulphuring. When the pest does not yield to this treatment a spray is recommended.

1999

S. ACCARDI. *Scolytus Amygdali*, an insect pest of Almond-trees in Sicily. (Lo *Scolytus Amygdali* è un parassita), pp. 2-15. — *Cattedra ambulante d'agricoltura per la provincia di Girgenti*. Girgenti, Marzo, 1911.

Italy:
Sicily

Considerable damage is done to almond-trees in the Province of Girgenti by *Scolytus Amygdali*, which, as the writer has shown by his investigations, is to be considered a parasite. It attacks healthy trees in full growth, and kills them in two or three years (1).

Two years after the attack the branches and trunk gradually die, whilst the foot of the trunk and the roots are still alive. For this reason the writer, who has obtained satisfactory results with the method he suggests, advises that the tree be felled and the trunk grafted on a level with the ground or at the roots. The shoots thus obtained are strong and healthy and begin to bear fruits as early as the third year.

2000

J. CHAPELLE. A New Enemy of the Olive in Spain (Un nouvel ennemi de l'Olivier). — *La petite revue agricole et horticole*, 17e. année, No. 397, p. 136. Antibes, 25 juin, 1911.

Spain:
Tarragona

The writer notifies that he recently had occasion to record in Spain, at Picamoixons (Prov. of Tarragona), the presence of *Aleurodes olivinus*, an olive pest.

He noted in a group of trees large numbers of leaves invaded by the larvae of this insect.

The trees thus attacked were distinguishable from their neighbours by their chlorotic appearance and lack of vigour. He was unable at first sight to determine whether this difference in growth was due to the attack of this new scale insect or merely to the cultural conditions.

Aleurodes olivinus has never been recorded in France.

---

(1) On *Eccoptogaster Amygdali*, or *Scolytus Amygdali* See : F. SILVESTRI e GUIDO GRANDI, *Dispense di Entomologia Agraria*, Parte speciale, Portici, 1911, p. 388. (*Ed.*).

How to Discover Whitefly (1). *California Cultivator.* Vol. XXVI, No. 18, p. 549. — Los Angeles, May 4, 1911.

2001

It is not always easy to discover the presence of whitefly when it is first- beginning to infest a grove. It is at this stage of infestation however that drastic measures for its control should be adopted in order to check its rapid spread. The following manipulation for loosening and making the larvae more easily visible is very useful. To loosen the larvae (not to remove them simply) grasp the end of a leaf with the thumb underneath and forefinger on top, turn it over, stretch it taut, and rub the free finger of the hand holding the leaf along the lower side. It is surprising how many more larvae can frequently be made visible by this means, and the whitefly traced far beyond the suspected limits.

United
States:
California

W. V. TOWER. **Insects Injurious to Citrus Fruits and Methods for Combating them in Porto Rico.** — *Porto Rico Agr. Exp. St. Bull.*, No. 10, pp. 7-35. Washington, 1911.

2002

The present condition of the citrus industry in Porto Rico is very promising. No insects are found in the groves that cannot be held in check by thorough treatment.

Porto Rico

For biting insects, arsenate of lead is the best spray for the conditions that exist on the island. Paris green has not the adhesive power of the arsenate of lead.

Sprays containing oils are used against scale insects, but they will also keep the rust mite (*Phytoptus oleivinus*) and red spider in

---

(1) Whitefly : *Aleyrodes* spp. See this *Bulletin*, December 1910, p. 124; Abs. 651, *ibid.*, February 1911; Abs. 1556 and 1562, *ibid.*, May, 1911.

Aleyrodes are Hemiptera related to the Scale Insects and Aphides. They are popularly known as snow, ghost and white flies. In some seasons the cabbages, broccoli, etc. are smothered with *Aleyrodes Brassicae*, especially from midsummer to the close of summer, when myriads of these little white insects start off the leaves when disturbed, making short flights. Several species occur in Britain, both in greenhouses and in the open. *A. vaporarium* (Westwood) is a pest on chrysanthemum, cucumbers, tomatoes, etc. Spraying with soft soap and quassia is the best treatment out-of-doors; fumigation with hydrocyanic gas under glass. F. V. THEOBALD in the *Standard Cyclopedia of Modern Agriculture*, 1910, vol. I, p. 101.

check.   However, where spraying is done for the rust mite and red spider alone it would be better to use sulphur sprays.

The purple scale (*Lepidosaphes Gloveri*) has been the worst enemy, but since windbreaks have been introduced, the beneficial fungi play a very important part in checking it.

The hemispherical scale (*Saissetia hemisphaerica*), and the Florida red scale (*Chrysomphalus*) are both held in check by the sprays used for the purple and white scales, and so is the white fly (*Aleyrodes Citri*).   It is very seldom that these insects need special treatment.

It is considered advisable to pick all the fruit before the new blossom growth starts, so that the sprayers may clean the trees well for the new crop.   If the trees are thoroughly cleaned in this way, there is very little chance for the fruit to become scaly.

A great deal of the cultivated fruit has been disfigured either by fungi, mechanical bruises, or insects.   Special attention is called to the last two causes of disfigured fruit.   The insects causing the worst scars on fruit are ants, the small orange leaf weevil, rust mites (*Phytoptus oleivorus*), and red spiders.

The two last mentioned rust the fruit.

All these insects, however, are held in check by sprays.

Mechanical injuries are caused by the fruit rubbing or hitting against some foreign object, as the leaves or branches.

2003   H. J. QUAYLE.   **The Orange Tortrix**. *California Cultivator*. Vol. XXVI, No. 18, pp. 548-549. — Los Angeles, May 4, 1911.

The orange tortrix (*Tortrix citrana* Fernald) was first described in 1889 by Prof. C. H. Fernald from specimens bred from oranges

United States: California

from Southern California.

During the season of 1909-10 this insect was the cause of no little concern in certain sections of the Southern California citrus belt. It seemed to be most abundant in Los Angeles County, from Glendale to Pomona.   In some of the packing houses during the early part of the shipping season the amount of wormy fruit ran between 5 and 10 per cent.

The larva has the habit of burrowing into the green oranges ; of course such fruit, when mature, is classed as culls.   The burrows in the fruit also cause it to drop prematurely, especially if the fruit is still small.   The eggs are laid on the leaves, more usually on the lower surface, and also on the fruit.   In a year there are probably three generations, or two with a partial third generation.

This insect appears to attack a wide range of food plants besides the orange. Coquillet states that it occurs on apricot, willow, oak (*Quercus agrifolia*), wild walnut (*Juglans californica*) and golden rod (*Solidago californica*) (1). It attacks also green-house plants, especially pelargoniums, and the larvae seem to work into the tips and branches of these plants, like a borer. Commonly they work in folds of leaves tied together by means of silk threads.

Two species of Braconids (species not yet determined) have been reared from the larva. As for control measures, spraying with an arsenical has been suggested, but the caterpillars would have to become more abundant than they have far to make this practical. Picking up and destroying of dropped fruit in the field, and destruction of the wormy culls seems to be the most feasible measure.

Cocoa-nut Insect Pests in the West Indies (2). — *The Agricultural News*, vol. X, No. 325, p. 138. Barbados, April 29th, 1911.   **2004**

In 1910 the following insects were mentioned as pests of cocoa-nuts in the West Indies: The Bourbon fly (*Aspidiotus destructor*), the cocoa-nut white fly (*Aleyrodicus cocois*), the palm weevil (*Rhyncophorus palmarus*), all of which are of general distribution.

The larger moth borer (*Castnia licus*) was stated to have occurred on cocoa-nut and other palms in Trinidad, and *Castnia Daedalus* in Surinam, while the cocoa-nut butterfly (*Brassolis so-phorae*) was reported as a pest in British Guiana.   **West Indies**

The *Proceedings of the Agricultural Society of Trinidad and Tobago*, for February 1911, contain notes on some Cocoa-nut pests by P. L. Guppy (3), in which it is mentioned that the cocoa-nut butterfly (*Brassolis sophorae*) occours in Trinidad, and that the caterpillars attack cocoa-nuts in the same manner as in

---

(1) See BAILEY. *Cyclop. of Americ. Horticulture.*   (*Ed.*).

(2) For a list of fungoid disease of the cocoa-nut palm, see p. 407 *Bull.* Dec. 1910.

(3) See Abstract 1058, *Bulletin* March 1911.

(4) See Abstract 354, *Bulletin* January, 1911. *Steirastoma depressum* L. (Cocoa Borer Beetle), should be added to the list of insects given here. 2040

               (*Ed.*).

British Guiana. Another caterpillar, the larva of a moth, *Hyperchiria* sp., also attacks the leaves of the cocoa-nut in Trinidad. The caterpillars of this moth differ from those of *Brassolis sophorae* in not building « nests », but resemble those of that species in being gregarious.

Mr. Guppy gives an account of the attack of a rhinoceros beetle (*Strategus anachoreta*) on young cocoa-nut trees in Trinidad.

2005   G. HERSCHER, L. MILLOT. **A new Enemy (*Hylecoetus*) of the Cocoa-nut Palm.** (Contribution à l'étude du Cocotier. Un nouvel ennemi : la « maladie » du Cocotier (*Hylecoetus*). Législation dans les Protectorats Malais). *Revue de Madagascar*, 13ᵉ année, No. 5, pp. 781-793. Paris, 15 Mai, 1911.

Madagascar.   The most formidable enemy of the cocoa-nut palm all along the north-west coast of Madagascar is a small nocturnal beetle, which has been determined only at Seychelles under the name of **Straits** **Settlements** *Melitomma insulare*, but is very little known, in spite of the havoc it does. It is a *Hylecoetus*, which may be placed in the family *Serricornia*, section *Xylotrogi*.

The female of this moth lays its eggs in accidental scars in the trunk and in the natural cracks in the bark, but it has a marked preference for the base of the trunk, laying them in the interstices between the roots at the base of the collet and also in the dead roots of trees which have been planted too near the surface of the soil, or which, for sundry reasons, send out ground roots.

The larvae penetrate into the trunk, at first almost horizontally toward the interior, when they describe a wide curve so as to approach the centre, whence they pursue their upward progress vertically.

Whilst tunnelling into the live wood the larvae emit a caustic liquid which attacks the cellular tissue for a radius of from 1 to 2 centimetres causing its rapid decomposition. The tunnel may attain a length of from 1 to 1.2 meters. When they have finished their ascent the larvae collect round the rotten parts and go through the pupal stage. Their transformation into adult insects is rapid. It is at the beginning of the rainy season (November or December) that the individuals of this beetle mostly attain their final stage.

The most serious damage done by these insects is in attacking the collet of the tree. After the first sèrious attack, the whole root system of the cocoa-nut palm, just where it joins on to the collet, is rapidly rotted by the presence of the larvae. The tree seems at first to react by sending forth new roots, but besides the fact that these rarely succeed in penetrating the soil, their restricted number cannot compensate for the loss suffered.

The result is, that after a momentary arrest of vegetation, often preceded by an abundant yield of fruit, the tree gradually decays, losing its bunches of fruit and its palm-leaves, until it falls to the ground, sapped by the rotting of its root tissues.

If energetic means are not resorted to without delay all the cocoa-nut plantations will be destroyed in a few years time. Preventive legislation might be modelled in its general outlines on the Ordinance of March 6th, 1890, completed by the Amendment of October 21st, 1895, in force in the Straits Settlements, where it has given the most satisfactory results, taking into account the following measures which apply more especially to the *Hylecoetus*.

1. Prevention :

a) it should be strictly forbidden to scar the trunks of cocoa-nut palms or to expose them to injury from brushwood fires ;

b) it should be made compulsory to keep the collet of the tree adequately buried to prevent the access of insects to the roots ;

c) all natural or accidental scars, cracks, fissures or excoriations of the trunk should be smeared with coal-tar ;

d) lime or ashes should be spread at the foot of healthy trees so as to keep insects off from the collet.

2. Treatment :

a) in the case of cocoa-nut trees belonging collectively or individually to the inhabitants of a village, the village head man must notify the competent authorities of those persons in charge of cocoa-nut palms who neglect or refuse to take the requisite steps for preventing the spread of disease to healthy trees, for the efficacious treatment of those known to be attacked, and for the destruction by fire of dead trunks ;

b) the culprits will be fined and the cocoa-nut palms in their care treated at their risk and expense by the village authorities ;

c) coal-tar is supplied free by the administration to the villages, so as to leave no legitimate excuse for neglect ;

d) in the case of private plantations the owners are compelled to take the same preventive and curative measure, and are liable to the same fines and penalties.

In conclusion, whilst it is true that *Hylecoxtus* is terribly destructive in neglected and ill kept plantations, still it must be remembered that its progress is slow, and that simple and inexpensive precautions suffice to obviate its inroads.

2006 'M. DE KONING. **A New Enemy of the Douglas Fir,** *Pseudotsuga Douglasii* Carr. (Een nieuwe beschadiging der Douglassparren). — *Tijdschrift der Nederlandsche Heidemaatschappij*, 23è Jaargang, Aflevering 6, pp. 177-179, ᴛ fig. Utrecht, I Juni, 1911.

Of late years Douglas firs in the province of North Brabant have been noted on which the annual shoots were almost all dead. Gradually the dead branches lose their needles and nothing remains but dry wood. Careful observation shows that the bark at their base has been eaten away.

Holland: **North** **Brabant**

This disease is due to *Strophosomus obesus*, an insect already recorded as an enemy of coniferous trees. It is grayish brown in colour. The larvae and pupae live underground. In the spring the insect makes its appearance and begins to do injury.

As the injured branches live on for some time, the sap which oozes out sometimes forms a thickening just above the wound.

This insect might become very destructive, especially as it also feeds on the needles of the Douglas fir. The young trees suffer most severely.

In its control advantage is taken of the fact that it cannot fly and that it readily falls when it thinks itself discovered. Trenches are dug round the young plantations to prevent the insects entering them. Grease bands can be put round the trunks of the trees to prevent their climbing up, and the insects in the top branches of the pine fall if the tree is thoroughly shaken.

200 **Larvae in** *Pinus insignis*. — *The Gardener's Chronicle*, vol. XLIX, No. 3679, p. 432. London, July, 1911.

Great **Britain**

The larvae attacking *Pinus insignis* are those of the Pine Shoot Tortrix Moth (*Retinia buoliana* Schiff). They attack the leading buds or whole whorls of buds which develop for a time, then the median one droops and dies, but now and then they survive and form distorted growths. The moths hatch towards the end of July, and lay their eggs on or near the tips of the shoots. The eggs hatch in autumn and the small larvae gnaw the buds from which resin exudes and covers them. Beneath this resinous house they live all the winter, and in spring, tunnel into the leading bud and feed until the end of June, and then pupate there. The moths come out of the pupae in about two weeks. Nothing but hand-pinching the attacked shoots in June can be done.

STEWART MAC DOVGALL. **The Alder and Osier Weevil** (*Cryptorhynchus Lapathi* L.). — *The Journal of the Board of Agriculture*, Vol. XVIII, N. 3, pp. 214-217. London, June, 1911.

2008

In the United Kingdom, particularly in Scotland, the Alder and Osier weevil (Cryptorhynchus Lapathi L.) injures Willows and sometimes also Alders, Birches, and Poplars. The larvae of this insect bore under the bark of the branches, destroy the cambium and tunnel long galleries in the wood. The branches so weakened are easily broken by the wind.

United Kingdom

The adult weevils eat the young shoots and the leaves, and gnaw the bark down to the cambium, thus preparing the way for cryptogamic diseases and other infection.

The most obvious symptoms of the attack are yellowing of the leaves, drying of the buds and discolouration of the bark over the larval tunnels.

Besides the usual insecticides and burning of the infected parts, the planting of a few Alders among the Willows to act as traps is recommended, as the insects prefer this tree to Willow.

2009 *Tylenchus devastatrix*, attacking Oats in Great Britain — See Abstract 1941.

2010 *Heterodera Schachtii*, attacking Hops in England. — See Abstract 1941.

2011 *Heterodera radicicola*, injurious to Cucumbers and Tomatoes in Great Britain. — See abstract 1941.

2012 M. SCHWARTZ. **The Eel-worms of Violet Galls and of Leaf-spot of Ferns and Chrysanthemums.** (Die Aphelenchen der Veilchengallen und der Blattflecken an Farnen und Chrysanthemum). — *Arbeiten aus der k. biol. Anstalt für Land und Forstwirtschaft*, VIII B., H. 2, pp. 303-304. Berlin, 1911.

Germany

Aphelenchus Ormerodi Ritz-Bos, causes galls to form on violet stalks. These galls, due to the simultaneous growth and thickening of several lateral shoots, prevent the normal development of the leaves, and when the attack is severe the whole plant is transformed into a mass of corpuscles resembling the inflorescence of cabbage. This species of nematode is hard to distinguish from others of the same genus which affect strawberries, chrysanthemums, and ferns.

The following remedial measures are suggested:

1) Watering with lime-sulphur mixture;

2) Uprooting and burning the diseased plants; the pots are then disinfected along with the implements and all other objects which may be infected.

2013 *Tylenchus devastatrix* and *Aphelenchus Fragariae*, Eel-worms injurious to Strawberries in Great Britain. — See Abstract 1992.

Protecting Plants against Slugs and Snails in British Guiana. —   **2014**
The Journal of the Board of Agriculture of British Guiana,
vol. IV, n. 4, p. 199. Demerara, 1911.

This is a description of a particularly effective and useful
method for protecting young tomato plants, cabbages, etc., from
slugs or snails.   **British**
The system is to spread sawdust soaked in phenol round the   **Guiana**
rows of plants to be protected.
The labour and cost involved are exceedingly small, and the
protective action is remarkable.

Mariaella Dussumerii, a Slug Pest of *Hevea Brasiliensis*. — See   **2015**
Abstract 1932.   **Ceylon**

H. RAEBIGER. The Destruction of Field Mice (1). (Zur Bekämpf-   **2016**
ung der Feldmäuse). — *Landw. Umschau*, 3 Jahrg., n. 21,
pp. 504-505. Magdeburg, 26 Mai, 1911.

In many countries, and more especially in Germany, the destruction of field mice has become one of the most important pro-   **Germany**
blems of rural economy.
Amongst the remedial measures recommended so far the most
practical and effective is undoubtedly Löffler's "Typhoid bacillus"
now prepared and sold by the Bacteriological Institute of the
Chamber of Agriculture of Halle.
Pieces of bread are infected with cultures of this bacillus and
placed at the entrance to the nests. The Field mice who eat them
die rapidly and their bodies, devoured by the other mice, become
in their turn centres of infection.
Good results are also obtained with carbon bi-sulphide, which
is however too expensive and very inflammable.
When the field-mice are not very numerous and the infected
area is restricted traps can also be used with advantage.

---

(1) See Abstract 362 *Bull.* Jan. 1911 and Abstract 1328 *Bull.* April 1911.
(Ed.).

2017   L. Testart.   **Destruction of Field Mice with Carbon Bisulphide**
(Destruction des Campagnols par asphyxie, à l'aide du sulphure
de carbone). — *La Belgique horticole et agricole*, 23ème année, n. 72,
pp. 190-191. Bruxelles, 65 juin, 1911.

Field mice can be destroyed (1) by suffocation caused by
fumigating their nests with sulphurous acid, by means of special bel-
Belgium   lows; or better still by means of bi-sulphide of carbon injected
with a syringe or a dropping tube.

Smoking by means of sulphurous rags has been tried with
success. This is done by driving the smoke from rags steeped in
sulphurous acid into the holes and tunnels of these vermin.

Bi-sulphide of carbon (the writer believes) does not injure the
soil or interfere with the crops. 1 liquid kg. costs 1 fr. and is
enough for treating 500 holes.

Care must be taken to treat the embankments of fields and
railways with the bi-sulphide, as these embankments are the
favourite resort of field mice.

2018   **Birds and Squirrels damaging Pears and Apples.** — See Abstr. 1941.
Great
Britain

Legislative and Administrative Measures for the
Protection of Plants.

2019   **Protection against Plant Diseases in Ireland.** — *Department of
Agriculture and Technical Instruction for Ireland, Journal.* Vol. XI,
N. 3, pp. 457-461. Dublin, April, 1911.

United   In 1877 the "Destructive Insects Act" was passed with the
Kingdom :   view of preventing the introduction of the "Colorado Beetle" (*Dory-*
Ireland   *phora decemlineata*). The Lord Lieutenant in Council was empowered

(1) See Abstract 362 *Bull.* Jan 1911 and Abstract 1328 *Bull.* April 1911.
(*Ed.*).

under this Act to make any Order considered expedient for the purpose of regulating or prohibiting the importation of potatoes and potato haulms, or other material, the landing of which might be likely to introduce this pest; and also of providing for the disposal or destruction of any crop which might become infected. Two Orders were accordingly issued in August 1877, " The Colorado Beetle (Ireland) Order, 1877 ", and " The Colorado Beetle, Customs (Ireland) Order, 1877 ". Subsequently, by Section 2 (b) of the Agricultural and Technical Instruction (Ireland) Act, of 1899, the powers vested in the Lord Lieutenant under the Destructive Insects Act were transferred to the Department of Agriculture and Technical Instruction for Ireland.

In 1907 the Destructive Insects and Pests Act was passed extending the provisions of the Act of 1877 to include all insects, fungi, or other pests destructive to agricultural or horticultural crops. The Department have availed themselves of their powers in this respect to make three orders :

· 1. " The American Gooseberry Mildew and Black Currant Mite (Ireland) Order, 1908 ', dealing with the diseases American Gooseberry Mildew (*Spaerotheca mors-uvae*) in Gooseberries, and Black Currant Mite (*Eriophyes* (*Phytoptus*) *Ribis*) in Black Currants.

2. " The Black Scab in Potatoes (Ireland) Order, 1908 ', dealing with the disease Black Scab (*Chrysophlyctis endobiotica*) in Potatoes.

3. " The Foreign Potatoes (Ireland) Order, 1910 ".

In these Orders provision is made to regulate the importation into this country of any bush, plant, or other material with which the diseases in question might possibly be introduced. Under the first-named Order, gooseberry or currant bushes may not be landed in Ireland without a licence from the Department. Under the two remaining orders, the importation of potatoes (including potato haulms, etc.) from the Continent of Europe and the importation from Great Britain of potatoes affected with the disease, Black Scab (*Chrysophlyctis endobiotica*) are absolutely prohibited.

In 1909, the " Weeds and Agricultural Seeds (Ireland) Act " was passed. Part I of this Act empowers the Department, with the consent of the County Council concerned, to make an Order declaring that throughout any county all or any of the plants, ragwort (*Senecio Jacobaea*), charlock (*Sinapis arvensis*), coltsfoot (*Tussilago Farfara*), thistle (*Cnicus* sp.) and dock (*Rumex* sp.) are noxious weeds for the purpose of the Act. The Department may require the destruction of these weeds within a specified time. The second part of this Act gives the Department certain powers in regard to the taking and testing of samples of agricultural seeds offered or exposed for sale, and the publication, with the names and addresses of the suppliers, of the results of such tests. This power indirectly checks the spread of noxious weeds, as it tends to check the sale of the lighter and cheaper classes of seeds, especially those mixtures sold under such names as " Hay ", " Brown Hay ", etc. which usually contain a large proportion of weed and other seeds injurious to agriculture.

The administration of these Acts and Orders is carried out by officers of the Department of Agriculture and Technical Instruction.

2020   F. W. DAFERT. **Report on Measures taken by the Austrian Government for the Control of Leaf-Curl in Potatoes** (1908-1910). (Bericht über staatliche Massnahmen anlässlich des Auftretens und der Verbreitung der Blattrollkrankheit der Kartoffel in den Jahren 1908 bis 1910). — *Zeitschrift für das landw. Versuchswesen in Oesterreich*, XIV, Heft. 5, pp. 557. Wien, 1911.

In 1907, when Leaf-Curl first seriously attacked the potato crops throughout Austria, the Ministry of Agriculture hastened to **Austria**   appoint a Committee to study the nature of the disease and the most appropriate remedies.

In 1908, under the direction of this Committee, and in accordance with a plan which it drew up, extensive studies and experiments were made at the Vienna Phytopathological and Agricultural Bacteriological Station as well as at the Station of Experimental Agricultural Chemistry.

These experiments have already supplied material for many valuable publications, which though they have not given a definite solution to the problem, have at least helped to place the work on a well-defined basis, and to accumulate a really remarkable mass of material (1).

---

(1) Leaf-Curl often accompanies attacks of insect pests, and occurs also in peaty and other damp soils, as a result of imperfect nutrition. Recent studies made by APPEL show that Leaf-Curl is a symptom of the " *Fusarium di-s ease* ", which can be recognized by the curling of the edges of the leaves; the younger leaves are the first to start curling about July, so that their lower and less pigmented surface is apparent to the eye and patches of leaves of a paler tint are noticeable in the field. These grow more and

The Work of the Department of Agriculture of Russia, in 1909, in the control of Plant Diseases and Insect Pests. (Borba s Vrediteliami Selskago Khosiaistva). — *Exegodnik Glavnago Upravlenia Semlieustroistva i Semledielia po Departementu Semledielia.* (Year-Book of the General Direction of Rural Organization and Agriculture of the Department of Agriculture), God. III, pp. 88-94. S. Peterburg, 1910.

2021

The work of the Russian Department of Agriculture in the Control of insect pests in 1909 took the form both of scientific investigations and the adoption of practical remedial measures. Several expert inspectors were appointed and sent to the localities more seriously affected; and the Bacteriological Department of St. Petersburg was provided with the requisite material for phytopathological investigations in the field.

Russia

Many studies on the life history of insect pests and experiments to find the best means for their control were carried out under the direction of specially appointed entomologists in the most varied localities of the Empire.

Thus an inspector was entrusted with the control of *Agrotis Tritici* in the Governments of Vladimir and Samara, and of *Agrotis segetum* at Tula and Twer. Another entomologist travelled, by order of the Department, through the Governments or St. Petersburg, Novgorod, Pskow, Podolia, and Volhynia, delivering lectures and organizing excursions so as to interest land-owners and rural agents in agricultural entomology and to instruct them in practical methods of control. In view of the very great destruction done at Tula and Orlov, in 1908, by *Agrotis segetum*, the Ministry decided, in 1910, on the proposal of the entomologist in charge, to open an entomological station in that district.

At the end of 1909, a grant of 475 800 frs was made to the Governor General of Turkestan to organize the control of the

more noticeable as the diseased leaves fade. If the stalks of these plants are cut it is seen that the vascular bundles contain a yellowish brown ring, discoloured by filaments of fungi, which spread to the tubers causing their discolouration. When the leaves are severely attacked the tubers are small and will probably be attacked by dry rot when stored. Next season the filaments of the fungus invade the young shoots, again causing leaf-curl; the disease is thus transmitted from one crop to another, and in a few years time a variety originally good may become valueless. W. G. SMITH, *Potato Disease*, in P. WRIGHT, *Standard Cyclopedia of Modern Agriculture*, Vol. X. p. 31, London, 1910. (*Ed.*).

locusts, and he was also supplied with 104,375 kgs of Schweinfurth Green and with one hundred horse-drawn spraying machines. Roughly speaking the zone invaded by the locusts covered an area of over 67000 hectares.

In the spring of 1909 the control of *Spermophilus* (1) was begun under the auspicies of the Department of Agriculture, by the use of bisulphide of carbon in five different parts of the Governments of Astrakan and Samara. 5,500 hectares were thus cleared, 324,000 holes were destroyed, and a considerable number of these destructive rodents were killed. The Imperial Governments also made vigorous and commendable efforts to put an end to the destruction done over a very wide area by voles. Cultures of Typhus bacilli were used with great success ; they are now prepared at the bacteriological laboratory of St. Petersburg, and forwarded to the most distant parts of Siberia. The great and growing demand for this preparation has led to the opening of special Stations and Laboratories for its preparation, 50 of which are now in regular work.

Besides this the Government has abolished import duty on Schweinfurth green, copper sulphate, and other insecticides sent from abroad to Societies or agricultural associations for use in the control of insect pests. Educational tracts drawn up by the Entomological Bureau have been distributed gratis to the rural population, such as the " Hand-book for the Collection and Study of Insects" by Sokolow; the " Sitotroga (2) of Cereals " by Porcinsk, etc.

As regards the control of fungoid diseases, the Department of Agriculture has recognized the need for energetic measures against *Sphaerotheca mors-uvae*, and has sent a specialist to the Government of Kursk to study the question and draw up a plan of action.

---

(1) The Sousliks (*Spermophilus*) are small rodents, something like Squirrels ; there are several species found in South Germany, Austria-Hungary in Southern Russia and across Siberia. R. LYDDEKER " *Souslik* ", in *Encyclopedia Britannica*, 11th. Ed., vol. XXV, p. 463. Cambridge, 1911.   (*Ed.*).

(2) *Sitotroga cerealella*, known as the " Angoumois Grain Moth ". See Abstract 1943.   (*Ed.*).

The Antiphylloxera Committee of the Caucasus and its Work.   2022
(Kavkaskü Gilloksemi Koimtet, ego Dieiatchnosti). — *Exeégod-nick Glaonago Upravlenia Semleustroistwa i Semledielia po De-partmentu Semledielia.* (Year-book of the General Direction of Rural Organization and of Agriculture), G. III, pp. 84-86. Peterburg, 1910.

As in previous years, the Antiphylloxera Committee has done active and valuable work in connection with vine cultivation, so widespread in the Caucasus, by encouraging the distribution of grafts on resistant American stocks, by training the natives in grafting,   **Russian**
and by sending inspectors to infected zones to survey such areas   **Empire**
and take the requisite steps fer eliminating the disease.

The five experimental nurseries opened in the principal vine-growing centres have been insufficient to supply the demand for American vine-stocks. Consequently six new nurseries have been opened this year, to allow of entirely restocking the vineyards. Practical courses of training in viticulture, with special attention to grafting and the control of plant diseases and insect pests of the vine were held in some Caucasian villages.

The expenses incurred amounted in all to 79 358 roubles (£ 8 389) and were met entirely by the Ministry of Agriculture.

Legislative Measures in the Straits Settlements for the Control of   **2023**
" Cocoa-nut palm disease " *(Hylocoetus).* See Abstract 2005.   **Straits Settlements**

An Ordinance to prevent the Introduction into Mauritius of Di-   2924
seases of Plants. — *A Collection of the Ordinances passed by the Governor in Council published at Mauritius during the Year* 1910. Pp. 18-19. Mauritius, 1911.

1) *Definition.* In this Ordinance " articles " is used to mean seeds, plants, fruits, soil, or other objects which have been in con-   **Mauritius**
tact therewith, coming from certain localities.

2) The Governor in Council is authorised to prohibit the introduction of such articles, which, coming from certain localities, might be agents in carrying fungoid diseases. The Governor is likewise authorised to fix the conditions regulating the importation of such articles.

2025

Noxious Plants. The Blackberry. — *Queensland Agricultural Journal,* vol. XXVI, Pt. 4, p. 200. Brisbane, April 1911.

Australia: Queensland

In February, 1911, the Home Secretary, in pursuance of the " Local Authorities Act 1902-1910", declared the plant known as Blackberry (*Rubus fruticosus*) to be a noxious weed or plant, and to be a nuisance throughout Queensland.

This plant is extending more and more, covering an area of some 350 sq. miles with brambles which prevent the normal growth of cultivated plants. The seed is distributed by birds, and streams also act as distributors, the seeds being carried by water to the deep soil deposits which form ideal spots for the propagation of this plant.

2026

The Importation into Algeria of Trees and Bushes other than Vines and Resinous Plants. (L'importation en Algérie des végétaux à l'état ligneux autres que la Vigne et les Résineux). — *Bulletin de l'Office du Gouvernement général de l'Algérie.* 17 année, n. 19, p. 155. Paris, 15 Mai, 1911.

Algeria

The Governor General of Algeria has signed a decree under date of April 21, 1911, whereby trees and bushes, (other than vines and resinous plants) palms, rooted or not, and fresh parts of such plants coming from abroad and from the French departments of Alpes-Maritimes, Var, Bouches-du-Rhône, Gard, Hérault, Aude, Pyrénées-Orientales. and Corsica, and citrus fruits from all parts, are not allowed to enter Algeria except through the ports of Algiers, Oran, Bône and by the station of Ghardimaou.

Such vegetables or fruits will be disinfected on their entry into the Colony by the agents of the anti-phylloxera service.

2027

The Importation of Plants and Seeds into Somaliland Forbidden. (Divieto d'introduzione di piante e semi in Somalia). — *L'Agricoltura coloniale,* anno V, nn. 4-5, pp. 212-213. Firenze, 31 Maggio 1911.

Italian Somaliland

The Regent of the Government of Italian Somaliland issued a decree, N. 646, from Mogadiscio, on March 6, 1911, to prevent the importation of insect and fungoid parasites injurious to the plants cultivated in this Colony. He decrees:

1) To prevent the introduction and diffusion throughout the Colony of parasites injurious to cultivated plants, the importation

of plants and seeds is forbidden without the authorization of the Government authorities. Such seeds and plants must be accompanied by documents (receipts, bills, certificates) stating the places from which they come.

2) When the Government authorities deem it desirable, seeds and plants must be disinfected by the parties concerned, in accordance with the instructions they will receive.

Abstract and Digest of Ordinances, Laws and Acts affecting Landowners, Farmers and Agriculturists generally in Natal. XII. Plant Diseases and Pests. — *The Natal Agricultural Journal*, vol. XV, N. 7, pp. 66-70. Pietermaritzburg, January 1911.

2028

This Act enables the Governor to prohibit from time to time the introduction of any plant into Natal likely to introduce disease. The destruction of plants in nurseries affected with any specified disease, or their isolation, may be ordered by the Governor.

Union of S. Africa: Natal

All nurseries have to be registered at the beginning of each year. The owners of nurseries are also required to provide fumigation chambers. The sale of any plant is deemed to be a guarantee in itself that the plant is free from disease.

The act is entitled : " To prevent the Introduction and Spread of Disease in Plants. " It contains, amongst others, the following articles :

3) *Definition.* — In this Act " plant " means any tree, shrub, or vegetation and the fruit, leaves, cuttings, bark, or any part or product thereof whatsoever, whether severed or attached. " Disease " means any of the insect pests or plant diseases mentioned in the Schedule of this Act, and any insect pest or plant disease which the Governor in Council may declare to be a pest or disease within the meaning of this Act.

4) *Inspectors.* — The Minister may from time to time appoint Inspectors and other officers necessary for the carrying out of this Act.

6) The Governor may, from time to time, by proclamation prohibit the introduction into Natal of any plant which may be considered likely to introduce any disease. Such Proclamation may either be absolute or subject to such conditions or exceptions as may seem proper, and may apply to the introduction of plants either generally or from any specified place.

7) *Destruction of Plants.* — The Governor, on advice of the Board, may order that all plants in nurseries throughout the Co-

lony which may be affected with any special disease be destroyed
or that they shall be isolated and treated in any specified manner.

10) *Inspection.* — An inspector may at all reasonable times
enter a nursery or orchard, with his assistants, for the purpose of
making inspection or carrying out any other duties therein.

12) *Quarantine.* — So long as an order of quarantine applies
to a nursery or orchard, it shall not be lawful to remove any plant
or any part or produce of a plant therefrom, except with the permission or under the direction of an inspector.

16) When any Disease considered by the Minister, on the
recommendation of the Board, to be a source of danger. is prevalent in any nursery or fruit garden, he may order the special treatment, and if necessary the destruction of any specific kinds of
plants therein, provided that compensation shall be paid for healthy
plants so destroyed.

22. *Offences.* — Every person shall be guilty of a contra-
vention of this Act who :

1) In any manner obstructs or impedes any person in the
execution of any of the powers conferred by this Act or refuses
any assistance which he is required to give; or

2) Disobeys or neglects to comply with any of the provisions of this Act or the terms of any regulation, order, or proclamation made thereunder.

The following insect pests and plant diseases are scheduled :

Insects : Codling moth (*Carpocapsa pomonella*) ; San José Scale
(*Aspidiotus perniciosus*) ; Pear Slug (*Selandria Cerasi*) ; Cape Fruit
Fly (*Ceratitis capitata*); Apple Mussel Scale (*Mytilaspis pomorum*);
Orange Mussel Scale (*Chionaspis citri*) ; Parlatoria of the orange
(*Parlatoria ziziphus* and *P. Pergandei*) ; Glover's Scale (*Mytilaspis
Gloveri*).

Plant Diseases : Orange Yellows and Peach Rosette; Crown Gall;
Fusicladium of the Apple.

202   **Legislative Measures for eradicating Burr Weed, *Xanthium* spp.
Abstract and Digest of Ordinances, Laws, and Acts affecting
Landowners Farmers, and Agriculturists generally in Natal. XI.
Noxious Plants.** — *The Natal Agricultural Journal,* Vol. XV,
n. 7, pp. 62-66. Pietermaritzburg, January, 1911.

Union
of S. Africa :
Natal

Law N. 38 of 1874 was framed to make provision for preventing the spread of the Burr Weed, (*Xanthium spinosum*) but the
provisions of this law were extended by Acts N. 20 of 1901 and
N. 12 of 1904 to *Xanthium strumarium* and *Cnicus diacantha*.

Law N. 38, 1874. 2) *Penalty for leaving Burr Weed growing.* — All occupiers of land allowing Burr Weed (*Xanthium spinosum*) to grow on their lands without taking the requisite steps for its destruction are liable to a penalty of not less than Twenty Shillings and not exceeding Five Pounds.

3) Should the owner refuse, or should the land be unoccupied, the Resident Magistrate is authorised to engage a sufficient number of labourers for the destruction of this weed. The cost thereof to be made chargeable to the owner or to the State.

5) When the said weed shall be found growing on Municipal lands, the Mayor and Council of the Borough will be liable to double the penalty by the Second Section provided, the provisions of Section 3 being also applicable.

7) The Colonial Secretary shall cause a notice to be published in the Government Gazette in August of each year, instructing Field-cornets and Constables to warn all persons against any infringment of this law; and these latter are required to give information to the Resident Magistrate of their Division or County of any occupier or owner on whose land *Xanthium spinosum* is found growing.

10) Every road-inspector shall cause the working parties under his direction to eradicate and destroy all plants of the said weed growing upon or within 100 yards of any road upon which said party is working.

11) The Lieutenant-Governor shall appoint one or more persons in each County as Inspectors to inspect all localities, to which they shall have free access.

12) The said Inspectors shall send in each month a detailed report of their proceedings.

Act to Provide for the Extermination of Locusts in Natal. — *The Natal Agricultural Journal*, Vol. XV, N. 7, pp. 59-62. Pietermaritzburg, January, 1911.

2080

Act N. 40. To provide for the extermination of Locusts. Any portion of a Province may be declared a locust area, and occupiers and owners of land therein may be ordered to assist in the extermination of the locusts, failing which the Chief Locust Officer may cause the lands of such persons to be cleared of locusts and recover any expenses incurred from the owner or occupier.

Definitions. " Locusts " means the insects called respectively " *Acridium pupuriferum* " and " *Pachytylus migratorius.* "

Union
of S. Africa:
Natal

5) The Governor in Council may, from time to time, appoint a Chief Locust Officer and such other officers as may be required to carry out this Act.

7) The Governor may at any time order the occupiers of any locust area to take such action as he may order for exterminating locusts upon their lands.

15) Any person who shall wilfully drive locusts off any property on to any neighbouring property shall be liable, on conviction, to a fine not exceeding Fifty Pounds Sterling, or to imprisonment with or without hard labour for any term not exceeding six months.

16) Every person guilty of an offence against this Act is liable to a penalty not exceeding Twenty Pounds Sterling, and, in default, shall be imprisoned with or without hard labor for any period not exceeding three months.

19) All ingredient and mechanical and other appliances, used in the destruction of locusts and in the carrying out of this Act shall be carried free of charge over the Natal Government Railways.